The Case Manager's Handbook

Third Edition

Catherine M. Mullahy, RN, BS, CRRN, CCM
President
Options Unlimited
Huntington, New York

with **Deborah K. Jensen**
President
An In-House Associate, Inc.
Huntingtion, New York

JONES AND BARTLETT PUBLISHERS
Sudbury, Massachusetts
BOSTON   TORONTO   LONDON   SINGAPORE

World Headquarters
Jones and Bartlett Publishers
40 Tall Pine Drive
Sudbury, MA 01776
978-443-5000
info@jbpub.com
www.jbpub.com

Jones and Bartlett Publishers Canada
2406 Nikanna Road
Mississauga, ON L5C 2W6
CANADA

Jones and Bartlett Publishers International
Barb House, Barb Mews
London W6 7PA
UK

The authors have made every effort to ensure the accuracy of the information herein. However, appropriate information sources should be consulted, especially for new or unfamiliar procedures. It is the responsibility of every practitioner to evaluate the appropriateness of a particular opinion in the context of actual clinical situations and with due considerations to new developments. Authors, editors, and the publisher cannot be held responsible for any typographical or other errors found in this book.

Library of Congress Cataloging-in-Publication Data

Mullahy, Catherine M.
    The case manager's handbook / Catherine M. Mullahy.—3rd ed.
        p. ; cm.
Includes bibliographical references and index.
    ISBN 0-7637-3188-9 (hardcover)
    1. Hospitals—Case management services—Handbooks, manuals, etc.
    [DNLM: 1. Case Management. WX 162 M958ca 2003] I. Title.
    RA975.5.C36M85 2003
    362.11—dc22

                                                        2003017850

Acquisitions Editor: Kevin Sullivan
Production Manager: Amy Rose
Associate Production Editor: Jenny L. McIsaac
Editorial Assistant: Amy Sibley
Marketing Manager: Joy Stark-Vancs
Marketing Associate: Elizabeth Waterfall
Manufacturing Buyer: Amy Bacus
Cover Design: Kristin E. Ohlin
Composition: Bookwrights
Printing and Binding: Malloy Inc.
Cover Printing: Malloy Inc.

Printed in the United States of America
07 06 05 04 03   10 9 8 7 6 5 4 3 2 1

Table of Contents

Foreword

Since the first edition of *The Case Manager's Handbook* was released in 1994, professional case managers as a group have seen dramatic industry growth and explosive change. Educational programs at the graduate and undergraduate level abound, as do niche market specialties including pregnancy case management, cancer case management, pediatric, elder care, and end-of-life care. There are now more than 23,000 Certified Case Managers (CCMs). The Commission for Case Manager Certification (CCMC) has celebrated the 10th anniversary of the CCM exam's first administration. Responding to the evolving and maturing case management practice, in 2002, the Case Management Society of America (CMSA) updated and revised its Standards of Practice for Case Management following an intense peer review and public comment.

Not surprisingly, the proportion of case managers related to managed care organizations is rising sharply. To meet the demand, as fewer women and men move into the nursing profession, licensed nurses are taking on a larger role across the care continuum. The nursing shortage impacts the role of case managers in several ways. One result is that the average health care experience of the frontline case manager is decreasing as nursing professionals come into the case management field earlier in their line of work. The vanguard of case management practitioners, those who founded the field in the 1980s after successful nursing and social work careers, are nearing retirement. Having inaugurated the industry, case managers must now reach out to colleagues in nursing and nonnursing allied health fields to recruit and mentor the case managers of tomorrow.

Health care is ever-changing. It is time to push forward, adapt to this continuing change, and perfect what we do as we move through this whirlwind. And with every change comes increasing recognition of case management as one of the premiere positive strategies toward the delivery of quality, cost-efficient health care outcomes. The success of case management has been recognized globally.

American case management has become an exportable entity, and our partners in health care management around the world are asking for the patterns of success as demonstrated by case management.

Cathy Mullahy has continued her consulting/teaching role in major health care corporations and associations across the country. As clinical, legal, ethical, and benefits issues intensify in health care, she has emerged as a national case management leader, speaking at numerous major health care conferences nationwide and contributing to a number of journals and books. Editor of *The Case Manager* magazine, Cathy Mullahy was 2001–2002 National President of the Case Management Society of America. She served on the CMSA National Standards of Practice Task Force and as Ethics Committee chair. In 2001, Cathy Mullahy was named as National Distinguished Case Manager of the Year by the CMSA. She is Past-Chair of the Commission for Case Manager Certification (CCMC), has chaired its Ethics Committee, the CCMC Certification Compliance Review Committee, and is the CCMC representative to the Foundation for Rehabilitation Education and Research. She has served on ongoing expert panels in connection with the development of the CCM credential since its inception, and was Chair of the CCMC committee that developed the case management Code for Professional Conduct. In addition, she is a contributing editor to *Case Management Advisor.*

One of the most widely recognized authorities on case management continues to share her knowledge and expertise with the industry. Yet this author speaks in a personal and direct manner as a mentor. This mentor's role is critically important when it comes to communicating the essence of case management: the care, the passion for quality, and the art of the business. This book is one such link between mentor and learner, written by an author who has experienced and developed case management at its finest and who shares not only the "stuff", but also her heart.

It was through a mentor-learner relationship that I first came to know Cathy Mullahy. Several years ago, half a continent away and in the midst of working cases, she offered the expertise I required to take what I had learned in other areas of case management and transfer it to the group health experience. It was during our crucial conversations that I discovered both her knowledge and her vision of case management. Well-versed in the ins and outs of claims, the nuances of benefits language, and the clinical and operations management of various reimbursement systems, she provided insight and direction. More importantly, she cared about people—the patient, the family, the provider, and the payer—and incorporated that concern into case management.

I have known Cathy when the status of her business was incredibly good and when it could not have been worse. It was in those "worst of times," when the desire and determination to make her case management vision work were about all that was left, that I came to recognize and respect her uncompromising ethics and values. In a number of ways, she has been, and continues to be, a mentor and has also become a coplanner, coconsultant, copresenter, and friend. All of this is to say that I can commend the author of this handbook as a trustworthy communicator and adviser, a teacher who has carefully crafted a significant part of case management practice. From her years as a staff nurse in emergency room and other critical care settings through the establishment of her own case management company, she has consistently applied new techniques and innovations, making her a leading case management professional and a well-received lecturer and commentator.

As you refine your own manner of case management delivery, you will be involved in a three-part pursuit: gathering medical and clinical expertise, learning the industry, and fulfilling your personal goals. This practical book, written by a pioneer who has creatively and compassionately addressed patient, provider, and payer needs via case management, will enable you to achieve peak collaborative performance in your practice setting, on behalf of your clients and in conjunction with the other professionals serving them. I believe you will find that its content wears well over time, through the tests of a changing health care system, and that it serves as a rich reference. Using this major tool prepared for practiced and novice case managers alike, you will be introduced to the basics and subtleties of the mentor's vision of truly meaningful case management.

Jeanne Boling, MSN, CRRN, CDMS, CCM
Executive Director
Case Management Society of America
Little Rock, Arkansas

Preface

When *The Case Manager's Handbook* first appeared, the case management industry was in its youth. With their ability to reinvigorate and support health care delivery, case managers now play pivotal roles in numerous provider, payer, and educational venues, and *The Case Manager's Handbook* has gone with them into case management department libraries, corporate boardrooms, rehab facilities, claims offices at Third Party Administrator offices, university classrooms, insurance firms, and other affiliated practices. Because it was one of the first comprehensive handbooks available to case managers, and because of the industry's explosive growth, valuable material and sections have been added. This third edition incorporates nuts-and-bolts information on managed care, disease management, capitated rate structures, new legislation, outsourcing, carve-outs, public sector case management, and case management credentialing and accreditation agencies, plus expanded sections on consumer-driven healthcare, e-Health, and formal educational programs for case managers. The ready-to-apply basics of case management remain, updated as needed for our changing practice environments. In response to these changes are new chapters in this edition that address HIPAA, end-of-life and cultural issues, behavioral health, and, as further acknowledgment of how technology is driving us, Internet resources.

Case management helps resolve one of the paradoxes of the current health care delivery system: Our technologically advanced medical facilities are staffed by highly skilled and trained professionals, yet we fall short in our efforts to provide optimum care to individual patients, especially those afflicted with multifaceted, problematic, chronic diseases, or disabilities. Patients enter a high-performance health care system so specialized and organ-specific that treatment is often fragmented and the overall quality of care is diluted. Serving as a vital connection linking all the private and public associations, agencies, disciplines, and practitioners within the delivery system, case managers are catalysts and communicators, advocates for patients, providers, and payers. They help focus the system for each person, facilitating the delivery of more individualized, coordinated care.

While working toward improved quality of care and better patient outcomes, case management professionals have also become recognized for their abilities as good financial managers, an expertise they have gained by fulfilling the role and function of their profession. However, it is both incorrect and unconscionable to equate case management with cut-rate health care. Finances should not drive case management systems, but the pressure for cost containment and some hefty greed have led to the creation of several large, financially focused case management groups. Applying case management solely to cut costs is just not an acceptable strategy.

Committed individuals, adhering to ethical case management principles, will deliver more cost-appropriate health care. Once case management methods of coordinating medical services are put in place, cost-effectiveness becomes ensured, as do quality and improved outcomes.

The discipline of case management is evolving as you read this. Because the need is so great, the escalation of medical costs so swift, and the application of case management strategies so effective in maintaining high standards of care while cutting expenses, case management has become an industry "overnight," although it has been practiced for years. It is an industry that is changing in response to modifications in the health care delivery system even as it influences those modifications. Accepted as an integral element in the health care system, it is attracting increased recognition as well as generating demands for a consensus on standards of practice, and just what constitutes *good* case management. Some who have only a rough idea of the nature of case management are claiming they are case management practitioners regardless of their expertise and the appropriateness of their interventions, one unfortunate result of the industry's rapid growth. Incredibly, there are still many professionals who believe they are case managers and organizations that confer this title upon them, yet never talk to patients.

Growth in the case management industry will be spurred by various sectors. As the number of insurance companies in the health care business decreases, due to mergers and acquisitions, and the trend among employer groups toward self-funded benefit programs increases, we will see more case management organizations within larger corporations. Smaller companies and entrepreneurs, realizing that claims administration services that lack cost-containment mechanisms do little to ease the burden of health care payments in the long run, will begin to self-administer their programs, relying on case managers to coordinate care delivery. As with other service areas in our changing economy, there are endless opportunities for entrepreneurs. Sensing that case managers are true advocates, individual consumers and communities will call on them directly for help in navigating the channels of health care support services, from selecting a suitable head trauma center to obtaining family counseling for those living with a terminally ill loved one to representing the estate of a disabled individual in court. Increased focus on consumer-driven health plans and direct-to-consumer advertising are certainly calling out to us...will we be ready to respond?

Before case management professionals will be accepted more completely as part of the mainstream of advanced medical care, a change will need to occur in current thinking regarding human resources and medical benefits. Case management must become a standard element in the administration of benefits. The concept driving case management is so straightforward, and the results of case management so positive, that it is difficult to believe we are still in the process of educating other medical professionals, insurers, corporations, communities, and politicians regarding its benefits rather than simply implementing its procedures.

A change also needs to occur in our own thinking. Health care policy has impacted case management, and in turn, case managers must take an aggressive and active role in influencing legislation and health care policy. Where were we when the guidelines for the day-op mastectomy were put in place? Why weren't we, who call ourselves patient advocates, taking the lead in voicing concern over issues that our patients and their physicians brought to light? With our silence, we forfeit valuable opportunities to position case management as the solution to a multitude of health care problems, including access to service, quality, and improved outcomes, coordination of care, patient education and emotional support, and continuity of care.

For years, it has been known that the greatest portion of health care costs is generated by the 3 to 5% of the patient population that are at high risk, critically injured, or suffering from a chronic disease. As an example, from January to October, one client firm spent over $1.8 million in health care benefits for its employees and their dependents (2,520 covered lives). One half of that dollar total was distributed to 30 individuals (4% of the employees). This means that one half of the benefit dollars spent, over $900,000, was focused on 1.1% of the total covered population. Twenty-two employees spent $588,702, meaning that 3% of the employees accounted for 32% of the group's total in paid claims. When one considers the covered lives, the figures are more remarkable: 0.8% (or less than 1 percent) spent 32% of the dollars. In an insurer's review of its plan year covering 11,000 employees, a report showed health benefits expenditures of $36 million. A program designed to pull out each case tallying more than $50,000 listed 35 cases responsible for a total of $5 million in benefits that year. Those 35 cases represent 0.3% of the employees, meaning that less than one half of one percent of the group spent 14% of the group's dollars.

By developing systems to identify and manage cases from day one, case management promotes quality care and contains costs. By wrapping the case management approach around all lines of medical coverage, case managers can be appropriately attentive to potentially problematic cases, more creative in problem solving, and better able to address spiraling expenses before they take off. As a byproduct, case management also tackles three other problem areas that push up employer costs and concerns: employee morale, decreased production, and absenteeism. A case manager's professional intervention and guidance improves employee morale by providing direct communication and personal attention, helps return employees to the job more quickly, and helps eliminate repeated occurrences of the same afflictions.

Case management, in conjunction with such programs as preadmission review, utilization review, disease management, absentee management, claims administration, and health care education for individuals and their families, can smooth the path of health care delivery. Patients and their families do not have to feel that they are being abandoned in the middle of an overwhelming and confusing system controlled by inaccessible authorities. Health care providers will rest assured that the individuals they treated will be tracked through home or hospice recovery and that fewer cases will be readmitted due to complications that could have been prevented. And insurers and employers can put the brakes on escalating health care claims by using backup data on where dollars are needed and where dollars are being spent.

True, money is pouring into our health care system. But improved treatment and services are not flowing out at the same rate. Acknowledgment of increased medical errors, a growing nursing shortage, and a lack of quality outcomes are just a few of the indicators of a system in trouble. Case management is one needed catalyst to push performance to more cost-effective levels. Although patient responses and cost-benefit analysis reports are proof positive of top-level treatment and bottom-line results, we must continue to demonstrate how the commonsense approach of case management can improve a potentially successful health care system that appears in danger of running into the ground. Our challenge is to maintain the high standards of care and commitment, backed by expertise and performed via repeatable and verifiable procedures, so that the industry we are creating will become standard operating procedure.

This handbook is designed to define good case management, examine the case management process in its entirety, and present practical procedural information. It reviews case management's current business applications and also discusses future possibilities as well as the expanding opportunities for professional case managers.

Capitalizing on my experiences, I have created a how-to manual. I had to learn through a great deal of trial and error because there was no Case Management University, no place to study the kind of case management that exists today. There was no case manager's reference guide to consult. Much of the information contained in this manual was developed through my own "pilot projects." I have shared my experiences, including my failures. Hopefully, these experiences will keep other case managers from repeating my mistakes. This text is filled with instances in which I was left with a dilemma because I did not think things through in advance or I did not plan sufficiently. It also incorporates methods that started as trials and became tried-and-true approaches to care and claims management.

Each person can do exactly what I have done. Given experience and time and grade in the health care business, much of what is contained in this book has immediate application. It can serve as a resource or inspiration when something that you have done does not quite work, when you are looking for an alternative. That is why I like including anecdotal information, and this third edition will certainly demonstrate that case management is a work in progress. While emerging from its adolescence, case management is not a perfect science. It is filled with individuals and systems, some of which function, some of which are so fraught with disaster that when you prepare a final report on a case, you wonder how you managed to promote anything good. This handbook was written to serve as a reference on those days when you become convinced there must be another way, a different approach. My answer will not always be the right answer, but it may provide a new perspective just when one is needed. Sometimes, just knowing that others "feel your pain" gives you that extra bit of encouragement to try a little harder, or to remember that it's always possible to back up and go down a different road.

The Case Manager's Handbook can be used as a training guide for new case managers or a teaching tool for client groups. It stands apart from other case management references, in that it is partly designed to function as a tool for *the business world.* Case management, besides improving health delivery outcomes, is also a financial and human resource tool that more businesses should be using. There are some strong examples in this book to help persuade and educate business executives who might be inclined to incorporate case management practices as a way of serving their employees better, containing the expenditure of benefit dollars, and getting more value for the dollars they do spend.

Other special features of this book include examples of usable forms, letters, and dialogues, tools that with modification may make sorting information, collecting data, or presenting material easier. Some will simply be ideas holding the seeds for new methods. You may look at a paragraph in the book and say, "Well, that's good, but . . ." These concepts have worked for me; they can be improved on by you.

Because so much of case management is specific to a patient, an insurance plan, the community where a patient lives, or the providers one works with, some of the examples are not going to be useful to all readers. The information in the manual is based on my own experience and may not have universal application. Case management is utilized in so many arenas today; it is difficult to give examples that fit every criterion. If you are a case manager, not everything in this book is going to be immediately appropriate for you in your current employment setting. However, the handbook will have something to offer for virtually every case manager. Is it the definitive book for case managers in a rehab facility? No, it is not. But are there some methods discussed that a rehab facility case manager is going to be able to apply? Yes, there are. If you are a provider-based case manager, your reports perhaps are not going to be useful to a claims department. However, you will still have to justify the amount of money that someone spent in your facility, perhaps to another case manager so that she will continue to refer people to you. So, when I talk about presenting a cost-benefit analysis (CBA) report to an employer group, this does not mean that employers are the only audience for CBAs. Many of the issues discussed have several different applications, and although the focus in a particular chapter or paragraph may be for one kind of case manager, another will be able to redirect it to her advantage.

I did not set out to write the all-purpose case management handbook. I never intended to try to incorporate all the answers in one manuscript—that would take a lifetime. I know there will always be new challenges for case managers, new hurdles caused by changing health care policies and programs. My goal was merely to create a compendium of knowledge for now and a vision for the future. What this book offers is the nuts and bolts of case management and a sense of where it can go. I want to empower the industry and the individual. I hope the work I have done and shared will encourage other case managers to create and be the difference in their health environment rather than waiting for someone else to incorporate them into the mainstream.

Author's Note: Because the majority of case managers are women, I have used the feminine pronoun throughout this book. No offense to our male colleagues is implied or intended. For your reference, terms of widely used health care field concepts that are abbreviated in the text are spelled out in the Acronyms and Abbreviations section of the book.

Acknowledgments

It seems hard to believe that more than eight years have passed since *The Case Manager's Handbook* was first written. So many changes have occurred in the field of case management that the original book has become a work in progress. Additionally, our world has been forever changed in the aftermath of 9/11, and the way we view ourselves as professionals, employees, family members, and citizens has been affected as well. In an effort to meet the unending challenges facing case managers, the third edition was prepared in response to and with much consideration to the many readers of the first and second handbooks. I would like to acknowledge and express my sincerest thanks to all of you who made the book such a success. Your kind comments, suggestions, and encouragement were invaluable as I began and completed *The Case Manager's Handbook,* Third Edition. You will see how many of them have been utilized as you note the many additions and improvements in this edition, including more case studies; new sample letters, forms, and guidelines; new chapters and sections on a range of topics, such as ethics, end-of-life issues, disease management, consumer-driven health plans, cultural diversity, and web reference sites; as well as case management and HIPAA, and revisions in virtually every chapter reflecting the changes in practice.

I also want to acknowledge and thank in advance the first-time readers of *The Case Manager's Handbook,* as well as those original readers who are adding this third edition to their resource library. You are the future of case management, and I hope this book contributes to an exciting, more fulfilling and rewarding career for each of you.

So many others have been involved in this undertaking. Without their assistance and support, this book would not have been possible. I especially want to thank Deborah Jensen for her talent and perseverance in pursuing this project with me. Her expertise as a writer and editor is truly exceptional and her enthusiasm and determination kept us on target and deadline. With recognition of her generosity and willingness to join me in the telling of the story of case management, Deborah in every respect has become an additional author of this text, and will always have my deepest gratitude. To Jeannie Boling, my friend and colleague, thanks for her ongoing support and encouragement. Her honesty, vision, and love of case management continue to inspire me. As we shared the loss of parents, we learned more than we cared to about end-of-life issues. Thanks to Alice Casey, who continues to provide me with her insight, experience, and unique views on the health care industry. To these three women in particular, I express my heartfelt appreciation. They have provided and continue to provide me with their strength, warmth, guidance, and that which I value most, their humor, in unending supply. As I faced business and personal challenges, especially the loss of my dad to Alzheimer's four years ago, these women cared for me as I tried to be his case manager...and helped to renew my spirit as I searched and found new solutions for my business. Along with the many others, these events have become part of the blended professional, personal, and business experiences that are so much a part of each case manager's journey.

There are others whom I would like to acknowledge for their support, belief, and promotion of the original book and their continued assistance with this third edition. To Kevin Sullivan, Jenny McIsaac, Amy Sibley, Eileen Ward, Linda McGarvey, Joy Stark-Vancs, Elizabeth Waterfall, Linda McKenna, Nicole Quinn, and the many others at Jones and Bartlett Publishers, my thanks to each of you for watching over this project. I would also like to thank Jane Garwood for her assistance, and the many individuals who reviewed the manuscript for content, accuracy, and their special perspectives, among them Tom Strickland and Karyl Thorn. I would also like to thank Kathleen Moreo, Anne Llewellyn, Sherry Aliotta, Linda Chalmers, Dr. Christopher Wood, and Michael Demoratz for sharing their thoughts on the waves of change in health care and their own experiences in responding successfully by creating systems and businesses to meet the emerging need.

I express profound gratitude to my staff at Options Unlimited for their understanding and support while this book was in development, to Julie Graziano, Kathi Norouzieh, Nancy Peters, Ann Bivona, and Judy Middleton who brought their case management expertise to the third edition in the form of insightful case studies, and to Mary Lou Beeck and Linda Mercurio for their assistance in preparing the manuscript. I also want to thank our client companies, our patients, and their families for according us the privilege of working with them; to all the many case managers who have been my colleagues and friends and the inspiration for this work, you too were part of this endeavor.

And finally I want to express my deepest appreciation to my husband, John, for his love, unfailing enthusiasm, and belief in me, and to my children, Michael and Aileen, their spouses Pam and Neal, my mother, family, and friends, who encouraged and allowed me the time to complete this handbook. And, with love, in memory of my father.

PART I

Profile of a Case Manager

CHAPTER 1

The Case Manager as Catalyst, Problem Solver, Educator

Case management is not for the faint at heart. It is not for those seeking to avoid the stress of a hospital setting or the stretch of working with patients and families in distress. Providing intervention on behalf of the patient, medical provider, and payer (insurer), a case manager must place herself at the center of the confusion in today's health care delivery system and be willing and able to ask the tough questions. Is that surgical procedure appropriate and necessary? Can we do better on the pricing for the TPN (total parenteral nutrition) infusion or the out-of-network rehabilitation program? Can we honor this patient's wishes and enable him to live his last days at home? And because case management is a process, a case manager must have commitment to go the distance, offering ongoing, on-site, individualized services and becoming involved in finding medical treatment alternatives, monitoring results, solving problems, and revising the treatment plan as needed. A case manager is the catalyst who sifts through the array of possible paths, selects the most appropriate plan, and then coordinates the expertise and support of other professionals, family members, agencies, and suppliers. Case managers are concerned with every detail, from the minute—is the noise from the oxygen concentrator disruptive, preventing the patient from utilizing it?—to the major—can the family member, home health aide, or registered nurse in attendance handle a patient emergency? Is the family rejecting the needed hospital bed because they don't want their den to have a "sick look"?

It is not an easy professional specialty, but it is a tremendously rewarding one. As a discipline, case management requires an understanding of how various medical, insurance, government, and corporate mechanisms affect the health care delivery system. Each of these areas influences the type of care available and how it will be administered. It is the case manager's responsibility to know the distinctions between acute hospitalization, subacute care, and specialized chronic care; the results and impact of federal legislation; and the coverage offered by different lines of insurance.

It is also the case manager's responsibility to make assessments and recommendations on an objective basis, having no vested interest in which rehabilitation facility or infusion service is selected. If it seems that case managers are held accountable not only for their academic credentials and work history, but also for their personal ethics, it is because they are. Often functioning without peer support or direction from an immediate supervisor, case managers must bring their own motivation, moral strength, independence, and confidence to each case. This is the personal profile needed to oversee a wide spectrum of activities with the sole focus of ensuring the best possible outcome for a patient in the most cost-effective manner.

The current nursing shortage has been widely reported. Nurses are working more overtime or double shifts, and are responsible for a greater number of patients than before, meaning they have less time to spend with each patient and to complete all their tasks to the standards they feel are important to maintain. Turnover is increasing, especially among the more experienced nurses. Many hospital nurses are concerned that these conditions have the potential to affect their early detection of patient complications and their ability to maintain patient safety.

In this environment, the case manager's role becomes increasingly significant toward ensuring appropriate, quality care. Case management intervention addresses the needs that arise as hospital staff, for example, is stretched to its capacity. Conversations between case managers and acute care nurses were never relaxed coffee klatches, but now have become even quicker exchanges of information. To obtain background that might not have been communicated verbally, our staff has begun looking more closely at nurses' notes, especially when the things we're hearing don't match up; the patient is saying he's fine, but he's experiencing complications. The insights gained from these notes, where treatment changes and patient reaction are recorded, enhance our ability to spot potential problems or a lack of progress, so we can intervene and redirect, as considered necessary.

Aware of the higher possibility of infections due to understaffing, a case manager will be more proactive, and assess skin integrity, on-site or through conversation, to avoid the development of decubitus ulcers. On behalf of a stroke patient, she might ask if hand splints are in place to prevent contracture, which would decrease hand mobility and a return to strength.

Exacerbating the shortage, hospital-based RNs have also become more involved in and accountable for activities not associated with patient care, such as budgets, coding meetings, staffing issues, and usage of quality improvement tools. Each of these is of value to hospital administration, but does not contribute directly to patient care.

Similarly, case managers are vulnerable to revisions of their job descriptions and responsibilities as hospitals and health care organizations face both economic stresses and this shortage of qualified nurses. In an article in *The Case Manager*, trends noticed by CMSA (Case Management Society of America) members included: the delegation of clerical responsibilities to case managers, delegation of patient interactions to non-case managers, an increase in the clinical condition responsibilities now falling to case managers, and a rise in caseloads.[1] (A closer look at changes in caseloads is documented in the American Health Consultants/Case Management Society of America 2000 Case Management Caseload Survey.) Each of these undermines the case manager's role by drawing her away from patient advocacy and coordinating care across the continuum, and siphoning off her time with secretarial duties, or loading up on her work responsibilities so that rushing through each task would be the only way to complete them all. This lessens the value and effectiveness of her contributions, and opens the door for complications. Would anyone knowingly hurry an analyst through reading a sonogram or a breast x-ray?

THE CASE MANAGER'S ROLE

Case managers are not the claims police. Ensuring cost-effective treatment does not mean that case managers are overrated number crunchers who review treatment alternatives simply to find the cheapest scenario. Case managers are coordinators, facilitators, impartial advocates, and educators. Their roles are as varied as the sites where they are employed and the job titles that designated their position in the past.

The case manager in an acute care facility may have been called a discharge planner a few years ago. In behavioral health facilities, the "Program Coordinator" or "Coordinator of Patient Services" may now carry the title "Case Manager."

Case managers in hospitals, rehabilitation facilities, home health agencies, and infusion care companies are in the provider sector of health services and may include nurses and social workers. They may oversee treatment while a patient is in a particular facility or receiving a certain type of service, such as infusion therapy, but not be involved with that same patient's care once the patient moves on to a different center or care program. Depending on the employer, a case manager may never make a home visit or manage care outside of a particular facility.

In the payer sector, both public and private, case managers may work through Third Party Administrators (TPAs), self-administered programs, health maintenance organizations (HMOs), preferred provider organizations (PPOs), point-of-service plans (POSs), military programs, or major insurance carriers. In these settings, case managers identify and track all hospital admissions and other events in which there is a likelihood of costly or high-exposure conditions. Although employer emphasis may seem to be on reducing overall costs, these case managers are also dedicated to assisting employees and their dependents in the utilization of services.

Because of financial organizational structure and administrative overhead, many organizations do not elect to maintain an in-house case management department or staff. This, coupled with the direct-to-consumer trend, is behind the growing and diverse opportunities for independent case managers. Those with strong expertise in neonatal, oncology, elder care, or organ transplants may find heightened demand for their services. One such source is stress-ridden baby boomers who call on independent case managers on behalf of their aging parents.

Independent case managers are outside both the medical care provider and the claims payer systems. All case managers are charged with the responsibility to make totally objective assessments and to coordinate a program of care. With no vested interest in the companies selected to provide this care or services, independent case managers can remain more impartial advocates for their clients and may have an advantage in exercising out-of-the-box thinking and solutions.

The focal point of case management in all of its roles is to empower patients, giving them and their families access to a greater understanding of their disability or disease, a larger voice in the delivery of their care, and more personalized attention to their particular needs. Obtaining data on the particulars of each patient's case, case managers enable patients and their families to make informed decisions. Through their role as advocates, they help patients deal with the complexities of the health care system.

CASE MANAGEMENT IS NOT EQUIVALENT TO MANAGED CARE

Managed care and *case management* are not interchangeable concepts. Managed care is a system of cost-containment programs; case management is a process. A global term, managed care consists of the systems and mechanisms utilized to control, direct, and approve access to the wide range of services and costs within the health care delivery system. Case management can be one of those mechanisms, one component in the managed care strategy.

Based on the use of cost-containment programs that include guidelines and criteria for health care delivery, managed care organizations (MCOs) incorporate a wide variety of options. These may include Pharmacy Benefits Management (PBM), POS plans, consumer-driven plans, HMOs, PPOs, direct contracting (in which an employer contracts directly with a hospital or other health care facility), bill audits, utilization review, preadmission authorization, concurrent review, retrospective review, second surgical opinions (SSOs), independent medical exams (IMEs), disease management, and case management. Whereas managed care programs strive to involve all potential users of health care services, case management focuses on certain individuals—the 3 to 5% of the patient population responsible for 60 to 70% of the expenditures in any health plan.[2]

Case management is a highly individualized process that aims to identify those most at-risk, vulnerable, or care- and cost-intensive patients; assess treatment options and opportunities to coordinate care; design treatment programs to improve quality and efficacy of care; control costs; and manage patient care to ensure the optimum outcome. Concentrating for the most part on catastrophic or chronic cases, case managers are called in to consult for diagnoses such as head injury, multiple trauma, cancer, AIDS, organ transplants, cardiovascular and respiratory disease, stroke, burns, spinal cord injury, premature infants, diabetes, and high-risk pregnancy.

In the Towers Perrin 2002 Health Care Cost Survey Report of Key Findings, company employers were asked to name the targeted disease/demand management programs they had implemented within the past two years, or were thinking of putting in place in the future, as steps to control costs. Catastrophic case management led the list, with 48% of respondents having adopted it within the past two years, and another 6% considering its near-term application. Other containment measures mentioned were chronic disease management programs, a 24-hour nurse line, the use of centers of excellence, on-site/near-site wellness features, and health risk appraisals.[3] A survey of 80 employers with a median workforce of 52,000 employees, conducted as a joint project by Watson Wyatt Worldwide and the Washington Business Group on Health, and reported on www.businessinsurance.com (posted by Michael Prince; February 13, 2003) found that 75% of surveyed employers utilized case management.

The trend toward greater use of case management is not new. In its 1996 Executive Opinion Poll (which introduced a new survey design and methodology), *Business & Health* asked respondents to name the management techniques applied by their health care plans, from a list including case management, utilization review, disease management, demand management, pharmacoeconomics, and outcomes research. Outcomes published in *"Business & Health* Executive Opinion Poll—1996" showed case management leading the other categories as the management technique most used by the health care plans of large and small companies combined (with 43% applying it) and by companies with 20 to 499 employees (with 42% applying it). Among larger companies employing more than 500 individuals, 73% of health care plans used case management techniques and 75% applied utilization review. In a note that should have been a wake-up call to chief executive officers (CEOs), even as it warmed the hearts of Third Party Administrators and insurers nationwide, the report mentioned that a substantial portion of respondents didn't know whether a particular technique was utilized by their health care plan(s). Nearly half of the respondents in many cases, and 60% of those asked about demand management, weren't certain whether that technique was being applied by their health care plan. This reinforced my concern (and continued amazement) that the majority of employers (those who ultimately pay for employees' health care coverage) do not know how that money, that resource, is being managed.

In 2001, URAC (originally incorporated under the name "Utilization Review Accreditation Commission," shortened to URAC, and now also known as the American Accreditation HealthCare Commission) conducted a national survey of more than 120 companies regarding trends and issues in medical management. Participants included HMOs, PPOs, stand-alone medical management companies, insurance carriers, and others. The study researched national trends and issues in medical management, and the white paper "2001 Trends and Practices in Medical Management: Implications for the Industry" reported that more and more companies were utilizing a combination of utilization management (UM), disease management (DM), and case management (CM). Of the 92 companies providing quantitative data, 52% offered case management as a stand-alone product, and 22% offered disease management as a stand-alone. Even those identified as UM stand-alone organizations had brought in case management and disease management to provide more integrated services.[4]

Case managers have long expressed the benefits of combining CM, utilization review (UR)/UM, PreCert, and—as new concepts in health care came on the scene—disease management, in a coordinated system to best provide for the patient and limit employer and payer risks. Now it seems that this type of system is becoming a reality. Fully 73% of Third Party Administrators also offer UM, 46% offer CM services, and often offer DM (35%), as noted in the summary "New Insights in Medical Management: Results of URAC's 2001 Study of Medical Management Practices," written by Liza Greenberg, RN, MPH.[5]

The positive piece that all case managers can embrace is that, within this comprehensive study, case management is perceived as a distinct role and function that is best applied in a coordinated program with UM, DM, discharge planning, and social work. Still, this collaborative model can be improved upon, and more information about case management needs to be communicated.

MEDICAL CREDENTIALS AND EXPERTISE

Agreed-upon credentials and criteria for what makes a good case manager and the level of preparation required to handle the usual responsibilities have long been established as part of the development of the Certified Case Manager (CCM) and other case management credentials. Predictably, the criteria caused an outcry from some individuals who claim to offer case management but discovered they are worlds apart from those case management practitioners who are eligible for certification. For example, there are individuals currently working as case managers who have no more experience than one year in a hospital and a weekend-obtained certificate in case management. Case management as a profession demands critical thinking skills, in-depth clinical knowledge, and extensive, diversified experience within the health care delivery system. It is an advanced practice, and as such, requires a high level of knowledge and competency.

Today's case managers come from diverse educational and clinical settings, many with broader backgrounds than a strict hospital environment. Generally, they are nurses, social workers, or rehabilitation counselors, and a number of them have had experience administering workers' compensation and disability cases involving catastrophic injury. Far beyond helping an individual recuperate and return to work, case managers address health and wellness within disease management and wellness programs, as well as the needs of those already experiencing costly medical conditions and their complications. They assist in everything from tertiary neonatal cases, premature babies, and healthy baby programs to geriatric cases, stroke victims, and living with diabetes. There is a need for broad clinical knowledge and standards of care for the less complicated conditions, and on to kidney failure and amputations, which is causing subtle shifts among case management practitioners.

Social welfare caseworkers, involved with programs like Medicare, originated some elements of case management procedures. They developed and perfected the skills involved in connecting people to their community resources and obtaining financial aid from federal and state agencies. Social workers will undoubtedly continue to make up a substantial portion of case managers. Although considerable supplementary training and experience might be required before they could manage complex medical cases, such as ventilator-dependent babies or an individual requiring infusion services, social workers with medical backgrounds can handle stable cases and provide assistance to our fast-growing "gray" population. They also take a significant role in behavioral health programs. And combining social workers and RNs in medical case management teams has already proven very effective, enabling speedier identification of solutions to patient problems. As professionals with a different focus, rehabilitation counselors have also become valuable members of such teams, with their emphasis on recuperation and the return to work.

Because of the medical problem solving and coordination responsibilities inherent in the case management role, the kind of experience and education that nurses possess becomes important. In addition to basic educational preparation—associate degree, diploma-school, or baccalaureate-level college—life experience counts for a great deal. But case management demands a greater depth and intensity of involvement than traditional nursing, as well as more advanced medical, psychological, and sociological training. Therefore, a case manager's educational process should be ongoing and, through continuing education studies or postgraduate work, should be directed toward achieving a master's degree in a clinical specialty, for example. Because continuing education is not mandated for updated RN certification in many states, a number of practicing case managers neglect their obligation to remain current in their field. Those selecting case management as a career owe it to their patients, their profession, and themselves to read, attend conferences, and sit in on seminars and lectures so as to broaden their knowledge base. The CCM designation requires case managers to take advantage of continuing education to maintain their credential status, as does the Care Manager Certified certification (CMC) and the Case Manager Associate (CMC-A) from the American Institute of Outcomes Case Management (AIOCM), the Certified Social Work Case Manager (C-SWCM) designation from the National Association of Social Workers, and many others.

Due to the tendency of multiple conditions, sometimes comorbid, in the case management patient population, the kind of clinical experience of greatest value is that of a generalist. Although there are case managers with a single practice area, such as those who specialize in high-risk neonates, head trauma, organ transplants, oncology, or hematology, most case managers should have experience with a variety of age groups, treatment facilities, and medical conditions. The majority of case managers will receive referrals requiring knowledge of a wide spectrum of medical practice specialties, and they will need to acquire a diversified clinical background to meet the challenges. Ideal clinical preparation includes in-depth exposure to medical-surgical treatments, intensive care, critical care, home care, psychology, obstetrics, pediatrics, and neurological care. Case managers must be able to distinguish good care from bad care, understand potential complications, and evaluate alternate treatment options. Working in one hospital unit for one year does not provide the range of cases and insight required of a good case manager. Even comprehensive hospital experience alone is insufficient preparation. In most hospitals, equipment and supplies are readily available. Leaving the safety and support systems of the hospital environment, we can appreciate how vulnerable our patients can become when necessary services are fragmented. Further, case management requires self-direction, critical thinking, and independent functioning and judgment, skills honed more readily in nontraditional health care settings. Experience in home health care, walk-in clinics, and occupational health nursing can provide a beneficial view of community health care options.

Because the work requires financial savvy, a business background is also helpful. Hospital nurses do not have to cost out the care they are administering, but case managers must be financially accountable. If they cannot demonstrate the positive impact of case management to its stakeholders (payers, providers, patients), they undermine the value of their industry and, therefore, their future. They need to know, for example, the cost of infusion care treatment so they can question payment on a creatively submitted invoice. Forget that they can help improve employee morale, can help a disabled person get back to work faster to continue a rewarding career, can locate an appropriate facility 10 miles from home rather than 550 miles away for a child with a head injury; if they cannot combine their healing skills with practical business skills, they will lose the opportunity to practice.

Case management work often places individuals in situations in which patients and their families are devastated by health-related problems. Beyond facilitating health care decisions on behalf of other human beings, case managers also face the type of intense social/dynamic family issues that never become "easy" to handle but can be approached with more empathy and grace by practitioners who have become acquainted with the emotions encountered in marriage, divorce, illness, and death. Less experienced practitioners are likely to have difficulty appreciating the significance of such issues. Five or more years of clinical experience helps develop a maturity and depth that makes it easier to relate to patients and understand their emotional state.

Case managers need personal stamina and strength. Most caseloads include tragic cases. Case managers cannot make a terminal illness fade away. They cannot fully empower a patient if the family is too broken to accept the necessary responsibility. Case managers, therefore, need personal resources and support from friends and family to meet the challenges each day will present. A can-do mentality, a ready sense of humor, and the gift of levelheaded self-affirmation to take personal note of the small successes every day are among the traits that boost a case manager's effectiveness.

A DEFINITION OF CASE MANAGEMENT

The Commission for Case Manager Certification (CCMC) defines case management as follows: Case management is a collaborative process that assesses, plans, implements, coordinates, monitors, and evaluates the options and services required to meet an individual's health needs, using communication and available resources to promote quality, cost-effective outcomes.[6]

The CMSA defines case management as "a collaborative process of assessment, planning, facilitation, and advocacy for options and services to meet an individual's health needs through communication and available resources to promote quality cost-effective outcomes."[7]

Although it is not in all the language referring to the role and function of case managers, and is not possible in all settings, for all case managers I would add that case management is most effective when provided across the continuum of care. When a case is opened and then worked as the patient moves from acute care hospital to a skilled nursing facility or rehabilitation center, and then home, case management can offer its greatest contributions to quality health care and the best use of health care dollars.

In the broadest sense, a case manager is the person who can make the health care system work, influencing both the quality of the outcome and the cost. In our country, health care delivery is fragmented and complex. Providers range from the walk-in clinics to exclusive provider organizations and centers of excellence, and care settings run the gamut from a patient's own bedroom, up through rehabilitation facilities, outpatient facilities, specialized long-term care sites, and nursing homes, to hospices, subacute care facilities, and hospitals. It is no surprise patients are confused.

Working as an advocate for the patient (always searching for and moving toward the most medically appropriate solution), an empowering agent for the family, and a facilitator of communication among the patient, family, care providers, and payers, the case manager is a sentinel for quality assurance and cost-effectiveness. Perhaps the case manager can effect an earlier discharge, negotiate a better fee from a medical equipment supplier, or encourage the family to assume responsibility for a portion of the day-to-day care the patient needs. She can be a catalyst for change by seeking solutions that promote improvement or stabilization rather than simply monitoring patient status. If the case manager performs all these functions well, quality assurance and cost savings fall into place as a matter of course, prolonging the life of benefit dollars for individuals and helping to free up health care monies for the 41 million uninsured in the United States today.

CASE MANAGEMENT ROLE AND FUNCTIONS

To be effective, case managers require broad-based knowledge. They need to be part general practitioner, part social worker, part psychologist, and part minister or rabbi. Even if the case management role never requires going beyond the boundaries of this specialty, a case manager needs to be aware of the psychosocial, environmental, family, economic, and religious dynamics that can impact patients. She also must have a diverse medical background; being a clinician is not enough.

Areas of general knowledge and the understanding of health care treatments and systems required by case management practitioners were encompassed in the preliminary 1992 CCM credentialing report. Suggested general knowledge included theories of family functioning; the characteristics of various stages of physical and psychosocial development; the traits of functional and dysfunctional coping and their implications for health; and resources, eligibility for services, and referral procedures. In the area of health care, first-draft credentialing criteria called for comprehension of "home health resources; strategies to access medical records; medical terminology; pharmaceuticals and pharmacological management; levels of care in acute and rehabilitative treatment; adaptive equipment and assistive devices for various disabilities and illnesses; issues involving experimental treatments and protocols; and competitive cost for medical and health care services, aftercare and independent living resources,"[8] in addition to other health care factors. Because of the case manager's role as a communicator and liaison, she must also be familiar with certain elements within the insurance, legal, and vocational disciplines. For example, to interact successfully with insurance and funding sources, a case manager must be facile with insurance terminology, the preparation of cost-benefit analyses for payers, the reporting requirements of various health care reimbursement and government agencies, disability compensation systems, extended medical or indemnity payments, and the coordination of benefits. To practice ethically and safely, a case manager should also be familiar with legal terminology, liability issues, use of depositions, confidentiality laws, and the accepted procedures and requirements for releasing or sharing information. To best meet patient needs, one must be familiar with cultural issues, complementary and alternative care, herbal medications, end-of-life concerns such as pain management, and specialty areas of case management. And finally, vocational and legislative protocols will govern care options and benefit plan dollar availability for some individuals. These areas of knowledge will encompass resources for reentry into the labor force, work evaluation processes, job accommodation principles, affirmative action, the philosophy of workers' compensation, the Americans with Disabilities Act of 1990 (ADA), Medicaid and Medicare provisions, and the rights of individuals under federal and state law (both the state in which a case manager practices and the state in which a patient is undergoing treatment).

All this said, it must also be noted that case management usually is not a hands-on role. Case managers, while continuing to be actively practicing nurses, clinicians, or caregivers, do not diagnose an ailment, prescribe a medication, or set the course of treatment. They do offer their observations on a patient's status and use their expertise to plan and suggest alternative care options. Using on-site visits as fact-gathering missions, a case manager can make sure a noncompliant patient is following the treatment plan outlined by the physician or note the possible complications from the medication recommended by the patient's ear-nose-and-throat specialist but never mentioned to his or her cardiologist. Case managers are consultants, advisors, and facilitators.

Although the majority of case managers do not offer hands-on care, neither can they be truly effective if they act in a totally hands-off manner. Telephone work, which is a part of case management, is necessary for keeping open the lines of communication without driving up costs. It is particularly effective for preventive and case-screening measures as well as for tracking low-intensity patients or patients whose conditions have improved to the point where in-person case management is no longer needed. However, strict telephonic case management, in which all the communication between the case manager, patient, family, physician, and payer occurs over the phone, can lead to major oversights in care unless skillfully conducted, especially in cases in which the patient is noncompliant, undereducated, or poor. The vulnerability of the patient, combined with the legal and monetary exposure of the case manager, provider, and payer, often necessitates on-site interaction.

Case managers fulfill a role not provided for elsewhere in the health care system. They become the eyes and ears for others, a resource for physicians and other members of the health care team, insurance groups, employers, and particularly families. Because people tend to picture described situations in terms of their own experience, they tend to make incorrect assumptions. A telephonic case manager might envision a patient's "home" as complete with a stocked refrigerator, adequate room for the ventilator or the motorized wheelchair modified with respiratory equipment, and clean sheets on the bed. During an on-site home visit, a case manager will be able to note the empty refrigerator, the two toddlers careening around the couch and bumping into the infant's oxygen-supply tubing, the unopened medication bottles, and the family in need of respite. Let's review a real case in which a gentleman suffered a left-sided stroke leaving him with right-sided weakness. The physician assured the case manager that the patient was fine upon discharge and didn't require any equipment or support services. The case manager never asked the patient: Can you walk comfortably? Will you need a cane for support? Will you be able to walk around inside your home? In the weeks following discharge, the man experienced complications and difficulty maneuvering around his house. His wife was upset with the case manager and the physician for their lack of support. A more complete telephone conversation and the appropriate follow-up calls would have solved these problems. (For more information on telephonic case management, please see Chapter 9 sections "Talking with the Patient," "Talking with the Family," and "Telephonic Case Management.")

Beyond the medical aspects lies another whole dynamic of an illness, the logistics of coping, which might require putting a caretaker's job on hold or a home up for sale. Here is where a case manager can help fill a void in the system by assisting the well persons in the family to deal with practical matters. The comatose patient does not need hand-holding, but the caretaker in the family might—or might need guidance from a person who can fully explain treatment options, a safe person to share emotions with, or someone to fill out the forms and help file the claims. When the claims department returns a form marked "incomplete," there is no note describing what information was omitted. Unfiled claims cannot be reimbursed, and the case manager can be the person to help pull the details together, to get the burned-out caretaker some part-time assistance, or to call the bank and request a payment plan for the home mortgage.

Again, once a basic assessment of the patient's condition and family and home setting has been completed, the case manager has established her role with the patient, treating physician, and nurses, and has set up the services to match the resources and needs of the patient and family, then the telephone can become a tremendous resource. The moment a case manager hears something during a telephone conversation that sets off an internal "red alert," an on-site visit should be made.

A CASE MANAGER'S EDUCATION, CLINICAL PREPARATION, AND LIFE EXPERIENCE

CCMC publishes the *CCM Certification Guide,* revised periodically to meet the changing roles of case managers in numerous practice settings within the evolving managed care industry. Every five years, representatives from the entire field of case management practitioners across the continuum of care are canvassed, and their conclusions are incorporated into the CCM exam content and credentialing criteria, leading to appropriate updates in the CCM role and function information. In this way, the CCM exam remains an accurate reflection of the field. The results also indicate areas in which case managers might require additional educational support and reference materials.

The Case Management Society of America developed the first set of Standards of Practice for Case Management in 1995. In 2001, it became apparent that an update was needed to bring the standards in line with the evolution of the case manager's role, the process of case management, and practice settings as the health care delivery system changes to meet our times. Following a rigorous peer review of the standards, public comment, and research, drafts and final versions were developed. Published in 2002 by the CMSA, the revised Standards of Practice for Case Management lists the primary case manager role functions as assessment, planning, facilitation, and advocacy.

URAC, a leader in the accreditation of health and managed care organizations, has created the URAC Case Management Core Standards, which also speaks to case management staff development, organization ethics, processes, and other issues that are involved in the provision of case management services. Taken together, these three new documents offer a comprehensive, detailed description of the case manager's purpose, goals, role, function, experience, performance indicators, and more. (The most recent versions of each can be obtained by calling or e-mailing CMSA, CCMC, and URAC at the numbers/addresses listed in Appendix A at the back of this book.)

The CCMC certification guide provides insight into the kind of education, clinical preparation, and life experience that will most benefit a case manager. The guide's "Licensure/Certification Requirements" section includes the eligibility standards, education, licensure, and certification criteria that applicants for the CCM credential must satisfy prior to sitting for the CCM examination (see Appendix 1–A).

In addition to CCMC's education, licensure, and certification criteria, applicants must meet the qualification of one of three employment experience categories. Category 1 calls for "12 months of acceptable full-time case management employment experience supervised by a Certified Case Manager (CCM). Supervision is defined as the systematic and periodic evaluation of the quality of the delivery of the applicant's case management services." Under Category 2, "24 months of acceptable full-time case management employment experience" is required. Supervision by a CCM is not requisite in this category. Category 3 lists employment experience of "12 months of acceptable full-time case management employment experience as a supervisor of individuals who provide DIRECT case management services." Verification of this status varies.

According to the *CCM Certification Guide,* applicants must perform the six essential activities of case management: assessment, planning, implementation, coordination, monitoring, and evaluation, and be able to demonstrate that they apply these six essential activities within at least five the of the six core components of case management (processes and relationships, health care management, community resources and support, service delivery, psychosocial intervention, and rehabilitation case management) across the continuum of care that matches ongoing needs of the individuals being served, with the appropriate level and type of health, medical, financial, legal, and psychosocial care. The employment experience regarding core components must also "involve interactions with relevant components of the individual's health care system such as physicians, family members, third-party payers, and other health care providers," and deal with the individual's broad spectrum of needs (see Appendix 1–B).

To clarify those health-related services that fit the description of acceptable case management employment as described in the guide, a flowchart is included. It delineates processes and services that clearly demonstrate the provision of case management activities applying the six essential functions across five of the six core areas beyond a single episode of care (see Appendix 1–C).

Alongside the CCM credential, there are several other popular case manager certification programs. These are discussed in Chapter 14.

NOTES

1. J. Boling and L. Hoffmann, "The Nursing Shortage and its Implications for Case Management," *The Case Manager* 12, no. 6 (2001): 53.

2. C. M. Mullahy and D. K. Jensen, "Case Management: The Cost-Containment, Quality and Employee Satisfaction Link for Self-Funded Employers," *The Self-Insurer* 19, (2002): 7.

3. Towers Perrin, *Towers Perrin 2002 Health Care Cost Survey Report of Key Findings* (New York, NY: 2003).

4. L. Greenburg with G. Carneal, M. Hattwick, "2001 Trends and Practices in Medical Management: Implications for the Industry," URAC (2001): 6.

5. Liza Greenburg, RN, MPH, "New Insights in Medical Management: Results of URAC's 2001 Study of Medical Management Practices," URAC (2001): 1.

6. Commission for Case Manager Certification, *CCM Certification Guide* (Rolling Meadows, IL: 2003).

7. K. Moreo, G. Lamb, "CMSA Updates Standards of Practice for Case Management," *The Case Manager* 14, no. 3 (2003): 54.

8. Certification of Insurance Rehabilitation Specialists Commission, *Case Management Role and Function: Knowledge of Health Care* (Rolling Meadows, IL: 1992).

Appendix 1–A CCM Eligibility Criteria for Certification as a Case Manager

SECTION 3: LICENSURE/CERTIFICATION REQUIREMENTS

To be eligible for voluntary certification as a case manager, an applicant must be of good moral character, reputation, and fitness for the practice of case management; must meet ALL of the licensure or certification criteria described in this section; and must qualify under one of the commission's employment experience categories in Section 4.

All licensure or certification criteria MUST be fully satisfied by the application deadline (November 15 for the spring exam or May 15 for the fall exam).

All requested documentation must be received before CCMC can determine your eligibility for certification.

Criteria

An applicant's license or certification must be based on a **MINIMUM** educational requirement of a post-secondary degree program in a field that promotes the physical, psychosocial, or vocational well-being of the persons being served. A post-secondary degree is defined as any nursing school, college or university diploma obtained after graduating from high school (nursing diploma or associate's, bachelor's, master's or doctorate degree).

The certification awarded upon completion of the educational program MUST have been obtained by the applicant's having taken an examination in his/her area of specialization. If you have successfully obtained licensure through your state, CCMC recognizes each state's criteria for licensure as fulfilling the licensure requirement.

Furthermore, completion of the educational program's licensing or certification process must grant the holder of the license or certification the ability to legally and independently practice **WITHOUT THE SUPERVISION OF ANOTHER LICENSED PROFESSIONAL.**

Definitions

LICENSURE: The commission considers licensure to be a process by which a government agency grants permission to an individual to engage in a given occupation, provided that person possesses the minimum degree of competency required to reasonably protect public health, safety, and welfare. To meet the commission's requirements, an applicant's license must be current and active in the state in which he or she practices. The applicant and license holder must be classified as being in good standing in the state in which he/she practices. Upon receipt of your application, CCMC will provide you with a verification form to submit to the grantor of your license. CCMC allows for Internet license verification; visit the agency's web site and print out the license verification. Then photocopy the front and back of your current license and forward both to the Administrative Office.

CERTIFICATION: The commission considers certification to be a process by which a government or non-government agency grants recognition to an individual who has met certain predetermined qualifications set by a credentialing body. To meet the commission's requirements, an applicant's certification must be current and active, and the holder classified as being in good standing by the credentialing body. Upon receipt of your application, CCMC will provide you with a verification form to submit to the grantor of your certification. CCMC allows for Internet verification so that you may visit the agency's web site and print out your certification verification. Then photocopy the front and back of your current certificate and forward both to the Administrative Office.

Source: Reprinted with permission from *CCM Certification Guide,* p. 3, © 2003, Commission for Case Manager Certification.

Appendix 1–B: CCM Acceptable Employment Experience for Certification as a Case Manager, Essential Activities of Case Management, and Core Components of Case Management

SECTION 4: ACCEPTABLE EMPLOYMENT EXPERIENCE

Categories

In addition to satisfying CCMC's licensure or certification criteria, applicants must qualify under **ONE** of the employment experience categories described below. For any employment to be considered, it must have been acquired after the ability to become a state licensed/certified professional, and must be fully satisfied by the application deadline (November 15 for the Spring Exam or May 15 for the Fall Exam). To be considered acceptable, the employment must be verified.

All part-time employment experience will be pro-rated based on a 37-hour full-time work week. All work experience, past and present, may be considered by the commission in determining a candidate's eligibility for certification. Internship, preceptorship, practicum, and volunteer activities are **NOT** considered acceptable employment experience.

The employment experience categories are as follows:

Category 1   12 months of acceptable full-time case management employment experience supervised by a Certified Case Manager (CCM). **Supervision is defined as the systematic and periodic evaluation of the quality of the delivery of the applicant's case management services.**

Category 2   24 months of acceptable full-time case management employment experience. (Supervision by a CCM is not required under this category.)

Category 3   12 months of acceptable full-time case management employment experience as a supervisor of individuals who provide **DIRECT** case management services.

Verification Process

The information requested is needed in order for the Eligibility Compliance Committee to take a consistent, objective approach to evaluating each application on its own merits. For an individual's employment as an employed or self-employed/

independently contracted case manager to qualify for review, the following conditions must be met:

For Case Managers Employed by an Agency, Institution or Corporation:

1. Each place of employment you list **MUST** be verified by a manager, supervisor, or employer on the employment verification forms that will be sent to you with the commission's acknowledgment of your application.
2. The case management employment verification form must be completed and signed by your manager, supervisor, or employer. It must be accompanied by an official job description (see next section titled Official Job Description) that also has been signed by the individual who signed the employment verification form.
3. **YOU MUST INCLUDE YOUR NAME AND CCM ID NUMBER ON ALL VERIFICATION DOCUMENTS.**

For Self-Employed/Independently Contracted Case Managers:

1. To verify self-employment (if indicated on your application), three purchasers of your services **MUST** complete the form titled Verification of Services Provided as an Individual Contract Case Manager. You will receive three of these forms from the commission. You must attach an official job description (see next section titled Official Job Description) to the form prior to requesting completion by the purchasers of your services. The form is to be completed by the purchaser of your services. The purchaser of your services **MUST** sign both the completed form and the job description.
2. You will also receive a form titled Self-Description of Activities as an Individual Contractor Case Manager that you must complete, sign, and return to the commission along with the job description for case management used in your practice.
3. You are encouraged to send the commission any materials that describe the type of case management services you offer.
4. **YOU MUST INCLUDE YOUR NAME AND CCM ID NUMBER ON ALL VERIFICATION DOCUMENTS.**

Official Job Description

The CCM designation is experience-based. Therefore, for your work experience to be considered acceptable, your official job description must reflect:

1. Your performance of the services encompassed by the six essential activities of case management described later in this section.
2. Direct client contact within a minimum of five of the six core components of case management described later in this section.

3. Your provision of services across a continuum of care that addresses the ongoing needs of the individual being served by the case management process (see next page).
4. Your provision of services that interact with relevant components of the client's health care system (see next page).
5. Your provision of services that deal with the individual's broad spectrum of needs (see next page).
6. That you spend **NO LESS** than 50% of your time on:
   a) the provision of direct case management services; or
   b) the supervision of those who provide direct case management services, in which case you must submit two official job descriptions: one for your position as a supervisor and one for the case managers you supervise. The person who supervises you should be the individual who signs your employment verification form and both job descriptions.
7. If your official job description is global in nature and does not identify all of the case management activities that you perform, have your employer/supervisor/purchaser of services write a letter describing your specific case management activities in order to clarify and expand upon your official job description. This letter must be on company letterhead, signed by your employer/supervisor/purchaser of services, and notarized.

Essential Activities of Case Management

1. ASSESSMENT
   Assessment is the process of collecting in-depth information about a person's situation and functioning to identify individual needs in order to develop a comprehensive case management plan that will address those needs. In addition to direct client contact, information should be gathered from other relevant sources (patient/client, professional caregivers, non-professional caregivers, employers, health records, educational/military records, etc.).

2. PLANNING
   The process of determining specific objectives, goals, and actions designed to meet the client's needs as identified through the assessment process. The plan should be action-oriented and time-specific.

3. IMPLEMENTATION
   The process of executing specific case management activities and/or interventions that will lead to accomplishing the goals set forth in the case management plan.

4. COORDINATION
   The process of organizing, securing, integrating, and modifying the resources necessary to accomplish the goals set forth in the case management plan.

5. MONITORING

The ongoing process of gathering sufficient information from all relevant sources about the case management plan and its activities and/or services to enable the case manager to determine the plan's effectiveness.

6. EVALUATION

The process, repeated at appropriate intervals, of determining the case management plan's effectiveness in reaching desired outcomes and goals. This might lead to a modification or change in the case management plan in its entirety or in any of its component parts.

Core Components of Case Management

Applicants must also be able to demonstrate that, as part of their employment, they apply the six essential activities detailed above within a minimum of five of the following six core components. More information on each component is found in Section 7: The Certification Examination (page 11).

1. Processes and Relationships
2. Health Care Management
3. Community Resources and Support
4. Service Delivery
5. Psychosocial Intervention
6. Rehabilitation Case Management

The core components listed above **MUST:**

1. Be applied across the continuum of care. The continuum of care matches ongoing needs of the individuals being served by the case management process with the appropriate level and type of health, medical, financial, legal and psychosocial care for services within a setting or across multiple settings.
2. Involve interactions with relevant components of the individual's health care system such as physicians, family members, third-party payers, employers, and other health care providers.
3. Deal with the individual's broad spectrum of needs.

In addition, the primary focus must be on case management practice.

Source: Reprinted with permission from *CCM Certification Guide,* pp. 4–6, © 2003, Commission for Case Manager Certification.

Appendix 1–C   CCM Acceptable Case Management Employment Flowchart

IS MY EMPLOYMENT EXPERIENCE ACCEPTABLE?

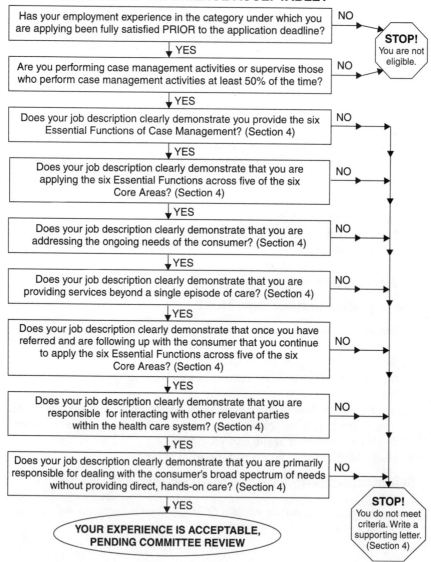

Source: Reprinted with permission from *CCM Certification Guide,* p. 7, © 2003, Commission for Case Manager Certification.

CHAPTER 2

The Case Manager's Universe

IMPORTANT CONTACTS AMONG HEALTH CARE PROVIDERS

The list of health care providers a case manager needs to know is as varied as the places these individuals work. Among a case manager's major contacts are physicians, surgeons, medical specialists, physical therapists, psychiatrists, pharmacists, behavioral health specialists, practitioners of alternative and Eastern medicine, discharge planners, rehabilitation nurses, rehabilitation and job counselors, nurse case managers, social workers, home health aides, family counselors, and medical equipment and service providers.

An addition to the provider group is hospitalists, general internists who practice only in the hospital. The concept was to improve care for hospitalized patients by having one physician on-site full-time at the hospital, responsible for most of their care, allowing office-based physicians to focus on their outpatients. Critics decry the further fragmentation of the health care delivery system. Concerned patients worry that they will not be able to see their own physicians, who are more familiar with their needs and medical history. Advocates point to the benefits of being tended by a specialist in hospital care and to the realities of today's health care system, in which internists no longer follow a patient through hospital care and discharge but refer to critical care specialists. Both sides are waiting to see how the use of hospitalists evolves. While we wait, case managers need to include these specialists in the care and communications loop. The range of facility resources includes hospitals, hospices, subacute care facilities, skilled nursing facilities, outpatient rehabilitation centers, nursing homes, and facilities offering illness-specific, chronic, or catastrophic care.

Case managers must be conversant with providers of specialized care, including, for example, neonatal teams that treat high-risk newborns at hospitals offering tertiary-level care. Centers of Excellence, which are designated areas within major university centers or other facilities that insurers have approved as providers of treatment, also offer specialized care. Also among a case manager's vital resources are specialized hospitals. There are, for example, fully accredited pediatric care facilities such as Stanford Children's Hospital in California, Children's Memorial Hospital in Chicago, and Schneider Children's Hospital in New York. Cumberland Hospital for Children and Adolescents has an Eating Disorders Program for patients ages 2–22 who not only have medical conditions but also are experiencing emotional and behavioral problems. The Mayo Clinic is noted for its team approach to diagnostic work ups, while Memorial Sloan-Kettering Cancer Center in New York City is renowned for its cancer research and treatment. Located in Denver, National Jewish Hospital/National Asthma Center is a diagnostic, research, and education facility that specializes in the treatment of asthma and pulmonary conditions, offering both adult and pediatric programs. Shriners Hospitals in Boston, Cincinnati, Galveston, and Sacramento have a threefold mission: treating severely burned children, conducting research and improving methods of burn treatment, and training and educating medical personnel in the care and treatment of burn injuries. Other specialized centers include Joslin Diabetes Clinic in Boston, Patricia Neal Stroke Center in Knoxville, Rusk Institute for Rehabilitation Medicine (New York University Medical Center), Bascom Palmer Eye Institute in Miami, and the M.D. Anderson Hospital and Tumor Institute in Houston.

Beyond acute care centers, case managers need to maintain an updated database listing facilities with accredited expertise and specialized programs for organ transplants; rehabilitation following head or spinal cord injury, burns, amputation, loss of sight or hearing; and other disabilities and diseases. In recent years, post-acute or subacute care facilities have gained recognition as lower-cost alternatives for those medically complex cases that do not require the depth of service offered by a hospital or specialized care center but demand more than home-based recuperation. Individuals who might benefit from treatment at a subacute facility include patients needing short-term care following surgery, patients with a chronic illness who require intravenous pain control and/or nutrition, patients needing extended or respite care due to permanent debilitating injuries, and patients in a transitional stage of rehabilitation therapy after a fracture, stroke, or amputation. Subacute care centers are designed for medically stable patients and generally offer services such as wound management, infusion therapies, respiratory care, nutritional management, dialysis, TPN, and physical, occupational, and speech therapy.

HMOS, PPOS, MCOS, IPAS, PHOS, IDSS, HCOS, AND EPOS

HMOs and PPOs were originally developed as alternative health care delivery systems, cost management strategies in which services are packaged for a group of insureds. The hope was that by shifting from a fee-for-service system to the use of payment schedules for packaged services, providers would have greater incentive to consider the appropriateness and costs of care when suggesting treatment. Today, PPOs are more prevalent, whereas the traditional HMO model is less common.

In the HMO arrangement, the physicians or practitioners within the HMO group agree to provide set benefits as needed by voluntarily enrolled members for a fixed dollar amount per member. Generally taking one of a few forms—staff model, group model, network model, or independent practice arrangement (IPA) model—an HMO usually offers members the choice of a primary care physician or other specialist from among those participating in the HMO. This primary physician then coordinates all the individual's medical care as well as any needed referrals to specialists and hospitals. Because they were losing patients, HMOs also created a service version allowing participants greater flexibility in choosing specialists and scheduling office visits without a referral, for an extra fee. The group HMO physician is usually employed by the HMO or receives most of his or her patients from the HMO. Staff-model HMO physicians limit their practice to the HMO and are salaried employees. In the IPA model, the HMO arranges contracts with physicians who also maintain their fee-for-service practice and who are paid a blend of fee for service and fixed fee. In a network model, two or more independent physician groups contract with an HMO to supply medical services. The HMO pays an established fee per employee per month, and the physicians or physician groups determine how those fees are split.

Most HMO services are generally covered in full or subject to co-payment. Limitations, restrictions, or nonreimbursement provisions come into play when services are sought outside of the HMO's geographical region of coverage or when medical treatment is obtained from nonparticipating providers. Waivers are usually granted if care given by a nonparticipant was received following an accident or the sudden acute onset of a life-threatening disease. The HMO will then retrospectively review the nonparticipant services and may provide coverage if the appropriateness of the care can be verified. Enrollment in health maintenance organizations has dropped from 80.8 million Americans in mid-1999 to 74.2 million in mid-2002, according to a 2003 update from The Bureau of National Affairs.[1] This is partly the result of HMOs ending their Medicare service to the poor and elderly, a trend that started in the late 1990s, and rising premiums for health care coverage, which compel the youngest and healthiest individuals to opt out, leaving a smaller pool of those who are older and in need of more care.

A PPO basically consists of a "limited provider panel," health care providers selected for their cost-effective style of practice. These providers also agree to lower their fees for services provided to PPO members. PPOs can be sponsored by medical providers, investors, or insurers. Some large national employers have created PPOs (and HMOs and HMO-PPO mixes) as nationwide networks of health care providers for their employees. In a PPO, members can choose to receive care from a provider outside of the PPO network, accepting reimbursement at levels similar to those received from traditional insurance coverage. (Network services may be provided with no deductible or for a lower co-payment than traditional insurance-covered services. Nonnetwork services may be subject to a deductible and higher coinsurance.) Nonnetwork emergency needs may be reimbursed at rates comparable to those for network services.

MCO (managed care organization) is a generic term that encompasses a variety of managed care plan types, such as an HMO, PPO, IPA, integrated delivery system (IDS), or an exclusive provider organization (EPO).

An IPA is a group holding a contract with a managed care plan to provide services in return for a single capitation rate. The IPA then arranges with individual providers to deliver the services on a capitation or a fee-for-service basis. Typically, an IPA encompasses all specialties, but one can be organized for primary care alone or another such specialty. An IPA may also exist as the "PO" element of a physician-hospital organization (PHO).

Often created to contract with managed care plans, PHOs are legal or informal arrangements that link hospitals with their attending staff as business entities. In some cases, any staff member may apply for inclusion in the PHO, or the organization may be closed to staff members who do not qualify or who are part of an overrepresented specialty.

The IDS is loosely defined as a system of health care providers organized to span a broad range of health care services. It is also referred to as an integrated health care delivery system, an integrated delivery network (IDN), an integrated delivery and financing system (IDFS), or an integrated delivery and financing network (IDFN). Anyone else have a headache now? This IDS is established to select from the broad health care provider market to "optimize cost and clinical outcomes, accept and manage a full range of financial arrangements to provide a set of defined benefits to a defined population, align financial incentives of the participants (including physicians), and operate under a cohesive management structure."[2]

Health care organizations (HCOs) are an outgrowth of California's 1993 workers' compensation reforms, which created a certification process for managed care companies, and seek to concentrate on applying the benefits of managed care strategies to work-related injuries. Disability insurers, HMOs, and other medical groups and providers may apply to become certified HCOs; the certification is not required to treat work-related injuries. HCOs are required to provide case management and return-to-work services.

An exclusive provider organization or EPO resembles an HMO; primary physicians are often gatekeepers, providers are often capitated, its provider group is often limited, and an authorization system is applied to care. The word "exclusive" is used to denote that members must remain within the network to receive benefits. Unlike HMOs, EPOs are usually regulated by insurance statutes.

MANAGED CARE

Managed care continues to evolve, as a health care service and as a business. More than 100 million Americans are enrolled in managed care plans.[3] Many new provider organizations have developed (dental care providers are among those moving into managed care networks), and case managers have significantly more entities to sort out and address, as players and "rules" change and the system becomes more convoluted.

Numerous and significant mergers and acquisitions among providers have blurred previous distinctions. In the past, hospitals were entities unto themselves and physicians maintained private practices. Doctors would hang out their shingles and determine the type of practice they would build and how they would treat patients. Today, to capture larger markets and to position themselves as one-stop providers offering a broad range of services, hospitals and physician groups have merged or formed partnerships, just as health care companies and durable medical equipment companies have joined. As hospitals scoop up physician practices, combining them into larger organizations that span communities, we move away from a traditional arrangement in which the physician had greater control over his or her business and often maintained close ties to a local hospital. The balance of power in medicine has shifted from the insurance companies to the large providers.

From the case manager's perspective, such mergers raise quality-of-care and negotiation issues. Case managers are aware of the strengths and weaknesses of the hospitals in their communities. A signed contract establishing a hospital network does not automatically upgrade the technical capabilities or medical expertise of the weaker hospitals. Although advertising slogans assure patients that they will receive the same quality care, in some cases prestigious, university, or teaching hospitals are carrying smaller, less accomplished hospitals.

Decreased competition also affects quality of care. Instead of a variety of providers, we have two or three major players, or less. In our area, for example, smaller religious hospitals are considering a merger with a nonsectarian group to combat a rival medical "dynasty." As providers seek advantageous alignments, care can be inadvertently leveraged out. We once had hospitals and their respective boards of directors responding to the particular medical, social, welfare, economic, or language problems of the community and developing the structure to serve those needs. Now, we have health care monoliths attempting to run "lean and mean." What chance does the smaller hospital's wonderful high-risk pregnancy management program have of being sustained if management perceives it as a duplication of services?

I've also found that case managers have lost some of the opportunity we had to negotiate certain services, and our ability to work with local hospitals is somewhat curtailed. We hear that as part of ABC Healthcare Corporation, the hospital doesn't negotiate with anybody. Visiting a hospital where we had enjoyed a good rapport and friendly relationship with the administration becomes a confusion of red tape. We call a discharge planner and are told that we have to go through ABC corporate, or there is a completely new system in place to navigate. It's very difficult for case managers (as well as physicians and others), and I question whether patients are really being as well-served as some facilities would have us believe.

The burgeoning PPOs and networks are another challenge for case managers. What guarantees that the PPO group in New York maintains the same criteria and credentialing standards as the network in Massachusetts? Case managers need to be aware that while working with one network may seem easier than dealing with numerous providers, we still have a responsibility to know the people we're dealing with, from the physicians to the hospitals to the home care companies. We have a responsibility to look beyond the recognized logo and ads for quality of service. The more complicated the system is, the more on notice we have to be.

Working state to state, case managers may be involved with in-network providers, out-of-network providers, and out-of-state providers. A company may employ many individuals across a state where there are no network providers, or it may use one network in three states, a second network in another five states, plus out-of-network services in all states. A case manager working in a centralized location would find it extremely difficult to sort out and coordinate among these plans. Adding to the challenge are the physicians, home care providers, physical therapists, etc., who may have been accepted to the network or switched to another network within the past months. The networks cheerfully suggest that case managers call them to check on the status of network members, not realizing that the request is an overwhelming administrative task.

For example, an employer group we have worked with for four years uses a network, and we work with its doctors, physical therapists, and others. In one region of a northeast state, the network mandated that all precertification (precert) calls and case management services go through the network staff, rather than the Third Party Administrator (TPA) staff as is customary for employee precert calls in every other region of every other state. We were working a case only to find that it was to have been a network case; we shouldn't have gotten that case. A case manager who is part of a large company that offers its employees many plan options, or a case manager working with 30 different employer groups, each with its own arrangements, faces a huge managerial problem. She must track the employer group, plan, or network, as well as the division of labor within the network.

One major telecommunications group offers its employees a choice among eight different health care plans. Within each plan are options for indemnity coverage, an HMO, a PPO with point-of-service arrangements, and more. Each plan's overall benefits are the same, but the several providers have individual claims processing formats, and they pay claims separately. How can the telecommunications company, concerned with quality-of-care issues and wise allotment of monies, possibly know what is going on when so many different players are spending its dollars? It's an administrative nightmare and extremely difficult for the case managers providing outcomes tracking and cost-benefit analysis reports.

I see the evolution of managed care and the trend of narrowing down providers creating more problems. Patients have less to select from, and already there seems to be less response to certain population groups. The one-size-fits-all concept doesn't work with health care.

MANAGED COMPETITION

Managed competition refers to the very real competition that HMOs, PPOs, and other managed care entities face in getting and maintaining business. Managed competition introduces new criteria for health care decision making and price evaluation, and puts control back in the hands of the purchaser. Within the last few years, the availability of outcomes data has made it possible to review and select a health provider facility based on quality of service and patient outcomes as well as pricing. It is no longer good enough to be price competitive; service providers have to demonstrate effective pricing and good outcomes without sacrificing the satisfaction of patients and their families.

When the term *managed competition* was first coined in the late 1970s by Alain Enthoven, he mentioned "sponsors," agencies that acted as brokers by examining all the health plan possibilities in the field and negotiating with those plans to help a client get the best mix of care and price based on the client's needs. More recently, the term *health insurance purchasing cooperative* (HIPC) has gained acceptance as a way of referring to brokering organizations that serve small employers and individuals. (In some managed care models, there is only one HIPC per geographical region, and all individuals purchase health insurance through that HIPC.) HIPCs and sponsors relate to that version of managed competition that is still in the theory stage. Yet, managed competition is already here, as is evident from the description of the managed competition model that follows.

It is generally agreed that there are four stages of managed competition. In the first, independent hospitals and physicians maintain profitable businesses without any organized purchasing payers. Provider networks begin to form in the second stage, called loose framework. Payments are structured in the form of discounts and per diems. The next stage, called consolidation, signals the emergence of a few large sophisticated purchasers and systems, and fewer private practices. In the fourth and last stage—managed competition—hospitals, physicians, and insurance companies form integrated networks to manage patient populations. Several large providers generally dominate markets. The rest of the providers have either sold their practices, merged with larger groups, or closed up shop.

Managed competition is here today in the form of managed care organizations. The PPOs that are successful are the ones that are able to deliver quality and good outcomes while holding down costs. At their origin, some argued that HMOs benefited from adverse risk selection, that healthier people usually opt for HMOs based on a belief they will not need catastrophic coverage. They are attracted by the lower premiums or have young children whom they can take to the doctor for a small fee per visit—a prime concern during the winter chickenpox-sniffles-and-strep school season. It was thought that the sicker people would tend to stay in the more flexible plans, PPOs, POS (point-of-service), and indemnity plans, which offer the most freedom of choice regarding physician selection, varying sites for care, different levels of co-payment, and reimbursement of customary fees. The challenge for HMOs became clear when the government, one of the nation's largest payer/providers through its Medicare and Medicaid programs, moved its sick and elderly into managed care plans. One can argue that a disproportionate share of high-cost patients was enrolled in HMOs, which reacted by restricting access. The biggest HMOs are the ones that are able to penetrate the market, and those that were and are well-managed are the ones that have survived.

Employer coalitions and business alliances are buying services and getting discounting arrangements from providers of prescriptions and durable medical equipment or from local rehab facilities. They say, "We'll send all of our people to you. What can you do for us?" Employers, insurance carriers, brokers, and TPAs are managing care and cost; they are being aggressive negotiators because of the law of supply and demand.

These changes signal the total management of the health delivery system, with employers sponsoring different levels of plans and consumers and providers sharing responsibilities for risk and choice, specifically in consumer-driven health care (CDH) plans, discussed in Chapter 4. Even when risk, which influences the payments an employer group makes, is a consideration, the employer group still has an edge. For instance, if a company has a high incidence of a particular disease, that is factored in to how the company is rated and the premiums it has to pay. But the company now has an ability to choose from a variety of health insurance programs and health providers and facilities, whether its health insurance network includes an HMO, a PPO, or whatever.

COMPLEMENTARY AND ALTERNATIVE CARE

The use of complementary and alternative care treatments is still considered controversial or "unorthodox" in some quarters; however, especially given the increased cultural diversity of our patient populations, they are among the most appropriate healing techniques for certain patients. Classified as mind/body/spirit treatment, holistic medicine, and Eastern medicine, these alternative approaches can refer to acupuncture, guided imagery, dietary therapy, Chinese medicine, spiritual healing, herbal remedies, homeopathy, meditation, craniosacral therapy, chiropractic care, massage including Reiki, fertility treatments, paranormal healing, Tai Chi, and Yoga, among others.

Premature infants are being aided by "kangaroo care" or skin-to-skin care. Mothers and fathers hold their baby, wearing a diaper, against their bare chests. These babies gain weight and thrive, and are also able to go home sooner in many cases.

The on-line Alternative Medicine section of Health Care Information Resources (http://www-hsl.mcmaster.ca/tomflem/altmed.html#gen) offers insight into treatments, resources for additional information, studies in progress and completed, and fraud issues. Included in the resources the site suggests are CAMline, the Complementary Medical Association, the Alternative Medicine Foundation, and Alternative Health News Online. (I especially like its note on the last references as one that helps us to separate the hogwash from the promising therapies in alternative medicine.) These sites are referenced in Appendix C.

Case managers also need to know about alternative treatment facilities and programs, such as residential and experiential programs for teenagers. Aspen Achievement Academy in southern Utah combines an outdoor therapy program with traditional mental health therapeutic interventions for 13- to 18-year-olds who suffer from psychiatric, emotional, and substance abuse disorders. Working with emotionally disturbed youths aged 10 to 17, the Eckerd Alternative Treatment Program blends reality therapy, behavior modification, individualized mental health services, group therapy, and problem-solving sessions in a wilderness camp setting. In addition, there are camps designed to meet the needs of patient populations, such as Western Pennsylvania Hospital's Summer Camp for Burned Children, held at the Emma Kaufmann Camp in the Blue Ridge Mountains; Camp Barnabas, near Monett, Missouri, for children 7 years old or older with terminal or serious, chronic diseases; and facilities like Gilda's Club in New York City, for men, women, and families coping with cancer. In the San Bernadino Mountains of southern California is the World's Greatest Camp, created for the families of children with cancer. The Adaptive Sports Center at Crested Butte, Colorado, offers outdoor recreation to people with developmental and physical difficulties. Instruction and equipment includes skiing, snowboarding, snowshoeing, ice dancing, dogsledding, snowmobiling, downhill mountain biking, hand cycling, canoeing, multiday river trips, white-water rafting, hiking, camping, and fishing. Designed for children between 5 and 21 who have mild to moderate neurological and developmental impairments, Camp Le Mar is an accredited coed facility in Pennsylvania. Teaching youths with diabetes to maintain good habits for a healthier lifestyle while having a great time is Camp Sweeney in Gainesville, Texas. The Double 'H' Hole in the Woods Ranch in the Adirondacks was founded for children with cancer, hemophilia, sickle-cell anemia, spina bifida, and AIDS. The Imus Ranch in New Mexico is a 4,000-acre working cattle ranch where children suffering from cancer or serious blood disorders, and children who've lost brothers and sisters to Sudden Infant Death Syndrome (SIDS) complete daily chores, are responsible for a horse, and are required to pitch in caring for the other animals.

Located near Malibu, Camp Bloomfield was created for visually impaired and multidisabled blind children ages 5 to 18. Dating from 1868, Vacation Camp for the Blind in Spring Valley, New York, is a year-round facility providing a rich array of sports, cultural, rehabilitation, and educational programs for blind and visually impaired adults and children with disabilities.

KidSource online (www.kidsource.com) lists resources and guides from associations and private organizations, such as Easter Seals and the Hemophilia Association. *Summer Fun: The Parents' Complete Guide to Day Camps, Overnight Camps, Specialty Camps, and Teen Tours* by Marian Edelman Borden is recommended by *Library Journal*.

Other resources case managers need to be aware of include nursing services, home health agencies, infusion and respiratory care companies, counseling centers, surgical supply firms, and a host of local, state, and federal agencies and associations targeting problems such as aging, learning disabilities, and physical disabilities. There are national organizations for most major diseases, and it is the case manager's responsibility to know about them. As an example, the National Head Injury Foundation will send on request a state-by-state listing of facilities treating head injuries at various levels, from the catastrophic stage through transitional stage to rehabilitative care. National organizations are invaluable for assistance in another area: education. The American Lung Association and the American Heart Association are two prime providers of free educational materials. The Alzheimer's Foundation offers articles on estate planning, Medicaid law, long-term care insurance, and other topics written by the foundation's legal advisory board. The YMCA runs a healthy back program and is willing and able to provide informational pamphlets.

Where can a case manager begin to locate these legions of specialists, services, and support personnel? *The Case Management Resource Guide,* updated annually, includes information on mail-order pharmaceutical companies, pediatric home care, hand rehabilitation centers, hotlines for physical and mental disorder, and auto remodelers that can fit a car for a wheelchair ramp. A national guide, it is divided into four regional volumes and is published by Dorland Healthcare Information and available from Amazon.

Other resource volumes include *How to Find the Best Doctors,* which includes hospitals, medical centers, specialties, specialists, and physician rating references. This series by John J. Connolly, Sandra Gainer, and others, offers editions for various parts of the country, updated on a rotating basis and published by Castle Connolly Medical Ltd. In addition, look for *America's Top Doctors: The Best in American Medicine,* second edition (by Castle Connolly Staff, Compiler, *et al.,* Castle Connolly Medical Ltd.), *Consumer's Guide to Top Doctors* (by Center for the Study of Services Consumer's Checkbook Magazine Staff), *America's Best Hospitals* (by editors of *U.S. News & World Report* with the National Opinion Research Center at the University of Chicago, J. Wiley & Sons), and *The Best Hospitals in America,* second edition (by John W. Wright, Linda Sunshine, Gale Group), and *Voluntary Health Organizations: A Guide to Patient Services* (Labe Scheinberg, Demos Medical Publishing; out of print but available). Also check for regional volumes that cover the array of facilities and services in your area.

As a case manager weighs the best solution for an individual, she must remember to examine all alternatives the patient is entitled to as well as possible overlapping resources. For example, if the case manager can refer a patient to one of the Lighthouse sites supervised by the Association for the Blind in the state, dollars may be conserved for insurer-provided care. For additional information on medical facility and service directories, please refer to Appendix A at the end of the book.

STANDARDS OF CARE

How does one distinguish the professionals from the we-do-that-toos? One method of evaluating an organization is to check whether there is a governing body or written standards of care. Today, there is a much greater emphasis on standards of care, facility accreditation, and the good standing of medical practitioners than existed a decade ago. For instance, rehabilitation facilities are accredited by the Commission on Accreditation of Rehabilitation Facilities (CARF). The National Committee for Quality Assurance (NCQA) provides accreditation for health care organizations, and for managed care organizations in particular. The Health Plan Employer Data and Information Set (HEDIS) is sponsored, supported, and maintained by the NCQA. It is a set of standardized, quality performance measures to help employers and other purchasers evaluate health plan operations.

We now have evidence-based medicine, and guidelines for care, and it is the case manager's responsibility to bring each patient as close as possible to these standards. It is our role to ensure that patients have access to information and can choose a physician, facility, and health plan, and evaluate them in light of others of the same class, to judge the methods and measures that have proven most effective. We want to move our patients into systems in which standards of care are utilized effectively.

When there are no recognized standards of care or when an individual is being evaluated, the best strategy is to combine available performance criteria information with a personal critique. Some case managers create their own facility or individual review form to separate core quality from showcase dressing. Questions might include these: How does the specialist or medical facility director answer questions—directly or by responding with his or her own questions? Is the facility truly open to sharing information on its programs or is it reciting the five-minute marketing speech? Is a request to attend a team conference met by resistance or a welcome? An individual or a group trying to control access to or hide background information should set off an alarm. The case manager should begin to suspect that getting complete reports on a patient's progress will be an onerous task.

Individual specialists should be board-certified in their field, have teaching experience, an active license, and a strong hospital or facility affiliation. Because there are subpar credentials, check the certifying agency. For example, in New York, the Medical Society of the State of New York has published a medical directory that lists credentialed practitioners in a number of specialties. The State Education Department can provide information on whether the physician is currently licensed and registered in New York State.

National medical societies can offer guidance on how to verify credentials. One can compare and research physicians at www.healthgrades.com, or contact the Board of Medical Specialties to confirm whether a physician is board-certified and to get the number of individual specialty boards. The Board can be reached at 1-800-776-2378. Found in the reference sections of most libraries, *The Directory of Physicians in the United States* (by the American Medical Association, 2000), the *Medical Directory of New York State* (Medical Society of the State, 1999), and *The Official Abms Directory of Board-Certified Medical Specialists,* 35th edition (by American Board of Medical Specialties, W. B. Saunders, 2003) list qualifications of individual physicians, including where the physician attended medical school and received residency training, board certification, hospital affiliations, type of practice, and other information. At HealthGrades, located at www.healthgrades.com, one can find a physician, physician in a specialty, and information on hospital outcomes, nursing homes, home health agencies, hospice, and other services.

Whether reviewing a person or an agency, ask for names and phone numbers of references. If a home health agency provides dated information—case managers it last worked with when an actor was in the White House—question its capabilities. If a physician is unwilling to give references, question his or her reliability (the same goes for an agency). Medical "report cards" for physicians and facilities exist for each state.

Another way case managers can educate themselves on the appropriate levels of expertise and service to expect from providers and suppliers is to become members of local and national associations. Meetings planned by professionals working within separate disciplines and condition- or illness-specific conferences are excellent sources of information and resources. At conferences with exhibitors, case managers should talk with adaptive equipment vendors, marketers of oxygen-supply devices, prosthetics designers—and ask every question that comes to mind, including costs of equipment and services. Then, when reviewing bids from suppliers, they will have enough background to spot the inclusion of unnecessary equipment or overzealous billing. They will be more savvy and capable of providing improved advocacy for patients and more effective use of resources.

NOTES

1. "National HMO Enrollment Decline Continues Through Mid-2002, Report Says," *Health Plan & Provider Report,* The Bureau of National Affairs, Inc. © 2003. http://healthcenter.bna.com/pic2/hc.nsf/id/BNAP-5MQRCE?OpenDocument

2. P. R. Kongstvedt, *Managed Care: What It Is and How It Works*, 2nd ed. Sudbury, MA: Jones and Bartlett Publishers, Inc., 2002.

3. "Health Care Overview: The Issue at a Glance," *Public Agenda Online,* Public Agenda, © 2003. http://www.publicagenda.org/issues/overview.cfm?issue_type=healthcare

CHAPTER 3

Insurance Providers and Administrators

When considering the world of insurance, including insurance companies, re-insurance companies, indemnity providers, self-insured firms, and self-insured/self-administered corporations, case managers are tempted to ask, "Who are those guys? What are the differences in their services and why is it important for me to distinguish between them?" Good questions.

The role of the case manager becomes more complex the larger the company that is insuring and the larger the group that is being insured. Size and type of both the insurer and the insurance administrative arm will impact the autonomy of the case management role, influence (if not dictate) the format and frequency of communications, and affect the case manager's ability to obtain approval for allowances or exceptions in coverage should the need arise. In a CIGNA or Aetna fully insured plan, a company customarily pays premiums based on expected case incidences and outcomes. Conversely, case managers often work with patients whose needs are not considered in the typical premium structure. Further, when employer groups are blended into larger groups (PPOs, multiple employer trusts, or business alliances, for example) to increase their purchasing power, case managers find themselves layers away from the decision makers—the chief executive officers (CEOs) and employers—who sometimes can help speed the approval process when plan dollars need to be utilized in a nontraditional fashion. A case manager might have more flexibility and success working with local or regional insurers and employers because of the closer contact with those capable and willing to make decisions regarding reimbursement.

Insurance companies vary in how they work with case managers. Some firms have in-house or affiliated case management capabilities (e.g., CIGNA has Intracorp and UnumProvident Corp. has GENEX Services, Inc.). Other insurers contract with several case management entities across the country by region, using one for all cases in the Northeast, for example, and another for cases on the West

Coast. Another insurer might contract by specialty, clinical expertise, or by market niche. The larger the insurer, the less likely it will employ an independent case management provider, unless the insurer is sophisticated and already has an in-house regional coordinator for case management services.

Are the insurer's operations contained within one state or does it have national capabilities? Because the activities of case managers are largely mandated by both federal and state regulations, it is the case manager's responsibility to know the effect of state regulations on different health insurance benefits. A state might require that x number of mammographies per year be covered for women in a certain age group as part of the regulations companies must follow if they want to write insurance in that state. (Under Employee Retirement Income Security Act [ERISA] guidelines, companies that self-insure are not compelled to hold to those same minimum benefits regulations and provide equivalent benefits. For example, employer groups can choose to limit their fiscal responsibility for HIV-related treatments over a claimant's lifetime.)

In the majority of cases, case managers are employed by the payers, the insurers, and their work is governed by the group, department, or agency carrying the fiduciary responsibility for the benefit plan. This entity defines what will be covered and when coverage will be cut or phased out to ensure that no one person or group of persons makes excessive claims that consume all the benefits dollars in the plan. As the plan or insured group becomes larger, the efforts to provide appropriate, timely, cost-effective care can become convoluted. With numerous layers of fiduciaries, insurers, administrators, and claims adjustors to contact for approval, the patient's experience is often over before a decision is reached.

BASIC INSURANCE AND ADMINISTRATIVE COMPANY PLAYERS

In traditional insurer-client relationships, a company or individual pays an annual premium to an insurance firm. The cost of any particular benefits plan is determined by the breadth and length of coverage that will be provided; the age, sex, and health of the individual at the time the plan is drawn up; and the statistical likelihood the individual will suffer from a disease or disability. Generally, group plans, in which insurers cover a body of employees or associates in the same industry along with their dependents, are available at a lower premium than plans for single individuals. The entire administration of the benefits plan is managed and handled by the insurance company. For example, when an individual makes a claim against his or her insurance plan, the claims department within the insurance firm processes the paperwork and arranges for full or partial payment or denies payment. Similarly, it is the insurance firm's responsibility to invest and manage the premium dollars it takes in to ensure its ability to pay claims.

In response to rising insurance costs, many businesses have pursued alternative financing methods, such as self-insurance. The switch to self-funding does result in a significant initial reduction in health care benefits costs for individual companies. Business executives nationwide find that self-insurance helps streamline company operations and offers better control over where their health care dollars were used. Overall, self-insurance has been a consistently growing trend, especially among large employers, which can be seen in the steadily increasing numbers of employer-funded PPOs, indemnity plans, HMOs, and point-of-service (POS) plans. In self-funding, companies assume dollar-for-dollar responsibility for employee health care and avoid the spillover of financial responsibility previously included in their premiums to cover other clients an insurer might be carrying. However, self-insured firms run a risk. By narrowing the universe of contributors to their health benefit fund (by eliminating the old insurer's other clients), companies also limit their payout capabilities. Financial liability is spread among a smaller group, often without the application of support systems, such as preadmission authorization, utilization review, claims review, or case management, to help manage the benefit program. A few catastrophic claims, such as for a premature infant, an organ transplant, childhood leukemia, a head trauma, or a burn or cancer patient, can sap a plan's resources and eliminate any bottom-line savings. Another version of self-funding, the consumer-driven health care concept, elicits more employee responsibility financially.

With the appearance of self-funded plans, two other types of service companies became more prominent: TPAs and firms offering administrative services-only (ASO) contracts. TPAs and those insurers or companies providing ASO contracts take on the administrative responsibility of handling claims for self-funded groups. They process claims, answer claimant questions, and act as the liaison between the offices and officers of the payer and the health care provider groups. There are a number of TPAs and ASO companies that at the request of their self-insured employers have begun to render claims management services (e.g., educating client company employees via wellness programs, assisting with medically fragile cases, tracking high-cost cases, and providing comprehensive cost-control programs). They provide these services by subcontracting with a case management or utilization review firm or by setting up an in-house case management or utilization review group. Some self-funded companies elect to self-administer their plans as well, processing all claims through their own claims group.

To handle an unexpected rise in health care costs or a number of catastrophic or chronic claims, self-insured employers often invest in excess or surplus lines of insurance such as reinsurance or stop-loss coverage. It is often purchased in combination with capitated payment arrangements to help protect employers against the fluctuating utilization within their employer groups, as well as those unforeseen, very costly cases. Premiums are paid to a reinsurance firm, establishing a plan that commits the reinsurance firm to step in and cover health benefits payouts in the event that claims should surpass a set dollar limit. "Specific" stop-loss protection becomes activated when an individual's claims reach the deductible level selected by the self-funding group; such protection usually covers up to one million dollars per lifetime per employee. "Aggregate" coverage, which kicks in when a self-insurer's total group health claims outstrip a predetermined level or percent of its annual estimated claims costs, is another form of stop-loss protection that is available.

Minimum premium is another means of financing medical benefits. In this method, an employer pays a segment of the regular premium to an insurer to administer the benefits program and provide specific and aggregate stop-loss insurance. The employer maintains a "bank account" that the insurance company taps for payment of claims. Minimum premium differs from straightforward stop-loss in that the employer maintains the funding source rather than purchasing stop-loss or reinsurance coverage from an insurer. It provides some of the economic benefits and tax advantages of self-funded plans without the deep restrictions that can be associated with fully insured plans.

Too often, employer groups assume that their insurers "know the business" and settle into a false sense of security. Granted, today's insurers are astute in the business of setting premiums and designing benefit plans, but they may not be well-versed in the business of properly managing available health care benefit dollars and the broad array of health care claims. Regardless of the size of the company and its method of insuring and administering health benefits, it is the case manager's responsibility to know the allowances and restrictions of the benefit plan. A case manager subcontracting with a TPA might find that of the TPA's eight clients, three are fully insured and the others are self-insured, each with a unique benefits plan design and claims administration package. Although working in-house with a major insurer and responsible for helping to manage the insurer's own employee benefits, a case manager might have to coordinate her work with the TPA overseeing payment of all claims. A large regional firm with thousands of employees and dependents might be self-funded but contract with an insurance firm for the administration of its plan.

In addition to the setup of the plan, a case manager needs to know the relationship of the referring party to the claimant: Was the request for case management the result of a red flag sent up by the stop-loss insurer? Was it made by the utilization review staff within the insurance firm? Or was it the suggestion of a human resources manager within the employer company? The referral source affects how the case can be managed and the amount of autonomy the case manager will have. Being in a position to ask direct approval to change a treatment plan from a corporate CEO is a far cry from taking a call from the claims department at a TPA—already once or twice removed from the benefit plan decision maker—on a case in which the claimant is covered by an insurer who does not offer reimbursement for case management services. Likewise, if a case manager needs allowance to spend a slightly higher portion of benefit dollars now to prevent spending a substantial amount of money for repeat hospitalizations for complications later on, the CEO of a self-insured firm looking at that scenario might be better able to appreciate the case manager's point of view than the three owners of an HMO, who see dollars spent on case management as an expense that directly diminishes profits because of the way the HMO's profit base is structured. The utmost in cost control and practice autonomy occurs in the self-insured, self-administered employer group that has hired its own medical administrator or case manager to track all stages of the health benefit process, from plan design through claims processing.

ADMINISTRATIVE AND CUSTOMIZED SERVICES

Along with claims payouts, many insurers, TPAs, and ASOs serve as "broker/ administrators" and provide a broad range of specialized or ancillary administrative services. These may include claims adjustment, claims analysis (medical, dental, and disability), risk control services, design and creation of national and regional networks, utilization review, Pharmacy Benefits Management (PBM), and disease management programs. TPAs can help redesign plan language, communicate to employees the items included in a Summary Plan Description (SPD) and their relevance, assist with COBRA administrations, and craft Medical Savings Accounts (MSAs) and 401Ks. Case managers can contribute effectively to each of these offerings.

Because of their clinical medical experience, case managers can evaluate a claims run, ascertaining those areas in which claims are excessive and perhaps indicating special needs (e.g., the need for an employee wellness program). Case managers can also analyze specific claims for use of services. Risk control requires a system to identify possible high-care, high-cost cases so they may be properly managed each step of the way. Again, case managers have the experience and expertise to review an employer's or insurer's covered lives and establish an appropriate "grading" system—not to pull out individuals for restricted coverage or treatment but to provide early warning so that each case receives the attention it needs.

The same skills make case managers particularly effective when an employer seeks or an insurer designs an HMO, a PPO, or a blend of the two. Using a geographical or medical services-based strategy, a case manager can help develop the provider profile most appropriate for the characteristics of the employer group being covered. Utilization review, rather than the lower service fees typically associated with HMOs and PPOs, is the ingredient that leads to reduced expenditures, although it has come under fire as a "gatekeeper" strategy that can prevent individuals from getting the care they need. In developing a utilization review program, case managers, because of their medical background and their tradition of managing each case individually, are in a position to elucidate the importance of establishing a treatment path for each patient. Putting the individual back into the care picture enhances the benefits of utilization review for both the patient and the payer.

THE CASE MANAGEMENT DELIVERY SYSTEM
AND REPORT CARDS

Employer groups are beginning to understand the complexities of the health benefit system, but there is still a need for more comprehensive employer education. The system is undoubtedly complex, and given the expanding numbers of providers and payers, it is not growing any simpler or more streamlined. Education remains an uphill struggle. When they discovered that their health benefit premiums were often higher than the coverage or reimbursement their employees received in return, many employers turned to self-funded plans, and the first- and second-year savings were substantial. On the flip side, any catastrophic case within the employer group became more keenly felt than before.

To control risk, some employers responded proactively by acquiring reinsurance. Those who took the unwise position that the money saved through self-insuring would cover any big cases that came along have learned otherwise.

Employers also had to manage employees' growing sense of entitlement in conjunction with their disconnect regarding risk factors and the true cost of health care. To bring employer-sponsored health care coverage more in line with reality, companies are beginning to share health care risks and costs with employees in the form of consumer-driven health plans, and are educating their covered populations on the importance of wellness.

Report cards were a direct response to employers' frustration with the burden of health care expenses. These tools compare health plan performance in key areas of accountability (quality, utilization, administrative responsiveness and performance, consumer satisfaction, cost control) and help answer the question: What are we getting for our money?

Similar concerns about the quality of health care prompted the Leapfrog Initiative, sponsored by The Business Roundtable in early 2000. It was formed in response to reports on quality in 1998 and safety in 1999 from the Institute of Medicine (IOM), a congressionally chartered, independent organization that gathers and reports objective information on health care. The IOM found that upwards of 98,000 Americans die every year from preventable medical errors experienced during hospital stays (outpatient settings were not included in this study). Not all these mistakes resulted in death; however, other results were similarly tragic—permanent disabilities and the need for additional treatment leading to longer hospital stays and recovery periods. The concept behind the initiative was that a large body of hospital service purchasers would have the clout to initiate improvements in the safety and quality of health care by taking its business to providers with proven records of strong performance in both areas, while at the same time educating consumers in making better choices on hospital care.[1]

A coalition of more than 135 public and private organizations providing health care benefits, the Leapfrog Group represents approximately 33 million health care consumers in all 50 states. It works with medical experts around the country to identify problems and suggest solutions in hospital systems to avoid preventable errors in patient care.[2] Those in the group, including IBM, PepsiCo, Verizon, Xerox, Empire Blue Cross/Blue Shield, and New York Business Group on Health, base their health care purchases on a hospital's progress in adopting three safety measures, or "leaps": computer physician order entry systems, evidence-based hospital referral, and ICU physician staffing. These leaps are considered by the Leapfrog Group to be a starting point toward improving care and will likely be broadened over the years.[3]

Payers want to know how successfully a case might be handled through case management prior to giving the go-ahead for its application. So, current standards lump all cases together. Any patient claim exceeding a specific dollar limit or falling into a specific diagnostic category is earmarked for case management. But what of the situations that lend themselves to case management more readily than the diagnoses would indicate? A pregnancy experienced by a healthy 22-year-old differs from that experienced by a healthy 14-year-old or 45-year-old. Because there is often little leeway in the standards set by payers for case management intervention and there are numerous restrictions on how and when case management can come into play, many opportunities to provide high-quality, cost-effective care are lost.

Case managers have created a win/win scenario; patients and payers are both well-served. Instead of routinely spending $50,000 on a treatment, employers, providers, payers, and case managers manage that money, putting it to its best use. However, case management has a distance to go before it is integrated as a routine element of a benefit plan rather than as an alternative treatment applied to specific cases upon request. Case managers need to expand their communication with employers and decision makers. (For more information on communicating with payer sources, please see Chapter 8.)

Case managers are providing services and working cases in many practice settings. When they are employed directly by an employer group, hospital, or insurance company, case managers have a greater opportunity to review medical care and benefit dollar protection issues thoroughly and to position case management as a solution to escalating health care costs. There are case managers holding positions now (registered nurses, occupational health nurses, social workers with teaching backgrounds), but only a few case managers are involved in marketing the service to CEOs and relatively none in the benefit plan design and decision-making loop. The next step in educating insurance providers and administrators is to convince these companies to put case managers in more pivotal positions and make them an integral part of higher-level management, able to report the true benefit of case management, to expand case management services to multiple lines of insurance, and to increase the value, marketability, and awareness of case management.

NOTES

1. "About Us," The Leapfrog Group, http://leapfroggroup.org/about.htm; June 10, 2003 and "BRT-Sponsored Initiative Focuses on Patient Safety," The Business Roundtable, http://brtable.org/press.cfm/375; June 10, 2003.

2. The Leapfrog Group home page, http://leapfroggroup.org/; June 10, 2003.

3. "NYBGH Board Votes to Become Leapfrog Group Member," *New York Business Group on Health Newsletter* 24, no. 1, Winter 2002: 1.

CHAPTER 4

Insurance Lines and Health Benefit Plans

What is the health benefit plan? And why does it matter? Often, what a case manager can accomplish and the positive impact she can effect upon a patient's outcome are dictated by the terms of the benefit plan under which an individual is covered. It is vital that case managers understand what their role is relative to the type of coverage in question. Some plans contain no provision for case management services, leaving case managers struggling for approval to implement alternative treatment strategies at the eleventh hour—with answers at hand but no means with which to put the care-at-home or subacute care scenario into action. In the optimum situation, case management services are covered by the benefit plan, enabling case managers to make the best use of one of their assets—the ability to respond quickly to complex problems.

Case management, disease management, and utilization review are product lines that may be offered to providers and members within a plan. Indemnity, consumer-driven, disability, and point-of-service are all insurance plans.

In all cases, a case manager must know a policy's caps on dollars or duration, service exclusions, and any specific treatments that may or may not be covered. Basic coverage terms of a plan are available in the Summary Plan Description, an easy reference guide written in lay language that describes the benefits. However, the master contract—called the plan of benefit or the policy of insurance—prevails in any matter. A plan of benefit is a technical and legal contract containing definitions of the terms within the text, all eligibility requirements, and a list of treatments that are not covered.

WORKERS' COMPENSATION

Workers' compensation was one of case management's earliest practice settings. Today, workers' compensation insurance costs are rising at the highest rate in almost 10 years. In June 2002, *The New York Times* reported that the system that covers 127 million workers nationally has seen the average cost of insurance climbing 50% in the last 3 years. *Employee Benefit News* cited insurer Liberty Mutual's 2002 Workplace Safety Index calculating disabling workplace injuries to cost employers $40 billion annually in direct wage replacement and medical payments, with indirect annual costs estimated between $80 billion and $200 billion. As noted in CMSA's National Case Management Week 2003 Media Kit, a 2002 Alexander and Alexander survey of more than 2,000 corporate executives found that 86% of them use case management to help control the upward spiral.

According to Tom Strickland, CRC, President of Systemedic Corporation and founder of the first case management association, conference, and *The Case Manager* magazine, the birth of modern-day case management can trace its roots back to the workers' compensation market in the early 1970s. A true pioneer in the field, George Welch was the driving force behind an in-house "rehabilitation nurse" program within the Insurance Company of North America (INA), known initially as the MEND program. INA's parent company merged with Connecticut General Corporation (CG Corp.) to become CIGNA. The early success of Welch's initiative evolved into a successful CIGNA subsidiary, International Rehabilitation Associates, still in existence today under the name Intracorp.

Describing the workers' compensation setting of a decade ago, Linda L. Chalmers, RN, CRRN, CCM, WCLA, Early Intervention Nurse Case Manager for Zurich Insurance North America, notes that case management started in the workers' compensation field with major insurance carriers, such as Liberty Mutual and Wausau Insurance, hiring "rehabilitation nurses" to help handle the medical aspects of work-related injury claims for the employees of its policyholders.

In those early days, Chalmers notes, the case managers were all RNs that "worked in the field." The registered nurses would meet with the injured employee, their physician, and the employer. The goal of this contact was to assess the injury, develop the treatment plan, implement the plan, coordinate the identified service needs, monitor the results, and evaluate the outcomes. The field grew tremendously during the early 1980s when carriers and employers realized that they could save dollars and get their employees back to work sooner while reducing their loss costs. The difference between the decades is that today there are many more carriers that have their own established programs with internal staff, or who use the services of a regional or national company offering a full menu of case management and managed care products.

The introduction and growth of the managed care model has impacted workers' compensation in many ways. Chalmers feels the change has been significant, saying,

> As states began to write rehabilitation benefits into their statutes, that actually fueled the need for medical and then vocational services and

personnel. While this was happening, the cost of medical care began to rise at an alarming rate. It was thought that a major reason for this was the cost shift that was occurring. The group health carriers were developing products to contain their costs, such as PPO and POS programs, usual and customary bill review, second opinion requirements, utilization review, pharmacy management programs, and more, while the medical providers were shifting their expenses to the workers' compensation carriers, with extended care, unbundled, or unnecessary care. This was happening, many thought, because the providers viewed a work-injured patient as a blank check; there were no cost or service controls, no bill review, no PPOs, and no utilization or any significant means of cost control. The first effort to control medical costs in the workers' compensation arena was the development and mandate for a workers' compensation fee schedule for physician services in a number of states.

As the cost of medical care continued to escalate, increasing the cost of workers' compensation premiums, many states stepped up their methods to control or at least try to manage the medical costs associated with work-injury care. States and carriers began adopting many of the strategies that were developed and implemented by the group health payers. Providers also began to create products that were specifically designed to meet the special needs of the workers' compensation carriers and their customers. For example, in the '80s, PPOs did not include the specialty care providers, such as orthopedic, occupational health, or physical therapy clinics, that are commonly needed and used by workers' compensation, but were heavily weighted with family practitioners, OB, or pediatric specialists, which were not the practitioners appropriate for the care of a work-related injury. Today's PPO looks entirely different, and offers specialty providers that are commonly utilized by workers' compensation carriers and their customers.

So today, even in a state such as Illinois, where the injured worker has 'choice' of their physician, cost management strategies can still be used, such as the provision of a list of PPO providers from which the employee can choose.

Looking at the past decade in workers' compensation, Christopher Wood, PhD, CRC, CDMS, President of Industry Management Resources, finds policyholders/insureds are more savvy as to what constitutes good service from claims organizations. He feels the level of service has improved, with injured workers receiving better care than they did previously. The much greater use of managed care tools (i.e., utilization management, provider networks, and telephonic case management) has encouraged earlier and improved management of provider resources and costs, and a more aggressive and successful constraint on fraud. Another significant change cited by Wood is the increased responsiveness in terms of recognizing and accommodating return-to-work needs, and a greater percentage of employers who have return-to-work capacity at less than full duty.

Strickland offers his insights into the transformation of workers' compensation and its effects on case management (and vice versa) and expands upon this in Table 4–1. He believes that there certainly have been a lot of changes in workers' compensation case management in the last 20 to 30 years. However, the philosophical foundation of this specialty remains basically the same—assisting the injured worker in maximum recovery, and cost containment for the carrier and/or employer by helping manage medical treatment, equipment, lost time, employee/employer relations, and more. Something else that has not changed over the years is the dominance of registered nurses in compensation case management. In the late 1970s and early 1980s, vocational rehabilitation counselors swelled the rank of compensation case management, with the increasing focus on return-to-work issues and several states going to mandatory vocational rehabilitation.

Currently, the specialty pendulum has swung substantially toward nurse case managers in workers' compensation, Strickland notes, and he predicts that nurse case managers will continue to be, by far, the specialty that manages a great majority of workers' compensation cases. He believes this is true for at least two major reasons. One is the substantial increase in health care and treatment costs in both compensation and health over the last 20 years. As these costs continue to rise, employers and compensation claims adjusters have personally seen the cost-containment impact of proactive medical case management. Vocational case management has also become established as an important resource in workers' compensation. However, the vocational percentage has decreased over the last several years relative to nurse case management.

A second reason Strickland sees for the success of RN medical case management has been its ability to consistently deliver the twin benefits of improved medical treatment for injured workers and the savings of claims dollars through a variety of methodologies. Case management (both medical and vocational) was saving money prior to what became the hot trend of "managed care." Case management held its own quite well through the managed care cycle and remains as strong as ever as an effective resource in workers' compensation, whereas many utilization review and discount network programs have come under fire and have diminished or significantly evolved.

According to Strickland, the diminishment of vocational case management in workers' compensation most likely comes from the fact that mandatory vocational rehabilitation services have changed their laws or have modified them to the extent that they are no longer as lucrative for vocational rehabilitation practitioners.

Table 4–1 Issues Impacting Workers' Compensation and Case Managers

There are areas now in workers' compensation that are somewhat new and different from the past, and which will impact the practice of comp case management for several years to come.

1. Work Setting – In the early days of comp case management, you had a relatively small number of case managers working within the insurance industry, but there was a rapidly growing private/for-profit trend which saw a proliferation of private case management companies formed by nurses and vocational counselors, or combinations thereof. Case managers doing primarily workers' compensation now find employment areas in four major categories:

   - Insurance Carriers – The cycle here has been from only a handful of case managers in the earlier days, to a move within the comp insurance industry to rely heavily on company-based case management staff, and now the trend appears more towards contracting out to large or regional case management companies. Many comp carriers have retained a significant number of telephonic case managers, and contract out on only the more complicated or serious injuries.
   - National Case Management Companies – National case management companies, such as Intracorp, Concentra, GENEX, CorVel, etc., retain a large portion of comp case management on the strength of multiple locations, standardized billing, one-stop shopping, etc.
   - Regional Case Management Companies – Usually strong entrepreneurial companies, with a long history of success and expertise in local markets.
   - Solo Practitioners – Individual RN or vocational professionals who usually do work for a smaller customer base of employers or TPAs.

   In all of the above settings, the case manager is generally required to know only the comp laws and regulations of one particular state. However, some comp case managers are called on to travel into adjoining states to provide services and it is critical that they have at least a basic understanding of the state's comp rules and regulations. As has always been the case, the legal and administrative rules of the individual states in comp can directly effect the development of rehabilitation plans and the feasibility of professional recommendations. Issues such as change of physician, impairment ratings, and time limitations on training programs, are examples.

2. Managed Care – Case management was established in workers' compensation well before the introduction of "managed care." The major financial crisis in American health care was in the area of *health* claims, and this was where managed care got its hold. After observing some of the successes that managed care brought to reducing health claims costs, the workers' comp industry began to adopt, on a state-by-state basis, various methodologies used in

continues

Table 4–1 continued

managed care. As is common in workers' compensation, the individual state laws and regulations concerning managed care determine to what extent, if any, the case manager's professional practice is impacted. In those states with minimal or no managed care in comp, the case manager's service – especially medical case management – remains essential for managing effective care and providing cost containment.

In those states that have been active in incorporating comp managed care methodologies, the case managers have to adjust and work with these other cost containment programs. This is true of both telephonic and on-site case managers, as well as those working for employers, carriers, or private case management companies.

In states that allow the use of managed care organizations, there are usually several preferred provider organizations that are utilized by the insurance carriers, employers or Third Party Administrators (TPAs). It is essential for the comp case manager to understand the benefits and structures of these net-works, as they are directly related to hospital and provider referrals, obtaining equipment discounts, coordinating physician care, etc. In states where in-patient (or outpatient) preauthorization is required, the case manager must understand the players and procedures to arrange for surgeries and other types of medical treatments.

Not working appropriately with these types of managed care programs can result in excessive and unnecessary expenditures by the payer/customer. The effective integration of these various managed care programs with case management can result in excellent outcomes and substantial cost savings. However, the issues of complex regulations, varying claims philosophies and a poor spirit of cooperation by other managed care professionals, can make case management more of a challenge.

3. HIPAA and Confidentiality – Since the beginning of the 21st century, privacy and confidentiality issues in the whole field of medical care have been a hot topic of conversation and legislation. Under the current HIPAA law, the field of workers' compensation has been excluded and the focus is primarily in the health insurance industry. However, this could change at any time, and it is wise for comp case management practitioners and their companies/organiza-tions to have clear policies, in writing, regarding their specific efforts to safe-guard the privacy and confidentiality of those with whom they work. Because of potential exposure to HIPAA guidelines outside the realm of workers' com-pensation, some case management companies are seriously considering restrictions of their areas of practice (such as group health, liability, etc.) and thereby not fall under the stringent rules and regulations that apply to com-panies who are a "covered entity" under HIPAA.

Even if your practice is restricted to workers' compensation, you should have in place confidential safeguard policies and abide by them rigorously. Exam-

Table 4–1 continued

ples of privacy issues in workers' compensation for case managers would be: not releasing any case management reports or medical records to parties outside the payer without obtaining a signed consent form; doing evaluations or discussing medical issues with a client in a public facility – such as a physician's waiting room; keeping case management records in locked file cabinets for non-working hours; file protection while traveling, i.e., keeping files in a secured trunk as opposed to public view and access in an automobile interior; a clear explanation to new clients at the time of the initial contact as to your role as a case manager and privacy rules that you and/ or your company follow.

Source: Courtesy of Tom Strickland, President, Systemedic Corporation.

In some ways, the success of vocational rehabilitation/return-to-work programs has impacted the demand, at least in the private, for-profit case management industry. Specifically, the trend with many employers toward self-insurance has slowed vocational referrals. This is not because return-to-work services are not effective, it is because many employers have observed the techniques and successes of vocational counselors over the years and have incorporated these techniques internally. Further, they have been much more proactive in bringing employees back to work on their own in modified jobs or transitional employment programs. The ADA has also had a major impact in getting employers to think in terms of "reasonable accommodations" for workers with residual physical limitations.

As previously mentioned, the basic philosophy of workers' compensation case management has not changed significantly over the years. And in reality, the methods and techniques that worked well 20 years ago still essentially work well today. Obviously, there are newer treatment modalities, improved surgeries, better medications, advanced equipment, funding shifts, and changing legal environments. However, success in workers' compensation case management remains firmly rooted in caring and competent case managers who can be sensitive, firm, creative, and frugal. Combine that with a working knowledge of claims/legal issues and written and verbal communication skills, then success in compensation CM will occur in most cases, comments Strickland.

Unlike group medical, long-term disability, or short-term disability insurance, in which a master plan is written for a national company and health benefits will be the same whether the employee of a California company lives in California, Minnesota, or New Jersey, workers' compensation falls under the guidelines of the state in which the policy is written. Workers' compensation regulations, therefore, vary from state to state for companies with coast-to-coast operations. Similarly, a case manager's activities will also be dictated by each state's workers' compensation process. The benefits an employee in Arkansas is entitled to will not match those for an employee in Delaware. The percentage granted for wage replacement funds may range, and can vary, within the same workers' compensation plan dependant upon the employee's selection of options for benefits only, benefits plus sick pay, or benefits plus sick and vacation pay. Rates and medical benefit exposure for the employer will differ as well.

The state workers' compensation guidelines also take precedence over the funding source. Employers must provide employees with the level of benefits the state mandates, not the level of benefits they can afford. Regardless of whether a company is self-funded, self-administered, or utilizing a traditional indemnity plan, workers' compensation cases fall under the jurisdiction of the state Workers' Compensation Commission, whose laws and regulations set the limits and extent of coverage. A liaison or intermediary agent between the claimant, employer, insurance carrier, and funder, the state Workers' Compensation Commission acts as an advocate for the claimant. It determines the level of benefits, the obligations of the employer, the responsibilities of the employee, and the level of capability and performance that constitutes "rehabilitation." In some states, the Workers' Compensation Board may list those doctors individuals may utilize.

Among the greatest challenges case managers face when working across state lines, according to Linda Chalmers, is keeping up with the regulations. One way that her company, Zurich Insurance, addresses this is by making sure that there are designated staff who are licensed to work cases in a particular state. They also assign designated teams to specific jurisdictions. This enables the RN to become a "specialist" for particular areas. The RNs have access to current information and jurisdictional requirements via Internet sites such as Workers' Comp Connection (http://workerscompensation.com), and are provided in-service training regarding the changes occurring in the industry and regions.

Another challenge has been the need to adhere to URAC standards in order to become and remain accredited, notes Chalmers. The workers' compensation carriers are now held to a much higher standard than in days past. Most recently, they have been required to develop programs and educate not only the health care professionals they employ but also claims personnel about the Health Insurance Portability and Accountability Act (HIPPA), and the importance of maintaining the confidentiality of the medical information that they handle.

Bound by a greater degree of legislation than group medical coverage, workers' compensation cases tend to be more legally involved and litigious than group medical cases. In order to sell group medical insurance, an insurance company must include certain benefits and coverage as designated by the state. Under ERISA guidelines, self-funded companies are exempt from meeting those same mandates for levels and provisions required of insurance firms covering companies paying premiums for benefits. This is what allows for the elimination of medical benefits or top-dollar caps on medical treatment for AIDS or psychological problems in some employers' group health plans. But workers' compensation cases are different. If state guidelines require that an out-of-work person be reimbursed for medical expenses at 100% of cost and for lost wages at 80% or two-thirds of preinjury salary, even self-funded employer groups must provide that level of benefits.

Case managers are also regulated much more by legislation in state-by-state workers' compensation cases than in group medical cases. For a time, South Carolina offered employers the option to leave the system but revised its law in 1996, mandating that employers return to the system by July 1, 1997.[1] Workers' compensation has always been elective in Texas for nongovernmental employers, but those who opt out expose themselves to tort law liability.[2] For certain industries, the state does provide for mandatory workers' compensation coverage, like that under Title 25 of State statutes regarding rules and regulations for "Carriers" (Article 911-A, Sec II, Motor Bus Transportation and Regulations by the Railroad Commission). In New Jersey, the complex workers' compensation law allows coverage to be terminated by either party upon 60 days notice in writing prior to any accident. Under Rhode Island's Department of Labor and Training Division of Workers' Compensation, employees are permitted to claim common-law rights and opt out of the workers' compensation system. (Another example illustrating state-to-state variations in insurance is a New Jersey statute allowing 10 or more employers licensed by the state as hospitals to group self-insure.[3])

Further, states are trying to control workers' compensation costs by limiting options for claimants in filing claims, qualifying for benefits, or attempting to change a negative compensation board decision. Arkansas has required workers to identify the day and time of an injury, rather than simply describing it in general terms. This straightforward measure has reduced fraudulent claims. Connecticut stopped awarding disability benefits for mental or psychological disorders unless they were caused by an injury. In Texas, restrictions were placed on legal appeals by workers on rulings by compensation boards. California established a fund, paid for by employers, that finances special teams to go after fraud.[4]

Those who have only worked group medical insurance cases need to be aware that in workers' compensation, most insurance companies and employers face a double exposure. Although states have varying levels of benefits, insurers and employer groups are mandated to reimburse both medical costs and lost wages. Therefore, a carrier is not only interested in optimizing the results from medical care, but also wants the patient back to work as soon as possible. As a result, case management professionals may find themselves asked to achieve inconsistent goals—medical health vs. a timely return to the workforce. It pays to be aware that an employer's first and only concern might be the return-to-work time frame because the replacement of salary is a greater expense than the actual medical care.

For example, imagine a case involving a back injury. The employee might see a doctor once every few weeks without undergoing any major surgical procedure or complex medical care, such as a laminectomy or extensive physical therapy. Nevertheless, the employer is getting hit and hit heavily by salary replacement benefits. In a group medical case, an employee either has sick leave or disability leave, but the employer is not paying a salary indefinitely. In most workers' compensation cases, the employer is required to keep the job open. Added to the employer's constraints is the fact that in workers' compensation cases, employees are more inclined to hire attorneys if they feel they are not getting the benefits to which they are entitled. The involvement of an attorney is sometimes perceived by a claims examiner or an employer as a roadblock: "Well, this guy has an attorney, so why bother with case management now?" However, this might be the juncture at which case management is most needed. In fact, when a case manager can convince a doubting group of liability examiners as to the value of their services, she might have a group that is dedicated to the use of case management for the enhanced ability to evaluate and control the damages associated with liability claims.

Recapping, the payer's exposure in a workers' compensation case can be much greater than in a group medical case, even though the illness or injury is less severe, and the involvement of attorneys sometimes complicates the situation. Complying with the regulations of different states compounds the difficulty for case management professionals, especially those working for a nationwide insurer. Other variables contribute to the challenge. In mandated rehabilitation states, patient report formats must follow stringent guidelines; case managers must also file specific forms for billing. Further, there are more players in workers' compensation cases. In addition to the claims department and medical rehabilitation professionals, there are administrative law judges, vocational counselors, and vocational rehabilitation boards. Working on such cases can be a nightmare for independent case management companies as they try to keep abreast of changes in workers' compensation regulations in all the states they serve.

On the other hand, there have been changes in the workers' compensation industry over the past decade that benefit case managers in their efforts to guide patients toward the best outcomes, while assisting employers with their staffing and disability pay issues (see Table 4–2).

A single group medical plan or MCO may offer the same benefits from state to state; however, these benefits will be supplied by different providers from state to state. Coordinating and assessing care and services remains a challenge. An independent case management company with licensed nurses in multiple states can work group medical cases in several states relatively easily. To be effective, case

Table 4–2 Improvements for Case Managers in the Workers' Comp Industry

---

Among the more significant improvements in workers' compensation case management according to Linda Chalmers are the following:

1. Employers are much more proactive and offer modified duty programs for early return to work for their employees. In the 1970s, the common reply I received from an employer was, "The employee must be 100%, or we don't want him/her back." Today, I see iron and construction workers returned to modified duty.

2. Employers finally understand the value of Early Return To Work programs and have developed plans and special handling protocols for carriers to help them implement those programs for their injured employees.

3. There is a greater acceptance and understanding of how an RN case manager assists the claims handler/adjuster with managing the medical aspect of claims. In the '70s and early '80s it was commonplace to get a case assignment months following an injury when it was nearly unsalvageable and the adjuster was asking for a "miracle recovery." Now, carriers are likely to offer Early Intervention services. The medical case manager will "triage" the case within 24 hours of the accident, assess its severity, and assist the claims professional with the medical management of the injury. This helps to ensure appropriate care and coordinate a return-to-work plan with the physician, employee, and employer. It is a win-win situation for the employer, injured employee, and carrier.

Source: Courtesy of Linda Chalmers, RN, CRRN, CCM, WCLA.

---

managers have to decide beforehand whether to tackle the workers' compensation arena or stick with group medical.

AUTO INSURANCE

Like workers' compensation regulations, auto insurance policy regulations vary from state to state in terms of medical coverage limits and lost-wage replacement. Some states pay medical costs from the day of the accident. In auto policies, this is called PIP (personal injury protection) or "no-fault" coverage. Whereas New Jersey might offer medical coverage up to $250,000, New York policies may generally cover individuals for $50,000. In North Dakota, PIP of at least $30,000 per person is required. There are states with very low caps, in which auto policies have perhaps $5,000 maximum medical exposure. Where does an individual go when that $5,000 is exhausted? To a group medical plan. Those states with generous medical coverage sometimes provide minimal salary replacement coverage.

Because these variations can create incentives or disincentives for individuals to get medical problems resolved quickly and return to work, case managers need to be aware of the fine points of auto insurance coverage. There are states where, as long as an employee can demonstrate some level of impairment, he or she can continue to remain off the job. This type of provision leads people to tend toward prolonging the recovery process.

Every case manager needs to know the terms of coverage for the line of insurance, the state regulations, and any other plans covering an individual to make the best use of time and dollars. As discussed previously, workers' compensation and no-fault auto insurance policies vary from state to state, but they also differ in structure. In a given policy, does the term "state" refer to the location where the accident occurred, or where the employee resides, or where the corporation has its headquarters office? For example, I have had case managers working a case in Arkansas under New York state regulations. A truck driver from Arkansas was injured in an accident in New York, where his company has its headquarters. The driver recuperated in Arkansas, but the case was treated as a New York workers' compensation case, not as an Arkansas resident compensation case.

INDEMNITY PLANS

The meaning of *indemnity* is determined by its usage. In general, *indemnity* refers to a traditional insurance plan in which reimbursement or compensation for loss or personal injury is provided via a contract. A company or individual pays premiums for a policy that outlines a contract of benefits and entitlements. The formation of HMOs, PPOs, and the applications of self-funded plans were responses to the escalating costs of traditional indemnity plans. Interestingly, we have returned to the same double-digit increases that led to the evolution of managed care as we know it today. *Indemnity* can also be used to describe legal exemption from liabilities—the "hold-harmless" clause.

GROUP MEDICAL PLANS

Whereas workers' compensation plans use terms such as *degree of disability* and *causally related,* and auto policies refer to PIP portions, group medical policies contain a different terminology: *caps, limitations, co-payments, coinsurance, pre-existing, exclusions.* Aside from knowing the exact meaning of these terms, a case manager needs to be apprised of the source of funding that backs a group medical policy. If it is a fully insured plan, the plan may have to meet certain conditions on a state-by-state basis. Is it a premium-rated plan or is it self-funded, PPO backed, or HMO backed? Because employees are able to choose the plan they want to belong to, one employer group can refer to a case manager individuals in any number of plans: fully insured plans, HMOs, PPOs, and so on. Some of these plans will have case management provisions written in; some might not utilize case management.

The business of health care has become so convoluted, created with such complexities, that business owners feel hard-pressed to point out the exact source of the problem. They no longer have long-term relationships with their providers or payers; often, they have a variety of providers and payers from state to state. It appears inevitable: health care rates continue to rise.

Case managers can break this pattern and mind-set. By working with patients, employers, providers, and payers across the continuum of care, case managers can demonstrate that there is not one source of high costs but rather a series of checks and balances along the way in which a case can fall through the cracks and spiral out of control. Case managers help to keep all parties informed and that patient at the appropriate level of care.

In my experience, employers tend to be less involved and less interested in the administration of fully insured plans. Some employers continue to pay the premiums and consider themselves done, paying little attention to the potential benefits of case management programs, wellness programs, cost containment, and management of claims. For these reasons, a case manager might find less flexibility for alternative care arrangements when working within a fully insured plan. On the other hand, I believe case managers will be utilized more and more in the self-funded and risk-bearing managed care entities. A case manager will often find a greater degree of flexibility within a self-funded plan, with its increased or direct contact with the employer chief executive officer, chief financial officer, and the human resources manager.

Case managers should be aware that the group medical benefit structure often changes as an individual moves from one level of employment to another. Is the patient an active or retired employee? A retired employee who has COBRA coverage and is now at the age of Medicare eligibility? On disability and moving into retirement? Adjustments may be triggered by the employee's age as well. A case manager working with a 63-year-old active employee who suddenly retires must have an answer to the question, "How does retirement change the patient's coverage?"

For example, under COBRA, the employer must offer terminated employees an 18-month continuation of benefits under the plan the employee had been covered by during tenure with the company. Coverage extends for 36 months to a spouse and all dependents on the policy at the time of termination. If the employee was disabled at the time of termination—an unlikely scenario—coverage continues for 29 months. The employee is responsible for meeting the premiums.

The extent of medical benefits, in terms of length of time, is subject to the determination of the employer group or union contract. Some companies only provide coverage to their active employees. Others offer benefits to retired employees for a specified period, or design plans with less generous benefits over a longer period of time; if an individual had been with the company for 5 to 10 years of continued service, he or she might receive an additional 3 years on the medical plan. The larger the firm, the more likely it is that retirees will leave with their benefits intact—because of management loyalty to senior staff. For those hired at a later date, and therefore younger, the benefits structure might have been revised to meet the expense constraints of the times.

DISABILITY PLANS

Disability plans can be very specifically worded according to the desire of the employer group or single employer. Self-employed individuals can hold disability policies on themselves. Short-term disability (STD) plans can transition into long-term disability (LTD) plans carrying a different level of provisions. Varying in terms—the policy definition of short-term, long-term, and total disability; the portion of salary replaced; the number of months or years covered—disability plans require individual review by a case manager.

Within an LTD policy, there are two major distinguishing provisions: HISOCC ("his occupation") and ANYOCC ("any occupation"). Under HISOCC, a person must be totally disabled from performing any and all aspects of his or her job. Even if the person can perform three out of four job functions, that one missing function entitles him or her to the replacement of salary. HISOCC usually carries specified time limitations, ranging from 1 to 5 years. In general, a HISOCC plan might state that a person totally disabled from performing any and all aspects of his or her job is entitled to receive a specified amount of dollars for no more than 5 years but no less than 1 year. LTD plans may also be group specific. Physicians and other professionals, for example, tend to establish well-worded policies and often "layer" their coverage, purchasing several policies to provide the salary protection necessary should illness limit their earning power. These multiple disability policies are designed to take effect as claims escalate, and because some higher socioeconomic groups readily pay the more expensive premiums necessary to fund such coverage, the entitlements are generally more generous than other ANYOCC or HISOCC plans.

The other portion of an LTD plan, the ANYOCC clause, is where the rubber hits the road. Under ANYOCC, an individual may not be able to perform all aspects of his or her previous job but may well be able to perform the tasks required in other occupations. Most LTD policies cover individuals up to age 65 totally disabled from performing any and all aspects of their jobs and provide perhaps two thirds of their salary. These policies are expensive, and employer groups are trusting the law of averages and an actuary that while all employee premiums are paying into the LTD plan, only a small percentage of the employees will require coverage under it. Therefore, when a patient has improved to the point of moving from HISOCC status to ANYOCC, LTD carriers get very aggressive. Often, case managers are not involved in any type of intervention until the end of the HISOCC stage, when a carrier feels, "Okay, it's been a year now" (or 3 years or 5 years) and takes a closer look at the particular circumstances of the case.

The trust in the law of averages when writing HISOCC policies has proven to be misplaced. Companies often believe they will collect many more premiums than the benefits they will have to pay out. Insurers thought HISOCC policies would be big moneymakers because of the large population of well-paid professionals who would be interested in the income protection and who could afford the premiums. Indeed, many people did invest in them. However, there are now a large number of policyholders claiming benefits, and insurers have to pay each individual until he or she is 65 years old, unless the patient moves from HISOCC to ANYOCC status.

We were called in by a payer to assess a 41-year-old emergency room (ER) nurse for a return-to-work status for her ER job. At the time of her ER injury, she was working 23 hours a week. The question is not, "Can the job be modified or can the hours be restricted?" Even if we could help her return to work in another capacity at the hospital, she would still receive her benefit from the payer (which is, of course, where the payer's interest is focused in this case) as long as she continues to be disabled for her ER job (HISOCC status). This means she will collect from that policy, receiving $2,000 a month, until she is 65 years old, even though she may be gainfully employed someplace else. Unless her physician releases her for the job description of an ER nurse, the payer is obligated to pay $24,000 a year for 24 more years. For this reason, some companies no longer write HISOCC policies that are open-ended until age 65.

Case managers, rehabilitation managers, and anyone else competent to intervene should know that sometimes STD and LTD policies are strictly wage-replacement plans and lack provisions for medical services. Obviously, it is much more difficult to work cases without that medical arm to put to good use. Despite knowing medical treatment could improve a patient's situation, a case manager might be stymied because medical benefits have been terminated or used up and the patient continues to linger on LTD. To cut short theft losses, other LTD carriers are much more willing to be creative and bend the rules. Such carriers, looking at risk management as well, will buy the motorized wheelchair or electrify the employee's van in order to move toward a solution. Carriers concentrating on vocational rehabilitation are more likely to pursue these alternatives.

As an example, when working with a major corporation that had self-funded all its lines of insurance for employees, I could call the benefits manager directly to arrange funding for medical treatment on behalf of an LTD employee. The benefits manager and upper management were familiar with case management and could see that such medical support would make sense.

In contrast, a fully insured employer might have Prudential as its LTD carrier while buying its major medical coverage from Blue Cross/Blue Shield or Aetna. Coordinating two different carriers adds levels of approval and discussion that hinder the case management-medical intervention process. I could get an LTD case and know exactly what needs to be done medically, but if the medical plan does not cover the intervention and the LTD claims examiner cannot see the need for it, I must make a very convincing argument for a medical course. This is where the financial planning capability of case managers comes into play. Depending on a carrier's exposure—the amount of money it is responsible to reimburse under the plan—the carrier can be willing to stretch provision boundaries to include medical treatment when a case manager can demonstrate that once x dollars are spent on medical treatment, an employee could be off LTD and back to work. Carriers are especially willing to look at a creative case manager's ideas when the employee is a heavy-hitting professional with LTD receipts ranging in the thousands of dollars per month.

Living and working in the real world, it must be acknowledged that not all companies are willing to consider an extension of benefits for their top professionals, even those who hit it out of the park on a regular basis. Mr. Belton, a 51-year-old male vice president in sales and marketing for a food distribution company, kept up a very demanding schedule of devising corporate strategies, heading up his department, attending trade shows where he would stand for long hours maintaining and building client relationships, and even lifting and loading heavy boxes to get the job done. He holds personal short-term and long-term disability coverage, as well as health care coverage through his employer. The same carrier holds Mr. Belton's personal health care insurance policies and his employer coverage. Overtaken by a very debilitating disease that made it impossible for him to continue the physically active aspects of his job, and during the waiting period for his corporate disability coverage, Mr. Belton was let go due to "poor job performance." Perceiving his call for disability coverage as an inflation of his needs in order to gain company benefits beyond what his personal coverage offered, his employer denied the existence of a disability and declined benefits. Our case manager has referred all parties to vocational counseling.

POINT-OF-SERVICE PLANS

Originating in 1988, POS managed care plans include a range of customized care plans most often offered by larger companies. They evolved from PPO plans as companies sought to combine employee choice, cost reduction, and efficient utilization. The most successful POS arrangements are characterized by effective providers, limited network size, and provisions requiring health care providers to share a portion of the payer's risk, making for a more realistic plan design. These plans run the spectrum from open-access HMO plans to gatekeeper PPOs. HMOs with open access tend to incorporate smaller network panels and to be more rigid in their procedures. Consequently, employee resentment is more likely to occur when an employer moves from a traditional insurance plan to an HMO-based plan. POS networks based on gatekeeper PPO models generally include broader network panels, impose fewer restrictions on patients and providers, and allow more range in plan design. Responsibility for overseeing a POS plan falls to a network manager within the company. The key feature differentiating POS plans from PPO arrangements is that a higher level of benefits can only be accessed if care is provided through a primary care provider, such as a pediatrician, an internist, or a family practitioner. (OB-GYNs are the exception to the rule.)

Case managers working cases that fall into the POS category need to ascertain the type of POS the employee is enrolled in—open-access HMO, gatekeeper PPO, or a hybrid falling between the two. To be in a better position to make a case in favor of an alternative treatment, a case manager should also be aware of which party within the network is responsible for what portion of the risk. Is the employer, provider, or payer most exposed to financial risk? The group with the highest exposure to financial risk is the group most likely to benefit from and be interested in case management services.

There is a growing attention being paid to coinsurance rather than co-payment, whether it takes form within indemnity or consumer-driven plans. This emerging option will be interesting to watch.

CONSUMER-DRIVEN HEALTH CARE PLANS

The convergence of several technological, financial, and administrative and provider trends has led to the growth of a new frontier in health care management: consumer-driven health care (CDH) plans. Born from consumers' ready access to Internet-based health information, employers' need to reign in steadily increasing health care costs, the cold reception to medical savings accounts and warm reception to health reimbursement arrangements, and restrictive plan language, consumer-driven health care plans are giving individuals greater choice, responsibility, control, and difficult decisions to make. These and other self-directed plans fall under the defined care or defined-contribution health care model. Essentially, CDHs allow (or require, depending upon individual reaction to the idea) consumers to decide how they want their available pool of health care dollars spent. In this way, the incentive to purchase wisely and limit unnecessary expenditures falls to the employee rather than to the employer.

To be successful, individuals who have no clear idea of the cost of medical care have to become educated consumers and smart shoppers. This is an issue I have addressed throughout my career (some would say, "yes, continually, from a soapbox"). We can recite from memory the price of a loaf of bread, a cell phone with camera capability, a new refrigerator, or a Lexus. How many of us can offer up the price of an MRI, heart bypass surgery, or anesthesia and the technician to provide it?

Early entrants into the CDH plan provider market include Aetna Inc., The Choice Care Card, Definity Health, Destiny Health, Flexible Benefit Service Corp., HealthAllies Inc., HealthMarket, Humana Inc., Lumenos, MyHealthBank Inc., Self Insured Plans Inc., Vivius, and a number of Blue Cross Blue Shield plans (Blues).

In general, consumer-driven health plans have high deductibles that assign the first several thousand dollars in medical expenses to employees, combined with an employer-funded health spending account. Each employee might receive an annual tax-exempt fund of $500 or $1,000 that he is free to spend on any medical expenses he elects provided by any physician or alternative provider, from dental work and cardiology to massage therapy. The employee may take any money left in this personal account and roll it over into next year's account, with no penalty.

When medical expenses top $1,000, the employee pays the deductible, approximately $500. When expenses reach $1,500, the employer coverage takes over, with 80% of costs being paid by the employer and the remaining 20% charged to the employee.

There are several variations on the basic plan. Flexible plans allow employees to earmark a portion of their pretax paycheck dollars for medical expenses that don't generally fall under traditional insurance, such as dental or vision care. In flexible plans, unused dollars must be forfeited at the end of the year.

Using another type of CDH, workers can personalize their coverage by selecting benefits from an on-line menu of coverage offerings. They balance deductibles, premiums, and co-payments to suit their individual needs.

Another plan variation offers a CDH tier inserted into a more traditional insurance policy. This type is favored by some Blues. The variables might include drug formularies, hospital networks, and benefit choice. Premiums are set according to the benefits an employee selects, and workers take on the financial risk for their choices when costs overrun the fixed contribution of the employer.[5]

At this time, providers and consumer groups alike are split on their response to CDH plans. Interest is widespread, although actual enrollment remains low. Cautioning voices cite high administrative costs, the possible loss of tax advantages and provider network negotiated savings, potential rising costs with broader enrollment, and the fact that employer savings are not ensured.[6] Although momentum seems to be building, the next 5 to 10 years will tell us whether this new product is here to stay.

DIAGNOSIS-SPECIFIC BENEFITS

There are conditions and diagnoses that may allow for additional funding through federal, state, and local programs. The availability of programs varies from state to state. A premature baby with developmental delays, such as those caused by cystic fibrosis, may be eligible for state early-intervention programs. Coverage varies from state to state. This can be checked through your state's health department, and other programs such as Children with Special Health Needs (formerly Crippled Children's Services and often called Children's Medical Services) and the state-administered cash grant program, Aid to Families with Dependent Children. Medicare automatically becomes the primary funding source for patients with end-stage renal disease, even those who are active employees, after 18 months of dialysis treatment, but only for services related to the renal condition.

For those with physical limitations or disabilities, such as the legally blind, there are also federal and state programs that help stretch funding dollars. Easter Seals aids those with muscular dystrophy; the Shriners have funds available for burn victims. As citizens and taxpayers, patients are entitled to the offerings of these and other programs. (Unfortunately, most case managers do not take as much advantage of these alternative sources as they could. This is an area in which case managers need to expand their activity.)

Admittedly, utilizing these funds is not always easy or straightforward. Working with state or federal funding sources is often more difficult for case managers because of the bureaucratic layering. In any state-operated or federally funded program, the rules are sometimes so stringent that they allow for no flexibility at all, even when it would seem that a more cost-effective solution is available. For example, some regulations force case managers to spend more money. Case managers are mandated to use only Medicare-certified agencies in some state Care at Home program cases despite the fact that such agencies may be as much as 50 to 100% more expensive than another home care agency. In its effort to protect both those people who might not be able to fend for themselves and the taxpayers, Medicare has adopted rules that are not always in anyone's interest.

Further, case managers will find that government billing and report formats are entirely different from those used in the private sector. Case managers with a high overhead might not be able to afford to handle mostly Medicare cases because of the significantly lower profit margins. In addition to generating an increased number of diverse reports and tracking down agencies that are delinquent in payments, case managers will have to contend with a high turnover rate among government staff (necessitating reintroductions to case management), regulatory changes, and midstream program cuts.

TRADITIONAL INSURANCE VERSUS SELF-FUNDED PLANS

In working with a number of major insurance companies that provide traditional insurance (a.k.a. indemnity plans and premium-based plans), I have found that there appears to be less willingness to be flexible with benefit alternatives. This may be because the premiums have been set based on known experience (the history of health benefit usage for that type and number of employees) and an anticipated projected cost for that employee group over time. The insurer has been investing or managing the premium income to make certain there will be enough funds to cover employee claims. A change in the benefit payout—even if it lessens the payout—is perceived as a disruption to the system. There also seem to be rigid constraints on adopting options that, even at first and second glance, appear sound from a business-management perspective. When case management might result in an extra expense or administrative cost that the insurer will have to absorb at the year's end, a traditional insurance company almost requires a guarantee of projected savings neatly spelled out, which is brought back to the employee group for review at a multitude of levels prior to taking action.

With one major insurer, I had to complete a cost-benefit analysis immediately following my initial evaluation before the insurer could determine whether it felt case management would be viable in each particular case. Instead of being able to blend our experiences, pulling on the volumes of past history, I had to justify case management again and again. While the reams of documentation were prepared for the claims managers and everyone else in the approval process, we were missing opportunities to help the patient and save benefit dollars. During the 3 to 4 weeks it took for all levels to decide that case management might indeed be a good idea, we missed more openings. I have no problem with the demand for a round-figure estimate of potential cost savings, but in these instances it seemed that the carrier was asking case managers to become actuaries.

The approval process itself is too convoluted, too enormous to be successful, fraught with so many players and layers, and "we-have-to-talk-with-legal" situations that case management options become too big a "problem" to be resolved. The "problem" is twofold: getting to the decision maker and presenting the information.

If case managers could go directly to the group paying the premiums and tell them their options and alternatives, they could snap the trap and get their jobs done. But case managers dealing with traditional insurance most often talk first to agents, then brokers, and case management reports are finally presented by marketing managers or claims managers instead of the case managers, who are of course closest to the issues. There seems to be insufficient education and preparation by case managers as to what case management can accomplish and an inability on the part of large insurers to take a successful pilot case management project and make the transition to a successful corporatewide program.

For example, suppose a case manager is assigned a case by a large carrier, a case that had been directed to the carrier by its preadmission/concurrent review contractor. By the time the case has come to the attention of the insurer and has been determined to be appropriate for case management, several days have passed. The patient has cancer and is in the hospital now. The insurance contract has an absolute limit on home health benefits, no more than 30 visits per calendar year, but unlimited dollars can be spent in hospital care. Other than a hospital, it seems there are very few places where this patient could be cared for—at a skilled facility or perhaps at home with multiple support services. The indicators seem to dictate that the person remain in the hospital.

After seeing the patient on-site, the case manager follows up her visit with a verbal report to the insurer's in-house case management contact. The patient wants to go home, and the case manager wants to move him out of the hospital as soon as possible. Such a move will not threaten his current medical status or recovery. The insurance contact has to discuss the plan with her manager, then bring it to the service representative who reviews it with the service manager to determine whether a plan exception can be made. The service manager wants to speak with legal counsel, and then there is the meeting of the trustees next week, where they will see if they can do something about it. Meanwhile, alternative care is in place, the patient is poised to go home, but the contract does not allow it. The case manager needs an exception but cannot get a decision, and the hospital charges are adding up.

Now consider the same basic scenario with the insurance provided by a self-funded employer group that has a TPA administering its claims. The benefit plan contains the same language limiting home health visits to 30 per calendar year and providing unlimited hospital benefits. Through the same process of identification—via a preadmission/concurrent review contractor—the case is red-flagged in the claims department of the TPA. Knowledgeable about case management, the claims adjuster contacts the TPA's case management contractor. Returning from her on-site visit, the case manager talks directly with the employer's service representative and the claims department within the TPA, outlining the alternatives for the patient, who requires support services and really wants to go home or at least into a less intensive care setting. With case management, a program can be constructed that results in the best care for the patient and saves the plan substantial benefit dollars.

The TPA's service representative contacts the fiduciary or controller of the benefit plan, who sees the economic sense of adopting the use of case management. (Fiduciary responsibility obliges the controller not only to meet the needs of the individual but to safeguard dollars for the needs of the entire benefit group.) By deciding for case management in this instance, the controller creates a win-win scenario—quality of care is increased and cost is decreased. The recommendation and decision take a few hours, as opposed to the days needed in a large insurance firm.

This is not to say all TPAs have seen the light and welcome case management with open arms. The issue really centers on a level of sophistication and the willingness to make decisions and assume a controlled risk regardless of the insurance benefit system. In general, the larger the organization, the more tortuous the decision.

Previously, TPAs tended to be small and local, whereas insurance companies tended to be larger and operate nationally from a central location. Through more recent mergers and acquisitions, there are now larger regional and national TPAs, although this in itself is not a guarantee of more seamless operations. A national TPA with a certain level of sophistication might contain its own case management group, contract with several case management companies across the country, or find a case management provider with nationwide capability. The role of case management within the TPA world is as variable as the TPAs and the organizations that employ them.

I believe my frustration with the convoluted decision-making process within some larger insurance firms remains an industrywide frustration. When I have the opportunity to work one-on-one with an employer group or a small group of payers, whether within a claims department or a TPA—or when I speak with CMs in a large company—and show them what a smaller firm has been able to achieve for patients and payers, their eyes light up. If we can restrict the players in traditional-insurance decision making to the key people, we have a chance at success. The difficulty of working with a larger complex bureaucracy provides a strong argument for becoming self-funded—it is the control of decisions and dollars that makes case management programs work. Case managers need to spend more time bringing their successful scenarios and pilot projects to the marketplace. Education and proof of case management's viability will make case management a more readily used medical- and business-management tool.

STOP-LOSS INSURANCE PLANS

Because of their position in the insurance industry, stop-loss insurance carriers (reinsurance carriers) are of special interest to case managers. They can see more clearly the positive effects of case management. Many employer groups, whether utilizing traditional premium-based insurance or a self-funded plan, set a threshold over which the financial responsibility for health benefits will be borne by a stop-loss carrier. Handling only the big-cost cases, stop-loss carriers absolutely see the benefits of case management. Customarily, a reinsurer requests a specific limit report—notification when a claim reaches 50 or 75% of the set threshold. At that point, the carrier might intercede and put case management in place or have written into the stop-loss agreement that a case manager be automatically assigned by the company when a claim hits its specific limit. In fact, many stop-loss insurers mandate cost-containment measures, agreeing to write reinsurance only if the company puts preadmission review, case management, and other managed care strategies in place.

Reinsurers are looking closely at how they can best protect their layer of coverage from exposure to financial catastrophe. A company might have health care benefits of a million dollars per covered life, with a threshold set at $100,000 with a reinsurer. This means there is coverage for patients for claims of $150,000 or $250,000, but the company only pays the first $100,000 out of its group coverage and is reimbursed dollar-for-dollar by the stop-loss carrier for any costs over the threshold up to $1 million. Therefore, reinsurers are very interested in using case management to keep benefit payouts beneath the level of stop-loss. If a case manager can help manage health care and costs, keeping benefits payouts from moving upward into the stop-loss range, the firm saves not only in its fiscal year but also in the next year, because premiums are based on claims experience. Just as the stop-loss carrier uses case management to protect it from high dollar losses, the employer group itself should be seeking the same protection.

Using this information, case managers can create opportunities by "creating the need" for case management (i.e., identifying the need and demonstrating it). When I talk to employers, I tell them that for many organizations, stop-loss coverage can be hard to obtain. The premiums can become so costly that company managers are forced to raise the group's threshold—the amount of money the company is responsible for—higher than the firm can actually carry. However, if an employer group can tell a reinsurer that it already has case management and other cost-containment strategies (preadmission review, concurrent review) in place in the first layer of coverage, the reinsurer might be more inclined to write coverage for the group, more assured that high numbers of catastrophic cases will not reach the stop-loss layer.

MULTIPLE-EMPLOYER BENEFIT PLANS AND TRUSTS

Prior to the passage of the Taft-Hartley Act in the 1950s, there was no mandated health care coverage for individuals who worked for multiple employers during the course of the year. Unlike the office workers employed year-round by a single firm, the organized laborers employed annually by various contractors (carpenters or painters who worked out of a union hall) had no single organization sponsoring a health benefit plan. The Taft-Hartley federal labor law included a number of citations, among them a provision allowing for the establishment of multiemployer benefit trusts (a.k.a. welfare funds). Funded by multiple employers, a trust of this type is regulated by a board of trustees (with union and employer positions equally represented), which determines the operative and administrative rules. As in a pension fund, the monies are gathered and placed in a trust overseen by a welfare plan administrator. The manager at ABC Building Co. will send in a monthly statement listing the individuals employed by ABC, the hours worked, and the amount ABC owes to the fund on the workers' behalf. There is then a pool, the "Carpenters Health and Welfare Plan" pool, for instance, from which health benefits can be drawn.

Unions and associations, such as the local truck drivers or Writers Guild of America also offers benefits to members. These groups are able to purchase services at discounted group rates.

Case managers with patients who are covered by a multiemployer trust should ascertain the name of the welfare plan administrator (or health and welfare officer) for assistance in clarifying benefits. Eligibility for these trusts is complex and can fluctuate from quarter to quarter. The hours a carpenter works in the first quarter will be applied to his or her coverage for the second quarter. If the carpenter does not have the required hours of employment to cover plan participation, he or she might have to self-pay for a quarter to maintain eligibility.

It is illegal to form a union for the sole purpose of providing or obtaining insurance benefits. Case managers can be involved unwittingly in a welfare fund or trust that is not sound. After negotiating a discount in good faith for prompt payment, and putting one's reputation on the line with a provider, it is a shock to find that there is no money to pay claims. It might be that the fund monies were poorly administered, or dollars fell short as unmanaged cases drove up costs and drained the fund. It is always wise for case managers to know as much as possible about the type and health of the welfare fund payer.

VIATICAL SETTLEMENTS

Originated in the late 1980s and very popular in the late 1990s, viatical settlements enable someone facing a terminal illness to utilize the present-day value of their life insurance policy to ease financial burdens. They are arranged when companies purchase life insurance policies from people with limited life expectancies (less than 8 years), offering the *viator* (the owner and potential seller of the life insurance policy) a cash settlement based on the policy's value and the viator's life expectancy, generally ranging from 40 to 80 cents on the dollar. Viators may also elect to collect an accelerated death benefit in cash and viadicate the remainder of the policy. Shorter life expectancies generally translate to larger viatical settlements.

A viator with 6 months to live might be offered 80% of the policy's face value, whereas a person who is expected to live for 36 months might receive only half of the policy's face value. This is because ownership of the policy and beneficiary rights transfers to the viatical company, which continues to pay the premiums. When the viator dies, the viatical company cashes in the policy for its full face value. Its strategy is to make a profit by reaping a higher return from the policy's face value than it paid out in premiums or to the viator. Although certain viatical companies will purchase insurance policies from people with life expectancies of more than 4 years, some only buy from viators with less than a 6 months' prognosis. If a viator lives longer than anticipated, the viatical company's profits diminish due to increased premium payments.

Viatical settlements offer viators—people with terminal illnesses who often are unable to continue working and are, therefore, financially squeezed—the funds to pay for food, rent, medical bills, unreimbursed medical expenses, the mortgage, or a vacation. Policy owners, rather than beneficiaries, benefit from the settlement, as is appropriate; a mentally competent person has a right to decide how and when to use his or her assets.

A person can decide to sell only a portion of his insurance policy value to the viatical provider and leave the remainder of its assets to beneficiaries. Using some or all of an insurance policy's worth can enable a person/family to keep a house, property, or an heirloom chest of drawers, rather than having to put them on the market to raise funds for health care, food, and the electric bill.[7]

Initially a response to the financial needs of people with AIDS, the viatical industry now is a resource for any terminally ill patient. As protease inhibitors and pharmaceutical cocktails have proven more effective in treating AIDS, fewer viatical companies are purchasing policies from people with AIDS, and some have stopped altogether. Those utilizing the settlements might have cancer, Alzheimer's, or other conditions.

Any individual, family, or group of friends coping with a terminal illness is obviously in a stressful and sometimes heartrending situation. When case managers are working with a client considering arranging a viatical settlement, they can assist by helping them obtain accurate information. Areas to cover include:

- Tax ramifications and the settlement's effect on other benefits, such as Social Security or Medicaid
- Alternatives, such as a personal loan, cash advance on credit cards, or liquidating other assets
- The viatication of a portion of the value of the life insurance policy according to the viator's needs
- A review of licensed viatical companies (some "companies" are merely brokers who connect a self-funded group of investors with an interested viator)
- A contract containing a reclusion clause of 15 to 30 days, which allows the viator to void the contract

- The assistance of a knowledgeable financial adviser
- The assistance of AIDS service organizations to identify reputable viatical companies
- Negotiations with at least four viatical companies

Resources for information on viatical settlements include the Viatical Association of America, National Consumers Helpline, National Viatical Association, viaticaladvocate.com, idealsettlements.com, and viatical-expert.net, listed in the book's Appendices A and C.

Similarly, life settlements create cash from a non- or underperforming asset, allowing policy owners to cash out of unwanted, unaffordable, or obsolete life insurance policies. Senior settlements and lifetime settlements are two forms of lifetime settlements that have become tools in the estate planning for seniors. Another option is the accelerated death benefit (ADB), discussed in Chapter 17.

NONTRADITIONAL POLICIES

There are also a number of nontraditional supplemental policies currently available that, although not necessarily recommended for purchase, are often selected by individuals seeking more comprehensive coverage.

Disease-Specific Policies

Covering a broad range of conditions (including, but not limited to, cancer, Alzheimer's, and asbestos exposure), such plans provide benefits upon a confirmed diagnosis of the specific problem by a physician.

Cancer Policies

While working on behalf of one patient, I discovered he had paid for a cancer insurance policy due to the high incidence of cancer in his family. This policy allowed for greater benefits than his health plan or an LTD policy would have provided. To receive the entitlements of a cancer policy, an individual must have a confirmed diagnosis of cancer as described in his or her policy. Although a broad number of cancer policies have been purchased, they are not recommended to the general public because of the limitation of the coverage. People are usually encouraged to put the money they might spend on a cancer policy toward expanded health plan coverage instead.

Alzheimer's Policies

These are seen as very limited and costly policies. The stated qualifications for nursing home coverage—a key issue with this type of policy—generally preclude any history of Alzheimer's within a family, eliminating the patient group most likely to benefit.

Occupation-Specific Policies

AIDS and HIV policies are sold to law enforcement officers and fire fighters, who, because of their occupation, are at a high risk of exposure to HIV infection through lifesaving efforts, resuscitation procedures, or hostile bites.

Care Settings: Long-Term Care, Home Care, and Nursing Home Policies

Long-term care plans (a.k.a. home-care policies) are now being perceived as an insurance vehicle that everyone in our society needs to look at and consider for themselves. We are now seeing high numbers of these policies, and will continue to see them as people age and face financial liabilities that could be devastating. Meant to meet the bulk of expenses for unexpected catastrophic events, such as a head injury, long-term care policies fill the gaps in a plan that might not cover custodial care or other treatments no longer considered part of a traditional health care plan. As employers look for ways to protect themselves from long-term health care responsibilities, medical policies—whether traditional indemnity plans or ERISA (self-funded) plans—are becoming more stringently worded. As an example, a group medical plan might cover 30 days of inpatient rehabilitation. However, if someone claims that this amount of rehabilitation is not sufficient to restore a patient to his or her prior degree of function or capability, the group medical response will likely be, "That's not restorative you're requesting, that's long-term custodial care, and we don't pay for that."

The long-term care policies being offered by some employer groups to employees and their immediate family or dependents do respond to a tremendous need in the health care marketplace. Unfortunately, even these policies are so narrowly written, restrictive, have many exclusions, and/or are expensive that they bar a great number of people from access to care or limit the actual length of care to be covered. The industry is just now seeing a gradual move toward more consumer-friendly long-term care policies.

Medigap Policies

Similar to long-term care policies, Medigap plans were devised as a safety net for those areas of coverage where Medicare stopped short. A Medigap policy is an independent policy purchased by individuals through an insurance agency to augment Medicare coverage. Launched in the marketplace with a great deal of hype, some Medigap policies are actually less than they appear. Guidelines on items that should be included in every Medigap plan can be obtained from the federal Department of Aging or the Department of Health and Human Services.

Dental Insurance

Dental insurance policies are currently popular in the marketplace. Further developments in this product line include a shift toward dental managed care networks, PPO networks, and POS arrangements as alternatives to "indemnity" dental plans.

RIDERS TO LIFE INSURANCE POLICIES

Individuals may also purchase additional coverage through a rider, material or paragraphs added to an existing life insurance policy.

Accelerated Benefits

Additional funds for terminal illness care may be obtained through a rider to a life insurance policy. Should a policyholder develop a terminal illness (as validated by a physician statement that the person is likely to die within a year), the person can gain access to approximately one half of the life insurance policy's benefits.

Accidental Dismemberment Clause

Also written as a rider to a life insurance policy, this clause has not come into common use. It provides for a flat dollar amount to be paid, regardless of the medical care delivered and its cost, if a person loses an arm, a leg, his or her vision, or suffers multiple losses.

COORDINATION OF BENEFITS

When there are two or more coverages on a claim—perhaps a wife and husband both work and are covered by their employers, a no-fault auto policy, or Medicare—there are rules governing which of the plans is primary and pays first and which pays second. In an "intact" family, an employee's plan pays first on that employee. When the claim is for a child covered by both parents' plans, the "birthday" rule comes into play. The plan of the parent with the earlier birthday, by month and day, not year, is utilized. If Mom's birthday is April 12 and Dad's birthday is August 20, Mom's plan is primary. (In the past, Dad's plan was always primary; some plans still hold the male parent as primary.)

Medicare is primary if a person retires on pension and his or her spouse is not an active employee with coverage as an active employee. However, an employer group health plan is always primary vis-a-vis Medicare. A 74-year-old active employee is entitled to Medicare, but his employer plan is primary. That same plan also is primary for his 69-year-old spouse named on the plan. If an employee is disabled but still covered by an employee group plan, Medicare is the secondary payer.

To clear up any unknowns and prevent future confusion, a case manager should always ask about all insurance in effect during an initial visit or telephone call. The source referring the case might not have all pertinent information on file. All findings regarding multiple coverage, coverage origin, plan sponsor, and who is insured under each plan should be recorded. In divorced families and step families, coordination of benefits becomes more intricate, as custody and court-order issues may be involved.

Coordination of benefits is always specific to the types of plan involved in a case, and a coordination of benefits statement is customarily included in each plan.

NOTES

1. M. Bradford, "Texas Employers Defend Workers Comp Opt Out," *Business Insurance* 31, no. 7 (1997): 18.

2. W. B. Conerly, "Is Workers' Compensation a Model for Unemployment Insurance?" *National Center for Policy Analysis Brief Analysis no. 435* (2003): http://www.ncpa.org/pub/ba/ba435.

3. Department of Labor, *State Workers' Compensation Statutes,* "Table 1. Type of Law and Insurance Requirements for Private Employment," John Burton's Workers' Compensation Resources (2003): http://www.workerscompresources.com/.

4. M. Quint, "Crackdown on Job-Injury Costs," *The New York Times,* CXLIV, no. 50,002 (1995): D1, D7, D9.

5. L. B. Benko, "Jury Still Out on Consumer-Driven Health Care Plans," *Business Insurance* 37, no.11 (2003): 16.

6. E. Kaplan, "Early Results Mixed for Consumer-Centric Plans," *Employee Benefit News*, (2003): 11.

7. D. Petrie, "Are Viatical Settlements Appropriate for Your Patients?" *The Case Manager* 14, no.4 (2003): 48.

CHAPTER 5

Legal Responsibilities of the Case Management Profession

To serve as an advocate for individuals in today's massive, intricate health care delivery system, a case manager needs to know the laws governing patient rights and entitlements as well as the criteria determining "fair treatment" under the law. This does not mean that case managers must have each minute detail of workers' compensation legislation committed to memory, but they do need to understand policies to know when it is appropriate to file for COBRA coverage or set an appeals process in motion. For self-protection and protection of her employer, a case manager must also be aware of any recognized standard of practice by which her work will be judged. Like nurses, physicians, social workers, and physical therapists, case managers now have protocols (practice guidelines) that are becoming the established benchmarks for appropriate case management services.

PATIENT BILL OF RIGHTS AND PATIENT CONFIDENTIALITY

Every hospital has a patient bill of rights that outlines the individual's prerogatives regarding care, including the right to emergency aid, the right to diagnosis and prognosis information, the right to unbiased treatment, and the right to voice grievances. Prominent among the items covered are the right to privacy and the right to confidentiality of all patient records. (Table 5–1 is a sample patient bill of rights from the New York State Department of Health web site (www.health. state.ny.us/nysdoh), Table 5–2 is another sample patient bill of rights created by the American Hospital Association, and Table 5–3 is a patient bill of responsibilities, a list of corresponding duties a patient is expected to fulfill.)

Table 5–1 Patients' Bill of Rights

As a patient in a hospital in New York State, you have the right, consistent with law, to:

(1) Understand and use these rights. If for any reason you do not understand or you need help, the hospital *must* provide assistance, including an interpreter.

(2) Receive treatment without discrimination as to race, color, religion, sex, national origin, disability, sexual orientation or source of payment.

(3) Receive considerate and respectful care in a clean and safe environment free of unnecessary restraints.

(4) Receive emergency care if you need it.

(5) Be informed of the name and position of the doctor who will be in charge of your care in the hospital.

(6) Know the names, positions and functions of any hospital staff involved in your care and refuse their treatment, examination or observation.

(7) A no smoking room.

(8) Receive complete information about your diagnosis, treatment and prognosis.

(9) Receive all information that you need to give informed consent for any proposed procedure or treatment. This information shall include the possible risks and benefits of the procedure or treatment.

(10) Receive all the information you need to give informed consent for an order not to resuscitate. You also have the right to designate an individual to give this consent for you if you are too ill to do so. If you would like additional information, please ask for a copy of the pamphlet "Do Not Resuscitate Orders—A Guide for Patients and Families."

(11) Refuse treatment and be told what effect this may have on your health.

(12) Refuse to take part in research. In deciding whether or not to participate, you have the right to a full explanation.

(13) Privacy while in the hospital and confidentiality of all information and records regarding your care.

(14) Participate in all decisions about your treatment and discharge from the hospital. The hospital must provide you with a written discharge plan and written description of how you can appeal your discharge.

(15) Review your medical record without charge. Obtain a copy of your medical record for which the hospital can charge a reasonable fee. You cannot be denied a copy solely because you cannot afford to pay.

(16) Receive an itemized bill and explanation of all charges.

(17) Complain without fear of reprisals about the care and services you are receiving and to have the hospital respond to you and if you request it, a written response. If you are not satisfied with the hospital's response, you can complain to the New York State Health Department. The hospital must provide you with the Health Department telephone number.

(18) Authorize those family members and other adults who will be given priority to visit consistent with your ability to receive visitors.

Table 5–1 continued

---

(19) Make known your wishes in regard to anatomical gifts. You may document your wishes in your health care proxy or on a donor card, available from the hospital.

Source: Courtesy of the New York State Department of Health, 2003, Albany, New York.

In its *Accreditation Manual for Hospitals*, the Joint Commission on Accreditation of Healthcare Organizations (JCAHO) identified privacy and confidentiality as two patient rights, entitling a patient to the following:

- To refuse to talk with or see anyone not officially connected with the hospital, including visitors, or persons officially connected with the hospital but not directly involved in the patient's care
- To wear appropriate personal clothing and religious or other symbolic items, as long as they do not interfere with diagnostic procedures or treatments
- To be interviewed and examined in surroundings designed to ensure reasonable visual and auditory privacy
- To expect that any discussion or consultation involving the patient will be conducted discreetly and that individuals not directly involved in the patient's care will not be present without the permission of the patient
- To have the medical record read only by individuals directly involved in the patient's treatment or in the monitoring of its quality, and by other individuals only with the patient's written authorization or that of a legally authorized representative
- To expect all communications and other records pertaining to the patient's care, including the source of payment for treatment, to be treated as confidential
- To request a transfer to another room if another patient or visitor in the room is unreasonable, disturbing the patient by smoking or other actions
- To be placed in protective privacy when considered necessary for personal safety[1]

(In 1995, the Joint Commission adopted new accreditation standards that addressed the ethical practices of health care organizations and implemented a code of behavior regarding marketing, admission, transfer, discharge, and billing practices, as well as the relationship of the organization and its staff to other health care providers, educational institutions, and payers.)

The American Hospital Association has adopted a Patient's Bill of Rights that encourages health care institutions to use a template, revise it for their patient community and populations, and simplify or translate language as needed to make it of best use to patients and their families.

Table 5–2 The American Hospital Association Patient's Bill of Rights

These rights can be exercised on the patient's behalf by a designated surrogate or proxy decision maker if the patient lacks decision-making capacity, is legally incompetent, or is a minor.

1. The patient has the right to considerate and respectful care.
2. The patient has the right to and is encouraged to obtain from physicians and other direct caregivers relevant, current, and understandable information concerning diagnosis, treatment, and prognosis.

   Except in emergencies when the patient lacks decision-making capacity and the need for treatment is urgent, the patient is entitled to the opportunity to discuss and request information related to the specific procedures and/or treatments, the risks involved, the possible length of recuperation, and the medically reasonable alternatives and their accompanying risks and benefits.

   Patients have the right to know the identity of physicians, nurses, and others involved in their care, as well as when those involved are students, residents, or other trainees. The patient also has the right to know the immediate and long-term financial implications of treatment choices, insofar as they are known.
3. The patient has the right to make decisions about the plan of care prior to and during the course of treatment and to refuse a recommended treatment or plan of care to the extent permitted by law and hospital policy and to be informed of the medical consequences of this action. In case of such refusal, the patient is entitled to other appropriate care and services that the hospital provides or transfer to another hospital. The hospital should notify patients of any policy that might affect patient choice within the institution.
4. The patient has the right to have an advance directive (such as a living will, health care proxy, or durable power of attorney for health care) concerning treatment or designating a surrogate decision maker with the expectation that the hospital will honor the intent of that directive to the extent permitted by law and hospital policy.

   Health care institutions must advise patients of their rights under state law and hospital policy to make informed medical choices, ask if the patient has an advance directive, and include that information in patient records. The patient has the right to timely information about hospital policy that may limit its ability to implement fully a legally valid advance directive.
5. The patient has the right to every consideration of privacy. Case discussion, consultation, examination, and treatment should be conducted so as to protect each patient's privacy.
6. The patient has the right to expect that all communications and records pertaining to his/her care will be treated as confidential by the hospital, except in cases such as suspected abuse and public health hazards when reporting is permitted or required by law. The patient has the right to expect that the hospital will emphasize the confidentiality of this information when it releases it to any other parties entitled to review information in these records.

Table 5–2 continued

7. The patient has the right to review the records pertaining to his/her medical care and to have the information explained or interpreted as necessary, except when restricted by law.
8. The patient has the right to expect that, within its capacity and policies, a hospital will make reasonable response to the request of a patient for appropriate and medically indicated care and services. The hospital must provide evaluation, service, and/or referral as indicated by the urgency of the case. When medically appropriate and legally permissible, or when a patient has so requested, a patient may be transferred to another facility. The institution to which the patient is to be transferred must first have accepted the patient for transfer. The patient must also have the benefit of complete information and explanation concerning the need for, risks, benefits, and alternatives to such a transfer.
9. The patient has the right to ask and be informed of the existence of business relationships among the hospital, educational institutions, other health care providers, or payers that may influence the patient's treatment and care.
10. The patient has the right to consent to or decline to participate in proposed research studies or human experimentation affecting care and treatment or requiring direct patient involvement, and to have those studies fully explained prior to consent. A patient who declines to participate in research or experimentation is entitled to the most effective care that the hospital can otherwise provide.
11. The patient has the right to expect reasonable continuity of care when appropriate and to be informed by physicians and other caregivers of available and realistic patient care options when hospital care is no longer appropriate.
12. The patient has the right to be informed of hospital policies and practices that relate to patient care, treatment, and responsibilities. The patient has the right to be informed of available resources for resolving disputes, grievances, and conflicts, such as ethics committees, patient representatives, or other mechanisms available in the institution. The patient has the right to be informed of the hospital's charges for services and available payment methods.

Source: Reprinted with permission of the American Hospital Association, © 2003. This document has been superseded by The Patient Care Partnership, available at http://www. hospitalconnect.com:80/aha/ptcommunication/index.html

As health care professionals, case managers are ethically charged to maintain the maximum amount of confidentiality possible on matters of health and finances on behalf of patients. Confidentiality touches on a number of issues and relationships. Regardless of the health plan and their health status, patients are equal. The getting of information is not an arbitrary and capricious procedure. It can be argued that providers, payers, case managers, and patients all have rights, and in fact they do, but in particular cases the rights of one group will override

Table 5–3 Patients Bill of Responsibilities

The Nassau County Medical Center recognizes the primary role its patients play with regard to their care, their safety and the safety of others, and the safeguarding of the rights of other patients and staff.

A bill of patient responsibilities describing this role is set forth below in the interest of promoting a safe, comfortable environment in which the best possible care may be rendered.

Patient Responsibilities:

NCMC patients shall be responsible:

1. To provide, to the best of his/her knowledge, accurate and complete information about present complaints, past illnesses, hospitalizations, medication and other matters relating to his/her health.
2. To report unexpected changes in his/her condition to the responsible practitioner, as soon as possible.
3. To make it known whether he/she understands a contemplated course of action and what is expected of him/her.
4. For following to the best of his/her ability the plan for medical care as recommended by the physician primarily responsible for his/her care.
5. To keep appointments and when unable to do so, to notify the hospital with sufficient time to reschedule.
6. For his/her actions if he/she refuses treatment or does not follow the practitioner's instructions.
7. For assuring that the financial obligations of his/her health care are fulfilled as promptly as possible.
8. For following hospital rules and regulations regarding patient care and conduct.
9. For assisting in the control of noise and the number of visitors.
10. To comply with the No Smoking Policy as posted and assist Medical Center staff in their efforts to provide a smoke free environment for all.
11. For being respectful of the property of other persons and of the hospital.
12. For being considerate of the rights of others.
13. To fill out the patient evaluation form to provide feedback to the hospital.

Source: Courtesy of Nassau County Medical Center, East Meadow, New York.

those of another. Each member of a health plan enjoys the same right to know about his or her condition, and the same protection must be given to the privacy of any member. A cancer or HIV-positive patient has the right to keep his or her health status from being known by anyone else; an employer requesting such particular information from a case manager is out of line.

However, some patients need to be educated on how far they can push their right to confidentiality. A case manager cannot forge a document or fudge a claims report, altering the diagnosis, treatment, or medication, for example, to cloud facts about an illness because it might be a tip-off to the patient's condition. Although claims forms generally include a patient's name, social security number, age, and illness, patient codes are utilized to help protect the patient's identity on reports that might be sent to a corporate office, such as cost-benefit analysis reports.

Jeanne Boling, the executive director of the Case Management Society of America (CMSA), assembled information on confidentiality issues that case managers typically must face. The material was adapted from "Confidentiality: An Issue CMs Must Understand," conference handouts developed by Susan Scheutzow. Case managers will ask themselves two very basic questions to clarify confidentiality concerns: When must information be disclosed? When must information not be disclosed?[2]

Following the principle that the sensitivities of patients must be respected while facilitating the truthful and complete disclosure of information necessary for proper health care determinations, Scheutzow says that information must be disclosed when a patient requests it (as qualified by state law). Many states have statutes requiring that any patient be given access to his or her medical records except when the content might be damaging to the patient. In the absence of statutes, courts generally hold that patients must be allowed to see their medical records.

Varying from state to state, statutes may require that the following events be reported: births; deaths; child or elder abuse and neglect; violent injuries; animal bites; contagious, infectious, and occupational diseases; certain conditions of newborns; abortions; impaired health care professionals; and breath, blood, and urine testing for alcohol and drugs. Federal law mandates the reporting of certain adverse transfusion reactions, certain misadministration of radioactive materials, and certain medical device defects and failures. According to Scheutzow, case managers have a duty to warn authorities in cases of communicable diseases or violent inclinations of the mentally ill. They are also compelled to respond to subpoenas and court orders; if information is privileged, a case manager should request a signed consent from the patient and consult a lawyer.

When can't case managers share information? When it comes from a drug or alcohol abuse treatment provider or a patient's mental health records or when it concerns AIDS or a sexually transmitted disease. As an example of why case managers should consult legal counsel, the list of confidential matters includes cases of abortion, in direct contrast to state statutes that might require disclosure of abortion. To help clarify such issues, Scheutzow recommends that case managers have a strict, well-defined confidentiality policy, operate with the informed consent of patients, and get adequate and valid releases or consent authorization forms for all disclosures of confidential information.

Confidentiality, privacy, and access to information are issues of concern at hospitals, within managed care organizations, and on Capitol Hill. Key pieces of confidentiality legislation were debated in 1996 and 1997, with elements of the Health Insurance Portability and Accountability Act and the Patient Right to Know Act opening up debate on how to prevent breaches of privacy. The overarching legislation now in effect is HIPAA, which calls for full disclosure to patients regarding how their health care information will be used and who might see it (see Chapter 7). It has been the position of the National Coalition for Patient Rights to point out that everyone wins in a system that improves health and prevents illness at the lowest cost. However, if employees and patients feel the health care system leaks personal information, they will begin to withhold that information, lying about their lifestyle and concealing their genetic background, resulting in delayed treatment, and, coincidentally, outcomes data based on erroneous input.

CONSENT/DISCLOSURE AND CONSENT AUTHORIZATION FORMS

Empowerment derives in part from awareness. Therefore, a case manager, as patient advocate, must have the utmost respect for a patient's right to knowledge. During a well-conducted assessment, the case manager will discover just how much the patient understands about his or her condition and prognosis. In most instances, not enough background has been provided to enable the patient to safely manage his or her illness or injury. The wife or husband or eldest child perhaps knows a few more details, but the patient remains in the dark. There must be a free disclosure of information so that an informed decision may be made.

When a case manager begins working with a patient, she should have in hand a consent authorization form (Table 5–4), signed by the patient or the person authorized to act on the patient's behalf, whenever arranging for an alternative care location or provider, considering an optional medical procedure, or developing a case management plan. This document provides for the release of information to the case manager and certifies the patient's permission to review case information with the treating physician, other health care providers, the payer, the employer group, and so on, when some data must be shared to further the case. It also incorporates permission for the provision of case management services. In a group medical plan, consent forms are not strictly required, although certainly recommended and increasingly a standard of practice. They are a necessity in a workers' compensation or no-fault case, especially in situations more prone to litigation than others. A consent form can be written very specifically or broad-based to cover a number of medical situations, but it should authorize access to information for the duration of the case. A copy of the consent form is kept on file and accompanies all case management reports sent to a physician, lawyer, claims examiner, and so on. For long-term cases, a consent form should be signed annually.

A case manager might think, "John is in the hospital and I need to see him." So off she goes, driving 45 minutes to the hospital. But John feels that case management intervention is not necessary and certainly does not want to sign any consent form. There is no other family member present. The case manager has

Table 5–4 Consent Authorization Form

CONSENT

Date: _____

To assure appropriate medical case management services, I, _____, authorize any physician, hospital, or other professional involved in my treatment to disclose medical, hospital, vocational, or related information. I authorize that the information may be shared with other professionals, agencies, or insurance companies who may be involved in the provision or payment of necessary services.

A copy of this authorization may be accepted, if necessary.

Signed   _____

Guardian _____

Witness   _____

Source: Courtesy of Options Unlimited, Case Management Services Division, Huntington, New York.

---

now trekked to the hospital and gotten nowhere because she was not prepared. It would have been better to have moved a little more slowly, but thoroughly, through the case management process. Perhaps the case manager is planning on seeing a man who is on life support; she needs to review his hospital records. The man's wife, authorized to sign for him, cannot meet the case manager at the hospital. The case manager may send the consent authorization form by mail, e-mail, or fax and have a signed copy with her when she visits the hospital. In essence, it safeguards the patient–case manager relationship, noting who the case manager is, those people she will need to speak with, and the records that will be discussed.

Perhaps the patient is in an intensive care unit (ICU). The case manager has spoken with the doctor and the family; both parties think case management is a great idea. She arrives at the ICU and a family member says, "Oh, we have an attorney. You'll have to show this to him." Unable to speak to the patient without the counsel's permission, the case manager is back to square one. To prevent this, the case manager will want to ascertain whether the patient is represented by an attorney. However, she will want to be careful not to put herself in the position of inadvertently "suggesting" that the patient needs an attorney. Instead of saying, "Do you have an attorney? I need to know because I will need his or her authorization as well," the case manager can call, explain her role, mention the use of a consent authorization that will enable her to speak to the doctor, and ask as an "afterthought" if there is anyone else who the patient thinks she might need to contact. The patient may respond, "Well, my lawyer already told me that I can't sign anything, so you'll have to talk to her." In this way, without asking directly, the case manager finds out an attorney is involved.

In some cases, a consent form is not critical but is used to give the patient confidence. When a case manager gets a referral from an employer group or an insurance carrier and the patient's diagnosis is a psychiatric disability, cancer, a degenerative disease such as ALS, or AIDS, a consent form offers the patient an assurance of confidentiality. (There is extra anxiety in the case of an AIDS diagnosis, and justifiably so, because insurers and companies have been known to cut benefits or employment for individuals with AIDS.) In response to this growing concern, some states have imposed additional mandates to ensure the confidentiality of HIV/AIDS status. I send a consent form with a brochure on my services and a note requesting the patient's signature so I can speak to the doctor, the therapist, and others, to help them work with the patient. With such a form, there is a record that a case manager is working in tandem with the patient and the doctor and that sensitive patient information will not be disclosed to a boss or an insurance representative.

Many case managers have difficulty with consent forms, feeling that as soon as they have to ask for a signature, the patient will respond negatively. It is true that many people are intimidated by anything requiring their signature. What I basically do is follow rules of full disclosure, explaining the authorization and telling the patient that it is good for his or her protection and for my protection. Often, case managers must call a doctor on the telephone for details of a treatment plan. Sometimes, broader background must be gleaned from patient records, or assistance is needed on an emergency basis. How can a case move forward if the patient must be contacted for each and every release? I tell each patient that the document is a simple statement showing that he or she is aware of what is going on, that it is similar to the form signed upon entering the hospital or when a doctor wants to forward patient records to someone else for review. I also explain that my ability to help might be severely compromised without the authorization. When the patient understands all this, consent is customarily given readily.

In her comments regarding consent and disclosure issues, Scheutzow outlines the process of informed consent:

- Give the information verbally and in writing.
- Offer an opportunity for questions and answers to clarify patient understanding.
- Witness the signing of the consent form and retain the current consent in case management records.
- Recognize the two legal standards for disclosure: Disclose the information that a reasonable medical practitioner would disclose under the same or similar circumstances, and disclose all the background needed to make the decision-making process meaningful.

When there is a question of a patient's competency (legal judgment rendered by a court after hearing evidence) or capacity (the patient's functional ability to understand the diagnosis, treatment, risks, and alternatives), the case manager should involve family members in the case management plan and also recommend that they seek legal help for purposes of establishing power of attorney, durable power of attorney, or guardianship.

MEDICAL RECORDS

Case management files are considered medical records and, consequently, must be retained for the period of time mandated by state and federal statutes. In most states, this period is 5 years or the period of time in which lawsuits may be filed, whichever is longer. Children's medical records must be kept until the children reach legal age, as defined by the state.

THE RIGHT TO KNOW VERSUS THE NEED TO KNOW

When case managers work directly with employer groups, especially self-funded employer groups, the issue of an employer's right to know (as opposed to need to know) comes to the forefront. Involved with the bigger, more expensive cases, charged with tracking a company's stop-loss ceiling, or facing an employer who can—if dedicated to the search and wishes to illegally sort through computer files or paperwork—identify a particular employee by matching a benefit claim to the corporate checkbook register or social security number, case managers find that their fiduciary relationship with patients can be compromised. (A fiduciary relationship is the legal relationship of confidentiality that exists when one person relies on another, as in the case manager–patient relationship.)

Despite the risks of a lawsuit, some employers might ask for specific information on a patient. Citing pending layoff, promotion, or management decisions that need to be made or the responsibility to protect dollars now that it self-funds and administers its health package, the employer might assert that it has the right to know which employee is costing the most. A CEO might say, "Before I can approve that home care alternative, I need to know who we're talking about here."

It is true that the boss does need to have a broad perspective on employee problems, but the "who" must be protected to the greatest extent possible. Without naming an employee or dependent, the case manager can respond in generalities. Cost-benefit analyses and other reports can give credible but not identifiable narrative data. John, the 45-year-old drill bit specialist who works in the machine shop, becomes a "middle-aged man." Further, the case manager can explain to the employer that it is in the employer's best interests *not* to know exactly who John is in the event of an unlawful discharge or workers' compensation lawsuit.

DISCLOSURE ISSUES

Issues of disclosure and confidentiality are not as clear-cut as they once were. Susan O. Scheutzow noted how changes in the ways in which society, the government, and the courts perceive these issues impact a case manager's responsibilities and liabilities. At her session, "Confidentiality: How a Case Manager Can Protect It," given at the Medical Case Management Conference V, she included these comments in her materials:

> The issue of disclosure of information includes mandatory reporting of information to the government, disclosure of information to protect third parties such as when there is a duty to warn third parties about the illness of a patient, and disclosure of information pursuant to judicial or quasi-judicial process. Information may be required to be released in these instances even if there is otherwise a general legal requirement to keep information confidential.

> Generally there has been a trend to increase mandatory disclosure of information. The physician–patient privilege, which generally came into being in many states over 100 years ago and protected confidential communications from release pursuant to judicial process, is largely inadequate today. The physician–patient privilege generally is limited to communications made to physicians. With the proliferation of licensed health care professionals rendering care in today's health care system the physician–patient privilege is inadequate to protect health care communications.

> The laws requiring confidentiality and requiring disclosure of medical records are on a collision course for health care providers as providers are increasingly required to release information to comply with the law yet are subject to liability for errors in making such disclosure.[3]

Given this environment, it is still the case manager's responsibility to protect the rights of the patients she is working with by keeping medical (as well as financial and emotional) information confidential unless required by law to disclose it. In questionable instances, case managers should consult legal counsel for advice.

ADEQUATE INFORMATION

Because they may be held legally responsible for their decisions, it is important that case managers make certain the information they use is accurate and adequate. Secondhand information, unless it comes from a reliable source, might not be good enough. Long-distance telephonic case management, conducted without on-site or in-person visits, can be dangerous if an element of the treatment plan is overlooked. In all cases, the case manager should document decisions, medical sources, transitions from one care facility to another, and so on, to support the selected case management plan.

CONTRACTS AND LETTERS OF AGREEMENT

Case managers working in-house for insurance carriers, HMOs, TPAs, and so on, will not have to consider this question, but those working independently as case management consultants should review the use of case management service contracts. As Thomas K. Hyatt pointed out in a presentation titled "Contracting for Case Management Services," the decision to utilize a formal business contract must be based on legal and practical considerations and the case manager's working relationship with the client. How frequently does this payer or client refer cases? What is the range of services the client is expecting and how much responsibility will the case manager have?

If a written contract or letter of agreement is used, Hyatt recommends that it include the following:

- A "due diligence" section. Basically, this section includes the practices, conduct norms, documentation, and so on, that both parties can reasonably expect from each other. As an example, the payer will expect the case manager to document his or her credentials and qualifications. The case manager will expect to receive the benefit plan (Summary Plan Description) and all amendments applicable to the beneficiary. The case manager should review the insurance contract for a statement giving the insurer the authority to perform case management and to delegate this function to an outside entity.
- Evidence of the payer's professional liability insurance. Does the insurance cover case management services and, if so, for how much?
- Specific terms, if any, between the payer and a TPA or any TPA terms for case management intervention
- Written releases allowing the case manager access to confidential medical information
- Any applicable medical protocols
- The payment structure
- A clear delineation of the duties of the payer and the case manager
- Confidentiality protection
- Physician and patient consent
- Professional liability insurance protection
- Compliance with laws

A case manager's ability to negotiate with a large payer might depend on her specialty, the needs of the payer, and a host of business circumstances, Hyatt suggests. In my mind, the most important requisite for negotiating is that the case manager adopts the firm position that she is a health care professional working to achieve a positive outcome for all parties. This stance enables the case manager to pursue the contract she deserves and to turn away contracts that are inadequate.

Hyatt also notes that case managers should read carefully any prepared written agreements presented by a payer and should not sign anything they do not fully understand. It is appropriate to line through any provisions that are unacceptable even if the agreement is subsequently signed and returned to the payer. If a payer rejects the need for a written agreement, Hyatt says, the case manager should consider developing a letter stating her understanding of the business terms and the case manager–payer relationship, including the case manager's duties, the payer's duties, compensation (per hour, per day), payment schedule (payment within 30 days of receipt of the case manager's invoice), insurance coverage and indemnification (e.g., a "hold harmless" clause to protect the case manager from claims, liabilities, damages, etc.), and the length of the term for case management services (for one particular case, a group of cases for 5 years, etc.).[4] See Appendix 5–A at the end of the chapter for Hyatt's sample written agreement.

LEGAL ISSUES IN CASE MANAGEMENT

Noted speaker Alice G. Gosfield, Esq., said, "Case managers are at the fulcrum of where the care management aspect of the health care delivery system currently is focused, and a great deal of what you do is going to get much more scrutiny as years go by. The concept of liability and accountability for the outcomes of care is not just going to be competitive but is increasingly going to be based on whether patients are harmed as a result of the choices that are made in this changing system." This means that case managers will not only need to document "controlled costs with appropriate outcomes demonstrated on the basis of data," but also that a case manager's recommendations for care might have to stand up in court.

Following is an overview of case management and the law. The basis of this section is a reference document compiled by Jeanne Boling titled "Legal Issues in Case Management." In her brief, Boling succinctly captured the range of diverse elements that may legally impact on a case manager's practice. (A section of this document appears as Appendix 5–B.)

The first focus is on a case manager's competence, noting that it must be and will be measured against accepted standards of care in the industry. Among the existing formal standards of care pertinent to case managers are those developed by the CMSA, URAC, the Association of Rehabilitation Nurses, the National Association for Social Work, the National Association of Rehabilitation Professionals in the Private Sector, The National Association of Geriatric Care Managers, the National Institute on Community-Based Long-Term Care, and the

American Nurses Association, as well as nurse practice acts and standards of care developed by individual hospitals or practice-based protocols, as well as the Department of Human Services or Department of Health in individual states. Corporate, organizational, and facility standards of care and protocol are other resources, including those from the NCQA referenced earlier and the HEDIS performance measures. Also appropriate are the Guidelines for Health Benefits Administration (a joint effort of the American Hospital Association, American Medical Association, American Managed Care and Review Association, Blue Cross and Blue Shield Association, and Health Insurance Association of America), the series of 19 Clinical Practice Guidelines created by the former Agency for Health Care Policy and Research and released from 1992 to 1996 (see the Agency for Healthcare Research and Quality), and the HEDIS performance measures and NCQA protocols noted in Chapter 2. The National Guideline Clearinghouse is a public resource for evidence-based clinical practice guidelines located on the Internet. Currently relevant certifications available to case managers are discussed in Chapter 14.

Beyond these protocols and certifications are the basic educational curricula and degrees for the various health care professions, continuing education credits, and the more informal standards of care "set" by peers in case management practice and other health care professionals. Taken together, such standards will be used as criteria to ascertain whether a case manager has the background and experience to practice case management.

From a legal standpoint, what are the questions of liability that may arise? Attorney Lynn S. Muller succinctly addresses the basics in "Legal Issues: An Ethical Dilemma" (Table 5–5).

Case managers may be held liable for negligence in the form of malpractice, bad faith actions, or for the actions of a certain provider or staff member, in the sense that the case manager was not sufficiently careful or knowledgeable about the selection of a provider or the competence of staff. Charges of negligence look at an individual's conduct, rather than state of mind or intent. Malpractice is seen as the negligent conduct of professionals, such as case managers, nurses, physicians, and others.[5] Malpractice includes any professional person's wrongful conduct, improper discharge of professional duties, or failure to meet standards of care that results in harm or undue costs to another person. Bad faith actions involve a breach of implied duty conducted in good faith and fair dealing as part of providing managed care services. There are a few relevant cases that help illustrate the implications for case managers regarding liability and malpractice. A number of cases that have passed through the courts focus on a payer's denial of claims, or the size of damage payments. Although a case might not include a case manager on the stand, case managers will want to be aware of trial process and outcomes.

Table 5–5 Legal Issues: An Ethical Dilemma

Legal Basics

By what standard would a nurse case manager be judged? In the absence of new case law, we must rely on history, as the law is based on what came before. *Res Judicata* is a fancy legal term for the idea that the thing has already been decided.

Professional Negligence arises out of Tort Law. Negligence is a tort, a civil wrong. This is distinguished from crimes.

Negligence is the conduct that falls below a standard of care required by the law for the protection of persons . . . from foreseeable harm. Negligence may result from an act or omission.

The Standard of Care applied to a tort suit is not normally derived from an external authority, such as a government standard. In the developing Case Management Field, as with other professionals, standards develop in a complicated way through interaction with leaders of the profession, professional journals and meetings and networks with colleagues. Over time, hundreds of separate statements and comments become the "Standard Practice." Eddy, *Clinical Policies and the Quality of Clinical Practice*, 307 New Eng. J. Med. 343 (1982).

Proving Plaintiff's Case: Standard or customary practice by those in a specialty area is normally established through the testimony of experts. The purpose of the expert is to assist the trier of fact, (usually a jury . . .). Such experts base their testimony on their knowledge, education, and experience. Fed. R. Evid. 703, 704, N.J.S.A. 2A:84A-2, *et seq.*

The Plaintiff must offer proof that the Defendant Physician (includes peer review), Nurse (including case managers, UR, QA, Discharge Planners, etc.), and Therapists (including all licensed therapists) acted contrary to the accepted standards of practice in the area.

Where do you fit into this picture?

Source: Reprinted with permission from L. S. Muller, Legal Issues in Case Management Practice, *An Ethical and Legal Roundtable, Questions and Quandaries in Case Management: Quest for Resolutions,* p. 44, © 1996, Case Management Society of America.

Discharge

The first four cases reviewed here concern issues that arise with regard to patient discharge. The first, *Wickline v. State of California* (1986, 1987), is one of the more widely known cases with elements pertinent to case management practice. Alice Gosfield summarized the basic message of the *Wickline* decision as follows: Anyone can be held liable for damages or harm to a patient when (1) services being provided in the utilization management environment are not in accordance with standards of care, (2) the attending physicians disagree with the utilization management function, or (3) appeals on a medical decision are not pursued or are arbitrarily ignored or denied.[6] For case managers in particular, these implications follow:

- Case management is a reasonable activity.
- Case managers can be held accountable when something bad happens to the patient.
- Case managers must meet a reasonable standard of care.
- Case managers must not conduct their activities in a way that corrupts medical judgment.
- Case managers must act within the scope of their licensure and their own competence and education.
- The case manager's role is as a consultant to clients and physicians (who make the final medical decision).
- Case managers should not practice medicine and should not interfere with the doctor–patient relationship.
- Alternative treatment plans should be placed in writing as much as possible and be signed by the physician.

In the light of legal ramifications and consequences, case managers must act on complete information. If contradictory information exists, it is the case manager's responsibility to determine what is true. The case manager should consider carefully whether sufficient information can be gathered over the phone or whether an in-person meeting is necessary. At a minimum, the case manager should work from a claims history and all available medical records, and the case management plan should be based on data that a competent professional in the case management role would deem sufficient for clinical decision-making purposes.

At the end of the day, the court decision placed responsibility for the *Wickline* discharge solely on the shoulders of the physician. However, because they may be held responsible for the patient's care, case managers should not comply with unreasonable third-party payer limits without written protest. Case managers are patient advocates foremost, and the courts demand that a patient's interests come first. Also, if employees make treatment decisions based on payment mechanisms or a fear of denial rather than on what is appropriate for the patient, the company may not be protected.

Protection against liability claims when dissent from a treatment plan exists requires that the case management review process be conducted by adequately qualified reviewers using valid medical criteria and include a thorough review of medical records and a discussion with the treatment team. If discharge is called for, the review should incorporate an assessment of the risk of discharge.

The second case with discharge issues at its center is *Wilson v. Blue Cross of Southern California and Blue Cross Blue Shield of Alabama and Western Medical*

Review (1990). This case involved the premature discharge of a patient from a psychiatric hospital. At the time of discharge, the physician had written in his notes that the patient was discharged on the recommendation of the utilization review company. The patient went home and committed suicide. The family did not sue the physician or the hospital; they sued the insurer and the utilization review company that had suggested the discharge. In court, the insurer and utilization review firm held that they were not responsible for the decision to discharge the patient and that the attending physician was responsible for making his own decisions and, if at all concerned, should have appealed the decision for discharge. The jury felt that the insurer violated three of the four elements of the case, and only held back on finding the insurer guilty of a "bad faith denial of claims." Because all four elements against the insurer did not hold up in court, the insurer was not held liable in this particular case. (Alice Gosfield commented, "Some in the industry now say, 'Oh good, we can't be held liable.' My view is that this was a squeaker and somebody better start paying attention to the processes by which these judgments are going to be made."[7])

As for the implications for case managers, there are two. First, case managers should check benefit plan contract language. Does it include coverage for case management? Has the insured authorized case management? If not, the case management entity can be charged with interfering with the insured's insurance contract and perhaps with liability for any harm resulting from that interference. Second, it is critical that a case manager's treatment plan have the approval of the treating physician and the patient or family.

Two additional cases of record with lessons for case managers are *Hughes v. Blue Cross of Northern California* (1989) and *Linthicum v. Nationwide Life Insurance Company* (1986). In *Hughes,* as noted by Marilou M. King, an appeals court upheld a trial court's award of $700,000 in damages, finding that there was a "defective determination of medical necessity because only a part of the beneficiary's medical records were reviewed by the utilization reviewer." This case also contained some "bad faith" implications for case managers. When a case management plan denies a patient access to the benefits of an insurance contract, it is usually the result of intentional and outrageous conduct, but to avoid any problem in this area, a case manager should thoroughly review and/or discuss contractual obligations with the insurer, should formulate a recovery plan or plan of care in concert with the treating physician and patient, and should ensure that it is satisfactory to them.

In *Linthicum,* the insurer was held liable for failing to consult the treating physician. The implications for case managers are as follows: All medical records must be reviewed and reflected in case management reports and recommendations, and a case manager must consult the treating physician. Consult the treating physician? Sounds like very basic advice, but someone somewhere along the line at Nationwide forgot and was held accountable.

These cases underscore the importance of one's ethical and clinical responsibilities, whether fulfilling the role of case manager, social worker, home health care nurse, discharge planner, or "other" in the discharge planning process. Over and over, I see case managers neglecting to cover the bases, not sweating the details. There are principles and guidelines that exist to help define the criteria for appropriate activities in discharge planning. (See Appendix 5–C for the "Evidence-based Principles of Discharge and Discharge Criteria" developed by the American Medical Association.)

Negligent Referral

The next legal area to be considered is negligent referral. When referring a patient to a facility or provider, case managers have a responsibility to act in good faith in the best interest of the patient, investigate the competency and qualifications of the facility or provider, and use reasonable care in making the referral. The more choices a case manager offers the patient or physician, the less her risk of being held liable for that referral.

When considering a practitioner or facility for referral, a case manager should examine current licensure and accreditation, the outcomes of cases similar to the one under consideration for referral, billing practices, insurance coverage, and the records of any previous pertinent malpractice judgments. The National Practitioner Data Bank, www.npdb-hidb.com, retains information on all malpractice judgments and settlements, catalogued by practitioner and institution. Although there is a recommendation currently under consideration to open these records to all inquiries, only those nurses and physicians with cases on file and hospitals can retrieve their own data. Thus, an independent case manager would have trouble checking a physician's record through the data bank.

The National Practitioner Data Bank (NPDB), the Healthcare Integrity and Protection Data Bank (HIPDB), and the Federal Credentialing Program (FCP) are managed by the Division of Practitioner Data Banks, a division of the Bureau of Health Professions (BHPr) within the Health Resources and Services Administration (HRSA).

Case managers should document their continuous inquiry into the credentials and performance of the practitioners and facilities to which they refer patients, offer the patients and families a choice of practitioners and facilities, and always follow up with patients who are referred to review their status and response. Further, a case manager should disclose any problems to the patient and physician for their informed consent and obtain the patient's and physician's consent in writing, keeping it on file in a case management report.

Relevant case law citations include the nationally publicized case of *Bergalis v. CIGNA Dental Health Plan* (1991). Kimberly Bergalis of Florida sued her dentist for allegedly infecting her with the AIDS virus and also sued CIGNA for

$20 million on the basis of a negligent referral to this particular dentist. According to Marilou King, "The claim is not that CIGNA knew the dentist had AIDS but that CIGNA should have undertaken a reasonable investigation to discover if the dentist to whom CIGNA referred patients had a disease that could be communicated like AIDS."[8]

Another case, *Moshe v. Rush-Presbyterian St. Luke's Hospital* (1990), alerts case managers to the fact that utilization review (UR) and case management activities may be interpreted as inhibiting the ability of physicians to render care. Therefore, in making a referral, a case manager must use a reasonable process for determining that the referral is in the patient's best interest, give complete referral instructions, and, if the agency or facility is providing questionable levels of care, take corrective action immediately.

This issue of access to care is also seen in *Nazay v. Miller*, a 1991 Pennsylvania case, in which the original court ruling supported a retiree who did not comply with PreCert/UR requirements and was subsequently penalized for noncompliance by the plan. A subsequent ruling reversed that decision. Even in a cost-containment environment, denial of access to care is a very sensitive issue. A case management plan should always be proactive and in the patient's best interests.

Bad Faith Actions

One of the tenets of ethical practice is veracity, telling the truth. A case manager preparing marketing materials should avoid overemphasizing capabilities or guaranteed results. In *Warne v. Lincoln National Administrative Services Corp.*, a jury awarded Warne $26.8 million for his school district's plan because it did not cover his liver transplant. The benefit plan language clearly stated that this surgery was not covered; however, the plan's benefit brochure included organ transplants as a covered procedure. The jury felt the plan's denial of payment was a bad faith action.[9]

Emerging Case Law

Lawyer Stephen J. Schantz has noted cases that fall short of what he calls "black letter law" but offer guidance and fuel for thought for case managers. In *California v. State Care Health Plan,* a husband and wife, members of a managed care plan, found through a series of referrals that their daughter had Wilm's tumor, which can be a problematic, dangerous diagnosis. Surgery was recommended. After many conversations with physicians, the plan, and various providers, the family found a multidisciplinary medical team that followed protocol developed by a prominent national body to treat Wilm's tumor. The family wanted the plan to approve surgery by this team. The plan had approved another surgeon, at the same hospital, even though the individual lacked the depth of experience or the exact same credentials. Timing became critical. There were discussions, appeals, and allegations that the evening before surgery, the health care plan called the parents to request their presence at a meeting. Bedside with their daughter, the parents declined. The family went ahead with the team, following its protocol. Afterwards, payment was denied became the procedure was not completed by a preapproved provider.

In California, the California Department of Corporations is the regulatory entity overseeing HMOs and managed care entities. It sought to institute a fine against the HMO for $500,000 on the premise that, if you say you are an HMO, you must have the ability to give ready referrals in a variety of specialties. That fine was appealed and upheld, based on extensive review of the referral process, expertise available, and who did what and when, indicating that, in California at least, the right to provide managed care services is predicated on the ability to fulfill the "care" element.

Another class action filed in federal court, *Drolet v. Healthsource,* includes a number of allegations, one holding that the physician–patient relationship is compromised by the various financial incentives the provider company provides to participating physicians to reduce specialty care expenditures and referrals. There is a growing concern that financial incentives within some managed care organizations almost serve as disincentives for referral care, diagnostics, and services. This area is ripe for litigation and bears watching.[10]

Providers are beginning to turn to the courts for protection against liability or claims that go unpaid. In a 2001 case, *Rogers v. Cigna HealthCare,* a group of physicians in Texas alleged that Cigna had evaded paying for medical services that had been provided. In a similar vein, the Maryland Insurance Commissioner in 2001 declared $1.4 million in administrative penalties plus disciplinary action to five health plans for allegedly neglecting to reimburse claims within the 30-day time frame allotted, and failing to comply fully with state insurance law.[11]

LEGISLATION

In addition to tracking case management protocols and practice guidelines, case managers need to monitor local and national legislative and regulatory changes and statutes to make certain their practice is in line with current regulations. This task can appear daunting. Major pieces of pertinent legislation include the following:

- The Employee Retirement Income Security Act (ERISA) of 1974 governs the majority of nongovernmental employee benefit plans. It exempts companies that self-insure from meeting the same minimum benefit regulations that govern insurance companies.

- The Tax Equity and Fiscal Responsibility Act (TEFRA) of 1982 amended the Social Security Act and made Medicare secondary to employer group health plans for active employees 65 to 69 years old and their spouses in the same age group. It also revised the Age Discrimination in Employment Act (ADEA) of 1967 by requiring employers to offer active employees age 65 to 69 and their spouses the same health benefits as those made available to younger employees.
- As a result of the Social Security Amendments of 1983 (Title IX), Medicare reimbursement shifted from reasonable costs to diagnosis-related groups (DRGs). The amendments also clarified professional review organization (PRO) functions.
- The Consolidated Omnibus Budget Reconciliation Act (COBRA) of 1986 eliminated the age cap of 70; made the employer's plan the primary payer for all active, Medicare-eligible employees and their spouses regardless of age; mandated the extension of medical plans after termination from a job and after a person becomes ineligible under medical coverage; required employers with health care plans to provide health care coverage to former employees, divorced or widowed spouses of employees, and former dependent children of employees at group rates over a fixed amount of time.
- The Omnibus Budget Reconciliation Act (OBRA or *oh boy, regulations again*, with a nod to Alice Gosfield) of 1986 made private employer health plans primary and Medicare secondary for claimants who were permanently disabled and were covered dependents under a working spouse's health plan or for claimants who returned to active employment.
- The Health Care Quality Improvement Act (HCQIA) of 1986 established the National Practitioner Data Bank mentioned earlier.
- The short-lived Medicare Catastrophic Coverage Act (MCCA) of 1988, which was repealed in 1989, mandated the largest expansion of Medicare since its introduction in 1965: a cap of $1,370 for personal expenses for physicians' services; elimination of all cost sharing for inpatient hospital care after the deductible; and revisions in skilled nursing, home health, and respite care benefits.
- AIDS-related legislation passed in 1988 by Congress provided funds for research, education, HIV testing, and home health demonstration projects.
- The Omnibus Budget Reconciliation Act (OBRA) of 1989 and 1990 included updates to HCQIA and required states to extend Medicaid coverage to all pregnant women and children up to age 6 with family incomes less than 133% of the federal poverty level.
- The Agency for Health Care Policy and Research (AHCPR) was created as a result of OBRA of 1989. The agency has developed the Office for Forum on Quality and Effectiveness to publish and disseminate national clinical prac-

tice guidelines. It is now called the Agency for Healthcare Research and Quality (AHRQ).

- The Civilian Health and Medical Program of the Uniformed Services (CHAMPUS) gives all active and retired military personnel and dependents access to treatment at any Department of Defense medical facility. Retired military personnel, their dependents, and dependents of deceased personnel are compensated by CHAMPUS if they are not eligible for Medicare.
- The Federal Employees Health Benefits Program (FEHBP) provides health insurance coverage for federal government employees. The coverage is voluntary and includes variable benefit and premium levels and a choice of competing health plans.
- The Federal Patient Self-Determination Act of 1990 required that adult patients be given written information about the state's policy regarding advance directives, living wills, and durable powers of attorney. The AHA Patient's Bill of Rights noted earlier in this chapter was an outgrowth of this bill.
- The Americans with Disabilities Act (ADA) of 1990 (federally enforced beginning in 1992) required that employers not prevent employees from returning to work even if they can no longer perform 100% of their jobs. In her presentation "Case Management & Alphabet Soup: Understanding FMLA, ADA, OSHA & DOT" at the CMSA's 1997 national conference, Deborah DiBenedetto noted that the ADA prohibits discrimination against "qualified individuals with disabilities," regarded as having an impairment and/or a record (or history) of impairment, and seeks to balance reasonable accommodation and undue hardship.
- The Family and Medical Leave Act (FMLA) of 1993 applies to companies and public agencies employing at least 50 people and enables covered employees to apply for 12 weeks of unpaid time off in each 12-month period, taken intermittently or in a block. This short-term leave is set aside for the care of themselves (in the case of illness or injury); a sick spouse, child, or infant; or for the birth of a child. During the leave, the employer must maintain health benefits as the worker desires. In a 1997 article, *Business Insurance* noted the interrelationship between FMLA, the ADA, and workers' compensation benefits. Citing expert advice from speakers at the Risk & Insurance Management Society, Inc. conference in April 1997, the piece states that benefits from other sources, such as short- or long-term disability and workers' compensation, may be used toward the 12-week FMLA limit. According to government rules, "workers' comp leave can count against the 12-week FMLA allowance if the absence is due to a qualifying illness or injury and the employee is properly notified in writing that the leave will count as FMLA leave." Also, "the employer is not required to pay health

benefits beyond the 12 weeks if the worker cannot return to his or her job; in that case, COBRA benefits should be assigned."[12]

- The Health Insurance Portability and Accountability Act (HIPAA) of 1996 (first known as the Kassebaum-Kennedy Act) curbs employers' ability to deny health benefit coverage to employees with preexisting medical conditions and allows Medical Savings Accounts (MSAs) on a trial basis for employers with fewer than 50 employees. It also included amendments that set a timetable for putting in place privacy regulations and electronic standards for medical record keeping, as well as penalties for breaking them. These went into effect mid-year 2003.

- The Health Centers Consolidation Act of 1996 included a definition of "required primary health services," incorporating patient case management.

- In 1996, more than a dozen states enacted legislation requiring health plans to provide inpatient coverage for at least 48 hours following normal childbirth and 96 hours following a caesarean section. Among these states were Alaska, Connecticut, Georgia, Illinois, Maine, Maryland, Minnesota, Oklahoma, Pennsylvania, South Carolina (72 hours for C-sections), South Dakota, and Washington.

- Federal legislation requiring health plans to provide at least 48 hours of inpatient coverage following a normal birth and 96 hours of coverage following a caesarean was enacted at the federal level in 1996, as well, as the Newborns' and Mothers' Health Protection Act. Federal regulations issued in late 1998, and put into effect January 1, 1999, provided guidance to employers on how to comply with the law. Approximately six states either passed or were considering bills to give managed care enrollees direct access to certain specialists, customarily obstetricians and gynecologists, without first having to see a primary care physician.

- Other federal legislation that would have impacted case management included the Comprehensive Long-Term Care Act of 1997, which would require case management plans under Medicare long-term care and permit a Medicare beneficiary to request case management assessment regarding one's status as a "dependent individual," and the Medicare Patient Choice and Access Act of 1997, which would require direct access to specialists as determined by the case manager and provider, and allow a specialist to serve as a case manager regarding chronic conditions, were actively debated with portions of each folded into the Balanced Budget Act of 1997.

- The Balanced Budget Act of 1997 established the State Children's Health Insurance Program (SCHIP), Medicare+ Choice plans, provider-sponsored organizations (PSOs), TEFRA limits, and other education programs, payment schedules, etc. It also mandated a demonstration of coordinated care in the fee-for-service Medicare program, the impetus for the Medicare Coordinated Care Demonstration Project.

- The Patient Protection Act of 1997 defined utilization review broadly, requires health plans to have utilization review programs that meet standards or are state certified, mandates provider credentialing, [13] and established The Health Care Consumer Advisory Board.

- The Children's Health Insurance Program, legislation dubbed "Kid Care," was passed by Congress in mid-1997 providing federal funding to the states to build programs offering health care coverage to children in low-income families who are uninsured and to those whose parents' employer plans don't offer family coverage. From 1998 to 2000, $3.2 billion in federal funds was left unspent, eliciting George Bush's proposal that states have until 2006 to use the money, before it's returned to the treasury. (Some states deliberately underused the fund to maintain their eligibility for other programs, as well.) Case managers will have to track their state's utilization of its portion of the $24 billion in block grants to ascertain how this safety net can be best used by their clients.

- In late 1997, President Clinton presented his health care agenda, outlining legislation he planned to pursue, including a ban on so-called drive-through mastectomies, when coverage is denied for an overnight hospital stay following a mastectomy. Clinton called on Congress to enact legislation for mastectomy coverage similar to the mandated 48 hours of inpatient/normal birth and 96 hours of caesarean coverage. In 1997 and 1998, several states (Connecticut, Oklahoma, Rhode Island) adopted Breast Cancer Patient Protection Acts requiring insurers to cover a minimum of 48 hours of hospitalization for mastectomies and 24 hours for lymph node excision. Introduced to the 106th Congress as part of H. R. 383 in 1999, the concept was referred to the Committees on Commerce, Education and the Workforce, and Ways and Means. Mastectomy length of stay was reintroduced in the 107th Congress and designated The Breast Cancer Patient Protection Act, H. R. 536. Let's fast forward. In 2003, legislation requiring a minimum hospital stay for mastectomies and lymph node dissections was introduced to the 108th Congress in H. R. 1886.IH (Breast Cancer Patient Protection Act of 2003) and H. R. 1448.IH (Women's Cancer Recovery Act of 2003), and to the Senate as S. 10 (Health Care Coverage Expansion and Quality Improvement Act of 2003). Let's see what happens next. In addition, Clinton also called for a ban on gag rules, a clause that was included also in the Patient Right To Know Act. He cited as problems the lack of early retiree health care coverage for those not yet eligible for Medicare and the need for subsidized health care coverage for the unemployed.

- In December 2000, President Clinton announced Patient Privacy regulations, issued under the authority of the bipartisan Health Insurance Portability and Accountability Act (HIPAA). President Bush authorized these early in 2001, with full compliance required by April 2003. Under the regulations, patients gained the right to see their own medical records and to limit what information doctors can give to insurance companies, rights that had been limited in some states.
- The Mental Health Parity Act of 1996 expired in October 2001. Lawmakers have extended it each year since then, and did so again in December 2002. The act calls for health plans to set mental health services reimbursement limits that are at least equal to those for medical and surgical care. As studies prove that mental diseases such as depression can be linked directly to genetic makeup, the call for mental health parity is becoming stronger.
- In mid-2003, President Bush's first proposal to give seniors a drug benefit by forcing them to move into managed care was dropped, following its poor reception. House and Senate representatives then passed bills for two different pieces of $400 billion legislation to add a prescription drug benefit to Medicare, the biggest expansion of the program since its inception in 1965, intended to take effect in 2006. Both bills included private, stand-alone insurance policies for drug coverage and similar deductibles. Lawmakers working to reconcile the two bills have hit a sticking point: finding a compromise for the way each bill provides extra assistance to low-income elderly or disabled. (In July 2003, the House voted to guarantee that Congress and civilian federal workers would be able to hold onto their prescription drug benefits when they retire, even if the final Medicare drug bill provides significantly lower benefits. In essence, they are working to pass a bill they hope never applies to them.)
- Medical Malpractice/Tort Reform was hotly debated in 2003, especially on the state level. Physicians in West Virginia reported a 150% increase in their medical liability insurance rates in 18 months and reacted by planning early retirement, moving to other states, and requesting state legislation to control escalating costs. In Pennsylvania, a general surgeon pays twice what his fellow surgeon in New Jersey pays in malpractice insurance premiums. Recruiting new doctors to the state has become a problem. Several states are pursuing tort reform as a solution, and setting caps on noneconomic (pain and suffering) damages in medical malpractice cases. We will be hearing more on this subject.
- Also in the pipeline are several bills concerning coverage for veterans: H.R. 533, the Agent Orange Veterans' Disabled Children's Benefits Act of 2003, H.R. 1048, the Disabled Veterans Adaptive Benefits Improvement Act of 2003, and H.R. 966, the Disabled Veterans' Return-to-Work Act of 2003.

DAY-TO-DAY PRACTICES

There are a number of areas in case management practice in which common sense and thinking ahead helps case managers prepare for liability claims (see also Appendix 5–B). As mentioned throughout this handbook, discussions and decisions regarding the case management treatment plan should be documented. If a patient, family member, or physician resents or is unhappy with case management intervention, this too should be documented, along with memos on steps taken to resolve any concerns or problems. Routine patient and provider satisfaction surveys will help monitor quality assurance and serve as an indicator of responsiveness to patient needs (see Chapter 9).

In practice, follow the agreed treatment plan. Noncompliance with the plan can be construed as mismanagement. In any publicity or marketing efforts, avoid puffery or claims that case management guarantees better outcomes or cost containment. In contract making, be very cautious of any type of incentive compensation arrangement with a payer or provider. Again, remember that case management is customarily administrative in nature. However, in rural areas and certain situations, a nurse case manager might provide hands-on care. Consequently, case managers should not insinuate that they are in any way determining the medical treatment plan.

Case managers should keep suspicions, conjectures, and allegations out of their correspondence and reports; these documents can be subpoenaed. A situation can be objectively covered in a report without accusation and without giving legal weight to either side in court. It is enough to record a patient's verbalized wish to return to work and the missed job interviews as well, letting the judge decide the motivations behind the actions. Similarly, a case management report can mention that a patient has stated his or her benefit payments have been significantly delayed, causing hardship; that the patient has been directed to contact a claims examiner; and that the case manager has undertaken to relay this information to the claims examiner—end of story. Case managers should consider what might happen if "the other side" sees the report.

Individuals and payers increasingly are suing plans for adverse decisions. Some UR nurses and individuals called case managers simply shorten length of stay (LOS) and deny benefits, which can be perceived (as well it might be) as harmless by patients, increasing the number of suits naming case managers.

Further, case managers may be requested by either party in a court case to appear as witnesses. (Although nurses are rarely called, the tide may be turning; certified rehabilitation counselors and vocational counselors can and do serve as witnesses in court.) If requested to appear in court, a case manager should consult with the client and a lawyer.

To defend her own interests, a case manager needs to remain involved in a case. If taken off a case ("We don't need you now; the home health company will take care of it"), the case manager should document the situation in an accurate and objective manner. The report might include language such as this: "Despite our suggestions that we continue to monitor this case actively and despite our concern for the patient, which was communicated to our client, the client has decided to end case management involvement in this case." Further, the case manager should file copies of the written notices to the patient, the medical provider, and all other members of the treatment team informing them that she is no longer involved at the client's request, not because the case manager thinks there is no need. The case manager should also make certain the patient knows whom to contact—the physician, therapist, claims examiner, and so on—if a problem arises.

GETTING LEGAL INFORMATION

No case manager has to be a lawyer, but it is important to be current regarding case management professional guidelines. There are conferences specifically for case managers, training seminars, a host of national conferences relevant to case management, and magazine coverage of pertinent issues. *The Case Manager,* for instance, includes a regular feature called "Laws, Liabilities & Legislation." Other publications, such as the *Case Management Advisor, Inside Case Management, Remington Report, Managed Care Interface, Care Management, Journal of Case Management, NARPPS Journal, Journal of the American Medical Association, Journal of Clinical Ethics, Continuing Care, Wall Street Journal, Rehabilitation Nursing Journal,* and the *American Journal of Nursing* also carry articles on medicolegal issues.

Unfortunately, much of the law that will eventually affect case management practice is currently in the process of creation. While clear codes of conduct are being formulated, case managers should do the following:

- Work within the guidelines that already govern case management practice settings.
- Develop a risk-management mentality. ("How do I protect myself, my company, and my patients against lack of knowledge?")
- Act according to their best judgment and keep apprised of changes in the profession. ("Is this how another prudent person in this profession would act in similar circumstances?")
- Use common sense and instinct. If something does not feel right, it probably is not. Network and ask questions of peers.
- Get a lawyer who is knowledgeable about case management.
- Document case management activities and decisions in an objective manner.

- Purchase professional liability insurance in the form of a personal or corporate policy.

NOTES

1. J. Boling, "Legal Issues in Case Management," in *Managing Case Management Seminar Manual* (Little Rock, AR: Individual Case Management Association, 1991), 183.

2. J. Boling, "Legal Issues in Case Management," prepared for the Individual Case Management Association, January 1994. (The material was adapted from "Confidentiality: An Issue CMs Must Understand," handouts developed by Susan Scheutzow for the Medical Case Management Conference IV in Orlando, 1992.)

3. S. Scheutzow, "Confidentiality: How a Case Manager Can Protect It," in *Medical Case Management Conference V Manual* (Little Rock, AR: Individual Case Management Association, 1993), 323.

4. T. Hyatt, "Contracting for Case Management Services," in *Medical Case Management Conference V Manual,* (Little Rock, AR: Individual Case Management Association, 1993), 395–398.

5. G. Carneal and L. Caprio, ed., *Case Management Trends: An Overview of Recent Industry and Regulatory Developments* (Washington, D.C.: URAC, 2002).

6. A. Gosfield, "Clinical Practice Guidelines and Managed Competition: Legal Implications for Case Managers," session audio tape recorded at the Medical Case Management Conference V, Orlando, Florida, September 1993.

7. A. Gosfield, "Clinical Practice Guidelines."

8. M. King, "Liability for Negligence," *Legal and Risk Management Issues in Case Management Seminar Manual* (Little Rock, AR: Individual Case Management Association, 1991), 87.

9. P. R. Kongstvedt, *The Managed Healthcare Handbook,* 4 ed. Gaithersburg, MD: Aspen Publishers Inc., 2001: 1227.

10. S. Schantz, "Legal and Legislative Aspects of Case Management," presented at Upward Bound, CMSA 7th Annual Conference and Educational Forum, Boston, MA, June 1997.

11. A. G. Hendricks and W. J. Cesar, "How Prepared are You?" *The Case Manager* 14, no. 3 (2003): 58.

12. R. Kazel, "Leave Act Shouldn't Scare Employers," *Business Insurance* 31, no. 17 (1997): 39.

13. Schantz, "Legal and Legislative Aspects of Case Management," 320–321.

Appendix 5–A Written Agreement: Some Typical Provisions

Caveat: While these provisions have been prepared by a professional attorney, they should not be used as a substitute for legal counseling in specific situations. Readers should not act upon the information contained herein without professional guidance.

1. *Recitals.*

This Agreement is entered into by and between _____ (Payer), a _____ corporation and _____ (Case Manager), an individual residing in _____.

Whereas Payer has entered into an agreement with one or more employee health benefit plans (the Plan) and thereunder has agreed to provide case management services to beneficiaries of those plans; and

Whereas Case Manager is a registered nurse licensed in _____ and certified by _____, who desires to perform case management services to beneficiaries of the Plan, as appropriate;

Now, therefore, for adequate consideration, the receipt and sufficiency of which are hereby acknowledged, the parties agree as follows:

2. *Duties of Payer.*

(a) Payer authorizes Case Manager to perform services defined in Section 3 for beneficiaries referred by Payer to Case Manager pursuant to _____.

(b) Payer shall provide to Case Manager current, accurate and complete benefit plan information pertinent to beneficiary and shall cooperate with Case Manager in explaining terms of such benefit plans and in supplying Case Manager with any information.

(c) Payer shall provide to Case Manager all necessary waivers of confidentiality for release of medical information, which it warrants, are valid for beneficiary.

(d) Payer represents and warrants that plan documents are sufficient to authorize the performance of the case management services to be performed by Case Manager pursuant to this Agreement.

(e) Payer represents and warrants that it shall maintain professional and general liability insurance coverage in the amount of _____, which shall provide primary coverage for any claims arising from the acts of Payer pursuant to its agreement with the Plan and this Agreement.

(f) Payer represents and warrants that it shall make and communicate to beneficiary all benefit determinations regarding beneficiary's health insurance coverage and that Case Manager's reports and recommendations shall be advisory to Payer and may form the basis, in whole or in part, of Payer's benefit determinations. Case Manager shall have no responsibility to make or communicate benefit determinations.

(g) Payer represents and warrants that as part of its benefit determination program it has in place an appeals process that complies with the Guidelines for Health Benefits Administration published by _____ _____.

3. *Duties of Case Manager.*

(a) Case Manager shall receive referral of beneficiary by Payer pursuant to _____.

(b) Case Manager will review beneficiary's coverage as supplied by Payer and necessary waivers of confidentiality. If this information is incomplete or inadequate, Case Manager shall contact Payer and shall not take any further actions until such information is complete and adequate.

(c) Case Manager will obtain pertinent medical information from beneficiary, facility or primary or admitting physician(s) as necessary and shall devise an alternative plan of treatment for beneficiary. Case Manager shall provide beneficiary and physician(s) with alternative plan of treatment and thoroughly discuss plan with same. If physician(s) and beneficiary competently agree with the alternative plan of treatment, Case Manager will obtain their written consent thereto. Thereafter, Case Manager will contact providers of such alternative treatment and secure rates.

(d) If agreeable to beneficiary and physician(s), Case Manager shall facilitate beneficiary's access to alternative treatment. Case Manager shall report in writing to Payer within _____ business days its recommendations and outcome with originals of all written consents by beneficiary and physician(s).

(e) If not agreeable to beneficiary and physician(s), Case Manager shall report in writing within _____ business days to Payer its recommendations and outcome. Thereafter Case Manager's responsibilities with regard to said beneficiary shall end.

(f) Case Manager represents and warrants that it shall maintain professional liability insurance coverage in the amount of _____, which shall provide primary coverage for any claims arising from the acts of Case Manager pursuant to this Agreement.

4. *Compensation.*

For the duties performed by Case Manager under this Agreement,

(a) Payer agrees to compensate Case Manager at a rate of $_____ per hour, which shall include travel time as necessary.

(b) Payer shall pay Case Manager within thirty (30) days of its receipt of invoice from Case Manager.

(c) [Penalty for late payment.]

(d) [Additional fees for expenses of Case Manager such as supplies and Xeroxing.]

5. *Relationship of Parties.*

Payer and Case Manager mutually agree that there shall be no relationship between them other than an independent contractor relationship, and nothing herein shall be construed to create a principal-agent, employment or partnership relationship. Payer shall neither have nor exercise any control or direction over the methods by which Case Manager performs its duties under this Agreement. Case Manager recognizes that Payer shall not pay or withhold on behalf of Case Manager any sums for income tax, unemployment insurance, social security or any other withholding requirement of any law.

6. *Indemnification.*

(a) Payer agrees to indemnify Case Manager and hold it harmless from and against any and all claims, losses, liabilities, suits, damages and expenses incurred by Case Manager, including court costs and attorney's fees, to the extent such claims, losses, liabilities, suits, damages, and expenses arise out of any acts or omissions of Payer, its officers, agents or employees, or arising from any breach or default on the part of Payer in the performance of its duties under this Agreement or under the Plan.

(b) [Only if Case Manager has to, insert corresponding indemnification of Payer by Case Manager.]

7. *Term and Termination.*

This Agreement shall commence on _____ and continue for a term of one year. Thereafter, this Agreement shall automatically renew each year for successive one-year terms. Either party may terminate this Agreement without cause upon _____ days prior written notice to the other. In the event Case Manager is in the process of performing services hereunder for referred beneficiaries at the time of termination, Case Manager shall complete such performance even if to do so extends past the date of termination. The right of Case Manager to be paid for services already performed hereunder shall continue past the date of termination of this Agreement.

8. *Miscellaneous.*

(a) Choice of law/venue;

(b) Assignment;

(c) Compliance with applicable laws;

(d) Entire agreement/amendment; and

(e) Other.

In witness whereof, the parties hereto have caused this Agreement to be executed on _____, 20_____.

Payer	Case Manager
Name:	Name:
Title:	Title:
Date:	Date:

Source: Reprinted from *Medical Case Management Conference V Manual*, pp. 399–404, with permission of ICMA and Thomas K. Hyatt, Esq., ©1993.

Appendix 5–B Legal Issues in Case Management Checklist

COMPETENCE OF THE CM

❑ 1. Are you properly trained and licensed? Have all qualifications been checked and documented?

❑ 2. Are you working toward the highest appropriate credential license or certification? Are you maintaining appropriate continuing education units to support the existing credential/license?

❑ 3. Are you first a client (claimant) advocate? Does your CM practice reflect this standard?

❑ 4. Are your case management plans created in concert with treating physician and client?

❑ 5. Are you familiar with your company's Job Description and Organization Chart and Policies and Procedures?

❑ 6. Is there anything in your current operations that seems inconsistent with existing formal standards for CM? (If so, discuss with your supervisor and/or legal counsel to resolve.)

CONSENT/DISCLOSURE

❑ 1. What consent form and written materials explaining case management services are you using? What is required? (Discuss any concerns about appropriate procedure or materials with supervisor and/or legal counsel.)

❑ 2. How do you explain CM services?
—by phone?
—by brochure?

❑ 3. Is your explanation consistent with staff, appropriate, and accurate?

CHANGE OF PROVIDER

❑ 1. Is your CM role empowering/facilitating to physicians and clients? Are you directing care or transfer without physician and/or client agreement? (If so, stop. Rethink and revise your role.)

❑ 2. Are you always acting within the scope of your licensure, your own competence and education? (If not, focus your CM practice on your area of competence and/or obtain additional supervision, education or experience to support you in an expanded role.)

In reviewing referral policy procedures

❑ 3. How are practitioners/agencies/facilities evaluated?

❑ 4. Is a continuous inquiry into credentials and practice of the above documented?

❑ 5. Is patient/family offered a choice? Are pros and cons reviewed with family appropriately? Is referral in patient's best interest?

❑ 6. Have you followed up after referral to assure good care?

❑ 7. Are referrals with knowledge of benefit/funding structure?

CONFIDENTIALITY

❑ 1. Do you know state legislation relating to confidentiality and reporting concerns, which apply to your CM practice?

Check Areas of Applicable Legislation
❑ Patient right of access to medical information
❑ Abuse/Neglect—Child and Elder
❑ Contagious/Occupational Disease
❑ Alcohol Treatment
❑ Chemical Abuse Treatment
❑ Mental Health Treatment
❑ AIDS/Sexually Related Disease
❑ Abortion

❑ 2. Do you know and/or have you reviewed and are you complying with your company's confidentiality policy? (Review and revise if necessary with legal counsel.)

❑ 3. Are you clear about the appropriate path of medical information in your office to assure confidentiality is protected?

❑ 4. Are discarded medical records shredded?

❑ 5. Are faxed medical records handled so they are only seen by appropriate people?

❑ 6. If CMs have field files away from office, are they locked at all times in car or home? Are they safe? Who might have access?

❑ 7. If electronic records, are they accessed only by appropriate people?

❑ 8. If information returns to employer, is it "sanitized" so individuals cannot be identified? Who sees this information?

❑ 9. Are CM files retained according to state law then destroyed as medical records? (Adults 5–7 years; Children, to age of majority)

❑ 10. Is documentation concise yet complete for CM assessment, plan, implementation, follow-up, and outcome?

❑ 11. Do you know clearly how to handle medical information with employers, self-insureds, families of competent clients, others requesting access to your files?

CONTRACTING

❑ 1. Are contracts or letters of agreement (LOA) in place for all major referring accounts?

❑ 2. Are these contracts or LOA reviewed by legal counsel before signing?

❑ 3. Do contracts clearly define
- your duties?
- payer's duties?
- your compensation and time of compensation?
- insurance coverage and identification?
- term for performance?

❑ 4. Do agreements/contracts avoid incentive compensation (or waste) arrangements? (May cause appearance of overemphasis on financial arrangements corrupting judgment regarding your primary responsibility of client advocacy.)

❑ 5. Do the entities referring cases to you have the authority to authorize you to perform CM services? Do they warrant that fact?

❑ 6. Do you understand the benefits and restrictions of different payer/ reimbursement systems? (i.e. group health, indemnity HMO, PPO, reinsurance, COBRA, work comp, liability, Medicaid, Medicare, CHAMPUS, military, etc.)

CLIENT CARE NEGOTIATION

❑ 1. Does state insurance law allow you to proceed with quality and cost negotiation for client care and services?

❑ 2. Do quality issues always supersede cost issues?

❑ 3. Are you operating in concert with the primary physician and client? With their understanding and support?

❑ 4. On major decisions, do you have client and physician written consent?

❑ 5. Have you documented referral data on all options being considered?

❑ 6. Is there a direct contract in place, which establishes a rate? Is this non-negotiable?

❑ 7. How and to whom will the agreed upon quality and cost of care be documented? Monitored? Concluded?

COSTUMER SERVICE/RISK MANAGEMENT

- ❑ 1. What's your company's Incident Occurrence Reporting System?
- ❑ 2. What is your CM quality assurance program? Do you keep routine patient satisfaction surveys as a quality assurance monitor?
- ❑ 3. Are all advertising/marketing materials and procedures fair and appropriate? (not overstated)
- ❑ 4. Is staff consistent in offering information describing CM services and CM company?
- ❑ 5. Are written materials and policy reviewed by legal counsel?
- ❑ 6. Who communicates benefits decisions? (Never communicate a payer benefits decision unless the payer indemnifies you for it.)
- ❑ 7. What are your corporate, personal liability, medical malpractice, and errors and omission policies? Do you review them regularly with the carriers?
- ❑ 8. Do you keep current by
    - • reading journals, medical, and general literature?
    - • attending seminars, conferences in your area of practice?
    - • networking with peers on local, regional, and national level?
- ❑ 9. Are potential clients transported by CM? (Be sure liability insurance is in place to support.)
- ❑ 10. Is there a policy regarding staff protection when there is possible exposure to violent and high-risk neighborhoods?

Source: Developed by Jeanne Boling, MSN, CRRN, CDMS, CCM for the "Case Management Practice" Seminar and used with the permission of the Foundation for Rehabilitation Certification, Education and Research, © 1994.

Appendix 5–C AMA Evidence-Based Principles of Discharge and Discharge Criteria

H-160.942 EVIDENCE-BASED PRINCIPLES OF DISCHARGE AND DISCHARGE CRITERIA

(1) The AMA defines discharge criteria as organized, evidence-based guidelines that protect patients' interests in the discharge process by following the principle that the needs of patients must be matched to settings with the ability to meet those needs.

(2) The AMA calls on physicians, specialty societies, insurers, and other involved parties to join in developing, promoting, and using evidence-based discharge criteria that are sensitive to the physiological, psychological, social, and functional needs of patients and that are flexible to meet advances in medical and surgical therapies and adapt to local and regional variations in health care settings and services.

(3) The AMA encourages incorporation of discharge criteria into practice parameters, clinical guidelines, and critical pathways that involve hospitalization.

(4) The AMA promotes the local development, adaption and implementation of discharge criteria.

(5) The AMA promotes training in the use of discharge criteria to assist in planning for patient care at all levels of medical education. Use of discharge criteria will improve understanding of the pathophysiology of disease processes, the continuum of care and therapeutic interventions, the use of health care resources and alternative sites of care, the importance of patient education, safety, outcomes measurements, and collaboration with allied health professionals.

(6) The AMA encourages research in the following areas: clinical outcomes after care in different health care settings; the utilization of resources in different care settings; the actual costs of care from onset of illness to recovery; and reliable and valid ways of assessing the discharge needs of patients.

(7) The AMA endorses the following principles in the development of evidence-based discharge criteria and an organized discharge process: (a) As tools for planning patients' transition from one care setting to another and for determining whether patients are ready for the transition, discharge criteria are intended to match patients' care needs to the setting in which their needs can best be met. (b) Discharge criteria consist of, but are not limited to: (i) Objective and subjective assessments of physiologic and symptomatic stability that are matched to the ability of the discharge setting to

monitor and provide care. (ii) The patient's care needs that are matched with the patient's, family's, or caregiving staff's independent understanding, willingness, and demonstrated performance prior to discharge of processes and procedures of self care, patient care, or care of dependents. (iii) The patient's functional status and impairments that are matched with the ability of the care givers and setting to adequately supplement the patients' function. (iv) The needs for medical follow-up that are matched with the likelihood that the patient will participate in the follow-up. Follow-up is time-, setting-, and service-dependent. Special considerations must be taken to ensure follow-up in vulnerable populations whose access to health care is limited. (c) The discharge process includes, but is not limited to: (i) Planning: Planning for transition/discharge must be based on a comprehensive assessment of the patient's physiological, psychological, social, and functional needs. The discharge planning process should begin early in the course of treatment for illness or injury (prehospitalization for elective cases) with involvement of patient, family and physician from the beginning. (ii) Teamwork: Discharge planning can best be done with a team consisting of the patient, the family, the physician with primary responsibility for continuing care of the patient, and other appropriate health care professionals as needed. (iii) Contingency Plans/Access to Medical Care: Contingency plans for unexpected adverse events must be in place before transition to settings with more limited resources. Patients and caregivers must be aware of signs and symptoms to report and have a clearly defined pathway to get information directly to the physician, and to receive instructions from the physician in a timely fashion. (iv) Responsibility/Accountability: Responsibility/accountability for an appropriate transition from one setting to another rests with the attending physician. If that physician will not be following the patient in the new setting, he or she is responsible for contacting the physician who will be accepting the care of the patient before transfer and ensuring that the new physician is fully informed about the patient's illness, course, prognosis, and needs for continuing care. If there is no physician able and willing to care for the patient in the new setting, the patient should not be discharged. Notwithstanding the attending physician's responsibility for continuity of patient care, the health care setting in which the patient is receiving care is also responsible for evaluating the patient's needs and assuring that those needs can be met in the setting to which the patient is to be transferred. (v) Communication: Transfer of all pertinent information about the patient (such as the history and physical, record of course of treatment in hospital, laboratory tests, medication lists, advanced directives, functional, psychological, social, and other assessments), and the discharge summary should be completed before or at the time of transfer of the patient to another setting. Patients should not be accepted by the new setting without a copy of this patient information and complete instructions for continued care. (8) The AMA supports the position that the care of the patient treated and discharged from a treating facility is done through mutual consent of the patient and the physician; and (9) Policy programs by Congress regarding patient discharge timing for specific types of treatment or procedures be discouraged. (CSA Rep. 4, A-96; Reaffirmation I-96; Modified by Res. 216, A-97)

Source: Council on Scientific Affairs Report 4. Evidence-Based Principles of Discharge and Discharge Criteria. American Medical Association, Annual Meeting, Chicago, IL; June 1996. Available at http:www.ama-assn.org/ama/pub/article/2036-2459.html. Accessed: July 18, 2003.

CHAPTER 6

Ethical Responsibilities of the Case Management Profession

Closely connected with questions of legality are questions of ethics or morality. In any health care delivery system, our primary motivation should be the health, welfare, respect, and dignity of the individual. The moral principles and ethical values attached to this—autonomy, beneficence, fidelity, justice, nonmalfeasance, and veracity—are at the core of patients' rights and case managers' responsibilities.[1]

Autonomy is a respect for the patient's right to self-determination; that is, we ought to respect his right, as much as possible, to make his own decisions about his care. Beneficence is our charge to promote and act for the patient's good, to further a person's legitimate interests, and to actively prevent or remove him from harm. Fidelity involves faithfulness, trustworthiness, and duty; keep your promises. Justice is the maintenance of what is right and fair, nonmalfeasance means to do no harm (and as ethicist Mark Meaney points out, repair harm caused), and veracity requires that we tell the truth.

It is not illegal for a case manager to accept a finder's fee from a durable medical equipment supplier, but neither is it ethical. There is no law prohibiting a case manager from taking the season football ticket from a rehabilitation center contact, but it does cloud the objectivity of the relationship. Whether self-employed or working in a health care setting or insurance firm, case managers have to make clear decisions regarding their ethical standing.

Money is shifting to case management. Providers understand the purchase power case managers wield and their ability to refer to one facility over another. It has been an accepted marketing strategy in the medical industry for providers and pharmaceutical houses to wine and dine physicians and others who might recommend their institutions or products. Given the relative newness of case management and its professionals (e.g., nurses just entering the field from hospital settings), such perks are unexpected and they look very good. To avoid the criticism that case managers have become just another part of the "fat" medical bureaucracy (and, even more important, to avoid the possibility of litigation), case managers must rely on their inner conscience to remain free from associations in which objectivity could be questioned.

As a stronger incentive, association directives and legislation are putting handcuffs on any type of overemphasis on a certain drug when the pharmaceutical company making the drug is sponsoring the conference on the condition the medication is used to treat. The Pharmaceutical Research and Manufacturers of America (PhRMA) adopted a voluntary code on Interactions with Healthcare Professionals in 2002 that includes comprehensive guidelines limiting offers of scholarships and educational funds, practice-related items, gifts (stethoscopes versus golf balls, for example), travel, lodging, use of a corporate box at a football game, and more.

There are ethical dilemmas on the patient side of case management as well. John appears fit, is begging to return to work, and has mentioned his readiness to his employer, who is eager to have him back in the machine shop at his old station—the only job station that is available to him at this time. However, John has not been able to control a hand tremor completely, which will jeopardize his safety at the drill. Does the case manager fudge her report on his capabilities and release him to work?

Jane, while recuperating from a skin graft, has returned to a drug habit she had kicked 3 years ago. Her employer and family are unaware of the problem. Does the case manager keep this "secret" to herself or take steps to enroll Jane in a drug rehabilitation program?

Mary has made it clear to her family and the case manager that she does not want her life prolonged by any artificial means under any circumstances. The treating physician has authorized the insertion of a feeding tube and family members are reluctant to challenge the doctor's authority. Does the case manager raise the issue or let it pass?

Three cases that involved ethical and/or moral concerns are included in Tables 6–1, 6–2, and 6–3. In each case example, we address the choices made to resolve the challenges we faced.

Table 6–1 Ethics Case Study 1

The case of a 29-year-old female with an extremely communicable disease was reported to Options Unlimited by the acute care treating facility, 1 day after admission. In speaking with the patient directly, we learned that she had recently been overseas, visiting her native country. She is married and has two very young children. One week after her return to the United States and her employment (through the client group with which we are affiliated), the patient

Table 6–1 continued

demonstrated symptoms of her illness and shortly thereafter, was admitted to the hospital.

During her course of treatment (while inpatient), questions arose at Options:

1) Was the case, with this diagnosis, reported to the Centers for Disease Control (CDC)?
2) What risk factors pertain to her immediate family and to her coworkers with whom the patient was in contact after her return to work?
3) Should measures be taken (and if so, what/how; with/to/for whom) regarding notification to the employer in order to prevent exposure to other employees, the patient's coworkers?
   a) How will this affect confidentiality issues with/for the patient?
   b) Specifically, what are Options Unlimited's responsibilities in this matter?
4) What, if any, responsibility does Options Unlimited have with regard to protection of the patient's immediate family (spouse and two very young children, ages 1 and 3)?

What we did:

1) Verified that the CDC was provided with appropriate, reported information;
2) Discussed with CDC and treating physicians and researched (from our end) the necessary precautions that must be taken by the patient, her family, her employer, and her coworkers to prevent spread of the disease;
3) Educated the patient and her family regarding the necessary precautions to take; verified understanding and willingness to comply/adhere to the necessary precautions;
4) Asked the patient whether she had discussed her illness with her employer/coworkers;
   a) We found that she had, in fact, discussed her condition with her HR Department and coworkers. (*This fact opened the door for us to then intervene in that regard.*)
5) Spoke with HR Department at the patient's job (with the patient's permission);
   a) Verified the necessary precautions/measures needed/taken to prevent contamination/spread of the disease.

Thought-provoking concerns/dilemmas:

1) What was the responsibility to patient versus responsibility to employer and/or coworkers had the patient not previously discussed her condition with them?
2) What should/could have been done with that scenario?
3) Did Options perform actions appropriately in this case as noted?
4) Is there something else which should/could have been done?

Source: Courtesy of Options Unlimited, Case Management Services Division, Huntington, New York.

Table 6–2 Ethics Case Study 2

A 50-year-old female was admitted to acute care for treatment of substance abuse, opioid dependence. During the course of her treatment in acute care, Options Unlimited learned of her history of drug use/abuse, which she advised began after a motor vehicle accident many, many years ago. Her "neck problems" continue, she is "in constant pain," and needs further care and treatment of her cervical disc situation. The MD who prescribed all of her addicting drugs was (per the patient) "recently brought up on charges for issuing too many prescriptions for drugs." We also learned that she was molested as a child, and that she is currently employed as an individual who works with mentally handicapped, young adults.

Concerns/questions that arose:

1) Ability of patient to perform her job requirements
2) Concern of abuse for those committed to her care:
   a) Neglect due to her drug use
   b) Possible physical abuse to those in her care due to her own history of abuse
   c) What, if any, responsibility/obligation belongs to Options in this matter?
3) Need to determine (or rule out) actual medical/surgical concerns that need to be addressed in addition to her substance abuse and psychological issues
4) Do we have any obligation with regard to the report about the physician who ordered the numerous addictive drugs?

Dilemma:

1) What are our responsibilities to the patient versus responsibility to her employer and the young adults in her care (as far as disclosure of our information obtained and the concerns that followed)?
2) What are the legal ramifications of any actions taken on the part of Options Unlimited in all regards?

What we did:

1) Consulted with psychiatrists and medical doctors to rule out any physical conditions that would/should be monitored/addressed
2) Followed case through discharge from acute care
3) Set her up with outpatient care for follow-up treatment regarding psych/substance abuse issues, and continued treatment of same
4) Negotiated fees for care and treatment by nonparticipating providers
5) Monitored monies used due to a limited dollar benefit in order to maximize her care and treatment
6) Reported the patient's information with regard to her past history (social and medical), job function(s) and her statement regarding her physician being brought up on charges to the benefit plan to note their system of same. We

Table 6–2 continued

also encouraged the Plan to have this physician removed from preferred provider listings.

What we wanted to do but did not (because of concerns over breach of confidentiality and legalities):

1) Report our findings about the patient's job functions and our noted concerns regarding same to the employer/HR department
   a) No evidence of abuse toward those in her care was found, therefore, tying our hands in this matter. We understand that without reported misconduct or question of abuse, there is no action possible.

Outstanding questions:

1) Should we/could we have intervened further; if so, in what regard and to what degree?

Source: Courtesy of Options Unlimited, Case Management Services Division, Huntington, New York.

PATIENT RIGHTS AND CASE MANAGER RESPONSIBILITIES

Case managers have access to a great deal of information. What will the decision be regarding the disclosure of someone's substance abuse or HIV status when the choice involves either compromising one's principles or losing a client? When the choice involves telling the patient's wife or not?

When I talk to case managers across the country about the push and pull of ethical issues, for instance, autonomy versus beneficence, sometimes the patient's right to autonomy is in direct conflict with some of the other principles. The individual has the right to make his own decisions about treatment, the right to refusal, the right to information, all rights we want to safeguard. Although that is true, questions arise with regard to beneficence, doing no harm, or promoting good. Does the patient have the right to select treatment even if it is going to drive up the cost? Does he have the right to continue poor health habits? In patient advocacy versus resource control, a case manager will advocate for the patient and protect his rights. How can one protect the life of a one-pound baby and still strike a balance vis-à-vis plan resource control? Questions arise regarding end-of-life issues: Does the 80-year-old person requesting an organ transplant have fewer rights than a 5-year-old child? How can one make those decisions?

It is a difficult, introspective challenge. You must know what your values are, and respect the rights and values of the individuals upon whose behalf you are

Table 6–3 Ethics Case Study 3

A 33-year-old pregnant female is deemed to be high risk for preterm labor/delivery, and is placed into case management to monitor and assist in coordinating care and treatment to prevent threat of complications, early birth of infant, etc. During our initial interview with the patient, we are advised that she is unmarried, but lives with the father of the child. She is HIV+, which she contracted from her deceased husband, who acquired the disease from a blood transfusion after injuries sustained in an MVA many years prior. The father of the child she is currently carrying (her significant other) is aware of all facts. The rest of the patient's family are aware of the pregnancy, but none are aware of the positive HIV status; that's the way the patient wants it.

As far as the patient's job function(s), she reported that she is employed in a manufacturing plant and works on a line in which small pieces of glass and/or metal frequently "fly off" and hit her in the legs, causing bleeding and the necessity for her to "pick out the pieces with tweezers." She states that she has "never put anyone at the job in risk." She adamantly wants any/all information related to her HIV status to be kept from her employer and especially the occupational health (OH) nurse in the plant, who is described as "too nosey."

Within a very short time of obtaining the noted information, the patient (unfortunately) informed our case manager that she did not want to continue with our intervention, as she had others (social workers, physician's nurses, supportive boyfriend, etc.) following up with her frequently.

We believe (but cannot confirm) that she became "skittish" over the fact that we were affiliated with the benefit plan whose client is her employer. We asked if that concerned her, but she denied same, and simply wanted her case closed.

We did so, reluctantly.

What we did:

1) Discussed the possibility of her transitioning into another job function, which would not expose her to flying debris; advised that in following that recommendation she could state that her request was due to her pregnancy status, to make it less taxing on herself by coming off the line, thus accomplishing that issue while also preventing any coworker, the OH nurse, or employer from becoming suspicious as to her HIV+ status
2) Role-played with the patient to empower her to have the confidence needed to have such a conversation with her employer/superior
3) Offered the possibility for psychological treatment intervention (to assist the patient in dealing with her family and their lack of knowledge of her condition, also to assist in her fears of OH nurse/employer finding out about her status)
4) Notified the benefit plan of the patient's status and job function
5) Notified the benefit plan and the physician of case closure per the patient's request

Table 6–3 continued

Dilemma/frustrations/concerns:

1) We believe that our first and foremost concern/responsibility is that the patient's confidentiality issues not be breached regarding her HIV. However, we are also very concerned over the risk of exposure to her coworkers. Are we appropriately prioritizing?
2) Is there a way of decreasing the risk of exposure to the patient's coworkers without breaching the patient's confidentiality? If so, how/what could we have done?
3) Is there anything else we should have done in this case?

Source: Courtesy of Options Unlimited, Case Management Services Division, Huntington, New York.

working. Ethical matters do not have easy answers, and the continuing emphasis on cost containment and our improving technical abilities contributes to the rising concerns of health care professionals. We have not anticipated the horrible outcomes that people live with as a result of some of the wonderful advances. To save that one-pound baby who then becomes dependent on his family for every activity of daily living may be acceptable for the family during the initial stages when the family unit can care for the infant. However, when the baby becomes a young adult and then a full-grown adult, the family and society shoulder a huge burden in caring for this individual. Technology creates both wonders and nightmares.

Many hospital networks today are very competitively pursuing profit margins, perhaps by discharging patients in a timely fashion so they may capture more of the resources, especially in capitated contracts. The hospital-based case manager or social worker involved in discharge planning may not feel comfortable sending a person home, yet there is a push on the utilization review (UR) team to free the bed, or there is a productivity level to be met (a certain number of cases to be carried). When does our professional concern for that patient outweigh the financial motivations and concerns of the institute that employs us? On one hand, the case manager's role and responsibilities have been defined by her employer; on the other hand, she knows how complex some of these issues are. When does she say, enough is enough? Not only is this not fair, it puts the patient, the hospital, and me at risk.

With home care contracts pushing more for the patient and family to become their own care providers, some case managers in home care agencies are being pushed to transfer patients to less supervised home care far earlier than we would normally deem wise. I think there are many home care case managers with very mixed feelings about the capabilities of patients and families to take on the care programs.

A case manager in a rehabilitation facility may find herself in a different situation. She may know that a person might well go home, deriving more use of the benefit dollars if discharged. Perhaps there are only $50,000 lifetime benefits in terms of rehabilitation needs. Yet the rehabilitation facility that employs her has a need to keep the beds filled as long as possible. Job viability and security might depend on it.

In a managed care organization, a case manager might find herself participating in a bonus arrangement for most number of days saved or highest dollar amount saved. With this incentive to cut days for a personal or team award, she might do something that is, if not illegal, certainly ethically questionable. At the very least, the bonus system creates competition rather than coordination among departments.

We were never divided in quite this way. Under the traditional health care system, there was no question that our role was as an advocate for the patient. I am not sure that nurses or employers (or patients) still wholeheartedly believe that we serve solely in the patient's best interests, especially for those employed by managed care organizations.

Many of these issues are money-driven. I believe most case managers feel the ethical pull now because of finances. As nurses and social workers, we never really had to be involved with money matters, never had to make those kinds of decisions, and were not directed to push patients out of hospitals. There was no reason for it. They remained in hospital care until they were well enough to go home. We did not have the technology to enable them to survive, so it was not an issue, and no one lived long enough to use a million dollars worth of benefits. Money is certainly driving many of the health care decisions being made, who gets it, for how much, and for how long. Health care professionals, physicians, social workers, nurses, and therapists now are all involved in these financial issues and are no longer so well-guided by the standards of practice and codes of conduct that gave us answers earlier in our more traditional settings.

Case management was a direct response to both technological advances and the monetary constraints and issues, but because we sit squarely in the middle of the health care process, we must deal with these ethical problems. Because health care is now managed like a business, health care professionals often find themselves reporting to business managers who might not understand or be sympathetic to the ethical dilemmas. We are working in buildings that look the same but are run quite differently. To survive, we must respond in kind. We need to know more about the financial issues of health care. Just as we want the CEO, hospital director, or medical director to understand our role, we have to compre-hend their need to balance the budget. They face the same ethical dilemmas and are as unequipped as we are to address them. Whereas earlier we experienced over-utilization of services, possibly driving costs up, now we have under-utilization as an area for fraud and abuse because patients are not being given access to ser-vices. Futility of treatment is another issue. Are we being empathetic profession-als? Is this patient really suffering, or are our actions really driven by another motive—profit?

More dialogue needs to take place between health care managers, financial managers, and case managers. Certainly, when dialogue happens, some of the issues are so confrontational and confusing that we need ethicists and legal pro-fessionals to assist us in the decision-making process. Are the treatment paths we are considering legal? What is the appropriate ethical choice? I believe our health care colleagues feel they are swimming in the same deep waters we are trying to navigate. On Long Island, New York, the Stony Brook University Hospital formed the nonprofit Long Island Center for Ethics, designed to increase the prac-tical application of ethics in the academic, medical, and business worlds.

Groundwork is being laid to bring outdated codes of conduct into line with the realities of the health care industry's day-to-day practices. The American Acad-emy of Physical Medicine and Rehabilitation Code of Conduct includes sections on ethics relating to the patient and patient's family, the practitioner's relationship with members of the rehabilitation team, physician-to-physician relationships, relationships with the community and government, and research and scholarly activity (www.aapmr.org).

The ethical challenges and responsibilities we face heighten in direct propor-tion to a patient's degree of impairment; when a patient cannot be a partner in care due to cognitive or speech difficulties, acting out, or inappropriate or impulsive behaviors, a case manager's ethical responsibilities increase. When cost-control issues are involved, ethical dilemmas multiply as well. If an insurance company initially refuses to pay for medically indicated treatment, is it ethical for a primary care doctor to lie to get the coverage for a patient? Should a doctor deceive an insurance company to gain coverage for bypass surgery for a patient with severe angina or chronic atherosclerosis? How many case managers might misrepresent a condition to get the coverage a patient desperately needs?

Our industry is focusing on these ethical dilemmas. John Banja, PhD, Assistant Director for Health Sciences and Clinical Ethics, Center for Ethics, and Associ-ate Professor of Clinical Ethics at Emory University, speaks and writes on the eth-ical accountabilities of case management and the medical industry in general. During one intense session, topics under discussion included futility of treatment, continuation versus withholding of treatment, the "injury of continued existence," and "distributed justice." The concept—that we, as case managers, take or do not take action based on our professional interpretation of ethical conduct—led to some passionate exchanges.

At issue was the case of a 4-year-old, unconscious and in a persistent vegetative state since age 2, loved by his family and fully treated as a family member, who develops frequent respiratory infections that require ventilatory support and occasional pediatric intensive care support. Further, the child is developing contractures that interfere with his home care and that physicians believe will require surgical intervention.

The child's physician is under pressure to de-escalate the child's treatment. Given the prognosis, the hospital staff questions the clinical appropriateness of continued ventilatory support and future surgery. Other physicians in the pediatrics group wonder about spending significant resources on a child who will not improve and whose care might have adverse repercussions on accessing care for other children in the plan. The HMO considers the proposed surgery to be heroic, whereas the family insists that everything possible be done.[2]

Selected responses from panel and audience members portray the multiple considerations that constitute an ethical dilemma and decision:

> It is true that case managers are often caught in the middle, and I guess that's where I think they ought to be. What I would like to suggest is that the case manager is going to have an increasingly important role as a mediator. You advocate for the patient, yet you also balance cost and quality. In the process of mediation, there is a lot of emotion. It is very important to provide a forum where we can vent these emotions and patients can voice their concerns.
> —*Mark Meaney, Executive Director, Institute for Clinical and Corporate Ethics*[3]

> This case is fairly typical of cases that we as case managers find ourselves in. In the previous fee-for-service system with unlimited funding available for care, anything that was clinically possible was considered clinically appropriate and necessary treatment. Now, we are hearing more discussion about whether or not care is futile, or inappropriate.
> —*Author as a panel member*[3]

> The whole idea of futility is important to look at, but I'd like to address two issues that relate to the family and the child. Is this child any longer a person? I would like to suggest that there is a philosophical difference between having a life and being biologically alive. [Also], it is not necessarily the responsibility of society to give that family everything it wants for this child. The family can elect to act with their own discre-

tionary resources. It is a harsh view, but we must also consider the obligations to the other siblings in the family. And, what happens to other members of the health plan if the resources are spent on this child? It is possible for people, such as these parents, to make themselves moral heroes at the expense of others.
—*M. Jan Keffer, assistant professor of family health nursing, Indiana University School of Nursing in Indianapolis*[3]

When case management is done well, it is pursuing at least two moral goods. One moral good is patient advocacy and the other is proper use of resources. The key issue is distributive justice. Whenever case managers are faced with a managed care case where the health plan is pushing for conservative care, they should ask the following questions before jumping to any conclusions: What is going to happen to the money and resources saved by our not doing this? Who said that doing everything possible for the patient is in the patient's best interests? Until we start making decisions about what constitutes good managed care and unethical managed care, and what constitutes good case management and unethical case management, any situation involving a health plan denying payment will be greeted by cries of "rationing" and I think that's bunk.
—*Emily Friedman, adjunct assistant professor, Boston University School of Public Health*[3]

There is suffering on the part of the family caregivers; there is suffering on the part of the professional caregivers, and there certainly seems to be suffering on the part of the child. There is a concept called "the injury of continued existence." Is there a point at which being dead is better than being alive?
—*Keffer*[3]

A couple of years ago I went back and looked at what my nursing license says I can do. All it says I can do is teach and advocate. That's all; teach and advocate.
—*audience member*[4]

How do we measure the worth of this little child against someone who may grow up to be 16, 17, 18, and who becomes sexually promiscuous, on drugs, and we're spending a lot for that as opposed to this?
—*audience member*[5]

There isn't one option; there are many options. Parents may opt for everything, but they need to know the consequences of what that every-

thing may be. Frequently they do not because no one has taken the time to explain it to them. Ethics panels help bring to the forefront all of those issues in making sure that everyone understands fully not only the rights and responsibilities, but the possible consequences as well.
—Author, during the keynote[6]

I also voiced my concern that many case managers seem reluctant to enter the ethical arena, to speak up, take a stand as the patient advocate, or blow the whistle on unbundled billing practices, upcoding, or Medicare fraud. We are waiting for a committee to be formed. We are waiting for someone else to take the first step. I would like to see a heightened empowerment of case managers, with an understanding that being a patient advocate is not something we do in name only. We must be willing to confront employers, confront physician groups, and confront plan administrators.

There is another issue often left unsaid but gaining importance. We live in the days of swift technological advances that can sustain life longer than was ever possible. We also live in the age of increasing medical errors. Who pays for the surgery that included a gross medical error—the insurance company, or is a bill ever sent back to the provider? In a pilot program, does a full-disclosure report go back to the insurer?

Case managers sometimes stumble across legal or ethical problems. Among those issues a case manager has an ethical responsibility to report are patients who are potentially or habitually dependent on their medication, who are overmedicated or overtreated by multiple physicians, or who are lying to their physicians regarding compliance. If a patient has not been receiving the treatment that claims are filed for, if an occupational therapist is treating a patient outside practice guidelines, or if a physician inappropriately refers a patient to a center he or she has a financial interest in, the circumstances should be reported to the plan administrator, the treating physician, or a peer review organization. A case manager must develop a knowledge of professional ethics, standards of practice, and the appropriate code of behavior, and must report through proper channels whatever is intolerable, fraudulent, or abusive in hospital or private practice.

CODES OF ETHICAL CONDUCT

To assist case managers in their day-to-day practice, our industry (as well as others) has responded with standards of practice and codes of conduct. The CMSA issued the CMSA Statement Regarding Ethical Case Management Practice (Appendix 6-A) to "provide guidance to the individual case manager in the development and maintenance of an environment in which case management practice is conducted ethically." The CCMC adopted its Code of Professional Conduct for Case Managers with Disciplinary Rules, Procedures, and Penalties, revised in 2001, incorporating three kinds of standards (Principles, Rules of Conduct, and Guidelines for Professional Conduct), along with guidelines and procedures for processing complaints and possible sanctions. In its preamble, it is stated that the Code was designed to achieve goals that include the following: CCM certificants accept the responsibility that their actions or inactions can aid or hinder clients in achieving their objectives; that they provide services in a manner consistent with their education, formal training, and work experience; and that they demonstrate their adherence to certain standards (see Appendix 6–B). In addition, CMSA's Standards of Practice for Case Management, revised in 2002, and *Case Management Practice Guidelines*, discussed further in Chapter 9, offer guidance to direct case management practice.

What I have yet to see is the real use of these documents to empower the case management community. I think if more case managers were to use these documents as they define roles and responsibilities within their departments and make them active, working documents, it would help eliminate some of the problems they are having. It would give them recourse when faced with a choice, presented by an employer, that they feel is unethical.

In early 1997, I developed, along with Mark Meaney, a survey instrument to solicit from case managers in a range of practice settings the scope and type of ethical issues by which they feel challenged on a daily basis. The purpose of the survey (Appendix 6–C), which was subsequently followed up by intensive one-on-one interviews with case managers of various expertise levels, was to establish a field-tested consensus on ethical dilemmas, enabling the CMSA to prepare training tools (a manual, video tapes, training guides) to address those most pressing issues and assist in the education of case managers toward more ethical practice.

LOOK TO YOUR RESOURCES

I have encouraged every managed care organization and every case management department to create an ethics panel or review board to help mediate some of these problematic cases. I do not think any single case manager should have to face alone the kinds of issues touched upon in this chapter. Mediation, collaboration, and input from other professional disciplines will assist in some of these tough calls. A case manager needs a network of people to bounce around ideas about ethical challenges. Perhaps there is an ethicist at a local college or other case managers not in direct competition who can act as sounding boards. The unexpected case will arrive, and case managers need resources for ethical counseling.

In addition to books such as Kenneth Blanchard and Norman Vincent Peale's *The Power of Ethical Management,* there are magazine and newspaper columns that address the issues of professional ethics. Look for a 2004 book titled *Medical Error and Medical Narcissism: Bioethical Explorations* (working title) by medical ethicist John D. Banja, PhD, an associate professor of clinical ethics education at Emory University Hospital, on the ethical issues that arise from medical errors. Ethics issues are also addressed consistently in *The Case Manager* and *Case Management Advisor.*

Books that are helpful in exploring ethical issues include *The Elderly: Legal and Ethical Issues in Health Care Policy* (M. L. Levine, ed., Ashgate Publishing Company, 2004); *Clinical Ethics: A Practical Approach to Decisions in Clinical Medicine,* 5th edition (A. R. Jonsen, M. Siegler, and W. J. Winslade, McGraw-Hill/Appleton & Lange, 2002); *Managed Care: Financial, Legal, and Ethical Issues* (D. A. Bennahum, Pilgrim Press, 2000); *Ethical and Legal Issues in Home Health and Long-Term Care: Challenges and Solutions* (D. A. Robbins, Aspen Publishers, 1996); *Ethical Decision Making in Nursing* (G. L. Husted and J. L. Husted, Mosby, 1995); *The Ethics of Health Care: A Guide for Clinical Practice* (R. Edge and J. R. Groves, Delmar Publishers, 1994); *Ethics on Call* (N. Dubler and D. Nimmons, Vintage, 1992); *Principles of Biomedical Ethics,* 5th edition (T. Beauchamp and J. Childress, Oxford University Press, 2001); *Clinical Ethics,* 3rd edition (Jonsen, Siegler, and Winslade, McGraw Hill, 1992); and *The Crisis in Health Care: Ethical Issues* (edited by N. F. McKenzie, Meridian, 1990).

NOTES

1. C. M. Mullahy, "Satisfaction of Persons Served," in *Ethical Dimensions of the CARF Standards,* ed. J. D. Banja (Tucson, AZ: Commission on Accreditation of Rehabilitation Facilities, 1997).

2. L. F. Hoffman, "Ethics Helps CMs Handle Difficult Cases," *Case Management Advisor* (8, no. 8 1997): 138 (for more information, please call 800-688-2421), and J. Banja, E. Friedman, J. Keffer, M. Meaney, C. M. Mullahy, "Ethical Accountabilities of Case Management," *Journal of Care Management* 3, no. 4 (1997): 4, 12.

3. L. F. Hoffman, "Ethics Helps CMs Handle Difficult Cases," 138.

4. J. Banja, E. Friedman, J. Keffer, M. Meaney, C. M. Mullahy, "Ethical Accountabilities," 24.

5. J. Banja, E. Friedman, J. Keffer, M. Meaney, C. M. Mullahy, "Ethical Accountabilities," 16.

6. J. Banja, E. Friedman, J. Keffer, M. Meaney, C. M. Mullahy, "Ethical Accountabilities," 17.

Appendix 6–A CMSA Statement Regarding Ethical Case Management Practice

INTRODUCTION

This statement is intended to provide guidance to the individual case manager in the development and maintenance of an environment in which case management practice is conducted ethically. Such an environment is one in which morality prevails and there is support for right (good) decisions and actions.

The statement sets forth ethical principles for case management practice. When applied in practice, these principles underlie right decisions and actions. Thus, they can be utilized by individuals or peers to judge the morality of particular decisions and/or actions.

Ethics is inherently intertwined with morality. In the practice of the health care professions, ethics traditionally has dealt with the interpersonal level between provider (e.g., case manager) and client, rather than the policy level which emphasizes the good of society. Ethics deals with ferreting out what is appropriate in situations which are labeled "dilemmas" because there are no really good alternatives and/or where none of the alternatives is particularly desirable. Thus, ethics addresses the judgment of right and wrong or good and bad.

ETHICAL PRINCIPLES IN CASE MANAGEMENT PRACTICE

As professionals emanating from a variety of healthcare disciplines, case managers adhere to the code of ethics for their profession of origin. In all healthcare practices certain principles of ethics apply. Case management is guided by the principles of autonomy, beneficence, nonmaleficence, justice and veracity.

Autonomy is defined as "a form of personal liberty of action when the individual determines his or her own course of action in accordance with a plan chosen by himself or herself" (Beauchamp and Childress, 1979, pg. 56). This is the fundamental ethical principle of case management practice. The role of case manager as client advocate arises from a commitment to the concept of client autonomy. The needs of the client, as perceived by the client, are preeminent. Thus the client is primary relative to decision-making. The case manager collaborates with the autonomous client with the goal of fostering and encouraging the client's independence and self-determination. This leads the case manager to educate and empower the client/family to promote growth and development of the individual and family so that self-advocacy and self-direction of care is achieved.

This implies informing and supporting the clients in their options and decisions related to their healthcare.

From application of the principle of autonomy, the practice of case management is concerned with preservation of the dignity of the client and family. The case manager is knowledgeable about and respects the rights of the individual and family which arise from human dignity and worth, including consent and privacy. The case management plan is individualized and constantly changing based on the needs of the specific client and family. The case manager does not discriminate based on social or economic status, personal attributes, or the nature of the health problems of the client.

Beneficence is "the obligation or duty to promote good, to further a person's legitimate interests, and to actively prevent or remove harm" (Fromer, 1981, pg. 317). In ethical case management practice the application of beneficence is balanced with the interests of autonomy in order to prevent paternalism and promote self-determination. The definition of the principle of nonmaleficence is related to beneficence. Nonmaleficence means refraining from doing harm to others (Frankena, 1973, pg. 5). The realization of this principle in case management practice involves emphasis on quality outcomes.

Although uniformity of thought about the practical application of the principle within our society does not exist, Frankena (1973) defines justice as maintenance of what is right and fair. The concept of distributive justice deals with the moral basis for dissemination of goods and evils, burdens and benefits. The concept of justice raises such public healthcare policy questions as: Who should receive services? Based on what criteria? Who should pay for services for the poor? What services should benefit from government funding?, etc. Case management practice brings the issue of comparative treatment of individuals into sharp focus because on a daily basis it deals with allocation of healthcare resources on an individual level. Case managers know firsthand the dilemmas related to relative access to care based on such factors as geography and ability to pay.

Decisions regarding such goods and benefits as access to healthcare services within a society with limited resources are initially analyzed based on individual need. Where a fundamental need exists, that is, in situations in which an individual will be harmed if a product or service is not provided, the case manager advocates for the individual to receive it. The case manager applies concepts of fairness so as to maximize the individual's ability to carry out reasonable life plans.

Veracity means truth telling. This is an essential operational principle for the case manager in order to develop trust. Trust is an essential forerunner of collaborative relationships between case managers and clients/families and between case managers, providers, and payers. Truth telling also is basic to the exercise of self-determination by the autonomous client/family.

CONCLUSION

The professional case manager strives for a moral environment and practice in which ethical principles can be actualized. Ethical dilemmas are identified and reasonable solutions sought through appropriate consultation and moral action. The ethical case manager is accountable to the client as well as to peers, the employer/payer and to him/herself and to society for the results of his/her decisions and actions.

CMSA Standards of Practice Committee
February, 1996

DEFINITIONS

Client:
The individual who is ill, injured or disabled who collaborates with the case manager to receive services.

Payer:
The individual or entity which purchases case management services.

Family:
Family members and/or those significant to the client.

Source: Reprinted with permission from Case Management Society of America, © 1996.

Appendix 6–B Excerpts from the CCMC Code of Professional Conduct for Case Managers

PREAMBLE

Throughout this document and for the purposes of this document, "client" is used to refer to the individual for whom a CCM certificant provides services; likewise, "payer" is used to refer to the CCM certificant's customer.

CCM certificants recognize that their actions or inactions can either aid or hinder clients in achieving their objectives, and they accept this responsibility as part of their professional obligation. CCM certificants may be called upon to provide a variety of services and they are obligated to do so in a manner that is consistent with their education, formal training, and work experience. In providing services, CCM certificants must demonstrate their adherence to the Committee on Ethics and Professional Conduct.

The basic objective of the Code is to protect the public interest. Accordingly, the Code consists of Principles, Rules of Conduct, and Guidelines for Professional Conduct, as well as the CCMC Procedures for Processing Complaints.

The Principles are fundamental assumptions to guide professional conduct and are advisory in nature. The Rules of Conduct and the Guidelines for Professional Conduct prescribe the level of conduct required of every certificant. Compliance with these levels of conduct is mandatory and will be enforced through the CCMC Procedures for Processing Complaints.

PRINCIPLES

Principle 1: Certificants shall endeavor to place the public interest above their own at all times.

Principle 2: Certificants shall respect the integrity and protect the welfare of those persons or groups with whom they are working.

Principle 3: Certificants shall always maintain objectivity in their relationships with clients.

Principle 4: Certificants shall act with integrity in dealing with other professionals so as to facilitate their contributions with respect to achieving maximum benefits for the client.

Principle 5: Certificants shall keep their technical competency at a level which ensures their clients will receive the benefit of the highest quality of service their profession can offer that is consistent with the client's conditions and circumstances.

Principle 6: Certificants shall honor the integrity and respect the limitations placed on the use of the CCM designation.

Principle 7: Certificants shall obey all laws and regulations, avoiding any conduct or activity that could harm others.

Principle 8: Certificants shall help maintain the integrity of the Committee on Ethics and Professional Conduct for Case Managers.

CCMC RULES OF CONDUCT

Violation of any of these requirements may result in denial or sanctions on the part of the Commission up to and including revocation of the individual's certification.

Rule 1: Intentionally falsifying an application or other documents.

Rule 2: Conviction of a felony that involves moral turpitude.

Rule 3: Violation of the code of ethics governing the profession upon which the individual's primary professional credential upon which eligibility for the CCM designation is based.

Rule 4: Loss of the primary professional credential upon which eligibility for the CCM designation is based.

Rule 5: Violation or breach of the guidelines for professional conduct (i.e., professional misconduct).

Rule 6: Failure to maintain eligibility requirements once certified.

Rule 7: Failure to pay required fees to CCMC.

Rule 8: Violation of the rules and regulations governing the taking of the certification examination.

SCOPE OF PRACTICE FOR CASE MANAGERS

I. Assumptions

- Case management is not a profession in itself but rather an area of practice within one's profession. It is collaborative and trans-disciplinary in nature.
- Certification determines that the case manager possesses the education, skills, moral character, licensing and experience required to render appropriate services based on sound principles of practice.
- Certificants shall practice only within the boundaries of their competence, based on their education, training, appropriate professional experience, and other professional credentials. They shall not misrepresent their role or competence to clients. They shall not attribute the possession of the certification designation to a depth of knowledge, skills, and professional capabilities greater than those demonstrated by achievement of certification.

II. Underlying Values

- Belief that case management is a means for achieving client wellness and autonomy through advocacy, communication, education, identification of service resources, and service facilitation.
- Recognition of the dignity, worth and rights of all people.
- Understanding and commitment to quality outcomes for clients, appropriate use of resources, and the empowerment of clients in a manner that is supportive and objective.
- Belief in the underlying premise that when the individual reaches the optimum level of wellness and functional capability, everyone benefits: the individuals being served, their support systems, the health care delivery systems and the various reimbursement systems.
- Recognition that case management is guided by the principles of autonomy, beneficence, nonmaleficence, justice, veracity and distributive justice.

III. Definition of Case Management

Case management is a collaborative process that assesses, plans, implements coordinates, monitors, and evaluates the options and services required to meet an individual's health needs, using communication and available resources to promote quality, cost-effective outcomes.

IV. Ethical Issues

Because case management exists in an environment that looks to it as a solution for many of the problems in the health care delivery and payer systems, case managers frequently find themselves in ethical dilemmas.

Each case manager must abide by the Committee on Ethics and Professional Conduct for Case Managers as well as by the professional code of ethics of their specific profession for guidance and support in the resolution of these conflicts.

GUIDELINES FOR PROFESSIONAL CONDUCT

G 1—Representation of Practice

Certificants shall practice only within the boundaries of their competence, based on their education, training, appropriate professional experience, and other professional credentials. They shall not misrepresent their role or competence to clients. They shall not attribute the possession of the certification designation to a depth of knowledge, skills, and professional capabilities greater than those demonstrated by achievement of certification.

G 2—Competence

Certificants shall not:

a) handle or neglect a case in such a manner that the certificant's conduct constitutes gross negligence (which for the purposes of this guideline shall mean willful, wanton or reckless disregard of the certificant's obligations and responsibilities).
b) exhibit a pattern of negligence or neglect in the handling of the certificant's obligations or responsibilities.

G 3—Representation of Qualifications

Certificants shall take the necessary steps to represent their qualifications and to correct a misstatement made by a third party with respect to the certificant's qualifications.

G 4—Legal and Benefit System Requirements

Certificants shall work in accordance with applicable state and federal laws and the unique requirements of the various reimbursement systems involved.

G 5—Testimony

Certificants, when providing testimony in a judicial or non-judicial forum, shall be impartial and limit testimony to their specific fields of expertise.

G 6—Dual Relationships

Certificants who provide services at the request of a third-party payer shall disclose the nature of their dual relationship at the outset of the certificant/client relationship by describing their role and responsibilities to parties who have the right to know. Dual relationships, other than payer/client, include, but are not limited to, certificants working with clients who are the certificants' employer, employee, friend, relative, and/or research subject, and must also be disclosed.

G 7—Description of Services

Certificants shall explain services to be provided to the extent reasonably necessary to permit the client to make informed decisions, understand the purpose, techniques, roles, procedures, expected outcomes, billing arrangements, and limitations of the services rendered and identify to whom and for what purpose the results of the services will be communicated.

G 8—Objectivity

Certificants shall maintain objectivity in their professional relationships and shall not impose their values on their clients.

G 9—Relationships with Clients

Certificants shall not enter into any relationship with any client, business, personal or otherwise, that will interfere with the certificant's professional objectivity.

G 10—Confidentiality: Legal Compliance

Certificants shall be knowledgeable about and act in accordance with federal, state, and local laws and procedures related to the scope of their practices regarding client consent, confidentiality, and the release of information.

G 11—Confidentiality: Disclosure

Certificants shall inform the client, at the outset of the certificant–client relationship, that any information obtained through the relationship may be disclosed to third parties. Disclosure of information shall be made only to clients, payers, service providers, and governmental authorities and limited to what is necessary and relevant, except that the certificant must reveal information to appropriate authorities, as soon as and to the extent that the certificant reasonably believes necessary, to prevent the client from: a) committing acts likely to result in bodily harm or imminent danger to the client or others; and b) committing criminal, illegal, or fraudulent acts.

G 12—Confidentiality: Client Identity

Certificants shall maintain the confidentiality of the identity of the client when using data for training, research, publication, and/or marketing unless a written release is obtained from the client.

G 13—Confidentiality: Records

Certificants shall maintain client records, whether written, taped, computerized, or stored in any other medium, in a manner designed to ensure confidentiality.

G 14—Electronic Recording

Certificants shall not electronically record communications with clients without first obtaining the client's written permission.

G 15—Reports

Certificants shall be accurate, honest, and unbiased in reporting the results of their professional activities to appropriate third parties, to avoid exerting undue influence upon the decision-making process.

G 16—Records: Maintenance/Storage and Disposal

Certificants shall maintain records necessary for rendering professional services to their clients and as required by applicable laws, regulations, or agency/ institution procedures. Subsequent to file closure, records shall be maintained for the number of years consistent with jurisdictional requirements or for a longer period during which maintenance of such records is necessary or helpful to provide reasonably anticipated future services to the client. After that time, records shall be destroyed in a manner assuring preservation of confidentiality.

G 17—Use of CCM Designation

The designation of Certified Case Manager and the initials "CCM" may only be used by individuals currently certified by the Commission for Case Manager Certification. The certificant shall not utilize the designation or initials as part of a company, partnership, or corporate name, trademark, or logo.

G 18—Research: Legal Compliance

Certificants shall plan, design, conduct, and report research in a manner consistent with ethical principles and federal and state laws and regulations, including those governing research with human subjects.

G 19—Research: Subject Confidentiality

Certificants who supply data, aid in the research of another person, report research results, or make original data available shall maintain the confidentiality of the identity of the respective subjects unless an appropriate authorization from the subjects has been obtained.

G 20—Unprofessional Behavior

It is unprofessional behavior if the certificant:

a) commits a criminal act that reflects adversely on the certificant's honesty or trustworthiness;
b) engages in conduct involving dishonesty, fraud, deceit, or misrepresentation;
c) engages in conduct involving discrimination against a client because of race, color, religion, age, gender, sexual orientation, national origin, marital status, or disability/handicap;
d) engages in sexually intimate behavior with a client; or
e) accepts as a client an individual with whom the certificant has been sexually intimate.

G 21—Conflict of Interest

Certificants shall fully disclose an actual or potential conflict of interest to all affected parties. If, after full disclosure, an objection is made by any affected party, the certificant shall withdraw from further participation in the case.

G 22—Termination of Services

Certificants shall recommend the termination of case activity when the certificant reasonably believes that the client is no longer benefiting or when services are no longer required.

G 23—Fees

Certificants shall advise the referral source/payer of their fee structure in advance of the rendering of any services and shall also furnish, upon request, detailed, accurate time and expense records. No fee arrangements shall be made that would reduce the quality of care.

G 24—Advertising

Certificants who describe/advertise services shall do so in a manner that accurately informs the public of the services, expertise, and techniques being offered. Descriptions/advertisements by a certificant shall not contain false, inaccurate, misleading, out-of-context, or otherwise deceptive material or statements. If statements from former clients are to be used, the certificant shall have a written, signed, and dated release from the former clients. All advertising shall be factually accurate and shall not contain exaggerated claims as to costs and/or results.

G 25—Solicitation

Certificants shall not reward, pay, or compensate any individual, company, or entity for directing or referring clients to the certificant. Nothing contained herein shall preclude certificants from making reasonable expenditures in entertaining individuals who have referred or may in the future refer clients to the certificant or from giving gifts of minimal value to such individuals.

G 26—Reporting Misconduct

Certificants possessing knowledge, not otherwise protected as a confidence by this Code, that another certificant has committed a violation of any provisions of this code shall promptly report such knowledge to CCMC and to such other authority as may be empowered to investigate or to act upon such actions or violations. Certificants shall not initiate, participate in, or encourage the filing of complaints that are malicious, unwarranted, or without a basis in fact.

G 27—Compliance with Proceedings

Certificants shall assist in the process of enforcing the Committee on Ethics and Professional Conduct for Case Managers by cooperating with investigations, participating in proceedings, and complying with the directives of the Committee on Ethics and Professional Conduct.

Source: Reprinted with permission from *Code of Professional Conduct for Case Managers with Disciplinary Rules, Procedures, and Penalties,* © 2001, Commission for Case Manager Certification.

Appendix 6–C　CMSA Ethics Survey

I. Your Practice Setting and Discipline

I am a:

❏ Nurse
❏ Social Worker
❏ Therapist
❏ Other _____

Employment Setting:

❏ Independent
❏ Facility-Based
❏ Home Care
❏ HMO/PPO
❏ Insurance Carrier/TPA
❏ Employer Group
❏ Other

My contact with patients/claimants is:

❏ Telephone only
❏ By telephone and on-site, as needed
❏ None, but I know of their status through physicians, providers

As a decision maker:

❏ I can assess, plan, recommend, implement and change services, levels of care for patients in conjunction with the physicians.
❏ I can monitor services, but others do the above.

II. Metaethical Analysis (what is important)

When you conduct yourself as an ethical and moral professional, rank your *goals* in *order* of importance (1 being MOST important, 5 being LEAST important):

___ patient outcome
___ quality of life
___ cost savings

___ professional reputation and success
___ appropriateness of care
___ advocacy of patient

III. Descriptive Analysis (how they work)

Which character traits are essential for ethical case management? List as many as you feel are appropriate.

_____
_____
_____
_____

To whom is a case manager responsible?

Assign to each: (1) important, (2) somewhat important, or (3) least important

___ Patient	___ Family of Patient
___ Self	___ Employer
___ Payer	___ Society

Decisions that case managers are asked to make frequently present ethical challenges. The following represent some of them. Please note your response when confronted with the situations below by writing in an a, b, or c:

a) I make the decision comfortably and unassisted.
b) I frequently consult with others.
c) I make the decision, but often or occasionally wonder if it was the right one.

Rank, a, b, or c:

_____ 1. When I have to provide a referral to providers about whom I know little

_____ 2. Referral to in-network providers (physicians, hospitals, home care, etc.) about whom I have reservations, but not doing so results in:
  increased costs to my patients _____
  employment problem for me _____

_____ 3. Family members ask me not to discuss the seriousness of a condition with the patient

_____ 4. Patients ask me to withhold information from their family members or employers

_____ 5. Called upon to manage cases beyond my comfort level or knowledge

_____ 6. When quality of care, poor outcomes or safety of patient is in serious jeopardy but confronting the provider or informing the patient/family of the situation can jeopardize my relationship with the patient or threaten my employment

_____ 7. When I have to balance quality of care with the need to demonstrate savings

_____ 8. Respecting patient autonomy when his/her choices may result in further deterioration and increased costs

_____ 9. Intervening on a patient's behalf whenever a physician continues aggressive treatment despite expressed wishes of the patient

IV. Normative Ethical Analysis (how we do things around here)

Have you ever:

- been offered bonuses directly tied to the amount of savings you or your department achieved?

  ❑ yes   ❑ no   ❑ not applicable

- been offered gifts, finder fees or other incentives for referrals to certain facilities, providers or dealers?

  ❑ yes   ❑ no   ❑ not applicable

- been asked to change contents of a report or other documentation to obscure facts or to remove "damaging" information?

  ❑ yes   ❑ no   ❑ not applicable

- been asked to report outcomes or cost savings that were greater than you felt you obtained?

  ❑ yes   ❑ no   ❑ not applicable

- Are there other ethical issues or dilemmas that you face that were NOT addressed in this survey?

  ❑ yes   ❑ no   ❑ not applicable

If your answer was yes, would you please describe in the space provided.

_____

_____

_____

I would be willing to be contacted for an interview or discussion or to assist as a member of the Ethics Committee:

  ❑ yes   ❑ no

Optional:

Signature: _____

Name: _____

Address/City/State/Zip: _____

Phone: _____

Are you a current CMSA Member?   ❑ yes   ❑ no

Source: Reprinted with permission from Case Management Society of America, © 1997.

CHAPTER 7

HIPAA: The Health Insurance Portability and Accountability Act

The Health Insurance Portability and Accountability Act (HIPAA), passed by Congress in 1966, has had the single greatest impact on the health care industry and the case manager's role; COBRA and Medicare legislation were also far-reaching. In my mind, the conditions of HIPAA touch more people right now and certainly relate more to every case manager's role.

The majority of HIPAA's provisions went into effect back in 1996, eliminating all medical underwriting and severely limiting the impact of exclusions for pre-existing conditions in those plans. The provisions relating to the confidentiality and privacy aspects of HIPAA had a long-deferred compliance date, so they were not the immediate focus of plan writers, providers, payers, or patients.[1] When the effective date in April 2003 for these elements was approaching, there was a wide-scale hiring of software developers, legal assistants, compliance officers, and individuals to oversee the privacy measures. The cost was high, but long-term savings generated by a uniform system for billing, claims processing, benefit coordination, utilization management, and other administrative and health delivery functions are estimated to reach into the billions each year.[2]

TITLE I AND TITLE II

Title I of HIPAA is not an insurance policy itself; instead, it provides rights and protections for individuals and group health plans. It protects employees and their families during times of job loss, pregnancy, moving, and divorce. For employers, it spells out rights when arranging for and renewing health coverage for their employees. Title I addresses portability—whether an individual can get coverage if he chooses to change coverage, availability—whether health coverage must be offered to an individual and his/her dependents, and renewability—whether one is able to renew his health coverage.[3]

Title II has three main components: these include a set of regulations and standards for transactions and coding sets, as well as a set for privacy and confidentiality of patient information. The third part is a set of regulations and standards for the security of this information. The security standards apply to data that is on file and/or during any type of data transfer or sharing with other professionals associated with the provision of care. (Data transfer or sharing can only occur with the signed acknowledgement of and permission for such from the patient).

The transactions and code sets provisions are designed to rid the system of a multitude of different forms that are used to record and transfer the same type of information by hard copy or electronically, and to transfer more of the information filing and data processing to electronic systems, rather than having file cabinets with reams of paper hand-placed into folders. As an example, there were approximately 400 various formats used for health care claims. Add to that the forms used for enrolling members, submitting claims, referring for specialist treatments, and more.

According to HIPAA, insurers and health plans may no longer use proprietary or local coding sets. The medical coding standards approved for use include five that have been in use for years in the industry: *The International Classification of Diseases, 9th Edition, Clinical Modification* (ICD-9-CM); *Current Procedural Terminology, 4th Edition* (CPT-4); *Health Care Financing Administration Common Procedure Coding System* (HCPCS); *Code on Dental Procedures and Nomenclature, 2nd Edition* (CDT-2); and *National Drug Codes* (NDC).

The privacy regulations grant consumers the right to control their medical information, how it is used and distributed. The HIPAA rules clarify the obligations of providers and others to guard the confidentiality of this information, referring to specifics such as the need for a privacy official, a notification of the privacy practice to consumers, signed consent forms from patients, and the consumers' right to see their medical records, and to request a record of where the information has been sent if sent for any reason other than treatment, payment, or health care operations.[4] A sample notice of privacy practices is included in Appendix 7-A at the end of this chapter.

RESOURCES

The Health Care Financing Administration (now called the Centers for Medicare and Medicaid Services) put together a booklet that provides informative details on the individual provisions of the HIPAA regulations and their interpretation. It is called "Protecting Your Health Insurance Coverage" and can be viewed at cms.hhs.gov/hipaa/hipaa1/content/protect.pdf.

Two other good resources are Section 5.0 "Privacy and Case Management: The Impact of HIPAA," written by Dennis Melamed in *Case Management Trends: An*

Overview of Recent Industry and Regulatory Developments, published in 2002 by URAC and available for purchase from CMSA's web site; and Peter R. Kongstvedt's comprehensive chapter in his book, *The Managed Health Care Handbook, fifth edition,* available from Jones and Bartlett (www.jbpub.com).

NOTES

1. J. B. Helitzer, "HIPAA Privacy Rule: A Primer for Plan Sponsors," *C&B Consulting Group, Inc. Update 11,* no. 11 (2002): 1.

2. D. C. Kibbe, "HIPAA Q & A: Just the Facts, Please!" *The Case Manager* 12, no. 6 (2001): 69.

3. N. Hudecek, "Are You Ready for HIPAA?" *Inside Case Management* 10, no 4 (2003): 12.

4. D. C. Kibbe, "HIPAA Q & A: Just the Facts, Please!" *The Case Manager* 12, no. 6 (2001): 71.

Appendix 7–A Summary—Notice of Privacy Practices

MOUNT SINAI
SCHOOL OF
MEDICINE

The Mount Sinai
Hospital
of Queens

A Division The Mount Sinai Hospital

North Shore
Medical Group

SUMMARY - NOTICE OF PRIVACY PRACTICES

THIS IS A SUMMARY OF OUR NOTICE OF PRIVACY PRACTICES, WHICH DESCRIBES HOW MEDICAL INFORMATION ABOUT YOU MAY BE USED AND DISCLOSED AND HOW YOU CAN GET ACCESS TO THIS INFORMATION. WE HAVE ALSO MADE AVAILABLE TO YOU A FULL VERSION OF THE NOTICE.

Our Pledge to Protect your Privacy:
The Mount Sinai Hospital and Mount Sinai School of Medicine ("Mount Sinai") are committed to protecting the privacy of your medical information. So that we can best meet your needs, we share your medical information with all the healthcare providers involved in your care. Only to the extent necessary, we also use and share your information to conduct our business operation, to collect payment for the services we provide to you and to comply with the laws that govern healthcare. We will not use or disclose your information for any other purpose without your permission.

You have the following rights to access and control your health information: (See Notice pp. 3-6)

- To inspect and obtain a copy of your medical and billing records, subject to some special requirements for substance and alcohol abuse, genetic, mental health and HIV-related data;
- To request restrictions on certain uses or disclosures of your medical information;
- To request an accounting of Mount Sinai's disclosures of your medical information;
- To add an addendum to your medical record;
- To request that we communicate with you in a certain way or at a certain location;
- To receive a copy of the full version of our Notice of Privacy Practices.

Examples of how we may use and disclose your health information : (See Notice pp. 6-10)

- To provide you with medical treatment and services;
- To bill and receive payment for the treatment and services you receive;
- For functions necessary to run Mount Sinai and to assure that our patients receive quality care;
- To provide only demographic information to our development office for purposes of fundraising for Mount Sinai;
- To support our research mission as an academic medical center with approval of Mount Sinai's Privacy Board;
- For workers' compensation or similar programs;
- For required public health activities (e.g., reporting abuse or adverse reactions to medications);
- For healthcare oversight (e.g., to the New York State Department of Health);
- For law enforcement in certain limited circumstances;
- To a coroner, medical examiner or funeral director as required by law;
- For organ procurement or transplantation, if you are a potential donor.

3/12/03

MOUNT SINAI
SCHOOL OF
MEDICINE

A Division The Mount Sinai Hospital

The Mount Sinai Hospital
Mount Sinai School of Medicine

NOTICE OF PRIVACY PRACTICES

Effective Date: April 14, 2003

Introduction

THIS NOTICE DESCRIBES HOW MEDICAL INFORMATION ABOUT YOU MAY BE USED AND DISCLOSED AND HOW YOU CAN GET ACCESS TO THIS INFORMATION. PLEASE REVIEW IT CAREFULLY.

The Mount Sinai Hospital (MSH), which includes The Mount Sinai Hospital of Queens (MSHQ), and Mount Sinai School of Medicine (MSSM), including its owned physician practices (Faculty Practice Associates or FPA and Northshore Medical Group or NSMG) (together, "Mount Sinai" for purposes of this notice) are required by law to protect the privacy of health information that may reveal your identity. Mount Sinai is also required to provide you with a copy of this notice which describes the health information privacy practices of its medical staff, and affiliated health care providers that jointly provide health care services with the institution, and to follow the terms of the notice that is currently in effect.

A copy of our current notice will always be posted in our reception area. You will also be able to obtain your own copies by accessing our website at http://www.mssm.edu/HIPAA, calling our office or asking for one at the time of your next visit.

If you have any questions about this notice or would like further information, please contact our Privacy Officer.

PARTICIPANTS

Mount Sinai provides health care to patients jointly with physicians and other health care professionals and organizations. The privacy practices described in this notice will be followed by:

- Any health care professional who treats you at any of our locations;
- All employees, medical staff, trainees, students or volunteers at any of our locations;
- Any business associates of the institution (which are described further below)

These practices will be followed at all of our sites:

Main Manhattan campus, The Mount Sinai Hospital of Queens, Mount Sinai School of Medicine (MSSM) including the Faculty Practice Associates. Off-site locations that are part of these institutions will follow this notice as well. A list of current locations is attached. (Attachment E).

These facilities and individuals will share protected health information with each other, as necessary to carry out the treatment, payment, and healthcare operations described in this notice.

IMPORTANT SUMMARY INFORMATION

What Health Information is Protected. We are committed to protecting the privacy of information we gather about you while providing health-related services. Some examples of protected health information are: information indicating that you are a patient at Mount Sinai or receiving treatment or other health-related services from our institution; information about your health condition (such as a disease that you may have); information about health care products or services you have received or may receive in the future (such as an operation); or information about your health care benefits under an insurance plan (such as whether a prescription is covered); *when combined with:* demographic information (such as your name, address, or insurance status); unique numbers that may identify you (such as your social security number, your phone number or your driver's license number); and other types of information that may identify who you are.

Personal Representatives. If a person has the authority under law to make decisions for you relative to Healthcare ("personal representative") Mount Sinai will treat your personal representative the same way we would treat you with respect to your PHI. Parents and guardians will generally be personal representatives of minors unless the minors are permitted by law to act on their own behalf.

Requirement for Written Authorization. We will obtain your written authorization before using your health information or sharing it with others outside Mount Sinai, except as described below. You may also initiate the transfer of your records to another person by completing a written authorization form. If you provide us with written authorization, you may revoke that written authorization at any time, except to the extent that we have already relied upon it.

Special Protections for HIV, Alcohol and Substance Abuse, Mental Health and Genetic Information. Special privacy protections apply to HIV-related information, alcohol and substance abuse treatment information, mental health information, and genetic information. Some parts of this general Notice of Privacy Practices may not apply to these types of information. Notices explaining how these categories of information will be protected by Mount Sinai are attached as Attachments A-D.

YOUR RIGHTS TO ACCESS AND CONTROL YOUR HEALTH INFORMATION

You have the following rights regarding your medical information:

Right To Inspect and Copy Records

You have the right to inspect and obtain a copy of any of your health information that may be used to make decisions about you and your treatment for as long as we maintain this information in our records. This includes medical and billing records. To inspect or obtain a copy of your health information, please submit your request in writing.

If you request a copy of the information, we may charge a fee, as permitted by law, for the costs of copying, mailing or other supplies we use to fulfill your request. The fee must generally be paid before or at the time we give the copies to you.

We will respond to your request for inspection of records within 10 days. We ordinarily will respond to requests for copies within 30 days if the information is located in our facility and within 60 days if it is located off-site at another facility. If we need additional time to respond to a request for copies, we will notify you in writing within the time frame above to explain the reason for the delay and when you can expect to have a final answer to your request.

Under certain very limited circumstances, we may deny your request to inspect or obtain a copy of your information. If we do, we will provide you with a summary of the information instead. We will also provide a written statement that explains the reasons for providing only a summary and a complete description of your rights to have that decision reviewed and how you can exercise those rights. The notice will also include information on how to file a complaint about these issues with us or with the Secretary of the Department of Health and Human Services. If we have reason to deny only part of your request, we will provide complete access to the remaining parts after excluding the information we may not let you inspect or copy.

Right To Amend Records

If you believe that the health information we have about you is incorrect or incomplete, you may ask us to amend the information. You have the right to request an amendment for as long as the information is kept in our records.

Your request should include the reasons why you think we should make the amendment. Ordinarily we will respond to your request within 60 days. If we need additional time to respond, we will notify you in writing within 60 days to explain the reason for the delay and when you can expect to have a final answer to your request.

If we deny part or all of your request, we will provide a written notice that explains our reasons for doing so. You will have the right to have certain information related to your requested amendment included in your records. For example, if you disagree with our decision, you will have an opportunity to submit a statement explaining your disagreement which we will include in your records. We will also include information on how to file a complaint with us or with the Secretary of the Department of Health and Human Services. These procedures will be explained in more detail in any written denial notice we send you.

Right To an Accounting of Disclosures

After April 14, 2003, you have a right to request an "accounting of disclosures" which is a list with information about how the institution has shared your information with others outside Mount Sinai. An accounting list will not include:

- Disclosures we made to you or your personal representative;
- Disclosures we made pursuant to your written authorization;
- Disclosures we made for treatment, payment or business operations;
- Disclosures made from the patient directory;
- Disclosures made to your friends and family involved in your care or payment for your care;
- Disclosures that were incidental to permissible uses and disclosures of your health information (for example, when information is overheard by another patient passing by);
- Disclosures for purposes of research, public health or our business operations of limited portions of your health information that do not directly identify you;
- Disclosures made to federal officials for national security and intelligence activities;
- Disclosures about inmates to correctional institutions or law enforcement officers;
- Disclosures made before April 14, 2003.

Your request must state a time period within the past six years (but after April 14, 2003) for the disclosures you want us to include. For example, you may request a list of the disclosures that we made between January 1, 2004 and January 1, 2005. You have a right to receive one list within every 12 month period for free. However, we may charge you for the cost of providing any additional lists in that same 12 month period. We will always notify you of any cost involved so that you may choose to withdraw or modify your request before any costs are incurred.

Ordinarily we will respond to your request for an accounting within 60 days. If we need additional time to prepare the accounting list you have requested, we will notify you in writing about the reason for the delay and the date when you can expect to receive the accounting list. In rare cases, we may have to delay providing you with the accounting list without notifying you because a law enforcement official or government agency has directed us to do so.

Right To Request Additional Privacy Protections

You have the right to request that we further restrict the way we use and disclose your health information to treat your condition, collect payment for that treatment, or run our business operations. You may also request that we limit how we disclose information about you to family or friends involved in your care. For example, you could request that we not disclose information about a surgery you had.

Your request should include (1) what information you want to limit; (2) whether you want to limit how we use the information, how we share it with others, or both; and (3) to whom you want the limits to apply.

We are not required to agree to your request for a restriction, and in some cases the restriction you request may not be permitted under law. *However, if we do agree, we will be bound by our agreement unless the information is needed to provide you with emergency treatment or to comply with the law.* Once we have agreed to a restriction, you have the right to revoke the restriction at any time. Under some circumstances, we will also have the right to revoke the restriction as long as we notify you before doing so; in other cases, we will need your permission before we may revoke the restriction.

Right To Request Confidential Communications

You have the right to request that we communicate with you about your medical matters in a more confidential way by requesting that we communicate with you by alternative means or at alternative locations. For example, you may ask that we contact you at home instead of at work.

We will not ask you the reason for your request, and we will try to accommodate all reasonable requests. Please specify in your request how or where you wish to be contacted, and how payment for your health care will be handled if we communicate with you through this alternative method or location.

How to Obtain a Copy of Revised Notice. We may change our privacy practices from time to time. If we do, we will revise this notice so you will have an accurate summary of our practices. The revised notice will apply to all of your health information. We will post any revised notice in our hospital reception area. You will also be able to obtain your own copy of the revised notice by accessing our website at http://www.mssm.edu/HIPAA, calling our office.

or asking for one at the time of your next visit. The effective date of the notice will always be noted in the top right corner of the first page. We are required to abide by the terms of the notice that is currently in effect.

How to File a Complaint. If you believe your privacy rights have been violated, you may file a complaint with The Mount Sinai Hospital (MSH), The Mount Sinai Hospital of Queens (MSHQ), or Mount Sinai School of Medicine (MSSM) including its owned physician practices (Faculty Practice Associates or FPA) or with the Secretary of the Department of Health and Human Services. To file a complaint please contact:

Department of Health and Human Services/Office of Civil Rights at: www.hhs.gov/ocr/hipaa

No one will retaliate or take action against you for filing a complaint.

How We May use and Disclose Your Health Information Without Your Written Authorization

Treatment. We may share your health information with healthcare providers at Mount Sinai who are involved in taking care of you, and they may in turn use that information to diagnose or treat you. A healthcare provider at Mount Sinai may share your health information with another healthcare provider for your diagnosis and treatment.

Payment. We may use your health information or share it with others so that we may obtain payment for your health care services. For example, we may share information about you with your health insurance company in order to obtain reimbursement after we have treated you, or to determine whether it will cover your treatment. We might also need to inform your health insurance company about your health condition in order to obtain pre-approval for your treatment, such as admitting you to the hospital for a particular type of surgery. Finally, we may share your information with other health care providers, payors and their business associates for their payment activities.

Business Operations. We may use your health information or share it with others in order to conduct our business operations. For example, we may use your health information to evaluate the performance of our staff in caring for you, to educate our staff on how to improve the care they provide for you or to conduct training programs for students, trainees and other healthcare practitioners. Finally, we may share your health information with other health care providers and payors for certain of their business operations if the information is related to a relationship the provider or payor currently has or previously had with you, and if the provider or payor is required by federal law to protect the privacy of your health information.

Appointment Reminders, Treatment Alternatives, Benefits and Services. In the course of providing treatment to you, we may use your health information to contact you with a reminder that you have an appointment for treatment or services at our facility. We may also use your health information in order to recommend possible treatment alternatives or health-related benefits and services that may be of interest to you.

Fundraising. To support our business operations, we may use only demographic information about you, including information about your age and gender, where you live or work, and the dates that you received treatment, in order to contact you to raise money to help us operate. We may also share this information with a charitable foundation that will contact you to raise money on our behalf.

Business Associates. We may disclose your health information to contractors, agents and other business associates who need the information in order to assist us with obtaining payment or carrying out our business operations. For example, we may share your health information with a billing company that helps us to obtain payment from your insurance company. Another example is that we may share your health information with an insurance company or law firm, or a risk management organization in order to obtain professional advice about how to manage risk and legal liability, including insurance or legal claims. We may also share your health information with an accounting firm in order to obtain advice on legal compliance. If we do disclose your health information to a business associate, we will have a written contract to ensure that our business associate also protects the privacy of your health information.

Patient Directory. If you do not object, we will include your name, your location in our facility, your general condition (*e.g.*, fair, stable, critical, etc.) and your religious affiliation in our Patient Directory while you are a patient at Mount Sinai or one of the facilities listed at the beginning of this notice. This directory information, except for your religious affiliation, may be released to people who ask for you by name. Your religious affiliation may be given to a member of the clergy, such as a priest or rabbi, even if he or she doesn't ask for you by name. If you wish to opt out or restrict access please inform the Business Associate at registration or your nurse.

Family and Friends Involved in Your Care. If you do not object, we may share your health information with a family member, relative, or close personal friend who is involved in your care or payment for that care. In some cases, we may need to share your information with a disaster relief organization that will help us notify these persons.

As Required By Law. We may use or disclose your health information if we are required by law to do so. We also will notify you of these uses and disclosures if notice is required by law.

Public Health Activities. We may disclose your health information to authorized public health officials (or a foreign government agency collaborating with such officials) so they may carry out their public health activities. For example, we may share your health information with government officials that are responsible for controlling disease, injury or disability. We may also disclose your health information to a person who may have been exposed to a communicable disease or be at risk for contracting or spreading the disease if a law permits us to do so. And finally, we may release some health information about you to your employer if your employer hires us to provide you with a physical exam and we discover that you have a work-related injury or disease that your employer must know about in order to comply with employment laws.

Victims of Abuse, Neglect or Domestic Violence. We may release your health information to a public health authority that is authorized to receive reports of abuse, neglect or domestic violence. For example, we may report your information to government officials if we reasonably believe that you have been a victim of such abuse, neglect or domestic violence. We will make every effort to obtain your permission before releasing this information, but in some cases we may be required or authorized to act without your permission.

Health Oversight Activities.   We may release your health information to government agencies authorized to conduct audits, investigations, and inspections of our facility.   These government agencies monitor the operation of the health care system, government benefit programs such as Medicare and Medicaid, and compliance with government regulatory programs and civil rights laws.

Product Monitoring, Repair and Recall.   We may disclose your health information to a person or company that is regulated by the Food and Drug Administration for the purpose of: (1) reporting or tracking product defects or problems; (2) repairing, replacing, or recalling defective or dangerous products; or (3) monitoring the performance of a product after it has been approved for use by the general public.

Lawsuits and Disputes.   We may disclose your health information if we are ordered to do so by a court or administrative tribunal that is handling a lawsuit or other dispute.

Law Enforcement.   We may disclose your health information to law enforcement officials for the following reasons:

- To comply with court orders or laws that we are required to follow;
- To assist law enforcement officers with identifying or locating a suspect, fugitive, witness, or missing person;
- If you have been the victim of a crime and we determine that: (1) we have been unable to obtain your agreement because of an emergency or your incapacity; (2) law enforcement officials need this information immediately to carry out their law enforcement duties; and (3) in our professional judgment disclosure to these officers is in your best interests;
- If we suspect that death resulted from criminal conduct;
- If necessary to report a crime that occurred on our property; or
- If necessary to report a crime discovered during an offsite medical emergency (for example, by emergency medical technicians at the scene of a crime).

To Avert A Serious And Imminent Threat to Health or Safety.   We may use your health information or share it with others when necessary to prevent a serious and imminent threat to your health or safety, or the health or safety of another person or the public.   In such cases, we will only share your information with someone able to help prevent the threat.   We may also disclose your health information to law enforcement officers if you tell us that you participated in a violent crime that may have caused serious physical harm to another person (unless you admitted that fact while in counseling), if we determine that you escaped from lawful custody (such as a prison) or eloped from a mental health institution.

National Security and Intelligence Activities Or Protective Services.   We may disclose your health information to authorized federal officials who are conducting national security and intelligence activities or providing protective services to the President or other important officials.

Military and Veterans.   If you are in the Armed Forces, we may disclose health information about you to appropriate military command authorities for activities they deem necessary to carry out their military mission.   We may also release health information about foreign military personnel to the appropriate foreign military authority.

Inmates and Correctional Institutions. If you are an inmate or you are detained by a law enforcement officer, we may disclose your health information to the prison officers or law enforcement officers if necessary to provide you with health care, or to maintain safety, security and good order at the place where you are confined. This includes sharing information that is necessary to protect the health and safety of other inmates or persons involved in supervising or transporting inmates.

Workers' Compensation. We may disclose your health information for workers' compensation or similar programs that provide benefits for work-related injuries.

Coroners, Medical Examiners and Funeral Directors. We may use health information to identify a deceased person or determine the cause of death or disclose health information to a coroner or medical examiner for such purposes. We may also release this information to funeral directors as necessary to carry out their duties.

Organ and Tissue Donation. If you are a potential organ donor, we may use your health information or disclose your health information to other organizations that procure or store organs, eyes or other tissues for the purpose of investigating whether donation or transplantation is possible under applicable laws.

Research. In most cases, we will ask for your written authorization before using your health information or sharing it with others in order to conduct research. However, under some circumstances, we may use and disclose your health information without your written authorization if Mount Sinai School of Medicine's Institutional Review Board (IRB), applying specific criteria, determines that the particular research protocol poses minimal risk to your privacy. Under no circumstances, however, would we allow researchers to use your name or identity publicly. We may also release your health information without your written authorization to people who are preparing a future research project, so long as any information identifying you does not leave our facility. We may share health information with people who are conducting research using the information of deceased persons, as long as they agree not to remove from our facility any information that identifies the deceased person.

Completely De-identified or Partially De-identified Information.

We may use and disclose your health information if we have removed any information that has the potential to identify you so that the health information is "completely de-identified." We may also use and disclose "partially de-identified" health information about you for research, public health and specific healthcare operations if the person who will receive the information signs an agreement to protect the privacy of the information as required by federal and state law. Partially de-identified health information will exclude all direct identifiers but may include zip code, dates of birth, admission and discharge.

Incidental Disclosures

While we will take reasonable steps to safeguard the privacy of your health information, certain disclosures of your health information may occur during or as an unavoidable result of our otherwise permissible uses or disclosures of your health information. For example, during the course of a treatment session, other patients in the treatment area may see, or overhear discussion of, your health information.

Attachment A

CONFIDENTIALITY OF HIV-RELATED INFORMATION

Effective Date: April 14, 2003

The privacy and confidentiality of HIV-related information maintained by Mount Sinai is protected by Federal and State law and regulations. These protections go above and beyond the protections described in Mount Sinai's general Notice of Privacy Practices (NOPP). *If you have questions about this notice or would like further information, please contact the Privacy Officer.*

We recommend that you also take time to review the Mount Sinai Notice of Privacy Practices for information about how your health information may generally be used and disclosed by Mount Sinai. The Mount Sinai Notice of Privacy Practices also provides information about how you may obtain access to your health information, including confidential HIV-related information. If there is any conflict between the Notice of Privacy Practices and this notice, the protections described in this notice will apply instead of the protections described in the NOPP.

Confidential HIV-related information is any information indicating that you had an HIV-related test, have HIV-related illness or AIDS, or have an HIV-related infection, as well as any information which could reasonably identify you as a person who has had a test or has HIV infection.

Under New York State law, confidential HIV-related information may only be given to persons allowed to have it by law, or persons you have allowed to have it by signing a written authorization form.

Confidential HIV-related information about you may be used by personnel within Mount Sinai who need the information to provide you with direct care or treatment, to process billing or reimbursement records, or to monitor or evaluate the quality of care provided at the hospital. Generally Mount Sinai may not reveal to an outside person confidential HIV-related information that the institution obtains in the course of treating you, *unless:*

- Mount Sinai obtains your written authorization;
- The disclosure is to a person who is authorized to make health care decisions on your behalf and the information disclosed is needed by that person to make his/her decisions;
- The disclosure is to another health care provider or payer for treatment or payment purposes;

- The disclosure is to a third party of the institution who needs the information to provide you with direct care or treatment, to process billing or reimbursement records, or to monitor or evaluate the quality of care provided at Mount Sinai. In such cases, Mount Sinai will have an agreement with the third party to ensure that your confidential HIV-related information is protected as required under Federal and State confidentiality laws and regulations;
- The disclosure is required by law or court order;
- The disclosure is to an organization that procures body parts for transplantation;
- You receive services under a program monitored or supervised by a Federal, State or local government agency and the disclosure is made to such government agency or other employee or agent of the agency when reasonably necessary for the supervision, monitoring, administration of provision of the program's services;
- Mount Sinai is required under Federal or State law to make the disclosure to a health officer;
- The disclosure is required for public health purposes;
- You are an inmate at a correctional facility and disclosure of confidential HIV-related information to the medical director of such facility is necessary for the director to carry out his or her functions;
- The patient is deceased and the disclosure is made to a funeral director who has taken charge of the deceased person's remains and who has access in the ordinary course of business to confidential HIV-related information on the deceased person's death certificate;
- The disclosure is made to report child abuse or neglect to appropriate State or local authorities.

Violation of these privacy regulations may subject the institution to civil or criminal penalties. Suspected violations may be reported to appropriate authorities in accordance with Federal and State law. To file a complaint mail completed form DOH-2865 (Complaint Report for Alleged Violation of Article 27-F) to:

NYS Department of Health/AIDS Institute/Special Investigation Unit
5 Penn Plaza
New York, New York 10001

Please refer to Mount Sinai's main Notice of Privacy Practices for additional information.

<u>**MOUNT SINAI**</u>

ATTACHMENT B

<u>**CONFIDENTIALITY OF ALCOHOL AND SUBSTANCE ABUSE TREATMENT INFORMATION**</u>

Effective Date: April 14, 2003

The confidentiality of alcohol and substance abuse treatment records maintained by Mount Sinai is protected by Federal and State law and regulations. These protections go above and beyond the protections described in the Mount Sinai Notice of Privacy Practices. *If you have questions about this notice or would like further information, please contact the Privacy Officer.*

We recommend that you take time to review the Mount Sinai Notice of Privacy Practices for information about how your health information may generally be used and disclosed by Mount Sinai. The Mount Sinai Notice of Privacy Practices provides information about how you may obtain access to your health information, including alcohol and substance abuse treatment records. If there is any conflict between the Notice of Privacy Practices and this notice, the protections described in this notice will apply instead of the protections described in the Notice of Privacy Practices.

CONFIDENTIALITY OF ALCOHOL AND SUBSTANCE ABUSE TREATMENT INFORMATION

Confidential alcohol and substance abuse treatment records include any information that identifies you as having been diagnosed with, treated for or referred for treatment of alcohol abuse, substance abuse or chemical dependency.

Information about you may be used by personnel within Mount Sinai in connection with their duties to provide you with diagnosis of, treatment for or referral for treatment of alcohol or substance abuse. Such use will be limited to the minimum amount of information necessary to carry out their duties. Generally Mount Sinai may not reveal to a person outside of Mount Sinai any information that would identify you as under treatment for alcohol or substance abuse, *unless*:

- Your written authorization is obtained;
- The disclosure is allowed by a court order and permitted under Federal and State confidentiality laws and regulations;
- The disclosure is made to medical personnel in a medical emergency;
- The disclosure is made to qualified researchers without your written authorization when such research poses minimal risk to your privacy. When required by law, we will obtain an agreement from the researcher to protect the privacy and confidentiality of your information;
- The disclosure is made to a qualified service organization that performs certain treatment services (such as lab analyses) or business operations (such as bill collection) for Mount Sinai. Mount Sinai will obtain the qualified service organization's agreement in writing to protect the privacy and confidentiality of your information in accordance with Federal and State law;

- The disclosure is made to a government agency or other qualified non-government personnel to perform an audit or evaluation of Mount Sinai. Mount Sinai will obtain an agreement in writing from any non-government personnel to protect the privacy and confidentiality of your information in accordance with Federal and State law;
- The disclosure is made to report a crime committed by a patient either at Mount Sinai or against any person who works for Mount Sinai or about any threat to commit such a crime; or
- The disclosure is made to report child abuse or neglect to appropriate State or Local authorities.

Violation of these privacy regulations is a crime. Suspected violations may be reported to appropriate authorities in accordance with Federal and State law.

Please refer to Mount Sinai's main Notice of Privacy Practices for additional information.

<u>MOUNT SINAI</u>

ATTACHMENT C

<u>CONFIDENTIALITY OF MENTAL HEALTH INFORMATION
AND PSYCHOTHERAPY NOTES</u>

Effective Date: April 14, 2003

The privacy and confidentiality of mental health information and psychotherapy notes maintained by Mount Sinai is protected by Federal and State law and regulations. These protections go above and beyond the protections described in the Mount Sinai Notice of Privacy Practices. *If you have questions about this notice or would like further information, please contact the Privacy Officer.*

We recommend that you also take time to review the Mount Sinai Notice of Privacy Practices for information about how your health information may generally be used and disclosed by Mount Sinai. The Notice of Privacy Practices also provides information about how you may obtain access to your health information, including mental health information. If there is any conflict between the Notice of Privacy Practices and this notice, the protections described in this notice will apply instead of the protections described in the Notice of Privacy Practices.

CONFIDENTIALITY OF MENTAL HEALTH INFORMATION

Mental health information about you may be used by personnel within Mount Sinai (or its Business Associates) in connection with their duties to provide you with treatment, obtain payment for that treatment, or conduct Mount Sinai's business operations. Generally Mount Sinai may not reveal mental health information about you to other persons outside of Mount Sinai, *except in the following situations*:

- When Mount Sinai has obtained your written authorization;
- To a personal representative who is authorized to make health care decisions on your behalf;
- To government agencies or private insurance companies in order to obtain payment for services we provided to you;
- To comply with a court order;
- To appropriate persons who are able to avert a serious and imminent threat to the health or safety of you or another person;
- To appropriate government authorities to locate a missing person or conduct a criminal investigation as permitted under Federal and State confidentiality laws;
- To other licensed hospital emergency services as permitted under Federal and State confidentiality laws;
- To the mental hygiene legal service offered by the State;
- To attorneys representing patients in an involuntary hospitalization proceeding;
- To authorized government officials for the purpose of monitoring or evaluating the quality of care provided by the hospital or its staff;
- To qualified researchers without your specific authorization when such research poses minimal risk to your privacy;
- To coroners and medical examiners to determine cause of death; and
- If you are an inmate, to a correctional facility which certifies that the information is necessary in order to provide you with health care, or in order to protect the health or safety of you or any other persons at the correctional facility.

CONFIDENTIALITY OF PSYCHOTHERAPY NOTES

Psychotherapy notes are notes by a mental health professional that document or analyze the contents of a conversation during a private counseling session – or during a group, joint, or family counseling session. If these notes are maintained separately from the rest of your medical records, they can only be used and disclosed as follows.

In general, Psychotherapy notes may not be used or disclosed without your written authorization, except in the following circumstances.

- The mental health professional who created the notes may use them to provide you with further treatment;
- The mental health professional who created the notes may disclose them to students, trainees, or practitioners in mental health who are learning under supervision to practice or improve their skills in group, joint, family, or individual counseling;
- The mental health professional who created the notes may disclose them as necessary to defend him or herself, or Mount Sinai, in a legal proceeding initiated by you or your personal representative;
- The mental health professional who created the notes may disclose them as required by law;
- The mental health professional who created the notes may disclose the notes to appropriate government authorities when necessary to avert a serious and imminent threat to the health or safety of you or another person;
- The mental health professional who created the notes may disclose them to the United States Department of Health and Human Services when that agency requests them in order to investigate the mental health professional's compliance, or Mount Sinai's compliance, with Federal privacy and confidentiality laws and regulations; and
- The mental health professional that created the notes may disclose them to medical examiners and coroners if necessary to determine the cause of death.
- The mental health professional who created the notes may disclose them to a health oversight agency for a lawful purpose related to oversight of the mental health professional.

All other uses and disclosures of psychotherapy notes require your special written authorization.

Please refer to Mount Sinai's main Notice of Privacy Practices for additional information.

<u>MOUNT SINAI</u>

ATTACHMENT D

<u>CONFIDENTIALITY OF GENETIC INFORMATION</u>

Effective Date: April 14, 2003

The privacy and confidentiality of genetic information maintained by Mount Sinai is protected by State law and regulations. These protections go above and beyond the protections described in Mount Sinai' s general Notice of Privacy Practices. *If you have questions about this notice or would like further information, please contact the Privacy Officer.*

We recommend that you also take time to review Mount Sinai's Notice of Privacy Practices for information about how your health information may generally be used and disclosed by Mount Sinai. Mount Sinai's Notice of Privacy Practices also provides information about how you may obtain access to your health information, including confidential genetic information

Under New York State law, special restrictions apply to (1) genetic testing of human biological samples and (2) the disclosure of information derived from genetic tests to any person or organization. Genetic test means any laboratory test of DNA, chromosomes, genes or gene products to detect a genetic variation linked to a predisposition to a genetic disease.

Mount Sinai will not perform a genetic test on a biological sample taken from you unless Mount Sinai obtains your written informed consent under NYS law. With your informed consent, Mount Sinai may use the results of your genetic test for treatment, payment and healthcare operations (See NOPP pp. 6-7). Any other uses or disclosures of the results of your genetic test will generally require your written authorization. This authorization is separate from, and may not be combined with the informed consent.

Authorization is not required if:

- The disclosure is to a person who is authorized to make health care decisions on your behalf and the information disclosed is needed by that person to make his/her decisions;
- The disclosure is required or allowed by law or court order.
- Mount Sinai's IRB has determined to allow the disclosure of information obtained about you from genetic tests on your stored tissue, or information which links you with specific test results and you have signed either a Research Authorization form or a Consent to Release Genetic Information form under NY Civil Rights Law §§ 79-l(3)(a) and 79-l(9)(d)].

Violation of these privacy regulations may subject Mount Sinai to civil or criminal penalties. Suspected violations may be reported to appropriate authorities in accordance with Federal and State law.

Please refer to Mount Sinai's main Notice of Privacy Practices for additional information.

NOPP
ATTACHMENT E

"Mount Sinai Off-site Locations"

I.   **Mount Sinai Hospital (Manhattan)**

- Primary Care Building (101st Street Manhattan)
  IMA
  Geriatrics
- Adolescent Health Center (94th Street)
- Sports Therapy (59th Street)
- Vocational Therapy (96th Street)
- Psychiatry OPD (1160 Fifth Avenue)
- Dialysis (94th Street)
- REAP (Madison Avenue/98th Street)
- School Based Clinics
- Northshore Practice
- Senior Outreach (5E 102nd Street)
- Visiting Doctors (19 East 101st Street)

II.   **MSSM FPA**

- Community Medicine (1391 Madison Avenue)
- Community Medicine (Astoria, Queens)
- Community Medicine (Yonkers, New York)
- WTC Recovery (1200 Fifth Avenue)
- Primary Care Building (1470 Madison Avenue)
  Geriatrics
- Primary Care Building (1470 Madison Avenue)
  General/IMA
- Psychiatry (1100 Park Avenue Suite 1B)
- Psychiatry (1160 Fifth Avenue, ground Floor, 1 South, 1 North)
- Psychiatry (1 West 85th Street, Suite 1A)
- Psychiatry (57-59 East 96th Street)
- West Side Practice

III. **Mount Sinai Queens**

- Senior Health Center
- Family Health Associates
- Industrial Health Center

3/3/03

PART II

Case Management Procedures

CHAPTER 8

Communications

Because case management has become an integral part of the medical mainstream, it is essential that new dialogues and heightened levels of communication be maintained. Case management is a person-to-person service, and open pathways must be laid for good interaction. More focused and conscious communication is needed between case managers and physicians, patients, families, payer sources, and related legal entities. To communicate effectively with each of these groups, case managers must recognize the obstacles to communication and strive to overcome them.

I think it is also important for case managers to make their letters, phone calls, and reports useful to the people they are addressing. It sounds simplistic, but it is appalling how many case managers totally ignore this basic rule of communication. Case management nurses in particular, more than rehab professionals or vocational counselors, tend to offer explicit, medically oriented information to individuals who have not the foggiest idea of what the terms mean, that this blood gas is saturated or unsaturated, elevated or unelevated. The data may be of some use to another nurse or physician, but they are of no help to an adult child of a patient or to a claims examiner. This does not mean that a case manager should never attempt to produce a professional-looking report or should never use medical terminology when speaking with a claims examiner, but I suggest reinforcing the medical terminology with remarks to further educate the referral source or recipient.

COMMUNICATING WITH PHYSICIANS

Working against positive communication between case managers and physicians are stereotypical judgments long held by each group about the other. In many ways, the stereotypes derive from the personality traits that cause an individual to become a physician or a case manager in the first place. Physicians tend to be results oriented, trained to "diagnose and treat," with only episodic patient involvement. Case managers, who usually come from traditional caretaker professions such as nursing and social work, maintain ongoing patient contact to perform their functions. Therefore, from the onset, case managers tend to view physicians as being less interested in their patients, whereas physicians tend to regard case managers as being overly involved or downright obstructionist.

A second obstacle to case manager–physician communication is the health care system itself. Churning with change, it is unwittingly pitting health care professional against health care professional. Despite a common cause (the well-being of patients), physicians and case managers are becoming adversaries in an eroding system in which territorial struggles run rampant. With the bureaucracy collapsing around them, physicians view case managers with a wary eye, wondering, "Are they going to take my patients away?" or "Are they going to try to tell me how to treat my patient?"

In addition to issues of care control, there are issues of cost control. Misperceptions and misunderstandings stem from the emergence in the 1980s of cost containment as a factor influencing health care delivery. Necessitated by advancing medical technologies with advancing price tags, a longer-lived population requiring care, and a shrinking pool of dollars funding both general and high-tech treatment, managed care practices have placed case managers and physicians in "uncharted territory." Neither group of professionals is accustomed to considering, much less negotiating, the cost of care.

Mistrusting them as "claims police" who deny patient access to needed care (and confusing them with "gatekeepers" who sometimes deny care based on computer software programs), some physicians perceive case managers as a threat to their medical judgment and their income. For example, when RNs began assuming clinician roles, establishing clinics in rural areas or in disciplines less attractive to MDs, the traditional physician–nurse relationship remained unchallenged. Nurses were making medical decisions and advising patients on their treatment plans, but there were no physicians in the picture. When case managers, on the other hand, began to be accepted by corporations, insurers, and the public and play an active and high-profile role in devising care plans, some MDs felt their medical opinions were being second-guessed.

Case managers can address both the stereotypes and the stresses of a shifting health care system by opening up positive dialogues with physicians. With a new case comes both the responsibility and opportunity to take a proactive stance and begin promoting better case manager–physician relations. The initial phone call is an example. It is important to communicate the purpose of that call—concern for the patient. Certain cases, by nature of their circumstances, may automatically cause a physician to be on guard regarding the case manager's intent. For example, a case manager may be called upon to intervene on behalf of a patient who has been in an acute care setting for 3 weeks and for whom new health care settings are being explored. The case manager needs to relay that there is a concern over the patient's limited policy and that she wants to work with the physician to make better use of the patient's benefit dollars so that funds will be available for a longer period of time. The communication is upfront and professional, and the case manager's role is clearly defined.

This kind of direct communication should not be confused with taking a militant or overly aggressive attitude. Too often, case managers starting out mistakenly believe that in speaking with physicians they need to validate their role—by emphasizing they are representatives of a large insurance company, for instance. However, they soon learn that, instead of causing physicians to acquiesce, this approach alienates them. The more secure case managers are in their role, whether speaking with physicians, hospital discharge planners, social workers, or patients, the better able they are to convey their objectives and all necessary information.

Because of the changing working relationship between case managers (nurses, social workers, and counselors) and physicians, the transition to full collaboration is often awkward. Involved are differences in orientation, training, spheres of influence, and recognition of each group's expertise. Generally, society conceives of physicians as being at the apex of medicine. Buying into this mythical pyramid, nurses, along with other health care professionals, have failed to recognize their own contributions to the system. Caught in their traditional roles by their own and others' perceptions, case managers are sometimes seen as "simply" nurses or assistants. As a result, case managers may not be confident in dealing with physicians and have difficulty assuming anything more than a secondary or tertiary function. Also hindering the establishment of a collaborative alliance with physicians is the so-called sacred physician–patient relationship and physicians' perceptions of their legal responsibility to protect confidentiality. This impediment can also be hurdled by empowering case managers to recognize the value of their role and to understand what their abilities have brought and can continue to bring to health care management.

Case managers have the kind of knowledge and insight into patients' needs that derives from a tradition of 24-hour patient attendance. Most also come with strong medical credentials and experience. Taking on a role that MDs were less inclined or less able to assume due to time constraints, case managers honed their skill in locating and recommending alternative treatment facilities and suggesting options for the provision of care via community services and resources. Some now feel their income and status as professionals are being jeopardized by MDs who are challenging their role in health care delivery and by medical directors at insurance companies and HMOs who do not appreciate or fully understand their contribution to care. It is difficult for case managers to have to confront such resistance and to feel they are being denied entrance into the "inner circle" as widely recognized medical professionals.

In working with physicians, case managers need to make it perfectly clear that their first and foremost concern is for the patients, that their interest is in ensuring the highest quality of care and the best possible outcomes. In addition, physicians must be assured that the case managers are not there to control or dictate patient treatment plans. Instead, the communication between the two groups should create an atmosphere of cooperation and collaboration. Case managers, after all, possess a different knowledge base than physicians (e.g., an understanding of the patients' insurance policies as well as information about various community resources that may be accessed to effect better outcomes).

In short, what must be conveyed is, "We are all focused on our patient." This statement not only sets the stage for a unified effort, but also communicates that the case manager will assume an integral role in the care of "our patient."

To facilitate physicians' receptivity to and cooperation with case managers, exchanges should occur in a certain order. First, case managers must clearly state whom they are representing. Because case managers come from diverse practice settings, ranging from within an insurance company to health care provider or corporate entity, they must establish whom they represent, the organization's interest, and what can be offered in the way of services. A waiver of confidentiality or consent from the patient or guardian should be presented to permit the physician to legally share the necessary information. This introduction should also include an explanation of the line of insurance involved, which shapes the case manager's objectives.

If the case manager comes from a payer group (e.g., an employer group, a Medicare/Medicaid plan, a company's premium or indemnity plan, or a workers' compensation carrier), it is important that she state, for instance, "I am the case manager representing John's employer group working within his workers' compensation plan. John was injured on the job, and my goal is to help your patient get the best possible results and return to work in the shortest period of time, as medically comfortable as possible. If he can't return to his previous type of work, I want to help him find other suitable employment."

Especially given the current chaos in the health care system, including the confusion between case management and managed care, it is critical that this complete introduction and communication of intent is done at the outset. Remember, not every call a physician has received from a case manager has been a positive one. The last "case manager" dealt with may in reality have been a clerk in the utilization review department of an insurance carrier. This individual may have called the physician to say that the carrier's software tracking system indicated that her patient's condition should only require a 3-day hospital stay rather than the 5 days the physician authorized. Understandably, the physician may recall the experience with anger. Because of the possibility of this kind of scenario, the case manager may want to try to establish rapport with the physician's nurse or office administrator in order to pave the way for better communication. This person will also be a tremendous resource in maintaining ongoing communication with the physician.

Timing the Initial Physician Contact

The means by which a case manager acquires a case often dictates the order in which the exchanges with a physician will proceed. Some insurance companies do not permit involvement of a case manager until the treating physician has approved case management. This is akin to putting the cart before the horse. It is also unfortunate, because most physicians, once knowledgeable about case management, welcome the case manager's intervention at the earliest possible stage of treatment. In addition, it is probably unethical, because patients, unless incompetent, should be empowered by the case providers to make decisions on their own behalf.

Typically, the case manager first contacts the patient or family, then the treating physician. In making the initial contact with the patient, and hopefully winning over that individual, the case manager can gain valuable information that can later be passed on to the physician. The preliminary contact can also be used to confirm the identity of the patient's physician and determine his or her schedule for visiting the patient. The case manager can enlist the patient to alert the physician to expect her call and to tell the physician, "I think it might be helpful to have you and this case manager working together." This plants the seed with the physician that the patient has accepted the case manager and supports a joint effort.

If a patient is in the hospital setting or critically ill with no family members in attendance, the case manager may need to contact the treating physician first (or concurrently with attempts to reach relatives). The first outreach to the physician should be well-planned and well-executed.

It is important to take into account that, like all professionals, physicians have their own work schedules and daily priorities. A surgeon's day, for example, may consist of morning rounds at a hospital, followed by surgeries, then time spent at the office for patient appointments or paperwork, and finally a return to the hospital for postoperative rounds. The case manager should be cognizant of this regimen and acknowledge it when contacting the physician's office. The case manager might say, "I understand Dr. Jones is very busy and may not have time to meet with me during his office hours. Would it be possible for me to call him after hours? Is there a particular time that is better for him?"

Once someone in the physician's office understands that the case manager is aware of the physician's busy schedule demands and is trying to be accommodating, he or she will usually be helpful in coordinating a meeting or telephone contact.

The information gleaned by the case manager in the initial exchange with the patient also influences how time-sensitive the physician communications must be. The case manager may have uncovered relevant information that the patient neglected to tell the physician and that may alter the treatment plan, but it is essential to use common sense in determining the appropriate urgency of the call. By understanding the importance of effective physician contact and properly timing dialogues, the case manager is more likely to make a real contribution toward a successful outcome for the patient.

Finally, in establishing good communication with physicians, case managers should not agonize over their knowledge of a particular medical specialization. Although some large insurance companies or provider organizations may have case managers who concentrate on pediatric or elder care, oncology or cardiac cases, head injuries, and so on, many very effective case managers are generalists. There is nothing wrong with saying to a physician, "I am really not that familiar with your patient's particular treatment plan. Would you explain it further?"

On the other hand, many nurses have had the opportunity to work with very fine physicians, renowned in their fields, and have in-depth experience in specialized areas. Drawing on these resources to gain better insight into a particular case can only serve to equip case managers for more effective partnerships with physicians.

When I started my case management company, I was asked to handle a case involving an infant with a brain stem aneurysm. He had survived an extremely intricate surgical procedure but was left with multiple problems. His neurosurgeon, highly respected and also a clinical professor in a university hospital, was very much in demand and maintained a full schedule. The family was insistent that the physician be involved in all aspects of their child's care. I realized that to gain their trust, I needed to establish a good relationship with the physician.

In trying to reach him, it seemed I was jumping through one hoop after another and getting nowhere. I eventually ended up calling him at his office on a Saturday morning and arranging to meet him the following week after his office hours.

When we met, he was very relaxed and helpful in providing information. He even took the time to draw medical diagrams to clarify his points. He was also outwardly appreciative of my involvement and admitted he did not really understand case management. In fact, he opened up and expressed some of his own difficulties. He said that he entered neurosurgery because of an infinite fascination with the brain, never considering that some cases would require him to give advice regarding a patient's long-term care. He helped me to see that, like many physicians, he just did not have the time or even the preparation for this type of case, one that called for ongoing participation on a number of levels. I, in turn, proved my value by recommending a state-funded early intervention program for the child. The neurosurgeon and I visited the facility and, along with the pediatrician, attended team meetings together. He soon became convinced that this program, by affording the right care and social interaction for the child while alleviating much of the family's stress, was the best alternative. Ultimately, he helped convince the family, who were initially reluctant to remove their child from a home care setting. In that case and others to follow, the physician became a strong ally. This example underscores how a free-flowing and solid case manager–physician relationship facilitates effective communication between the case manager and the patient or family.

Practical Steps to a Win-Win Relationship Between Case Managers and Physicians

The following list details some practices case managers can put into play to better their working relationships with physicians and improve the standing of the entire case management community.

1. Develop an understanding of the physician's practice setting. When is the physician in OR? When is the best time to call the physician's office? Who is the best contact in the office? Sometimes, a nurse or receptionist can provide a quick answer if you frame a clear question over the phone.
2. Go in as a savvy professional. Send the physician credible information on you and your role. Include your credentials.
3. Use your business card. Giving out your card facilitates Rolodex® reference and supports your presentation of yourself as a professional.
4. Assure the physician that you will not be talking to him or her every day about every patient. Present yourself as a collaborative partner, a right-hand associate.
5. Reassure the physician that you will never presume that you can put a better treatment plan into action. You care about license liability and patient outcome as much as he or she does. State that you recognize the need to back up your assessment, and plan to review your findings, concerns, and suggestions with the physician.
6. Never drop in on the physician unannounced. Confirm all your appointments. Emergencies do arise.
7. When you attend a meeting with the physician, state how much you appreciate the time being given. Time is a valued commodity among physicians.

8. Make it easy for the physician to give you the information you need. Often, physicians lack the time to meet in person. Type a questionnaire requesting specific information and enclose a self-addressed, stamped envelope for the reply. Include a copy of an appropriate signed release of information from the patient. In preparing your questions, remember that you are trying to avoid responses that will have to be dictated to a receptionist and typed, delaying a prompt response. Do everything you can so all the physician has to do is generate clear answers. Use e-mail as a communications tool, if the doctor prefers it. (See the introductory letter and questionnaire samples in Chapter 9.)

9. Attend the physician's hospital visits. It underscores your dedication and gives you the opportunity to directly ask the physician, "How can I help you?"

10. Let the physician know you are a resource: "I have this brochure with specific and clear information on open-heart surgery. Would you mind if I pass it along to Mr. Jackson?"

11. Express your recognition of excellence and a job well done. A brief note (with copies sent to the insurance carrier and the patient, if appropriate) can make a big impact. Writing such notes tells the physician that you value his expertise and effort and communicates to your client company that you and the physician are working well as a team.

12. Make it clear that you are also a resource for referrals. After a successful effort on behalf of a patient, let the physician know that you are aware of and value his or her care and concern and that you will certainly make patients in similar straits aware of his or her skill and manner.

13. Get to know the physicians in your community and develop a good relationship with a support person in each office.

14. Do not trust your memory. Maintain a physician database to document specialty areas, preferred communication patterns, and previous experience.

15. You know how to problem solve with other case managers, so use the same techniques in your associations with physicians. For example, every case manager and every physician struggles with patient compliance, so let physicians know you will be their eyes and ears to ensure that treatments are carried out. For a broader perspective, attend a physicians' conference or pick up publications written for physicians, such as *Physicians Practice Digest.*

16. Maintain the collaboration. Offer to give the physician an update after your house call or hospital visit.

17. When apt, provide the physician with copies of your case management report, enclosing an authorization release. Such updates can be particularly helpful for the physician seeing a patient on a consultation basis.

18. Hone your diplomacy skills and try to handle any problems in an ethically and morally responsible manner. Perhaps you discover a patient is taking medication that has an adverse effect in combination with another pill. He may be using over-the-counter medication or have forgotten to mention a drug he has been on for 10 years. Make it clear that you are interested in the best outcome, not in pointing a finger, when you uncover a bad situation. Document your concern as a partner, without laying blame, unless you are confronted by overt negligence.

19. Do not undermine a physician's position in front of patients. Request a moment in the hall or office afterward.

COMMUNICATIONS WITH PATIENTS AND FAMILIES

The timing of a patient's referral to a case manager helps describe how her role should be introduced and explained to the patient or family. For instance, consider this workers' compensation case. The patient has left the hospital, has completed a physical therapy program, and is now involved with various follow-up services. He has not returned to work, prompting the case to be referred to a case manager. Understandably, the patient may view this intervention less than positively. In fact, all parties may have been better served by earlier involvement of the case manager. Helping to educate clients as to the ideal time for case management intervention should be a constant objective of all case managers. However, because case managers cannot always influence when a case is referred, they must learn how to establish good patient communications regardless of the circumstances. Empathy is the key.

Case managers should put themselves in their patients' shoes. For instance, a case may have been referred within 24 hours of a catastrophic event—a massive stroke, an explosion, or the severing of a limb. Or, perhaps a patient has just entered a rehabilitation center or experienced a difficult or dangerously premature delivery. To facilitate the best possible exchange, the case manager needs to have as many facts as possible about the patient and the reasons for the referral. The case manager should be aware that the patient and family may be experiencing much more than a medical crisis and should take the time to consider the patient's and family members' feelings. The medical circumstances may have created financial difficulties, marital problems, role reversals, and so on. Knowing this, the case manager should not simply pick up the phone and dial.

The person receiving the call may be waiting for news from the treating physician or the hospital. The case manager may be calling the wife of a patient who was involved in a head-on collision and is in a hospital 300 miles from home. Consider the impact of a call by a case manager who begins by introducing herself as a representative of the insurance company for the driver whose car struck her husband. The case manager must understand that there will probably be negative feelings and low receptivity and try to surmount these obstacles by using good communication skills.

Similarly, if it is a workers' compensation case and a patient was injured on the job, the case manager should recognize that management–employee or management–union relations may affect the patient's response to the case manager. The individual may have been injured in a plant recently cited for hazardous working conditions. If the patient was a new employee, he or she may be somewhat threatened and skeptical of the employer's position, fearful that management is questioning the veracity of his or her accident report. Conversely, a key senior employee of a company may have none of these concerns owing to his or her more secure position and possibly positive experiences relating to past insurance claims.

Something as simple as whether or not a company has sent flowers and cards to an injured worker can also influence how the case manager will be received. Although some organizations act in a humane way toward employees—sending gifts, calling on family members to express their interest, and setting up a "sunshine organization" to help maintain contact—others do not. The case manager should bear this in mind and try to get a sense of the company's corporate culture before calling on an employee. Especially in programs in which the case management service is new, the case manager might want to make a joint contact with the claims department or the employer benefit department to help ease patient concerns.

After introducing herself, the case manager should ask, "Is this a good time to talk?" The case manager must appreciate the suffering going on and offer support by asking how the family is, what information they have been given by the hospital, and so on. It is not a good strategy to assume family members know everything about the case and launch into the specifics of changing the treatment plan before giving them time to accept the involvement of someone new in an emotional and intense family crisis. If the case manager flounders, she can lose the family's good will before she begins her work.

Group medical cases also introduce special challenges to patient communication. Consider a patient who was just diagnosed with brain cancer. He comes from a rural community and was transferred to a major metropolitan hospital for optimum care. His family is distraught, shocked by the news. Family members may be completely out of their element, not knowing what to ask or whether they are making the best decisions. When the case manager comes on the scene, they may believe she is there to control things or keep down the high medical costs. She is looked upon as an unwanted intruder. Particularly in such situations, it is imperative that the case manager make a timely introduction and state something like this: "It may be possible, after we have spent a little more time talking and

I've visited with your husband, that my assessment will be that he is receiving the best possible care and we will not be suggesting any changes. My role is to act as a coordinator of medical services and a resource for additional alternatives. Your insurance company (or employer) does not require you to accept case management. It is totally up to you."

Our health care system has been a very paternalistic one; we believe we know best what the patient needs. But we assume this without input from the patient. From a patient's perspective, a good scientific outcome may not be relevant. Patients do not have access to clinical research data; they are not familiar with care maps or care pathways. Have we asked: Are you comfortable? Did you understand this recommendation? Do you want to die at home?

A May 2003 Commonwealth Fund/Harvard/Harris Interactive survey of patients with health problems in the United States, Australia, Canada, New Zealand, and the United Kingdom showed poor communication between doctors and patients, high rates of medial errors, lack of coordination in patient care, and barriers when accessing care. The findings, published that same month in Health Affairs and available online at The Commonwealth Fund site (cmwf.org/media/releases/), points out missed opportunities for improving care. The survey report authors suggest that reforms targeted to populations with health problems could reap systemwide improvements in quality of care and potential cost savings (here, case managers around the world are replying, "You rang?").

The report notes that U.S. patients were more likely than those in other countries to mention communication problems with their doctors. "Three of ten respondents in the U.S. (31%) said they left a doctor's office without getting important questions answered." In Australia and New Zealand, the ratio was one in five (21% and 20%, respectively); in the United Kingdom it was 19%; and in Canada, 25%. Fully half of those adults with health problems in the United States, Australia, Canada, and New Zealand, and two-thirds of those in the United Kingdom said their regular physicians do not ask for their ideas and opinions about treatment and care, and one-fifth to one-fourth of physicians did not provide information on their goals via the treatment they recommended. Again, half the survey takers in the United States, Australia, Canada, New Zealand, and two thirds of United Kingdom adults reported that their doctors never discussed the emotional problems associated with their condition.[1] Certainly sounds like a communication breakdown to me.

Such statistics are telling regarding the state of the industry. As health care professionals, we really have been functioning all by ourselves. A case manager should interview a patient and family members for their expectations regarding the future: What do you think this rehab program is about? What do you hope to gain from this medical procedure? Patients should be encouraged to participate and collaborate in the process via the use of open-ended questions. Further, open-ended questions can be used to delve deeper than check-off questions, and in some cases, fill-in-the-blank queries.

Then, the case manager can begin providing the family with educational materials that describe this next step in the healing/recovery phase. This grants the patient and family the chance to form realistic expectations. My company worked with a 39-year-old corporate vice president who had a massive stroke. He and his wife were a career couple. He entered a world-renowned rehabilitation facility and his wife really felt that within the 30-day stay covered by her policy, he would improve sufficiently to come home and "be fine." Adequate information regarding his status was not communicated or, if communicated, was not reviewed for perception. In this case, her misguided perception was her version of reality.

I believe that people view acute care hospitals as the dramatic stage of recovery: They have survived. From my conversations, I gather that rehab is seen as fine-tuning. They feel that "when I leave rehab, I'm not going to have my slurred speech any more, I'm going to have complete mobility, although I may be a little bit slower." These and other care expectations are far off the mark. Case managers need to better understand a patient's perspective and help clarify reasonable goals. Has his experience been either very negative or positive? Are his goals realistic? That's not only the caring thing to do, in fact it's the ethical thing to do, because it gives patients the information they need to know about the decisions that they need to make. Tell them the dollar amount of coverage their policy offers, the length of time provided for rehabilitation facility or nursing home care coverage, what they can reasonably expect medically, and the program's parameters; in a word, assist them with patient goal setting.[2]

The care program coordinated by the case manager may be far off the mark from the patient's perspective. Now is the time to address that. "Okay, John, these are your short-term goals; these are the physician's short-term goals for you— how far apart are you? What do we need to do to bring them back together again? Were they reasonable or not? Let's review long-term goals; are there any shortcomings? How many days does your health benefits plan give us?"

Here is an opportunity to share with the patient. "John, it seems like you are plateauing at the rehab facility. This may be a slow process. Because you only have 2 or 3 weeks of rehab coverage available, maybe it would be better for you to go home for a while and practice on some of these exercises until you reach the next stage. How do you feel about this?" This encourages a more collaborative process with that patient. Patients will see that someone really respects their needs or desires. Perhaps John was in an acute care hospital for 3 or 4 weeks with a horrendous illness. From there, he entered the rehab facility. Now, he is lonely for home and really wants to get back into more normal surroundings.[3]

Communications with a family are as important as those with the patient. There is a saying in case management, "If you lose the family, you lose the patient." It is often a good idea for case managers to give the patients and family members examples of how they have worked with other people in similar circumstances. This helps families perceive case managers as caring human beings and not just additional bureaucrats in the health care system.

The Patient Communication Chain of Command

Communications between a case manager and a patient should ideally follow a certain sequence. However, many factors can alter this sequence. Today's society has introduced new family units, including step-, mixed, common-law, gay, and multigenerational family units, creating different hierarchies for patient communications. The case manager needs to remember that communications with the patient and family might affect and be affected by numerous other people. Generally, the patient communication chain of command is as follows:

1. Patient (if of legal age)
2. Spouse (if married)
3. Parent or legal guardian (if patient not of legal age)
4. Oldest child (if patient widowed or divorced)
5. Significant other (if patient has an alternative lifestyle)
6. Individual with power of attorney (if patient is incapacitated)

A caveat exists in regard to the "significant other" category. Although new legislation has begun to clarify the legal rights of close companions, it is important that case managers adhere to what society and the legal community recognize to be the significant other on behalf of a patient. Also, in many workers' compensation or auto cases, although the referral may come from the carrier or the employer group, if an attorney represents the individual, the attorney, not the individual, is contacted first. For legal reasons, the case manager must explain the role of a case manager and obtain the permission of the attorney before contacting the patient.

Elder care cases in which only one sibling is represented or cases involving children whose parents are divorced may also have a skewed communication sequence. The oldest child in a family might not be the most appropriate child to assist a needy parent, being too distant physically or emotionally or being simply unable to take on the responsibility of making a life-and-death decision. At some point, the case manager might want to suggest that the on-site child contact any brothers or sisters for additional support in dealing with a parent who is critically ill.

When the Family Becomes a Patient

Many medical cases, particularly those of a catastrophic nature, will devastate a family. In tough medical situations, all attention is focused on the ill or injured person, even though the caretaker or family member might be hanging from a thread. Case managers must understand that their role includes advocacy for the families. Family members should be encouraged to say what is on their minds and be reminded to ask for help if they need it. Keeping a family intact through a difficult period can ultimately be one of the case manager's greatest achievements in managing a particular case. The case manager should communicate to the family that she is there to assist in any way possible, whether that means helping the family sort through accumulating bills or preparing for the patient's return home by providing information about special equipment or home care services.

Case managers have to meet people where they are. One of my very first cases—and probably one of the biggest challenges to communication that I have had in case management—involved a gentleman who was injured in an automobile accident and rendered a quadriplegic at a C-4 level. He was on a respirator. His daughter, a nurse on a neurosurgical unit in a major metropolitan hospital, worked over 100 miles away. Although she was absolutely devastated by the situation, as the nurse in the family, she had a great deal of responsibility thrown at her. All the relatives were asking her all their questions. She felt that she had to make all the decisions, and she was having tremendous difficulty dealing with the pressure. Although she probably was very capable, she was beset by conflicts. What if she chose wrongly? She remained confident in making determinations for her own patients, but in this case, she was a daughter and not simply a nurse on the case.

Many of the medical professionals supposed that because she was a neurosurgical nurse on a unit, she knew everything she needed to know. They were talking to her not as a family member, but as a peer. I, as the case manager, became the claimant's advocate and his daughter's advocate as well, making it easier for her to be just the daughter in this particular situation. I acknowledged that she had certain expertise, but I did not make further assumptions regarding her knowledge and skills. For example, when we were researching rehabilitation facilities for her father so he could go into a weaning program and eventually get off the respirator, I gave her detailed information. I did not presume that she knew all the various types of mechanical ventilators, or could, in her current state of mind, distinguish the benefits of one rehabilitation program over another. I put myself in her place—and now I've been in that place.

When my mother had a massive coronary and was rushed to the hospital at 3 AM, the family looked to me to make all the decisions, especially because I had worked as a nurse in a coronary care unit. I had not been as intimately involved with the intricacies of coronary care for a while, and I would have liked to have had someone who could reassure me. Yet my family said, "You're the expert. Tell us what's going on." I was panicked, I was panicked to death. Some case managers might assume that they can take less of a role in such situations because of a family member's medical background, but I would alert them to the possible need for more tailored assurance and support.

With the C-4 case, I spoke to the physicians involved and reminded them that this nurse was a daughter first, that she had doubts and questions and required shoring up. This intervention was effective and in fact became very important because this was a liability case. A municipal vehicle that was being used for something other than official town business had struck the father. I was referred by the insurance carrier that represented the town, so I was on the absolute opposite side, giving the daughter and her family a reason to doubt my intentions. But because I was able to work nurse to nurse and person to person, I helped her see that I really was not there just for the town, just to cut dollars; I was interested in maximizing the auto policy resources. There was a limit to certain benefit dollars, but there was also a huge lawsuit involved. While communicating with both parties and both parties' attorneys, I kept myself from taking a side. It was a difficult situation, but if case managers keep their goals straight and remember exactly what they are contributing, they can handle such challenging cases successfully.

The Question of Confidentiality and the Question of Cost

In their communications, case managers must assure patients and families that their discussions will be held in confidence. Certain diagnoses (substance abuse-related illnesses, cancer, AIDS, depression, etc.) in particular cause patients to worry about others' knowledge of their condition. Although case managers must tell patients whom they represent (an employer's group medical plan, workers' compensation, etc.), they must also make it clear that certain information will not be communicated to employers or supervisors.

Along with issues of privacy, there may also be worries about the cost of the case manager's involvement: "I don't have the money for this. Who's going to pay for this help?" The case manager should explain how the intervention is being funded and indicate that it does not represent another bill to the patient or family. In most lines of insurance, case management is a claims administration expense and the cost is not deducted from the patient's benefits. Regardless of how the service is being funded, some patients consider it unnecessary. They may also sense that the case manager's involvement reflects another agenda (that of the insurance carrier, workers' compensation plan, etc.) and be wary.

Some referrals may in reality be thinly disguised requests for case managers to serve as medical investigators. Soul-searching is in order here. Case managers have to decide whether these assignments are really the ones they want to take on and recognize the consequences of their decision. Particularly in smaller communities, where everyone knows everyone else, being regarded as the individual who interrogated the local grocer about his back injury can definitely cause future patients to become close-mouthed, preventing effective communication and case management. It is appropriate to tell a potential client that claims investigation is not a case management role.

Documenting the Patient Contact

Case managers should document all of their patient communications, whether in-person or telephonic, regardless of the patient's acceptance or refusal of services. Beyond chronicling a case manager–patient exchange, correspondence can be used to reinforce important messages. For instance, the document may highlight certain aspects of the conversation, such as the statement that the services will not cost the patient anything, thereby offering reassurance to the patient and family.

Communication should flow between case managers and patients and families whenever appropriate: at the time of referral, after the referral, and when new information becomes available. Case managers should write to keep lines of communication open—to reassure an invalid parent's adult child who wants to remain in the loop or to document a change in treating facilities. Sometimes, a case manager needs merely to send a simple reminder, "I'm writing to confirm that I will accompany you when you go to therapy next week." Letters can help establish consensus among those involved in caring for a patient and create the impression that the case manager, far from being an intruder, is one of the team.

Form letters can be used, but they should be personalized. Easily produced using word processing programs, the customized letter projects a personal interest rather than one governed by routine. The case manager might include words that focus on the patient or family: "I hope your husband is recovering comfortably from his back injury by the time you receive this letter." Or, "I just wanted to elaborate on our discussion. I know we covered a lot of information about burns in a short period of time. I thought this might be helpful." Throughout their communication with patients and families, case managers should strive to position case management as apart from the medical bureaucracy.

The case manager–patient correspondence should document the patient's acceptance or refusal of case management services. In the case of refusal, it should note patient and family concerns and their reasons for declining the service, address them, and leave the door open for future dialogue and possible reconsideration.

The correspondence should reinforce and redefine the role of the case manager. It should explain who is being represented and how the services will be paid for, and it should underscore the point that the purpose of case management is to facilitate a positive outcome for the patient. The case manager might well include some promotional material that is user-friendly and helps the patient better understand case management's role and objectives. The initial letter might close with a statement such as this: "I am sending you this letter and brochure to better acquaint you with our services. I will call you in a few days when, hopefully, we can further discuss some of your concerns." Or: "I look forward to seeing you again at the hospital with Dr. Johnson and your husband. In the meantime, one of our brochures is enclosed to give you a better idea of our services." The letter should indicate that the referral source has been provided with a copy. (Sample patient letters appear in Chapters 9 and 10.)

COMMUNICATIONS WITH PAYER SOURCES

Each payer source or line of insurance (whatever entity is referring the case for case management) places certain restrictions or obligations on the case manager. For instance, workers' compensation in one state may mandate that a case manager perform stipulated duties in a set time period, use specific forms, apply stated criteria in an evaluation, and charge only a fixed amount. In other cases, the case manager has to listen very closely to what the payer is requesting and not begin a program that she considers ideal. Specifically, what does the payer expect? What are they asking for? The semantics of the communication must be clarified at the outset.

Following referral, a group medical carrier usually wants to know how big the case is going to be. Is this long-term, or is this short-term? If it is a plan with stop-loss insurance, another umbrella of insurance coverage, is it likely to reach the stop-loss threshold? If so, maybe the group medical carrier is required by the nature of the policy to advise the stop-loss carrier when the accumulated benefits reach 50% of the threshold figure. Part of the case manager's responsibility might be to predict when that will occur.

For each of the various lines of insurance, the case manager needs to be able to help the referral source to know which are going to be the big cases in terms of time and dollars and what case management can do to improve the situation. Can the case manager get John out of the hospital sooner, move him into a more aggressive rehabilitation program, or work with his employer to modify his job site according to his needs?

In their communications, case managers need to make the effort to tell the whole story and illuminate the issues that do not come across on a piece of paper or a claims form. I think case managers too often report major problems and think the job is done. They say, "Oh, this is horrible," without saying, "Listen, you have a problem case here, but I really think we can make this a better scenario" or "I've found the patient is giving us more to work with than we might have thought initially."

For example, if a patient is getting reimbursement for disability care or income replacement, the physician might not distinguish in his or her reports between stages of disability. My office handled a disability case in which the individual had a diagnosis of postmeningitis syndrome. Month after month, the doctor continued to rubber stamp "totally disabled" on the claims form. Well, the guy was totally disabled for his job at the time, but he was absolutely desperate to go to work again. Nobody knew that, nobody took the time to make a telephone call, and when our case manager went out and saw how motivated this guy was and how hard he was trying, we got him into a computer training program. He made arrangements for his own transportation and attended classes like clockwork. All we needed to do was to get out there and see him and bring back the unknown information. Prior to that, the diagnosis was that his disability was forever, based on the lack of knowledge within the claims department. He had gotten lost in the system, he was labeled "postmeningitis" and "neurological disorder" and everyone assumed his condition was permanent.

Group medical cases are the same. It may well be a horrible situation, but the family members are very supportive, they really want the patient home, services can be put in place, and some serious cost containment and positive results can be achieved simultaneously. Again, case managers must realize they are problem solvers. They must not cut short their communications with payer sources by saying, "Just let me know what you want." They do a disservice to the patient, the payer, themselves, and the case management industry.

The following list describes typical challenges for case managers in communicating with payer sources:

- Because of prior experience with case management services, a payer might have assumptions about what case management can and cannot do.
- Lack of medical knowledge within a claims department can slow a case manager's progress. This is where the role of educator is vital.
- The line of insurance might present problems. A fully insured plan can be more difficult to work with than a self-funded plan, due to restrictions prohibiting some of the more creative interactions between the referral source and the case manager.
- Sometimes, the size of the company can be a hindrance. I often find the bigger companies are not willing to explore the what-ifs of case management, to take a risk. They say, "We've always done it this way and that's it."

Case managers can clarify a number of issues for employers to keep them better informed regarding case management and its benefits. Employer groups have become increasingly concerned about their possible liability when another individual, such as a case manager, becomes involved and perhaps "interferes" in the patient–physician relationship. To address this, case managers would do well to position themselves as a solution within the complex and complicated system. They should stress their advocacy role—that in general they do not provide "hands-on" care—and that only a very small percentage of employees within a given group require the services of a case manager. Those selected are exactly those who an employer would want to receive special attention—the sick, absentee employee (or dependent) who has multiple problems and whose family is suffering because of it.

It is very difficult for the average case manager to have a conversation with an employer group, especially within large managed care organizations, because there are so many layers of administration between the on-line case manager, the one who develops a working relationship with the employee or a family member, and the actual employer. There are account coordinators, marketing people, sales representatives—chains of people on both the employer group and the managed care side. Case managers could break through this communication barrier if they were more actively involved in the marketing and account coordination meetings between the managed care company and the employer group. The director of a case management department can speak to the issues of case management at a board meeting or annual review and open a different dialogue with CEOs and CFOs, enabling them to better understand the role and process of case management.

One way to delineate the benefits of case management to employers is to highlight its risk management contributions. Every organization today is familiar with the principles of risk management and with reviewing its overall exposure to prevent occurrences and contain loss. The case manager needs to walk in the employer's shoes and use a comparative example to make her point. How does the employer protect itself against disaster or risk? A manufacturing company executive uses risk management tools such as routine safety inspections, employee instructions on driver and/or plant safety, and procedures to prevent injuries and fires or to maintain OSHA compliance. In the same way, health care management includes risk management strategies used to maintain and grow an industry, minimizing loss and damage to your resources—your employees. Case management is one such strategy.

Case managers can ask questions at that board meeting. What presents the biggest risk to your health plan or the greatest use of your valuable health care dollars? Here is what we can do to maximize the use of your dollars and minimize the spiraling costs. An integrated multilevel case management program will manage that small portion of people who present the biggest exposure to your plan and who are driving up costs. As the group entrusted with the fiduciary responsibility of administering your plan and safeguarding your benefits, we target these populations and manage them.

Employers and payers at this meeting should be asking the case manager, managed care organization, or TPA the following questions: What strategies do you have in place to identify these cases? When you identify them, what do you do? Are they selected by a computer system? Do people call them on the phone?

What red flags do you use to apply industry standards to an employee group to protect my plan assets from known problems? How do you practice case management? The director of a case management program can explain to an employer how an out-of-work employee with multiple diagnostic conditions moves through the managed care system.

For many companies, the first results of switching to managed care were strong and satisfactory. Large savings were realized as healthy people and young people moved into managed care, drawn by the options and benefits, including mammography, new baby care, wellness programs, and prenatal coverage. The sick tended to stay in traditional plans. Now that HMOs and PPOs have had several years' experience *and* are picking up the Medicaid and high-risk Medicare population group, they are experiencing much more dramatically the effects of adverse selection, and they face what insurance plans did years ago. The catastrophically and chronically sick are using up the greater portion of benefit dollars. A database or outcomes profile will not help deal with these people. We still have to work on our delivery system and use the tools, such as case management, that have proven effective in managing high-cost patient populations.

Case management needs a more widespread and ongoing voice in the boardrooms, managed care businesses, and homes as the personalized, proactive benefit that it is. Too often, people first hear of case management when they or a family member are in critical care. Case managers can take advantage of company newsletters and brochures reviewing benefit plan provisions to introduce case management in a consumer-friendly vein. When case examples are communicated on a regular basis, the real work and role of case management are evident.

The value and benefit of case management also needs to be communicated to the employee. As an example, our company routinely sends out patient satisfaction questionnaires. A local union we were working with sent out its own participant survey on its provider groups. A board of trustees member responded to both questionnaires, and his quotes were used in a report to members emphasizing the case management element of the union's health care network.

COMMUNICATIONS WITH LEGAL PROFESSIONALS

Attorneys are rarely called on for case-managed group medical claims, with the exception of certain HIV cases, but are frequently contacted in workers' compensation and short- and long-term disability cases and sometimes contacted in auto liability cases. Above all, a clear explanation of the case manager's intent and role, along with an honest and straightforward manner, goes a long way toward overcoming an attorney's concern regarding case management intervention. Anticipating questions, all communications should underscore the case manager's proactive involvement in a complex delivery system.

During the early years of case management, case managers allowed attorneys to state the case for case management to clients. Intimidated by attorneys (as some still are), case managers had no comfort level for butting heads with a lawyer who portrayed case managers as out to find fault. When legal counsel said no to case management, there was little further discussion. Today, case managers are more apt to use a negative response as an opportunity to begin a brief public relations campaign. "Why are you denying case management on behalf of your client? I'm really surprised. Most attorneys I know have no problem with the service."

The reasons behind a refusal might have merit. Perhaps the carrier has acted in bad faith; perhaps the client's lost-wages payments or a physician's invoices are being held up unreasonably. If the case manager can resolve the problem, she should do so, thereby demonstrating to the attorney that case management can be a catalyst for positive change.

When an attorney refuses to allow case manager–client conversation, we want to know why. Sometimes it is helpful to write a letter to the attorney, with a copy to the patient/client, to again explain as a matter of record the benefits of case management services, the intended proactive role of the case manager. This letter calls the patient's attention to the attorney's denial of services, should he not already be aware.

There are some attorneys who do not understand case management or who are aggressive and challenging. Case managers have to be articulate and assertive in return. The more comfortable they are with their role, the better job they can do as case managers. If they do not challenge a refusal and transform it into an assent, they are walking away from work and very possibly from a career.

There are stereotypical judgments on both sides. Some lawyers think case managers are claims investigators in disguise, and some case managers see lawyers as litigation hounds. And of course there *are* both case managers and lawyers who are less than professional. On the other hand, there are law firms that are interested in case management and how it can benefit their clients. We need to move past the us-versus-them mind-set. Attorneys want patients to get the best from the health care system, and this is what case managers want, too. They want patients to be able to go back to productive lives; so do case managers.

In some instances, the time frame in which a case manager is contacted can confuse communications. When a case manager is brought to a case early on, patients and lawyers alike tend to view case management intervention as more beneficial, and some of the long letters of introduction and initial lawyer–case manager meetings can be avoided. If an insurance carrier refers a case 1 year after the fact because the individual is still not at work and the care costs are piling up, a case manager might have more difficulty portraying the payer as truly concerned and herself as an objective advocate. The claimant is likely to ask, "Where were you 6 months ago?" and an attorney would be smart to ask, "Why weren't you offering help when John had his accident?" A more wary lawyer might question the case manager's intent: Is it advocacy or investigation? Case managers must be aware of politics; the carrier might well intend to tap her for information—for example, What is the HIV status of the ill employee? Is she an alcoholic? Is this a case the case manager wants to take? Can she be credible when the payer's motives are so suspect?

In another scenario, an attorney, unbeknownst to the carrier, might become involved several weeks after an accident. The case manager should obtain the attorney's written permission to work with the patient before continuing on the case.

Case managers will want to maintain ongoing communications with attorneys involved in their cases. Especially when a case manager has a particular concern about a claimant, an attorney can be quite helpful (by obtaining, for example, better cooperation from a patient who insists on drinking or smoking in direct opposition to the doctor's recommendation). By sharing information with and giving credit to attorneys, case managers make them a part of the care team.

As with contracted medical services, the case manager should track whether the claimant is well served by his or her attorney. Many attorneys are cooperative and interested, whereas others are aloof and detached. If the claimant voices a concern regarding the attorney's representation, the case manager can suggest that there are alternatives but should stop short of recommending specific replacements, just as she should not name a certain physician as the best choice.

COMMUNICATION SUBTLETIES

Not everything a case manager communicates is verbal or written. The case manager's overall demeanor projects a message to patients, physicians, and social workers. For instance, many nurses in the habit of wearing comfortable clothing in the hospital environment adhere to the same dress code in their role as case managers. They might wear a skirt and blouse with sneakers rather than pumps. Or, they might go to the extreme of wearing a warm-up suit. At the other end of the spectrum are case managers who don the complete "corporate look" (tailored suit and briefcase) without considering that it could intimidate a patient. Minor modifications, such as not wearing the jacket and walking in with an envelope rather than a briefcase, can soften the image and signal a more approachable person.

Case managers also need to know their audience. When visiting a patient whose home is in a low-income neighborhood, it is preferable not to march in dressed to the hilt in designer labels and expensive jewelry. For appointments with physicians or corporate representatives, the power look not only is appropriate, but also places the case manager on a par with other professionals, affording greater credibility.

Demeanor also extends to behavior. Upon entering a patient's home, a case manager should remember that he or she is a guest. Extending courtesies such as complimenting the decor, taking note of photographs, or kneeling down to greet a young child communicates a genuine interest. Commenting on a patient's new level of skill (such as moving from wheelchair to walker) further assists in projecting the image of a caring professional. When meeting a physician or human resources manager, it is a good idea to express awareness of how busy the office seems to be or to request literature regarding the practice or company.

THE RIGHT MIND-SET

A positive attitude and confidence in one's role are essential for good communication. Case managers who are motivated and even proud of their role as catalysts for change will convey the value of case management. Those who chose the profession merely to escape a battered existence in another health care role are likely to suffer from low self-esteem and be ill-equipped to meet the challenges that case management presents.

The case manager's role can be extremely difficult and, depending on the motives of others involved, quite disheartening. In fact, certain lines of insurance will present case management assignments that may be layered with bureaucracy and rifts between medical personnel, payer groups, and legal entities. Such cases cause some case managers to be timid and even apologetic. Case managers who feel powerless may resort to an opposite tactic. Rather than withdrawing and becoming subservient, they ride roughshod over patients or others, drawing their "authority" from what they perceive to be the powerful "big business" or insurance company. This approach only serves to alienate people, creating barriers to effective communication.

Case managers need to accept the fact that their job will not always give them warm feelings and provide professional satisfaction. They also need, however, to keep feelings of frustration and disappointment in check, particularly when communicating with patients. Usually, the difficulty with making certain calls to patients lessens as a case manager's experience builds. Moreover, if a case manager views each case as a new opportunity to improve a situation, communication can become a more agreeable aspect of providing assistance.

COMMUNICATIONS AND CARING OVERLOAD: BURNOUT

Simply because of the nature of the work, most case managers' caseloads consist of tragic cases. Many are life-and-death situations; the bulk of them have no happy ending. Yes, the high-risk pregnancy often results in the birth of a healthy infant, and getting a partially disabled person well-situated in a new job is especially rewarding, but the balance between success and tragedy that exists in more traditional health care delivery roles is not part of case management. Often, case managers deal with people who are angry at the system, at God for allowing this terrible thing to happen, at themselves for not handling it better, or at the patient for getting ill in the first place. Angry patients and families tend to voice their opinions to case managers rather than physicians. Case managers who try to distance themselves emotionally by totally walling themselves off from the pain their clients feel will lose their ability to be effective because they will stop interacting with those clients. They must create for themselves a balance between success and tragedy by finding an appropriate level of involvement.

There is a fine line between "I have a no-hands-on role" and "I am totally responsible for this person," and case managers must be able to walk it by knowing where the function of case management begins and ends. They must take on enough of the responsibility to help fix problems while acknowledging their limitations. In their former roles as practicing nurses, many case managers were able to offer a quick solution to pain; the proper medication "made it better." But case managers cannot deter a terminal illness or make a dying child well; they cannot keep contracted services or equipment from failing; they cannot absorb everyone's woe. Despite the day-to-day challenges, case managers need to maintain their equilibrium and a strong sense of their role; otherwise they will become overwhelmed and burn out.

When a case manager begins to blow up at associates, dreads the next call or any further involvement in a case, is unable to see any positives in her work, and grinds through cases that appear completely hopeless, she needs to step back and get help on the cases that seem overwhelming. Usually, a case manager is burned out on a few cases rather than on the job as a whole, unless she has pushed herself long beyond the point where she needed to take a break.

One way to avoid taking on too much responsibility for a case's progress is to draw on the knowledge and experience of peers, even peers in another state. By calling, putting thoughts and concerns out in the open, knocking ideas around and getting feedback, it becomes easier to see a situation clearly. Perhaps there is a personality clash with the patient, or maybe the case manager has simply run out of ideas for a successful intervention. Sometimes a case has to be given over to an associate or back to a supervisor. How can a case manager turn over a case to someone else and not lose face with the client? Nothing works better than honesty. Some cases benefit greatly by another's expertise in an area; sometimes all that is needed is a better patient–case manager match.

To prevent burnout, a case manager would do well to understand the parameters of the job and not glamorize it. An RN trying a utilization review or case management role needs to prepare for the role's requirements. Many professions have hazards, and recognition of them is three fourths of their solution.

One problem is isolation. Case managers are often on their own, enjoying minimal interaction with other case managers. They are no longer on the nursing team, and they are not physicians, claims adjusters, or rehabilitation specialists. They interact with all these specialists, but their work places them outside the "inner circle" of an office or professional group. This can lead to a lack of input when facing a problem and a lack of recognition for a job well done. There may be few or no peers providing the "safety valve" of shared laughter or griping. Case managers can combat the isolation by creating a case management "team." They can talk to their contacts in the claims department about their lives and interests. They can make an effort to observe and discuss improvements in patient abilities with the family, choosing to dwell on the joy of progress after all the time spent on the tougher aspects of an illness.

Case managers also need to get out of the case management cycle. The job allows for flexibility, and because the job includes great tension and stress, it is vital for a case manager to use some of that flexibility to provide "fueling up" time. Instead of writing all the necessary reports during the 9–5 workday, the case manager might take time off to attend a child's scout meeting, visit a museum or park, water the garden, or exercise, completing the reports in the evening or on a Saturday morning. Regularly going out to lunch, taking no-work-allowed coffee breaks, and attending at least one annual case management conference are the types of activities that can help keep burnout at bay.

NOTES

1. The Commonwealth Fund, "Medical Errors, Lack of Coordination, and Poor Physician-Patient Communication are Pervasive in Health Systems of Five Nations." Available at http://cmfw.org/media/release/blendonhaitl645_release05062003.asp.

2. C. Mullahy, "Satisfaction of Person Served," in *The Persons Served: Ethical Perspectives on CARF's Accreditation Standards and Guidelines,* ed. J. Banja (Tucson, AZ: Commission on Accreditation of Rehabilitation Facilities, 1997): 55.

3. C. Mullahy, "Satisfaction of Person Served," in *The Persons Served: Ethical Perspectives on CARF's Accreditation Standards and Guidelines,* ed. J. Banja (Tucson, AZ: Commission on Accreditation of Rehabilitation Facilities, 1997): 55.

CHAPTER 9

The Case Management
Work Format and Process

When a case manager receives an assignment, she will make a series of contacts, including one with the patient and family, the treating physician(s) and medical facility staff, the employer, and, if the patient is involved in or considering a lawsuit, an attorney. The information gathered is reported in writing, and planning is coordinated with the payer. The process of case management can be broken into categories: case finding and targeting, gathering and assessing information, planning, reporting, obtaining approval, coordination or putting the plan into action, follow-up, and evaluation. Each step of the case management process involves medical, financial, behavioral/motivational, and vocational management activities. It is vital at each phase that case managers analyze and not simply record or report their findings. (See the case management flowchart presented in Figure 9–1.)

Case finding and targeting encompasses the determination of eligibility and the identification of high-risk or high-cost clients. The way in which a case manager approaches a new case is influenced by the referral source (generally the payer) and the line of insurance. The referral source might be an insurance company with clients covered under workers' compensation, auto, or group medical plans, a Third Party Administrator (TPA) that is paying claims for a client company, a hospital discharge planner, a corporate human resources manager, or a home health services agency. It might be a state Medicaid office with case management services within a line of insurance or a population segment, such as high-risk newborns or children who are dependent on technological medical assistance. In today's growing and diversified market, cases may also come directly from consumers. An individual might contract elder care services and request that a case manager evaluate a family member's capabilities and needs. For the independent case manager, the case might be referred as a "trial run" by a new client she has been soliciting.

Figure 9–1 Case Management Work Format Flowchart.

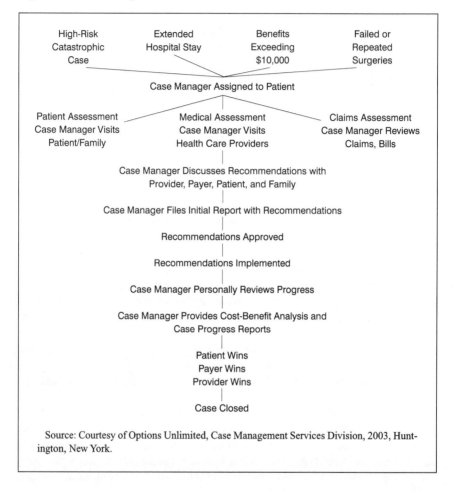

Source: Courtesy of Options Unlimited, Case Management Services Division, 2003, Huntington, New York.

Within some larger case management, insurance, TPA, and employer firms, computer software programs are utilized to flag potential cases appropriate for case management intervention. For example, system software can be programmed to pull out every individual with claims totaling over $5,000 or $10,000, each individual with claims bearing the ICD-9 or CPT codes indicating a certain type of illness or condition, or each patient experiencing three or more hospitalizations over a set period of time. (*2003 ICD-9-CM: Professional for Physicians: International Classification of Disease, 9th Edition, Clinical Modification,* one of the ICD-9 code reference books, is published by Medicode Inc.

Current Procedural Terminology CPT 2003 is published by the American Medical Association, which also publishes *ICD-9-CM 2002: International Classification of Diseases, 9th Edition* (Volumes 1 and 2). Medicode publishes *ICD-9-CM Spiral Expert for Physicians, Volumes 1 and 2, 2002, International Classification of Diseases, 9th Revision, Clinical Modification.*)

Other artificial intelligence systems screen cases through a series of reviews. Generally, on the first review level, nurse reviewers might ask 10 standard questions regarding a patient's file. If any of the 10 questions is answered yes, the computer system presents a series of new questions to help single out those cases needing immediate case management attention. The system is making its "decisions" based on data taken from interviews with specialists in various medical fields. The system operator, usually a medical review specialist, answers the computer's questions. Cases are forwarded for case management by the system itself and by the system operator.

There are a range of software programs available, some designating specific illnesses or designed to track progress through a care plan. Computer software can be of significant assistance in finding and targeting cases for case management intervention, but it should not be the sole instrument for reviewing information. It requires the support of a personal interview with the patient, knowledge of the patient's prior history, or an independent professional judgment regarding the data. In other words, the use of computer software should be regularly combined with a case manager's personalized contact.

The variety of referral sources is enormous, as is the variety of backgrounds in case management that referral sources may have. A company recently mandated to offer case management services might be referring its first case and have little or no understanding of case management. A claims examiner might have been told to refer the case and have scant knowledge of what type of report or data to request from a case manager. The source of the case might be another health care professional. Large companies and insurance carriers often have in-house medical directors who refer patients for case management. The referral may come from a senior claims person, a physician, or a nurse familiar with case management who coordinates all vended-out services. The source and his or her background will partially determine the information requested, expected, and provided. Case managers must take clues regarding assessment and reporting from the referral source.

GATHERING AND ASSESSING INFORMATION

The accuracy of the entire case management process depends on the information gathered. The process of collecting information might include scheduling a conversation with the referral source (payer), determining policy limits and coverage, interviewing the patient and family, interviewing the physician(s) and the key members of the medical treatment team, reviewing the medical records, holding discussions with employers and attorneys as needed, and determining the availability of community resources.

I always suggest to case managers that they conduct assessments as a reporter first and then as an analyzer of the information. Too many nurses and other case management professionals have functioned like journalists, writing wonderful documentaries about patients but not really telling and selling the role of case management. Because of this, too many client companies and organizations see case managers as observers of care rather than contributors to the care plan. All case managers must be observers, but they must be much more as well. If they never looked beyond "what is wrong with this picture" to "what can I do to improve this," if they never envisioned the contributions they could make—to better the patient's condition, support the family, stretch the dollars, tighten up the treatment plan, coordinate the activities of the providers—then they would be merely a group of reporters who call themselves case managers. With the various functions of case management in mind, case managers should approach each case with an open mind and an eye for problems that must be addressed.

THE R.I.P. METHOD OF CONDUCTING INTERVIEWS

This approach was developed by the Foundation for Rehabilitation Education and Research for a seminar section titled, "Interpersonal Skills for Case Managers."

R is for rapport, the essential connection made by the case manager with the person being interviewed. That connection, which can last 10 seconds or 30 minutes, might take the form of a brief and pleasant introduction, a quick statement of purpose, or a warm comment or observation about the individual, his or her situation, home, or busy schedule.

The *I* in R.I.P. refers to information, the purpose of the communication, be it approval for a previously submitted case management plan, permission for a hospital discharge, or knowledge of the specific medication a patient is receiving. The case manager must focus on the objective of the contact and maintain the contact until she has the background needed to continue the case management process.

Even if the involvement of the interviewed party will be minimal, the conversation should not end before that individual completely understands the next step in the process or the plan *(P)*. The case manager might conclude by saying, "Thank you for letting me visit with you in your home. My report goes to the insurance company shortly, and I'll call you with their comments in 2 weeks." To a physician, she might say, "Thank you for your time (on the phone), Dr. Reynolds. I'll confirm your approval by letter and do everything I can to assist you in making certain John follows his treatment plan."

TALKING WITH THE REFERRAL SOURCE

Prior to beginning an assessment of a case, a case manager (CM) provides a clear definition of assessment and a description of the report she plans to file based on the needs of the referral source (claims examiner, vice president of human resources, corporate CM department head). Not every client wants the same type of initial needs assessment, nor does every client have the same document in mind when an "initial needs assessment" is requested. Because responsibilities for administering claims within an insurance policy are different, client requirements are different. The case manager might work for a company that considers an initial evaluation an on-site personal contact with the claimant, an on-site personal contact with the employer, and an on-site personal contact with the treating physician—a three-point, on-site contact. Another company's "initial evaluation" may be either an extensive phone call or an on-site contact visit with the claimant only.

What is the referral source being asked to do? What is the problem that case management might have a role in solving? Perhaps the case will not merit case management intervention. There is no plain vanilla case management and no plain vanilla initial needs assessment.

Depending on the case manager's type of employment—whether working for an insurance firm, within a TPA, or self-employed as an independent CM, for example—and the kinds of clients served, request-for-service referral forms may be forwarded for completion. Some case managers have developed their own forms, but corporations often have a "Directive for Service" that is mailed to the case manager to utilize at the outset of a case. Perhaps the case manager works in a branch office of a company with national accounts, providing case management services for a large client group. The company might have its own referral intake sheet incorporating very specific data regarding past medicals, file numbers, and so on. A form designed and used by an independent case manager might also function as a marketing tool and include information on the range of services.

Referral form data can be taken in person, by phone, by e-mail, or sent by fax. Again, there are numerous variations that influence how and what information is obtained.

In a workers' compensation case, the payer might ask the following questions: How extensive is this injury? What is my exposure in terms of dollars? How long is this individual likely to be out of work? If the client is paying medical costs and replacement of salary and is also handling liability issues, there may be multiple concerns, with the medical portion being the least important. A case manager accustomed to delivering an intense discourse on clinical aspects of the case will be preparing an initial assessment report that is of little use to this client.

In other situations, the case manager might be called in as an intermediary, perhaps to confirm the status of a case. In an auto liability case, a client might request that the case manager call two doctors or visit the hospital to determine the extent of an injury. If the policy carries $50,000 in benefits and the injury is so severe that the patient will be in an intensive care unit for two months at $3,000 per day, the benefits dollars are already spent. The client may decide that there is no action a case manager could take to save any money at this juncture. In a disability case, the client may have little interest in the course of medical treatment but be especially concerned with whether the disability will be permanent. Therefore, the case manager may be asked to conduct a telephonic assessment rather than make an on-site visit.

Imagine a situation in which a case manager works for a company that has a set policy on procedures and a referral comes in regarding a workers' compensation case:

Case Manager: Kate, you've asked for an initial evaluation of John Jones. Does that mean you want us to visit John, his employer, and his treating physician, or are you just interested in a visit with John?

Payer: We'd like you to conduct a visit with John only.

Case Manager: All right. Are you interested in our customary initial evaluation with a claimant, Kate? It includes a medical history, a current medical status, a vocational history, and a financial profile. It's fairly extensive. I anticipate that it will take me an hour and a half or two hours, and John is an hour away. [If John is represented by an attorney, there is a whole new angle and additional time required for an initial assessment.] Is that what you're interested in?

Payer: No. All I want you to do is go to the hospital and find out what's going on right now. Write it up and get me a report.

Case Manager: OK. Do you have a time limit, Kate, on when this needs to be done, or a specific format for that report? Do you want just a phone report, do you need a letter, or do you want this to be a full report? Do you have any benefit limits? What are you really looking for here? [Again, the case manager needs to find out the desires of the particular client and get as much of the client's agenda on the table as possible. The first case from a referral source is a key case: If the case manager messes it up, she may not get another referral from that payer. If the case manager goes on and on about what "we always do" but the payer has different requirements, the case manager runs the risk of losing the opportunity for future work. She should not make the assumption that she knows what is best for the client; the client is buying her services.]

Case Manager: Does the report need to be completed in 72 hours? Do you have to reserve dollars on this case? Is your home office looking for this information quickly?

Payer: As a matter of fact, I need to get someone out on it right away.

Case Manager: I am sorry, the staff that I have right now that's closest to John already have appointments. If you can wait a little while, I can get one of our other case managers to do it, but it won't be until the end of the week. [A case manager should never, just to get that first case, make a promise that cannot be fulfilled. A broken promise will definitely destroy any hope of future referrals.]

Payer: Well, I am sorry, Jessica. I'll have to get someone else, but we'll give you all another opportunity in the future.

Are there any limits on travel time? The call may come from a regional office in Atlantic City: "I hear you do great work in New Jersey. I need you to send somebody out as soon as possible on this person." Maybe the case manager has a representative in Paterson, New Jersey. She should say, "We can take that, but are you concerned about travel-time expenses? This particular case is 3 hours away from our office. Do you have a problem with that?"

Or, a client may request a particular case manager for the case: "I want Jack to work this case. He did a great job for me on a head injury 3 months ago." The fact that he lives 2 hours away and his travel time will be factored into the case management fee might not matter to the client, but the case manager ought to verify this.

All business details—fees, how much is charged per hour, what service elements are charged (travel, phone, fax, postage), what service elements are not charged (report copies), the length of status reports—need to be clarified. The case manager might give a synopsis: "Our initial evaluation with these parameters probably will take from 6 to 8 hours. Is that in the ballpark of what you would expect?" The payer may feel that is agreeable or excessive. The payer might have been expecting to be charged for 4 to 5 hours tops or might say, "We never pay for travel time" or "We only pay half the rate for travel time." The case manager must then decide whether to work within those guidelines.

It may be that the case manager is busy working a broad client base and may choose not to reduce any of her fees, including those for travel time. It may be that the case management company is big enough, good enough, that it does not need to compromise on prices. The response could be, "Listen, I'm sorry, but our expenses are such . . ." or "In this part of the country, costs are such . . ." The case manager would then close with a request that the payer keep the firm in mind for other cases. On the other hand, the case manager might have been looking for the chance to work with that individual or payer company and say, "Our fees for this are $100 an hour. I understand that seems a little bit high, but I'd like you to see what we do. If you like what we do, maybe we can negotiate a lower cost another time."

Fees can be discussed on a case-by-case basis or can be set, for example, through the establishment of a 2- or 5-year contract. The important thing is to discuss fees openly at the beginning of the relationship and, if rates are raised over the course of the relationship, to communicate that as well.

A case manager should make certain that she is comfortable delivering the type of job a client is requesting. If the case manager feels incapable of completing an accurate and objective assessment of a particular case via the telephone, for example, or thinks there might be liability concerns with a particular assessment issue, the concern must be broached ("I only conduct on-site assessments" or "I've found that all physicians on a case must be consulted for an assessment"). When the criteria are clear, then information gathering may begin.

Prior to beginning an assessment, eligibility for coverage under the specific line of insurance paying for case management should be defined. The case manager needs to discover the client's responsibility on this case, for this individual, under this policy. She needs to have contact information for the employer, the plan administrator, and the stop-loss carrier, if there is one. Often, eligibility has not been ascertained, so the case manager must ask, "What is the line of insurance?" and "Is this individual covered under this policy?" "Is there stop-loss coverage?" (See Figure 9–2.) Suppose the case manager works in the preadmission and concurrent review department of a large company and receives a call that James Jones is in the hospital with multiple injuries. James is named on the policy of his father, employee John Jones, and covered under the company's medical plan. But in talking to John Jones, the case manager finds that James was involved in an auto accident or hurt at work. Therefore, James is not eligible for benefits under his father's group medical plan, because it is an auto insurance or a workers' compensation case.

In the event that a child is covered under a parent's policy, other questions arise. Many insurance policies include a "birthday rule," a clause that states that the insurance of the parent whose birthday falls earliest in the calendar year is considered the primary coverer and the other parent's plan is used as secondary coverage. Perhaps James Jones fell off a ladder while putting up an antenna on the roof of his parents' house. John Jones's birthday is in August and his wife's birthday is in March. In this instance, the wife's coverage is primary and John's is secondary. John's company may have referred James's case to the case manager under the illusion it was the responsible carrier. During a preassessment review, the case manager discovers the correct status and refers the case back to the wife's insurer.

At the outset of a case, the case manager should ask, "How long has the patient been ill?" or "When did the accident or injury occur?" to review the case for the potential of high-risk or long-term cost factors. In general, the more severe the event is in terms of injury, accident, or illness, the more likely the case will be

Figure 9–2 Employer Group Information Sheet

OU Group Number: _____   ABR's Group Number: _____

Employer Group Information Sheet

Group Name: _____Effective Date: _____

Subsidiary of/Parent Organization: _____

Main Address: _____

Phone: (800) _____Fax:_____E-mail_____

Web Site: _____

CEO: _____ CFO: _____

Director of Human Resources (Benefits Manager): _____

Phone:_____ Fax: _____E-mail: _____

Other Location(s) and/or Site Addresses: _____

Contact: _____ Title: _____

Phone: _____Fax:_____ E-mail:_____

Tax ID #: _____ Type of Industry: _____

No. of Employees: _____ No. of Covered Lives: _____

Number of Plans: _____

Type of Coverage:

Hospital (only) _____ Major Medical (only) _____ Comprehensive _____

Short-Term/Long-Term Disability _____ Workers' Compensation _____ Other _____

Funding Category:

Self Funded: _____ Minimum Premium: _____ Fully Insured: _____

continues

Figure 9–2 continued

Bill to #: _____

Health Plan Administrator: _____

Address: _____

Phone: (800) _____ Fax: _____ Web Site: _____

Contact: _____ Title: _____

Phone/Ext: _____ Fax: _____ E-mail: _____

Consultant/Broker: _____ Fax: _____ E-mail: _____

Modem Dial-Up Capability: Yes _____ No _____

Customer Service Line: (800) _____

Billing: _____ Title: _____

Phone/Ext: _____ Fax: _____ E-mail: _____

Case Management: _____ Title: _____

Phone/Ext: _____ Fax: _____ E-mail: _____

Claims: _____ Title: _____

Phone/Ext: _____ Fax: _____ E-mail: _____

COBRA Issues: _____ Title: _____

Phone/Ext: _____ Fax: _____ E-mail: _____

Eligibility: _____ Title: _____

Phone/Ext: _____ Fax: _____ E-mail: _____

Prenotification: _____ Title: _____

Phone/Ext: _____ Fax: _____ E-mail: _____

Reports: _____ Title: _____

Phone/Ext: _____ Fax: _____ Email: _____

Figure 9–2 continued

Stop-Loss Issues: _____ Title: _____

Phone/Ext: _____ Fax: _____ E-mail: _____

Specific Limit Reports: _____%

Type of Plan:

Indemnity: _____ PPO: _____ EPO: _____ POS: _____ Other: _____

Networks:
Name: _____ Phone: _____ Web Site: _____

Prescription Drug Card: Yes _____ No _____

Name of Plan: _____

Contact: _____ Title: _____

Phone: _____ Fax:_____ E-mail: _____

Mail Order Plan: Yes _____ No _____

Name of Plan: _____

Contact: _____ Title: _____

Phone: _____ Fax: _____ E-mail: _____

STOP-LOSS INSURANCE INFORMATION

Name of Group: _____

Carrier: _____ Policy #: _____

Address: _____

Contact: _____ Title: _____

Phone: _____ Fax: _____ E-mail: _____

Managing General Underwriter (if applicable): _____

Limits: Specific: _____

          Aggregate: _____

continues

Figure 9–2 continued

Does Carrier Require Case Management? Yes _____ No _____
Does Carrier Request Contact from Case Manager? Yes _____ No _____
Does Carrier Request Stop Loss Advisory: Yes _____ No _____

ATTACHED ARE:

Plan group number for each division: Requested: _____ Received _____
SPDs—2 copies (for each plan/division): Requested _____ Received _____
Cheat Sheets (for each plan/division): Requested _____ Received_____
Large Claims Info, if available: Requested: _____ Received _____
Paid Claims History (prior year): Requested _____ Received _____
VIP List (if applicable): Requested _____ Received _____
COBRA Enrollees: Requested _____ Received _____

Source: Courtesy of Options Unlimited, Case Management Services Division, 2003, Huntington, New York.

long-term. Rarely does a person in a coma wake up in a day or two and go about the normal business of life. Based on diagnosis alone, a case manager can outline short- and long-term needs. Even if the referral source has little information other than "it's a spinal cord injury" or "it's a traumatic brain injury," the case manager can ascertain that this is a complex case and prepare the referral source for long-term case management involvement. In the meantime, the case manager identifies those actions that can be taken immediately. Then, once the likely scenario becomes clear based on the present state of the individual or illness, the case manager can evaluate the long-term impact of case management on the situation. The line of insurance and the dollars available may determine what can be done. The case manager may devise an appropriate long-term plan but be unable to actualize the plan because of insufficient funds.

Therefore, the next question is, "What dollars are available to this individual within the policy?" For example, an individual holds an auto policy with only a minimal amount of coverage ($25,000). He has multiple injuries and multiple problems and has been in a hospital intensive care unit for 3 days. Would case management be effective in controlling costs? No. The claimant's injuries are severe, he requires high-level care, and all medical treatments being delivered are necessary. The benefit dollars have been spent, but spent wisely.

On the other hand, a group medical plan providing up to $50,000 worth of rehabilitation care may not stipulate that those dollars have to be spent in an inpatient setting. If the claimant has had a stroke, the case manager looks at the available dollars and determines how to maximize benefits while containing costs.

In addition to the dollar amounts, a case manager must ask about limits and restrictions on types of care, care facilities, and lengths of stay. Is there $100,000 or $500,000 for medical coverage? Is coverage limited to 1 year or is it open-ended until a cap of $1 million is reached? Are there restrictions on the number of days the individual will be covered for hospital care? Perhaps the individual is in a coma in an acute care hospital. The case manager should then ask, "Are there any limitations on inpatient rehabilitation? What are the benefits for a skilled nursing facility?" A benefit cap of $1,000,000 may appear adequate to cover all needs, but the policy may dictate very specific ways in which those dollars may be spent.

There are times when case managers can foresee an unsuccessful intervention despite a policy generous in dollars and services. A case manager may not be able to make a meaningful impact because of the limits of a line of insurance; because a number of attorneys have become involved with a case that is in litigation, requiring the case manager to obtain the approval of each lawyer prior to speaking with the patient and in some cases to have the lawyer present for each conversation; or because of a preexisting condition. Case management is undertaken on a voluntary level; a patient pleased with the medical services he or she is receiving may not be interested in any changes. Sometimes, a patient is so heavily invested in a particular team of physicians that he or she discourages or even refuses case management involvement.

Beyond the type of policy, line of insurance, dollars, and limitations, the data that case managers request from referral sources varies slightly depending on the line of insurance. In a workers' compensation case, the case manager needs to know not only the date of the injury, but also the employee's "time and grade," the length of time the individual has been an employee at the company, and his or her position and job responsibilities. How vested is the company in this employee? The founding fathers of a firm may be more likely to make special allowances for a key employee than for a short-term employee with under a year at the company—less is known about him and his contribution.

Salary and the person's status as a union or management employee also become issues in workers' compensation cases, and the case manager needs to be aware of this aspect of finances. Workers' compensation salary replacement regulations vary from state to state. Further, every union negotiates its own salary replacement. A union may dictate that an injured worker receive full salary for a year. This type of financial arrangement impacts a person's motivation and inclination to return to the workplace. Receiving 100% of normal salary can be a strong disincentive, even when the person is well enough to perform a portion of his or her job or work half-days. Lack of income also influences a person's decision to return to work. Perhaps the individual on disability gets full salary for a month and then goes on state disability and receives only two thirds of salary. This may be financially devastating for the family, to the extent that the person might attempt to return to work prematurely. Premature return to a hazardous environment is of as much concern to case managers as individuals who draw benefits for too long. Not everyone reacts the same way to financial stress, and not every family faces the same amount of stress. Some employees are the sole support, and others have partners who work full- or part-time. In the latter case, a role reversal often takes place, and the partner assumes the role of sole support for a time, easing the financial problem.

One question a case manager needs to ask in a workers' compensation case is, "How did the injury happen?" The idea is not to launch an investigation into who was at fault or to elicit background information for use in court but to prevent a recurrence of the incident. Sometimes, an employee will say to a case manager, "I told my boss that this piece of equipment was falling apart" or "I knew the belt on that sander needed to be replaced and I reported it." This may be the third worker injury at that job station in 2 years, causing the case manager to go back to the claims examiner and urge that a risk management team be sent to the job station before another employee is disabled.

There may be litigation pending or in place. If a claimant begins to volunteer information, the case manager must stop him or her from inappropriately discussing the case. The case manager can acknowledge the claimant's anger, state that she cannot get involved in the legal issues, and put the focus back on the case management program. However, certain circumstantial questions may be appropriate. Has the injury impacted the individual's mental comfort level with his or her job? Is the individual concerned about safety back at the sander belt? Seeking answers to these types of inquiries, the case manager can then help put services or worksite modifications in place that will help the patient overcome his or her fear.

Some workers' compensation issues can hinder the case manager's ability to be effective on behalf of the patient and the referral source because they point to hidden agendas being played out. The mentality that leans toward suing and retiring on the proceeds is an obstacle to successful case management intervention, as is a lawsuit involving a piece of equipment or a manufacturer. The case manager might know from the get-go that a company is mistreating its workforce and that the patient's anger is such that the case manager's efforts will be sidetracked. If the role is to minimize the disability and improve the return-to-work outlook, the case manager needs to take an objective look at the situation, realize its lack of potential, and discuss with the referral source whether the continued use of case management is appropriate.

In group medical plan cases, case managers are only responding to medical care issues; there are no return-to-work or lost-earnings-replacement issues. A carrier will not be asking, "When can I expect John back in the office?" Again, key points will be the type of policy, the dollars available, the dollar limitations, the services included in the plan, and the plan's flexibility. Some group medical plans are very, very generous, incorporating provisions for home care, skilled nursing facilities, rehabilitation facilities, and rehabilitation, especially when provided outside of an acute care facility. On the other hand, other policies may include generous benefits for inpatient care and hardly any language supporting an alternative setting. Such limitations may dictate a case manager's degree of success. If the case manager uncovers these limitations as she is collecting information from the referral source and begins to see the intended care plan unraveling, what are the options? Work with half the case management plan? Work the case any way possible? The case manager might go ahead with the full assessment and offer options after ascertaining that there are decision makers who would consider covering benefits that are not outlined in the policy but that are more appropriate to the case and potentially less expensive as well. In group medical plans and fully insured plans, there is often less flexibility, as plan language has been set in stone because it is formulated based on group experience (e.g., premium rates are assigned based on age, sex, and lifestyle). With self-funded or employer-funded plans, even though the plan language may not include provisions for alternative care, there may be more willingness to consider other possibilities.

Like workers' compensation cases, auto insurance and disability insurance cases are governed by state regulations. When taking notes on an auto policy case, a case manager should request information on medical and lost-wages provisions, the amount of dollars available, the covered years, and whether the carrier has direct control of the policy. Is an individual covered for any medical treatment wherever it may be administered? If the auto accident happened out of state, which state's laws take precedence? It may be the state in which the injury occurred, the state in which the policy is written, or the state in which the employer's headquarters office is located. In short- or long-term disability cases, the extent and framework of the policy must be known before the case manager can begin an assessment.

A Wrap-Up of Referral-Source Communication Steps

1. A referral call to the case manager is made.
2. The case manager gets the appropriate business details and confirms the needs of the referral source (e.g., expectations, fees, format, and time frame for reports).
3. The case manager requests case background (e.g., the status of the patient, the diagnosis and prognosis, the type of insurance coverage, the patient's

eligibility under the policy, the policy benefit limits, the plan's flexibility, and the restrictions on care).
4. The case manager confirms the initial assessment and report parameters in writing to the referral source and/or payer.
5. The case manager makes a follow-up call to review the confirmation letter.
6. The case manager documents all conversations.

CASE FINDING AND TARGETING

Sometimes, cases are targeted for case management via referral, some are flagged by a software system, and some are spotted by nurse reviewers and case managers during admissions, intake interviews, or initial assessments. To assist our nurse reviewers and case managers, I developed a case management identification worksheet, guidelines, and a "Red Flags" list, which together form an information-gathering tool. Applicable for use in precert departments, managed care organizations, insurance company offices with nurse reviewers, and a variety of other venues in which case management and utilization review/precertification is practiced, the tool's main purpose is to help more selectively identify those cases with the optimum potential for successful case management.

The Case Management Identification Worksheet (Figure 9–3) is used to tally up all our case management indicators; the Case Management Identification "Red Flags" List (Figure 9–4) lists indicators that should "flag" a case for case management review. The Case Management Identification Worksheet Guidelines (Figure 9–5) are exactly that, an explanation of those issues listed under "Reasons for Referral" on the worksheet, such as a request for or need for a service, complications, financial/insurance issues, family/social issues, and paid claims to date.

We have developed advisory forms for case management intervention and stop-loss notification. (Figures 9–6 and 9–7). Our nurse reviewers and case managers fill these out when a case is identified for case management services, or when a case needs to be presented to a department manager, claims department, or referral source for approval, prior to initiating case management services. This form includes diagnosis, reasons for referral, type of insurance, our particular case management goals, and whether a claims examiner has been or needs to be notified. The basics of this advisory can easily be reworked to meet the needs of internal or consultant case managers when communicating with internal or client management.

Our Case Management Audit Tool (Figure 9–8) is used as an evaluation tool to track the progress of the patient and our services. The line of questioning it presents promotes quality improvement initiatives by helping the case manager think in new ways about the case, in some cases inspiring alternatives if the patient has plateaued or seems stuck. It also helps us monitor the capabilities and development of a new hire.

Figure 9–3 Case Management Identification Worksheet

Date:_____

Nurse reviewer: _____

Patient: _____ D.O.B. (age): _____

Insured: _____ Date of adm.:_____ Date of discharge: _____
                                                           (or unknown)

S.S.#:_____ Admitting diagnosis: _____

Group: _____

    Surgical procedure:_____

    Hospital: _____

    Physician(s)/specialty:_____

Reason for referral for case management—check all that apply

     A ❑   B ❑   C ❑   D ❑   E ❑   F ❑

A. Request or need for: SNF ❑   Rehab ❑   Hospice ❑

                   HHC ❑   Infusion ❑   Extended hosp. ❑

                   Other ❑

B. Prior admissions & LOS*:_____

C. Complications (existing or potential): _____

D. Financial/insurance issues:_____

E. Family/soc. issues: _____

F. Paid claims to date (if known): _____

          <u>Reviewer</u>   <u>Date</u>

*Attach or refer to system notes _____

* *

<u>Management review:</u>

Accepted   ❑

Denied   ❑

    (Reason): _____

Assigned/referred to: _____

Manager: _____ Date: _____

Source: Courtesy of Options Unlimited, Case Management Services Division, 2003, Huntington, New York.

Figure 9–4 Case Management Identification "Red Flags" List

Diagnosis or Illness:

AIDS	End stage or other organ	Neuromuscular diseases
Alcohol and substance	failure/transplant	Parkinson's disease
abuse	Hepatitis C	Psychiatric (anorexia,
Cancer	Head injury	bulimia, substance
Cardiovascular	High-risk infant	abuse, etc.)
Chronic respiratory	High-risk pregnancy	Rheumatoid arthritis
Chronic obstructive	Hip fracture	Severe burns
pulmonary disease	Leukemia	Sickle cell
(COPD)	Liver disease	Spina bifida
Crohn's disease	Lyme disease	Spinal cord injury
Cystic fibrosis	Morbid obesity	Stroke
Diabetes	Multiple trauma	Transplants
		Tuberculosis

Potential Treatment:	Chemotherapy	Monitors (uterine, apnea, etc.)
	Extended ICU	Oxygen (concentrators,
	Home care services	ongoing O_2)
	Hospice care	Pain management. programs
	Insulin pump	Rehabilitation (inpatient
	IV antibiotics/IVIG	or day program)
	(other injectables;	TPN/enteral
	Heparin, Lovenox)	Ventilator dependent

Frequent hospitalizations or prolonged confinement:	• Three admits same year for same or related problem • Confinements exceeding 10 days
Cost of claims:	• Same illness over $25,000 year to date
Patterns of care:	• Failed or repeated surgeries, hospital-acquired infections, malpractice concerns (quality-of-care issues) • Multiple providers, medications, outpatient surgeries, admissions to a skilled nursing facility
While patient still hospitalized:	• Consider response to treatment: multiple providers, prior compliance issues, family support, responsibilities issues, complications
After patient has been discharged:	• Consider patient knowledge of illness, medications and medical directions, involvement of patient/family (have they scheduled follow-up appointments, testing, second opinions, etc.?), satisfaction with medical care —Does patient/family know what to report, to whom, and when?

Figure 9–4 continued

	—Do they know the treatment plan for the future . . . do they have the ability and inclination to follow it?
Location:	• Complex care delivered in rural setting, small hospital, or facility with poor outcome history
Pharmaceutical profile:	• Multiple providers/drugs, drug interaction potential, abuse patterns, disease management potential

Source: Courtesy of Options Unlimited, Case Management Services Division, 2003, Huntington, New York.

TALKING WITH THE PATIENT

Following the initial conversation with the referral source, the first person the case manager interviews is the patient. The object is to obtain an overview of the patient's current medical history, the particular individual, and the situation. The case manager must be proactive and nonthreatening, perceived as an advocate and viewed as a benefit. The case manager must also encourage the patient to be participatory, which is done by being supportive and not being overly presumptive or controlling. Because the first contact is the key to future success, the case manager must take the time to lay the groundwork. To set up the first meeting or telephone interview with the patient, the case manager should telephone or, in cases where the patient has no phone or contact number, send a letter (see Tables 9–1 to 9–5 beginning on page 217).

Telephone Call to Patient To Set Up Initial Visit

Case Manager: Ms. Williams, this is Ann Sanders and I am a rehabilitation nurse [medical case manager, nurse case manager, counselor, etc.] here in the Brownsville area. I work with people who have had serious illnesses or injuries. Your workers' compensation carrier [health insurance carrier, etc.] asked me to visit with you to see if I can be of assistance during your recovery. How have you been feeling today?

Case Manager: It sounds like you're still having a few problems. I am going to be out in the Hampton area next Tuesday morning. Would 10:00 A.M. be a convenient time for me to drop in and visit with you for a few minutes? [I'm planning to be at the hospital around 9:30 tomorrow and will plan to visit you. As far as you know, will that be a convenient time for you?]

If the patient seems hesitant or has questions about what the case manager will be doing in working with her/him, the case manager should briefly explain her

Figure 9–5 Case Management Identification Worksheet Guidelines

---

Instructions for Use

Purpose: The Case Management Identification Worksheet is intended to standard-ize and ease the process of identifying the most appropriate cases for case manage-ment. The upper section of this form has the usual demographic data and needs to be completed by the nurse reviewer.

"Reasons for Referral": This section has a concise "Red Flags" list. Each one of the areas needs to be considered and obviously, if several or all of these are checked off, it is likely to be a serious case, both medically and financially.

A. Request or need for: During the review process, has there been a direct request for any (or several) of these services? Or, does the reviewer anticipate the need for any?

B. Prior admissions and LOS: All prior admissions *and* the length of stay for each should be noted. If there are reference notes or comments, this, too, should be noted, e.g., ". . . see PreCert # 1234 and notes . . . etc."

C. Complications: The presence or potential for complications is always a "red flag" to alert us to quality-of-care issues and/or *other* medical conditions, for example, a post-op wound infection—is it a nursing issue, a compromised immune system, or a matter for an infectious disease specialist? Because case management should be *preventing* complications, we need to be aware of the potential for them, for example, a patient with a stroke returning to a home with-out other adults *may* be at risk for falls and reinjury. *State the complication.*

D. Financial/insurance issues: Having too little insurance benefits is as much a problem for the case manager as those contracts with very generous benefits and ambiguous language. *State the issue specifically,* for example, traumatic brain injury—only 30 days inpatient rehab *or* 365 hospital days but no sub-acute hospital benefits.

E. Family/social issues: Patients living alone, patients in rural areas, patients in high-crime, inner city areas, patients with aging spouses, or families in the midst of emotional crises (death, divorce, etc.) are all issues that could signal a need for case management. *State concisely and specifically.*

F. Paid claims to date: When there is access to claims data, it is helpful as a con-sideration to know how much has already been spent. Enter the dollar amount.

The "Management Review" section is intended to be another screening level to ensure that *appropriate* cases and those with the most opportunity for a successful outcome by a case manager are actually accepted and assigned.

Note: Those cases denied by a member of the management staff need to have the rationale for the denial, for example, family refused.

Source: Courtesy of Options Unlimited, Case Management Services Division, 2003, Hunt-ington, New York.

Figure 9–6 Advisory: Case Management Intervention

Options Unlimited, Inc.
76 East Main Street
Huntington, NY 11743
Tel: (631) 673-1150
FAX: (631) 673-8369

ADVISORY

CASE MANAGEMENT INTERVENTION

Advisory Date: _____

O.U. File #:

Name:	Title:	S.S. #:

Company Name:	Employer. Group:
Address:	Insurance Coverage & State

City:	State:	Zip:	Tel:	Insured:

Name:	Diagnosis:
Address:	Co-Morbidities:

Tel:	S.S.#:	D.O.B.:
Hospital:	Date of Admission:	Date of Discharge:

Approval For Case Management:

Claimant:	Case Management Approval from other than claimant:
YES: ☐ NO: ☐	Name:
	Relationship:
Potential For Cost Containment:	Tel. No:

Reason for Case Management Intervention: (Please check one or more of the following)

Complex Medical Diagnoses: ☐	3 admissions within year with same diagnosis: ☐
Prolonged Hospitalization: ☐	Transitions to appropriate level of care: ☐
Multiple Treatment Providers: ☐	High Risk/Cost to Plan: ☐

Plan Approval:	Reason for Denial:
Date:	Date:

Notify Plan Via:	Group Renewal Date:
Re-Insurer:	Member Effective Date:

INDIVIDUAL LIMITS:	**AGGREGATE LIMITS:**
Re-Insurer Notified:	Date Notified:
Plan to Contact Re-Insurer:	

** IF THIS INTERVENTION DOES NOT MEET WITH YOUR APPROVAL, CONTACT OPTIONS IMMEDIATELY **

Date Received:	Date Assigned:	Assigned To:	Completed By:

Source: Courtesy of Options Unlimited, Case Management Services Division, 2003, Huntington, New York.

Figure 9–7 Advisory: Stop-Loss Notification

Options Unlimited, Inc.			**ADVISORY**			
76 East Main Street						
Huntington, NY 11743					Advisory Date:	
Tel: (631) 673-1150						
FAX: (631) 673-8369		**STOP LOSS NOTIFICATION**			O.U. File #:	

Name:		Title:			S.S. #:	
Company Name:				Employer. Group:		
Address:				Insurance Coverage & State:		
City:	State:	Zip:		Tel:		Insured:
Name:			Diagnosis:			
Address:			Co-Morbidities:			
Tel:		S.S.#:			D.O.B.:	
Hospital:		Date of Admission:			Date of Discharge:	

Approval For Case Management:

Claimant:		Case Management Approval From other than claimant:
YES: ☐ NO: ☐		Name:
		Relationship:
Potential For Cost Containment:		Tel. No:

Reason for Case Management Intervention: (Please check one or more of the following)

	Complex Medical Diagnoses: ☐	3 admissions within year with same diagnosis: ☐
	Prolonged Hospitalization: ☐	Transitions to appropriate level of care: ☐
	Multiple Treatment Providers: ☐	High Risk/Cost to Plan: ☐

Plan Approval:		Reason for Denial:
Date:		Date:
Notify Plan Via:		Group Renewal Date:
Re-Insurer:		Member Effective Date:
INDIVIDUAL LIMITS:		**AGGREGATE LIMITS:**
Re-Insurer Notified:		Date Notified:
Plan to Contact Re-Insurer:		

** IF THIS INTERVENTION DOES NOT MEET WITH YOUR APPROVAL, CONTACT OPTIONS IMMEDIATELY **

Date Received:	Date Assigned:	Assigned To:	Completed By:

Source: Courtesy of Options Unlimited, Case Management Services Division, 2003, Huntington, New York.

Figure 9–8 Case Management Audit Tool

Options Unlimited
Case Management Audit Tool

Auditor: _____   Case Manager: _____   Pt. Initials: _____

Audit for month of: _____   Date: _____   OU File #: _____

Quality Item			YES	NO	N/A
1. Is the Advisory form current and complete?					
2. Was the case opened in a timely manner, consistent with criteria?					
3. Has the modem sheet been completed, or are the benefits documented in the nurse's notes?					
4. Are all entries in the nurse's notes dated, with billing sheets and noted?					
5. Are patient centered, short- and long-term goals documented?					
6. Documentation of appropriate actions to meet these goals?					
7. Are goals of plan reflected with each patient/family contact?					
8. If a message was left, is there documentation of the nature of the message?					
9. Patient or family contact documented?					
10. Documentation of explanation of CM services?					
11. Documentation of verbal or written permission to initiate case management services?					
12. Documentation that patient information was mailed?					
13. Medical record release of information obtained? (if required)					
14. Is appropriate physician contact documented? (within 72 business hours)					
15. Documentation of diagnosis specific information? i.e., DME, Home Care/Hospice, Physicians, Social Issues					
16. Was contact with the discharge planner/hospital case manager noted? (if appropriate)					
17. Medications noted?					
18. Is there a fax or notation of computer system entry noted within 24-48 hours after receipt of referral?					
19. Were contacts with the frequency appropriate for the level of the case?					
20. Is there documentation regarding whether providers are in-plan?					
21. If providers are not in plan, are there documented attempts at negotiation?					
22. Are fee agreements/alternative treatments present if negotiations were successful (or notation in computer system of same?)					
23. Are fee agreements clear?					
24. Are appropriate records from providers in the record?					
25. If there was drug coverage noted, is there documentation of notification of the needs to use the drug plan coverage?					
26. Is there drug documentation, if appropriate? Re: off-label use of drug, chemotherapeutic agents, atypical treatment, FDA approval.					
27. Is verification of plan language in transplant cases noted?					
28. Re: DME: Is there documentation of provider notification of rental to purchase price only with documentation of both rental and purchase price?					
29. Were outpatient therapy/home care/hospice/SNF/inpatient rehabilitation notes requested and reviewed on a regular basis?					
30. Is there a timely transition to self/family care noted?					
31. Was the initital report done within a month of opening the case?					
32. Were subsequent reports done in a timely manner?					
33. Was a subrogation referral made if potential liability for injuries was involved?					
34. Was the case closed in a timely manner consistent with criteria?					
35. Is there documentation that patient goals have been met?					
36. Re: Case closure: Is there documentation that the appropriate notification was sent to patients/families and clients?					
37. Were case management functions conducted within scope of licensure?					
Comments:					

continues

Figure 9–8 continued

Comments and/or Corrective Action Plan with Timeframes

_____
_____
_____
_____
_____
_____
_____

_____   _____
Case Manager Signature   Date

_____   _____
Director of Case Management Services   Date

COB:ja
Revised 12/2002
MSExcel/P:Reports/URAC file:Case Management Audit.xls

Source: Courtesy of Options Unlimited, Case Management Services Division, 2003, Huntington, New York.

role but try to direct the greater portion of her answers to the personal visit. A personal visit, if possible, can help develop good rapport.)

Case Manager: OK, fine, I'll plan to see you next Tuesday around 10:00 A.M. Let me give you my telephone number so if your plans change, you can just call me collect at my office. If I don't hear from you, I will look forward to meeting you next Tuesday.

Case Manager: I have your address in my file, but let me get directions to your house. Can you name any landmarks or stores I can note along the way, so I know I'm still going in the right direction?

Case Manager: Those are good directions, thanks. Mary,[1] I've enjoyed talking with you and I'll see you next Tuesday morning.

It is often advisable to send a brief letter, postcard, or handwritten memo to remind the patient of the case manager's pending visit, especially if considerable travel time and mileage are involved.

Initial Evaluation or Assessment

At the initial visit, the case manager's first questions should center on the patient's comprehension of his or her medical condition. What does the patient see as the problem? The patient might say, "My doctor told me I had a heart

Table 9–1 Sample Letter to New Client Who Does Not Have a Telephone

---

Mr. John Williams
132 E. Main Street
Brownsville, TX 84362

Dear Mr. Williams:

I am a rehabilitation nurse [case manager] and I have been asked by your insurance company [name] to meet with you and see if I can provide additional information about or be of assistance in your recovery from your injury [present illness]. In the information that was sent to me, I did not find a telephone number for you. I need to talk with you so that we can arrange a convenient time to meet.

When you receive this letter, would you please call my office collect at (999) 999-9999. If I am not in the office, please leave a message that you called and also a telephone contact number where I may reach you.

I am looking forward to working with you and I hope to hear from you in the next day or two.

Sincerely,

Angie White, R.N.
Medical Case Manager

Source: Courtesy of Options Unlimited, Case Management Services Division, 2003, Huntington, New York.

---

attack." The case manager can then elicit further information by asking, "What do you think that means? Will it change your lifestyle?" By encouraging the patient to use his or her own words, the case manager can get a reading on the patient's level of understanding and acceptance (or denial) of his or her situation. Perhaps the patient minimizes the illness. The referral source may have told the case manager that the patient has a malignant tumor that has already metastasized to other organs. But the patient says, "Well, I had a growth and the doctor removed it and he said that I should be fine now." It might be that the referral source, the physicians, and the case manager all know the patient's true medical condition but the patient and family do not have a clue. Perhaps the family wants to isolate and protect the patient from knowing his or her true health status. It is the case manager's job to ascertain the reality of the situation by speaking to the treating physician and family members and by getting documentation from the referral source.

Table 9–2 Sample Letter of Introduction to Insured for High-Risk Pregnancy Management

---

Date

Dear Ms. _____:

I enjoyed speaking with you today and, as promised, this letter is to reexplain what my call and our services are all about. As discussed, _____ is a private consulting firm used by _Third Party Administrator_ on behalf of your employer group to provide assistance to individuals who may experience difficulties with certain medical conditions.

Diabetes can _sometimes_ make a pregnancy difficult and what we want to ensure is that you and your baby come through it healthy and happy. Our nurse case managers work with patients, their physicians, and families in coordinating the necessary care and services that may be needed both now and in the future months.

This service is at no cost to you and is provided through the benefit plan. It again is not a "hands-on" service, nor is it intended to interrupt or interfere with any care you are now receiving.

In order to determine just how we may be of assistance, one of our nurses would like to meet with you at your home. Because they are often out visiting patients, we ask that you call collect at (999) 999-9999 so that we can put her in touch with you.

Please accept my personal assurance that every effort will be extended on your behalf and our best wishes for a happy, healthy pregnancy and a very healthy, happy baby for you and your husband.

If you have any questions or concerns, please feel free to contact me at any time at the above number.

Warmest regards,

Case Manager

cc: Claims Department

Source: Courtesy of Options Unlimited, Case Management Services Division, 2003, Huntington, New York.

Table 9–3 Sample Letter of Introduction for Services Requested for Insured's Child

---

Date

Mr. Thibault Queyroy
13 Bree Lane
Siddleton, New York

Dear Mr. Queyroy:

Please allow this letter to serve as an introduction and explanation of services that have been requested on behalf of your son, Anthony, by _____ Managed Care Services, Group Health Insurance.

Case Management Company is a private consulting firm utilized by Third Party Administrators on behalf of their insureds who may be experiencing difficulties with a variety of medical, psychiatric, and other complicated situations.

These services are provided at no cost to you and are offered to provide assistance and coordination of services that will be necessary both now and in the future. Our role is not intended to interrupt or interfere with any care or therapies that your son is now receiving, nor will our nurse consultants be providing any direct counseling or "hands-on" care. We work with physicians, therapists, the family, and patient, in order that the best outcome is obtained in a manner that is caring, appropriate, and cost-effective.

In order to determine just how we may help, would you please call us collect at _____. One of our consultants would like to arrange an appointment to meet with you, your son, and physician, if available.

Enclosed, please find one of our brochures that describes our services further. Please accept my personal assurance that every effort will be extended on behalf of your son and we look forward to working with you.

Thank you very much for your time and anticipated cooperation.

Very truly yours,

Source: Courtesy of Options Unlimited, Case Management Services Division, 2003, Huntington, New York.

A case manager should never assume a patient has the ability to accept a diagnosis. Some of the most brilliant medical professionals are uncomfortable hearing about their own health problems. Patients and their families can block out information or deny the obvious. Case managers must take each person where they are at the time of the assessment and explore his or her view of the situation.

Table 9–4 Sample Letter of Introduction for a Workers' Compensation Case

---

Date

Dear Mr. _____:

Please allow this letter to serve as an introduction and explanation of services that have been requested on your behalf by _____, the Workers' Compensation Administrator for your employer.

Case Management Company is a private disability management consulting firm that works with individuals such as you who have sustained injuries in the course of employment.

This is not a "hands-on" service, nor is it meant in any way to interrupt or interfere with the care you are currently receiving. The role of our consultant is to work with you, your physicians, therapist, and other health professionals who may be involved to ensure that you derive the best results from these efforts. Our goal is to assist you with a return to a medically stable, comfortable, and productive lifestyle in an employment situation.

In order to determine just how we may be of assistance, one of our consultants, _____, R.N., would like to meet with you at your home. If you have not heard from our consultant, would you please call us collect at _____ in order that we can put her in contact with you.

Enclosed, please find one of our brochures that describes our services. Should you have any questions or concerns, please feel free to contact me directly.

Mr. _____, we look forward to working with you and please accept my personal assurance that every effort will be made on your behalf.

Very truly yours,

Source: Courtesy of Options Unlimited, Case Management Services Division, 2003, Huntington, New York.

Does this particular patient understand that he has had a serious or a minor illness? Does he understand how it is impacting his life now and will impact it in the future? Does he have any knowledge about that part of his body? If surgery was performed, does he understand why? Has his doctor been communicating with him? If he is on medication, does he know what it is for? If he is in the hospital and about to go home, is he knowledgeable about his discharge plan and what he needs to do? What does he need to be watchful for? Does he understand any specific limitations he may have now? Does he accept these? Many patients intellectually grasp such limitations but do not take them in emotionally.

Table 9–5 Sample Letter of Introduction for Services Provided Through a Third Party Administrator

---

Date

Dear _____:

Please allow this letter to serve as an introduction and explanation of services that have been requested on your behalf by _____ of *Third Party Administrator* (TPA), which is the company administrating the health care benefits on behalf of your employer, _____.

_____ is a private consulting firm utilized by TPA on behalf of their insureds to assist them with the problems resulting from a variety of medical conditions. This service is at no cost to you, and is a benefit provided by the company.

Our nurse consultants work with you, your family, and treating physicians in coordinating whatever care and services are necessary in order that you may receive the best results possible. This intervention is not intended to interrupt or interfere with any care you are currently receiving, nor is this a "hands-on" service.

In order to determine just how we may be of assistance, one of our consultants, _____, would like to meet with you at your home. Because our consultants are frequently out of the office, would you please call us COLLECT at (999) 999-9999 in order that we can put her in touch with you.

Enclosed, please find one of our brochures that further describes our services. Should you have any questions or concerns, please feel free to contact me directly. Please accept my personal assurance that every effort will be extended on your behalf.

Very truly yours,

Case Manager

cc: Claims Department

Source: Courtesy of Options Unlimited, Case Management Services Division, 2003, Huntington, New York.

A patient might say, "Yes, I've had a heart attack and I understand that the major wall of my heart was involved." When the case manager asks, "Do you think you can resume all your regular activities?" the response might be, "Oh, yeah, no problem." But the case manager knows that this is not the case. The patient has heard a portion of the doctor's answer, has been selective in listening, and does not have a total grasp of what he or she needs to know to be a cooperative, compliant participant in his or her health care plan.

Whereas some patients may be in denial, others are overly dramatic and intent on being a long-term part of the health care system. Some patients who have relatively minor problems try to boost them into life-threatening disorders. Having a major illness allows them a respite from life's burdens.

The ideal patient, after having been given good information about his or her condition, accepts that information and is realistic about possible treatments and likely outcomes. Unfortunately, the typical patient in the kind of cases that case managers tend to get may be physically or emotionally overwhelmed as a result of the severity of the condition. The patient might be a poor historian, might be unable to recall information, might be on a life-support system and unable to communicate easily, or might be very young. In a pediatric case, even though family members will be making the "life-and-death" decisions on treatment alternatives and surgical recommendations, the case manager should find out what the child understands. It is part of the case manager's role to make sure every patient has all the information he or she wants and needs about his or her case.

Because past medical history may impact the present, the case manager must also ask leading questions about other medical conditions that might, from a medical management perspective, affect recovery. This is best done by example, as the patient may not perceive how another condition (one that seems minor or that the patient has lived with for years) might influence treatment. For instance, the patient might decide his or her high blood pressure is "nothing" and never mention it. In the case of a patient about to undergo surgery to repair multiple fractures to a leg bone, the case manager might ask, "Have you ever had problems with your circulation, any bone disease or diabetes? Is this a recurrence of an old injury? Have you had prior surgeries or prior hospitalizations?" A person with a healthy, active lifestyle suffering a first injury should be able to recover in a reasonable amount of time given good medical care. An individual who has been through it all before, especially with a knee or back injury, or even one who has suffered similar work-related injuries with the same employer, might experience delays in recovery.

Another important query centers on medications. This area is crucial, and too little attention is paid to it by all members of the medical delivery system, including case managers. A case manager should ask a patient to bring out all the pills and medications being taken, including over-the-counter medications and herbal vitamins, whether or not the patient thinks they factor into his or her condition. There is a gap between what a patient perceives as a problem and what the medical profession knows is a problem.

I was working with a gentleman in New Hampshire who was diagnosed with cellulitis and thrombosis. Recently starting a new job as a security guard, this 275-pound man had been given a brisk physical and had been hired with this pre-existing condition because no one really looked at his legs. A member of an HMO plan, he had been seen by a different physician every time he had an appointment, and no one was tracking his needs and care. My role was to evaluate his status as a short-term disability patient.

At my on-site home visit, I found him living alone in a filthy house where he had just shared a can of stew with the cat. One leg was propped up on a chair and the other was on an ottoman. I asked if he had any other medical problems. The answer was no. I then requested that he show me any pills or medications he took.

He pointed to a shoe box filled with bottles, "Well, I've got these water pills here and my sugar pills. . . ."

"What are these for?"

"My diabetes, but that's nothing. I've had it for years." In fact, he also had been diagnosed as having hypertension and emphysema in addition to the diabetes, was supposed to be on a low-sodium diet, and had just consumed a high-sodium lunch.

"And what's this bottle for?"

"I take those when I feel my blood pressure is high."

"How do you know when it's high?"

"Sometimes I get a headache."

It seems that when he was diagnosed as having hypertension, the presenting problem was his headaches. In his mind then, he had high blood pressure on the days he got a headache. In other words, high blood pressure was not a serious condition he felt he had, but a minor problem that might occur on one day or another. We repeated the question-and-answer scenario until we had reviewed all the bottles in the box.

People tend to follow their own rules for taking medications. Case managers need to ask not only "What are you taking for this diagnosis?" but also "Are you taking any other medications?" And as I found from experience, the question needs to be pursued. I might note a medication in the physician's report. When I ask the patient if she's taking it, she will say she is not. Why not? She does not like the way it makes her feel, she doesn't want to become dependent on it, she doesn't want to be taking it forever, or she simply got tired of taking it. Has she told her physician this? No, but she will tell him when she sees him. Her next appointment is scheduled for six months later.

In good situations, the medication manipulation has no unfortunate conse-quences; however, the ill effects of overmedication or lack of medication can be harrowing. Even if the patient appears to be progressing well, it is important for the case manager, as an individual charged with preventing patients from slipping through the cracks in the medical delivery system, to check this aspect of the care profile.

Another part of a case manager's assessment centers on socioeconomic and psychosocial factors. What are the family dynamics at work? Is the patient a child or an adult, married or single, single and living alone? A person with many contacts, active in the community and church, might have a vast network of coworkers, family, and friends who can become caretakers for a time. A single person new to an area is more isolated and will need, for example, an entirely different medical support system for home care.

What is the patient's vocational status? An active, valued member of a company tends to want to resolve any medical problems as soon as possible. A person recently fired or with a bleak economic outlook reacts to treatment differently. An upbeat, optimistic, well-adjusted patient is more likely to follow a treatment plan. A person whom life has beaten about the head and shoulders could be on disability or workers' compensation for years, electing a "disability mentality" in which the illness becomes his or her job and social life. It is also important to find out about the patient's prior jobs in the event the patient is not able to return to his or her most recent type of employment.

Avocational interests and hobbies also influence a patient's recovery curve. If a patient enjoyed a number of active physical pursuits, such as skiing, golf, and horseback riding, but can no longer engage in them, the case manager should help the patient develop other ways of expressing an interest in those pursuits and remain mentally stimulated during recovery (e.g., an avid golfer might be encouraged to read the biography of a golf pro). Generally, those with the most avocations are more likely to be responsive to treatment. People who are not participatory by nature sometimes have to be encouraged to take charge and fight for their health.

To assist the case managers in my office to conduct effective initial assessment/evaluation interviews, I developed an Initial Evaluation Guidelines and an Initial Evaluation Worksheet (Tables 9–6 and 9–7), which take them through each step of the assessment process, recording the vital medical, socio/environmental, vocational, motivational/behavioral, and financial information needed to create a valid case management plan. The use of this worksheet as a tool for collection of the data also ensures an organized, easily accessible location for referral back to the information. The worksheet coincides with each section of the Initial Evaluation Report Format (see Table 9–20 later in this chapter); therefore, following the worksheet also assists in writing the initial report. I encourage my case managers to review the initial report format before meeting with the patient so that they are familiar with each section of the report and the information to be covered. This preparation helps the initial interview proceed more smoothly, achieving its two main goals of gathering data and establishing a sense of trust and rapport with the patient and family.

Table 9–6 Initial Evaluation Guidelines

There are several parts to the initial evaluation process.

1. Meeting with the claimant/family.
2. Contact with the primary attending physician.
3. Contact with other key team persons.

There are two basic goals for each of these contacts. First, we need to *gather* as much information as possible from them; second, we need to *establish rapport* with the individuals involved.

The satisfactory meeting of these two goals can be a difficult task, and it requires a combination of empathy and listening skills, adequate preparation, and clear note taking. The difficulty lies in letting the relevant individuals feel important (by the use of eye contact and/or verbal techniques) while obtaining the necessary data. (Remember: the data is indispensable for a valid case management plan, but without the establishment of some degree of trust, it will be very difficult to work with the relevant individuals to actually carry out the plan.)

The Initial Evaluation Worksheet should be utilized as a guideline when meeting with and interviewing the claimant and speaking with other team members. Although certain cases may require additional data collection, obtaining at least the information required by the form guarantees the information needed for the development of a viable plan of action. The use of this worksheet as a tool for collection of the data ensures an organized, easily accessible location for referral back to this information.

The worksheet coincides with each section of the Initial Evaluation Report Format (Table 9–20). Therefore, following the worksheet should make it that much easier to write the initial report. We suggest that the consultant review the Initial Evaluation Report Format prior to meeting with the claimant in order to become familiar with each section and the information required.

In general, the referral of a case entitles us to meet with the claimant and the physician if deemed necessary. Usually, the contact should be made, and a case management plan determined within 2 weeks of receipt of the case. If there is a valid delay in this time line, a *brief* letter should be written to the client (referral source) addressing the reason for the delay.

If the claimant is located farther than 1 to 1.5 hours from your location, the visits to both the claimant and physician should be scheduled to occur in the same trip. The purpose of this is to save the client dollars. This requires appropriate scheduling, with assertive encouragement to busy physicians. Any exception to this should be well-documented and possibly cleared or approved by the client.

Should the consultant deem that multiple physician visits are a necessity, the consultant should inform the client of the additional visits required to perform an adequate initial assessment.

Source: Courtesy of Options Unlimited, Case Management Services Division, 2003, Huntington, New York.

Table 9–7 Initial Evaluation Worksheet

DATE:

CLAIMANT:

CASE SUMMARY:

Date of interview:
Place of interview:
Individuals present:
Medical diagnosis/status/reason for case management intervention:

INTRODUCTION

Sex:
Race:
Age/date of birth:
Height:
Weight (prior and current):
Physical appearance (pale, weak, etc.):
Sensorium (alert, confused, cooperative, etc.):
Signed authorization? (if not, reason):

MEDICAL

Recent medical history

Recap of events for this illness only (events leading to point we are at now):

Previous medical care

Prior medical/surgical history including diagnosis, medications, dates, physicians, outcome:

Current medical status and treatment

Current treatment plan, review of medical record (if indicated):
(What is actually being done medically for claimant at this time, related to current diagnosis):

Table 9–7 continued

If appropriate, complete a body system review:

Neurological

Gastrointestinal

Cardiovascular

Urological

Dermatological

Respiratory

Psycho/Social

Orthopedic

Endocrine

Medications

(Types, dosage prescribed, actual dosage taken, reason for medication):

Medical team

(List current treating physicians, addresses, telephone numbers, specialties):

Physician consultation

(Summarize the physician/case manager personal meeting, or telephone consultation):

Date of contact:

Pertinent data:

Physician plan of care:

SOCIO/ENVIRONMENTAL

Family makeup/position in family:

Extended family/friend support:

What is family's apparent understanding and feeling regarding illness and treatment:

Religion notes:

Cultural/Language notes:

Description of home/neighborhood:

continues

Table 9–7 continued

VOCATIONAL

Occupation:

Education:

Impact of illness on work status:

[In Workers' Compensation - Accident and Health and LTD, vocational will be more involved.]

MOTIVATIONAL/BEHAVIORAL

Claimant's apparent behavior:

Understanding/acceptance of current problem:

Claimant statement regarding compliance:

Subjective emotional adjustment data:

Psychological issues:

Substance abuse issues:

FINANCIAL

Apparent financial difficulties?

Retired or active employee?

Medicare eligible?

Disability:

Workers' Comp.:

Multiple insurance policies:

If not a problem, can be stated as such:

SUMMARY/IMPRESSIONS

Subjective data regarding your personal observations regarding the claimant and issues. Put concerns, positive aspects, and case management goals. (If having difficulty creating case management plan, list problems here.)

RECOMMENDATIONS:

1.)

2.)

3.)

Table 9–7 continued

4.)

5.)

ESTIMATED

Estimated hours plus expenses:

Source: Courtesy of Options Unlimited, Case Management Services Division, 2003, Huntington, New York.

Before closing the personal meeting with the patient, the case manager should obtain a signed Medical Authorization Release form (Table 9–8) from the patient or the patient's guardian. Required to review medical records and to share information with the patient's physician(s) and attorney if the case is in litigation, a consent form allows the case manager access to medical data regarding the patient.

TALKING WITH THE FAMILY

After talking with the patient (when possible), the case manager should interview the family for their perception of the situation. Again, it is essential to explain the role of case management, citing examples of activities with other patients in order to help illustrate the case manager's potential contribution.

Due to the stress of an illness or injury, particularly in long-term cases, the family will undergo role changes, dependency shifts, anxiety, anger, and an inability to make decisions. Therefore, the case manager must get a clear picture of the family structure and function prior to and after the illness.

When meeting with a patient and his or her family, it is important to observe the personal dynamics. As an illness progresses, some family members may foster a mentality of dependence on the part of the patient. Although well-intentioned, they are so frightened by what has happened that they become overprotective. They no longer allow the patient to participate in conversation; talk goes on around the patient as if he or she were not even there. "He needs to eat more." "She feels uncomfortable." Sometimes, this is the fault of the health care system. Assuming that a patient is too weak or tired or medicated, professionals and family talk about, but not with, him or her. The patient lies in bed and is discussed as if lacking the will or desire to be involved in his or her own care. Such behavior, rather than protecting a loved one, is dehumanizing. If the patient cannot converse, of course, another person becomes the historian, but if the patient can

Table 9–8 Medical Authorization Release

MEDICAL AUTHORIZATION

I, _____ , hereby request and authorize any hospital, physician, or other person who has attended or examined me, or who may hereafter attend or examine me for _____

_____

_____

to disclose any and all information obtained thereby, relative to this injury or illness, to Options Unlimited. I further authorize that this information may be shared with other professionals, agencies, or insurance companies who may be involved in the provision or payment of services that may be necessary.

(Date)   (Signature of Party)

(Date)   (Signature of Guardian)

Witness: _____

Source: Courtesy of Options Unlimited, Case Management Services Division, 2003, Huntington, New York.

---

communicate, the case manager really needs to involve and empower him or her. In no way would a case manager want to demean a family member or friend, but it must be remembered that the patient is the patient.

One objective of the initial assessment is to determine how family members perceive their roles. If a case manager sees that one person seems to be taking over the conversation and correcting other family members, some questions must be directed at that person. Perhaps this person has a completely different understanding of the problem than the patient; perhaps the physician has talked at greater length with him or her. If this person will be the primary caretaker at home, he or she might feel a responsibility to be the spokesperson for the family.

The case manager needs answers to the following questions: What was the primary caretaker's role in the family prior to this illness? Did the primary caretaker run the household? Hold down a job? Does the caretaker still have those responsibilities in addition to caring for the patient? Will the caretaker's job be jeopardized by this illness? How is the caretaker reacting to the illness? Will he or she be a willing participant or be frightened by the disease? What is the caretaker's intellectual and emotional capability? The caretaker might understand the situation intellectually but be emotionally devastated and barely able to cope.

Referral for case management intervention might come 3 months or 3 years after an accident or the onset of an illness, and the case manager might be confronted at the initial assessment with a family member who has been handling stressful physical, emotional, and financial aspects of an illness every day and is now burned out and about to walk out the door. (It is not uncommon for the spouse of a person with multiple sclerosis, after managing the disease for years, to suddenly cave in and leave the marriage.) The family member has used all his or her personal resources and unless someone does something soon, the case manager will no longer have an intact family with which to work.

The case manager needs to look at all the members of the family and determine their physical and emotional health. If children are involved, how has the situation affected them? Is there an older child who is now going to have to assume the responsibilities of one parent, perhaps taking time off from school to help? Are the children really worried because mom or dad may be dying? Is a brother or sister irrevocably injured to the extent of being unable to resume his or her prior place in the family? Depending on their age, children may develop symptoms or illnesses or engage in emotional outbursts as they try to come to terms with the changes in their lives. Even very young children, unable to talk, will sense that some acute changes have occurred and will react in some way.

It is important to ask the family members about their own health as well as the patient's health. Especially if the case manager anticipates that a family member might become the primary care provider at home, even if that possibility has not been discussed, questions regarding this person's medical status are in order. Is the person healthy enough to assist or overwhelmed by his or her own illness? The case manager should also compile a "medical family tree." Are parents and grandparents still alive and well? Do they have medical disorders? In talking to a 42-year-old man recovering from a heart attack who says, "Well, yeah, my father died from heart disease when he was 53," the case manager will know that this individual is not only coping with the fact that he now has a problem, but is also facing his own mortality because of a strong history of cardiac disease in the family.

All these elements—the illness or injury, present condition, medical history, current medications, family dynamics, vocation, and avocation—help point up the pluses and minuses of the treatment plan and help the treating team do their best work on behalf of the patient.

TALKING WITH THE TREATING PHYSICIAN

In 2003, an expert panel of medical directors and directors of case management for leading health care organizations across the nation met in a Physician and Case Management Summit, cosponsored by the CMSA and Professional Resources in Management Education, Inc. Dr. David B. Nash, MD, MBA, FACP, of Jefferson Medical College, Thomas Jefferson University and Kathleen Moreo,

RN, Cm, BSN, BHSA, CCM, CDMS, of P.R.I.M.E. Inc. cochaired the meeting. The panel had reviewed intellectual and scientific data, and case studies exploring successful collaborations between physicians and case managers. Their goal was to design a framework to establish and improve working relationships between the two groups. The panel identified both facilitators and barriers to effective physician–case manager collaborations. Kathleen Moreo brought their findings together in the "Consensus Paper of the 2003 Physician and Case Management Summit," which appeared in the September/October 2003 issue of *The Case Manager*.

To set the stage for a good working relationship with the treating physician, the case manager should explain the role of case management and communicate a desire to work with the physician to ensure the best outcome for the patient. The physician should be made to realize that help is available for dealing with any problems with the patient that may occur. The more a physician understands about case management, the more collaborative the partnership can be.

One thought toward building better professional relations is to focus on the aspects of the doctor–patient relationship primarily related to health care quality. In the paper "Doing Well by Doing Good: Improving the Business Case for Quality," Alice G. Gosfield, JD and James L. Reinertsen, MD note that a core activity of physicians is to take health care information and transform it into a "higher order of information," to satisfy the fundamental needs of explanation for understanding, prediction of the course of health care, and description of needed change. Here is a meeting place for physicians and case managers, a goal they both share.[2]

When I am introducing myself and the case manager's role to physicians, I find it helpful to mention that I have no intention of calling regarding many patients. In general, less than 7% of a patient population needs case management, and that number might be high for some populations. I also note that my job is to support the physician in communications with the patient, to ensure medications, dosages, and the treatment plan is understood and followed. We are patient advocates; at the same time, we assist all members of the care team.

Finding a good time for a personal meeting with the treating physician can be a challenge. A case manager can attempt to reach the physician at the hospital when he or she has just met with the patient or can telephone the physician's office to set up a visit. To smooth the path, it is a good idea to become friendly with a receptionist or nurse in the office.

Initial Phone Contact with Physician's Office to Set Up Personal Consultation

In setting up a consultation with the physician, it is best to address the receptionist or nurse by name if possible:

Case Manager: Good morning. My name is Sandi Miller, and I am a case manager [rehabilitation nurse, rehabilitation specialist, etc.]. I'm calling in reference to Dr. Brown's patient, John Fuller. I've been asked by Mr. Fuller's insurance company, U.S. America, to develop a rehab plan with him. To make sure my plan for him is appropriate, I need to schedule a brief personal meeting with Dr. Brown. [OR: I wonder if you can help me. I'd like to speak with Dr. Brown regarding Mr. Fuller today or tomorrow if at all possible. What would be the best way to contact him?]

[The receptionist or secretary advises that Dr. Brown does not see rehabilitation nurses and she requests that a letter be submitted.]

Case Manager: In some cases, a letter is adequate for a rehabilitation plan. However, in Mr. Fuller's situation, his medical care is very complex, and there are several issues that can't be adequately resolved by letter, because we are coordinating communications with his rehab and physical therapists, as well. I understand that Dr. Brown's time is valuable but it's critical that I have several minutes of his time.

Case Manager: I am willing to flex my schedule as much as possible to get this consultation. Would late afternoon be my best possibility?

Case Manager: Well, because Thursday afternoons are better for you for these kinds of meetings, could I come in about 3:00? I promise I will be brief and to the point.

Case Manager: Fine, I appreciate your help. I will be in next Thursday at 3:00. I'll mail you a confirmation letter with a medical release for Dr. Brown's file. Could you give me your name please in case we need to get back in touch with you?

Case Manager: Jill, thanks again for your help.

Table 9–9 contains a sample conversation of the actual visit to discuss Mr. Fuller's case.

Initial Phone Contact to Schedule Phone Consultation with a Physician

When the case is medically less complex or the physical distance great, a phone conversation with the treating physician is sufficient. Again, it is unusual to reach a physician by phone on the fast call, so developing rapport with the office personnel can speed the establishment of a phone consultation date and time.

Case Manager: Good morning, this is Sandi Miller and I am a rehabilitation nurse. I'm calling in reference to Mr. John Fuller, who I believe has been a patient of Dr. Brown's for the past 4 months.

Table 9–9 Sample Doctor Contact Script

INTRODUCTION

"Hello, Dr. Brown." (Shake physician's hand, comment about office.) "I'm the Medical Case Manager working with Mr. Fuller. I saw him for the first time on Tuesday and he seemed to be:

- getting along well."
- having trouble with his medication, his diet, restrictions on his activities . . ."
- anxious to return to his work doing construction, tree trimming, tennis instruction. . ."

If case manager has met with another doctor, briefly review conversation. (Case manager should offer specific information. If possible, offer it in a way that complements the doctor's treatment.) "In order to plan appropriately with you for Mr. Fuller's recovery [return to work, most comfortable and fullest quality of life], I need your direction. I'll be brief; I know you are quite busy. I just have a few questions."

CURRENT MEDICAL STATUS

"How do you see Mr. Fuller's current medical status? Where are we now with him medically?" (Case manager should listen for projected treatment plans and current limitation/abilities, filling in answers to as many questions as possible.)

FUTURE TREATMENT PLANS

"What are your future treatment plans for him [medication, length of treatment, surgery type and timetable, physical limits and duration, etc.]?"

LONG-RANGE PROGNOSIS

"You would anticipate maximum medical recovery when?"

VOCATIONAL ISSUES

"Mr. Fuller's job has been _____. He needs to be able to [case manager describes physical requirements of job]. His employer will let him return with half day/full day/limited activity [describe]. I'd like to set a target date when that might be possible. Would [date] be realistic?"

RESIDUAL DISABILITY

"At this time, do you anticipate any permanent disability from the injury? If you anticipate permanent disability, what is your estimation of the percentage of this disability after maximum medical recovery?"

Table 9–9 continued

LONG-TERM DISABILITY

"I will continue to stay in touch with you through his recovery process."

CLOSING COMMENTS

"That answers all my initial questions. Is there anything else you can think of that I may have overlooked? Is there any way I can be of assistance to you with Mr. Fuller?

"What is the best way for me to contact you [phone, day of week, time of day, through nurse/receptionist]? Thank you for your time."

Source: Reprinted with permission from Interpersonal Skills for Case Managers, *Case Management Practice,* pp. 120–122, © 1993, Foundation for Rehabilitation Education and Research.

Case Manager: I'm putting together a long-term care management plan for Mr. Fuller, and I have several medical questions I need to discuss with Dr. Brown as soon as possible. Would I be able to speak to Dr. Brown this morning about Mr. Fuller?

Case Manager: Let me check my calendar. I'm going to be out of the office this afternoon after 3:00. If I called around 4:00 tomorrow, would that work?

[Next day]

Case Manager: Yes, Jill, good afternoon. This is Sandi Miller. We spoke yesterday regarding Mr. Fuller, and you asked me to call back at 4:00 for Dr. Brown. Is he available to talk?

Case Manager: Yes, I'll be glad to hold for a minute. I appreciate your time.[3]

What is the physician's orientation to the patient? How long has the physician been treating the patient? Is this a recent illness or has the physician been overseeing the treatment plan for some time? Is the physician new to the patient or does he or she have a longstanding relationship as the family practitioner? The physician may have cared for a brother, sister, mother, or father and thus have some insight into the health needs of the patient. Is he someone who is trusted by the family or is he, as in many cases today, a consulting physician who saw the patient for the first time in the hospital and does not yet have a feel for the patient and family? Maybe the physician had an assistant conduct the patient history.

The case manager should hear the patient's status in the physician's own words. I encourage case managers to pursue details by saying, "Doctor, I am going to be asking you some questions that I've already asked your patient. Although you believe you have already done a thorough job of explaining his condition to him, we find that when it all settles in, the information retained is very selective. Patients understand some elements and let others drift away. I need to find out in your words what his problem is. What have you told him? What do you think he understands?"

If I am able to reach the physician prior to speaking to the patient, I explain my reasons for asking about what has been said. "I need to know what you've told your patient for my own information and because, after speaking with you, I plan to talk to your patient and I don't want to tell him anything that you have not. If you feel he has a certain understanding, and when I speak to him I find that it seems to be lacking, I hope you don't mind if I call you. I feel it might be important. Sometimes, we find that patients minimize their disease or choose to 'forget' the parts they can't cope with. This will impact your treatment plan. I want to make sure that we're all speaking the same language—that he has all the information you need him to have to be able to cooperate and follow your care plan for him."

Of course, it is also important to ask the following questions: What is the diagnosis? What is the treatment plan and prognosis? What do you think is going to be the outcome for this individual, both in the short-term and long-term? Do you anticipate any complications? Is there anything you feel you might need assistance with—patient information, lifestyle changes, or diet modifications? The whole physician–case manager introduction process should focus on eliciting and sharing of information and jointly establishing the best way to provide proper care.

The physician also needs to know how the case manager fits into the picture. "I represent the workers' compensation carrier," "I represent the employer group," or "I represent the employer group's insurance carrier for the medical plan, and I wanted you to know that the patient really has limited benefit dollars for inpatient care. Let's make those dollars stretch for the long-term. May I suggest alternatives to you? You may be more comfortable with one rather than the others. Do you have any alternative-care ideas you'd like to suggest?"

When the case manager knows upfront there is a limit on care dollars, he or she has a responsibility to make the physician aware of the limit and share in the goal of using the money in the best way. Although some care options may be ideal, the expenses connected with them make them poor first choices. An alternative plan may not be the ideal, but it will not pose any risk to the patient and may buy care and services over a longer period of time. It also helps to give the physician examples of the kind of work case managers do and to suggest alternatives in a professional but noncombative manner. "These are the kinds of things I have done with other doctors before to help them with patients and they have appreciated it. It is not the patient's fault that there are limits on his benefits dollars. To ignore that reality is to deprive your patient of an alternative that will provide care over the longer term."

Letters of Introduction and Physician Questionnaires

Tables 9–10 to 9–13 consist of sample letters of introduction to a physician, several of which are designed to be sent accompanied by a physician questionnaire, a good tool for obtaining information for an initial needs assessment, as well as for follow-up reports. Table 9–13 includes an attached physician questionnaire, Table 9–14 is a blank physician questionnaire, and Table 9–15 is a completed physician questionnaire with an introductory cover letter.

When there is more than one treating physician, the case manager needs to touch base with all those having an active and ongoing role. The case manager might also discover during the family interview that there was a prior treating physician who may have some very valuable information that even the current medical team does not know.

TELEPHONIC CASE MANAGEMENT

The increasing practice of telephonic case management is not in itself alarming; however, the increasing practice of poor-quality telephonic case management does bother me. I always advocate the in-person visit as an integral element of good case management, yet I understand that in the current managed care environment, such in-person contacts are not always possible. We have case managers overseeing huge caseloads in geographically distant areas; the increasing use of e-mail, facsimiles, and teleconferences; plus the push to manage more cases more cost-effectively, all moving our industry toward the greater application of telephonic case management strategies. I wholeheartedly advocate the telephone as one of the strong and effective tools of our trade. However, my concern is that much can be lost unless the individual practicing telephonic case management is very skilled and devoted to the small particulars of the job.

I believe it is difficult and, in some cases, impossible to provide the tight management required for good basic care unless a case manager is able to meet the patient, see his home environment, and hear how he interacts with his family. But not all of us have the opportunity to manage a case in the best of all possible words. Some view on-site as the most costly case management intervention. They would be correct. An on-site visit can be extremely expensive. However, in the long run, I believe it may be the most effective step to take because the case

Table 9–10 Sample Letter of Introduction to Physician (Neonatal Case)

Date

Dr. _____
Neonatology
17 Smith Street
Morristown, NJ 07960

Re:
Insured:
S.S.#:
Employer Group:

Dear Dr. _____:

As per our previous conversations, I would like to take this opportunity to express my appreciation for your input with regard to the above referenced infant. As you are aware, I am the Nurse Case Manager that was following his mother prior to her delivery. I would further appreciate a few moments of your time to become familiar with Case Management Company.

The services of Case Management Co., a private medical case management firm, were requested by the administration of Mr. _____'s group health policy to assist this family with any problems or needs experienced during the course of this high-risk pregnancy. This benefit also extends to the infant that was delivered as a result, especially in light of his premature birth.

My role as the case manager is not to interfere with but to complement your prescribed plan of care. Having a neonatal nursing background, I can certainly appreciate the complications attendant to a premature birth. By coordinating with you, should the discharge plan include home services of any type, I would be able to arrange for those services while not creating additional stress for the family, and in many cases with minimal out-of-pocket costs to them.

I realize that at this time, it may still be premature to discuss the discharge plan, though a periodic update will enable me to anticipate possible needs and be prepared to implement ways of meeting those needs. As I believe that our mutual goal is to help this family and infant achieve the most optimal level of well-being available, your professional expertise and opinions are greatly appreciated.

I also realize that your time is at a premium, and am grateful that you have made it possible for me to obtain the updates from your office. It would be very helpful for further communication to occur as discharge becomes imminent so that any posthospitalization care could be put in place in as expedient a fashion as possible.

Table 9–10 continued

I thank you for your assistance with this case, and appreciate that you have taken the time to consider the information in this letter. I am enclosing a copy of our brochure to further explain our services, along with my business card. Should you have any questions about this material, or concerns about your patient that you feel we need to discuss, please feel free to contact me at (999) 999-9999.

Very truly yours,

Case Manager

cc: Claims Department

Source: Courtesy of Options Unlimited, Case Management Services Division, 2003, Huntington, New York.

---

manager can establish a rapport with the patient and family, and learn much from the interactions (or lack of them) between family members.

I understand many case managers are hard-pressed to convince their referral sources that on-site assessment is a necessary element of the case management process. I would ask the bean counters, do you have an idea of how much money your plan pours out each year for noncompliant patients? Other compliance studies show that as many as one half of patients who begin taking antihypertensive medication stop within a year. Twenty-nine percent of people 45 and older stop taking their prescription medication early. Over 10% do not fill their prescription orders, and another 13% receive their prescriptions but do not take them.[4] Such patients' compliance might be better tracked were on-site visits a possibility.

To get the most out of telephonic case management, I encourage my case managers to get behind the "no." If they ask a patient if he experiences any difficulty testing his blood sugar level, and he says no, I have them ask him to give them his readings for the last 2 days. If he can not provide this, or his response is inappropriate, there is a good chance he is either having difficulty or no longer testing his blood sugar level. In training sessions, I tell case managers to try to avoid asking questions that can be answered by yes or no. Instead of asking, "Are you changing your dressings every day?" ask, "Who is helping you change your dressing every day?" Explore the patient's answer by asking another leading question. Perhaps the patient has said that his rehabilitation experience has been "okay." Ask him, "Are you where you want to be with your new prosthesis? Can

Table 9–11 Sample Letter of Introduction to Physician to Be Sent with Questionnaire

---

Date

_____, M.D.
_____ Pediatric Association
P.O. Box 5
417 State Street
Oklahoma City, OK 73101

Dear Dr. _____:

Claimant:
Insured:
Employee #:

I have been asked by _____ Companies to provide medical case management services to the above named patient and to assist with any needed medical services. I met with Mrs. _____ and _____ at their home in _____ on July 11th for an initial evaluation.

My business card and brochure describing *Case Management Company* and our services are enclosed, in order to better describe my involvement with the _____. Mrs. _____ referred me to you on details regarding _____ past and present illness, as she was unable to recall specific details.

For your convenience, I have prepared and enclosed a questionnaire that I ask you to complete, along with a stamped and self-addressed envelope. Enclosed, you will find a signed release of medical information form.

Thank you very much for your time and assistance in answering these questions. I look forward to working with you and the _____ and assisting with any needs or services that may become necessary, both now and in the future.

I extend my sincere appreciation for your time and valuable input and I look forward to our future contact. Should you have any questions or concerns, please feel free to contact me at _____.

Very truly yours,

_____, R.N.
Rehabilitation Consultant
RC:co
Enc.

Source: Courtesy of Options Unlimited, Case Management Services Division, 2003, Huntington, New York.

Table 9–12 Sample Letter of Introduction to Physician to Be Sent with Questionnaire

---

Dr. Timothy James
10 Smith Street
Chicago, IL 60611

Re:
S.S.#:

Dear Dr. James:

Please allow me to introduce myself as the case management consultant, with _____, who is currently following the progress of your patient, _____.
The services of _____, a private medical case management firm, were requested by the administrators of Mr./Mrs. _____'s group health policy, on his/her behalf, to assist him/her with any problems or needs that he/she may experience during the course of his/her illness.

My role as Mr./Mrs. _____'s case manager is not to interfere with but to complement your prescribed plan of care. This is accomplished through my interactions, not only with this patient, but also with you, his/her physician, as well as all other health care providers involved with his/her care.

I believe that our mutual goal is to help Mr./Mrs. _____ achieve the most optimal level of well-being available to him/her. To do so, I must anticipate his/her needs based on available medical data and physician input. Your professional expertise and opinions, on behalf of this patient, would be greatly appreciated.

Would you kindly take a few moments of your time to complete the enclosed questionnaire? Please return this to me, at your earliest convenience, to _____, in the enclosed stamped, self-addressed envelope. Also, please find a signed release of medical information.

If you have any questions regarding this matter, please do not hesitate to contact me at _____.

Thank you for your anticipated cooperation.

Very truly yours,

Medical Management Consultant

Source: Courtesy of Options Unlimited, Case Management Services Division, 2003, Huntington, New York.

Table 9–13 Sample Letter of Introduction to Physician with Specific Questionnaire Attached

---

Date

Dr. Frederick Zimmermann
_____ East 37th Street
New York, NY 10016

Re: Claimant

Dear Dr. Zimmermann:

As I explained to you in an earlier conversation, I am the Nurse Case Manager who is working with _____ at the request of _____, the Third Party Administrator of his health care benefits. As his case manager, I have followed him now for approximately 9 months. In that time, I am aware that he has recently had a liver biopsy and is presently awaiting the results. Because of this, and also because he has informed me that his T-Cell count is at 56, I am enclosing a questionnaire that I would like you to complete. I feel that the time for additional intervention may be coming and in order for me to be as effective as possible, it is important that I have some additional information.

Because of the sensitive nature of this diagnosis, I am also including a copy of the authorization that the claimant signed enabling me to obtain such information. You will also note a copy of the _____ brochure, which I hope will help to answer any questions you may have with regard to my role, is also enclosed. Should you have any questions, I would welcome hearing from you.

I thank you very much for your time. I know that your time is a very valuable commodity. I trust that this information will help me in assisting _____. I also hope that this letter will provide an introduction for you so that you will contact me when I can be of assistance to both you and _____.

Should you have any questions or need to reach me with regard to my interventions on behalf of _____, please contact my office at _____ and leave a message. I will contact you as soon as possible.

Very truly yours,

_____

cc: Claims Department

Table 9–13 continued

QUESTIONNAIRE

1. What is Mr./Mrs. _____'s specific medical diagnosis and extent of metastases?
2. In your medical professional opinion, what is the anticipated progression of this cancer?
3. Is his/her condition terminal in nature? As Mr./Mrs. _____'s case manager, I am responsible for providing qualitative yet cost-effective services when needed. This will help to reduce the family's stress levels as well as keep their out-of-pocket expenses to a minimum.
4. What types of therapies are being planned to treat the patient's disease?
5. In your opinion, is Mr./Mrs. _____ a candidate for any home therapy services, i.e., chemotherapy, pain management, hospice care?

Dr. Zimmermann   Date

Source: Courtesy of Options Unlimited, Case Management Services Division, 2003, Huntington, New York.

Table 9–14 Sample Physician Questionnaire

---

1. What is the primary diagnosis?
2. Does the patient have any secondary diagnoses?
3. Do you think the patient might benefit from a cardiac rehabilitation program as an outpatient?
4. What are the prescribed medications?
5. What is the specific diet of the patient?
6. What, if any, are the limitations or restrictions?
7. What are your further plans for the patient regarding his rehabilitation period?
8. What is the prognosis?

                                                  Date

Source: Courtesy of Options Unlimited, Case Management Services Division, 2003, Huntington, New York.

Table 9–15 Sample Letter of Introduction to Physician with Completed Physician Questionnaire

---

A. Edwards, M.D.
808 Olive Avenue
Sand City, CA 91313

Re: S.R.
S.S#:

Dear Dr. Edwards,

Please allow me to introduce myself as the case management consultant with OPTIONS UNLIMITED who is currently following the progress of your patient, S.R.

The services of OPTIONS UNLIMITED, a private medical case management firm, were requested by the administrators of Mr. R's group health plan, on his behalf, to assist him with any problems or needs that he may experience during the course of his illness.

My role as Mr. R's case manager is not to interfere with, but to complement your prescribed plan of care. This is accomplished through my interactions, not only with this patient, but also with you, his physician, as well as all other health care providers involved with his care.

I believe that our mutual goal is to help Mr. R achieve the most optimal level of well-being available to him. To do so, I must anticipate his needs based on available medical data and physician input. Your professional expertise and opinions, on behalf of this patient, would be greatly appreciated.

Would you kindly take a few moments of your time to complete the enclosed questionnaire? Please return this information to me by fax at my office. I have enclosed a copy of the signed authorization for release of medical information for your records. My fax number is (999) 999-9999. Please feel free to call me if you have any questions regarding this letter or my role. I look forward to working with you.

Thank you for your anticipated cooperation.

Very truly yours,

Sandra T., R.N., C.C.M.
Medical Management Consultant

ST:lm
Enc.

Table 9–15 continued

QUESTIONNAIRE

Patient: S.R.

1. What is Mr. R's specific medical diagnosis?
   Papillary thyroid carcinoma metastatic to lung and multiple lymph nodes.
2. Does Mr. R have metastases of his original thyroid cancer?
   Yes.
3. In your professional opinion, what is the anticipated progression of this cancer?
   Sparse data are available; however, disease recurred quickly postoperatively and tumor progressed under treatment. This makes the anticipated progression rapid.
4. Could you please explain the prognosis at this time? As the case manager, I will assist the family with supportive services, when and if the time comes. The information you can supply me can help me with anticipating care needs.
   Have recommended one-on-one counseling for Mr. R, for his wife too, with Liza G., RN, MS Oncology Counseling & "Friend to Friend" Cancer Pt Support Group Program @ Good Samaritan Hospital.
5. What is the current treatment plan?
   Radiation therapy and chemotherapy.

A. Edwards, M.D.   Date

Source: Courtesy of Options Unlimited, Case Management Services Division, 2003, Huntington, New York.

---

you see your level of improvement?" Whatever the response is, you will have more information to work with, and your instincts will pick up on a false answer or potential problem if you are asking thoughtful questions.

The *Case Management Advisor* offered practical tips to help case managers master telephonic case management:

- Be cognizant of how your own experiences and personality affect your impressions of your patient. Have you had a similar experience? How quick are you to make judgments based on your patient's responses? Are you allowing her to speak? Have you made any assumptions about her before placing the call?
- If you are in a hurry, your results will be poor.

- Reschedule the conversation if your patient is under severe stress or in pain.
- Answer her immediate questions before proceeding with other treatment issues.
- If you do not know the answer to a patient question, admit it. Tell her you will get an answer for her, or have another person who knows call her back.[5]

INDEPENDENT MEDICAL AND SECOND OPINION EXAMS

In some cases, an independent medical exam or a second opinion exam is requested. A case manager's involvement is linked to the type of exam performed (see Figure 9–9). An independent medical exam is generally utilized by insurance carriers to determine the diagnosis, the need for continued treatment, the degree of disability (partial or total), the duration of a disability (temporary, long-term, or permanent), and the patient's ability to return to work. Customarily arranged by the carrier (see Table 9–16), it is often seen by the patient as an exam he or she is required to undergo. The physician most often remains in a nontreating role. Depending on the circumstances, a rehabilitation nurse or a case manager may assist in setting up the exam and may accompany the patient, but in most instances, neither the nurse nor the case manager is present at the exam.

When should a case manager expect an independent medical exam to be requested? Such exams are used routinely by some carriers when treatment appears excessive (e.g., prolonged duplication of services, such as physical therapy or chiropractic manipulation), when the recovery time from an accident or injury appears overly extended, or when there is a delay in the patient's return-to-work schedule. They are also employed upon request to authorize surgery, expensive equipment, or unusual diagnostic testing or when there is an increase in the number of treating professionals. Certain diagnostic conditions (e.g., stress disorders) might also signal use of an independent medical exam.

Sometimes, the ordering of an exam results from one of a few administrative practices. Many examiners work selected cases using a "diary" system, in which files are reviewed once monthly. In the third or sixth month, they schedule an independent medical exam if the case is still active. Similarly, if a workers' compensation hearing is scheduled, an independent medical exam is often automatically ordered.

Also used to determine a diagnosis, a second opinion exam is performed to help clarify a complex medical picture or to prepare alternatives to the current or proposed treatment (see Table 9–17). It is typically presented to the patient as a proactive exam, and the insurance nurse or case manager who arranged for it is usually in attendance. In group medical plans, a second opinion exam is often required prior to certain surgical procedures that the carrier or the latest utilization review statistics show to have a high usage rate (e.g., hysterectomies, hip replacements, cardiac bypass, disc surgery). Often, the physician conducting a second opinion exam will become a treating physician.

Figure 9–9 Comparison of Independent Medical Exams and Second Opinion Exams

Independent Medical Exams	Second Opinion Exams
Utilized by carriers to determine:	Utilized to:
1. Diagnosis 2. Need for continued Rx 3. Degree of disability (total, partial) 4. Permanency of disability (temporary, total) 5. Ability to return to work	1. Determine diagnosis 2. Clarify a complex medical picture 3. Propose alternatives to current or proposed treatment
Would prefer this physician remain in nontreating state.	Often becomes treating physician.
This physician often becomes involved as an expert witness once litigation occurs—and appears *for* the carrier.	This physician often refuses to do exam if testimony may be requested.
Often viewed as an "ordered" exam by the claimant.	Presented as proactive examination.
Rehab nurse often does not attend (depending on circumstances, however, may assist in arrangements and may accompany claimant). Usually arranged *by* the carrier.	The nurse/case manager usually attends and, in fact, arranges this exam, obviously with carrier approval.

Source: Courtesy of Options Unlimited, Case Management Services Division, 2003, Huntington, New York.

A second opinion exam is called for when there is a conflict between potential treatment plans (surgery versus conservative treatment), when the patient requests one, when there is a multilayered medical scenario or a questionable treatment underway, or when the existing treatment plan is not achieving the expected outcome. The diagnosis may call for a second opinion exam, as when the need for a physician with more or different expertise is indicated. Considering the increasing, documented incidences of medical errors, it may be the wise choice to seek a second opinion. In some cases, a second opinion exam is ordered if a treatment is deemed inappropriate or excessive (e.g., when multiple drugs have been prescribed and all of them have the potential for abuse).

To get the most benefits from independent medical and second opinion exams, a case manager should thoroughly understand the purpose of any exam ordered and be specific as to what should be addressed in the physician's report. The physician most appropriate for the diagnosis of the patient should conduct the

Table 9–16 Sample Letter to Physician to Arrange an Independent Medical Exam

---

Date

Robert Jones, M.D.
42 Amsterdam Avenue
New York, NY 10002

RE: James Williams
Insured: ABC Woolens
Carrier File #: 110-24
Date of Accident: 2/2

Dear Dr. Jones:

Please allow this letter to serve as confirmation with Jane in your office today regarding the above captioned claimant.

World Insurance Company is the Workers' Compensation Carrier for ABC Woolens where Mr. Williams is employed as an assistant manager in the Shipping Department.

He sustained an injury to his back on 2/2 and has been in treatment with a number of physicians and therapists. Surgery has been performed, followed by a course of physical therapy. For your review, I am enclosing reports from his treating physicians, hospital records, and diagnostic studies. Mr. Williams will also be bringing with him various X-rays and CAT scans pertinent to this event.

We are at this time 1 year postinjury requesting that you examine this claimant and note your findings with specific attention to (1) current status; (2) objective findings; (3) subjective symptoms; and (4) need for continuance of PT and massage therapy and enrollment in a health spa.

You will also find enclosed a copy of a Job Analysis by our medical management consultant. Please note as you review this that the claimant has a mix of sedentary and physical labor, and the owner can accommodate some restrictions in activity. Following your examination of Mr. Williams and review of the Job Analysis, could you comment on his ability to perform in this job? For your convenience, there is enclosed a physical capacities form, which may be useful in your determination of his actual ability to perform the various tasks.

I have advised Mr. Williams of the scheduled date of his appointment, March 30th at 10:00 A.M., and have requested that he confirm this with your office.

Table 9–16 continued

Thank you very much for your assistance and I look forward to receiving your report.

Very truly yours,

Jane Ellis
Workers' Compensation Examiner

Source: Courtesy of Options Unlimited, Case Management Services Division, 2003, Huntington, New York.

---

exam; a general orthopedist is not the most appropriate physician if the claimant is using an acknowledged expert in hip replacement or needs specialized treatment. The examining physician should be provided as much information as possible, including operative reports, diagnostic test reports, X-rays, CAT scans, MRI, treating physician reports, and other independent medical exams, and be given enough time to review all the data prior to the actual exam. When appropriate, the case manager should arrange to discuss findings with the physician in person or over the phone following the exam. After reading the physician's report, the case manager should again speak to the physician if the report is not specific and responsive to the initial request for information.

TALKING WITH OTHER PROFESSIONALS

In addition to the treating physician, the case manager may need to contact facility staff nurses, attorneys, therapists, and other professionals involved in the patient's care. If the role of any individual is not understood, the case manager should ask questions. In all cases, the case manager should introduce herself and explain her relationship to the patient.

Initial Phone Contact with Medical Professionals to Set Up Personal Consultation

Case Manager: Phil, my name is Angie and I'm working with your patient [Dr. Smith's patient], Ann Simpson, in developing a rehabilitation [case management] program.

Case Manager: I met with Ann last week and she told me that she was seeing you two times a week for physical therapy [occupational therapy, speech therapy, etc.].

Table 9–17 Sample Letter to Physician to Arrange Second Opinion Exam

---

Date

Adam James, M.D.
Director of Orthopedic Surgery
Long Island Central Hospital
New Hyde Park, N.Y. 10021

Re: James Williams
Insured: ABC Woolens
Carrier File #: 110-24
Date of Accident: 2/2

Dear Dr. James:

After discussion with your office today, I am referring Mr. Williams to you for a "second opinion" evaluation and consultation. The appointment is scheduled for June 20th at 1:00 P.M. With your permission and with Mr. Williams' approval, I will attend this appointment.

As a medical management consultant working with this man at the request of World Insurance Company (the Workers' Compensation Carrier for his employer), I am in the process of developing a plan to assist Mr. Williams with a return to a productive and comfortable lifestyle once again.

To date and following an injury to his back on 2/2, he has been receiving treatment and testing from a number of professionals, including an orthopedic surgeon, neurologist, chiropractor, and his family doctor.

He has received conflicting opinions as to the suggested course of treatment, including a recent one for a laminectomy. Mr. Williams has, as would be expected, questions and concerns regarding surgery that he feels were not explained to his satisfaction by his doctor.

As a medical management consultant, it is not our intent to interfere with or interrupt current medical care; however, we do assist individuals in obtaining sufficient information in order for them to make informed decisions about their treatment.

I am enclosing prior to our visit copies of various medical reports and diagnostic tests.

Thank you very much for your kind assistance and I look forward to meeting you.

Very truly yours,

Medical Management Consultant

Source: Courtesy of Options Unlimited, Case Management Services Division, 2003, Huntington, New York.

I would like to meet with you briefly to get a better understanding of her current treatment program. Your input is very important in developing a recovery plan.

Case Manager: Ann said it would be fine if I met with you, and I'll have a signed consent form for your file. Would there be any possibility of meeting with you either next Tuesday or Wednesday, preferably sometime in the morning? I only need about 10 minutes of your time and I promise to be very brief.

Case Manager: Next Wednesday at 9:30 is fine. I'll put this time on my calendar and if there is any change, I will let you know. Please do the same.

Case Manager: Thanks again for your time. I'm looking forward to working with you.

After the appointment is set, the case manager might want to compose and send a brief letter, postcard, or handwritten memo as a time-efficient way to reinforce the date of the meeting and help ensure the medical professional will be there.

Part of the case manager's role may involve a review of hospital medical records. To facilitate this, the case manager needs a consent form signed by the patient or the patient's guardian. Next, the case manager must determine the hospital's procedure for medical record review and/or visit. Some hospitals are very formal, requiring that all medical record reviews be completed through the medical records department. Others require a form of photo identification, proof of immunizations, and a signed consent form be presented to the primary nurse, head nurse, or hospital contact. If the case manager meets any challenge to her right to examine the patient's medical records, she should ask to speak with supervisory personnel or the hospital administrator. Case managers do have the privilege of reviewing medical records if they have a signed consent.

In an acute care hospital, the case manager should ask to speak to the primary or head nurse, introduce herself, offer a copy of the signed consent form and her card, and ask about the patient's current condition and any concerns or key issues. The case manager should then request to review the medical records. In a rehabilitation facility, the contact person may be the social worker on the case, a discharge planner, or the primary nurse.

Staff nurses are good sources of information. Physicians have one window; nurses see the patient from a different perspective. They can be good historians. "Yes, we know John says he can test his urine to monitor his sugar level for his diabetes but he really doesn't do it. He's noncompliant. His family brings him treats and we see him sneaking things." Realizing the extensive demands made on hospital RNs, case managers should make it clear to the nursing staff that they are available for use as resources.

Another person to contact is the discharge planning coordinator, who is responsible for posthospital patient services and timely discharge. The case manager should let the discharge planner know that she is involved with the case, will be arranging for the patient's home or rehabilitation facility services, and will get coverage approval from the payer for those services. This frees the discharge planner to devote more time to other cases. Social workers involved with the family can also make a contribution by adding valuable background to the patient profile; they might even have a completed profile already prepared.

In workers' compensation or disability cases, the employer is a chief contact for the case manager. What does the employer know about the patient? How secure is the patient's job? Will the patient have a job to return to? Is the employer willing to modify the work site? Will the employer allow the patient to return on a part-time or reduced-hour basis? What is the employee's value in the eyes of the employer?

To obtain answers to these questions, the case manager should call the employer. If it is fairly clear that the patient's limitations will prevent a return to work, it may not be necessary or appropriate for the case manager to spend time arranging and attending a personal consultation. If the case manager feels that there is a reasonable possibility of a patient taking up a previous or modified job with the employer, a personal visit should be requested. In asking for time to meet with an employer, the case manager should never give the impression that she is coming to try to force an injured worker back to the job.

Initial Phone Contact with an Employer

Case Manager: Mr. White, my name is Cathy Simpson and I have been asked by your health insurance carrier [name of company and/or adjuster] to assist Mr. King in his recovery and then back to work. The records that I have show that Mr. King had been working for you up until March 12th and that he has not returned since his injury. Does this sound about right?

Case Manager: I'm in the process of completing my initial evaluation of Mr. King and I would appreciate having your input on some work-related matters.

[for a personal visit]

Case Manager: I am going to be in the Lakewood area next Tuesday. Could I see you for just a few minutes while I am in town?

Case Manager: OK, what would be a better day? I'll see if I can rearrange my schedule.

Case Manager: I really appreciate your help with this. I'll see you next Wednesday at 1:00 P.M.

An employer can also be part of the treatment plan. The case manager might request the employer's assistance for a patient facing a long recovery process. Fellow workers are usually great at sending flowers and cards at the beginning of an illness; can some contact mechanism be established to help maintain morale over the long haul? Is there an employee newsletter that the patient can receive so he or she will feel involved with the company? Does the company have a sunshine fund, a program that reaches out to injured employees so they do not lose touch with fellow workers?

In some cases, particularly when workers' compensation, disability, or liability claims are at issue, an attorney will also be contacted. (Case managers working a group medical case rarely see an attorney involved in the case before getting in touch with the patient.) In some states and among some employer groups, lawyers are called on regularly for minor cases—a neck sprain or a knee injury and the talk is lawsuit. Some attorneys are very hesitant to allow case management involvement; others approve the service right away. The concern stems from the fact that a case manager representing the employer or insurance carrier might pursue a hidden agenda and quiz or interrogate the client regarding his or her accident or illness.

Lawyers can deny a case manager the opportunity to work on a case, approve the case manager's involvement but refuse personal access to the patient, or allow access but deny full cooperation, setting strict stipulations for case management intervention: "You may only talk to him about medical issues, and you may not discuss his job." Or, "Every time you make a phone call, you must call me and get my permission first." Or, "Every time you have a meeting, I'm going to be there and we're going to tape it."

Obviously, the case manager's contact with attorneys is critical. Regardless of the injury, any time there is an attorney of record on a case, the case manager must contact that attorney and state very clearly who she is, whom she represents, and the purpose of her involvement. It is very important to position case management as a proactive service and to make it clear that the case manager's role is not to investigate the accident, not to find out who is at fault, nor to discuss the circumstances and details of the accident with the patient. (Obviously, it follows that during an assessment the case manager will steer clear of questions regarding the circumstances and events leading up to an accident and avoid trying to establish who was at fault.) The object of case management is to assist with the patient's recovery and eventual return to a productive lifestyle. It is often helpful, prior to calling the attorney to answer any questions he or she might have, to send a letter clearly stating the case manager's role (she is not a claims investigator or a hands-on provider of services), along with a brochure describing case management services and a copy of the authorization the patient will be asked to sign.

Initial Phone Contact with an Attorney

Case Manager: Mr. Anderson, my name is Sarah Craig and I am a case manager [rehabilitation nurse, rehabilitation counselor] with Professional Case Management. I'm calling regarding your client, John Roberts. I have been asked by American Insurance Company, the company carrying his workers' compensation [or auto insurance], to visit with Mr. Roberts to see if I can be of assistance to him in his recovery. I'm calling to ask your permission to contact him and proceed with an assessment of his condition.

Attorney: What's the purpose of your service? What do you plan to do to help John?

Case Manager: My meeting with him and my initial assessment would be to determine if his recovery is proceeding well, if there are any additional medical services which may be of benefit, or if we can provide for his needs in a more efficient manner. I'm not really able to tell you anything specific at this point as I have not had a chance to meet with him and discuss his current medical status. Hopefully, after I talk with him and review the various medical reports that I have, I will be in a better position to determine what services he might need to maximize his recovery. I know you also share this goal.

Attorney: I don't see why his doctor can't handle his medical treatment.

Case Manager: His physician is certainly the one in charge of his treatment plan. However, because I work in his community, I can assist the doctor and help him to fully understand Mr. Roberts' special areas of need in regard to follow-up treatment, his home environment, the type of work he's done, his family support system, and things of that nature. I am part of the physician's team, and we all work to provide the best recovery possible.

Attorney: I want a copy of every report you make.

Case Manager: That's fine. I'd like you to be aware of my work with your client. I'll be glad to check with the insurance company; it's not usually a problem to copy a patient's attorney on our reports.[6]

Sometimes, attorneys request copies of a case manager's reports to the referral source before they will approve case management involvement. When this happens to me, I tell the attorneys that the reports belong to the referral source. If that company or insurer allows reports to go out, I ask them to forward a copy of the report or I send a copy from my office given the go-ahead. However, I suggest that case management companies or departments working with lawyers always first give the report to the client (i.e., the carrier group or the employer) and let the client review it before making the final decision on whether to send it to the lawyers. This is because there might be something in the report that is not as objectively stated as it might have been or that perhaps compromises the client's position. Attorneys should never automatically receive a copy of a case manager's reports; they should be forwarded only with the client's approval. Case managers practicing in states with mandatory rehabilitation programs may have to follow specific requirements in reporting to attorneys.

An attorney may ask a case manager to sign a statement that the case management reports will not be used against the client in a court of law. Such stipulations should be referred to the carrier. It is the carrier's role to agree or disagree with the attorney's terms before case management involvement continues.

If an attorney questions a case manager's qualifications, the case manager should respond to this issue and perhaps ask for a brief personal visit to discuss the role of case management. There are some attorneys who really have not heard of case management before, have no idea what case managers do, and need an overview of the profession. The case manager should outline her experience and education, provide examples of case management work with other attorneys, offer to send literature on case management along with a personal résumé, inform the attorney that a refusal of services is very unusual, and address any objections.

The case manager might ask if the attorney would like to be present at the initial meeting of the case manager and the claimant; sometimes this allays fears that the case manager has an unwritten agenda as an investigator. When an attorney insists on being present at any case management meeting, the attorney's office can be used as the meeting place unless the patient is confined to a hospital or another care facility, is homebound, or needs to be seen by the case manager in his or her work environment. If a meeting time and place can be agreed upon, the case manager should let the attorney know that the initial interview may require up to 2 hours. The attorney may demand that he or she be present at every single meeting. This may not be possible given the case manager's schedule, nor be conducive to the most honest exchanges with the claimant.

In one case I had, the first such meeting was not very productive. The attorney stopped the patient every time I asked a question. The second meeting was a repetition of the first. At the third meeting, the lawyer had a tape recorder running with a microphone attachment. He continually interrupted my conversation with the patient. When I asked how the patient was feeling, the lawyer said, "Don't answer that!" I knew that we were getting nowhere. Because the atmosphere, due to the attorney's level of involvement, was no longer supportive of an effective case management intervention, I suggested to the referral source that we close the file. I believe case managers can meet lawyers more than halfway, but they cannot work around the obstruction created when patients are being coached on their answers.

If an attorney denies case management services, the case manager should try to find out the specific reasons behind the decision and address them. If further consideration is refused, the case manager should thank the attorney for his or her time and close the conversation. Some law firms have a reputation for sending patients to certain physicians and therapists, allowing no other involvement.

To keep all lines of communication and participation clear in a legal case, the case manager should document any acceptance or denial of service in a brief but specific letter to the insurance carrier or payer and the employer group. In addition, the attorney should be sent a letter either acknowledging appreciation for his or her approval of case management involvement or noting his or her refusal. In the instance of a denial, the case manager should document for the record that the attempt to institute case management was a good-faith gesture on the part of the employer or carrier. This demonstrates that help was offered, and it also may alert the Workers' Compensation Board that they may be dealing with an uncooperative attorney.

In my letters, I begin by reiterating the lawyer's refusal of case management services, along with the reasons given, noting that of course I will abide by the decision (see Table 9–18). To make a point, I include direct quotations: "You said you 'believe our involvement will jeopardize a fair hearing,'" or "I never work with case managers." I'm not courting a lawsuit myself, so I am careful in my use of quotation and synopses. If someone slams down the phone in my ear, I may write, "You abruptly terminated our conversation despite the fact that I assured you that I was contributing medical expertise to the case and was not a claims examiner." I also include an example of how I have worked successfully with an attorney in the past.

I have also started sending the claimant copies of letters of approval or denial that go directly to the attorney in workers' compensation, auto, or other liability cases. Several times, once an attorney's concerns or agendas were addressed (or the attorney was no longer on the case) and I was able to speak to the claimant, the claimant asked, "Well, where were you when I needed you 2 months ago?" I was there 2 months ago, trying to get in touch with him or her, but the claimant never knew because the attorney did not relay the information. Not every attorney shares everything with his or her clients. I feel that if it is the client's insurance policy, he or she has a right to know that case management is being offered; the client deserves access to information that can directly impact on his or her physical well-being. The attorney should be sent copies as well, giving him or her an opportunity to clarify any misunderstanding regarding the refusal of case management services on behalf of his or her client.

When an attorney denies case management intervention in a particular case, this does not close the door on an association with a case manager in another case. Case managers are wise to inform attorneys about the range of their work. For

Table 9–18 Letter to an Attorney Who Has Denied Case Management Services

---

Mr. John Smith, Esq.
456 Main Street
Buffalo Grove, IL 34678

Re: William Jones

Dear Mr. Smith:

Please allow this letter to serve as a confirmation of our telephone conversation today and your declination of services that have been requested on your client's behalf by Jane Brown of ABC Insurance Company. You have indicated that you ". . . never allow companies such as ours to work with your clients. . . ."

As you may recall, OPTIONS UNLIMITED is a private consulting firm utilized by ABC Insurance Company and other companies to assist individuals with the problems that may occur following accidents, injuries, or illnesses.

Our goal is to ensure that your client receives the best results possible from the services that are available and is able to return to a medically stable, comfortable, and, hopefully, active lifestyle once again.

Ms. Brown had requested that one of our nurse consultants meet with your client in order to determine how he is recovering from his accident and if he would benefit from our intervention.

Our role is not intended to interrupt or interfere with any care or services he is currently receiving, nor do we provide any "hands-on" services. We, hopefully, serve as a resource for your client and his family in resolving and preventing any further difficulties.

Because our services are at no cost to your client, and can only serve to enhance his recovery process, we were hopeful of obtaining your approval; however, we will abide by your refusal.

Should you wish to reconsider or if I can answer questions or concerns you may have, please feel free to call me. Also enclosed is one of our brochures, which explains our services further.

Thank you once again for your time.

Very truly yours,

Catherine M. Mullahy
President

CMM:lm
Enc.
cc: William Jones

Source: Courtesy of Options Unlimited, Case Management Services Division, 2003, Huntington, New York.

---

example, case managers with expertise in life-care planning are often sought by attorneys looking to settle a claim on behalf of a catastrophically injured child. A life-care plan developed by a case manager includes the probable costs of supporting that child throughout his or her predicted life span (medical services, care providers, improving technologies, and inflation costs are all figured in).

The time taken to perform an assessment depends on the needs of the patient and the severity of the injury or illness. A half hour might be required to speak to the recovering patient before preparing a 2-month postoperative update; a half hour might be all the time allowable for an easily tired patient in an acute care setting or all the time appropriate for a patient in the last stages of a terminal illness. To conduct a more comprehensive assessment (e.g., for a patient 3 months into a head injury rehabilitation program following a horrific accident), at least 1.5 to 2 hours should be allotted, especially if the evaluation will include a facility walk-through with a discharge planner. The more providers involved, the more time-consuming the assessment will be. Similarly, more recent injuries and singular injuries often require less time than recurring or multiple illnesses. The case manager needs to review the history involved with events in the patient's care plan, because that information impacts the scenario faced today and the plan for tomorrow. From a liability standpoint, the case manager needs to gather sufficient background for a responsible assessment, uncovering everything that will affect her ability to plan intelligently and completely for a patient's anticipated problems and the attainment of the treatment goals.

Factors to consider in estimating the time necessary for an assessment include the line of insurance, the state of health of the patient (a complex medical chart takes time to digest), the site where the interview will take place, and the number of people involved (e.g., the patient, family members needing support, discharge planner, physicians, nurses in the unit). After a case manager determines the amount of time needed, it is important to inform the referral source.

PLANNING

Case management is a process of identifying and solving problems. The first and key issue is whether the treatment is appropriate and being provided in the best possible setting. Given the patient's diagnosis, current medical status, and prior medical history, is the treatment plan attaining the most desirable results? Does it appear that it will lead to an eventual recovery or have there already been too many complications?

Is the treatment plan sound? Is it appropriate, reasonable, and really necessary for this patient? Is it forcing the patient into any undue hardship or discomfort? Case managers might come across situations in which treatment may be deemed questionable based on their experience or knowledge. Some cases may be outside the limits of their expertise. In medicine today, there are numerous breaking technological advances, therapies, and medications. If the disease is an unfamiliar one, the case manager has a responsibility to become knowledgeable about it. When things look questionable, when results are uncertain, it is appropriate to ask the treating physician or to acknowledge a need for more information. It is also the case manager's responsibility to comment on treatments that, based on her experience, may seem unusual or strange. Of course, tone is vital; no one should blurt out an accusation of mismanagement. The case manager might say, "Listen, I'm familiar with this, this, and this, but I've never heard of this. Is this something new? Is this something that you've had good results with? Why is this patient being referred for this particular therapy? I've seen more situations in which patients are treated with another therapy."

If a case manager notes that a patient is in a poor system of care—the physician is not communicating, the patient is having multiple complications, the therapists are unapproachable—part of the case management role is to serve as a patient advocate. The patient's interests definitely should come first. If the patient is not being well-served, the case manager can help create a better system of care. Patients do not always have the information they need to see their position clearly. They often are not even aware of what constitutes proper care. They might not know that they can access a second opinion, that they do not have to stay in a hospital where the ministrations are miserable, that they do not have to put up with what is going on. A key tactic is to present information to a patient in a way that does not overtly interfere with the patient–physician relationship but allows the patient to understand that this is not the only "game in town." I have had patients who really did not know that their care was horrible. I have posed questions to lead them to acknowledge that, although perhaps the physician was doing fine, two heads are better than one and they might want to talk to another physician. For example, I might ask, "Don't you feel that maybe you should be getting better by now? Are you concerned?"

When it comes to making recommendations to patients, case managers must protect themselves against the liability that could result from steering them toward particular choices. I caution case managers not to make direct endorsements but instead to present numerous alternatives to patients. "You have these kinds of facilities to select from; these are physicians who are board-certified; these are home health agencies that can provide the type of care you need." Obviously, if a case manager knows a particular physician in the community is absolutely wonderful, there is nothing wrong with saying, "I hear this physician is excellent. Here are two others as well. You are free to select anyone you want." Even though the choice ultimately needs to be the patient's, I try to select from physicians that

I feel are the most qualified. Knowing people's inclination to grab on to the first name suggested, I might tend to arrange the order in which I present the three options, but I never commend one practitioner to the exclusion of all others.

Is the patient in the most appropriate setting for his or her problem? If, for instance, the patient has a rare or difficult disease and is in a small, local hospital picked by the patient for its proximity to home, could he or she be better treated in a university hospital that perhaps has an entire department dedicated to that disease? Maybe the patient's treatment would be more medically effective (and more cost-effective as well) if provided by health care professionals who are more knowledgeable about the patient's condition. Is the care setting the most appropriate and most cost-effective? Could care be given anyplace else? John is in the hospital, his surgery has been completed, and now he is being observed and receiving medication, pain or infusion care services, or physical therapy. Does he have to be in a hospital? Could the case manager arrange for the same kind of services in a less costly and even more appropriate setting? In some cases, a patient may recuperate well at home through the use of support services at far less cost and with better results both emotionally and physically for the patient and with less stress on the family.

It may be that during the acute phase of his illness, John was absolutely in the best possible place, but now he needs rehabilitation and that particular acute care hospital may not be the best for rehab. This is especially true for some traumatic brain injury patients, for spinal cord injury patients, some amputees, and some burn center cases. When the acute phase is over and a patient needs focused rehabilitation, he or she is probably best served in an area or center that has personnel trained and equipment designed to deal with the specific disorder. Acute care hospitals are geared to address the acute phase of a range of conditions, medical problems occurring in episodic fashion. They are not well-suited for individual, long-term care. Individuals may go from the emergency room to an intensive care unit. After they achieve stability in intensive care, they belong on a medical or surgical floor. At the earliest opportunity, once they can be effectively managed without all the expensive support services of a hospital, they should be moved to a more appropriate and less costly arena for care—the home or another setting.

How motivated are the care provider and the patient in the current setting? Is the provider looking after the interests of the patient or trying to keep beds filled and services going?

During an assessment, a case manager should also be evaluating the money available and the exposure faced. Whose pocket is it and how large is it? Is there a pile of money, or are there piles and piles of money? If unlimited dollars are available, should they be spent whatever way the providers want regardless of necessity? Sometimes that attitude does prevail. People will say, "I have $2 million worth of coverage" or "I called my insurance company and they said I have lots of insurance dollars and I don't have to worry." In my mind, it is not responsible in the health care delivery system today to spend money just because it exists or just to line the pockets of providers. I look for the "value-locked dollar"—for a demonstration that the treatment is necessary, reasonable, and will achieve good results and that the treatment plan is the most cost-effective way to provide the requisite care.

What impact will the costs of medical equipment, supplies, and therapies have? During an assessment, one indicator of greater exposure is any ongoing condition requiring home care services, infusion care services, total parenteral nutrition (TPN, which can run from $165 to $450 per day depending on the provider), pain control medication (for cancer or chronic pain patients), inpatient or outpatient rehabilitation services, or any other intervention that lasts more than a few episodes. Case managers ought to pay particular attention during an assessment in which such services are involved because their price, quality, and delivery sites vary so greatly. For example, the intensity and frequency of activity multiplies when a patient is moved from the hospital to a home or alternative care setting. This is because the case manager must contract for bits and pieces of services as well as rent or purchase equipment. The case manager must examine what is already in place, look at ultimate costs, and evaluate where and how her time can be best spent. Can the cost of the facility, of equipment, or of drugs be negotiated or bid to bring it down? The expense in time and energy, however, might make haggling a $100 item down to $75 virtually wasted effort. (Note that case management should never be driven solely by costs. If a case manager starts operating with the mind-set that everything is too expensive and that the role of case management is just to save money, then she is laying the groundwork for potential legal action.)

In some cases, cost is not the determining factor. For a patient with a brain injury, an acute care hospital may be the best setting for the first several days or weeks of care. Then, the patient needs to be placed in a traumatic brain injury or coma stimulation recovery program. This might not be less costly and, in some cases, is even more expensive. The case manager must look at the patient's needs and how they can be best met in terms of quality and cost. One factor should never drive the others; there must be an equilibrium among the three. If John is going to be at risk as a result of moving him out of a hospital and bringing him home, with services, obviously the move home is not an acceptable alternative. If he can be moved to a less costly setting where the same results can be achieved in a more cost-effective manner, the case manager should try to get the patient and treating physician to agree to that move.

What is going to happen to the patient and how much is this case going to cost the payer or employer if there is no case management intervention? Is it a good case for such intervention? What can the case manager bring to the table? Is the patient's condition and the patient–family support system going to improve with case management, or will case management be just another layer of expense? The system of care already set in place might be good, medically sound, and conservative in its use of care dollars; the patient may be willing and able to follow care instructions, complications may be minimal at present, and the family may be aware of who to call for help. What more could case management offer? In these instances, a case manager must be honest and admit case management has no real role to play.

Sometimes, however, case management, although having no current value, could offer support down the road when the patient's condition is likely to deteriorate. The medical care required will become more complex, and additional services will need to be coordinated. In the meantime, the case manager does not want to drive up costs by going out to visit the patient every month, but neither does she want to totally pull back and be out of communication, waiting for complications to occur. The lost connection could mean less effective management. In such a situation, the case manager might suggest maintaining contact through regular semimonthly, monthly, or bimonthly phone calls.

In light of the information gleaned through conversations with the patient, family, and members of the care team, what is the most reasonable approach to each problem or issue? What are the alternatives to the current care plan? What are the options for future care? How much will the current or alternative plans cost?

Sometimes there are so many problems that a case manager hardly knows where to begin. Often, newer case managers become overwhelmed, thinking they have to identify every single complication or need and come up with all the recommendations for treatment forever. In reality, a case manager simply must show that there are going to be some long-term problems that eventually need to be dealt with by the case management plan and that there are short-term needs that can be addressed immediately and resolved. Long-term plans for chronic cases include short-term goals and long-term vision. The case manager's job is to know where everyone wants to go and then, in measurable steps, follow the procedures necessary to ensure that the ultimate goals are attainable.

REPORTING

As mentioned previously, the nature of the referral source or payer subtly affects communications from the initial assessment through the reporting stage. The focus should be on client needs at all times, and the information must be balanced to present an accurate picture. A report back to the client should include those things the client is most concerned about. In a disability case in which the client is the employer and the case manager goes on and on about the patient's medical condition but ignores return-to-work issues, the case manager has not really met the client's needs. However, when reporting to a claims supervisor or a workers' compensation examiner, a case manager should include specific medical information in the form of parenthetical explanations to help the readers properly interpret the medical terms they will see in other case reports regarding the diagnosis or prognosis. Even if a case manager is not obligated to send out a report (less and less likely, as outcomes management is an important part of health care delivery and our role in the system), such documentation is required for internal accountability.

A case manager in a case management company will probably get referrals from different lines of insurance. If the case manager works in an insurance company and the insurance is basically group medical, she will address medical issues for the most part. However, occasionally the case manager might be required to handle a case referred for workers' compensation evaluation or long-term disability evaluation in which the focus is not necessarily strictly medical.

In workers' compensation cases, carriers are responsible for both medical costs and lost earnings. There usually is "reserving of dollars," in which money is put aside to pay for long-term expenses incurred in big cases. Most workers' compensation administrators or claims departments want to know the extent of medical involvement, the severity of injury, the likelihood that there will be some permanent incapacitation, the potential for a full recovery, the length of medical treatment (episodic or continuous), and the need for long-term or enduring medical services.

The first question might be, will the person be able to go back to his or her prior job? If so, at what point is that likely to occur? If John cannot go back immediately, will he be able to go back at some point? In the meantime, can he return to a modified version of his job, perhaps part-time (reduced hours or reduced number of days per week)? Maybe he could work full-time but with one aspect or task taken away? If he cannot go back to the same employer in a modified job (likely in the case of catastrophic injuries), what past vocational and current avocational capabilities does he possess? What is the likelihood that some kind of employment will be possible for him? Did he only possess specific physical skills? Can he use his work knowledge in some other kind of job? Some people lack transferable skills, have only minimal skills, or have transferable skills but no job site in their part of the country where they can be applied. Then, the case manager needs to look at other alternatives. Past skills or hobbies often have the potential to be developed into viable job skills.

In long-term disability cases, the payer is mainly concerned with disability issues. Many policies have HISOCC (how long he will continue to be disabled for his own job) or ANYOCC (how long he will continue to be unable to work in any job) provisions. (For a more extensive discussion of HISOCC and ANYOCC, please see Chapter 4.) These issues are critical because, unlike workers' compensation, a long-term disability carrier does not pay for medical expenses. Disability insurance replaces lost wages, period. Therefore, the payer is less concerned with the intricacies of medical problems, even though the medical condition is often at the base of any disability. While focusing on work-related issues, case managers also need to keep long-term disability carriers aware of unresolved medical issues because managing those often brings a speedier resolution to the lost-wages situation.

Conversely, group medical payers are not particularly interested in return-to-work or socioenvironmental issues. However, from a case management perspective, these issues impact an individual's recovery ability. A group medical carrier may not require a great deal of information but should get some basics (e.g., the injury occurred at work, the claimant is a valued member of the workforce, she is going to be able to go back, her employer has already told her there is a job for her). These things make a big difference in how a person views him- or herself and are absolutely integrated with recovery from injury or illness.

The frequency and length of case management reports should be confirmed with the referral sources. The nature of the reports is an area of concern for many payers today because of their cost and perceived usefulness.

There are some case management companies specializing in workers' compensation that have a report format that everyone uses for workers' compensation cases. When a group medical case comes in, however, the same report format is used. This format might include a vocational assessment section that calls for a lengthy discussion of work site, transferable skills, return-to-work potential, and so on. As a result, a report on an employee's wife, for example, might include a description of transferable skills and her ability to push and pull and bend. Who cares? Return-to-work issues have no relevance. Someone was on automatic pilot, and the group medical payer has been charged for wasted case management assessment time and report-writing time. Case managers must concentrate on the particular situation, the particular line of insurance, the payer, and the particular needs of the patient. There is no all-purpose case management report.

In my opinion, reports should be written at least once a month. All pertinent case activity should be recorded in a specific, regular format. Clients should not be punished with months' worth of case work attached to a large invoice. Most of the discussion will be old news. By reporting in manageable increments of 3 weeks or a month, case managers gain better control of client files and their cash flow. Significant activity or events requiting clarification should be reported in a timely fashion, first by phone and subsequently through written documentation (within a few days). For example, a case manager who has visited a patient ready for discharge from the hospital and noted that everything is in place at his home does not need to generate another lengthy report on the patient's status. An addendum to a previous report will suffice. This type of reporting should continue for the length of the case and be modified according to the level of involvement.

How extensive should reports be? Some payer organizations have very specific guidelines, limiting initial report writing time to 2 hours or even half an hour. Others request a verbal report, asking that the case manager not take the time to send a document, even an e-mail or fax. In this type of situation, the case manager has to educate the referral source. Case management reports have value as documents chronicling case management activity. I know some of our client companies do not read our every report, but the reports do become a matter of record.

Suppose the case manager, during a phone conversation, reports to the payer a previously undocumented call to the patient or the physician. Will either of them remember this exchange of information? What if the case moves into litigation? What if the patient takes a turn for the worse? Especially when planning services, negotiating services, or putting alternate plans in place, case managers need to document decisions and their implementation. This is just good case management administration.

I confronted the issue of reporting in conversation with a client, a Third Party Administrator, who was seeking to cut administrative costs across the board. I used an example from his office to make a point. Most claims departments will pay for a surgery. But if a claim comes in for $10,000, it goes unpaid unless that surgical bill is accompanied by an operative report. The claims adjuster does not necessarily understand the medical jargon, but the report is requisite and accepted as documentation for a surgical procedure. I reminded the Third Party Administrator that he was paying for those operative reports that no one in his office read, yet they were considered a part of good claims administration. I then noted that case managers had procedural guidelines as well.

Just like physicians (who keep notes and dictate reports) or corporations (which maintain minutes of board of directors meetings), case managers need to document their work. Not everyone will read case management reports, but the medicolegal environment surrounding case management and the high cost and high risk associated with typical cases requires case managers to report their activities carefully and comprehensively.

I believe case managers need to explain our position and insist on providing full documentation because it helps validate and legitimize case management intervention. Case management is being requested by payers, and this is key. Case managers, to justify their involvement and demonstrate their contributions, need to be able to document what they did and how it affected treatment outcomes. Simply stated, case managers might be doing important work, but if they do not record it, it did not happen. Reports need to cover not just cost issues, but medical, physician, patient, and family issues as well, and also individuals consulted, actions agreed upon, actions taken, and the results.

Case management needs to put its principles and guidelines on record. I feel that too many case managers go along with every whim of their clients, putting themselves at risk. Far too many people are willing to conduct case management according to someone else's agenda. This is not to say that clients should have no input or be unable to restrict the length of time taken on a report, but case managers must do their job responsibly.

Regardless of the client's (payer's) needs, the report a case manager creates should follow a certain format. It should adequately catalog the generic information and capture the specific nature of the case as well. The case manager serves as an objective observer, weaving the role of case management into the picture. Although most case managers tailor their reports to meet the special requirements of clients, each report should include the same basic information: the name of the referral source, the mailing address and phone number for reporting, the line of insurance, the date of occurrence of the accident or injury, the name of the insured, a code for and the name of the claimant or patient. Each report also includes data obtained from the payer source, the patient and family, medical records, the treating physician, and other medical professionals; a review of the policy coverage and limits; any suggested alternative treatment program; and a discussion of relevant community resources. If an emotional or psychological component of the case is powerful enough to affect other care issues, it must be included as well.

Documentation attached to a report might include copies of the patient's past medical records, consulting reports, reports transferred from another treatment facility, questionnaires the case manager might have sent the treating physicians, letters confirming the agreement of the treating physicians with recommendations made by the case manager—anything that substantiates the case manager's activities and the unfolding of the treatment plan. In addition, the case manager should add information (e.g., brochures on diagnostic conditions, equipment, facilities) that might help the claims department or plan administrator better understand the patient's condition and needs, and should append the patient authorization form affirming the patient's permission for the information to be shared.

I usually suggest to newer case managers that each time they write a report, they first ask themselves, "Why am I not writing my successful closure report today? Why is this case still open?" This can help clarify the case's most pressing issues. The short-term situation should be presented along with solutions or responses, and then long-term needs should be cited.

A case management report should present the basics in a brief format using statements that leave room for clarification or follow-up. The first assessment report might be in outline form, but there should be a clause affirming that as the potential for case management involvement becomes more defined or the patient's condition becomes more stable, a more complete report will be filed.

Perhaps the client was anxious to receive something on paper for a synopsis to the home office before the case manager was able to speak with the patient or before all medical personnel involved could be contacted. In such cases, the case manager should describe the situation ("This information was gathered in an interview with the family; the patient was unconscious") and add that a broader report will be forthcoming.

The language of reports is different from phone conversation vernacular. No one would write that a patient's house "was a wreck." Rather, it was "in need of repair." Reports also must consolidate communication. It is impossible to portray the living environment of a low-income neighborhood in a heavily urbanized area to a claims examiner in a small, Midwestern city; a few well-chosen words can convey the needed information. Because a range of people might be reading case management reports, they should be understandable to the layperson. Apnea should be described as "the absence of respiratory activity" or "a frequent respiratory distress of infants with an underdeveloped brain center," not as "a low CO_2 level." A report also might be subpoenaed and have to stand up to scrutiny in court, and, therefore, positive and negative observations should be backed by objective statements. The comment "John is not making progress because he's not motivated" would need to be supported by the fact that John has not attended his physical therapy sessions for the past 2 weeks even though he had transportation and was fit enough to do so. Hearsay should be avoided.

Developing prompt reports requires knowledge of community resources, service costs, and appropriate medical responses. The presentation of a report is particularly important when recommending an alternative to the existing treatment plan. Suppose the patient is in a hospital. The case manager calls the billing department: "John's been in the hospital for 15 days. I'm the case manager. We're working here with a company that really doesn't have a lot in terms of benefits. Could you tell me what the interim bill is right now, the billing to date? What's it likely going to be?" Then, the case manager begins to draft a report taking into account quality of care and cost factors as well as patient and family receptivity to the situation. A day in an intensive care unit in this particular hospital may be $3,400. A physician is going to visit every single day (maybe several physicians every day) at $150 a day, 5 or 7 days a week. Add that. The projected stay in the hospital, if no change is made in the treatment plan, is likely to be another 3 weeks. The case manager calculates the per diem cost and then, multiplying that cost by 3 weeks, presents the cost of Plan A.

Then Plan B is described. "I think we could bring John home, but we can't bring him home with anything less than 24-hour care. His wife can take care of him perhaps for the first 4 hours of the morning, but then she has other responsibilities. We'll need to put in an LPN or a home health aide." Knowing that the patient and family will need someone, either an RN or LPN, to provide assistance around the clock, the case manager investigates the cost per hour of such service in the area and multiplies it by 24 hours a day. That may not be the only needed service. John may also need physical therapy. The case manager might need to rent equipment (e.g., a hospital bed and wheelchair). In analyzing the second scenario, the case manager must include as many of the variables as can be predicted.

The case manager should present every alternative that seems plausible. One might be to put the patient in a rehabilitation center or a skilled nursing facility at a fixed, all-inclusive, per diem cost negotiated to $325 per day. How does the case manager get that figure? By calling the facility and saying, "I'm trying to draw up a plan so I can submit it to an approval source. The last time I had someone in your facility it was x dollars per day. Is that still in the ballpark? I won't hold you to those exact dollars. I realize that this patient may be different, requiring other services, but this is an employer group and it's the first time they're seeing figures. I'm just trying to give them round numbers on which to base a decision."

Is this report communicated by letter, fax, or telephone? It may need to be communicated quickly, which means telephonically. The case manager gets the client on the phone and relates her findings: "I called up the billing department. It's $3,400 per day, and if we don't do anything, John will be there another week in ICU, with a possible additional week on a regular floor for $1,500 per day. It will cost $34,300, not including physician visits.

"We can move him to St. Jude's Rehab Facility in Yonkers. I had a person there 6 months ago; the outcome was really good. I was able to get a rate of $600 per day, including physical therapy, for a total of $8,400. Obviously, I will make certain the plan is approved by the treating physician.

"There is another possibility. John wants to come home. That's his preference, but to do it, we're going to have to add 24 hours of care because his wife can only do 4 hours. After we add physical therapy, the costs of bringing him home will be less than keeping him in the hospital but not as economical as the rehab facility, where he will get more services and better results. I have to let you know that home is where he wants to be. However, he and his family will have to look at what they want to do and how they want to use his benefit dollars."

When a report is drawn up and all this information is documented, the tone becomes more formalized and the case manager includes a projected analysis of predictable costs. Noting that these quotes may vary due to a change in the patient's condition or an unforeseen complication, the case manager would list costs for the current Plan A and alternate Plans B and C. A paragraph or two would follow offering the case manager's opinion as to what is best for the patient and why.

The body of a case management report should not include an emphasis on costs. If such a report should go to court, the case manager might have a problem defending what appears to be "bottom-line" health care. It is more appropriate to incorporate financial information by stating that the provider was selected for its quality, ability to meet the patient's needs, and to make the best use of benefit dollars after a review of several providers was conducted. Other financial data, that is, the range of fees offered by the providers, should appear apart from information on the patient's progress in a Cost-Benefit Analysis Report (see Chapter 12).

Ultimately, the choice is the patient's, but the case manager can present to the patient and family what she believes will be the best in terms of quality, outcome, ease of provision of services, and cost of services. The case manager can make it clear that John has x benefits but will use a greater proportion of dollars by coming home. She should also portray the realities of home care: "It sounds really great, but if the RN or LPN doesn't show up for a shift or gets sick, it can be complicated." Patients, especially when they are in a known and comfortable situation, are threatened by the thought of having to leave, and some will be more vocal than others. "Is this going to be okay with my doctor? Why would you want to have me moved? I really don't know; this is kind of far away from my family." The more vocal ones might be a problem for case managers who are unused to patients becoming so involved.

Introducing the alternative of a less-expensive but equally proficient facility can cause concern when the patient or family is attached to a care center because of its name or price tag. People may equate "less expensive" with "inferior quality." A case manager should never talk about cost eyeball to eyeball with a patient and say, "It's too expensive here and I've got to get you out." That sets up an adversarial relationship and increases the case manager's liability exposure. Family members might counter, "Well, okay, but if anything happens. . ." When recommending a site change, I use the Hyundai/Rolls Royce approach: Everything has a price tag, and it does not necessarily follow that expensive is always good and inexpensive is always inferior.

"Listen, this is a really good center here. I know you're very satisfied. You need to be aware, however, that your wife may need 6 months of these kinds of services. At $1,200 per day, this only buys us 2 months of care. Here's another site, where costs will be $500 per day for appropriate services. I'd like your input; I can't mandate that you go there. But I will assist in helping to see that it gets you the results you need, and I will confer with your doctor about it."

Enabling a patient to focus on long-term gains rather than short-term obstacles can help him or her make a decision. "Yes, the new facility is farther away, but even though you'll be away from home for 3 more weeks, remember that in 3 weeks you'll be so much closer to returning to life as usual." Giving the patient an example can be beneficial. "I hear what you're saying because of another patient I worked with. This was his situation, but actually when he got here. . ." A patient needs to hear some of the positives to be able to appreciate the case manager's vision. If the patient, by looking at a brochure or going on a tour, can see the facility is really nice and designed to meet his or her needs, he or she will be more inclined to "buy in."

No one is really comfortable with change. A case manager has to help people see the pros and the cons and allow them to voice their concerns and problems. If their objections can be dealt with, the case manager should follow through. If someone says, "Absolutely no, under no circumstances," the case manager should not try to force a change. The case manager should also never create a situation in which she, the employer group, and the carrier are at odds, because the patient will be more tempted to say, "Well you said I had to do this and now look what happened. I'm going to sue you." In addition, it is important to be wary of a patient or family who wants to turn over all authority to the case manager, because this also places the case manager at additional risk for a lawsuit. Each patient really needs to be involved in planning and be aware of why decisions are made.

The initial report sells the case management plan. A report can and should be used to bring something else to the picture—to provide the client with a vision, to demonstrate the more complex uses of case management, or to create new opportunities for case management work. Even a brief report can include under-lined or bold sections that emphasize the philosophy behind case management and its role in solving problems. Report-writing at its best includes creative, ana-lytical thinking that anticipates objections in order to win approval.

To maintain quality services, to better track our cases, and to assist our case managers in creating reports that served as valuable case management tools in and of themselves, I created guidelines for on-site and telephonic initial evalua-tion reports (Table 9–19), a sample on-site and telephonic Initial Evaluation Report (Table 9–20), guidelines for writing progress reports (Table 9–21), and a sample on-site and telephonic Progress Report (Table 9–22). The guidelines offer direction on what information is needed and, in some cases, why it is important to include certain references or nuances. The sample reports indicate the content and formats that I have found effective when communicating the process and ben-efits of a beneficial case management plan.

OBTAINING APPROVAL

After the case management plan has been devised and the report has been sent to the client, the case manager must then obtain approval to proceed with the rec-ommendations in the report.

Case Manager: Betty, this is Pat Sanders with Professional Case Management. How is your morning going?

Case Manager: You sound very busy. I'll be brief.

Table 9–19 Initial Evaluation Report Guidelines

Initial Evaluation Report
(On-site and Telephonic)

Guidelines for use (*see attached Sample*)

Referral Reason: The *major* reasons why case was identified for case management. Examples: long-term care placement, home uterine monitoring, TPN services, etc.

Current Medical Status: A narrative yet *concise* and *specific* paragraph about the claimant's medical status at the time of referral. If hospitalized, include the reason for that admission, course of treatment, complications, dates, care needs, future treatment plan, and expected outcome. You should also include physical descriptions of claimant (if visit occurred) or current height, weight, race, sex, and other physical characteristics.

Past Medical History: A *short* paragraph that should describe conditions, prior surgeries, etc. Include prior admissions, surgeries, and medications *as they impact* on current status and/or future recovery.

Treating Physicians/Other Professionals: A list of *current* treating MDs and perhaps others *if* they will continue to be involved. List name, specialty, address, and phone number.

Medications: A list of medications that the claimant is or will be taking: name, type (i.e., sedative, chemotherapy), dose, and frequency.

Socio/Environmental: A *short* description of claimant's family/work and home situation. Include marital status, family support, any cultural, language, or religious factors that may impede recovery, *or* those factors that will assist in promoting a favorable outcome.

Financial/Insurance: A statement of those issues or limitations that might adversely (or, perhaps, positively) affect outcome.

Case Management Intervention: A *short* paragraph to describe what you have done since the file was opened. It should include how initial assessment was conducted (i.e., phone, visit), who was contacted, authorization documentation, and receptivity to case management. Also state any particular activities/accomplishments.

Problems Identified: An *extremely important* section that serves as the *basis* for your case management intervention and recommendations. If there are no problems, then we don't need a case manager (. . . *and* if that *is* the case, we need to state so and recommend closure). Assuming that we have done a good job in assessing potential for case management, opened the file, etc., then *list those*

continues

Table 9–19 continued

---

problems that need to be resolved and that, when resolved, will bring us closer to a successful closure. No need to list any and all at this initial stage, just those requiring immediate attention and that you can address until the next report date.

Case Management Recommendations: A list of recommendations that is *action* oriented, defines what you plan to do, and is absolutely the logical connection to the problems you have identified. They should also lead to *measurable* outcomes, that is, improving medical outcomes, appropriate and cost-effective use of services/benefit dollars, empowerment/compliance of patient, etc. These recommendations are those you will or plan to accomplish until next report.

Estimated Hours for Case Management: The number of hours that you will expend until the next report (including time spent on your report).

Source: Courtesy of Options Unlimited, Case Management Services Division, 2003, Huntington, New York.

Case Manager: I just wanted to make sure you got my last report, which was dated March 14th. [If report has been received but not yet read.] Well, good, I'm glad to know you received it. Because you haven't had a chance to read it yet, can I call you back tomorrow? I just wanted to get your thoughts on my recommendations to see if I should proceed. I'll give you a quick call on Thursday.

Case Manager: [When report has been received and read.] As you may have read in the report, Mr. Williams is considerably improved from the time of my last report. I think our physician change was a good idea; he seems to be responding real well. Did my two recommendations look good to you? One involved a personal consultation with Dr. Friedman, and the second was getting three bids on the hospital bed. If Mr. Williams is going to need the bed for more than 3 months, we may come out better by a purchase, but I can make some calls on that and let you know.

Case Manager: OK, great, I'll go ahead and get started on this tomorrow, and I'll probably have another report to you in about 3 weeks. I'll also check on those medications you questioned and give you a call when I have some answers. Thanks for your time.

There are always going to be times when case managers have to use their own judgment and consider who they are representing. A case manager might receive direct communication from an employer or referral source: "I want John out of that facility; it's too expensive." If the case manager feels that the patient is in the

Table 9–20 Initial Evaluation Report (On-site and Telephonic Reports)

Date of Report:
SS#:
To: Jane Smith, Acct. Manager   Employer group: ABC Auto Corp.
Claimant: Sara Green   Diagnosis: Cerebral vascular accident
Insured: Same   (stroke), diabetes, hypertension.

Referral Reason: Options Unlimited's services requested based upon multiple diagnoses, need for inpatient rehabilitation, ongoing home care and therapy, and limited benefit provisions.

Current Medical Status

Information in this report obtained by telephone/fax. Signed release in file. The claimant is one week post right CVA at New City Hospital. She had sudden onset of left-sided weakness, slurred speech, and suffered a fall in her home. Upon her admission through the ER, the claimant was also found to be diabetic with blood glucose at 280 and her blood pressure elevated to 200/120. She remained in ICU for 3 days and then transferred to the neurological unit, where she is at present. There is significant paresis (weakness) of left upper and lower extremity, speech remains slurred but understandable. Blood glucose levels responding to insulin but dosage requires more regulation as does her blood pressure medication. Prognosis is guarded at this time with return to pre-illness status questionable.

Past Medical History

Prior to this hospital admission, the claimant had two previous admissions: in 2000 for cholecystectomy and in March 2003 for hypertension. She acknowledged a "touch of diabetes," a "little problem" with her weight (175 pounds, height 5′4″) as per the hospital admission note. As per her daughter, claimant took her antihypertension medication, ". . . only when she had a headache. . . . didn't want to get too dependent on drugs. . ."

Treating Physicians

Dr. Al Jones	Dr. Bob Brown	Dr. Sam Smith
(neurologist)	(internist)	(endocrinologist)
120 Main Street	100 Main Street	200 Old Street
Nice Town, USA	Nice Town, USA	Fine Town, USA
400-123-4567	400-123-8910	400-321-9876

Medications

NPH Insulin, 40 U, OD
Reg Insulin, 5 U for glucose level between 160–180 mgm, 4× day

continues

Table 9–20 continued

Lasix, 20 mgm., BID
K-Dur, 20 mgm., OD
Lopressor, 50 mgm, BID

Socio/Environmental

Mrs. Green is a 58-year-old Caucasian female, widowed for 2 years. She lives alone in an eight-room home in a rural area. Adult daughters (two) while having a close, supportive relationship with their mother, live 2–3 hours away and with family and work responsibilities, are unable to provide care or assistance other than occasionally and via phone calls. She admits to being shy and private with no real friends in the area, a few close coworkers but they are 1 hour away, close to the supermarket where the claimant works as a cashier. In conversation with the oldest daughter (Mary White, 400-000-0000), it appears that the claimant's house has become "very rundown" since her husband's death, resulting in embarrassment and reluctance to having "outsiders" in the home.

Financial/Insurance

Due to the claimant's long-term employment, she will receive full pay for the next 3 months. Although meeting normal expenses is NOT an immediate problem, there is concern that some benefit limitations and apparent need for long-term rehabilitation may give rise to financial concerns (60 home care visits up to 4 hours; rehab $50,000 total lifetime).

Case Management Intervention

Since this case was opened, Options Unlimited has conducted an initial assessment of the claimant through telephone contact with her daughter, the discharge planner, and Dr. Brown; and has begun research for rehab facility admission. Signed authorization has been obtained, and claimant and family are receptive to our assistance.

Problems Identified

1) Needs inpatient rehabilitation services; as per MD, 30–45 day period.
2) Limitation of benefits; @ a nonnegotiated cost/day of $1500 × 30 days—$45,000 would be spent with only $5,000 remaining; home care limit, 60 visits.
3) Somewhat medically stable; in addition to CVA, diabetes, hypertension, and weight reduction will require medical direction.
4) Patient by history is poorly educated about her condition and noncompliant due to lack of understanding.
5) Will need home care and/or physical therapy once home; patient is presently unreceptive, unrealistic regarding future and very anxious.
6) Patient lives alone.

Table 9–20 continued

Case Management Recommendations

1) Begin to research and negotiate fees for transfer to rehab facility; with MD and rehab facility, explore feasibility of 1- to 2-week admission to conserve benefits. Assist with discharge/transfer plans to rehab facility.
2) With treating MDs, determine who will provide follow-up medical care and/or referrals to appropriate MDs in claimant's area.
3) Enlist family assistance in preparing home for patient's return to allow for necessary home care in a safe environment.

Estimated case management hours: 6–8 hours.

Mary Smith, RN, BS
Medical Case Manager

Source: Courtesy of Options Unlimited, Case Management Services Division, 2003, Huntington, New York.

---

most appropriate center and there is no less-costly setting, she cannot allow the employer or client to override her professional judgment. The case manager cannot serve the client first and the patient last; the interests of the patient must always predominate. Case managers are not in the business of slashing away at the federal or corporate health budget at the sacrifice of patients' well-being and safety.

COORDINATION: PUTTING THE PLAN INTO ACTION

Plans are sometimes put in motion as early as the initial evaluation stage. The case manager may not have completed gathering all the information or submitted a report when she gets the go-ahead to put services in place. When a big, involved case has been referred by a client company the case manager has worked with before, the company might request a verbal report from the site. During that telephone call, the case manager might say, "This person could go home. I could set up some services. Do you want me to continue with case management intervention?" And the response will come, "Yes, go ahead. Do what you have to do."

Whatever the working arrangement is, whether the case manager is representing an insurer, HMO, PPO, TPA, or is part of an independent case management company, she should be aware of the voluntary guidelines that have been issued

Table 9–21 Guidelines for Writing Progress Reports (On-site and Telephonic)

Date of Report:

To: Jane Smith

SS#:

Claimant: Sara Green   Employer group:

Insured: Same   Diagnosis: Stroke

Medical Status

This should be a *narrative,* yet short and very specific summary of the claimant's medical status since the last report. Include in this section any hospital admissions, surgeries, complications, new conditions and/or diagnostic findings. If there has been notable progress, quality-of-care issues, or other factors impacting on claimant's medical status, it should be included in this section. See Example.

Problems Identified

In order to assure that case management is goal-directed, rather than a reporting of events, *list* in this section those problems that need to be addressed or resolved and that you will be working on during the next month (or report period if on extended diary). Because goals for case management should be directed toward the improvement of medical outcomes (or stability), appropriateness of care and services, and cost containment, we should be looking at the problems or factors that would interfere with this. See Examples.

Case Management Intervention

This should be a short *narrative* section as to what *you* as the case manager actually did on this case since the past report. There should be a demonstration in this section of your *action* and *involvement* in moving this case toward improved medical outcomes, involvement by the patient and family, interaction with the medical team and providers, and an ongoing ability to achieve quality outcome *and* savings or cost-effectiveness. Note: this is *not* to include date-by-date, activity-by-activity reporting of events, phone calls, etc., but rather a more global description of evidence of your impact on the case. This should clearly illustrate why case management is involved, what we've done and/or need to do. Use of "Options Unlimited" or "this case manager" and action verbs should be evident. See Example.

Recommendations

In this section, list those activities that you will do within the next month (or extended diary report period). Remember that these activities should have a relation or connection to the issues you have noted in the *Problems Identified* section. What do you need to do to solve the problems? See Examples.

Table 9–21 continued

Estimated case management hours: Note here the number of hours (including your report) that you will expend until the next report.

Source: Courtesy of Options Unlimited, Case Management Services Division, 2003, Huntington, New York

---

to promote consistency in managed care, including case management. Jointly developed by representatives of the American Hospital Association, the American Managed Care and Review Organization, the American Medical Association, the Blue Cross and Blue Shield Association, and the Health Insurance Association of America, these guidelines for the most part cover the conduct of concurrent review (see Chapter 10).

Although the concurrent review guidelines may be voluntary, such protocols are becoming part of the case management practice, and case managers could be held responsible in court for applying and utilizing them. In 1986, *Wickline v. State of California* established that any professional involved in making a health care recommendation could be held liable for damages or harm to a patient that occurs when services in a managed care environment are not provided in accordance with accepted standards of care. In 1989, Congress created the Office for the Forum on Quality and Effectiveness within the Agency for Health Care Policy and Research (AHCPR), now known as the Agency for Healthcare Research and Quality (AHRQ), and gave it a mandate to publish and disseminate national clinical practice guidelines. Cutting across populations, ages, problem areas, and delivery sites, these national guidelines, now developed for more than 19 clinical subjects, are systematic statements of what is appropriate in specific clinical terms when delivering care to patients. They are accessible on-line through the National Library of Medicine's Medline service. The last areas of care covered included low back pain problems, cardiac rehabilitation, depression, management of cancer-related pain, evaluation and management of early HIV infection, cataracts, and postoperative pain management. What case manager has never worked on cases involving these areas of care? Another task force at AHCPR developed a methodology to translate clinical practice guidelines into medical review criteria—guideposts used to judge the appropriateness of health care decisions.

AHCPR looked to the Institute of Medicine (IOM), an arm of the National Academy of Sciences, for advice on how to implement its guidelines program. The IOM, defining the standards for guideline development, devised eight attributes of good clinical practice guidelines: (1) validity (do they lead to the health and cost outcomes projected for them), (2) reliability/reproducibility (a similar

Table 9–22 Sample Progress Report (On-site and Telephonic)

Date of Report:
To: Jane Smith

SS#:

Claimant: Sara Green   Employer group:
Insured: Same   Diagnosis: Stroke

Medical Status

Mrs. Green continues to recover from her right CVA (stroke) and is now in the second week of her inpatient rehabilitation at Valley Rehabilitation Center. She is actively participating in the program; however, she remains anxious about her return home. Her diabetes is better controlled with insulin and diet but still requires close medical supervision and a change in her medications has brought her hypertension closer to normal range (last reading 130/90, lower than her prior 180/100.) There has been an additional weight loss of 10 pounds since her hospital admission 3 weeks ago, with another 15 pounds to go until her target of 140 pounds.

Problems Identified

- Patient lives by herself and will require assistance once home. Adult children (two) live 2–3 hours away.
- Patient is being cared for by three MDs: Dr. Jones (neurologist), Dr. Brown (internist), and Dr. Smith (endocrinologist). All MDs are 1+ hours from the patient's home and she will require frequent medical follow-up.
- Patient has benefit limits for home care and rehabilitation services (60 home care visits of 4 hours each, $50,000 rehab, lifetime).
- Patient is a very private person and resists "outsiders" in her home.

Case Management Intervention

Since our last report, Options Unlimited was able to expedite Mrs. Green's discharge from New City Hospital to Valley Rehab Center. This case manager researched the facilities in the area, assisted the family in evaluating each and then, upon agreement of all and selection of Valley Rehab, negotiated cost-effective, all-inclusive daily rates. Because of the Plan limit (lifetime) for rehab benefits ($50,000 total), Options Unlimited is working very closely with the staff of Valley to extend these available dollars. We are discussing a shorter inpatient stay in order to use the remaining dollars for a longer period of treatment once the claimant is home. We have also begun to research home care providers and DME dealers in her area.

Recommendations

1) Obtain progress reports from rehab team within next week; determine potential and date for transition to community-based day program and then home physical therapy.

Table 9–22 continued

2) Determine level of function and assess home care needs, for example, equipment care, services, etc. Arrange care, negotiate fees, and prepare provider agreements.
3) Contact all MDs. Determine current medical status, share concerns regarding follow-up, and obtain recommendations for appropriate medical care.

Estimated hours for case management: 5 hours

Signature
Medical Management Consultant

Source: Courtesy of Options Unlimited, Case Management Services Division, 2003, Huntington, New York.

group of experts would incorporate the same elements within their guidelines), (3) clinical applicability (the guideline specifies applicable populations), (4) clinical flexibility (details common, expected deviations for the clinical condition), (5) clarity (the language is clear, terms are defined precisely, and the presentation is logical and easy to follow), (6) multidisciplinary process (the guideline reflects input from the various practitioners who treat the condition), (7) scheduled review (guidelines are regularly reviewed for medical advances and new treatments), and (8) documentation (statements clearly addressing the evidence, assumptions, and rationales used to develop the guidelines).

There are, however, any number of practice guidelines and standards of practice that have been developed that do not directly address all of those eight criteria. The AMA's directory of guidelines estimates that over 1,700 different practice guidelines are in circulation.

In 1995, the CMSA published its first Standards of Practice, guidelines for practicing case management. Although they are not clinical in substance, these nationally recognized standards define case management, case manager functions, settings for case management services, relationships with clients, purposes and goals of case management, standards of care, and standards of performance. The standards of care identify activities incorporating assessment/case identification, problem identification, planning, monitoring, evaluating, and outcomes measurement criteria. Within the standards of performance are included measurement criteria for quality of care, education/certification qualifications, collaborative activities, legal compliance, ethical conduct, advocacy, resource utilization, and research utilization. When examined in light of the IOM definitions, these

CMSA standards hold up as standards of conduct for case managers, illuminating the role, describing functions, and setting boundaries for appropriate behavior.

Aetna Health Plans and the ICMA (now merged with CMSA) developed Case Management Practice Guidelines, published by Mosby-Year Book in 1996. These guidelines come closer to the IOM's definition of clinical practice guidelines. Like the CMSA standards, they offer general case management guidelines, but also provide condition-specific case management recommendations for 10 clinical or practice areas: AIDS/HIV, brain injury, high-risk neonates, high-risk pregnancy, low back injury, oncology, pediatric care, spinal cord injury, transplants, and workers' compensation.

In addition, there are the Standards of Practice for Case Management (CMSA), a section of which appears as Appendix 9–A, CMSA Statement Regarding Ethical Case Management Practice, Code of Professional Conduct for Case Managers (CCMC), Code of Professional Conduct (Certification of Disability Management Specialists Commissions; CDMS), Code of Ethics (American Nurses Association; ANA), the Standards of Occupational and Environmental Health Nursing (American Association of Occupational Health Nurses; AAOHN), Code of Ethics (AAOHN), Code of Ethics (National Academy of Social Workers; NASW), and standards of care in several practice settings from the NASW.

With legal precedent for potentially holding case managers accountable even though they are not hands-on care providers, it behooves every case manager to become familiar with these practice guidelines. Alice G. Gosfield, a lawyer very familiar with health law issues and a board member of the National Committee for Quality Assurance, said at a Medical Case Management Conference that guidelines such as the AHCPR offerings are readily available to practicing case managers; no one has an excuse for not applying them, when appropriate. However, they are not rigid rules, but rather standardized suggestions for actions given a certain diagnosis or clinical condition. For example, a past Milliman and Robertson (M&R) cataract guideline engendered such resistance and disagreement that major insurers who otherwise used the M&R guidelines refused to apply it as issued. Gosfield suggests that case managers should document both their adherence to and reasons for deviations from guidelines. If a case manager can demonstrate that she has conscientiously followed a national case management guideline or national clinical guideline, she provides herself with an additional shield against potential claims of negligence. The question asked in cases of professional liability is, did you behave as a similar practitioner would under similar circumstances? Attorneys are not attracted to cases in which the fact of negligence can be disproved by documented guideline adherence.[7]

Although we need guidelines and should certainly practice in accordance with the high level of standards in our fields, I caution case managers to call on their professional knowledge and experience in translating guidelines into action. I have seen any number of requests for proposals that call for "state of the art," "best in practice," or "best in class" procedures. A guide is a guide; it is not a mandate. Some guidelines are restrictive; some are dangerous. We all remember the swift outcry when the "drive-through" mastectomy guidelines were published and the legal actions that were taken to require more reasonable time frames for inpatient care following the procedure. The key point regarding use of guidelines is to apply them wisely, fully document your choices and actions, and clearly communicate your reasoning to the appropriate parties.

FOLLOW-UP

Attention must be paid to each detail. Any time a case manager has any responsibility for making recommendations for services or putting services in place, the case manager owes it to herself, the patient, and the client company who referred the case to make sure that what has been put in place is working, remains quality in nature, is cost-effective, and is necessary. Obtaining approval for monitoring from a client company can be difficult; managing a case without monitoring it can lead to liability exposure.

Sometimes a client company wants a case manager to make a one-time visit, put services in place, and be done with the case. No one is watching for changes in the patient's needs or tracking and assisting with increases or decreases in services. No one is gauging the continued effectiveness of the physician's treatment plan. What worked well in the hospital may not work at home. After 5 days, the patient is readmitted to the hospital. What happened? It may be that the patient initially followed the physician's recommendations to the nth degree, then became lax with dressing changes, and now has a dangerous infection. Especially when involved in helping a patient make the transition from one care setting to another, the case manager must make sure that the outcome for the patient will not become compromised.

The monitoring process varies from case to case. It may include semimonthly home visits by the case manager or periodic phone calls placed by the patient to the case manager. In active cases in which multiple services are in place, the case manager must make monthly on-site visits. It may be that there are no services in place but the patient has been discharged and asked to take specific medications or dress a wound a certain way. The case manager will not go out and watch the patient take pills but will ask for a check-in call to see how the patient is coping. If the patient sounds poor or acknowledges problems, the case manager should call the physician and assess the situation. Perhaps the treatment plan needs to be reevaluated.

When there are multiple services in place, the patient continues to recover, or the family resists any suggested decrease in service hours, the case manager may need to make an on-site visit to ascertain the true situation. It may be that the family members are not good communicators and things have taken a rapid turn for the worse. Without access, the case manager cannot determine whether continuing to adhere to the treatment plan is in the best interest of the patient.

Continuing follow-up and reports are especially important because they help maintain the case manager's link to the patient and support the case manager's role throughout the case. Rather than simply someone who sets up services or assists with hospital discharges, the case manager is perceived as someone who contributes to the entire treatment plan.

EVALUATING THE PLAN

Along with monitoring the medical treatment plan and its effectiveness, the case manager evaluates and reevaluates her own case management plan over the course of the intervention. Is the treatment working? Is the patient cooperating? There will be a flux in case activity and intensity.

Periodically (at least once every 30 days), the case manager should review the treatment plan and the patient's progress. Short-term referrals, which generally run less than 3 months and are characterized by intense activity at the outset that tapers off as the patient improves, are always reassessed prior to the patient's discharge from a facility or program. Long-term programs, such as geriatric care, are evaluated at intervals of 3, 6, or 9 months, or as in a brain trauma or SCI (spinal cord injury) at 1-year intervals. Long-term care evaluations can become challenging because the goal of case management is stability; in some cases, things can hum along for quite a while and there will seemingly be nothing to report.

Further, quality of life is less easily measured than the quantity of money spent on care. Is a continuation of the program warranted? Are the dollars spent on John's care every day worth it? What can the case manager use as a yardstick to measure care progress? Is John experiencing big gains? Perhaps the first month John could not walk alone; this month he walks unaided but his gait needs correction. Or, the first month John remained comatose; the second month he was alert but experienced memory loss. As long as improvements are ongoing, the treatment course can be justified.

The patient might be in a facility for a proposed 6- to 9-month stay at a cost of $1,000 per day. A monthly visit by the case manager can be extremely effective in monitoring the need for continuing placement. (If the patient has been placed in a facility in another state, the case manager may rely on the facility's case manager to keep her updated rather than making a personal on-site visit.) Treatment might be necessary for a 6- to 9-month period, but the patient might not require facility services for the entire time. Although making great strides the first 2 months, the patient may show no further improvement after 3 months. Perhaps the patient has hit a plateau and needs a break from the rigorous therapies. This is something the case manager cannot ascertain from facility reports. The case manager might have to decide whether a $1,400-per-day facility fee is justified when there is a day program available to the patient that costs $500 per day. The next step might be to place the patient in the day program, then perhaps return him or her to the inpatient facility for another round of more intensive therapy if improvement again becomes noticeable.

Over the course of care, the case manager maintains communication with the treating physicians to share concerns and observations regarding developing conditions. The case manager may need to reestablish ties to a specialist to request assistance. As a treatment facilitator, the case manager keeps in touch with everyone who can make a contribution toward the desired outcome for the patient, including physicians, physical therapists, social workers, employers, and community center personnel.

REPEATING THE PROCESS

Each case goes through modification, redevelopment, and reevaluation stages. Changes in patient status will require new measures of care.

I do not think a case manager can ever be certain that a case that appears short-term is not going to become problematic. Some conditions seem very straightforward, and then, for whatever reason (family dynamics, financial difficulties, new symptoms), the initial diagnosis is changed. Case managers should always allow for extenuating circumstances, unforeseen events, and as much as possible, they should try to prevent complications from occurring. Yet, despite the best of care and intentions, short-term problems can become long-term problems.

SPECIFIC CASE MANAGEMENT ACTIVITIES

Throughout the course of care, the case manager will be working in four major areas of activity: medical, financial, behavioral/motivational, and vocational. In "Job Descriptions and Standards of Care" in its *Case Management Practice* publication, the Foundation for Rehabilitation Certification Education and Research included the following descriptions.

Medical Activities

Into this category fall all those activities a case manager performs to ensure that the patient receives the most effective medical and nursing care, including the following:

• Contacting the patient in the hospital, in the rehabilitation unit, or at home.

- Contacting the members of the medical treatment team (the physician, nursing staff, rehabilitation therapists, etc.) to discover the patient's course of progress and needs and utilizing the information in discharge planning and the initial needs assessment.
- Arranging for all services required for discharge or relocation (equipment, home nursing care, therapy, transportation, transfer to another facility, home utilities, etc.), and coordinating efforts with the primary RN, discharge planner, or social service administrator to eliminate duplication of service and conserve benefit dollars.
- Visiting with the family.
- Checking the home for safety factors and architectural barriers and arranging for any needed safety aids and modifications.
- On follow-up, reevaluating equipment, ensuring supplies are replenished, monitoring home nursing services, and arranging for equipment repair; evaluating activities of daily living, home programs, and modifications to treatment.
- Identifying problems, providing health instruction, and referring the patient back to the physician or other health team member when appropriate.
- Identifying plateaus, improvements, regressions, and depressions; counseling accordingly or recommending help.
- Making personal visits or contacting the physician to clarify the diagnosis, prognosis, therapy, activities of daily living, expected permanent disability, limitations, and so on.
- Assisting in obtaining payer authorizations for any modalities of treatment recommended.
- Acting as a liaison between the physician and the insurance company when necessary.
- Sharing pertinent information about the patient with the physician and working together with the physician to achieve the best outcome.

Financial Activities

Some of the specific services a case manager might perform on behalf of a patient are as follows:

- Assessing the benefit plan for coverage and limitations; negotiating out-of-plan coverage to conserve dollars.
- Negotiating for more cost-effective rates for supplies and services.
- Counseling the patient or family on budgeting and notifying creditors.
- Identifying financial distress and referring the patient or family to appropriate community resources.

- Helping the patient or family sort and prioritize unpaid bills.
- Acting as a liaison between the insurance company, referral source, and patient to alleviate financial and other problems or misunderstandings.

Behavioral/Motivational Activities

Behavioral/motivational activities include these:

- Exploring the patient's feelings about him- or herself and his or her injury or illness and helping the patient with the associated trauma and frustration.
- Monitoring the family's feelings regarding the patient's illness and observing the family's ability or inability to manage under new emotional stress.
- Offering reassurance and information about the patient's condition.
- If qualified, counseling in the areas of marital discord, role reversal, dependency, and sexual problems arising from the injury or illness.

Vocational Activities

Possible vocational activities include the following:

- Obtaining a history of past education, employment, hobbies, and job skills and uncovering vocational interests and future goals.
- If appropriate, overseeing psychovocational testing, work evaluations, schooling, transportation, on-the-job situations, and anything else needed to assist the patient in becoming or remaining gainfully employed.
- Assisting the patient in using the recuperative period in a constructive fashion (studying, upgrading skills, preparing for job interviews, etc.).
- Visiting the patient's place of employment and talking with the personnel director or immediate supervisor about the employer's expectations and the patient's needs.
- Completing a job analysis and discussing the possibility of the patient's return to work in the same job, perhaps after job modifications or lightening of duties.
- Sharing the previous information with the physician at an appropriate time.

STAY ON POINT

Case managers always need to remember why they are part of the health care system. They are there to empower patients, to involve patients in their own treatment and destiny, and to help the very young and the very old live as best they can. During an initial assessment, a case manager might foresee some difficulties in affecting change for the better. The adult children of an elderly patient might be arguing among themselves regarding the best course of care; an HIV-positive patient or a patient with terminal cancer (some companies will not refer a cancer patient until he or she is a hospice candidate) is to be interviewed; a family might be devastated by their child's spinal cord injury. Often, the more catastrophic and irreversible the situation, the more strategic the case manager's planning has to be. Can that family remain intact as a unit? In the face of these odds, sometimes the best thing a case manager can do is ask the patient and family, "What is it you want? What do you hope to get from this care? If you could change the patient's care, how would you do it?" By finding out where their heads and hearts are, the case manager can often make an important difference in their ability to cope with a tough situation.

CASE MANAGEMENT SCENARIOS

Following are several brief case management scenarios, all involving employee–employer relationships that outline the case management process and when and how the various elements of the process take place.

Case #1

A 32-year-old office administrator has been out for 5 days due to exacerbation of pain in her wrists over the last 4 months and a sensation of her wrists falling asleep at night. She is currently 12 weeks pregnant and has a history of being hypothyroid and overweight.

Case Analysis

From the information provided, it would appear that this woman may have carpal tunnel syndrome. This condition's predisposing factors include pregnancy, hypothyroidism, and obesity, all conditions that this employee also has. Our goal would be to obtain an accurate diagnosis, appropriate treatment (which would not interfere with her pregnancy), and facilitate a timely return to work.

Further Information Needed

From the employee. The case manager (following explanation of our role) would determine employee's physical status, what testing or treatment has occurred, how pregnancy is progressing, prior medical history (including obesity and hypothyroidism), and treatment for these conditions. We would also discuss return-to-work issues (i.e., transitional assignments), and then determine response to these questions. We would advise her that we will be conferring with her physicians and working with them to assist her in resolving these problems, keeping her healthy during her pregnancy, and returning her to work.

From the physician(s). We would obtain medical information from her obstetrician, internist, and/or neurologist or orthopedic physician who may be treating the wrist pain. We would request objective information from any diagnostic examinations, laboratory testing, and other significant findings. We would determine the treatment plan, duration of disability, ability to return to work, and physician's willingness to cooperate in a return-to-work process. There would be discussion of her obesity as well because this is problematic for her pregnancy and her probable carpal tunnel syndrome.

From the employer. We would briefly discuss medical issues (respecting patient confidentiality) that are present and explore potential for a transitional assignment that would allow for early return to duty. We would enlist cooperation in this and assure that we would continue to be involved to assist with problems and eventual return to full duty.

If the employee had not yet been referred to a neurologist to evaluate her for carpal tunnel, we would suggest this and assist with this evaluation for appropriate treatment. Other than suggestion for further evaluation for carpal tunnel, no other referrals would be made.

Using *The Medical Disability Advisor* guidelines (by Presley Reed, Reed Group), we would estimate a maximum period of 3 weeks' length of disability/duration with conservative medical treatment; however, with transitional employment, a return much sooner is possible. If diagnosis of carpal tunnel is confirmed and assuming conservative management with splinting, compression, and localized treatment, the case manager would negotiate avoidance of prolonged and repetitive activities, brief rest periods to elevate hands intermittently, or reduced hours.

We would advise employer that employee is being evaluated and, hopefully, treated and suggest that work restrictions may be necessary. If known, we would advise as to possible return-to-work date. This case would not qualify for leave under FMLA and would not require consideration for reasonable accommodation under ADA because the condition is assumed to be temporary.

The next case management follow-up would be made with the patient, physician, and employer, who would be contacted within 5 business days. To facilitate return to work and case closure, we would maintain ongoing communication with the involved parties.

Case #2

Approximately 1 month ago, a 48-year-old boiler repair/field tech was lifting a box weighing approximately 50 pounds at a neighbor's yard sale and developed nonradiating low back pain. He has been working, but now has lost 4 days of work due to progressive back pain. He has had occasional backaches in the past; however, he denies any previous back injuries. He had a previous work-related shoulder injury, which was settled under workers' compensation. His past medical history includes peptic ulcer and obesity. His doctor has advised he be off work for the next 2 weeks to rest, start physical therapy, and use Tylenol for pain relief and a muscle relaxant as needed for back spasm. The physician has told the employee that he may need to be off work for as much as 6 weeks. The employee is concerned about his ability to work with his back pain and reports that his supervisor is not sympathetic. He states that he often drives his repair truck into desolate areas and is required to lift and move heavy boiler parts weighing upwards of 60 pounds.

Case Analysis

From the information provided, it would appear that this man has sustained a back strain in a non-work-related lifting incident. His prior history of occasional backaches, peptic ulcer, and obesity are factors to be addressed, as is his work, which would be classified as "heavy." Because of his prior peptic ulcer, treatment with nonsteroidal medications may be contraindicated, and conservative treatment needs to address back strengthening and weight reduction. Due to the physical demands of his job, a period of disability seems warranted to allow for healing and treatment of the strain. However, an extension of 6 weeks is excessive at this stage.

Further Information Needed

From the employee. The case manager would explain her role and inquire as to current status. Is the pain subsiding? How often is he taking a muscle relaxant and Tylenol? Are they effective? What is he doing now? (watching television, walking, resting) Has he started physical therapy, and what is his perception of it? She would determine his current weight and discuss weight factor influence on his back problems; she also would encourage weight reduction. In addition, she would discuss potential for early return to work and his response to this, and encourage contact with supervisor.

From the physician(s). Determine specialty (if not an orthopedic physician, consideration for referral may be warranted). Obtain objective findings noted during physical exam, reports of any diagnostics (i.e., X-ray, MRI), type of physical therapy program recommended, frequency and duration, and name and dosage for muscle relaxant. Inquire as to feasibility of release to light or sedentary work and when this may occur. Provide MD with job analysis for employee position and alternate or transitional position as well. Discuss/suggest back strengthening programs as part of the physical therapy.

From the employer. Advise as to role of case manager; determine impression of employee (Is he a satisfactory employee? Any other problems? Willing to return him to alternate job?). Encourage contact with employee. At this stage, no further medical evaluation is warranted.

Using *The Medical Disability Advisor* and the information obtained (assuring these are objective findings), the estimated length of disability/duration is 1 week (less if appropriate alternate or light-work position is available). We would advise employer as to current status, plans for return to work, estimated time frame, and suggested alternate position(s). We would recommend a transitional position with no heavy lifting, bending, climbing, etc. No consideration for FMLA; however, reasonable accommodation may be appropriate. If there is no improvement, referrals to orthopedic/neurologist for further diagnostic evaluation and treatment would be considered.

The next case management follow-up would be made with the patient, treating physician, and employer within 1 week. To facilitate return to work and case closure, we would encourage appropriate treatment of condition, communication between employee and supervisor, and provide support and direction to employee.

Case #3

A 28-year-old secretary slipped on a wet floor and twisted her neck and upper back. She's been out of work for 6 days and reports pain in the posterior cervical area and left upper back. She has vague complaints of discomfort going into her left arm. Her doctor has told the patient she should avoid using her left arm and "take it easy." Her doctor's lines state: "Employee may return to limited duty: no excessive use of left arm, no lifting over 15 pounds, no excessive phone use, sitting or reaching above her head." She wants to get back to work but feels she may not be able to meet her department's performance expectations if allowed back to work with these restrictions.

Case Analysis

It would appear from the information provided that this young woman has sustained a cervical strain, similar to a "whiplash" injury following a slip/fall accident. The case manager would have to ascertain whether treatment with her physician is ongoing and the diagnosis that was made. Because of her young age, we can assume that this is an acute problem and that with appropriate treatment, her ability to return to preinjury state and productivity is excellent. Although the doctor has released her to work, there are limitations, which are vague and in need of more specifics (i.e., what is meant by "excessive").

Further Information Needed

From the employee. Following an explanation of our role, we would inquire as to the current status, treatment to date, and results—is condition improving? Any cervical collar? Medication and results? We would also determine prior problems with neck or back, other medical problems, any other lost-time incidents, how she relates to her supervisor, and whether there's been any contact since the accident. (We would encourage this.) We would also discuss return-to-work issues, possible transitional assignment until she feels better (for example, perhaps as a receptionist—assuming she's right-handed, she *would* have use of *this* arm—with use of telephone headset, etc.), and determine her response to this. Advise her that we will be contacting her physician and supervisor and will follow up with her as well.

From the physician(s). Explain role of case manager and our interest in assisting with resolving medical problems and an early return to work. Determine diagnosis, results of any diagnostics, treatment to date, plan for future treatment, etc. Discuss limitations as stated in release to limited duty note, offer to send job analysis for review or share actual physical requirements of employee's job as well as a modified or transitional one. Obtain more definitive information. Determine when employee is scheduled for next visit and advise that we will follow up after that.

From the employer. Determine relationship with employee (i.e., is she a good worker, length of employment). Obtain physical requirements of position (Job Analysis, if available) to be able to share with treating MD. Determine willingness to have employee return to work in a transitional assignment (i.e., reduced hours, varied job duties—employee could use calculator with right hand—perhaps a project involving adding columns of numbers, or filing, taking dictation). Discuss reduced hours/days (which would also allow for treatment), avoidance of typing, use of headset for phone time, etc. Advise that we will be back in touch as soon as we have additional information.

Using the *Medical Disability Advisor* as a guide for estimated length of disability/duration, this woman has approached the estimated 1-week duration. However, if no treatment has occurred, then additional time may be warranted. If no improvement has occurred, discuss with MD the possibility of referral to orthopedist or neurologist for further evaluation. There is no consideration under FMLA and no protection under ADA because injury is of limited duration and does not interfere with major life activity.

The next case management follow-up would be made with the patient as soon as information is obtained from the MD and employer, with the treating physician following the employee's next appointment and with the employer as soon as more is known regarding a return to work (3 to 5 days). We would encourage the supervisor to contact employee and vice versa.

Case #4

A 40-year-old male began an absence 2 days earlier after a driving while intoxicated (DWI) episode. The patient reports he has been ordered by the court to undergo treatment for a cocaine and alcohol problem of some 20 years' duration. In speaking to the patient, the case manager learns that as a result of angry and threatening outbursts against several coworkers and his manager, he was referred 3 months earlier for outpatient assessment and treatment. A psychiatric consultant concluded the patient suffers from a personality disorder in addition to chemical dependency. The employee indicates that after several weeks he discontinued outpatient treatment and resumed his use of alcohol and cocaine. Recently, he has had increasing displays of anger both at home and on the job, and his wife of 18 years is planning to leave him. There are no friends or family who are close to the employee, who reports that he has always preferred solitude. At the present time, the employee is experiencing disappointment and anger against company management in general, indicating they have not been supportive. He adds that he feels his anger would be overwhelming were he to lose his job.

Case Analysis

From the information given, it would appear that this 40-year-old man has a long-standing history of alcohol and cocaine abuse with at least one episode of treatment that was terminated by the employee. With a diagnosis of personality disorder, DWI, arrest and court-ordered treatment, this man is clearly a danger to himself, others, and a threat to the workplace. The goal here would be to determine whether potential exists for treatment, rehabilitation, and return to work. Clearly, more information is needed in order to assess viability of this case. We do not know if this individual is a union employee, nor is it clear how long this individual has been an employee or whether his substance abuse problems have resulted in work-related problems. In this instance, and to determine extent of the problem prior to contact with the employee, the employer would be contacted first.

Further Information Needed

From the employer. We would determine prior lost-time incidents, any involvement with an employee assistance program, union versus management status, any prior alcohol/substance abuse treatment, length of employment, and any prior disciplinary actions. Assuming that there have been no prior disciplinary actions, we would attempt to proceed with resolving the multiple problems.

From the employee. We would contact the employee, explaining our role and the purpose of our intervention. We would express our concern for him, emphasizing the seriousness of the situation and its impact on his well-being and his job. We would determine his interest in accepting help and pursuing discussion of an inpatient program to address his substance abuse and other emotional issues. Because he has been ordered by the court into a program, we would assist him with compliance and entry into an appropriate program. An outpatient program will not be successful, and it will be important for him to recognize this and the responsibility he must now assume to confront and resolve these issues. We would assure him that our involvement will continue and, when appropriate, a return to work would be considered.

From the physician(s). We would contact the treating psychiatrist and obtain prior history, treatment, etc., explaining our role and expressing the concerns of the employer and its interest in attempting to assist in expediting appropriate treatment and possible return to work. We would determine the duration of in-patient and outpatient treatment needed and advise that we would assist as indicated. We would also contact the court officer to determine whether a specific facility/program was mandated and coordinate referrals as needed.

We would suggest 4 weeks to allow for treatment. At this time, the employee is not an appropriate candidate for return to work; he is a danger to himself as well as his coworkers. Assuming his supervisor has been advised of the DWI and related problems, he or she would be told of the planned treatment and proba-ble duration of disability. This individual would not qualify for leave under FMLA; however, if he successfully completed treatment, he may qualify for ADA rea-sonable accommodation.

The next case management follow-up would be made with the patient in 1 week or sooner, as indicated, and with the treating physician and employer in 1 week. To facilitate return to work and case closure, we would maintain contact, encour-aging communication among all parties.

Case #5

A 42-year-old male employee has been absent for 7 days. The employee is being treated by a psychiatrist who indicates he is "not fit for duty" because of stress. Upon initial contact, the employee states he had worked as a manager for 5 years, applied for a manager's position with the same company but at another location within the state, and was hired. However, his local management stated they couldn't transfer him for business reasons. The employee decided to return to his former craft position, which was approved by management. After the employee worked as an operator for approximately 3 months, he announced his intentions of running for a union position. A week after this announcement, local management informed him they had erroneously approved his retreat to his craft position and that he must be reinstated to his former managerial posi-tion. The employee feels angry and humiliated. He states "this situation is a con-spiracy" and that both "management and the union are after me."

Case Analysis

It would appear that the employee's disability status is interestingly related to a labor relations matter. "Not fit for duty" is an ambiguous term and would not sup-port a continued period of disability. The case manager would work quickly to address and hopefully resolve the issues. However, further information is needed. This would appear to be a nonmedical issue with the potential for being problematic without prompt resolution.

Further Information Needed

After we have spoken with the employee and explained the role of case manager, we would proceed with a call to the employer. We would discuss the information as told by the employee with our contact at the employer and/or its labor relations person (if known), and advise that this is a possible labor/management issue requiring some mediation. We would request employer assistance with this prior to further involvement. Because the employee is already feeling that "management and the union are after me," further contact with his treating psychiatrist may be viewed by this man as "harassment."

If the labor/management issue was irresolvable or would be over a protracted period of time, then, as directed by the employer, we could proceed with disability determination. We would advise, however, that an independent medical exam, etc., could heighten employee anger. There is no consideration for FMLA or ADA.

The next case management follow-up would be made with the employee and the treating psychiatrist as directed by the employer, and with the employer within a few days. We would continue to assist the employer with mediation efforts as directed. If indeed this is a labor issue, we would close the file.

NOTES

1. Excerpted from *Case Management Practice,* "Interpersonal Skills for Case Managers," Foundation for Rehabilitation Certification, Education, and Research, pp. 120–122, © 1993.

2. The Reinertsen Group, *Doing Well by Doing Good: Improving the Business Case for Quality* (Alta, Wyoming: 2003).

3. *Case Management Practice,* 118.

4. G. Dearing, "Improving Patient Compliance in the Best Interests of All," *Managed Healthcare News* 12, no. 12 (1996): 1, 15–16.

5. L. Hoffmann, "Practical Tips to Help You Master Telephonic CM," *Case Management Advisor* 8, no. 2 (1997): 29–30. (For more information, please call 800-688-2421.)

6. "Interpersonal Skills," 119.

7. A. G. Gosfield, "The 1995 Legal Clinic," presented at the Medical Case Management Conference VII, New Orleans, LA, October 1995, and Gosfield, "Guidelines," 106.

Appendix 9–A CMSA Standards of Practice for Case Management

II. Standards of Care

A. Client Identification and Selection for Case Management Services

The first step in the case management process is to identify those individuals who can most benefit from case management services. Identification of clients for case management services is accomplished through methods and tools that include, but are not limited to, health-risk screening tools, evidence-based criteria, risk stratification through data management, and referrals.

Determining whether a client is appropriate for case management services is achieved by gathering and critically assessing relevant, comprehensive information and data, so that clients are selected according to case management potential to influence positive outcomes. The case manager may or may not participate in client identification or in determining whether the client meets criteria for case management services. Rather, clients may be mandated to receive case management services based upon disease state, age, payer, potential for high cost, etc.

MEASUREMENT GUIDELINES

The case manager will seek to:

1. Evaluate pro-active triggers (such as criteria related to diagnosis, clinical condition, complications, or cost) to identify potential clients suitable for effective case management intervention

2. Consider strategies of predictive modeling, when available, including emerging technologies (i.e., neural networks that predict high-cost populations)

3. Conduct a thorough and systematic evaluation of the client's current status using standardized tools when appropriate, including the following components:

   - Physical/functional
   - Psychosocial
   - Behavioral
   - Environmental/residential
   - Family dynamics and support
   - Spiritual
   - Cultural
   - Financial
   - Vocational and/or educational
   - Recreational/leisure pursuits
   - Caregiver(s) capability and availability
   - Learning capabilities/self care
   - Health status expectation and goals
   - Transitional or discharge plan
   - Legal

4. Assess resource utilization and cost management; the diagnosis, past and present treatment course and services; prognosis, goals (short/long term), treatment, and provider options

5. Engage reliable and valid assessment steps to identify and select clients for case management services

B. Problem Identification

Utilizing objective data gathered through careful assessment and examination of the potential for effective intervention, the case manager identifies problems requiring case management intervention, reflecting practice patterns and trends wherein client outcomes can be positively influenced. Client/family participation is an essential element in problem identification.

MEASUREMENT GUIDELINES

The case manager will seek to identify opportunities for intervention, i.e., when there is:

- Lack of an established treatment plan with specific goals

- Compromised patient safety

- Over-utilization of services or use of multiple providers/agencies

- Under-utilization of services

- Premature or delayed discharge from appropriate level of care

- Use of inappropriate services

- Ineffective treatment plan

- Permanent or temporary alterations in functioning

- High-cost injuries or illnesses

- Non-adherence to treatment or medications

- Medical/psychological/functional complications

- Lack of education of disease course/process

- Lack of resolution in meeting health needs

- Lack of family/social support

- Lack of financial resources to meet health needs

The case manager will also seek to determine patterns of care that may lead a client into a case management program, which may include involvement in analysis of the patterns of care or behavior that may be associated with progression to severe disease.

C. Planning

The case manager, in collaboration with the client/family and members of the healthcare team, identifies immediate, short-term, and ongoing needs as well as develops appropriate and necessary case management strategies to address them. The case manager communicates with the client/family about which case management strategies will be implemented in the plan of care. The case manager assists the client/family in making informed decisions when developing this plan of care. The case management plan identifies measurable goals and time frames for achieved goals that are appropriate to the individual, his/her family, and agreed to by the client/family and treatment team. Distinction should be made between process and end-point goals. The case manager identifies funding and/or community resources that are available to implement the plan.

MEASUREMENT GUIDELINES

The case manager will seek to:

1. Interview, research, and otherwise gather relevant, comprehensive information and data to establish the factual and clinical basis upon which to develop an appropriate plan of care

2. Understand the client's diagnosis, prognosis, care needs, and outcome goals of the plan of care

3. Implement cost-savings strategies when possible, while considering the policy/benefits available to the client

4. Proactively identify situations that are, or may become, barriers to goal attainment

5. Work toward resolution of conflicts and problem solving

6. Involve the client/family and the healthcare team in the ongoing plan of care

7. Identify goals and related indicators for successful planning and implementation, such as clinical stability or client adherence to treatments and medications

D. Monitoring

The case manager employs a process of ongoing assessment and documentation to monitor the quality of care, services and products delivered to the client to determine if the goals of the plan of care are being achieved, whether those goals remain appropriate and realistic, and what actions may be implemented to enhance positive outcomes.

MEASUREMENT GUIDELINES

The case manager will seek to:

1. Maintain professional collaboration and communication with the client and family to the extent possible, so that important information regarding the client's health status and the impact on the goals and outcome of the care plan can be disclosed

2. Maintain professional collaboration and communication with the members of the healthcare team so that the plan of care can be discussed objectively, problems can be identified, and adjustments can be made to the plan as needed

3. Maintain regular communication with pertinent healthcare providers regarding client transition across settings, barriers to care/services, and strategies or plan revisions that are needed. Ascertain that the goals of the care plan are appropriate, understood, documented, and are being met. Also advise the providers of adjustments or revisions to be made in the care plan

4. Compare the client's care plan to evidence-based guidelines, when available, to determine variances and offer solutions or adjustments to the plan of care when variances exist or when otherwise appropriate

5. Review pertinent statistics to perform a comprehensive and independent assessment of the client's status and progress toward reaching the goals set forth in the care plan

6. Implement a data-tracking mechanism, when available, to determine goals that were met versus not met and to review safety indicators

E. Evaluating

The case manager employs a methodology designed to measure healthcare and case management processes focusing on the client's response to the case management plan. The evaluation process occurs over specific time frames and is a continuous process. The evaluation engages the client/family whenever possible, as well as the healthcare team, to appropriately determine the impact of case management and healthcare interventions on outcomes.

MEASUREMENT GUIDELINES

The case manager will seek to:

1. Identify when a client's condition has reached a static or regressive situation and proactively facilitate adjustments in the care plan, providers, and/or services, when possible, to promote enhanced outcomes

2. Focus efforts on maintaining the stability of the client's/family's home environment

3. Utilize knowledge of patterns in the stabilization, recovery process and resource use of individual clients to help revise standards of care for populations of clients

F. Outcomes

Case management is a goal-directed process. The case manager identifies and implements changes in practice patterns and in the plan of care to produce outcomes that are positive, measurable and goal-oriented.

MEASUREMENT GUIDELINES

The case manager will seek to:

1. Plan with the client/family using a goal-oriented care process that analyzes and gives direction to a plan of care that moves the client toward health, wellness, safety, adaptation, self-care, and/or (re)habilitation

2. Establish measurable case management goals which promote evaluation of the access, cost, and quality of the care provided

3. Identify the achievement of goals and differentiate those goals that directly resulted from the case manager's interventions

4. Report quantifiable impact, quality of care, and/or quality of life improvements as measured against the case management goals

5. Focus on accountability for quality care and/or cost benefit to clients that are reasonably consistent with payer, provider, and consumer expectations

6. Recommend referral sources based on evaluation of the provider's quality of care and the ability to meet the client's needs

7. Maximize client outcomes through incorporating community-based and non-benefit related services whenever possible

---

Source: Reprinted with permission, Case Management Society of America, 8201 Cantrell Road, Ste 230, Little Rock, AR 72227-2448; www.cmsa.org.

CHAPTER 10

Integrated Case Management: Preadmission, Concurrent Review, Utilization Review, Disease Management, and Case Management

There are several methodologies available to identify individuals who could benefit from case management intervention. The line of insurance and the structure and sophistication of a claims department affect which "red flags" are used. Some claims departments contract for review services, whereas others depend on in-house capabilities.

Generally speaking, reviews are either prospective (before the event, called preadmission or precertification), concurrent (during the event), or retrospective (after the event). All these types of reviews are basically forms of utilization review. The purpose of utilization review is to evaluate the necessity, appropriateness, and efficiency of the use of medical services.

Each type of review utilizes certain criteria to determine whether there is a need for further action, decision, or intervention. For instance, an organization that provides retrospective claim review services might review all surgical claims that are over $10,000 and include more than three Current Procedural Terminology (CPT) codes. These factors suggest a potentially unbundled claim, and the action warranted is a review by a utilization review nurse or physician. Another indicator might be an inpatient hospital bill with a disproportionately large pharmacy charge, which suggests a potential overcharge; the action warranted is a hospital bill audit. The review process itself can also be used to identify cases for case management if the organization reviewer is aware of the red flags (e.g., multiple hospital admissions, certain ICD-9 diagnostic codes, claims for apnea alarms, electric hospital beds, infusion care services).

The problem with retrospective reviews is that the services have already occurred and are now being billed. Occasionally, the best that can be gained is a minimal discount, perhaps for a prompt-pay arrangement (invoices earmarked by the case manager to be paid within 2 or 3 weeks). It is always preferable to be positioned from strength, and this is the case if one is aware of services *before* they are implemented rather than after. From a case management perspective, the opportunity to explore alternatives is already absent when the case manager is confronted with a claim for $60,000 resulting from a hospital stay of 28 days. Could the patient have gone to a skilled facility for two of those weeks? Were nursing and other services in the home a possibility? And with these as alternatives, would there have been fee negotiations as well? These are now questions without answers. What to do with the $60,000 bill? Can the carrier get a prompt-pay discount? Was there overbilling? These savings, if possible at all, pale by comparison to what could have been!

Review of services prospectively and concurrently, on the other hand, presents the best opportunity for a successful case management intervention. How this process works varies from company to company, but in my mind there is no reason to have preadmission or concurrent review other than to identify at the earliest opportunity potentially high-cost cases and then intervene.

It is amazing to me that carriers, Third Party Administrators, managed care organizations, and employer groups often set up a precertification or preadmission review* program without linking it to some kind of case management program. They perform reviews in a management vacuum and then assume that there are no savings to be gained. Several companies have discontinued their use because "they didn't save us any money." And, indeed, they will not, other than those possibly realized through the denial of a few days in a hospital or avoidance of an inpatient stay when a day-op procedure is indicated. (However, day-op procedures at ambulatory surgicenters are often much more costly than an inpatient stay would have been. This is because of the lack of reasonable and customary charges for surgicenter facilities.) Without a connection to case management, preadmission review accomplishes nothing more than maintaining a census of inpatient admissions. And preadmission review alone, without concurrent review, is incapable of reducing lengths of stay or allowing alternative care plans to be considered.

Let us assume that there is an understanding of the value of preadmission and concurrent review and a case management program, which is now the case where managed care is well-established. Many companies are looking for care networks

---

*In my company, we have avoided the use of the term *precertification* because it implies approval or denial of the proposed admission and related services and payment for them. As we believe the Plan makes these decisions, ours is an advisory notification program.

in which utilization review is offered as part of a health care package, including some type of preadmission review and case management, and many UR providers that began as companies offering retroactive review of medical bills now offer case management, disease management, demand management, and provider profiling. Who should provide the services, how should they be provided, and what, if any, should the guidelines and procedures be? Are there standards of practice, and what should the results be? Fortunately, there are some established standards and guidelines as well as organizations that continue to evaluate and review existing and developing programs. Now in its eighth edition, *Milliman Care Guidelines* includes clinical indications, care pathways, benchmarks, nationally recognized guidelines, and current medical research. Other groups providing care guidelines include the National Institutes of Health, the National Committee for Quality Assurance, Value Health Sciences of Santa Monica, California, and Interqual. The Agency for Healthcare Research and Quality web site (www.ahcpr.gov) offers an online database of health care quality measures (National Quality Measures Clearinghouse™), studies and projects on measuring health care quality and quality indicators.

I believe that the maximum opportunity for success exists when one organization provides preadmission and concurrent review along with case management services. Too often, one company does the reviewing and another provides the case management. The delays that inevitably occur between identifying a high-cost case, referring it to a case management vendor, assigning the case, and actually managing the case make the system ineffective, rather than an ongoing process of evaluation, identification, assessment, planning, and implementation that could be the ideal. The key in case management is how the case manager gets involved and how soon. For example, one has missed an opportunity if a case manager starts working with a spinal cord-injured patient 20 or 30 days after the initial hospitalization. Earlier involvement could have resulted in a transfer of this patient to a spinal cord injury treatment center and the prevention of some of the complications that have now occurred, which will be more costly to treat and prolong the period of rehabilitation.

So, let us once again make some assumptions and create the ideal program within one organization. To illustrate how this process could work, let's "take a walk through" the system.

INTRODUCING UTILIZATION REVIEW TO CLIENT GROUPS AND PLAN PARTICIPANTS

Let us suppose that a single organization intends to offer a combination preadmission review, concurrent review, case management, and disease management program. The first step in selling and implementing this program is to explain it to potential clients and the plan participants. If these individuals do not understand its purpose, its full benefits will not be realized. Over the years, I have seen various techniques utilized in an effort to implement such programs. These range from mandating cooperation, to penalizing by reducing the percentage of benefit reimbursement, to denying benefits altogether. Although the policy language needs to have some "teeth" to encourage participation, I think proactively positioning the services has a better chance of achieving success in the long run.

In today's environment, in which virtually everyone appreciates not just the cost of the health care system but its complexity as well, communicating the concept of a preadmission, concurrent review, disease management, and case management program is not really difficult. The intent very simply is to very proactively identify at the earliest opportunity patients or situations that could benefit from the intervention of a case manager. The program should be flexible and fast-moving enough to move the patient who needs it into case management as soon as possible. If concern for patients is seen as the focus, then enlisting cooperation becomes easier.

Case managers should be positioned as advocates and facilitators who have the expertise to understand and the ability to effect change. They assist patients by getting information and expediting the delivery of services. To perform their functions effectively, they need a system that allows involvement to occur at the optimum time. Because a seemingly simple admission or "routine" operative procedure can unexpectedly become complex and expensive, each admission needs to be reviewed as it occurs. This does not mean that each will require intervention by a case manager; in fact, most will not. But the strategy of reviewing each leads to the best outcomes for patients and payers.

Not long ago, I was meeting with two client groups. The first was considering having their claims staff handle all of the preadmission notification calls; they would refer to our case management department those cases they thought would be appropriate for our case management services. The second client group was prepared to suggest to its employer groups that they should notify its preadmission and concurrent review providers only of "serious conditions." It became clear to me that we, as the case management providers, were going to be disadvantaged by this incorrect perception of the process. Some further education was obviously necessary.

I took a sampling of the first client group's preadmission forms. It was soon apparent that some of the cases it would have identified were not appropriate for case management, whereas others that would have been overlooked required intervention. As an example, one admission for "abdominal pain" turned out to be a malignancy of the pancreas; the patient eventually went home after a 3-week hospital stay, with nursing and infusion care services arranged by the hospital (the infusion care services were referred to a physician-owned provider). Appropriate case management intervention would have served both the patient and the payer in this case.

The second client group, after a similar discussion, soon realized that each individual has a different perception of what constitutes a "serious condition" and that, in fact, it was not only the "condition" that might signal a problem, but other factors as well (e.g., multiple admissions, several seemingly "minor" medical conditions but only one admission, prior history). Through an education process, both client groups were soon able not only to understand the scope and value of an integrated preadmission and concurrent review and case management approach, but also to develop an appreciation of its complexity, which allowed them to implement a total and integrated system.

Whether by brochure, newsletter, flyer, meetings, or some other format, a program overview needs to be communicated. The sample cases presented in Figure 10–1 and Figure 10–2 were created for our clients to illustrate what would probably occur with and without an integrated system in place. Table 10–1 is a letter designed to be sent to plan participants to acknowledge notification of hospital admission and explain the advocacy role of the case manager and the nature of the case management process. Table 10–2 is a description of our company and its services that we send to communicate to employees, in layman's terms, the process of case management when a union, TPA, or insurer puts case management services in place. This always accompanies a letter such as the one shown in Table 10–1.

THE PREADMISSION AND CONCURRENT REVIEW PROCESS

Each preadmission and concurrent review process differs depending upon client group specifications and the line of insurance involved. For example, a nurse reviewer for workers' compensation may inquire as to the estimated return-to-work date or work restrictions (e.g., no lifting), whereas a nurse reviewer for a group medical plan does not need such information. (However, some information is requested in both types of review.) It is essential to develop a format to gather the necessary data and organize them so that they will be useful in evaluating and identifying cases with potential for case management intervention. There are software systems that have been developed for this purpose, although an organization might elect to develop its own system.

Each system, manual or computerized, should allow for the input of a professional (nurse or physician). Although standardized questions and data are useful, each patient presents unique problems and symptoms. There needs to be sufficient flexibility to accommodate the differences. If a form or artificial intelligence (computer) system includes only set questions, it is impossible to discover

Figure 10–1 Case Sample with and without Preadmission Review, Concurrent Review, and Case Management

Exhibit A

Mr. Jones enters the hospital as recommended by his physician for diagnosis of pneumonia. As prescribed by his medical plan, he contacts ABC Insurance Co. to advise of his scheduled admission. ABC's representative obtains basic information concerning hospital, treating physician, and possibly the proposed length of stay for this admission (5 days).

The notification procedure is completed, there is no follow-up of this patient, and eventually this individual will be discharged.

The hospital claim is eventually received by ABC, and it is then noted that the actual stay was for 21 days at a cost of $45,000.

Exhibit B

Mr. Jones, as prescribed by his medical plan, contacts ABC Insurance Co. to advise of his scheduled admission, and the representative obtains information concerning diagnosis, length of stay, name of treating physician, hospital, etc. This information is then faxed to Options Unlimited, where it is screened for follow-up.

The Options Unlimited nurse contacts the patient and treating physician, and obtains additional information, including prior medical history, other hospital admissions, etc. She is in agreement with the treating physician for length of stay (LOS for this man would be 5 days).

Now on day 5, Options Unlimited nurse contacts hospital utilization review nurse to determine if, in fact, patient will be discharged. Utilization review nurse advises that there was not a good result thus far with current antibiotic and further hospitalization was indicated. Options Unlimited nurse confers with treating physician, who discusses further and hopes that an additional 3 days will result in success.

Options Unlimited nurse contacts treating MD who reports continued lack of response and additional complications. He will try a different antibiotic, will need perhaps another 7–10 days of hospitalization.

Due to extended stay, requests for additional days, and uncertain treatment plan, decision made to refer for on-site case management assessment.

Figure 10–1 continued

Visit by case manager to patient and treating physician uncovers additional problems but result is that MD agrees to discharge patient home on IV antibiotics (rather than continue inpatient stay).

The patient is discharged to his home on day 9 of this hospital admission. Antibiotic therapy and nursing services are provided in his home. The Options Unlimited case manager has arranged the services with the input from the MD, negotiated the fees for these services, and monitored the patient for the desired outcome and eventual discontinuation of these services. Following a 10-day course at home, he is switched to antibiotics by mouth and permitted to return to work.

Results

Action:	Pay claim (obtain discount if possible, audit the claim) of $45,000.00
Savings:	None
Questions:	1) Were all the costs necessary?
	2) Was a 21-day stay necessary?
	3) Were there other alternatives?

Results

Pay:	Hospital claim of $19,278.00
Pay:	Claim for home antibiotic therapy and nursing services of $3,000.00 ($300/day × 10 days).
Pay:	Case management fees of $800.00
Total:	$23,078.00
Savings:	$21,922.00
Questions:	Were the costs appropriate? Yes
	Were the patient and the plan well served? Yes

Source: Courtesy of Options Unlimited, Case Management Services Division, 2003, Huntington, New York.

Figure 10–2 Case Sample with and without Preadmission Review, Concurrent Review, and Case Management

Exhibit A

Mr. Jones sustains an injury to his right knee following a fall from a ladder and reports the injury. He is out of work for 1 week and his supervisor has not heard from him or when he is coming back. The worker's family MD is treating the injury conservatively with rest and minimal activity. It is 3 weeks later and the supervisor now hears from the worker's coworkers that there is an infection in the knee and the worker is scheduled for a surgical procedure. No date for return to work is known. Another week passes, the worker is out of the hospital but still having problems. The supervisor does not know what the problems are but the worker's prolonged absence is increasing the workload on the department, and the supervisor is behind on his work (trying to keep peace and help out himself). It is now 6 weeks since this "little fall" (as per the supervisor) and it has gone on "too long." The treating MD has told the worker that he can go back to "light duty" and maybe his old job in another month. The supervisor tells the claims examiner there is no "light duty" and the worker continues to remain home. Someone sees the worker mowing his lawn, word reaches the employer, who notifies the claims examiner and requests surveillance. We all know where this is going, don't we?

Exhibit B

Mr. Jones sustains an injury to his right knee following a fall from a ladder. As is required, he reports the injury to his supervisor. The supervisor advises him that a case manager will be contacting him to help him get appropriate care, answer questions he may have, and assist him in returning to work. Options Unlimited's case manager contacts the injured worker and learns that he has sustained a 4-inch laceration to the knee, which required several stitches in the Emergency Room. She also learned during her phone assessment with the employer that he was unclear as to the care of the wound, what dressing was needed, or how often it should be changed. He also did not know the signs of infection to check for and had not yet scheduled a follow-up visit with his family MD. Because the case manager asked about prior medical history, she discovered that the worker had a "little bit of diabetes" (this as per the worker) and was lacking knowledge about this disease and, in fact, was told he had cataracts and that his vision is a little "blurry."

The case manager assessed the following as problems:

• A large laceration, requiring daily dressing changes and inspection of the wound
• Condition of cataracts that resulted in blurred vision and the inability to detect subtle changes in the wound
• Unmanaged diabetes, which prolongs and complicates the wound-healing process

Figure 10–2 continued

The case manager implemented the following:

- Skilled nursing visits daily to inspect wound, change the dressing and assess diabetic care needs
- Referral to physician the following day (after explaining risk factors for infection to office nurse)
- Call to supervisor apprising him of status of employee. During this call, obtained description of employee's job (physical demands, etc.), discussed some possible modifications to be considered, and suggested a call to the worker by the supervisor to "touch base," assure concern, and wish well.

Within a week, healing was progressing well and following calls to employee and treating MD, it was determined that worker could return to work as long as he did not have to use a ladder or work in a crouched position.

The supervisor was able to modify worker's position (climbing the ladder was needed only occasionally and another worker could do this; crouching position was done rarely and this, too, could be done by another). Employee could also be checked daily by the company nurse, who will also monitor his diabetes.

Eleven days after the injury, the employee returned to a modified form of his job. The case manager maintained contact with all parties, insured that the wound was completely healed in 3 weeks, and the worker could return to all of his duties.

continues

Figure 10–2 continued

Exhibit A

Costs:
Medical: Hospital admission for wound infection and IV antibiotics; wound incisions and drainage.
Hospital @ $1500 × 7 days = $10,500
Surgery: $2,500
Physical therapy, 3 times a week × 4 weeks (and continuing) = $900.00
IV antibiotics @ home following hospital stay @ $550/day plus nursing visit @ $140/visit × 7 = $4,830
MD fees = $2,000
Replacement of earnings @ $450/week × 6 = $2,700
Medical: $20,730.00 and continuing
Lost earnings $2,700.00 and continuing
Total costs $23,430.00
Indirect costs:
Decreased productivity
Litigation
Employee morale
AND IT'S NOT OVER.....!

Results

Increased costs
An employee with continuing medical complications
Adversarial relationship between employer/employee
Pending litigation
Decreased productivity
Decreased morale

Exhibit B

Costs:
Medical: Nursing visits for wound care/dressing changes @ negotiated rate of $75 × 10 days = $750.00
MD fees—2 visits for wound care/diabetic management = $200
Replacement of Earnings @ $450/week × 2 = $900.00
Total Costs: $1,650.00*

Results

Savings (Net): $20,780*

Actual costs and case management fees were deducted from costs of case that would have occurred **as in Exhibit A.**

A **productive employee** with a better outcome and the recipient of a true advocacy program.

A business that can return to its own business needs and goals.

*Case management is another cost consideration, but in this kind of case, managed early would be less than $1,000.00.

Source: Courtesy of Options Unlimited, Case Management Services Division, 2003, Huntington, New York.

Table 10–1 Letter Acknowledging Prenotification of Hospital Admission and Explaining Case Management to Plan Participants

---

Employee's ID#:
Physician:
Hospital:
Date of Admission:
Employer Group:

To:

We received notification of the above hospital admission on _____. Please be advised that this is an advisory notice only and does not imply payment of the claim/bill that will be received for this hospital confinement. It further does not imply payment for any of the services that may be related to the confinement, for example, surgeon, anesthesia, and so on.

A Nurse Case Manager will be following the patient's progress during the hospital stay. It is also possible that a Nurse Case Manager may be in contact with you either via telephone or in person, should this seem appropriate.

All claims received by the plan administrator for _____ will be reviewed and considered and will be subject to the terms of your medical plan. This includes but is not limited to preexisting conditions, plan limitations and exclusions, cosmetic vs. medical need, uncovered services, etc., co-payments and deductibles.

If there are any changes in the case-related information above, please notify the Nurse Case Manager at 1-800-555-1212. If you have any additional questions or concerns about this or other medical matters, please feel free to call us.

Thank you in advance for your anticipated cooperation.

Very truly yours,

Nurse Case Manager, Options Unlimited
cc: File @ S.L.01437

Source: Courtesy of Options Unlimited, Case Management Services Division, 2003, Huntington, New York.

---

all the situations and variables that might demand special attention. Even some very sophisticated software programs do not, unfortunately, allow for a patient-specific approach, thereby preventing consideration of the kinds of factors that would indicate the need for additional intervention. Systems cannot manage all people appropriately and successfully all the time. Case management addresses those issues that care paths and care maps can often overlook: multiple conditions, financial funding problems, and social/cultural issues.

Table 10–2 Sample Description of Case Management Services for Employee/
Patient Populations

OPTIONS UNLIMITED

Solving Problems Is What We Do Best

At Options Unlimited, we've been helping people across the country understand
their medical choices, evaluate their care options, and find solutions in tough
medical situations for over 20 years. We're a full-service medical case management and benefits consulting firm. We work with you, your employer, and your
insurer to make sure your medical treatment is appropriate and progresses as it
should.

You might talk to one of our nurses on the phone regarding a hospital admission
of an anticipated birth. In complex cases such as cancer, cardiovascular disease, AIDS, a stroke, transplant, head or spinal cord injury, or a high-risk pregnancy, one of our case managers will arrange to meet with you personally to
help coordinate care for you or someone else covered by your health care plan.

You don't pay for our case management services; they are offered in conjunction
with your health care plan. And our services are voluntary. We *can help* you get
the best, most appropriate, and most cost-effective care, but you do not have to
use our services. Most important to you, we keep all personal information
regarding you and your health in strictest confidence.

We work as advocates for patients, focusing on each individual case to explain
the diagnosis and what it means for today and tomorrow. We take the lingo out
of insurance plans and forms, arrange for home-care services, locate alternate
treatment facilities or rehabilitation service—sometimes we even help sort out all
the medications, or the bills! The one thing we don't do is provide hands-on
care. We don't take the place of your physicians; we work as partners with your
physicians, making sure that you and your family members get all the care you
need when you need it.

We look forward to helping you receive more personalized medical care.

Source: Courtesy of Options Unlimited, Case Management Services Division, 2003,
Huntington, New York.

All too often, we see utilization reviewers in a care management department
talking to the utilization reviewers in the hospital. Most UR reviewers never see
the patient. Utilization management looks at fees, access, frequency, and duration
of care and services, and identifies which services, providers, and patients are
most costly. To do this, standards, guidelines, and criteria are used to authorize
and manage the delivery of services. Among the drawbacks of utilization man-

agement without preadmission review is that it is reactive and often retrospective. It invites litigation, lacks consistency in administration from company to company and region to region, and views the service and costs (benefit management) rather than patients (care management). No one is talking to the patient, getting a history of the case, learning what the prognosis is, or introducing the role of a case manager.

Notification that a patient is about to enter the hospital, or that a physician has called in for a plan member's hip replacement, is an ideal time to bring in a case manager. A hip implant is not, generally speaking, emergency surgery; however, the case manager might discover that this individual is also a diabetic with hypertension, and at risk for deep vein thrombosis or a pulmonary embolism. She can help prepare the patient for surgery, discuss expectations and post-op recovery time frames, and educate him toward compliance with the treatment plan.

If a healthy baby program is not in place, or the preadmission plan requires only that patients call 2 weeks before their due date, the care management team misses a chance to assist mother and fetus. A quick conversation during the first trimester can uncover any risk factors and identify those pregnant women who should be in case management.

Each case will not call for case management intervention, but being part of the review process early on allows a case manager to determine this in a timely manner.

A key to success is the reviewer's skill in conducting a more comprehensive questioning process. Beyond the general concern (and regrettably, sometimes the only concern) for length of stay, it is important to look for comorbidities. Is there another condition already present that might lead to difficulties or episodes that can be prevented before they happen? What is the medical history attached to this case? Is this a readmission for a chronic condition? We will want to assign the same reviewer to a case that has frequent readmissions; this person knows the patient, family, and history, and can be more effective more quickly than someone taking the information for the first time.

Some plans include a prenotification requirement for certain high-cost equipment and services: all monitors, oxygen contractors, apnea alarms, infusion services, chemotherapy, and more. The emphasis today, and the reason behind the requirement, is eligibility for coverage. Our reasoning should be, is this the beginning of a problem? With a call for such types of equipment, we know something is going on. Get behind the request. Is the equipment needed for a lung cancer patient or is it for short-term use? Perhaps the equipment or service is for therapy, but it might be for someone in the final stage of cancer whose family is actively seeking admission to a hospice program.

After the basic information is obtained (including admitting diagnosis, length of stay, and treatment plan), there needs to be a determination as to follow-up in the review process. If a length of stay is estimated to be five days, there should be a follow-up call on day four, or certainly day five, to determine whether, in fact, the discharge will occur as planned. Although some management groups review every case every single day, I believe this to be extreme and, in many cases, a waste of time almost bordering on harassment of the hospital staff, especially when individuals designated as "case managers" are doing nothing more than tracking LOS for the sole purpose of denying days. Further, an administrative clerk lacks the expertise to recognize possible red flags in the hospital nurse's responses, ask the appropriate follow-up questions, and get more involved in the case. In both cases, every opportunity has been lost for intervention and potential improvements in patient care and expenditures in the long term.

We want to review the appropriate case at the appropriate time for the appropriate reasons. Could anything different be done toward a positive result? A diary system, whether electronic or otherwise, helps schedule and manage hospital reviews. If it becomes obvious during the first call that the patient will require ICU care for the next 3 days, a call can be "diaried" for day four.

If discharge is scheduled, will there be a need for any further services at home (e.g., nursing visits, physical therapy, or chemotherapy)? How was the hospital stay? Were there any problems or new conditions discovered? Is further testing required? What are postdischarge arrangements? Is a transfer to a different facility now scheduled? Is a follow-up call to the patient or to family members indicated to determine their understanding of the diagnosis or ability to cooperate with the discharge instructions? Were they, in fact, even aware of follow-up care instructions?

This kind of involvement by a nurse reviewer can often prevent a hospital readmission resulting from the patient's lack of knowledge. Two studies reported in *The New York Times* showed that nurse home-visit programs had lasting and positive effects. In one, visiting nurses discussed nutrition, prenatal care, child development, and other issues over a 2.5-year period with women following the birth of their first child. The home visits resulted in fewer and less closely spaced pregnancies, fewer cases of child abuse and neglect, and fewer emergency room visits. In a second program, nurses visited young, poor, unmarried, pregnant women and discussed prenatal health, parenting skills, birth control, education, and job skills. At age 2, the children were less likely to be injured or hospitalized, and mothers were less likely to have pregnancy-induced high blood pressure. Overall, compared with other poor, unmarried mothers, the women in the study had 69% fewer arrests, 46% fewer reports of child abuse or neglect, 44% fewer behavioral problems linked to drug or alcohol abuse, and used 30 months less of Aid to Families with Dependent Children.[1] The benefits consulting firm Hewitt Associates reports 77% of companies offering programs including well-baby or child care, prenatal care, disease management, and flu vaccinations, up from 71% in 1996.[2]

(For every $6 flu vaccination, $40 is saved because employees are at work, not home in bed.[3])

A follow-up call to the treating physician by a nurse reviewer to share a discovered problem is always welcome and helps establish a productive collaboration between two professionals who want a good outcome for the patient. Necessary services can be arranged with the client group's PPO network or at a negotiated rate. Continued case management involvement additionally provides the ability to oversee treatment effectiveness and continued need.

As noted earlier, it is not necessary to review every hospitalized patient every day, especially in a routine case such as a C-section or hip replacement. It is understood that the length of stay will be more than 1 day, and progress will follow a certain sequence. The situation in a catastrophic case is quite different. Here, day-by-day review is appropriate and beneficial, as patient events often lead to changes in treatment.

In situations in which the planned discharge will not occur, the nurse reviewer must uncover the reasons for the continued stay. Perhaps the patient developed a postoperative complication or the diagnostic studies have revealed other conditions that need further evaluation. Perhaps the patient remains medically unstable and requires the services and monitoring that only an acute care hospital could provide. For these and many other reasons, continued hospitalization is certainly warranted. Most review groups today inquire at this point as to the expected length of time that hospitalization will be necessary. Again, there are some software programs that have "built-in" norms for typical admissions, and as long as the responses fall within the norms, the stay continues to be "approved" or "certified." For the most part, hospitals and physicians are no longer guilty of over-utilizing inpatient stays. There are those patients who for a variety of very understandable reasons do not fall within the "norms." It is for these patients that discussion between nurse reviewers and/or physician reviewers and the treating physicians becomes extremely important. It usually resolves confusion and leads to a better understanding of a complex treatment plan.

Occasionally, however, a continued hospitalization is requested because of factors that could be addressed using an alternate care plan. The patient, for example, may need IV antibiotics or has no one at home to change dressings or monitor medications. Solutions in such situations include arranging for home infusion services, skilled nursing visits, and home health aide services. The expense is considerably less than a continued stay in the hospital. If the nurse reviewer determines the need and proposes an alternative to the treating physician and patient, more often than not it is approved. Knowledge of the case's status at the right time is crucial, however, to the solution and the realization of savings. Without case management review, notification of circumstances might occur but the ability to alter events will be lacking.

I have seen employer or insurer groups that have preadmission and concurrent review and case management programs but also have language in their benefit plans that works against the goal of better management of patient outcomes. For example, a plan might offer unlimited benefits for inpatient stays, payable at 80% for the first $5,000 and at 100% thereafter, but limits nursing visits to only 20 per year, 4 hours per visit, or allows nursing only if implemented within 3 days following a hospital stay. Although the group might have intended to prevent overuse of nursing services, its self-funded plan language pushes claimants and providers toward overuse of the much more expensive hospital services. An experienced case manager recognizes this as an obstacle and can assist in a modification or revision to the plan that allows more cost-effective solutions. For example, a plan could stipulate that with case management approval, certain benefits may be made available to participants. Other groups have preadmission and concurrent review nurse reviewers continue to track a lengthy hospital stay week after week, but provide no mechanism to refer patients to case managers who could implement changes.

TIMING DISEASE MANAGEMENT AND CASE MANAGEMENT INTERVENTION

At what point in the review process should a referral be made for disease management and/or case management intervention? There are some basic indicators or red flags to look for, and there are other less specific, more individualized considerations for both of these interventions. Some indicators may actually be evident during the very first call from a hospital admissions department, treating physician, or patient's family to a preadmission review department or company. Once a red flag surfaces, it is necessary to apply an amount of risk assessment to move the case into the care management program that best matches the need.

A preterm delivery, a high-risk pregnancy, a cerebral vascular accident suffered by a teenager, a spinal cord injury, or a traumatic brain injury with coma are all conditions for which there is a high probability of a lengthy hospital stay, a need for additional care and services upon discharge, high costs, and benefits to be gained through case management. For the most part, it is appropriate to refer any of these as soon as possible to case management.

Other conditions and circumstances also merit an early referral, not necessarily because of a particular diagnosis but because of surrounding circumstances. For instance, diabetes is not by itself a condition that would prompt a case management referral, but the fourth hospital admission in 2 months of a patient with diabetes might. Why are these admissions occurring so frequently? Is the patient noncompliant or noneducated? Has the patient been treated in a clinic by a different physician each time? Is the treating physician a retiring family practitioner? Perhaps an endocrinologist is needed. Is it reasonable to wait until there are additional complications? A referral to case management at this point does seem appropriate and indeed should be made.

A newly diagnosed diabetic exhibiting no problems and experiencing no episodes is a prime candidate for disease management. This program will provide the kind of assistance, resources, and education that can help avoid escalation into the following situation.

A patient with an admitting diagnosis of cellulitis may not at first glance seem appropriate for referral to case management. However, imagine that as the patient's stay in the hospital continues, more becomes known about this 46-year-old woman: She is also hypertensive, had a coronary bypass 2 years earlier, is diabetic, and weighs 320 pounds, clearly morbidly obese for her height of five feet six inches. The case is obviously complicated. For one thing, the woman eventually might require a below-knee amputation secondary to her multiple conditions. Doesn't the potential of this occurrence at least warrant an assessment by a case management professional? This patient is an ideal candidate not only for case management, but also for disease management, where she could benefit from a combination of ongoing education and behavior modification, in addition to regular, ongoing case management. Patients like this woman would likely be overlooked by a system for case management referral that was driven solely by one ICD-9 code or one set dollar limit. Yet each similar case presents such substantial opportunities for improved outcomes, prevention of complications, and reduction of expenses that not referring becomes a costly risk.

When approval for a case management referral is needed, a presentation of all pertinent information should support the request. A claims examiner or other approval source might be inclined to refuse case management for the cases just described, for example, because they do not fit the notion of an appropriate case. To avoid refusal, the case manager should be prepared to outline the problems, the costs that will be incurred if nothing is done, the solutions that could be applied, the approximate costs of the solutions (including case management fees), the length of time intervention will take, and the results that will be obtained. The object is to make the rationale clear, the savings obvious, and the approval much easier to justify.

When preadmission, concurrent review, disease management, and case management functions are provided by one organization, the transfer of information and concerns is better coordinated and can actually provide ongoing knowledge and improved control of cases. Such coordination can also avoid duplication of involvement, help a claims department manage its workload, assist in the development of prevention and wellness programs, support the evaluation of benefits use, and expose the need to redesign plans. When a nurse reviewer who has been involved throughout a complicated patient admission can share the background information she has acquired, the case manager is able to "hit the ground running."

On the other side of the "effectiveness" spectrum are disease and case management programs working in two separate silos with no coordination or communication between them. The case managers don't ask if the patient is in the disease management program, and vice versa, depriving both groups and the patient of timely intervention. Unable to track the patient fully, the potential optimal benefit from both is lost. If an organization or plan elects to use two different providers for these services, every effort should be made to integrate the knowledge and activities of both.

As a case manager, I once received a referral from a claims department after it was notified by a provider who had conducted the preadmission review 7 weeks prior and noted a diagnosis of cancer of the stomach. The end-of-the-month printout was now in the hands of the examiner, who had also just received a claim for 1 week of TPN and "other" services costing $25,000. The examiner thought a case management referral was appropriate. It was, but it came a little too late. The services continued for a second week as arranged. The provider refused to negotiate retrospectively to lower costs; he knew the services were payable at 100%. (He knew the patient's benefit plan would pay the full price for his services because he called the claims department and learned this from a customer service representative.) The patient expired following a second and final admission to the hospital. Perhaps the TPN services could have been negotiated more cost-effectively; perhaps a hospice program could have been arranged, allowing the patient to die at home with his family around him; perhaps money could have been saved, too. Perhaps, but the lack of an integrated approach prohibited the pursuit of these options. In this instance, there was preadmission and concurrent review and case management and a benefit plan that would have permitted alternatives, yet because each system functioned independently of the others, in a vacuum, realizing the alternatives was not possible.

It is clear that these utilization management functions (preadmission, concurrent review, case management) need to exist side by side, with cognizance of each other's role and an ability to interact when necessary. In addition, the newer model, disease management, needs to be an integral part of such a quality-of-care and cost-containment program.

PREADMISSION AND CONCURRENT REVIEW REPORTS

Preadmission and concurrent review summary reports (see Figure 10–3) and other documentation of case events constitute an ongoing profile of a case. Case-specific reports that include nurse case manager or case manager notes establish a case history and can be used to track the details of a case, which is especially helpful if the case changes from being low risk to being high risk. Produced for all hospital admissions, all scheduled pregnancies, and all emergency cases, case-specific reports incorporate ongoing notes made by nurse reviewers. They are valuable for internal use in a preadmission and concurrent review department, provide the rationale for case management referral, contain the background for the case manager assigned to the case, and are also forwarded to the claims examiner. (Options Unlimited developed the software for the computer-generated report presented in Figure 10–3. Not all case management departments and companies have similar computer capabilities, but the form itself is a useful tool whether it is created by a computer or not.)

The review summary report (Figure 10–3) shows that only one patient out of ten was referred for case management. One review summary report showed that there was a surprisingly high incidence of admissions for complications of pregnancy for this employer group, consisting mostly of women, and it led to the development of a maternity screening and management program and the prevention of two premature babies. The savings to the group far outweighed the costs of the managed care program.

Figure 10–3 Preadmission and Concurrent Review Summary Report

Group # - 001   Third Party Administrator   1/1/03-1/31/03

Date Reported	Emp ID#	Diagnosis	Type	Admission Date	Discharge Date	Status
1/2/03	000	Fracture	Emerg	1/1/03	1/2/03	Closed
1/3/03	000	Norm Delivery	Emerg	1/25/03		Open
1/5/03	000	Lump in Breast	Sched	1/8/03		Open
1/7/03	000	Myocardial Infar	Emerg	1/11/03	1/18/03	Refer CM
1/12/03	000	Herniated Disc	Sched	1/21/03	1/25/03	Closed
1/14/03	000	Miscarriage	Emerg	1/13/03	1/14/03	Closed
1/16/03	000	Appendicitis	Emerg	1/15/03	1/18/03	Closed
1/18/03	000	Derangement Knee	Sched	1/25/03		Open
1/25/03	000	Depression	Sched	1/28/03		Psych
1/28/03	000	Pregnancy	Sched	3/25/03		Open

Total Admissions for Period = 9   Total Discharged = 5
Total Referred for Case Management = 1
TOTAL CASES FOR PERIOD = 10

Source: Couresy of Options Unlimited, Case Management Services Division, 2003, Huntington, New York.

ESTABLISHING AN EFFECTIVE PREADMISSION REVIEW, CONCURRENT REVIEW, CASE MANAGEMENT, AND DISEASE MANAGEMENT SYSTEM

To be effective, a preadmission and concurrent review and case management system or department requires flexibility and cooperation on the part of payers and providers, benefit plan language that supports case management, and a claims administrator who understands the difference between managing benefits and managing cases. As stated previously, the only way case reviewing and case management can become truly potent is when each element is applied as part of a unified system. How should the system be set up? The first step is to look at what is in place in order to determine what is needed. Whether one is working with a Third Party Administrator, an insurance company, or a self-administered plan, the signs of a benefit and claims system in trouble are the same.

Most health insurance plans today (and with growing frequency, workers' compensation plans as well) have some form of review system in place, especially for hospital admissions. Unfortunately, too often the "notification of an admission" is the only step rather than the first step in an integrated system of review and case management. What value is it to those companies who pay for such services to require individuals to call an "800" number prior to entering a hospital or within 48 hours of an emergency admission? What purpose does it serve and what should be the result of such a notification system? It is interesting how many claims departments, Third Party Administrators, and employer groups require such a system, put one in place, and then have great difficulty describing the results. Over the last several years, it has almost become a "we have to have it" kind of service, but run with little accountability, and showing still less in terms of results.

So how can one determine whether a company or department needs a better preadmission and concurrent review and case management system? By asking the direct questions listed in the following sections.

Preadmission Review Services

Are patients required to call someone before entering the hospital? If the answer is no, then you know that there is no system in place. The result is that individuals can enter the hospital as often as they or their physicians want, stay until someone questions the hospitalization, and spend as much as may be available for hospital services.

If a notification call is required, to whom is it made? If it is to a claims department, does a claims examiner or a medical professional take the call? If it is a claims person, is the information intended to be used to decrease lengths of stay or costs, improve outcomes, or identify high-cost, complex cases? If the call goes to a medical professional in the claims department, what is done with the information? Are potential long-term cases flagged for any kind of action? Does the person taking the call have the ability to authorize case management, or is there a mechanism established to suggest a referral for case management? Dehydration or vomiting will not be a certain "red flag" to a nonclinical administration person, but an RN or case manager hearing that would pursue it with the caller to get more information, just in case there is a deeper problem.

If this kind of preadmission call is directed to a review organization, what are the results? Is the organization simply advised of the admission? Does anyone review the admissions as to their appropriateness? Are patients allowed to remain in hospitals for a fixed number of days, are they allowed to remain as long as their physicians want them there, or is each stay checked every single day, every other day, or after 7 or 10 days? In my mind, a call to the hospital every single day is a waste of time. If there is a day one, you can be assured there will be a day two.

Prenotification for all high-cost services, even if hospital admission does not occur (e.g., pregnancy monitoring, apnea alarms, IV therapy), is valuable because such services frequently signal other problems that can be successfully resolved by case management.

Proactive management of cases in the preadmission/concurrent review stage helps identify potential cases before they spiral out of control. All high-cost/problem cases eventually enter the hospital. This is an opportunity to speak to the patient, family, and physician from the start, introducing and explaining the role of case management, and if appropriate, disease management.

Concurrent Review Services

Does anyone review a hospital stay during the confinement? If so, how often are such calls made?

Does anyone from the review group ever speak with the claims department staff? Are reports available to indicate the number of admissions and readmissions and the average stay? Does a review of these reports indicate any problems (e.g., unusually long stays, unusually frequent readmissions)?

Does anyone authorize continued stays and, if so, what criteria are utilized? Again, some review services have a software program that uses a series of questions; depending on the answers, the system allows or denies extra days. Other review services utilize predetermined medical criteria and a professional reviewer. Use of software systems alone may result in arbitrary decisions and prevent consideration of individual patient needs. The ideal review program assessment combines industry standards and norms and professional interaction with the patient, physician, and family.

What happens beyond hospitalization, when the patient returns home? Is concurrent review extended? Does anyone track the patient's progress to prevent readmission?

Case Management Services

Assuming that the preadmission and concurrent review services are appropriate, what happens when a "red flag" indicating a possible need for case management is identified? What are the red flags? To whom is the information communicated and when? Is the claims department notified by phone or by report? What then is done with the information?

If there is some kind of notification, is the case referred to case management services? Are the case management services affiliated with the review group or provided by another company?

How long does this process take? Too long an interval reduces the opportunities for timely intervention and cost containment.

How many cases are actually case managed? Does this match the industry standard (3% to 5% of a group have potential for case management), or is the number higher or lower than would be expected?

What kinds of cases are managed? What are the results and the costs? Are any arranged services discounted or are fees negotiated? Are savings reports submitted? What are the costs for case management compared with the savings attained? If several nurses in several departments are each performing an activity of case management for one or a series of patients, case management is not being practiced. Case management is practiced when all activities of case management are integrated into one care plan, directed by one case manager across the continuum of care for an individual. (Working as a consultant, I met a hospital case management team "working with" an insurer case management team. The hospital team used Interqual's standards for length of stay and reasonable and customary fees; the insurer team referred to Milliman's standards. Relationships were strained, as you can imagine.)

Critical care paths, "best in practice" plans, care maps, and guidelines all help us to know about appropriate and successful procedures. However, systems can't manage all people appropriately and successfully all the time. Case management addresses those issues that care paths and care maps can often overlook: multiple conditions, financial funding problems, social/cultural issues, etc.

Exploring the answers to these questions one at a time will be effective in determining the structure, function, and, more importantly, the results of any cost-containment program. Obviously, when the answers indicate a poorly designed or managed program, they also indicate minimal savings. The lack of savings places the review group in the unenviable position of trying to justify the costs to their clients without being able to point to significant performance results. Again, this does not mean that these services do not yield savings, but they do not produce the savings that a well-designed, well-managed, and fully integrated program does.

Let us assume that the claims department, Third Party Administrator, or employer group has determined that there is a need to design and implement a fully integrated preadmission and concurrent review and case management program. One question that then needs answering is whether to do the work in-house or hire an outside company or freelance professionals to develop a program to meet specific client group needs.

In-house programs usually offer greater control, but the expense and increased management burden of adding review and case management professionals to existing staff may not be justified. Some considerations for in-house programs include these:

- Who will hire the staff?
- Who will train and supervise the staff?
- Who will define the responsibilities?
- Who will integrate claims and medical activities and responsibilities?

Employer-funded and employer-administered plans, whether workers' compensation or medical, tend to be better suited for the in-house staff approach. The companies that have such plans have already made the commitment to actively participate in their benefit plans. Larger employer groups are moving steadily toward integrating all of their employee lines of insurance, including short- and long-term disability and workers' compensation insurance, for reasons other than direct control. They are finding that a well-coordinated benefits philosophy and integrated 24-hour coverage are necessary elements of a truly cost-effective care management program. Third Party Administrators and insurance carriers are exploring the feasibility of coordinated, in-house programs as well.

For groups that choose not to use in-house staff, collaboration with a full-service managed care organization provides cost-containment capability and the flexibility to design company-specific programs. As employer groups have become knowledgeable about cost containment, they have become more vocal about what they want and do not want for their employees. The ability of a review organization or case management service to be responsive to these requirements or preferences is one factor to consider in designing a program.

Disease Management Services

Case managers are the creative minds of health care, monitoring those who otherwise fall through the cracks, making the best use of dollars spent across the provider continuum, and maintaining an unwavering commitment to quality care. The benefits of case management increase exponentially when CMs integrate their programs across utilization management, disease management, discharge planning, rehabilitation, outpatient, transition to home, hospice, and other services.

Although the majority of case management programs have focused on the management of the sickest and costliest individuals in a group, most would agree that earlier, more creative, and nonepisodic management presents far greater opportunities to prevent these health care disasters. Health care organizations and the payers have been striving to improve the quality of care, to control costs, and to actively involve plan members in this process. Whereas case management focuses efforts on an individual patient, disease management targets groups of individuals with diagnostic conditions that have historical and financial evidence of being costly and that will be significantly improved with more integrated and systematic management. It can assist in identifying cases earlier, an important asset to care, and pulls people who might otherwise go undetected back into the health care system for needed attention, using standards and guidelines to educate and help individuals better manage their disease state.

Several diseases have already been identified as having the greatest potential for change: asthma, diabetes, high-risk pregnancy, cardiovascular, and chronic neuromuscular. Companies are now looking at a broader spectrum of degenerative conditions, including diseases such as multiple sclerosis, amyotrophic lateral sclerosis (ALS), hemophilia, and cystic fibrosis, as well as chronic back pain and arthritis. Pharmacy benefits are also a growing field under the disease management umbrella. Disease management programs can also benefit those with behavioral disabilities and substance abuse or addiction problems.

In 2002, URAC approved national accreditation standards for disease management programs, a sign that it is becoming a fundamental part of managed care offerings. The URAC standards note six areas of disease management: disease management scope and objectives, administration and staffing, performance measuring and reporting, consumer rights and responsibilities, methods for managing eligible populations, and disease management program design.

Disease management programs seek to target these individuals at the earliest stages of known high-cost conditions. By providing ongoing information and intervention, these programs can prevent, or at least minimize, the problems that eventually result in chronic and costly complications. Among the drawbacks in disease management as it is now practiced are the following: It more often addresses a group profile rather than an individual's needs; it often does not track patient's progress or lack of progress; it lacks consistency in administration from provider to provider and region to region; it does not show all comorbid conditions; and in many cases it does not provide for the neediest cases, those who are noncompliant, unable to respond to phone calls, or illiterate.

The three cases described in Figures 10–4, 10–5, and 10–6 are examples of the benefits to both the patient and payer when precertification, case management, and disease management services are integrated. Figure 10–4 illustrates how a Precert nurse, asking questions that dig deeper to elicit more than a simple "yes" or "no" response, can uncover and address a problem when working with a patient who seems to have a good understanding of his disease and was practicing effective self-management. In Figure 10–5, the importance of knowing about a patient's current lifestyle and any recent changes in it become clear. The combination of precertification and disease management programs assists this individual in taking better care of herself.

The role that integrated precertification, case management, and disease management programs can play is shown in Figure 10–6. The case management intervention continues for 5 months, and when combined with disease management, effectively removes the patient from a high-risk status for developing further, life-threatening complications.

We have assisted several clients by adding a disease management program to the services we were already providing to them, such as preadmission, utilization review, and concurrent review. To introduce the disease management program to employees, a letter describing the service is sent to each individual (Table 10–3), accompanied by a questionnaire we developed to gather preliminary information regarding those with diseases or conditions that require self-management. The letter states very clearly that the program is voluntary, and that all health information they share will be kept strictly confidential. Our questions were carefully worded to help us design a disease management program that would meet the needs of the employees, given their disease, its progression, and need for additional education and possible case management intervention.

The major thrust of effective disease management programs is in the prevention of acute episodes. According to Margaret Flaum, RN, Director of Population Care Client Management at McKesson Health Solutions in Broomfield, Colorado, the care providers in McKesson's Disease Management program have seen a 33% increase in glucose monitoring among diabetic participants, a 33% decrease in hospitalizations, and 28% fewer missed workdays. For enrolled individuals with congestive heart failure, the disease management program has lowered readmissions for cardiac-related symptoms by 30.4% and inpatient readmission rates have plummeted 73%.[4]

In 1997, the Diabetes Treatment Centers of America in Nashville, Tennessee, successfully reduced hospital admission rates for patients enrolled in its program to 67.3% below the national average for diabetics nationwide.[5] Another successful program at the Denver-based National Jewish Center for Immunology and Respiratory Medicine reported in 1995 that asthma hospitalizations decreased 83%, emergency department visits decreased 45%, and hospital days decreased 82% for this high-cost patient group.[6]

Figure 10–4 Level I Integrated Precert/Disease Management Program

Mr. B, 30-year-old African-American male
DX: DM2

PRECERT	CASE MANAGEMENT	DISEASE MANAGEMENT
01/08/03 - Precert nurse contacted by patient to advise of elective admission for inguinal hernia repair. Questioned patient as to etiology. Patient states is "loader" at factory and recently felt "pull in groin" while loading truck at work. Precert nurse advised patient to report to worker's comp through employer as most benefit plans do not accept responsibility of coverage for work-related injuries. Further assessment of medical status revealed 30-year-old African-American male was diagnosed with type 2 diabetes 8 months prior. Has strong family history of same (both parents and two sisters with diabetes). Is currently under excellent control with oral medication, diet, and exercise program. Patient has no comorbidities. Precert nurse contacts plan to notify of information received from patient regarding work-related injury. Precert nurse initiates referral to disease management due to diagnosis of diabetes.		01/08/03 - Disease manager contacts patient to provide thorough assessment and learns was referred by primary care physician to endocrinologist who practices out of diabetes center affiliated with local hospital. Received appropriate education from CDE and RD. Attends weekly diabetes support group at center where receives ongoing education. Exercises 5/7 days per week by walking 5K. However, assessment revealed patient experiencing hypoglycemic episodes frequently during walk. Has tried adding snack to prevent episodes to no avail. Very good knowledge base regarding self- management. Supportive wife and family. Compliant with plan of care. Disease manager initiates referral to endocrinologist requesting visit with RD and/or CDE regarding hypoglycemic episodes. Disease manager contacts patient after visit to verify understanding of treatment plan.

Figure 10–4 continued

Mr. B, 30-year-old African-American male
DX: DM2

PRECERT	CASE MANAGEMENT	DISEASE MANAGEMENT
		Disease manager will monitor patient on a level I tier through telephonic contact every 6 months, receive seasonal condition-specific participant education materials, and be given access to condition-specific 24/7 nurse line.
		RESULTS
		Effective disease management prevented an acute episode from occurring by promptly intervening and coordinating appropriate measures to address the patient's hypoglycemic episodes early on. This serves both the patient and the plan well.

Source: Courtesy of Options Unlimited, Case Management Services Division, 2003, Huntington, New York.

Figure 10–5 Level II Integrated Precert/Disease Management Program

Mrs. M, 55-year-old white female - DX: DM2

PRECERT	CASE MANAGEMENT	DISEASE MANAGEMENT
03/31/03 - Precert nurse notified by hospital of admission for uncontrolled blood sugars. Precert nurse contacts UR and requests clinical review. Precert nurse contacts physician and requests C/B. Precert nurse contacts patient at bedside and learns this 55-year-old white female was diagnosed with type 2 diabetes 1 year earlier. Further conversation revealed good glycemic control initially. However, recently developed problems. Had appropriate referral to endocrinologist year prior and she continues to see every 3 months. Has received past education from CDE and Registered Dietitian. Checks blood sugars 4X/day and keeps log. Verbalizes understanding of diabetic self-management and meal plan. Subscribes to diabetes magazine and reads religiously. However, has had recent lifestyle changes which are adversely affecting glycemic control. Was not working when originally diagnosed,		03/31/03 - Disease manager contacts patient to conduct thorough assessment. Through this intervention it is learned the patient was recently widowed, necessitating her need for employment. She states she is under the care of an endocrinologist whom she sees regularly. Mrs. M has had adequate diabetes education in the past and has a good knowledge base of diabetes self-management. Feels she would benefit from a "refresher" class and behavioral modification training. Both are available through her endocrinology office. In addition, she is interested in a support group and agrees to level II tier participation. Disease manager sends assessment report to primary care physician and endocrinologist identifying need for additional education and support group. Disease manager contacts physician to verify receipt of assessment report and obtain agreement to facilitate appropriate referrals.

Figure 10–5 continued

Mrs. M, 55-year-old white female - DX: DM2

PRECERT	CASE MANAGEMENT	DISEASE MANAGEMENT
but recently accepted job as cook at local grade school. Often is too tired to take her usual walk after work. Also, states job as cook has presented a problem with dietary compliance as she often "tastes" too much. Has gained 20 lbs. and blood sugars have been recently elevated to 160–200 range. However, today elevated to 405 and experienced acute visual changes and headache which caused her visit to the ER. Precert initiates referral to disease management.		Disease manager contacts patient within 1 week to confirm arrangements for recommendations are in place. Reinforces availability of 24/7 nurse line. Educational materials sent. Disease manager will monitor patient's plan of care to prioritize and manage identified problems and risks as needed. Patient will receive appropriate nurse follow-up based on clinical activity and personal care goal status. Disease manager will send patient seasonal condition specific education and risk specific materials as needed, customized to her unique needs. Evaluation for case management will be assessed on a quarterly basis. **RESULTS** By addressing identified problems early on, disease management was able to greatly decrease the risk of current and future diabetic complications. This action enhances the efficiency and effectiveness of delivering health care. Again, the patient and the plan were well served.

Source: Courtesy of Options Unlimited, Case Management Services Division, 2003, Huntington, New York.

Figure 10–6 Level III Integrated Precert/Disease Management Program

Mrs. S, 58-year-old white female
DX: CVA, DM2, Obesity, Tobacco abuse, Hypothyroidism

PRECERT	CASE MANAGEMENT	DISEASE MANAGEMENT
11/27 - T/C from hospital; gave admit info. Admitting diagnosis right hemiplegia. 11/28 - T/C to hospital UR and clinical review requested. T/C from hospital UR: patient admitted 11/25 with c/o numbness face, jaw & right arm. Dizziness, right hemiplegia. MRI = left thalamic CVA. B/P 149/99 Rehab eval done. Diabetes mellitus type 2 diagnosed 3 years ago. Has not seen a physician in 1 year. BS on admission 525. Diabetic teaching started. Cholesterol 221, triglycerides 450. Heparin drip, Plavix started. Social: Single, lives with daughter, son-in-law, grandchildren. Prior to event employed as factory worker on evening shift. Precert nurse verified rehab benefits. Supplied network participating rehab facility with needed information. 11/29 - Precert nurse received and reviewed PT, OT, ST evals. Medical necessity for acute rehab verified. Secondary Medicaid verified.		

Figure 10–6 continued

Mrs. S, 58-year-old white female
DX: CVA, DM2, Obesity, Tobacco abuse, Hypothyroidism

PRECERT	CASE MANAGEMENT	DISEASE MANAGEMENT
11/29 - Precert nurse contacts patient at bedside. Only medical care from local D.O. Lives in rural area of Tennessee. Had been on oral antidiabetic (Glucophage) but stopped taking it 1 year ago because thought was causing diarrhea. Never notified MD of problems. Also stopped all other meds at same time, including thyroid medication. There has been no medical management of her diabetes. States she would occasionally check her blood sugar. Received no formal diabetic teaching at time of diagnosis. Current weight 179, height 5'. Smoked 1 ppd prior to admission. Precert nurse noted claimant has no understanding of the impact uncontrolled diabetes has on body or disease process. She is agreeable to case management. T/C from Rehab. Patient transferred from acute care to network participating rehab. 11/30 - Assigned to case manager.		

continues

Figure 10–6 continued

Mrs. S, 58-year-old white female
DX: CVA, DM2, Obesity, Tobacco abuse, Hypothyroidism

PRECERT	CASE MANAGEMENT	DISEASE MANAGEMENT
	12/1 - Learns from rehab case manager family is bringing food to patient. Rehab MD was notified and he discussed this with patient.	
	Case manager contacts patient to discuss status, care plan, and compliance. Reinforces education and asks questions to verify understanding of same. Patient unable to verbalize understanding of meal plan. States "they gave me a piece of paper with my diet on it. I will read it when I get home."	
	Case manager contacts rehab case manager and requests RD see patient/family to continue meal plan education.	Case manager verifies patient and family educated regarding meal plan and importance of same. Stressed need for compliance to decrease risk of future complications.
	Case manager contacts attending physician. Learns admitting HbA1c was 14.3% (N=≤ 7%). Learns diabetic teaching is continuing daily by CDE and RD. Discussed plan of care for diabetes management. Case manager asks if endocrinology consult might be helpful.	Case manager notes that MD agrees insulin will likely be needed to achieve glycemic control and reduce risk of future complications. Discussed triad of diseases DM, HTN, Hyperlipidemia and difficulty to control any if all are not in control. Will order endocrinology consult.

Figure 10–6 continued

Mrs. S, 58-year-old white female
DX: CVA, DM2, Obesity, Tobacco abuse, Hypothyroidism

PRECERT	CASE MANAGEMENT	DISEASE MANAGEMENT
		Case manager learns Endocrinology consult done and aggressive medication management started, including insulin regimen.
	12/4 - Case manager contacts rehab case manager. Learns patient does not have own glucometer with her. Requests family bring and that at least one family member is taught to check blood sugars, as well as patient.	
	Case manager learns family/patient cannot locate glucometer. Requests RX for new one be given to family.	Case manager verifies new glucometer/supplies purchased by family and brought to facility. Education done. Successful demonstrations returned by patient and family member.
	12/7 - Case manager contacts attending physician regarding medical status and care plan.	
	Case manager contacts endocrinologist and discusses current control and plan of care. Agrees with plan to increase insulin.	
	Case manager contacts rehab case manager and recommends family member learn insulin administration as well as patient.	Case manager verifies patient and daughter have learned to administer insulin.
		Case manager has frequent discussions with claimant regarding level of diabetic management needed at discharge and importance of same to decrease risks.

continues

Figure 10–6 continued

Mrs. S, 58-year-old white female
DX: CVA, DM2, Obesity, Tobacco abuse, Hypothyroidism

PRECERT	CASE MANAGEMENT	DISEASE MANAGEMENT
	Case manager learns compliance improving and BS readings improved. 12/7 - Case manager locates outpatient diabetic center/classes and verifies benefit for same. Verifies clinic is ADA recognized. 12/10 - Case manager learns patient's blood sugars under excellent control. Has been compliant with management and able to verbalize understanding of same. Case manager contacts endocrinologist and obtains orders for outpatient diabetes class. Diabetes center contacted and patient enrolled. Case manager receiving ongoing status reports regarding PT, OT, ST progress. Arrangements finalized for continued outpatient therapy in anticipation of upcoming discharge. Case manager contacts network participating home health agency and arranges for f/u visit after discharge to monitor status.	Case manager contacts patient to discuss need for continued outpatient rehab and diabetes education after discharge. Patient verbalizes understanding of importance of same and agrees to comply. Has stopped smoking since admit. Verbalizes understanding of relationship to stroke and plans to remain smoke free. Declines offer of nicotine patch.

Figure 10–6 continued

Mrs. S, 58-year-old white female
DX: CVA, DM2, Obesity, Tobacco abuse, Hypothyroidism

PRECERT	CASE MANAGEMENT	DISEASE MANAGEMENT
	12/13 - Patient discharged home. Rehab LOS = 14 days	
	12/14 - Case manager contacts patient at home. Learns blood sugars remain under control. Patient able to verbalize principals of diabetic self- management and importance of maintaining compliance with outpatient plan of care.	Case manager learns patient compliant with appropriate and medically necessary MD appointments with specialists, including endocrinologist and gastroenterologist who will evaluate problems with chronic diarrhea. Patient attending outpatient PT, OT, ST.

12/19–20 - Case manager notes patient attends two-day diabetes class at center with family member. Remains smoke free. |
| | 12/15–2/20 - Case manager maintains regular contact with patient, physicians, and therapists to monitor medical status, coordinate care, and intervene as indicated.

02/20 - Patient has met outpatient rehab goals and is discharged by PT, OT, ST. OT from rehab will meet with patient and Occupational Health Nurse at plant to evaluate work station for safety in anticipation of returning to work. | |

continues

Figure 10–6 continued

Mrs. S, 58-year-old white female
DX: CVA, DM2, Obesity, Tobacco abuse, Hypothyroidism

PRECERT	CASE MANAGEMENT	DISEASE MANAGEMENT
	03/06 - Patient returns to work half days.	Case manager learns patient continues to be compliant with outpatient care. Blood glucose remains under control. Remains smoke free.
		04/08 - Case manager learns patients current HbA1c reported at 7.8%.
	04/08 - Case management closed. Case manager initiates referral to disease management.	
		Disease management continues to contact patient periodically to monitor status, identify potential problems early, and identify case management needs.
		RESULTS
		Had Options Unlimited not been involved with this case the patient would have continued to poorly manage her diabetes and not receive appropriate care. This would have placed her at a high risk of developing further life-threatening complications. In addition to the significant cost savings recorded by aggressive utilization management in this case, it is likely multiple future hospitalizations were avoided.

Source: Courtesy of Options Unlimited, Case Management Services Division, 2003, Huntington, New York.

Table 10–3 Letter Introducing Disease Management Program to Client
Employees

Dear _____,

Options Unlimited, on behalf of Tele Electro, Inc., is very pleased to offer
Healthy Options, a wellness program that provides a personalized approach to
those patients with conditions that require self-management. *Options Unlimited*
is the organization that provides Tele Electro with hospital prenotification, case
management, and other services. We are the 800 # on the back of your medical
card. The goal of the *Healthy Options* program is to assist you and your family in
enjoying optimal health by providing information, resources and, in some
instances, coordinating health care services. In these busy days, we don't
always take the best care of ourselves, as we should.

Healthy Options is designed to help you better understand and manage some
conditions and illnesses you might have. This program is entirely voluntary and
strictly confidential. Enclosed is our Health Assessment Questionnaire. We hope
that you will take this opportunity to fill out the questionnaire and return it in the
stamped envelope provided. This assessment will come directly back to *Options
Unlimited* and be reviewed and evaluated by our professional staff to determine
if one of our programs is right for you. You will then be given the option of participating in this program. If you choose to participate in one of the targeted programs, you will receive communications on a continuous basis so that you can
become more proactive in your care.

Some of the conditions covered in our programs are diabetes, heart disease,
asthma, obesity, and cancer. It also covers pregnancy with its *First Breath* program. *First Breath* is designed for women who are pregnant or thinking of
becoming pregnant. It offers personal care plans, a 24/7 nurse hotline, access to
specialized care materials, articles, and more.

We hope that you will take advantage of this added benefit and complete the
enclosed questionnaire. Please remember this is strictly confidential and personal information will not be shared. The sole purpose of this program is to
assist you and your family with resources and tools to make sure you enjoy the
best health you possibly can.

So, please fill out the questionnaire, return it in the envelope provided, and get
started in taking charge of your health! If you have any questions about this program or filling out the questionnaire, please give us a call at 1-800-555-1212.

Sincerely,

Catherine Mullahy, RN, BS, CRRN, CCM

President

Source: Courtesy of Options Unlimited, Case Management Services Division, 2003,
Huntington, New York.

Given such good statistics in its early days, it is surprising to learn that less than one in ten employers now use disease management programs, although there is great interest and growing demand.[7] On the other hand, that fact will sound sweet to any case manager or case management company looking to build its book of business by offering disease management services.

Admittedly, the design and implementation of disease management programs will necessitate substantial commitment of resources and a true partnership among providers, payers, and plan participants. Change will be necessary at every level; for those case managers (working with the sickest individuals) who may be frustrated by the referral of patients too late for either prevention or effective management, these programs are certainly welcome news.

Risk assessments and the stratification of services play a significant role in a successful disease management program. Thoughtful assessment of risks to the patient and to the plan allow departments to apply the program at the level that best meets identified needs. Here are simple guidelines:

Level 1: Low-risk individuals can get by with frequent mailings and occasional phone contact. Basic information about disease and community resources should be made available.

Level 2: Medium-risk individuals often require frequent phone contact, alone. Determine level of understanding of disease (beginning, midway, end knowledge), impact of the disease and consequences, and the ability of the patient to be compliant. This level might last 3 to 6 months.

Level 3: This patient is suffering a more severe or chronic disease, or the consequences of noncompliance in managing the disease. High-risk individuals receive more frequent telephone contact, as well as occasional home visits and medical monitoring, reeducation, and coordination.

PREADMISSION REVIEW, CONCURRENT REVIEW, DISEASE MANAGEMENT, AND CASE MANAGEMENT CHECKLIST

The ideal program has the following elements and characteristics:

- Full integration of preadmission, concurrent review, case management, and disease management services, with coordinated communications and integrated databases between departments
- Knowledge of the plan and its provisions and restrictions
- Consensus on how and when cases are opened
- An outside company or an in-house department with nurses, physicians, and clerical and administrative staff who understand each other's role and function, have ongoing interaction, and operate as a unit in pursuit of quality outcomes and cost-containment results

- An established communications link with the claims examiner or claims staff administering the plan
- The ear of the CEO or a decision maker regarding specific allowances to be made on a case-by-case basis
- Preventive interventions (interventions at regular intervals) to catch problems before they happen; most DM programs have little or no interface with the enrolled population
- A regular reporting system charting active case management cases by type, duration, expenses, outcomes, and savings
- A process of continual program evaluation and the capacity to revise the program year to year. If, for example, the program initially included only cases over $100,000/year, criteria might be refocused to target another specific disease, red flag, goal, or group.
- A case management closure protocol. It is highly unethical to keep patients in disease management for the revenue stream, but it is commonly done. Only the truly catastrophic cases will have a case manager on board long-term. Once a case is stabilized, the patient no longer deemed at risk, and savings are no longer realized, the case manager should consider closure. The patient and family become, in essence, their own case managers. That being said, a periodic reevaluation of closed cases would seem appropriate as a continuing risk assessment tool to protect both patient and payer.
- A schedule to evaluate the computer systems that are used to capture potential cases or target needy patients, allowing program managers to improve the case selection basis
- A mechanism to direct cases into disease management programs. Not all diabetics need DM; some are well-educated, compliant, and self-manage very well.
- A mechanism to learn from past experience. Has the company or department ever had a preadmission and concurrent review and case management system in place before? If not, there should be a mechanism to track one year's performance against the next and determine how well the program has functioned.
- A mechanism that stratifies and allows for change in the level of disease education and behavior modification. Most individuals enrolled in disease management programs do not remain at the level at which they entered the program. In many cases, we expect to see a person move from a higher rate of management to a low-maintenance level of intervention as he becomes his own case manager and health care advocate.
- A schedule of preenrollment or postenrollment goals, so that a person's progress is tracked

FEES: CAPITATED, HOURLY, OR PER CASE

Once the hurdle of setting up the preadmission and concurrent review and case management system is gotten over, there is another potential stumbling block——the fees. Companies accustomed to buying preadmission and concurrent review services customarily purchase these services at capitated rates (a predetermined per-employee, per-month cost) ranging from $.85 per employee per month to $2.00 and on up. These become set fees, varying only by the number of employees or covered lives, and have nothing to do with office visits or hospital admissions. Therefore, fees for a group remain relatively constant if there are 20 or 60 or 200 admissions to a hospital. It is important, therefore, to determine an expected hospital experience for a group prior to establishing fees so that the fees charged will at least meet the expenses incurred in providing services (e.g., payroll, phone, computers, software).

Capitation as a system for reimbursement is gaining popularity among payer groups. Getting its start with HMO plans, capitation certainly places all kinds of risk on those who accept it as payment, rather than its predecessor, the "fee-for-service" arrangement. In a fee-for-service system, providers charge for a service as it is rendered, whether offering hospital, surgical, home health, pharmaceutical, or other medical care. With the inception of HMOs, there was a change in how service fees were paid. Given a certain number of employees and/or covered lives, HMOs consulted actuaries to review the group's prior health history, health care activity, and group demographics and to estimate the percentage of the group that would need certain services. The actuaries help set a capitated fee—a charge per employee or covered life for care or services to be provided over a period of time (usually 1 year).

Capitated fees are now applied by the range of managed care providers, including case management services. Many smaller case management companies break out preadmission/concurrent review services on a capitated basis, but because they do not feel as skilled in setting capitated case management fees—predicting how active a case is going to be or how much of a nurse reviewer's time it will need—case management remains a fee-for-service arrangement. Within larger managed care organizations such as HMOs and PPOs, where it is standard to have capitated arrangements with insured groups for purchased services (whether it be a mail-order prescription plan, a vision plan, or case management), capitated fees are more the norm.

Moving from fee-for-service to a capitated rate structure in case management is not easy. There may be considerable risk to the case management provider unless there is knowledge of the insured or self-funded group. In case management, especially with a new patient population or client, and considering marketplace volatility, we are seeing employer groups that are not staying with a particular insurer for any length of time. Therefore, the caseload is inherited with little knowledge about previous experience; the case managers don't have the ability to look back and review prior experience from 2 to 3 years for big cases. The patients may be coming to an HMO, PPO, or POS plan from another company, and the first company's claims department is not going to be sharing its claims information. The case manager then has to project, using standardized information, that perhaps 3% to 5% of the group may require case management; she also must know what her expenses might be to manage a case for the life of that case. Is the average case open 3 months or 6 months? How much activity does a case manager expend on a case? How is it charged out?

In capitated structures, if the industry norm shows that 3% to 5% of the group will be responsible for spending the larger share of the health benefits dollars, those are the individuals to manage. One must decide if it is best to manage all of them or manage 1% of the group very intensively with on-site case management and another 3% telephonically. Rates are then set based on how much it would cost to pay a case manager by the hour to manage those cases. That total fee is then broken into months and divided by group members to determine a capitated fee structure.

Industry norms for preadmission/precertification programs average $1.50 per person per month. Concurrent review services range from $1.50 to $4.00 per person per month, depending on the depth of the follow-up (telephonic or personal visit, for example). The per-person per-month fees for disease management programs (level 1 and level 2 intervention) vary with the disease state. Although diabetes disease management might be charged at $90 per person per month, the cost for chronic obstructive pulmonary disease (COPD) disease management might approach $130 per person per month.

Fees range widely, to put it mildly. Some companies use physicians as case managers, and their fees obviously are going to be higher when figured into a capitated rate, possibly throwing the per-member per-month rate considerably higher. Those companies that do all their case management telephonically may quote fees to manage the life of a case at a lower rate because a case manager can manage many more cases, there is no time on the road or in the hospital, caseloads tend to be higher, and the amount of time spent per case tends to be less. The capitated fees will reflect those givens.

Capitation does seem to be the wave of the future, but it is not without its problems. If those running the department and negotiating the contracts do not have an actuarial or underwriting background, it is very problematic to project group experience. An individual might know case management but not be able to predict group experience and set fees. However, reasonable projections can be made. If prior group experience is unknown, it is advisable to place some risk projections into the contract or to consider the purchase of stop-loss or reinsurance coverage.

(HMOs, payers, providers, and case managers may take responsibility for a certain dollar threshold when providing or paying for health services, and purchase stop-loss insurance or reinsure themselves to protect against financial risk and loss. A group might set a specific stop-loss threshold, with a payer covering perhaps $50,000 per case, or an aggregate stop-loss threshold, with the same payer saying it will pay up to $2 million in health care fees for the entire covered group. The payer then purchases stop-loss insurance for a predicted caseload above that threshold, as determined by an underwriter or actuary.)

Another fee system is modified fee-for-service. In this system, providers are paid on a traditional fee-for-services basis, with specified maximum fees for each procedure.

The following examples are offered as illustrations. The cases used are for illustrative purposes only, because the range and complexity of case management services may vary from company to company.

It is reasonable, and I strongly recommend, that at a *minimum,* 1% of covered lives in a group be case managed. For one union plan that my company managed, we quoted a capitated rate structure based on numbers from the union's records compared to our other groups with similar experiences. Let us assume the group contained 2,500 members. Using 2.3 as a factor to determine covered lives, and multiplying by the 2,500 members, we determined a given of 6,250 covered lives. One percent of this group (the minimum to receive case management services) is 62 cases. Given assumed lifetime case management fees of $2,500 per case per year, multiplied by 62 cases, we have a total of $155,000 for the year. To structure this contract on a capitated basis, we took the total of $155,000, divided it by 2,500 employees, and divided it again by the 12 months in a year. This determined a capitated rate of $5.16 per employee per month—the fees we would receive to case manage the covered lives associated with this employee group. (This fee could be quoted with one "carve-out," which would occur when capitated fees would be dropped for a fee-for-service structure, perhaps for an extraordinary experience such as more than the projected number of cases or cases requiring more intensive or lengthier intervention, such as transplants, traumatic brain injury, or preemie babies.)

My company had a year's experience with this particular group, so we were relatively comfortable moving into a capitated arrangement with them. Compare this with a smaller group with which we have a contract. Less than 4 months after we assumed responsibility for its case management services, the group had an extraordinary experience. The group of 350 employees provides services to nursing homes in the New York metropolitan area as nurse's aides, housekeepers, and porters. Using the same 2.3 as before to factor our covered lives, we set 805 lives as our covered group. One percent of this group (the minimum to receive case management services) is 8 cases. Given our formula, we would expect to manage

8 cases a year, give or take a few. We have already identified 10 cases and placed them into case management. There are 8 more months in our contracted year, however, and this group appears to be sick!

Had we made our usual assumptions and set capitated rates (1% of covered lives with case management fees of $2,500 for the care lifetime of the case), we could be experiencing a substantial loss. We would have set our fees to manage 1% of the covered group or eight cases for the year, with average fees of $2,500 per case, for a total of $20,000. A capitated rate would be $4.76 per employee per month ($20,000 divided by 350 employees, divided by 12 months, equals $4.76). If the experience of this small group continues as it has, there could be another 20 cases by year's end, with a total count reaching 30. For 30 cases at $2,500 each, we might be providing $75,000 worth of case management services for a capitated rate based on a projected experience costing $20,000, at a loss to us of $55,000. One can easily appreciate how financially problematic capitated rates can be, as well as the importance of establishing a fee structure based on a group's previous experience.

We were contracted to provide services for another group that had a substantial language barrier. Although communication materials were distributed to the members informing them of the need to notify our preadmissions department prior to all hospital admissions, calls were few. Perhaps the language barrier, or culture barrier, was greater than anticipated, or preadmission was not recognized as important. The union's experience, although it should have been the same or greater than other of our groups, was one quarter of the caseload we expected. I informed union management that our capitated rate was set too high. I took back the capitated rate structure and proceeded on a per-case basis until we discovered the true caseload experience for that group. We must be fair. Every company wants to make a profit. If case managers make an unearned profit, and the client company discovers the inflated charges, as companies will, the service provider loses all credibility and trust in the relationship.

Another trend instituted by HMO plans is to put a portion of their fees *at risk*. In most arrangements, the managed care company sets capitated fees assuming the experience of the group. Customarily, if the group has a worse experience than anticipated, the onus is on the managed care company to oversee the costs or perhaps create a carve-out arrangement and renegotiate the fee. An option is to risk a portion of the MCO's fee payment. This means that if quality assurance goals are not met, if patient satisfaction surveys are not completed, if outcomes do not improve, or if costs do not decrease as established in contract negotiations, the client does not pay the MCO fee in full. For example, a company with an HMO that has a disease state management program for asthma patients may go in saying we are going to reduce the cost of your asthma cases by 15%. If we do not, we will risk 2% of our fees. They will have examined their abilities and outcomes and the client's history and will have drawn a line in the sand, saying we can do this and if we do not, you do not have to pay us.

Case management companies are being asked to put a portion of their fees at risk. Setting fees at risk or setting capitated rates can both be risky maneuvers. It is unwise, to say the least, for a case management department or program to blindly set a capitated rate structure with no idea of what the group's experience has been or can be. We once managed two groups of the same size—2,500 members. One group had 40% more hospital admissions than the other group due to age and industry demographics. The first group's members tended to be more sickly, less educated, did not take care of themselves, did not have continuous medical care, did not follow diets, and were not compliant with medication. This again illustrates how a smaller group can have a worse experience history than a larger group. A case manager or department can choose to manage a certain percent of the high-cost cases or go back to the client and renegotiate based on their experience. We have done both. I recommend that case managers leave some room to negotiate either up or down when setting fees, capitated or otherwise.

Common problems of our immature capitation market include the use of multiple carve outs, which becomes an administrative nightmare. Some providers, seeking to keep their services in line with the capitated fees they are receiving, might opt to eliminate services for the problematic, catastrophic patients. And what happens when all the services provided within a facility are not included in the capitated contract? Does the case manager have to pick from the list of available options?[3] For example, a case manager may be instructed by a payer to use ABC Rehabilitation because a contract exists with that group. When the case manager is preparing to place a traumatic brain-injured patient in the facility, she discovers that this diagnosis is not covered under the capitated rate structure. She must address the issue straight on and negotiate coverage and fees or negotiate for approval of another rehabilitation facility. As patient advocates, we must remember that we manage care. Included within that job is our responsibility to consider benefit restrictions, allocations, and their impact on patient care and outcomes.

Some companies, believing that their employee groups (including dependents) are basically healthy, may elect to purchase services on a "per-case" basis. Fees may be calculated on an hourly basis for the time each reviewed case would take or on a flat-fee basis (i.e., a set fee is established for each review).

This covers the fees for the "small stuff." When such fees are quoted, they seem almost painless to the client groups. And, in fact, many client groups consider preadmission and concurrent review services to be case management. They truly believe that "review" and "manage" are one and the same, so discussions about case management fees often generate resistance. If a client group already thinks it is getting review and case management services for a capitated rate of $2.00 per employee per month, then it is necessary to redefine the terms, explain the differences, and determine the services actually being provided. Case management services are usually billed on an hourly basis or deemed "out of contract" or "extracontractual" services. When the services and fees are discussed, the group may decide to forgo them or to use them sparingly, only for catastrophes. ("We've only had one or two of these, thank God, our people are healthy!") Quite apparently, the group needs a little more information about case management, the kinds of cases typically managed, and how case management differs from preadmission and concurrent review.

Case management fees, if billed hourly, do get noticed. A case manager needs to discuss the fee structure and reach an agreement on it with the potential client group or payer prior to invoicing for these services. Hourly fees vary depending on the geographic location, whether services are provided telephonically or on-site, as well as the size of the case management company or department, and its client base. Case management provided within a specific market niche, such as oncology or premature babies, may warrant higher hourly fees due to the expertise and experience of the practitioner. In general, case management hourly fees can fall between $75.00 and $150.00.

Full acceptance of these fees is not automatic, nor is explaining them an easy process. They need to be presented as individualized and time intensive. A description of the kind of work that is involved is helpful and provides an understanding not only of the process, but also of the time required for visits, arranging for services, negotiating fees, monitoring, and so on. It should be pointed out that if a case is unmanaged, the costs will go unchecked and might indeed prove to be catastrophically expensive. A side-by-side comparison of patients that are case managed and those that are not is extremely valuable in demonstrating potential savings. Because some cases can generate thousands of dollars in invoices, there needs to be a thorough discussion and acceptance of the case management concept before work begins.

Trusting that a payer will automatically perceive the value and accept the costs of case management services is not a risk worth taking. It often results in having to justify expenses after the fact, which places one in the position of "putting out fires." There may be resistance or lack of understanding, but it is better to confront problems before services are initiated than to be well into a program and faced with a client who feels misled.

Because case management is largely intangible, educating prospective or current client groups takes time, energy, and verbal skills. One successful method of education involves the sharing of cost-benefit analysis reports. When these reports are reviewed case by case, it becomes evident that the investment in case management is worthwhile. Presenting case management as "the" solution to high-cost cases allows even the dubious to consider it, if only on a one-case-at-a-time basis.

Once aboard, "converts" become "zealots" as success after success is documented. Of course, there will be cases that do not yield as large a savings as others, but overall effective case management programs will always result in considerable savings. The bottom line should be that the dollars spent on case management are far less than the savings realized.

NOTES

1. "Studies Show Nurses' Visits in Pregnancies Helped Later," *The New York Times,* 27 (1997): A18.
2. Reuters News, "Most Employers Still Offer Health Programs," *Bio/Analogics* 1, no. 5 (2001). Available at www.imakenews.com.
3. K. Bliss, and E. Mischler, "Planting the Seeds for Improved Health and Productivity: Disease Management Programs," *Continuing Care* 21, no. 6 (2002): 22–25.
4. M. Flaum, "Comorbidity and DM," *Health Management Technology* 22, no. 10 (2001): 28.
5. "Proactive CM Improves Outcomes for Diabetics," *Case Management Advisor* 8, no. 3 (January 1997): 1, 22. (For more information, please call 1-800-688-2421.)
6. "Asthma Program Slashes Hospitalization Costs," *Disease State Management* 1, no. 3 (October 1995): 31.
7. R. Ceniceros, "Employer Interest in Disease Management Growing," *Business Insurance* 36, no. 6 (2002): T4, T7.

CHAPTER 11

Working Effectively with Claims Departments: Case Managers in Consulting Roles

There have been many changes in the ways health care claims are paid, yet in some fields there are still few incentives to watch out for costs. As long as there is coverage available and a doctor's prescription or a letter of medical need accompanies a claim, it will be paid because most claims examiners and departments do not have the sophisticated medical knowledge to know whether a procedure is really necessary. Once coverage starts, who in the claims department can say when it should stop? Is the claims staff supposed to decide the beginning and end points in medical care? One would not assume so, but in terms of payments for health care delivery, much has been left in the hands of the providers and claims personnel. Certainly neither individuals nor corporations really want to turn over their checkbook, especially in areas in which there are no reasonable and customary charges established for medical services, yet they do, daily. When a bill comes in, it gets paid at 100% or 80% of the submitted amount despite the fact that charges are all over the map; some people are paying what they should be and others are billed far above what is even deemed profitable. So, do we leave everything to the free market—let the buyer beware and hope that care costs eventually stabilize? I don't think so.

Let the buyer beware? Patients are often too weak, too compromised, or too distraught to look out for themselves. Savvy corporate managers, as well as smart homemakers, get thrown into the middle of the convoluted delivery-payment system and must gear up to act as self-advocates. The more complex their needs, the less likely it is they will be well-served by the system. The more providers involved, the less likely it is that there is one person looking out for the patient. Fortunately, all kinds of state, federal, and independent organizations, as well as consumer advocates, are providing health care financial information to patients via books, newsletters, and the Internet. Employers across the country are ramping up their initiative to encourage their employees to be educated consumers.

Still, we work within a system in which, despite dollars being spent, no one person has the responsibility of trying to ensure that the outcome will be desirable and the services will be quality.

This is the case manager's opportunity to create collaborative roles with employers, payers, and providers as they work in their patients' best interests. With a better understanding of the claims world, joined with their knowledge of how the health care delivery system works, case managers can get the most and best use from plan dollars and often extend the length of time care can be provided through the judicious use of available funds.

A nurse in a hospital would never decide to get involved in a patient's care just by reviewing the case while sitting at a desk. The nurse would walk down the hall and visit that patient, talk to the physician, and talk to the family. A case manager would do no less. There are too many liabilities and too much at stake. Similarly, shuffling claims (or even speeding claims) through the system for payment is not enough. Patient information is not enough. A physician's operative report is not enough. It is the combination of information and what the case manager does with that information that makes case management a valued service.

Understanding the roles and responsibilities of claims personnel and working in concert with claims staff can help a case manager improve patient outcomes and enhance a payer's bottom line. It can help her build a more successful case management program and achieve a better position in the marketplace. The line of insurance, the entity retaining the case manager's services, and the case manager's position dictate how close a case manager's contact is with a claims department. Some case managers never talk to a claims person, ever. They might converse with the case management department in XYZ insurance company, and that department then perhaps communicates with a claims department. Unfortunately, for far too many companies, the case managers work in a vacuum with no claims interface at all.

The amount of interaction with a claims department also depends on the structure of the case management department or company. The individual case manager may have more or less freedom to communicate directly with a claims department, benefit examiner, or claims adjustor. The bigger the company and the more case managers there are, the less likely it is a particular case manager will have ongoing contact with a claims adjustor. Sometimes, the supervisor of a case management company is afraid that a case manager will get too close to accounts and decide to start her own company, taking the accounts along. Case management and claims services are rarely integrated, and both the patients and the program suffer.

In short, the ideal does not exist. Not every case manager has ongoing communication, nor does every case manager who makes a recommendation see it put into place. A report may go to claims supervisor Jane Jones, but never past her to the claims examiner. Or, the report may go directly to a home office, because in this particular company only the home office assigns cases for case management; the local claims department may never see the report or know about it. There is no universal ideal for the interface between case managers and claims departments. However, this does not mean that case managers should ignore the benefits of this liaison or hesitate to establish it. The "norm" does not free a case manager from the responsibility to know claims issues and claims personnel, because whatever work a case manager does is eventually forwarded to a claims department.

CLAIMS DEPARTMENT STRUCTURE AND OPERATIONS

To make the most of their relationships with claims departments and to benefit patients and payers, case managers should distinguish the main players in the claims arena. What are the reporting relationships within the office? How does this person fit into the loop? A person's title may convey how much or how little control he or she has over processing a claim. It is also vital to determine the concerns of the claims staff: What is the real reason a claim was referred for case management? What is the claims manager looking for from the case manager? How can the case manager get timely, accurate answers to her questions in an effort to address claims concerns? Finally, case managers will want to discover their own process of working with claims staff to get the best for their patients and clients while creating more advocates for case management.

The Players

Job functions vary from claims office to claims office. Titles such as *processor, examiner,* and *adjustor* may be interchangeable, or each may denote different jobs with different responsibilities. In general, there are some titles and activities that are fairly consistent across organizations:

- A customer service representative is the first person an insured speaks to regarding eligibility, coverage issues, and plan allowances.
- A claims processor may not be a decision maker, but does put claims into the system. Edits to claim entries may occur after processing. This title is usually used in a high-volume claims environment.
- A claims examiner is a claims processor who has the necessary skills to examine claims and make decisions whether to approve, investigate, or deny them.
- A claims supervisor is usually in charge of work flow, examiner production, and the first level of management decision making.

- A claims manager usually makes the final decision regarding claims. Directors and vice presidents may be involved in decisions.
- A plan administrator has responsibility for overall administration of the plan, handling appeals and plan design and changes. Within a self-funded plan, there is a designated management-level person with responsibility for stop-loss advisories. This person notifies the stop-loss carrier when a call point is reached, usually when 50% of the dollars allotted to the primary insurance plan have been spent, and is the person responsible for allowing an override of the cover to pay a high-cost claim. The case manager is often involved in some of the conversation between the stop-loss carrier and the claims department liaison.
- An account manager with insurance and marketing skills is the direct interface between the client group and the claims department. This individual handles service issues, complaints, funding issues, and may report regularly on the claims experience.

These are the people charged with making claims payments and enforcing whatever insurance benefit contract might be in effect. Their responsibilities include the accurate and timely payment of claims in a manner that follows contract language and documents their activities. In most claims offices, there is also a productivity quota that must be met. When working for a self-insured employer group (in-house or self-administered claims), the staff reports to the employer's CFO or CEO. In the case of a Third Party Administrator, the claims staff answers to the Third Party Administrator's CEO or vice president. Claims personnel employed by an insurance carrier report to the insurance company's CEO or president.

The expertise and background of claims personnel vary widely. Some claims examiners have minimal experience in claims; some processors are experienced in data entry and are trained as they work their way up the claims staff ladder. In larger companies, an individual may begin as a file clerk, take on data entry, become a processor, and then become, over the course of several months, an examiner adjudicating and paying claims. Most claims personnel have a high school degree at least. Again, the bigger and more established companies tend to have many more in-house people experienced in claims issues. Newer firms and groups often begin their claims operations on a smaller scale, bringing in more expensive, more experienced senior people once their client base is more stable.

Broadly speaking, claims examiners have no background in medical terminology, and any experience they do get will come from day-to-day job-site training or from courses they attend in medical benefits administration. There are videos and seminars available covering workers' compensation, liability, and group medical coverage as well as the more complex topics (e.g., co-payments, coinsurance benefits, and statutes and regulations) they will encounter as they move up to become senior-level examiners.

Case managers and examiners view each case from totally different perspectives. Whereas case managers view a case globally and consider the patient's entire medical history and experience, claims examiners are presented with cases on an item-by-item basis, checking one ICD-9 or CPT code or R & C charge at a time. Further, examiners are productivity driven. The money that is going to be made by their employer is made by getting the claims in, getting them quickly and fairly administered, and getting them out. There is not a lot of time to be spent on the phone or deliberating over single claims.

Unaware of this, case managers sometimes get exasperated at the gaps in claims examiners' knowledge of cases. Claims examiners rarely get the opportunity to handle all the claims for one patient, never mind the claims for one entire family.

There is no staffing pattern common to all claims departments, and there may be little true account dedication. A claim comes in and anyone in a room of examiners may process it. Some companies do set up account-specific groups; an insurance company handling 500 different employer groups may have one set of individuals processing claims for ABC, Inc., but they handle the auto, group medical, and workers' compensation claims for all of ABC's 1,200 employees. Another department may section its staff by procedure; surgical claims staff, dental claims staff, and anesthesia claims staff, for example, administer surgical, dental, and anesthesia claims for the entire covered population.

The case manager trying to find out "why was this claim paid this way?" might have a long wait, depending on the claims department's line of business. Because its has direct contact with the employer, a Third Party Administrator usually has many more customer service and account representatives right in the claims department. The Third Party Administrator's representative may be in daily contact with the employer's human resources manager. In a large insurance firm, however, contact may be far removed. The employer group might call its insurance agent or broker, who in turn calls a customer service representative, who brings it to the attention of an account representative, who hopefully talks to a claims manager.

The diversity of claims operations makes a case manager's job more difficult; any assumptions she makes about a claims department usually turn out to be erroneous. Whereas a nurse in a coronary care unit in New York is likely to have had the same experience as a coronary care unit nurse in Nebraska, a claims examiner paying medical claims in a building in Chicago may not have had the same experience as the claims examiner at the next desk. Adding to the challenge for case managers are the reams of claims forms and the computer technology endemic to claims departments.

The Paper Trail

A claims department is a paper-intensive environment. One claims history can have hundreds of pieces of paper and electronically submitted documents, along with actual claims submitted by various providers. And, depending on the structure of the department, one claimant may have his or her claims paid by no fewer than 5, 10, or 20 individuals, none of whom may have any understanding of what is going on in the case. Because these pieces of paper and e-mails relate to only a small segment of the patient's overall condition, and because claims departments can be huge, it is a paper trail that is virtually impossible to track. Who has which claims, how were they processed, and what does this claimant's record look like when it is all assembled? The payment system is convoluted and fraught with regulations; every claim has to be submitted with this attachment and that notice, and because a consensus is lacking on how to handle claims, it takes one person minutes just to decide how to process a claim, which slows down the whole payment sequence. This is what the industry is complaining about, it is what providers are complaining about, and it is what the federal government and the states are complaining about.

And if the payment system is a challenge for the claims industry, it is a source of confusion and anxiety for the patient. For the most part, there is no one person to speak to if a patient has a problem. John Jones says, "Last month, I got my claims paid fine, and 2 weeks later I sent in a claim from the same provider, but now it's been paid differently. Why did that happen?" There do not seem to be any hard-and-fast rules, and claimants seemingly have no redress. And because of cutbacks in most companies, John can only "speak" to a telephonic mail system. The non-computer-savvy person or the person with a language barrier or a disabling condition is left hanging with no way to resolve major problems.

COMPUTERIZATION

The growing use of computers has alleviated a portion of this mess for some individuals. A patient's entire claims history can be keyed into a computer system and be pulled up on a computer screen. Many claimants, especially those insured by large plans, can see their plan on-screen and check coverage. People can enroll on-line and make changes in their enrollment as the plan allows. Technology is allowing enhanced access to check the status of a claim, whether it has been submitted, and where it is in the claims system.

Computers ease some of the confusion, but there are issues remaining that must be reviewed with a live person. This is why more patients are bringing case managers into discussions about claims. Sometimes, the case manager is the only person the patient feels he can talk to because she knows all his medical needs. I would advise all case managers to increase their understanding of insurance operations, plans, and the claims process. It is another area in which case managers can make themselves indispensable.

The majority of today's computer systems are set up in such a way that the problem has worsened. Claims examiners are no longer looking at actual pieces of paper. A claimant, who has been told to save a copy of everything, might have a copy of the claim but is talking to someone who is looking at a computer screen containing numbers, ICD-9 codes, and that is all. Even if the claimant had attached an explanatory note to the claim, there will be no corresponding explanation on the screen. So the claimant might have gone through laborious steps to clarify his or her situation but no one has recorded it. This is extremely frustrating for everyone involved.

Yet most lines of insurance today, including long-term disability, workers' compensation, and group medical insurance, are administered by software programs. Some insurance company departments and Third Party Administrators still administer claims by hand, but most large, competitive companies have computers assisting in the processing of claims. Various indicators can be programmed into the software to alert a claims examiner or consultant to a claim that may be problematic. Insurance companies or administrators handling claims for several employer groups need to be able to report back to those employer groups when an individual appears to be filing high-cost claims consistently. This allows the insurance company to control their present claims experience better and also plan for their future benefit needs. Actuarial professionals have been using these same techniques for years, garnering information from software programs to rate groups more appropriately and accurately. These reports also highlight information of interest to risk managers.

Employers in a particular industry purchase insurance at rates based on the industry's experience. In some industries, there may be an abnormal number of back injuries or a high incidence of lost-time accidents anticipated due to the type of work employees perform. Risk managers advise employer groups and insurance underwriters on how to decrease employee risk, prevent accidents from occurring, and contain the associated costs once they occur. Can a different therapy be used to shorten the rehabilitation period? What preventive or safety mechanisms can be installed to decrease the incidence of injury at that work site?

Most often, risk managers are consulted by companies that offer property, casualty, and liability insurance, yet are rarely approached by group medical carriers. To my mind, it makes good sense to apply risk management principles to all lines of insurance. I am certain that the trend toward moving patients from high-cost care settings to outpatient settings resulted from the examination by consultants of data runs showing the average length of hospital stays. A consultant would look at a benefit plan, see that there was little coverage available for outpatient care, and approach the company about ways to change the plan language to integrate outpatient care and make the whole experience a better one for the employer and insureds alike. In this way, software programs and risk management principles can be utilized for every line of insurance.

In some respects, there is an overreliance on software by managers and employer groups, who are understandably impressed by software capabilities. But software programs can tell just so much about what is really going on. No matter how sophisticated, software cannot keep up with all the elements involved in claims payment. Sometimes, employers rely on software to tell them what the problems are and how to solve them. They create great reports that give the percentage of people who generated a certain percentage of benefit dollars, but the software provides no clues on how to help those people or lower costs.

There is a common misconception that the speed and efficacy of a software system will now solve the problems that insurers thought they had (e.g., the relatively long time it might take to pay a claim). Now, perhaps claims are paid too quickly. They do get paid faster, but more important pieces fall through the cracks because of the speed. For example, fraudulent claims are less apt to be picked up. Examiners are no longer looking at a claim and saying, "This looks doctored to me." We have lost some of the familiarity and hands-on knowledge regarding problem claims or people who might benefit from a one-on-one relationship with the claims examiner, but we have gained the ability to process the volumes of simple and complex claims that are submitted. Nothing would ever get paid in some cases without the use of software, yet perhaps it is relied on too much in the identification of problem cases. Software alone cannot really tell us what the problems are.

CLAIMS ISSUES

Case managers need to be aware of the concerns of claims personnel. These individuals have their own set of criteria that they must meet on the job, and case managers can create much better relationships by taking the time to understand claims issues. Some of these issues are preexisting conditions, the funding vehicle (self-insured, fully insured, administrative services only, reinsurance, cost plus), insurance contract language, and coordination of benefits (if there are two medical plans in a family). Is COBRA coverage involved? Is the claimant in the midst of an eligibility change: active to retired, active to disabled, active to Medicare eligibility, or active to COBRA? If the insurer is an employee group, return-to-work issues are important to the claims staff, as are ERISA concerns.

INDICATORS FOR CASE MANAGEMENT

Sometimes, the best teachers for a case manager are the cases that came to her too late, in which she envisions all kinds of possibilities, if only she could have had this case earlier, when the home care first started. Now, it's 6 months later and she's wondering how to get the family unhooked from their services. Some services are difficult to "undo." By looking back at some of those cases, a case manager can develop her own red flags. The "I could haves" turn into red flag indicators.

Cases that benefit most from case management commonly involve the most expensive services. Use of these services is, thus, a red flag. Other indicators include a high frequency of admissions in a short period and an unusually long hospital stay. It is usual, perhaps, for certain surgical procedures to require 5 to 7 days hospitalization. (A stay of 10 days or longer for a surgical hospitalization indicates multiple problems or complications now and points to problems down the road as well.)

This is where a case manager's clinical knowledge comes into play, her feel for what constitutes a big case. Having developed a set of indicators, the case manager then needs to communicate them to claims personnel. The object is to get them to understand which cases to bring to the case manager's attention so she can at least follow up with a phone call and find out what is being recommended. If the treatment plan includes 12 hours per day of home nursing services or infusion care services for someone with a chronic infection, the result could be 30 days of services at $700 or $800 per day. With negotiation and appropriate service arrangements at the beginning, the case manager can get the patient what is needed and really demonstrate cost savings as the service is being put in place. It is very difficult to renegotiate a bill for $24,000 after the fact.

One new client handed me bills for $24,000 and $50,000 and asked, "Can't you do anything about this?" I informed the client that it is hard to do anything about such bills once the services have been provided. I said that similar cases, however, if referred early on, would benefit from case management and the costs could be reduced. The claims department, for example, was confronted with a claim for payment of monitoring services provided in the home of a woman with a high-risk pregnancy. They were looking at a red flag but did not know it. Instead of asking if the woman was covered, the claims personnel should have been asking if it is normal for a pregnant woman to be monitored at home. I needed to educate the claims department. Fetal monitoring is not usual for most pregnancies, and by informing the claims personnel of this fact, and showing them that abnormal means big costs, I was able to get them to tell me about such cases upfront, when case management could have a more positive impact.

It is important to let the claims personnel know that they really can make a difference. I have tracked a case without case management, run it through the case management process of negotiation and active intervention, and then shared the results with the claims staff. I tell the managers of the Third Party Administrators I work with, "Listen, if you get your people involved, if you give them some kind of incentive, let them become the ones who refer cases, who are given the credit for savings, you will see a marked difference in the reports to your clients." Empowering everyone and giving each person insight into his or her role in the team effort makes for a better claims team and more effective claims administration.

With regard to another service our company provides, claims review, we faced a problem with the wrong kind of incentive. There was an administration quota, and for every claim that claims personnel paid over and above a certain number, they were given a monetary bonus. Obviously, this encouraged them to pay claims quickly. I said, "Do you understand what you're doing here? You're pushing things through the system. It takes your examiners time to pull aside a claim and give it to me for possible case management intervention or review. Yes, you want prompt payment of claims but you don't want to pay everything without consideration. If you can put a monetary incentive in place for those claims examiners who refer claims that actually result in savings, you'll have the proper emphasis. As a Third Party Administrator, you're charged with the responsibility to save money, and your people should be rewarded. Not only is it part of their job, but ultimately it will be part of whether or not you get a contract renewed to pay a client's claims again."

The education process continues, little by little, case by case. Figure 11–1 is a "tip sheet" I developed for the claims department of one client Third Party Administrator. It includes red flags for case management intervention as well as indicators for claims review.

Different red flags should be used for different lines of insurance. Looking for case management indicators, a case manager will not apply the same dollar limit per claim in a workers' compensation case as in a group medical case. In workers' compensation, for each lost-time injury there is an established guideline, and if the injured person is still out of work a month beyond the date calculated using the guidelines, then that fact becomes a red flag. (Physicians use the reference *The Medical Disability Advisor: Workplace Guidelines for Disability Duration,* written by Presley Reed and published by Reed Group Ltd., to find out about injuries common to different job descriptions, including typical recuperative periods and return-to-work time frames.) On most workers' compensation claims forms, physicians are usually asked to note the date the claimant can return to work. If a physician has left the space blank or puts down "undetermined" month after month, that is a definite red flag. To my mind, a physician avoiding a return-to-work date indicates a problem. On the other hand, the physician might write in

Figure 11–1 CareSolutions™ Red Flags and AccuClaim™ Red Flags

CareSolutions™ Red Flags

• **Diagnosis:**	Cancer	Alcohol and	Chronic Respiratory
	AIDS	Substance Abuse	Conditions
	Stroke	Cardiovascular	Psychiatric
	Transplant	Head Injury	Multiple Trauma
	Neuromuscular	Hepatitis C	High-Risk Infant
	Diseases	Severe Burns	Lyme Disease
	Spinal Cord	High-Risk	
	Injuries	Pregnancy	

• **Potential Treatment:**   Ventilator-dependent   Extended ICU
                             IV Antibiotics   Home Care
                             TPN/Enteral   Chemotherapy

• **Frequent Hospitalizations:**   Three Admits Same Year/Same or Related Problem

• **Cost of Claim:**   Same Illness over $25,000 Year-to-Date

• **Location of Claim:**   Complex Care Delivered in Rural Setting, Small Hospital, or Facility with Poor Outcome History/Diagnosis

• **Patterns of Care:**   Failed or Repeated Surgeries, Hospital-Acquired Infections, Malpractice Concerns

• **Diagnostic Codes:**   ICD9CM - Case Management Referral Indicators

042–044	HIV infection	330–337	Hereditary and degenerative diseases of CNS (Alzheimer's, Huntington's chorea)	644	Early or threatened labor
140–239	Neoplasms (cancer)			655–656	Fetal abnormality
250	Diabetes with complications			710	All collagen (SLE+)
277	Cystic fibrosis, polyarthroporphyria, metabolic disorders (mult. hosps.)	340–349	CNS disorders, MS, CP, quadriplegie, paraplegic, anoxic brain damage	714	Rheumatoid arthritis w/ inflammatory polyarthropathies
279	Immunity deficiency disorders (repeat hosps.)	358	Myasthenia gravis (repeat hosps.)	740–759	Congenital anomalies, spina bifida, cardiac septal defect
286–287	Coagulation defects (repeat hosps.)	359	Muscular dystrophy (repeat hosps.)	760–763	Maternal causes of perinatal morbidity and mortality
290–299	Psychoses	430–438	Cerebral vascular disease, car. hemorrhage	765.1	Premature birth
300–316	Neurotic personality and other nonpsychotic mental disorders	496	COPD	800	Fracture vault of skull

continues

Figure 11–1 continued

850–854	Intracranial injury excluding those with skull fracture	501–503	Asbestosis and silicosis	806	Fracture of verte-bral column w/SCI
860–869	Internal injury of chest, abdomen, and pelvis	584–586	Renal failure		
		925–929	Crashing injury (may involve extensive trauma)	994	Effects of ex-ternal causes— lightning, drowning, strangulation
870–879	Open wound of head, neck, and trunk	948	Burns over 25% of body		
		952	SCI without spinal bone injury	996–999	Complications of surgical and medical care

AccuClaim™Red Flags

- **Surgical and Anesthesia Claims:** All provider claims over $10,000 and all cases with more than two line items should be referred for a medical review. Alert for GYN, Orthopedic, Plastic Surgery. If the surgical claim is referred, corresponding anesthesia claims should be referred also to verify complexity of claimed procedure. Information to obtain: 1) Operative report; 2) Anesthesia time; 3) R&C charges for each CPT code.
- **Podiatrists:** All claims that exceed $1,000 should be referred. Information to obtain: 1) Operative report if a surgical procedure is being billed; 2) R&C charges for each CPT code.
- **Physical Therapy and Occupational Therapy:** Claims that exceed 6 weeks of treatment should be referred. Information to obtain: 1) PT evaluation; 2) Therapy progress notes that include long- and short-term goals and the range of motion results; 3) Letter of medical need from treating MD with diagnosis, frequency of treatment, and estimated duration.
- **Chiropractic Care:** Claims that exceed $500 should be referred. Information to obtain: Complete copy of the medical records; NO summaries. Include diagnosis, treatment plan, frequency of treatment, estimated duration.
- **Durable Medical Equipment:** This is an area of extreme abuse and overutilization of services and fees. The following claims should be referred: oxygen concentrators and related equipment, hospital beds, wheelchairs, any monitors, respirators/ventilators, bone stimulators, insulin and lymphedema pumps, requests for home modifications (ramps, etc.).
- **Home Health Services:** All claims for nursing, aides, or related services should be referred. Information to obtain: 1) Itemized bills; 2) Nursing notes.
- **Infusion Care Services:** All claims for the following infusion services should be referred: IV antibiotics and other medications, TPN (total parenteral nutrition), chemotherapy, and analgesia (pain medications). Information to obtain: 1) MD's prescription; 2) Itemized billing for medications, nursing, and related services and supplies.
- **Any of the following should be referred:** 1) Appeals; 2) Difficult providers; 3) Ambulatory surgical centers; 4) Large hospital bills: over 7 days LOS; to review for LOS, medical needs vs. custodial.

Figure 11–1 continued

- **Procedure Codes:** CPT AccuClaim Referral Indicators

Integumentary System

11000–11044 For cosmetic vs. medical
15780–15791 For cosmetic vs. medical
15810–15840 For cosmetic vs. medical
17304–17310 For cosmetic vs. medical
19318–19500 For cosmetic vs. medical

Musculoskeletal

27590–27598 Amputation

Pulmonary System

30400–30630 For cosmetic
31300–31660 Laryngectomy-
             tracheotomy, etc.
32310–32545 Lung surgery

Cardiovascular

33200–33220 Pacemaker surgery
35450–35458 Vascular vs. cosmetic
37799 Unlisted procedure
38999 Unlisted procedure
39599 Unlisted procedure

Digestive

41100–41155 Mouth, tongue (for cancer)

43600–43630 Stomach (biopsy, etc.)
44100–44340 Intestinal
47100–47135 Liver

Urinary System

50200–50380 Kidney, including
             transplant
51550–51597 Bladder (especially for
             cancer)

Maternity

59000–59100 High-risk procedures
59120–59140 High-risk procedures

Nervous System

61340–61576 Craniectomy
62180–62258 Spine
64999 Unlisted procedure

Eye and Ear

65771 Radial keratotomy
69300 Cosmetic
69399 Unlisted procedure
68899 Unlisted procedure

Source: Courtesy of Options Unlimited, Case Management Services Division, 2003, Huntington, New York.

that a workers' compensation claimant should be able to return to work in 4 to 6 weeks. Four to 6 weeks go by, then another 4 to 6 weeks, then the patient needs another month of physical therapy three times per week. This kind of extension of treatment also indicates a problem. (Further, if the physical therapy is provided in a physician-owned facility, it may be a red flag.) Other indicators are: if the case continually passes by established goals; if the claimant is going to one doctor, and a month later he's going to another doctor who provides a similar service; or if the patient is receiving physical therapy and chiropractic manipulation at the same time. Or, the case manager might discover the patient is taking large numbers of pain medications and antidepressant medications, indicating the existence of new emotional components such as depression or lack of concentration, or that a seemingly simple injury has assumed grandiose proportions, with the patient seeing a variety of practitioners.

Other cases that need to be watched include those in which a new employee suffers a serious injury. One major concern is that the employer might not feel a commitment to get the employee back on the job, especially if modifications are required. New injuries to persons with prior claims for back or other workers' compensation injuries should be treated as red flags. (There is usually a state data bank that claims departments can use to research a claimant's prior workers' compensation injuries with other carriers or with other employer groups.) Indicators also include injuries to claimants nearing retirement age, injuries to part-time employees who might also work full time someplace else, or injuries to employees who could do work off the books. The insurer may be paying for an injury that occurred but not on the site the insurer is responsible for, or the claimant might still be able to work his or her main job but not the secondary job. For example, the claimant might work full-time as a file clerk in a corporation and part-time as a supermarket bagger. While recuperating, the claimant may be able to do filing but not stand for 4 hours and bag groceries, yet the workers' compensation carrier is still responsible.

Personnel issues can become reasons for people to go on short-term or long-term disability, and case managers need to devote attention to cases involving employees who are nearing retirement age or have both short-term and long-term disability policies (allowing a short-term leave to turn into a long-term leave, which is especially common in departments or companies facing layoffs). Employees who are at risk for being laid off or who have been passed over for promotion sometimes stay on short-term or long-term disability for security, using the insurance payments as a salary replacement. Obviously, the higher the salary replacement within a long-term plan, or the longer the HISOCC clause (see Chapter 4) in a long-term disability plan, the more quickly a case manager should review the claims. On the whole, the higher the policy benefits offered, the more bells and whistles should be going off.

In group medical coverage, the concerns are different. Group plans cover employees and their dependents, and a case manager might target catastrophic illnesses, premature deliveries, cancer cases, plus other chronic and devastating long-term diseases, such as AIDS or multiple sclerosis. Other things to watch for include multiple hospitalizations, multiple physicians, expenses beyond a certain threshold (e.g., $10,000), and particular kinds of services such as chemotherapy, radiation therapy, and infusion care.

Because medical professionals do not staff most claims departments, I encourage case managers to include visual aids or informative material to help illustrate the conditions of claimants when they are first introducing red flags and when they are working on a weekly basis with claims personnel. A case manager can discuss ICD-9 codes and CPT codes until next week and never make the impact that one good picture will create. For example, imagine a case involving body burns. The case manager may say, "There are substantial body burns, but they are confined to the trunk and upper extremities," and then shade those areas in on front- and back-view line drawings of the type supplied by most medical companies. The case manager, without spending much time, has enabled the claims staff to feel they know what the case is about.

I see articles all the time in consumer publications such as *People, TIME, Newsweek,* and *The Ladies' Home Journal* that can serve as terrific teaching aids. I might tear out a piece on breast cancer or cystic fibrosis and send it along to a claims examiner with a note. I have also purchased medical dictionaries and reference books designed for laypersons and handed them to my claims associates. Specific examples include *The Pill Book, Tenth Edition* (Bantam Books), *The Merck Manual of Medical Information, Second Edition* (Simon & Schuster), and the *Mayo Clinic Family Health Book, Third Edition* (Harper Resource).

The more complex and complicated the medical picture, the more user-friendly the explanation has to be. The goal is to get claims personnel to understand the reasons behind the need for case management and the decisions of the case manager. I have gone to the extent of taking a claims representative to a rehabilitation facility. I have also used videos from a rehabilitation facility showing pieces of equipment as well as videos taken by parents showing their child in a walker. I use videos and photos to give a clear impression of a given situation. I do not do this for every case or claim, only for those requiring special attention while we try to resolve their problems. Sometimes, word pictures suffice: The patient is down a country road six miles from his nearest neighbor, his family is dispersed across the nation, and he lives alone. Word pictures can humanize a case.

I have found all these methods of education extremely beneficial. They not only improve my relationships with referral sources but also enable me to do a better job for my patients, because I now have the understanding of the people who sent me out in the first place.

THE CASE MANAGER AS CONSULTANT

Case managers are an asset to a claims department. Bringing to the table their knowledge of clinical needs, medical procedures, and costs, they are a significant support toward maintaining cost-effective health care programs.

Claims Software

Working directly with a claims department on specific limit reports, group claims runs, and individual claims runs is a facet of the case manager in a consultant role. She becomes a hands-on team member, sitting alongside the employer group, the Third Party Administrator, or the insurer to capture those claimants in need of case management intervention. Using these tools, computer-generated claims runs, and creating the reports that follow from them, the case manager expands upon her case management activities and involvement with clients. These activities constitute the next step beyond noting red flags, but it is not a step every case manager may want to or be able to take (due to restrictions in her job description, the level of her interaction with the claims department, or the lack of computer technology sophisticated enough to generate claims runs). I include it here because I believe such consulting work is a vital part of case management capabilities, profile, and marketing strength.

Specific limit is the term I use to signify a computer-generated report that consolidates a particular type of information or claims run from all the claims experiences of a group of covered individuals. Such reports help pinpoint problem areas in which case management can effect a great change in case outcomes and dollar expenditures. If a company's employee base is predominantly female, I might want to see a specific limit report tracking pregnancy-related claims and benefit dollars spent. From this report, I could tell if there was a high incidence of problem pregnancies or premature births among these women. Perhaps the company needs to offer prenatal counseling or well-mother and well-baby seminars. At the least, it needs to make sure its female employees know they should be seeing a physician or nurse-midwife throughout their pregnancies, and it should give them clear information on what their benefit package covers regarding childbirth and infant care.

A case manager or claims manager can set a specific limit "marker" for any time, dollar, or medical treatment indicator. A specific limit report can cover any dollar amount one wants to establish, or it can be a hospital report with three admissions or more. Ideally, because everyone is concerned about dollars, the marker is a dollar amount, but it could also be time or an ICD-9 code. It might be appropriate to spin off a report on everyone in a group who has a diagnosis of cancer. Perhaps the case manager notices cancer cases are typically expensive and, in her role as consultant, wants to see who else in the group is likely to draw substantial benefits.

I might see that I seem to have an unusually high number of diabetes risks. In this situation, I will want to hone my data and look at everyone with diabetes who has spent $5,000, for example. I will want to know if they are in good systems of care. Is there something that should be done? Should the company establish a diabetic management program? Why is there such a high number of cases? This puts the risk management principle into case management, exactly where it belongs.

The object of tracking claims is not to dump a report in an employer's lap that announces that the firm has experienced *x* number of lost-time accidents in the past year, each requiring a recuperation period averaging 6 months and running up benefit expenses averaging $15,000. The purpose of claims tracking is to assess the information and utilize it proactively to design solutions. Case managers can help employers and Third Party Administrators create cost-containment claims administration programs to meet their particular needs. Does a company or a community have a particularly high rate of oncology claims, due perhaps to environmental conditions or job-site chemicals? Is a company experiencing an unusual rate of complex pregnancies or premature births? Once the presenting problem is pinpointed, a software program can be created to help find potential cases before complications are manifested.

A case manager consultant looking to interface more directly with claims personnel as a way of increasing cost-management capabilities first needs to understand the client company's claims system and computer and software systems. Five workers' compensation carriers may each have a software program capable of manipulating data in distinct ways and creating various report printouts. Can the system generate a report that breaks out cases with claims totaling over $10,000 or $20,000? Can it separate out all claims paid for lost-time injuries? Can it provide a run (list) of all claims filed by one claimant in the last 18 months?

The person to contact for this type of information is the claims manager. The claims manager may not be the programmer or the in-house computer wiz, but he or she is first in the line of communication. If the company has purchased software from an outside consultant, there may be reports already produced for the client that the case manager can use as a resource. There also may be an in-house capability to design almost any report the case manager might request. The extent of this capability varies from company to company and from line of insurance to line of insurance.

I sometimes ask to look at a run of workers' compensation cases in which the employee is still on salary replacement after 3 months, for example, regardless of the injury. Then I often note the amount of dollars that have been spent. If there is an explanation for big dollars spent, everything is fine. It is understandable that someone with a serious injury will be out of work a long time and will have high medical bills. On the other hand, if someone has only claimed a few hundred dollars in workers' compensation medical benefits yet is still off after 3 months, I want to know what is really going on. So, sometimes low dollars can be an indicator. Is the person really being treated? Is the person just sitting out there waiting for someone to say, "Hey, go back to work"?

In group medical coverage, a case manager can ask for a run of all claimants with three or more hospitalizations in a calendar year, all claimants with multiple medical procedures, or all claimants with home health services in place. The marker or specific limit might be a claims total of $50,000 or more (or $25,000 or $15,000). It doesn't take several years for some claimants to reach the $75,000 level; costs of this nature can add up within 1 or 2 months, and these cases would be among the ones called up for review.

TRACKING CLAIMS BY GROUP

The real key to consulting in case management is demonstrating to a client that only a small percentage of any employee group is responsible for generating the majority of claims and the bulk of benefit payouts. A case manager cannot attend a client conference, announce this fact, and expect the client to jump on the case management bandwagon. The case manager must be prepared to present concrete and objective information and offer a way to identify the relevant cases and improve the overall claims experience for the entire group. Nothing speaks louder to a client than a report taken from its own group experience. With a claims run, the case manager can show that out of a group of 500, with total claims paid of $200,000, fewer than 20 individuals (4%) filed claims totaling 80% ($160,000) of that sum. And nothing positions a case manager better than to work with a client as part of a team dedicated to helping better the claims experience.

With documentation, the case manager works with the claims department or Third Party Administrator to sell case management to the employer group. Because corporations often assume case managers work on all cases, it is important to emphasize that they focus on just a few; not everyone can benefit from case management. It is also appropriate to remind CEOs that case management is not a punitive investigative process, but a service whose purpose is to recognize and resolve health care delivery problems.

A computer run can be conducted to include all individuals covered by a policy. Perhaps a case manager is working with a company on its workers' compensation coverage. The first step is to define a benchmark, a worst-case marker, to find the cases in need of case management intervention. The class picked out might include those who have been out of work for 2 months or longer or those who had a lost-time accident resulting in a year or more of disability leave. (Employers with workers' compensation coverage pay medical as well as lost-wage expenses, so long absences are a big issue for them.) If there are no year-long cases, the case manager searches for absences lasting 9 or 6 months. To create a report, the case manager needs to work with the total number of covered lives, the number of individuals with major claims, and the kinds of injuries typical of the group. Are the injuries often catastrophic, such as traumatic brain injuries, or are they mostly unresolved back injuries? Using the data from a computer run, the case manager can determine that indeed 5% of the workers' compensation cases accounted for 83% of the claims dollars and that the majority of the individuals filed claims for complex, unresolved back injuries.

Figure 11–2 is a group claims run, a "hospital claims register," that includes all claims for hospital admissions. This run was requested as a means of focusing on those patients in need of case management intervention; a broad net (all hospital admissions) was used for the first cast. Such a run could also be conducted using

Figure 11–2 Hospital Claims Register

Cert #	Rel	Claim #	Type	Days	Incur	Paid	Charges
11355	4	1025022919	I/P	4	02/01/12	02/04/05	5,137.66
42093	4	1026501411	I/P	6	02/02/09	02/04/05	4,484.93
62164	4	1023703222	I/P	4	02/01/16	02/04/05	4,101.34
36014	4	1024502223	I/P	12	02/01/14	02/04/05	2,827.41
36014	4	1026602508	I/P	4	02/02/10	02/04/05	5,021.73
47794	4	1023021212	I/P	4	01/12/31	02/04/05	2,840.07
91247	4	1026502210	O/P	1	01/12/18	02/04/05	829.58
92247	4	1026502211	O/P	1	01/12/12	02/04/05	101.02
42376	4	1026602617	I/P	3	01/12/29	02/04/05	3,372.96
60170	4	1022021123	I/P	3	02/01/07	02/04/05	3,492.97
02136	4	1025701314	I/P	2	01/12/19	02/04/05	1,530.28
02136	4	1026502028	I/P	21	02/01/17	02/04/05	3,845.77
81182	6	1027202404	O/P	1	02/01/14	02/04/05	236.60
39464	1	1024501916	I/P	6	02/01/21	02/04/05	3,033.81
52052	5	1024402713	I/P	2	02/01/18	02/04/05	2,580.59
67116	4	1022020309	I/P	6	01/12/28	02/04/05	3,840.88
01212	5	1024502323	I/P	3	02/01/22	02/04/05	1,914.24
11093	4	1024402712	I/P	4	02/01/28	02/04/05	2,206.92
62129	4	1025021223	O/P	1	02/01/21	02/04/05	367.02
74120	5	1025802404	I/P	7	02/02/05	02/04/05	2,922.12
23269	5	1024402202	I/P	2	02/01/26	02/04/05	1,705.08
88196	5	1025802408	I/P	5	02/02/06	02/04/05	2,063.55
67198	1	1026601017	O/P	1	02/02/10	02/04/05	185.02
43282	1	1027302218	I/P	2	02/01/10	02/04/05	5,085.52
08551	5	1026601523	O/P	1	02/01/05	02/04/05	261.53
06055	6	1026701502	I/P	3	02/02/18	02/04/05	1,645.75
06055	4	1026701504	I/P	3	02/02/18	02/04/05	3,110.40
11038	6	1027302508	I/P	3	01/12/20	02/04/05	1,352.50
46230	4	1026701402	I/P	3	02/02/08	02/04/05	2,181.82
41144	5	1027202102	I/P	3	02/02/15	02/04/05	4,366.21
02812	4	1027101011	I/P	4	02/02/09	02/04/05	4,355.95

continues

Figure 11–2 continued

Cert #	Rel	Claim #	Type	Days	Incur	Paid	Charges
06326	4	1028102021	I/P	2	02/02/26	02/04/05	1,763.56
21139	1	1024502309	I/P	11	02/01/11	02/04/05	19,462.06
64552	4	1026602517	I/P	5	02/01/08	02/04/05	12,848.09
30252	4	1026602519	I/P	5	02/01/19	02/04/05	6,102.62
52232	1	1025021124	O/P	1	02/01/12	02/04/05	1,011.10
10102	5	1026602812	I/P	3	01/12/10	02/04/05	2,103.41
10301	6	1023703010	I/P	2	02/01/16	02/04/05	1,852.32
64984	1	1024402705	I/P	5	02/01/15	02/04/05	3,270.81
88292	1	1027302406	O/P	1	02/02/15	02/04/05	78.02
10283	4	1025021714	I/P	5	02/01/10	02/04/05	3,075.54
Month Total							132,568.76

Source: Courtesy of Options Unlimited, Case Management Services Division, 2003, Huntington, New York.

length-of-stay data. The computer run could then be narrowed and patients be better targeted by adding a specific limit (e.g., hospital admission stays of 10 days or more only).

Figure 11–3 is a report generated from a group run. This type of quarter evaluation report breaks out the high-cost cases over a calendar or fiscal quarter and can be used to demonstrate that only a handful of claimants need case management intervention. If these few cases are properly managed, the whole group benefits from lower claims costs. In April, 1% of the group generated 34% of the claims; and in May, 2% generated 67% of the total. In June, 2% of the group was responsible for 73% of the benefit dollars paid, and .3 percent (three employees) actually accounted for 44% of the total. This run also tracked cases that continued to require costly care from one month to the next. It clearly shows the need for case management.

Regardless of the reimbursement system or type of policy, once the case manager has identified a group of patients that could benefit from case management intervention, the focus turns toward setting up a preventive cost-containment program to reform the group as a whole. After intervening at an early stage in the treatment of a complex, unresolved back injury, for example, the case manager, by pointing to the improved outcome, shortened time, and reduced cost, can gain the confidence of the claims department.

Figure 11–3 Quarter Evaluation

Medical Claims—ABC Corporation - April   843 Employees—2,213 covered lives

Claim Number	Amt. of Claim	Diagnosis
0421160	$3,800	OBS-GYN
0743221	2,100	Deceased—in C.M., ovarian cancer
(W) 1501617	4,028	Psych—ALC
(H) 2214689	3,615	Anthroscopy
1821041	6,437	OK
1847756	4,100	OBS
1523314	4,580	Vasc. dis., diab. in C.M.
1015252	1,800	OK
5830764	3,958	Fx nose
0962140	9,200	HIP, CVA in C.M.
	$43,618	

Total claims: $129,575
1% of group generated 34% of claims

Medical Claims—ABC Corporation - May   858 Employees—2,262 covered lives

Claim Number	Amt. of Claim	Diagnosis
(M) 1356602	$ 2,732	
(W&D) 1516758	5,008	
(M) 2083312	25,571	
(M&S) 4373029	1,881	
(M&W) 0917462	4,923	
(M) 1503327	3,100	
(M) 2543178	1,644	
2594622	1,522	
1296654	7,521	Referred to case management but pt. declined
3601744	2,320	
3237161	1,500	
5237708	1,646	
*1523318	3,918	
(D) 3541006	25,073	We have in C.M.
(M) 0929763	7,770	
*(M) 0962143	1,800	
	$97,929	

Total claims: $146,800
16 employees (2%) generated $97,929, or 67% of total
*Also in April report.

continues

Figure 11–3 continued

Medical Claims—ABC Corporation - June   864 Employees—2,291 covered lives

Claim Number	Amt. of Claim
(S) 0543112	$6,417
(W) 0677896	2,324
** (M)1371818	3,907
(M) 5221021	1,459
(M) 1147786	17,103
** (W-Heidi) 2594638	2,914
(M) 1821053	3,451
** (M) 1296685	2,675
Miller, M. (M) 1703217	1,690
** (W&S) 1814437	3,085
(W&D) 1516992	4,682
** (W) 5237718	7,525
*** (M) 1523319	1,452
** (D)3541008	14,632
(M) 3202772	2,050
(M) 2567131	4,328
*** (M) 0962144	50,737
(W) 5818753	2,280
(M) 2501763	5,692
	$138,403

Total claims—$188,704
*In April report
**In May report
***In April, May & June
Note: W = wife; H = husband; M = member; D = dependent; S = spouse
19 employees (2% of group) expend $138,403, or 73% of total
3 employees, .3% expend 44% of total

ABC Corporation - 2nd quarter

		Employees	Covered Lives
April	$129,575	843	2,213
May	$146,800	858	2,262
June	$188,704	864	2,291
TOTAL	$465,079		

34 Employees (4% of group) expend $280,121, or 60% of total.

Source: Courtesy of Options Unlimited, Case Management Services Division, 2003, Huntington, New York.

TRACKING CLAIMS BY INDIVIDUAL CLAIMS HISTORIES

A case manager can also track individual claims histories. In particular, she may want to look at the claims histories of the few individuals responsible for the bulk of the claims for a given period.

In looking at a particular claims history, the case manager may first identify the dollar amount and then fine-tune the review to see if this is a case in which case management could make a difference. Suppose the individual has reached the specific limit of $75,000. The case manager might note that the claims were for one hospitalization and one major surgical procedure, a colostomy. The procedure is completed, there were only minor post-op problems, so there is no real opportunity for case management to have an impact. Another individual who has reached the $75,000 specific limit may have a series of claims for treatment of an unresolved ulcer of the foot, diabetes, hypertension, and vascular disease. Taken together, these claims indicate a health care time bomb. What is the real problem here? Why isn't the ulcer resolving? Is this person getting appropriate care?

Figure 11–4 presents an excerpt from an individual claims report. This report, which breaks out the claims history by ICD-9 and CPT codes, was requested because a set dollar limit had been reached. The question was, what were the charges for? By checking each diagnosis, it was discovered that the medical problems ranged from a stroke to respiratory and vascular difficulties to depression. By reading this history, the case manager is in a much better position to provide assistance.

Another step in the case management consultation process is to review the actual claims in particular files. (Access to files might be possible if the case manager and claims manager have a good relationship.) A computer provides just so much information: coding information, dollars, and where the money was spent. By looking at an actual file, the case manager might discover that the patient is on several medications, each prescribed by a different physician. Are the physicians aware of one another and of the other medications the patient is taking? Admissions and complications can be caused by interactions between medications. Perhaps the patient is having difficulty describing his or her symptoms or understanding the prescribed treatments and is consequently going from physician to physician. This is the type of case in which the case manager might be able to make a major contribution.

Although helpful information is usually plentiful, a case manager has to know exactly what data are available and how they can be used to help patients, providers, and payers. The claims department should ideally perceive case managers as a tool to better their service, whereas case managers use the tools of the claims department to help them resolve some case management problems.

Figure 11–4 Subscriber History File Accessing Report

Worksheet Inquiry

Group   930656 Hampshire Cty (Actv/Ret/COBRA)
Enrollee   e123-45-6789
Member   e123-45-6789
Enter latest incurred to date _____

Claim no.	Statuses	Incurred dates	Benefit	Diagnosis
e 94009618-01	f f	01/11–01/11	M1	CVA/EQU/ACERMAN MED SUPPLY
e 93051425-11	f f	08/11–12/31	M0	93¢RX/X-8 FARMING, FPO PHARM.
e 93099250-02	f f	12/01–12/31	M0	RB/MS/ATLANTIC REHAB/CVA
e 93086701-13	f f	12/22–12/29	M0	CVA/PTHD/ROCHE LAB
e 93086701-12	f f	11/29–12/21	M0	CVA/PTHD/ROCHE LAB
e 94004825-01	f f	12/20–12/20	M1	GI TRACT DIS/ERH/ KIMBALL MC
e 94004825-02	f f	12/20–12/20	M1	GI TRACT DIS/ INEL 12/KIMB PHY
e 93086701-14	f f	12/01–12/15	M0	CVA/PTHD/ROCHE LAB
e 94001820-01	h	12/05–12/05	M0	TRACHEST/ERH/ KIMBALL MED CT
e 94001820-02	h	12/05–12/05	M0	TRACHEST/ERD/ KIMBALL EMERDR
e 94001820-03	f f	11/16–12/05	M0	TRACHEST/VARIOUS PV'S
e 94001820-04	f f	12/05–12/05	M0	TRACH/INEL#12/MOOSA JAFFARI,M
e 93086701-15	f f	12/01–12/01	M0	CVA/XRAY/JERSEY SHR MC
e 93086701-09	f f	11/30–11/30	M0	HEMIPLEGIA/INEL#69/ JERSEY SHORE
e 93099250-01	h	11/26–11/30	M0	RB/MS/ATLANTIC REHAB/CVA
e 93086701-08	f f	11/22–11/26	M0	HEMIPLEGIA/PVIM/AHN
e 93086701-10	f f	11/04–11/26	M0	RB/MS/RUSK INST/ HEMIPLEGIA
e 94004825-04	f f	11/02–11/26	MI	GI TRACT/XRYD/JERSEY SHORE R
e 93086701-16	h	11/25–11/25	M0	CVA/CON/LOUIE MD
e 93067106-72	f f	10/07–11/24	M0	VASCULAR/RDO/ NYU RADIOLOGY

Figure 11–4 continued

Claim no.	Statuses	Incurred dates	Benefit	Diagnosis
e 93086701-11	f f	11/23–11/23	M0	ABDOM PAIN/ SRI/PTI/ASHA MD
e 93094583-02	f f	10/11–11/22	M0	DEPRESS/MPVO/ OLLINS, MD
e 93086701-07	f f	11/08–11/19	M0	HEMIPLEGIA/PVI/ AHN, MD
e 93091059-02	f f	11/16–11/18	M0	CHOLELITH/PVI/ PFEFFER, MD
e 94004825-03	f f	11/12–11/12	MI	GI TRACT DIS/PVO/ PARRY, MD
e 93094583-01	f f	11/02–11/11	M0	DEPRESS/MPVI/ FRANK, MD

Enter worksheet to inquire into (r)estart or (c)ontinue Alt-Z=Help COM1 9600 8N1 VT102

Source: Courtesy of Options Unlimited, Case Management Services Division, 2003, Huntington, New York.

MOVING INTO THE CONSULTANT ROLE

I have had terrific opportunities to put these theories into practice in my associations with Third Party Administrators. As a consultant, I help Third Party Administrators track claims and increase the efficiency of their administration services. We have become a value-added service in ourselves, and are now part of the Third Party Administrator's marketing strategy in reaching new clients.

My development and use of claims tracking reports and computer runs was motivated by my frustration at not being able to reach claimants who needed case management in time to make a difference. After convincing the TPA president to allow my company's staff to show how case management can resolve problems and reduce payouts, we were given access to the Third Party Administrator's claims staff and began training them in case management concepts and delineating the kinds of cases we wanted to see. I created red flags and the claims review tip sheet shown in Figure 11–1 as well as a "Request for Service" form (Figure 11–5). The claims personnel were to fill out this request form and leave it in my in-box whenever they came across a claim fitting the red flag profile or had a question concerning a case's suitability for case management or claims review. (I made it a practice to be in the Third Party Administrator's office once a week to review these requests and to be available to the claims staff as an associate and assistant.) Figure 11–6 is a form we designed for TPAs to use when they have a question or a claim to review on a case now in case management, or when they

Figure 11–5 Request for Service Form

OPTIONS UNLIMITED
HEALTH CARE & DISABILITY MANAGEMENT SERVICES
76 East Main Street, Huntington, New York 11743
(631) 673-1150 FAX (631) 673-8369

DATE

------------ REQUESTED BY: --

NAME		PHONE	YOUR FILE # (SS #)
COMPANY NAME		LOCATION	INSURED
CLAIMANT			INSURANCE COVERAGE & STATE
DATE OF DIS.	DIAGNOSIS		EMPLOYER GROUP

REQUEST FOR

PLEASE CHECK ONE
❏ CareWatch - UTILIZATION REVIEW: PREDETERMINATION, PRE-ADMISSION, CONCURRENT
    REVIEW, IDENTIFICATION FOR CASE MANAGEMENT, SPECIFIC LIMIT REVIEW
❏ CareSolutions - MEDICAL CASE MANAGEMENT
❏ CompSolutions - WORKER'S COMPENSATION
❏ AccuClaim - CLAIMS REVIEW
❏ Other Questions _____

IF NECESSARY, HAVE YOU INCLUDED:
❏ PRE-AND POST-OP PHOTOS   ❏ MD/PT OR CHIRO OFFICE NOTES (ATTACHED)
❏ OPERATIVE REPORT (ATTACHED)   ❏ R&C CHARGES (LIST HERE):
❏ ANESTHESIA REPORT (ATTACHED)   CPT CODE   R&C CHARGE
❏ ITEMIZED BILLING   _____
❏ NURSING NOTES (ATTACHED)   _____
                                     _____

CONSULTANT RESPONSE

SAVINGS:
SIGNATURE: DATE:

Send Original and one copy to   REFERRAL SOURCE COPY - YELLOW
                                 OPTIONS UNLIMITED COPY - WHITE

Source: Courtesy of Options Unlimited, Case Management Services Division, 2003, Huntington, New York.

Figure 11–6 TPA Claims Review Sheet

OPTIONS UNLIMITED CLAIMS REVIEW SHEET
FOR
_____

Date: _____   Claims Examiner: _____
                            (Last, first name, ext:)   _____

Employer Group: _____   Network: _____

Insured: _____   Please check one:
                                    □ Care Watch - To Identify Case Mgmt.
Patient: _____   □ Care Solution-Case Mgmt.
                                    □ Accuclaim-Claims Review
S.S.#:   _____

Address: _____   City: _____   St. _____   Zip: _____

Provider In or Out-of-Network: _____   Is this an appeal?   Yes   No
How much was paid on claim? _____

Please Circle:
Reason claim is being reviewed: Chiro PT -   Surgery -   Pre-Determination -   Dental -   Cosmetic
HHC/Nursing -   Worker's Compensation -   Coverage/issue -   Podiatry -   Diagnostic -   Other

If Any: Please include: Pre-and Post-op Photos - Operative Report - MD/PT or Chiro Notes/Itemized
                        Billing/Other

CPT CODE	AMOUNT CHARGED	R&C	REPRICED AMOUNT

Is there a co-pay? Y N   How much? _____   Deductible Remaining: _____
What would the claim normally be paid at: 70%   80%   90%   100%   Other: _____
Has the deductible been satisfied?   Y   N

Questions/Comments for Reviewer:

Source: Courtesy of Options Unlimited, Case Management Services Division, 2003, Huntington, New York.

Table 11–1 Claims Contact Letter

Date

Ms. Sue Ying, Claims Examiner
Third Party Administrator
One Chamber Plaza, Suite 1413
Cheyenne, WY 82001

Claimant: John Doe
Insured: Susan Doe
Group: Seventy-Seven Slides
S.S.#: 999-99-9999

Dear Claims Examiner:

Please accept my appreciation for referring the above captioned file for case management services.

_____ [Case Manager] will be handling this case. She will conduct an initial evaluation and will contact you with a verbal report to be followed by a complete written report with our impressions and recommendations.

Should you have any questions about this file, please don't hesitate to call me at (516) 555-5555.

Very truly yours,

President

KB:cs

Source: Courtesy of Options Unlimited, Case Management Services Division, 2003, Huntington, New York.

---

question a possible reentry into case management for a case that has been in the program.

When a case is referred to us for case management or claims review, a letter similar to the one appearing as Table 11–1 is sent to thank the claims examiner and to give him or her the name of the case manager assigned to the case. This promotes a more open and communicative association.

How did we convince the Third Party Administrator's president of the benefits of case management? We selected our trial group by requesting a quarterly report with a specific limit run of $100,000. (This was the stop-loss insurance benchmark for one of the Third Party Administrator's client companies.) When preparing a "mock" report like this to explain the value of case management, I've found it makes a deeper impression if we use the client's own cases and actual dollars spent to show the potential savings when case management is applied.

We as case managers were looking for all claims over $25,000, which is our company's own marker. We looked at every month to see whether the total number of cases over $10,000 increased and if the same individuals were consistently filing the larger claims. Once we identified several cases, we asked to see the actual claims files. In one instance, we found that the claimant had run up a claims total of $30,000, most of it in pharmaceuticals. There were pages and pages of claims on file for drugs prescribed by different physicians. Reviewing the prescriptions, we searched for drugs recommended for the same or related conditions, side effects, drug interactions, and drug combinations, and we also tried to determine whether the drug combinations were contributing to the patient's medical problems. In this case, we found there was reason to be concerned for the patient's safety. Because the Third Party Administrator fully supported our endeavor, we contacted the individual and his physicians to share our concern, finding that the physicians were unaware of each other and the prescription "overdose." We were then able to establish one primary physician who acted as the sole dispenser of medication. The example proved a perfect one for showing the benefits of case management to both patients and the bottom line.

In another instance, we saw a total of $50,000, but what really caught our eye were the three inpatient hospitalizations. Dollars are a case management indicator, but the truly important factor is always going to be how those dollars are spent. What is driving expenses up? Did these three admissions occur over a long period of time, or were they a series of closely spaced, short-stay admissions? When I see three or four admissions within a short time period, I wonder whether there is something wrong with the discharge plan or whether the individual cannot sustain the level of stability at the time of discharge once he or she reaches home.

Case managers working with claims departments become detectives. Using curiosity, instinct, and a paper trail, they look for items to uncover potentially serious cases. Obviously, the more experienced the entire team, the better they are at following the paper trail. But any case manager and any group of claims personnel can make a difference, a major difference, for their clients and the covered patients.

PART III

Case Management Administration and Financial Considerations

CHAPTER 12

Financial and Quality Assurance Reporting

Everyone flinches at the very sound of the words "the cost of health care." Not far behind the direct costs are the administrative or management expenses that are impacting all of us as we attempt to brake this "running train." While we individually and collectively grapple with these fees, those of us providing or managing case management services need to realize that our interventions are an addition to an already costly system. Cost of care is an issue that has to be faced head on. Case managers need to deal with the financial ramifications of care and alternatives. To make recommendations for care that the benefits dollars will not cover is ridiculous, and to not know how costly one facility is in comparison with another is not doing one's job.

If a case manager is going to put together a set of recommendations or alternatives, she needs to cite costs. Further, the case manager needs to involve the patient, family, physician, and other members of the health care team in financial matters. I think we have all been insulated from financial concerns for far too long. At some point early on, it is essential to sit down with paper and pencil and a family and say, "If your dad has three more hospitalizations at $1,500 per day, this is how quickly his benefits are going to be eaten up. If we can keep him out of the hospital longer and put services in the home, if you'll be willing to help with some of the care as well, we can get him care and services over the projected length of this illness, which is certainly what our goal needs to be here. We don't want to run out of benefits before he runs out of problems."

Although it would be nice if all consumers and health care professionals perceived the medical and monetary value of case management, unfortunately not everyone does. To avoid being seen as merely part of the "medical-insurance bureaucracy," case managers need to play an active role in communicating the benefits, in health management and dollar terms, of their services. Because most case managers come from nursing or social work backgrounds, they tend to resist talking about the financial aspects of health care.

DOLLARS AND HEALTH CARE

The majority of health care professionals today probably entered the field with a desire to help others. We were the actual hands-on providers of the services deemed necessary. No one questioned our motivation, methods, or outcomes. We were acknowledged as professionals and were generally assumed to adhere to the strictest of practice standards and to want only the best for our patients. But then money got in the way, and health care professionals were called upon to balance treatment and cost. Why health care costs became so unmanageable will, I suspect, be left to historians. In any case, there are now so many interest groups that sorting out truth from fiction will perhaps be an insurmountable task. Clearly, the health care system is undergoing profound changes. The system many of us trained in is a thing of the past. Cost is an issue for all of us, consumers (employers and employees) and health care professionals alike. And because cost is an issue, the transition for health care professionals continues to be a struggle. Why is it such a problem?

To develop a better understanding of the current situation, it may help to examine the health care system of yesterday. Those who entered medical and related fields had much in common. They shared, among other things, a desire to help, a need to contribute, and a willingness to comfort and counsel others in distress. They did not share, by and large, an interest in or talent for financial management. In fact, most health care businesses or practice settings have someone other than the physician, nurse, or therapist keeping the books. It was generally accepted that if medical professionals did have responsibility for financial matters, it might influence their decisions and cloud their perceptions of what was best for their patients. For many, many years, it was considered perfectly all right to protect professionals from having to deal with money issues.

Add to this society's idealized view of medicine and health care and its tendency not to question health care costs. Interestingly, we demand to know the price of almost everything, from houses to cars to airfare to hotel rooms and college tuition. Some of these items, when advertised, have their price tags clearly visible. Other items, such as designer clothing or jewelry, have their price tags more discreetly placed, but the prices are still discoverable through a little effort. This is not the case with health care services, undeniably among the most expensive commodities.

When was the last time you saw a price tag on an MRI (magnetic resonance imaging), saw, or were quoted, the fee for a specific surgical procedure, or chose Hospital A or Hospital B because the service was equal but one was more reasonably priced? Although most of us are facing higher deductibles and co-payments, we are still not asking the dreaded question, "How much will this cost?"

For example, imagine someone who needs surgery. The medical plan providing benefits reimburses at 80% of the reasonable and customary charge for the procedure. The surgeon selected has quoted a price of $9,200; the plan has established that the reasonable and customary fee is $7,500; the reimbursement, at 80% of $7,500, is $6,000; and the remaining balance is $3,200. Quite clearly, the time to resolve the discrepancy between the price and the payout is before the surgery takes place, not after. What can be done? The person can choose another qualified surgeon who charges less; discuss the matter with the current surgeon, who might be willing to negotiate or reduce the fees; or decide to proceed with the current surgeon despite the additional costs. But at least the decision will be an informed one, with all results and consequences evident.

When I hear providers criticizing case managers for "talking about money" and "asking prices," I realize they may resent having to compete and having to defend their prices. The old days of automatic acceptance of charges are gone forever. And this really is better for all of us. Medical professionals are intelligent consumers, and they do know how to make decisions that benefit their patients while preserving valuable medical resources.

The merger/acquisition activity among providers has created somewhat of a monopoly in health care, with the advantage to make more money weighted to the providers. Hospitals and specialists are following the direction of pharmaceutical coverage, offering boutique and "concierge" service in several tiers of health care packages. These out-of-network examinations and follow-up are for those patients who can and will pay a higher price. Case managers can look into such high-end marketplaces. The "sandwich generation," caring for their children and parents at the same time, needs elder case management, too.

Case management does become involved not only with the outcomes of care, but also with the many alternative levels of care and with the financial aspects of care. In fact, to address quality and outcomes and the alternatives without paying attention to the costs is doing a disservice to patients, payers, and, yes, even providers, who will also be losers if costs go unchecked.

Because of its role in cost containment, case management focuses on catastrophically ill patients (acute and chronic) and high-cost cases, as well as those predicted to be, for example, disease management cases. As defined and practiced, it addresses costs, but never at the expense of patient safety or quality of care. If case managers do not communicate both its cost-containment benefits and its quality-improvement benefits, case management could well become eliminated as a tool in the treatment of patients.

There are many experienced case managers who initially worked hard to demonstrate their effectiveness to their client companies. After their clients became believers, the case managers no longer felt the need to push the potential benefits. Case management departments were created, staffed, and supplied with computers and other equipment by major insurance carriers and Third Party Administrators, and hundreds and thousands of dollars were spent, month after month, until another someone at the senior level closely examined the figures. Then, questions were asked: "What does this department do?" "Is it making us any money?" "Does it save us or our clients any money, and if so, how much?" There were no answers because the case managers had stopped documenting their efficacy.

Discussion of fees and costs should be part of any case management program. Financial issues need to be examined and debated before a company implements such a program or contracts with a case management provider, or before a professional decides to be a provider of case management services. There must be an acceptance of financial accountability for the costs being added to the system. Individuals or departments who are not able to demonstrate cost-effectiveness will not survive, and their demise will be their own doing.

So, how do case managers prepare information or reports that will support continued case management involvement? How can they consider or suggest alternative care plans if they do not know the costs involved in the current system of care? How should the subject of costs be approached? What questions need to be asked and to whom should they be directed? Are prices negotiable? Should discounts be requested? How do case managers know what is reasonably priced and, at the other end, what is an exorbitant fee? Does cost have anything to do with quality or outcome? Just as with other products and services, it is best to be prepared with information beforehand. How is this information acquired? By acknowledging that the whole subject of health care costs is uncomfortable, especially for practitioners, and by asking questions over and over to compile provider cost-of-service lists.

There are several ways to obtain pricing information while learning about a company and its services. One of the easiest is to attend local, regional, and national conferences. Most conferences include provider exhibits as well as sessions conducted by provider companies. Such sessions offer marketing and educational opportunities for those who might either have influence on or direct purchasing capabilities. For example, a firm might present a session titled "Respiratory Management of the HIV Patient at Home." Although the information may be generic, the presenters are typically available afterward to provide specifics regarding the credentialing of staff, the accreditation of the firm, the location of its offices, the scope of its services, plus all of the other "need to know" information, such as "How much will this cost? Are there additional considerations for all-inclusive, for prompt-pay, for volume, for exclusive, or for PPO arrangements?" (And are these questions not the same kinds of questions we all ask before making other kinds of purchases? Is anything here "unprofessional"?) Most providers have ranges of fees and negotiating options and are better prepared today than 10 years ago to discuss fees. So go ahead, ask.

The larger the conference or the more diversified the subject matter, the more opportunity there is to meet with multiple providers of a wide range of products and services. A conference titled "The Rehabilitation of the Alcoholic Adolescent" will include presentations on topics of interest, such as "Peer Pressure," "Tough Love," or "Family Dynamics." Further, the exhibit hall is likely to feature providers such as inpatient programs, day treatment centers, and residential long-term centers, all utilized in the care of the alcoholic adolescent. If teenage rehabilitation is going to be a strong component of one's practice or department focus, this is an important conference to attend. On the other hand, a conference titled "Managed Care: Health Care Reform and Self-Insured Groups" will provide the opportunity to acquire an incredible amount of information in one setting. Featured will likely be HMOs, PPOs, home care agencies, rehabilitation facilities, head injury programs, pharmaceutical companies, equipment manufacturers and dealers, hospitals, computer software and hardware companies, consulting firms, infusion care services, and so on. This type of conference offers a nonstressful environment in which to learn about the whole range of services and providers available to case managers and, equally important, to begin discussions about costs. (One way of mitigating some of the anxiety caused by having to discuss fees and other costs is to examine the decision-making process for other purchases and then apply some of the same skills and methods to purchase agreements for health care services. This is a very concrete way to demystify some of the fear that has crept into this arena. I believe that this transition is possible if one approaches it in increments of time and information. In the process, our decisions will not only be safe and quality-assuring ones, but will also be cost-conscious and cost-effective.)

When the necessary cost information is acquired, what should be done with it? For the small company or independent practitioner, perhaps keeping a separate "provider book" will be sufficient. Dividing the book into sections by provider type or service or location allows easy access to the data. For instance, under "Infusion Care Services" should be listed companies that are quality providers; their strengths, weaknesses, and areas of expertise; special offerings that are of particular interest; and the costs of the services. Other categories might be high-risk pregnancy management, home care, subacute hospitals, durable medical equipment dealers, and so on. The information should be updated continually, eliminating providers that are no longer viable, adding new services, and changing contact names or the location of offices. Provider information needs to be current so that the time spent selecting providers and services is kept to a minimum.

In a larger organization or case management department, serious consideration should be given to putting such information in a computer database. Each case manager would then have access to it and would be able to update and change it according to departmental guidelines, obviously adhering to provider selection criteria applicable to that particular area. The accumulated information would not only be useful in actual case management activities, but could also serve as the database for cost-benefit analysis reports (discussed later in this chapter).

In addition to conferences, there are several other resources that can be utilized in developing provider information: government organizations and publications, travel and professional associations, and periodicals that publish data on costs and trends. Publications such as *Business & Health* (now online at businessandhealth .com), *Business Insurance, The Wall Street Journal, Medical Economics,* and *The Case Manager* frequently list costs of hospitals per day, average lengths of stay, fees for procedures, and high-cost organizations. They also sometimes publish lists of rehabilitation facilities, skilled nursing facilities, and other types of organizations and evaluate rates, services, and so on. *Newsweek* and *Time* run special issues on health care as a whole and often examine a disease state in-depth.

NEGOTIATING SKILLS

Once armed with information about services and fees, a case manager is better able to arrange for services and negotiate fees. Negotiating is an acquired skill and does require thought, and there are books written on the subject and guidelines developed especially for case managers (see Table 12–1 for a list of gender-related communication problems). William Ury, cofounder of the Program on Negotiations at Harvard Law School, has written two of the definitive books on negotiation: *Getting to Yes: Negotiating Agreement Without Giving In* (Houghton Mifflin Company and Penguin Books editions) and *Getting Past No: Negotiating with Difficult People* (Bantam Books). *Getting to Yes* is also available in a video workshop format. National conferences almost always have a session or more devoted to negotiating skills. The newsletter *Case Management Advisor* as well as journals *Harvard Business Review* and *Continuing Care* frequently incorporate tips for case managers.

The first thing to keep in mind in negotiating is that there are ranges in price for everything in health care. This does not mean that we aim for the least expensive category or that selecting a "Rolls Royce" price tag guarantees excellence—high price tags only guarantee a big bill. The goal is to try to fulfill the patient's equipment and service needs in a cost-justified manner.

The first roadblock case managers and product or service suppliers commonly confront is the difference in background, orientation, and industry jargon each party brings to the negotiations. For example, a home medical equipment supplier

Table 12–1 Common Female-to-Male Communication Obstacles and Solutions

---

Problem: Women tend to take too long to get to the point, using too many details.

Solution: State your main point up front, using few details. Be brief and precise.

Problem: Women tend to use soft, tentative, unassertive voices, especially in talking to men.

Solution: Practice speaking in a firm, moderately loud, confident voice.

Problem: Women often allow themselves to be interrupted by men in conversation.

Solution: Try one or several of these: (1) Keep talking in a firm, louder voice. (2) Stop in mid-sentence and wait in silence till the interrupter has stopped, (3) Say politely, "I'll be happy to continue when you're finished."

Problem: Women often end statements in a questioning tone of voice, with a rising inflection.

Solution: Speak in firm, declarative sentences that sound like clear statements, not tentative questions.

Problem: Women tend to seek consensus and agreement by ending sentences with "question tags," such as "don't you agree?" or "am I right?"

Solution: Drop most of those question tags from your speech, especially when talking to men.

Problem: Women tend to hedge in conversation instead of stating firm opinions.

Solution: Mentally define your message clearly, then state it assertively.

Problem: Women have learned to communicate in a way that builds friendship and agreement, while men are more action-oriented and directive.

Solution: Be aware of the differences in male-female communications styles and learn to match your communications style to men's when talking to them.

Problem: Women too often preface remarks by actually asking their listener not to take them seriously. ("This probably isn't a very good idea, but . . ." or "I don't know a lot about this; however . . .")

Solution: Never apologize or discount what you have to say. Believe in yourself and your statements and speak accordingly.

Source: Reprinted from *Medical Case Management Conference V,* p. 187, with permission of ICMA and Nancy N. Bell, © 1993.

---

may be well-versed in the features and functions of the equipment, but may not understand why certain models are problematic or inappropriate for a patient. The case manager knows the patient's diagnosis and needs, but is not necessarily familiar with the technical capabilities of equipment. To overcome this and other snags, it is best to take an honest and open approach to communications.

I have found it helpful to work exclusively with one representative at a durable medical equipment, home medical equipment, or home health care agency. First, this allows me to review equipment, services, contracts, and billing in a single call, and, second, it helps me get answers when I need them. Just as I want to know all the options included with a piece of equipment that might assist a patient, I am also interested in terms—lease, rent, rent with option to buy, and outright purchase and service costs. The various options often affect my decision.

Case managers and product and service providers alike are looking for long-term working relationships. An otherwise good relationship will be undermined if the case manager accepts a price break on a 1-year rental agreement knowing the patient probably has only 3 months to live or if the agreed-upon equipment arrives with expensive optional features that were sold to the patient without the case manager's knowledge. In their pursuit of high-quality health care at an affordable cost, both providers and case managers can benefit by serving as resources for each other. Dealers can take the confusion out of techno-speak; case managers can alert suppliers that certain bed features are not recommended for people with a particular back problem. By working as partners with service and equipment providers, case managers can build beneficial business associations and stronger resource bases.

Negotiating is a specific form of educational communication. As Louis Feuer has noted, negotiation allows for an open discussion of issues at hand, enables all parties to freely discuss their objectives, and helps all parties understand the implications of the plan. The more we know, the better decisions we can make. Here is a synopsis of some of Feuer's suggestions for successful negotiations outcomes:[1]

1. Define the limits, including time limits on a contract and time relative to the patient's illness, financial resource limits, and medical resource limits.
2. Know your power—in personality, expertise, situation, and sharing of information. (I would add the flip side, know your limits.)
3. Be aware of hidden agendas—was a decision made before negotiations began?
4. Know when you will walk away—what is your bottom-line?
5. Never take the first offer—go through the process.
6. Know that negotiations have stages: establish the criteria, exchange information, and then reach compromise.

7. If you reach an impasse, set aside that issue and concentrate on smaller issues to create a momentum of agreement that will carry you through the critical issue.
8. Be aware of changes in demeanor, in both you and your "opponent"— physical reactions, need to negotiate, more or less willing to negotiate.
9. Never assume that something will not work.

To assist case managers in establishing a negotiating process and evaluating service providers and facilities, two documents were developed: "Service, Equipment, and Supplies Placement Guidelines" (Table 12–2) and "Program Questionnaire and Facility Review for Case Managers" (see Appendix 12–A at the end of this chapter). These were designed to serve as standard tools for selecting providers and vendors and evaluating facilities, and they include criteria to facilitate the making of informed decisions based on the needs of the patient. The forms should be customized by the addition of the case manager's own criteria. Is there one person to contact for financial questions, or one contact for patient updates? This can save a lot of time otherwise spent playing telephone tag or holding on the line while someone who can answer a query is found. Does the vendor return phone calls? What is their level of service? All these elements play into the making of a good service match.

The following negotiating guidelines originally appeared in *HomeCare* under the title "Simple Negotiations." Although designed for home care providers, they are applicable to the types of negotiations in which case managers engage: [2]

1. For patients on long-term therapies, implement a reverification process.
2. Negotiate the payment terms. A good general rule is the deeper the discount offered, the sooner the provider should be paid.
3. Ask if a fax of the claim or other documentation can be sent to speed claims processing.
4. Always confirm verbal agreements in writing. Include in the confirmation letter the effective date of the agreement, the full name of the person who conducted the verbal negotiation, a complete description of the products and services agreed upon, the agreed-upon discount, the agreed-upon payment terms, the net payment after the discount, the agreed-upon type of claims submission form, and notification that the agreement will be considered mutual unless the supplier states otherwise in writing within a certain number of days.

I would add:

1. Remember to negotiate on a case-by-case basis. No two cases are alike, and no two negotiation processes will be alike. There are always things you can bring to the table from your past experience. However, each payer and

Table 12–2 Service, Equipment, and Supplies Placement Guidelines

---

1. Evaluate client to accurately determine his needs:
   - Personally assess client/family/home.
   - Review evaluations and recommendations of others—PT, OT, physician, etc.
   - Secure physician's order, if required.
   - Recommend or confirm the correct equipment supply or service.
2. Determine whether rent or purchase is more cost-effective.
   Consider:
   - Length of service
   - Availability and cost of service/maintenance contracts
   - Comparative costs of rent/purchase
3. Secure payer authorization (approval of claims professional).
4. Bid equipment, supplies, or service.
   - Requests for bids from providers must be uniform.
     —May be requested by phone (occasionally written)
     —Outline:
   - Specific item or service requested
   - Date to begin/deliver
   - Duration of service
   - Means and percent of payment from insurer
   - Date and time bid will be closed
   - Seek to determine the provider's
     —Ability to deliver service
     —Follow-up plan
     —Type of supervision
     —Teaching support
     —Reputation for dependability and quality of service
   - Request that providers convey bid figure by phone—with a written confirmation.
   - Vendors should be contacted once only with an accurate and identical description of the item/service needed. Failure to respond by bid closing time will constitute a "no bid."
   - Provided all key issues (service, delivery, and quality) are equal, the business is awarded to the lowest bidder. If not equal, the decision will be at the case manager's discretion/judgment and will be final.
   - Bid information may be available to participants only after the bid is awarded—and only at the case manager's discretion.
   - Providers should be requested not to actively market their equipment or services with case management clients, but rather to forward observations, suggestions, and recommendations to the case manager for consideration and coordination with the medical team and funding agency.
5. Follow-up to ensure:
   - Item (or service) is appropriate

Table 12–2 continued

- • Timely response or delivery is provided
- • Instructions are adequate
- • Service to equipment is available
- • Item (or service) is retained only as long as needed
6. Summarize bids (and logic behind choice if not lowest bidder), with attention to cost saved in report.

Source: Courtesy of Case Management Society of America, Little Rock, Arkansas.

---

provider has his or her own feelings and concerns, and even these may vary from case to case.

2. Negotiating is a subtle art, and it is all about listening. First, you learn the real concern behind the words when you listen carefully and watch for body language, and second, the people you are working for want to know you are paying close attention to them.

3. Negotiations can get testy. Keep your mind on the overarching goal, and gently position conversations (that is, remind participants) so that all involved are pursuing the best solution for everyone concerned.

4. There is something to be said for using a "most favored nation" negotiating strategy if this is a provider you will be working with on a regular basis.

5. The opposite of that is to negotiate from a one-case basis: "This is a singular need. We are not going to be seeing 20 or 30 more patients in this situation. How can we make it work?"

NUANCES BETWEEN NEGOTIATING WITH PROVIDERS AND PAYERS

Case managers are in a different position and, therefore, employ varying strategies in discussions with payers as opposed to providers. When negotiating with a provider, such as a home care agency, the case manager most often is one health care professional talking to another, using similar terms supported by shared understanding. Further, it is assumed that the case manager has the authority to approve or decline the price quote given; if she is not the decision maker, she is certainly a strong influencer in the process. It is also assumed she has a wide variety of providers to access because of the number of quality providers available, although the range of price quotes she receives may or may not be as varied. She may have the time to choose among the various proposals. The gathering of information from providers helps make her a more effective negotiator.

Negotiating with a payer for approval requires a different tack, and tact. The case manager is no longer the decision maker. Whether it is an insurance carrier, self-funded employer, or a Third Party Administrator, the health care dollars and ultimately the decision are the payer's. The payer may not have the medical knowledge or expertise to know what it is the case manager seeks, and why. The payer negotiator might be a chief financial officer (CFO) or a human resource manager who is uncomfortable with the responsibility of making the health care decision. Case managers have to help them arrive at an understanding of the situation to enable them to feel good about making the decision, which requires skill. They are concerned with a number of issues. How long will this alternative care last? If I do it for this case, will I have to do it for all the others?

Perhaps the case manager wants to place a patient in a subacute facility; this particular payer has no language in its plan to cover such facilities and it is the first time the case manager is approaching the payer to consider the issue. The payer's first reaction might be, "We don't allow for subacute care." To help the payer better understand the case so she can negotiate more effectively, the case manager needs to educate the payer by listing the alternatives and the consequences of not approving the suggested facility in terms that are meaningful to the payer. This means illustrating that financially, approval of another level of care or a more appropriate center for care is in the payer's best interests.

I had a case in which I negotiated with a payer on behalf of a youth hospitalized with a traumatic brain injury. The boy was beginning to come out of his coma but had developed bed sores, pneumonia, and an infection. The payer's plan provided unlimited days of coverage for hospital care and the boy met its criteria to remain there; however, I knew if he did, he would deteriorate further. We hoped to take him to an out-of-state, long-term care facility that had the ability to wean him off the respirator and address his rehabilitation needs. There was no plan language for that type of facility. I had to show the plan that the acute care facility was well equipped to manage his initial trauma but lacked the range of resources to manage his optimum recovery. I introduced the human aspects of the decision. Yes, they had hospital coverage, but this young man's condition would definitely worsen there. He had already experienced far too many complications; I felt we would lose him if he remained hospitalized, and we wouldn't have anyone left to rehabilitate.

I negotiated by being very patient with that payer who had every right to say, "No, there's no language in the plan, and we're not doing it." I had to help them understand that this young man was being harmed by every extra day he was there, that we would have a much better chance of getting him out of any kind of center for care if we brought him to a facility that could more appropriately meet his needs. I explained that hospitals are not set up to do long-term rehabilitation care. I showed them in real dollars how much continued hospitalization was going to cost. If he stayed in the hospital and had a decubiti, and needed skin grafting, he would face more infection and IV antibiotic treatment, and this is what it will cost in dollars and cents. By the time we get him cleared from the skin graft and infections, he will have lost whatever gains he had made. He already had a number of physical problems to overcome. I suggested that the faster we could get him to a place with expertise in managing his complications and rehabilitation needs, the faster he would improve and heal.

If case managers encounter resistance, I encourage them again to "get behind the no." Identify the payer's concern and continue to address it. Help them understand that a case manager is looking out for their interests in terms of medical and financial risk. Payers often buttonhole nurses and social workers as employee advocates and may become concerned that we give equal thought to the employer's needs as well. The case manager must be able to take herself out of the patient advocate role and be a strong advocate for the payer group as well. She can make the decision-making process a little less overwhelming for them, showing the payer group she understands that this is new territory for them and that she respects their questions. Make the payer part of the process; report every 2 weeks on money actually saved and the patient's status, which is what our office did in the previously mentioned case.

Not every case is successful. We explained to one payer that we were aware of its limitation of 60 home care visits in a calendar year, which the individual had exhausted. If we didn't go outside those limits, the patient would be back in the hospital again. The payer held to its plan language. In another instance, we were negotiating with a union for hospice benefits. A few members of its Board of Trustees had personal feelings that in essence set up a roadblock, so a reasonable discussion could not take place. They were almost sending up emotional flares. We knew allowance for a hospice benefit would best meet the patient's desires and needs, while saving expenses for the union. There was no way to win the group over to this decision.

Sometimes, case managers just have to wait for the disaster to happen. Then, they can return to the payer, not to gloat, but to ascertain if the decision remains unchanged.

NEGOTIATING IN A MANAGED CARE ENVIRONMENT

It is becoming more likely for case managers to negotiate an out-of-contract benefit in the managed care environment. HMOs and PPOs are realizing that although they may have contract limits and established contract language, in some very high-cost cases, they may have to do more creative and unusual things. More MCOs have determined that they do not need to change their contract language for all covered lives; however, especially when their dollars are funding a risk-based contract, and when they realize it is their money, they will respond to the best interests of their own bottom-line or profit margin.

A case manager may not receive approval for an alternative to a plan on the first phone call. I have found that a "no" does not mean I cannot get approval; it might mean that I am not speaking to the right person. If I can contact someone who is financially responsible for what goes on in the plan, I meet with greater willingness to negotiate. The key lies in how information is presented. I present the cost-effective care alternatives in financial terms first, and then discuss the fact that it is good for the patient and the right thing to do.

Negotiating in a Capitated Contract

This willingness to listen to options extends to payers and providers in capitated arrangements. Managed care is putting more of the responsibility on the providers to achieve the results. I've talked to nurses in HMO plans who years ago could not negotiate care alternatives. Now, because the HMO is contracting with a physician practice group that receives x dollars per month per employee to provide a range of services, these providers are doing whatever they can to keep patients healthier and to minimize hospitalizations.

Hospitals, home care agencies, and rehabilitation facilities all negotiate for services that help their entire organization run more efficiently. Those in home care might notice certain cases requiring a greater portion of its services, more of its nurses' time. The nurses are experiencing difficulty moving these patients toward independence or self-care, and the cases require numerous home visits. It may be that the agency is stretching to provide a service that it does not normally offer. Perhaps the agency does not go into the in-depth educational visits that these patients need to progress into self-care or to reduce the number of hours the nurse is working the case; this service will have to be added.

We will see fewer practice variances among providers, and greater acceptance of critical care paths, because we will have established the best treatment paths for pneumonia, for example (which is now treated differently by every provider in town). In part, this is because of the maturity of the marketplace, the business side of managed care. There is also growing acceptance and recognition among medical professionals, who have had a difficult time with loss of autonomy during the transition to managed care, to accept a medically appropriate, cost-effective option.

Negotiating for Carve-Out Services

Negotiating for carve-out services varies with the practice setting. Large payer groups, such as HMOs, PPOs, or employer groups, have contracts with rehabilitation facilities or hospitals. The hospital provides specified general services at a set rate per day. Services such as an organ transplant or bone marrow transplant are carved out and negotiated directly. We have a network of hospitals we are working with now. If we have an admission in a plan provider hospital, we do not negotiate hospital costs, unless the patient requires care that is not subject to the plan rate (such as head trauma care, certain surgeries, and organ transplants). We then negotiate a plan rate.

The same applies for a nurse's visit by a home care agency. For a patient who presents with complicated problems, requiring more than the standard nurse's visit (or physical therapist's visit), the price would be negotiated separately, or carved out.

In the same way, high-cost procedures, such as a transplant, are sometimes negotiated as a carve-out. Particularly with self-funded groups, the stop-loss carrier might have negotiated separately with Centers of Excellence if there appears to be a potential for one or two employees to have a such a need. These "laser-out" agreements serve as an umbrella policy on insurance, setting coverage at $250,000 and superceding the basic stop-loss agreement of $150,000. A case manager will want to ask about any laser-out agreements that the self-insurer might have struck with its own network providers.

Perhaps the all-inclusive case rate provides 21 days of coverage for a bone marrow transplant. The patient you are advocating for demonstrates a strong recovery rate and is discharged at 14 days, or it goes the other way, and the length of stay increases to 28 days. Worse, the transplant fails and a retransplant is mandatory. If the stop-loss insurer, as the risk-bearer, has negotiated with Centers of Excellence, the carrier might take over negotiations at this point. The case manager will continue providing care management services on the case, as before.

DOCUMENTING NEGOTIATED ARRANGEMENTS

Assuming that a case manager has selected the most appropriate service for the patient and negotiated a different fee structure than the one quoted originally, what is the next step? I believe it is important to document and communicate the terms of agreement that case managers arrange with providers.

It should be reemphasized, however, that prior to negotiating or arranging for any service, the case manager must have received approval to do so from the payer source. To begin with, the case manager needs to check that there is language in the plan contract that allows case management. Reviewing the details of the plan contract is especially important when arranging for services, selecting providers, seeking discounts, and so on. Will what the case manager arranges for actually "hold up" when the claim for services finally arrives in the claims department? Will it be paid on a "prompt-pay" basis (that is, within 2 to 4 weeks of arrival at the department)? Will it be paid even though language in the plan may not mention or may even exclude such services? Will it be paid at 100% of the submitted charge, rather than 80% of what is reasonable and customary? Will it be paid even if the plan maximum for the services has already been reached? Who knew about the services, who approved them, who will pay for them, and if no one else will, is the case manager now responsible?

Failure to get answers to these questions before starting work on a case or for a client company puts everyone at risk—the patient, the provider, the carrier or payer, and the case manager. Acting on mere assumptions in this extremely important area can result in legal consequences for all involved.

When entering into a relationship for the provision of case management services, the case manager needs to describe the scope of the services in sufficient detail to permit a complete discussion of how case management will interface with the department or individuals who will have the ultimate payment responsibility for what could best be described as "alternate care plans." It is essential to lead a potential client group through a typical case, one that illustrates just how case management works. The presented scenario should include referral, assessment, the care setting, the exposure the group has for this particular area of service within the patient's insurance plan contract, alternative care plans, and the details of the insurance plan contract that apply to these alternatives. For example, the alternatives presented might include sending the patient home and providing round-the-clock nursing care at $45 an hour ($1,080 a day) or placing her in a skilled nursing facility at a cost of $285 a day. The plan contract allows a maximum of 40 skilled nursing visits of up to 4 hours each, does not mention coverage for skilled nursing facilities, but does state nursing home custodial care is not covered. The case management proposal is for 30 days of care in a skilled nursing facility at a negotiated rate of $285 a day (not the usual $425) if the claim can be paid within 2 weeks of receipt. The other option is a continuation of the patient's stay in the acute care hospital at a rate of $1,500 a day, minimum, which the treating physician favors and for which there is coverage available. However, once apprised of the skilled nursing facility alternative, the treating physician switches his allegiance, and the patient and family also prefer this option.

The portrayal of a fairly typical case allows a client group to begin to understand the nature of case management and to realize how expensive the restrictions in a given plan contract can be when they prevent certain options from being approved. In the preceding scenario, the difference between 30 days of hospital care and 30 days of skilled nursing facility care is $36,450. Hopefully, such examples give client groups the determination, creativity, and sound business/financial rationale to allow the "insertions" of such solutions not just in one case but for as many times and situations in which not doing so would be deemed as fiscal irresponsibility.

Case managers need to be able to present this kind of information to client groups in order to create the right environment for case management and the system or pathways that will allow it to be used successfully. Health care cost "problems" are not without solutions. The important thing is to uncover, discuss, and resolve pertinent issues prior to the institution of an in-house case management program or the establishment of a working relationship between an independent practitioner or small company and a client group. There is no point in developing plans that might work "if only." This is why it is imperative that case managers understand and appreciate the various payer systems, plan contracts, and the claims payment process for the various lines of insurance. Inadequate understanding leaves the case manager functioning in a vacuum outside of the system instead of as an integral player within it.

After the case manager has made the client group understand what is required for the implementation and approval of suggested plans, payment issues need to be addressed again. I developed a heightened appreciation for the importance of developing a good relationship with a client's claims department when some claims for services I had arranged and received approval for (from the claims manager) did not get paid and then were "lost." At the same time, other claims were being paid but not at the rate I had negotiated, nor in the desired time frame. This resulted in embarrassment for me, with the provider and with the client group, who questioned the savings I had reported. On a closer look, a claim for a higher fee came in and was paid, because it was billed from the provider's regional office rather than from the local office with which I had "successfully negotiated." For these and many other reasons, I determined that there needed to be a more formal, accountable, and credible way of securing payment arrangements.

To better track and manage case negotiations and claims processing in my office, I designed provider agreement forms to be utilized for each provider and each service. Psychiatric, durable medical equipment, infusion, nursing care, therapy, rehabilitation hospital, and skilled nursing facility services all have separate provider agreement sheets (see Appendix 12–B at the end of the chapter), which are sent with a cover letter explaining their use (Table 12–3). For our staff, I developed guidelines to assist them in filling out the forms and in applying them to different situations (Table 12–4). All these forms are designed to be revised whenever necessary to meet our own needs or the needs of a client company.

These forms can be used for any number of distinct negotiations. They are not used for every X-ray or every piece of durable medical equipment; rather, they are used for high-priced items, for benefit plan exceptions, and so on. Perhaps the payer has a preferred provider arrangement that allows patients to receive a discount, or we have agreed on a prompt-pay discount of 3% if I can ensure that the invoice will be paid in 2 to 3 weeks (which qualifies as early in claims circles). Especially helpful when an alternative care plan is created, a provider

Table 12–3 Provider Service Agreement—Cover Letter

Service Agreement

Date: _____

Patient: _____

Insured: _____

Emp. Group: _____

S.S. #: _____

Dear _____:

OPTIONS UNLIMITED is a case management consulting firm retained by

_____.

Attached hereto is a description of the services and/or supplies that you agreed to furnish to _____ on _____.

In order for you to receive payment from the Plan for the services and/or supplies furnished to the Patient, you must submit each claim/bill to Options Unlimited with a copy of this letter and the enclosed Service Agreement, using one of the enclosed envelopes. This will ensure special handling and payment by the Plan subject, of course, to co-payments, deductibles, and other limitations of the Plan.

Any claim/bill received without a copy of this letter, with Service Agreement, will be returned with a message: "Please resubmit with Service Agreement."

Claims/bills received in amounts greater than allowed by this Service Agreement will be reduced to the agreed amount with the following "explanation of benefits" message: "Claim reduced to amount agreed to in the Service Agreement."

Claims/bills for services and/or supplies not covered by this Service Agreement should be sent to the Patient, who must then submit a claim to the Plan in the customary manner.

If you have any questions regarding this Service Agreement, please contact immediately the case manager identified below.

This Service Agreement is entered into by Options Unlimited on behalf of the Plan. This Service Agreement is a contract between you and the Plan, *not* between you and Options Unlimited, or any other person or entity.

We thank you in advance for your anticipated cooperation.

Very truly yours,

Options Unlimited

By: _____

Case Manager

(631) 555-1212

Table 12–3 continued

I have reviewed and am in agreement with the above arrangement.

Provider: _____

Name/Title: _____

Signature: _____

Date: _____

Source: Courtesy of Options Unlimited, Case Management Services Division, 2003, Huntington, New York.

---

service agreement documents case manager, provider, and payer approval for a specific care procedure so that the claims examiner is not put in the awkward position of having to "authorize" a treatment.

Following negotiations with the provider, the case manager completes most portions of the form, which is sent by fax to the provider for an approval signature. Then, a hard copy of the agreement is sent to the provider with a cover letter, which notes that any invoices must accompany the form. A copy of the agreement is also sent to the claims examiner; that particular claim will then be flagged manually or by computer for special handling so that the negotiated price, time frame, or exception is not lost. Given that five or more different examiners or different claims departments might cover one claimant, such tracking is vital.

My company manages the tracking and payment in two different ways. Sometimes, the case manager becomes the "clearinghouse" for every invoice received on behalf of a particular claimant and will hand the negotiated claim to an examiner for processing. In other instances, the provider company sends in its customary bill, knowing it will be reduced as per our agreement (for example, from $410 to $280).

Whatever type of provider agreement format a case manager uses, it should incorporate specifics of the arrangement: the time frame (beginning and end dates), the fees, and any conditions (for example, "payment at 100%" or "payment within 30 days," or "per diem rate is all-inclusive; no other charges to be billed"). The information needs to be documented and communicated to the provider and the payer source (claims department). In addition to all pertinent data, such as the patient's name, insured's name, group policy number, social security number, and physician, the form should include a space for the contact person, the case manager, and phone numbers where they can be reached. Each case management department or company needs to develop a method or

Table 12–4 Provider Service Agreement Guidelines

Subject: Provider Agreements

Purpose: To document service agreements with providers with the specifics of the arrangement clearly outlined.

Procedural Guidelines

1. Certain cases may require the utilization of specialized services, equipment, and therapies. Through ongoing assessment and in conjunction with the treating physicians, the case manager will identify the needs, select the appropriate services and providers (using the attached guidelines to assist you), negotiate fees and arrangements, and continually monitor patient status, appropriate use of goods and services, continued delivery of services and equipment, any complications or changes in patient, and timing of possible discontinuation of services and equipment use.

2. Source of Agreements
   —Nursing (RN, LPN, Home Health Aide)
   —Durable Medical Equipment (including apnea alarms, wheelchairs, hospital beds, oxygen, etc.)
   —Infusion therapy
   —Other therapies (PT, OT, Speech)
   —Rehabilitation facility, SNF, Psych, and Substance Abuse programs

3. Responsibilities
   —The case manager will fax form and letter of agreement to provider, requesting their signature to acknowledge acceptance of the terms. When signed, the case manager will send out the hard copy with a supply of envelopes with the case manager's return address.
   —The case manager will receive claims, accompanied by the agreement form, will review for adherence to the agreement, and will forward to the claims department for payment.
   —Note: Once the services are in place, it is the *case manager's* responsibility to monitor for quality/outcome and determine on an ongoing basis the need for less (or more) services.

In addition to requesting the claim for review, any notes related to these services must accompany the claim, for example, nurses' notes, PT evaluation and notes, and so on.

It is also the case manager's responsibility to monitor the reevaluation and/or expiration dates of these agreements and follow through with whatever is indicated. You will be in jeopardy of services being discontinued even if still needed, due to failure to renew an agreement.

Source: Courtesy of Options Unlimited, Case Management Services Division, 2003, Huntington, New York.

---

system consistent with its administrative capabilities and client base. For case management departments in insurance carrier groups, notes entered into a computerized claims system might suffice. Companies working with several carriers might find that mail or fax communication works best. When established, the system should enable accurate payments to be completed in a timely manner and also allow tracking of some of the savings realized by case management.

COST-BENEFIT ANALYSIS REPORTS

Documenting savings from case management intervention is a necessary component of case management work. One method of documentation is to use cost-benefit analysis reports. These are reports that serve to illustrate in financial terms that the costs spent on case management services (and the services that are implemented as part of an alternate care plan) translate into dollar savings, or dollars spent versus dollars saved. Each case management program should have from its very inception a mechanism in place to demonstrate savings to all who will pay for the services. The report format may vary from company to company, and it can certainly be customized or modified to meet client company needs. Report variables may change as a case management program develops.

A cost-benefit analysis report is so specific that I believe it is best prepared by the case manager who works the case. This individual possesses knowledge about the patient, the problems, and the care plan in place at the time the referral was made. She also identified solutions; prevented additional problems; and selected, arranged for, and negotiated the services that were utilized. As a consequence, she is in the best position to evaluate the intervention's success.

Cost-benefit analysis reports are not extended narratives, nor do they include ongoing documentation. They are concerned with the financial aspects of case management and, in my view, should not be included among the monthly progress reports. Because it is possible for certain cases to be in litigation (in particular, workers' compensation, auto, and disability cases), the financial aspects of case management should generally not be included in the patient-centered reports. Although it is expected that costs will never be the focus of case management decisions, there is concern that any mention of dollars (even alongside all the other reasons for a particular treatment decision, such as higher quality care, patient preference, etc.) might be misconstrued or misrepresented by those who view case management intervention solely as a means to control costs.

Some client groups, claims departments, and other purchasers of case management services would prefer to receive reports that deal exclusively with numbers, but it is my contention that this does a disservice to case management. By only portraying savings, one virtually eliminates all of the other contributions of case management. It would seem highly desirable, therefore, to develop a report format that can not only demonstrate savings, but also communicate the impact of case management and illustrate the process.

The data in these reports can be realigned to provide clients with insight into the workings of their benefits plan, successful or otherwise. They can serve a claims function by signaling a potentially greater risk and spurring a response before it occurs. Monthly, yearly, or reports over 1 or more years can be used to analyze benefit usage, group experience, and possible stop-loss needs. Documents can also be formatted by provider (is one much more costly than the other?), diagnosis (is a disease-state management program indicated?), or hospital claims (is billing accurate for services rendered?).

Whatever format is chosen, it is important that each case within a grouping is presented similarly. Following is a list of items that should be included in each case presentation:

1. Identifiers (file, case, or social security number; carrier; employer group; date case opened; date case closed; total weeks or months in case management; diagnosis)
2. Overview of case management intervention
3. Summary of intervention
4. Case management fees
5. Savings
   • Avoided charges
   • Potential charges
   • Discounts and/or negotiated reductions
   • Reductions in services, products, and equipment
6. Actual charges
7. Gross savings (potential charges minus actual charges)
8. Net savings (gross savings minus case management fees)
9. Status of case (open or closed)

Table 12–5 is a worksheet that can be used for each case, and Table 12–6 is a set of guidelines that explains how the worksheet sections should be completed.

A word about actual versus potential savings: Fortunately, there are many opportunities for case managers not only to improve the quality, outcome, and lifestyles for our patients, but also to become better at attaching value to what we do—as we perfect our skills and realize our worth. To cite an example, new case managers may be comfortable suggesting and then arranging for home care as a way of saving money, but experienced case managers know that they can realize additional savings by asking for prompt-pay discounts, reducing levels of care or hours of care through continual assessment of the patient's progress, and so on.

Table 12–5 Cost-Benefit Analysis Worksheet

Quarter _____

Re:

File #:

Carrier/Client Group:

Date of Referral:

Date of Closure:

Total Weeks/Months of Case Management:

Diagnosis:

Case Management Fees:

Summary of Intervention:

Avoidance of Potential Charges:

Total of Potential Charges:

Alternate Care and Related Charges:

Total Charges for Alternate Care and Case Management Fees:

Net Savings:

Source: Courtesy of Options Unlimited, Case Management Services Division, 2003, Huntington, New York.

Reductions, discounts, negotiated rates, all-inclusive per diem rates, and "freebies" are examples of actual savings.

Potential savings are more difficult to quantify but also need to be reported. For instance, a case manager is referred to a patient who, in prior months, had an admission every 1 or 2 months for diabetic complications and an emergency hospital stay of 5 to 7 days. At the time of the initial evaluation, the case manager determined that this patient did not understand his diagnosis, was minimally compliant, and, in fact, frequently ignored dietary restrictions and urine and blood testing requirements. During the 3 months of case management intervention, the case manager communicated these problems to the physician, referred the patient for formal education and a diet counseling program, and involved the patient in the daily monitoring of his own progress. She successfully resolved what would have been a continuing pattern of admissions and complications. In fact, in the 6 months of case management involvement, there were no further hospital admissions. This is the kind of potential savings that should be noted in cost-benefit analysis reports.

Table 12–6 Cost-Benefit Analysis Guidelines

Re: Assigned system number.

File # (SS #): Insured's social security number.

Carrier/Employer Group:

Date Opened: Date opened for case management.

Date of Closure: If applicable.

Total Weeks/Months in Case Management: How long case has been active.

Diagnosis: Major categories only, for example, Cancer of Liver, Right Side CVA (Stroke).

*Remember that these will be utilized by "lay" people mostly, so keep this understandable.

Case Management Fees: Related case management expenses for report time frame.

Summary of Intervention:

Note: This is not to be a discussion of the patient's entire medical history, symptoms, or surgeries. This will have occurred in initial and progress reports and should not be repeated here.

This is a summary of *your* intervention on this case. How did you make a difference in the quality, eventual outcome, patient compliance, patient and family support, prevention of complications, better/more appropriate use of resources, service, and dollars?

*See example reports for further illustration of this section.

This is the "proof" statement for case management, the justification for it on this case! It is *your* turn to cite *your* accomplishments, and give evidence of the need for our services, and the fees for our services.

Avoidance of Potential Charges: This section lists by specific service *and* possible charges (if there is a range put the range, for example, $750 per day–$1,000 per day) that *could* have occurred if this *case* did *not* have your intervention. Remember that you would not have been there to suggest home IV antibiotics versus continued stay in the hospital, or to negotiate rates for services (for example, fees for home IV and nursing services that could have been charged and paid for because there is no R & C for these, anything goes!), or to reduce RN visits from 3 × per week to 1 × per week to discontinuance. List *each* of these services or hospital admissions for the complications that you prevented or equipment, therapies, etc., that would have occurred and (probably) continued if you did not intervene during this quarter. Your list should look something like this:

1. Continued longer stay in hospital

5 days × $1,500 per day = $7,500

Additional MD visits while patient in hospital @ $150 per visit × 5 days = $750

Table 12–6 continued

2. Home care services—discharge planner & MD request hospital-based home care services following patient's discharge.

RN visits 1 per day × 14 days @ $160 per visit = $2,240

HHA 6 hours per day @ $20 per hour × 14 days = $1,680

PT 3 × per week × 2 months @ $115 per visit = $2,760

Total of Potential Charges: This should be a combined dollar figure for the preceding charges, e.g., $14,930.

Alternate Care and Related Charges: This is a list of *specific* services and charges for each that *you* put in place, negotiated rates, effected purchase versus rental, usually instead of the potential charges. For example:

Home care services by community-based, Joint Commission-accredited agency at following rates and with MD approval:

RN visits 1 × per day × 7 days @ $100 per visit = $700

then RN visits 3 × per week @ $100 per visit = $300

HHA 6 hours per day @ $18 per hour × 7 days = $756

then HHA 4 hours per day @ $18 × 5 days (family helped on weekends) = $360

PT 3 × per week × 1 month @ $85 per visit = $1,020

then PT 2 × per week × 1 month @ $85 per visit = $680

Total Charges for Alternate Care and Case Management Fees:

The sum total of charges compiled from preceding listing, e.g., $4,666.

Net Savings: This is a *dollar* figure to be calculated from the potential charges *minus* the charges incurred from the "Alternate Care and Related Charges," e.g., $10,264.

Note: Occasionally, it will not be possible to claim savings; you may not yet have had an opportunity to reduce the level of care or services, because the patient's condition worsened or the patient had to be readmitted to hospital, or you have just put the services in place, but no claims are in yet and savings are "to be determined." You may, however, state an approximate dollar figure that you expect will occur.

Actual Savings

Fortunately, there are many opportunities not only to improve quality, outcome, and lifestyles for our patients, but also (as we perfect our skills and realize our worth) to become better at attaching value to what it is that we do. To cite an example—experienced case managers may be comfortable suggesting and then arranging for home care versus continued hospital stays, but newer case managers may not know that there is still an ability to realize additional savings

continues

Table 12–6 continued

by asking for prompt-pay discounts, reducing levels of care or hours of care by assessing patient progress and needs frequently, etc. Such reductions, discounts, negotiated rates, all-inclusive per-diem rates, "freebies," etc. are *actual* savings.

Potential Savings

This is more difficult to quantify and qualify but *needs* to be stated. For instance, you have been referred a patient who in prior months of referral had an admission of 1–2 months for diabetic complications and the emergency hospital stay was 5–7 days. At the time of your initial evaluation, you determined that this patient lacked the understanding of his diagnosis, had minimal compliance, and, in fact, frequently ignored dietary restrictions, urine and blood testing requirements, etc. During the 3 months of case management intervention, you have communicated the problems to his MD, referred the patient for formal education and a diet counseling program, and involved the patient in a daily monitoring of his own progress. You have successfully resolved what *would* have been a continuing pattern of admissions and complications; in fact, in the 6 months of case management involvement, there have been *no* hospital admissions. The potential charges that *would* have occurred without case management intervention and savings could be stated in the following manner.

Summary of Case Management Intervention:

Case manager during this quarter identified and then implemented solutions for this man who had been referred due to recurrent hospital admissions. Patient was poorly informed and because of this was noncompliant following a diagnosis of diabetes. Further complicating this was prior history of increased blood pressure and angina. Case manager advised treating physician and with his cooperation arranged for diabetic education and counseling program; patient was directed to monitor his own progress and report problems to case manager and MD. Programs were available through community hospital outpatient program with considerable savings and good results. There have been no further admissions during this 3-month period and the patient feels more in control. This man was at absolute risk for increased problems and costs.

Avoidance of Potential Charges:

2 hospital admissions @ 5 days for each × 1,500 per day = $15,000

MD visits while patient in hospital @ $150 per visit × 10 days = $1,500

Diabetic Management Program @ $1,000 per private outpatient program

Total of Potential Charges = $17,500

Alternate Care Charges:

Diabetic Management Program @ $750 per program = $750

Table 12–6 continued

MD visits—1 per month @ $75 per visit = $225

Total Alternate Care Charges = $975

Total Savings $17,500 – $975 = $16,525 plus additional savings over several more months.

The preceding is an example of what a group might determine to be "potential savings"; *however,* positioned with expertise and stated strongly and authoritatively, it becomes highly credible.

Note: If there are *no* savings to be claimed, either actual or potential, then state *none* or *to be determined,* with a brief (few word) statement; for example, patient still in hospital, savings will be realized next quarter.

Source: Courtesy of Options Unlimited, Case Management Services Division, 2003, Huntington, New York.

THE COST-BENEFIT ANALYSIS SUMMARIES

After each client case has been outlined, there needs to be a summary of the case management program for the particular client group—a total financial analysis of dollars saved versus dollars spent for case management services for the quarter, 6 months, or year. Examples of such summaries are provided in Appendix 12–C and Appendix 12–D at the end of the chapter; these are expanded versions prepared for two different clients, one a union group and the other a self-funded employer utilizing a TPA. The former shows an annual summary as well as semi-annual summaries and reports. The latter shows a quarterly summary and cost-benefit analysis reports, including a difficult pregnancy case, which is discussed in the sections that follow: "Quality Assurance Programs," "Explaining Difficult Situations," and "Feedback from Patients." The reporting format that should be used for each client depends on the needs of the client group and the structure of the case management program, among other factors. These serve as a representative sampling of cases worked; not all cases that were worked are reported for this time frame.

These reports are tools that help make case management services more vital to a client. Pulling a diagnosis summary report allows a case manager to show a CFO the costs of a specific disease state, perhaps caused by an upswing in diabetes among the worker population, indicating the need for disease management or a wellness program. What is driving hospital admissions? A diagnosis summary report correlated to a hospital admissions report (using numbers, not names, to indicate cases) might reveal that there are a select few with that disease who are at the top of the group's benefits outlay. These few need to be in a case management program; the others might improve their health with the help of an educational program. A case manager delivering this type of report is pointing out the areas in which the employer is vulnerable to risk, a constructive and looked-for service.

It is recommended that some kind of financial analysis of case management programs be performed on a regular basis, whether quarterly, semiannually, or annually. Because dollars can add up quickly, especially in very active cases, preparing cost-benefit analysis reports on a quarterly basis is appropriate. Frequent reporting not only makes the compiling of information a more manageable task, but also allows on-line case managers and the supervisor or program director to evaluate the effectiveness of services before too much time has passed and too many dollars have been spent. Not all cases yield savings, and some are more successful than others. What is important is that a timely evaluation of services (which in essence is what this is all about) allows for earlier recognition of problems and the prevention of bigger ones. If case management fees are high and savings on several cases drop each quarter, the problem may be a case manager who is not using time appropriately or does not know how to capture savings. She may require additional training. It might also be a signal that some cases need to be closed.

Preparation of cost-benefit analysis reports is one of the more difficult tasks for many case managers. For several years, I assumed the responsibility for my staff. However, as business increased, this reporting became a larger part of my job, and I learned that I no longer had the kind of day-to-day knowledge of the cases that allowed for a more accurate capturing of savings. Eventually, it was decided that the best person to prepare each individual cost-benefit analysis report was the case manager who was working the case. Instruction in cost-benefit analysis writing became necessary and has now become a part of our training program. (Depending on the size of the case management company or department, preparation of the client group summary is probably a management task, which is relatively straightforward if all the case managers' summaries are in hand.)

QUALITY ASSURANCE PROGRAMS

Financial accountability is perhaps the greatest contribution that cost-benefit analysis offers. Although the reports are appreciated by clients and are useful as marketing tools, they are also useful as quality assurance tools. Further, the process utilized in the preparation of cost-benefit information becomes an empowering experience. Individuals come to appreciate the real value of case management and recognize their own contribution to each success. In instances of limited success, they are able to understand the reasons and develop different strategies to meet them. This kind of self-evaluation promotes excellence and allows the ongoing monitoring of case management services.

EXPLAINING DIFFICULT SITUATIONS

Almost every case manager will at some time be called upon to explain case management fees. Why are the case management fees so high this year compared to last year? Why does your time cost so much? Cost-benefit analysis reports can be a very effective tool for addressing such queries.

In one such instance, my company was providing case management services for a self-funded employer (Sam's, the firm in Appendix 12–D) through a TPA. One day, my contact at the TPA called, very disturbed. The human resources manager at Sam's had called her, ready to terminate his contract with the TPA due to our "increasing" case management fees. He was indignant that our fees had risen substantially in one year, and he and the TPA were looking for an explanation.

A review of several months from the previous year against our current experience with the Sam's employer group provided immediate, clear reasons for the increase in our fees. My letter to the TPA, along with a comparative analysis of the two blocks of time, appears in Table 12–7. The problem was more sick people and greater medical costs. The company's employees and their dependents had experienced a 51% increase in hospital admissions, a 120% increase in pregnancies, and a 400% increase in cardio/respiratory conditions. Using the cost-benefit analysis reports we had prepared, I was able to support the fact that the financial exposure to the employer's plan without case management intervention would have been disastrous.

I outlined one case in particular (included in Table 12–7 and listed as Case 0003 in Appendix 12–D) in which a diabetic woman, already diagnosed with kidney and eye damage due to years of noncompliance, became pregnant against the advice of her physician. This high-risk case included emotional/marital, cultural, and religious issues that had to be addressed. In addition, she lived in a remote, rural area of Washington State, 1 hour plus a ferry ride to the closest university hospital. Our total net savings for this case alone were $168,625, to say nothing of the improved life expectancies of this woman and her newborn.

FEEDBACK FROM PATIENTS

Owing to their lack of understanding of case management services and to their perception that employees might view such services as intrusive or interfering, carriers and employer groups have been concerned about and occasionally have

Table 12–7 Sample Letter Addressing Client Cost Concerns with Comparative Analysis

---

MEMO

DATE:

TO: Tami Monk

FROM:

RE: Case Management Fees and Group Experience for Sam's

Following a telephone conversation, and your expressed concerns regarding our case management fees, I researched the situation thoroughly and have prepared an analysis of my findings.

It was said that these increased costs were of concern to Sam's, and there was discussion of terminating their contract with the TPA.

Following is a more detailed breakdown; however, the major problem *does* appear to be one of more sick people and more costs. I reviewed the hospital admissions for the same period of time for last year and this year (January 1–May 16). **Sam's had a 51% increase in the number of admissions, a 120% increase in the number of pregnancies, and a 400% increase in cardio/respiratory conditions.**

The individuals who are in case management have extremely complex cases, and, unfortunately, have required a good bit of professional time. The financial exposure to the Plan *without* this intervention would be disastrous.

Consider the following . . . of the cases we now have open, there are:

1. A 17-year-old, now on dialysis awaiting a kidney transplant. Because of language and cultural differences and the multiple providers involved, we have had to maintain extremely close connection in order to ensure appropriate treatment and cost-effective use of services (we are negotiating/reviewing dialysis claims).
2. Two premature infants—one that we successfully closed with savings and one that was born prior to group coming to TPA that is now closed and has a conservative savings estimate of $101,491.
3. A 35-year-old gentleman for whom we expedited hospital discharge and successfully transferred safely and with no interruption in services or care from Georgia to N.Y. (for extended recovery at his mother's home). We coordinated airlines, physicians, continuous oxygen therapy, and transition to specialists using network providers. **This man weighed 454 lbs. at time of our initial involvement and was in hospital with heart failure, pneumonia, morbid obesity, and pulmonary emboli (life-threatening blood clots in the lung). This claimant to date and with our ongoing intervention is more medically stable and has lost 115 lbs.**
4. A 22-year-old woman, native of Guam with longstanding history of diabetes, pregnant with her second child who was admitted to hospital in her second

Table 12–7 continued

month with markedly high blood sugar. She is known (prior to pregnancy) to be noncompliant and was advised not to become pregnant. We have needed to follow her extremely closely due to risk factors (claimant already had kidney and eye damage due to years of noncompliance) and religious and cultural differences. She requires Insulin 4× daily (she often fails to administer this), and medical monitoring (several medical emergencies have occurred, and with our intervention these have been resolved). She lives in remote, rural area of Washington (1-hour drive plus ferry ride to closest university hospital). Case manager has maintained contact with multiple specialists and has arranged for nursing and monitoring services. Delivery date is 6/20 and we are cautiously optimistic of safe delivery. We are also considering placement of this young woman in hospital for duration of pregnancy if noncompliance continues . . . because of risks to infant and mother.

5. A 23-year-old woman with a brain tumor, for whom we have already obtained more appropriate treatment and expertise with renowned neurosurgeon, who will perform surgery with expectations for favorable prognosis. Claimant was being treated in community hospital and we were concerned about the appropriateness of her care. Through our intervention, we have avoided several hospital admissions and an extended inpatient rehab program, as well as obtained significant savings in fee negotiation with providers. Although this has been time-intensive, the exposure to the Plan was significant and, certainly, consequences for this young woman with inappropriate treatment could be devastating.

Tami, I hope you can appreciate that each one of these cases is far from "routine" and *none* can be resolved with just a few phone calls. We have already achieved significant savings and do what we can to provide *our* intervention in the most cost-effective manner.

I trust that the aforementioned will allay your concerns. Should you need further information, please feel free to call me.

Sam's

Analysis of Medical Experience

Last Year: January 1–May 16

39 Admissions
14 Employees

continues

Table 12–7 continued

---

16 Spouses
9 Dependents

Diagnostic Breakdown

10 Pregnancy & Related Conditions (26% of the admissions)
3 Cancer Admissions (on same patient) (8% of the admissions)
5 Psych/Alcohol (13% of the admissions)
2 Cardio/Respiratory (5% of the admissions)
2 Kidney-related (on same patient) (5% of the admissions)
17 Miscellaneous Surgeries/Medical (44% of the admissions)

This Year: January 1–May 16

59 Admissions
22 Employees
22 Spouses
15 Dependents

Diagnostic Breakdown

22 Pregnancy & Related Conditions (37% of the admissions)
2 Cancers (2% of the admissions)
4 Psych/Alcohol (7% of the admissions)
10 Cardio/Respiratory (17% of the admissions)
3 Kidney/Urinary (5% of the admissions)
18 Miscellaneous Surgery/Medical (31% of the admissions)

Conclusions

• Sam's had a 51% increase in the number of admissions.
• Sam's had a 120% increase in the number of pregnancies.
• Sam's had a 400% increase in cardio/respiratory conditions.

Source: Courtesy of Options Unlimited, Case Management Services Division, 2003, Huntington, New York.

---

resisted implementing case management programs. When my office began working more directly with corporate decision makers on group health cases, I could better appreciate the employers' position. Although interested in cost containment, they did not want to upset the favorable employer–employee relationships they had established. There was also unease expressed about the potential for liability. Would case managers or treating physicians be directing care? What if something negative happened to an employee as a result of a case manager's recommendations?

Case management requires direct interaction with patients and in some respects does interrupt their access to care and services. Frequently, the arrangement for case management services occurs too late for maximum benefits. For instance, one referral to our office was made because for more than 1 year postinjury the claimant was still in active medical treatment and had not returned to work. The claimant viewed this "reactive" referral by the claims department somewhat disdainfully. Where were we before when he needed us? For the most part, however, patients and their families have welcomed case managers. It is important for others to know this.

I first began conducting surveys of patients when I worked primarily in the areas of workers' compensation and auto insurance, prior to my expansion into the group health market. I wanted to be able to improve the delivery of our services not just for our client groups, who were satisfied as long as we were able to save money, but also for the recipients of our services—claimants and their families. We developed a questionnaire that was sent at the close of each case; for those cases that remained open for a long time, one was sent out every 6 months. The questionnaire, which has been revised in light of our increased experience, has helped assure our client groups that case management does make a difference, is well-received, and, as a valued employee service, can be used to improve public relations.

The questionnaire is sent with an explanatory letter (Tables 12–8 and 12–9). It combines a "check the box" format with blanks where individuals can enter their own responses, suggestions, or criticisms. It does not have to be signed but most are, and we further encourage a response by including a self-addressed stamped envelope. Over the years, we have reworked this letter and questionnaire, designing questions that encourage patients and their families to respond with examples of how and when the case manager made a difference, and whether the case manager affected an improved understanding of their disease/condition and treatment plan, health, outlook on life, and quality of living. These are views that we can gather as percentage points and present to clients, showing that a certain percentage of our patients who answer do so with positive comments. For employers, the employees' feedback often indicates that case management is viewed as a value-added benefit. Combined with cost-benefit analysis reports, such patient/family responses give us records on the benefits case management brings to health care, family support, and financial outcomes.

Table 12–10 is a quality assurance cover letter we use in cases in which the patient has passed away. We always make certain an appropriate amount of time has gone by before sending this on to the family.

Table 12–8 Quality Assurance Questionnaire Cover Letter

Date

xxxxxxxxxxxxxxx
xxxxxxxxxxxxxxx
xxxxxxxxxxxxxxx

Dear _____:

In an effort to improve the quality of our services, OPTIONS UNLIMITED is conducting periodic surveys.

_____, RN was assigned to your case to provide case management services as requested by _____, the company administering benefits for _____. At the onset of Case Management Services, our goal is for you to have a better understanding of your health needs and management and to assist you and your family to have better communication with your health care providers. The goal is also for you to be able to access appropriate health care as required.

In order to assess the quality of our services and our patient's satisfaction, we are asking that you complete the enclosed questionnaire and return it in the self-addressed, stamped envelope. Your candor and cooperation is appreciated.

If you have any questions, please call me at (631) 673-1150.

Very truly yours,

Catherine M. Mullahy
President

CMM:mm
Enclosure

Source: Courtesy of Options Unlimited, Case Management Services Division, 2003, Huntington, New York.

We are also working on a "Preinvolvement of Case Management" questionnaire to give us a "before case management" history that can be compared with the "after case management" perceptions. We anticipate that this will reveal a more in-depth and accurate look at the differences case management makes.

I am hearing more questions and demands from consumers, yet I do not believe our industry has recognized that they have a right to their questions and to

Table 12–9 Client Satisfaction Survey

OPTIONS UNLIMITED CLIENT SATISFACTION SURVEY

Was your first contact with OPTIONS UNLIMITED:
_____ Friendly
_____ Supportive
_____ Helpful
_____ Informative
_____ Other   Please check all that apply.

At what point of your health care status were you contacted by OPTIONS UNLIMITED:
_____ Newly diagnosed
_____ Hospitalized
_____ At home
_____ Presurgical
_____ Other   Please check all that apply.

	Strongly Agree	Agree	Disagree	Strongly Disagree	Not Applicable
1). The case management services were helpful for me.	5	4	3	2	1
My family	5	4	3	2	1
2) Case management helped me with the needs I feel are important.	5	4	3	2	1
3) The role of case management services was explained to me, my family, and my physician.	5	4	3	2	1
4) My case manager was helpful in thoroughly explaining my diagnosis and treatment options.	5	4	3	2	1
5) My case manager was helpful in obtaining the services I required.	5	4	3	2	1

continues

Table 12–9 continued

6) My case manager and providers worked well together caring for me.	5	4	3	2	1
7) Using what I learned from my case manager, I believe I am more able to access medical services on my own.	5	4	3	2	1

My case manager paid attention to my needs:
_____ Physical
_____ Safety
_____ Communication
_____ Nutrition
_____ Emotional
_____ Spiritual
_____ Understanding of medications   Please check all that apply.

What did you like about case management services?

What areas do you feel would have made a difference in your care?

Thank you for taking your time to complete this survey. We appreciate your input and we value your comments.

_____
Printed Name (optional)

_____
Signature of Claimant or
Significant Other (optional)

Source: Courtesy of Options Unlimited, Case Management Services Division, 2003, Huntington, New York.

Table 12–10 Quality Assurance Cover Letter Used When Patient Has Passed Away

Date

XXXXXXXXXXXXXX
XXXXXXXXXXXXXX
XXXXXXXXXXXXXX

Dear _____ :

We are aware that _____ has passed away and if we have not yet conveyed this to you, please accept our sincere sympathy. OPTIONS UNLIMITED had been providing medical case management services to _____ in order to assist with the coordination of care and services, to provide information and support, and hopefully, to ease some of the other burdens that often accompany illness. At the onset of Case Management Services, our goal was for _____ to have a better understanding of his/her health needs and its management and to assist _____ and your family to have better communication with your health care providers. The goal is also for you to be able to access appropriate health care as required.

These services were provided at no cost to the patient (or insured) and were at the request of _____, the Plan Administrator for the employer group medical plan. It is our hope to continually assess the quality of our services and, as needed, to improve or change certain aspects of them.

_____, RN was the case manager who was assigned to _____ and we are interested in any comments you may wish to offer regarding her role, as well.

Once again, thank you for your assistance and should you wish to contact us directly, please feel free to do so.

Very truly yours,

_____

Catherine M. Mullahy
President

CMM:xx
Enclosure

Source: Courtesy of Options Unlimited, Case Management Services Division, 2003, Huntington, New York.

carefully considered responses. The attitude has been, "Well, we're providing this highly sophisticated care, we're sharing what we've created, why seek their counsel?" We have been very late in the game to ask ourselves, "Is this really what a patient wants?" For instance, consider shortened maternity stays in a facility: This decision was not in the patients' best interests, and it was dangerous. This is a very clear-cut and simplistic example of how policy is established in hospitals, HMOs, insurance carriers, and employer groups across the country with little regard for the patient. It was quite obvious that no one had consulted new mothers, women who had experienced the birthing process, regarding the 24-hour return to home.

If we really are operating with an awareness of those characteristics that constitute health care ethics—respect for the patient, patient autonomy, dignity, veracity, beneficence, nonmalfeasance—we need to actively solicit patients' input in the health delivery process. And we must seek their comments before and during the process, not only after they have left us, after we've had all the control and authority over their lives at a point when they were very emotionally and physically vulnerable.

Particularly within critical care settings, case managers often minister to a substantial number of patients who are, in addition to their physical challenges, emotionally and cognitively impaired due to a head injury, stroke, multiple sclerosis (MS), and other neurological conditions. As difficult as it may be to meet the health care needs of our more able hospital or clinic patients, how much is our obligation heightened when the individual is struggling against communication deficits, including aphasia or locked-in syndrome? We must recognize that these persons have little or no ability to express their degree of satisfaction or dissatisfaction, and should expand our efforts to communicate as we design patient satisfaction questionnaires and incorporate patient/family responses into our programs.

To better plan a course of treatment, we need to ask, before patients are admitted or as soon as possible upon admission: What are your goals? What do you hope? Your doctor thinks that you should be here for 4 weeks. What do you think you will be able to accomplish in 4 weeks? What kind of care do you expect? What kind of professionals do you think are going to be working with you? Do you want an explanation of your therapy or the test? Would that make you feel better?

The answers to these kinds of questions help us understand what a patient knows about his condition and also what his prior education has taught him, what his prior experience in a health care delivery system has prepared him for, and how much you need to address some of his misunderstandings or misperceptions before you can create what both patient and provider hope will be a successful outcome. Our treatment is not ethically sound if we once again operate in a vacuum, as we in health care tend to do, outlining our best practice program, our state-of-the-art care maps and plans for day one and day two, without taking into consideration the needs of the patient. Addressing patient concerns when planning our programs elevates quality of care while elevating the ethics of care because we have asked, is this care palpable to patients?

A physiatrist (a specialist in physical medicine and rehabilitation) may have what he or she deems to be the ideal program to address a stroke, MS, or traumatic brain injury patient, but is that what the patient and his family are expecting? Is it in their best interests? The physiatrist may feel that 3 weeks or 4 weeks is enough to stabilize that patient, but does the patient see that? Maybe the patient's perception is based on an experience with a parent years before who was in a facility 2 or 3 months. Shouldn't that be addressed? Because of new technology or improved therapeutic moralities, or because he had a better surgical result than his parent, you are going to be able to move this patient along much faster. Here is the opportunity to calm any alarm, the chance to say, this is now the normal treatment program.

The patient questionnaire becomes a quality assurance tool, a marketing tool, an outcomes report tool, and a business tool. These are strong playing cards in this very complex system. From an operating perspective, it is an invaluable indicator to help fine-tune a program, to better train professionals, to more adequately meet the needs of patients, and to address the expectations of payers as well. With these uses in mind, it is appropriate to conduct segments of a patient questionnaire before admission, upon admission, midway through treatment, at discharge, and at postdischarge to discern how well the patient's needs were met.

The design of a questionnaire must be made as objective as possible. Anyone can create a market survey instrument without ever placing the facility or service in an unfavorable light by asking questions that elicit only favorable responses, never enabling a patient to give "undirected" input that might include negative comments. Perhaps the patient satisfaction questionnaire design group should include persons outside the facility itself, other providers such as physicians who refer to the facility, selected staff members, patients and family members who have been in your facility, and certain payers who meet the expenses of your facility. Anticipate what some of the negatives might be, and allow for that kind of response from a patient. We have a responsibility to make the survey instrument as patient-focused as possible. This is achieved by incorporating statements such as, "We would appreciate any comments you may have to improve our service. What would you like us to have done differently? What things that you experienced were not positive for you?"

SHARING QUESTIONNAIRE RESULTS

Care is a collaborative process, so survey results should be shared with internal staff. If responses are funneled only to the public relations or marketing department, for instance, how do people ever know whether they are improving? How do you evaluate the success? How do you propose change unless you have a benchmark? After the information has been applied during internal evaluation and planning, then it is appropriate to communicate selected comments and how the facility or service responded to prospective consumers; they need to understand that a group is invested in its patients, that services are patient-driven.

A sensitive area regarding implementation of the patient questionnaire involving both patients and staff is confidentiality. It is now a legal responsibility, as well. Patients should feel free to say negative things without a fear of untoward recriminations or legal action. Elements of the satisfaction survey might be completed anonymously, or the instrument might include a statement verifying that all information is confidential and will only be used to improve programs. Patients, especially those who will return, should be welcome to share whatever concerns they have. You also want to receive honest answers. Some groups code patient surveys so that they are completed anonymously but allow the patient or staff member to be identified should something problematic occur.

In the same way, staff confidentiality can become an issue. Positive feedback from a patient in a questionnaire can be shared; we want people to know when they have done a good job. However, when it is negative feedback, it should be handled between supervisor and staff member, never naming the patient. The information becomes an instructional vehicle; the patient might have a real issue with a staff member, a legitimate complaint that needs to be addressed. Patient questionnaires become the vehicle giving further assurance to both current and future patients that quality-of-service standards will remain high.

Effective means for linking patient satisfaction surveys back to the planning and provision of services include written documentation and regularly scheduled planning meetings among appropriate individuals. Results can be made part of a monthly or quarterly review of all programs. Beyond that is the peer review concept. A patient advisory board might be a huge asset. How often have hospital space planners designed a whole new wing without ever asking a head nurse about patient- and workflow on the floor? An ad for an HMO organization announced evening and Saturday hours and invited community members to stop by for a visit. This HMO is reaching out to meet local families where they are by making the medical staff available when the potential customers have free time. Instead of once again getting all the medical professionals together in a room to redesign a program, why not invite patients in? Tell them that the response to the orientation program was 50% favorable, and ask their opinion on how to raise that to a 98% positive response rate.

Ongoing methods of communicating the results of patient questionnaires to your staff professionals are a newsletter or bulletin board posting complimentary or grateful letters from patients so everybody can see them. Letters might be forwarded to a unit or program via administration or department directors. Negative comments should be handled in a different way. The need to communicate patient concerns may be fulfilled in a departmental meeting or performance review. Perhaps some comments can be used as a teaching or supervisory tool so staff becomes more aware of how their actions are being perceived by others.

Those preparing a patient questionnaire must think very carefully about the range of questions asked, and be prepared for the responses. Patient input on operations and the resulting internal review can prompt staff morale problems, liability, and issues of risk management, purchasing, profitability, and public relations.

After a problem is disclosed, a company or case manager has an ethical responsibility to address it. Criteria should be established for possible liability situations. No one wants to find out years later that a serious charge was reported and just left on file. Although patient confidentiality must be respected, a case manager is also charged with the additional responsibility of correcting injustices or infractions. Should a similar incident occur and be reported publicly while a former patient's comment on his previous similar experience was reported and went unheeded, the department or group might be held liable. To prevent such problems, the decision might be made to send reports through a risk manager, to corporate counsel, department heads, or a peer review. The choice of procedure is less vital to the health of the case management department or company than the fact that there is such a plan in place.

Questionnaire surveys are useful not only from a marketing perspective, but also in the evaluation of staff members and in the identification of problems with service. Many suggestions offered by our patients have become incorporated into our current services. When our case managers are given praise for their assistance, they receive a copy of the document for their records and it becomes part of their personnel file. Criticisms are also taken seriously, obviously allowing for personal preference, personality clash, or a situation that places the case manager in a position of reducing home care services or confronting noncompliant behavior. Criticisms also sometimes point to areas in which additional training or supervision might be helpful.

Whenever a questionnaire is returned, everyone is eager to see the results. Staff and administration want to know the positives and the negatives. If 80% of respondents thought a program was good, it means that 20% found it lacking, and some individuals will be very concerned about that 20%. What if a company delivers quality services and is the most cost-effective act in town, but patients have legitimate concerns about their care at the facility? Corporate counsel might well be up in arms. What if someone says something? Then we are required to take action. You mean we actually have to record negative comments? How many negatives are we getting? What is our insurance cost going to be like if x number of patients report an accident in our facility? How happy will our underwriter be about writing liability insurance now?

We provide summaries of the responses to the client groups and usually include actual samples. This has been most helpful, especially with those groups that were initially concerned about the receptivity of their employees. After seeing employee reactions, they soon start calling to suggest cases they now think should be case managed.

COMMUNICATING SUCCESS

Cost-benefit analysis reports and quality assurance surveys need to be communicated appropriately. They should be provided on a regular basis and ideally are presented in personal meetings. Cost-benefit analysis reports in particular need to be explained, because the information, when taken out of context or reviewed by individuals unfamiliar with the process or results, can easily be misinterpreted. Certain terms (for example, *avoidance of potential charges* and *prevention of complications*) and the method of calculating savings (*gross* and *net*) should be discussed. Reviewing a few or all of the individual cases within a group is also helpful. It enables a client to understand the case management process and raise questions regarding the accuracy of the figures and the credibility of the savings—all important steps. If case managers are not willing to explain and inform, then the whole purpose of reporting is subverted.

Usually, the individual representing a client group in its relationship with a case manager is the CFO, an insurance professional, or a human resource professional. In most instances, this individual does not have a medical background and is unwilling to accept everything the case manager feels justified in claiming as savings. To illustrate, several years ago one of my first major clients was a large health insurance carrier that contracted with my company to develop a case management program for it and its client groups. As part of the program, we obtained early discharges from hospitals, negotiated fees with facilities and providers, arranged home care, and prevented the kinds of complications that would have occurred had case managers not been involved.

Feeling very positive about our services and the results, I looked forward to sharing our first quarterly report with this group. The results were impressive, a 1:23 ratio (that is, for every dollar that this group spent on our case management services, we were able to save $23). Quite respectable, I thought, especially as we were somewhat conservative in our calculation.

At the meeting, the carrier's representatives included an underwriter, an actuary, the corporate counsel, and the claims director. Not one case manager! I started with the summary page, concise data, and the kind of "number crunching" that this group could really get into. Questions began: Where were the actual claims that we got these savings from? If we were saying that they never had claims (avoidance of potential charges), then how could we calculate a savings? How could we prevent a hospital admission or complications? This was going to be harder than I thought. How could I help them understand?

Case by case (fortunately, there were only eight that quarter), I led them through the case management process. I described each case at the time we received it, gave the claims history prior to our involvement (three hospital admissions for 3 to 5 days each on a noncompliant diabetic), reported what we learned at the time of our assessment (this patient had been treated in a city hospital, had a different physician each time, no family physician, was trying to stretch his insulin to last because finances were tight, never did get around to getting his glucometer), and described what the case manager did (referred him to a local endocrinologist, arranged for insulin and supplies to be billed directly to the carrier instead of the patient having to pay first and then wait to be reimbursed, obtained a glucometer at a discounted rate, arranged for diabetic training and diet plan by a nurse clinician in a physician's office, and referred him to a local diabetic support group, which he could participate in at no cost).

Finally, I summarized the results. There were no admissions during the quarter. With this scenario as described, was there any doubt that without case management intervention, the revolving-door admissions to the hospital would have continued and additional complications occurred due to noncompliance? This overview and walk-through demonstrated the problem, the solutions, and the savings.

We discussed all eight cases, and although there was some disagreement over whether something would or would not have occurred, at the end of this meeting all the representatives were enthusiastic about the accomplishments, including the containment of costs. For several quarters thereafter, interest in case management increased and more people attended the meetings, often contributing their own ideas as to what else could have been done and reporting that more of the client groups wanted this case management "stuff." This carrier group became so convinced of the merits of case management that it eventually developed its own department and retained us to work cases it could not handle.

Case managers are experts in assessing and resolving problem cases. Others cannot be expected to understand the case management process as well as we do. It is not enough to manage the case; we need to manage our relationships with clients as well. Educating clients allows them to "buy into" case management and helps avoid micromanagement discussions (for example, questioning whether the 5 minutes spent on a phone call was really necessary). To make case management more successful and established as an industry, each case manager not only needs to work effectively but also needs to articulate her achievements—walk the walk and talk the talk.

NOTES

1. L. Feuer, "Manipulative Negotiations: Winning and Loving It!," presented at the Medical Case Management Conference VIII, Orlando, FL, September 1996.
2. L. Thomas-Payne, "Simple Negotiations," *HomeCare* 14, no. 11 (1992): 104.

Appendix 12–A Program Questionnaire and Facility Review for Case Managers

PROGRAM QUESTIONNAIRE

Name: _____

Address: _____

Phone: _____

E-mail: _____

Contact Person: _____

Medical Director/Specialty: _____

Number of Beds: _____ Age Range of Patients: _____

Specialty Areas: _____

Per Diem Cost	$ _____	Cost varies per program and per individual need. Case managers call the
All Inclusive	$ _____	facility for an estimate of cost for care. Following an evaluation of specific
Room & Board Only	$ _____	need, the facility can issue a letter confirming cost for care.

Approximate Therapy Cost per 30 Minutes

Physical	$ _____	Vocational	$ _____
Occupational	$ _____	Cognitive	$ _____
Speech	$ _____	Psychological	
Recreational	$ _____	Counseling	$ _____
Prosthetics	$ _____	Drivers Ed	$ _____
Respiratory	$ _____	Audiologists	
		(Screening)	$ _____
		Therapeutic Recreation	
		Outings	$ _____

Comments:

Accredited by: _____ Joint Commission _____ CARF

Written Reports Rendered:

Insurance Company Representative included at staffings

_____ Yes _____ No

Case Manager or Insurance Representative permitted to:

_____ Attend staffings _____ Participate in staffings

Will the facility provide statistical data on length of stay, average costs, distribution of discharge placements?	( ) Yes	( ) No
Will the facility negotiate costs?	( ) Yes	( ) No
Does the facility have fax capability?	( ) Yes	( ) No
If so, fax #: _____		
Will the facility provide written reports no less often than 30 days?	( ) Yes	( ) No

Staffing

Board-certified medical director?	( ) Yes	( ) No
Physician/psychiatrist team leader?	( ) Yes	( ) No
Is the physician (the team leader) on premises?	( ) Yes	( ) No
Is the physician out-of-facility consultant?	( ) Yes	( ) No
24-hour skilled care available directed by RN?	( ) Yes	( ) No
Team is multidisciplinary, including representatives from all therapies?	( ) Yes	( ) No
Do patients have the same therapists and team members throughout their stay?	( ) Yes	( ) No
Are the majority of employees on staff and not contracted from an outside agency?	( ) Yes	( ) No
Are therapists registered or certified?	( ) Yes	( ) No
Does the facility have access to consulting physicians?	( ) Yes	( ) No
Is list of consultants available?	( ) Yes	( ) No

Additional questions for subacute facility:

Board-certified medical director with acute care experience?	( ) Yes	( ) No
Is there 24-hour physician coverage?	( ) Yes	( ) No
24-hour acute care nursing specialists directed by nurse/clinician?	( ) Yes	( ) No
(Nursing staff may include RNs specializing in medical/surgical care, critical care, home care, pulmonary rehabilitation, and oncology.)		
Is there 24-hour access to medical specialists certified in		
internal medicine?	( ) Yes	( ) No
pulmonary medicine?	( ) Yes	( ) No
critical care?	( ) Yes	( ) No
family practice?	( ) Yes	( ) No
Does the on-site support staff include		
registered dietitians?	( ) Yes	( ) No
respiratory therapists?	( ) Yes	( ) No
physical/occupational therapists?	( ) Yes	( ) No

speech pathologists?   ( ) Yes   ( ) No
social workers?   ( ) Yes   ( ) No
grief/bereavement counselors?   ( ) Yes   ( ) No

Clinical Care Available
Is a rehabilitation plan tailored for the patient's specific needs?   ( ) Yes   ( ) No
Are team conferences held: _____ weekly _____ every two weeks
Do all members of the team, including patient, family,
  and insurance representative, attend?   ( ) Yes   ( ) No
How many hours of therapy/rehab services does patient
  receive per day? _____
Are personal hygiene assistance and meals considered therapy?   ( ) Yes   ( ) No
Are the patient's therapy prescriptions appropriate?   ( ) Yes   ( ) No
Are therapies offered daily, and if patient conditions warrant,
  are therapies offered twice a day?   ( ) Yes   ( ) No
Weekends?   ( ) Yes   ( ) No

Check therapies available:

Physical _____   Speech & Language _____
Cognitive _____   Orthotic Services _____
Occupational _____   Psychological Counseling _____
Recreational _____

Additional questions for subacute facility:

Check treatment categories available:

Pulmonary care _____   Infectious disease _____
Wound management _____   Pediatrics _____
Rehabilitation _____   Oncology _____
Orthopedics _____   Cardiovascular _____
Neurology _____   Nutritional support _____

Check 24-hour capabilities for:

Laboratory services _____   Radiology _____
Pharmacy _____

Check service capabilities for:

Pain management _____   Hydrotherapy _____
Superficial wound debridement _____   Bowel/bladder training _____
Electrical stimulation _____

Check equipment capabilities for:

Telemetry _____   Piped-in suctioning _____
Ventilator support _____   Hemodialysis _____
Piped-in oxygen _____

Discharge Planning and Coordination of Follow-up

Is discharge planning instituted early in the hospitalization? ( ) Yes ( ) No

Is there a tentative discharge date set early in the
hospitalization? ( ) Yes ( ) No

Is patient/family education ongoing throughout the
hospitalization? ( ) Yes ( ) No

Does the family education include assisting the family to
realistically consider the client's long-term physical and
cognitive prognosis? ( ) Yes ( ) No

Is there a prescribed continuum of family ed? ( ) Yes ( ) No

Is there continuity of care and follow-up after discharge? ( ) Yes ( ) No

Will staff perform on-site evaluation for home
modification needs? ( ) Yes ( ) No

Will equipment and home modification needs be discussed
with insurance representative before purchase or direction
to the family? ( ) Yes ( ) No

Will several bids for DME be acquired if requested? ( ) Yes ( ) No

Will physician team leader refer patient to a local physician
for follow-up and act as a resource as needed? ( ) Yes ( ) No

Are outpatient services available? ( ) Yes ( ) No

Please detail living arrangements for outpatient program below.
Are patients encouraged to complete trial home visits prior
to discharge? ( ) Yes ( ) No

Will the facility provide a written discharge plan, including
level of care required, number of hours per day assistance is
required, abilities in ADLs, equipment needs, medications,
return-to-work/vocational potential, specific follow-up
care required? ( ) Yes ( ) No

Additional Comments:

Reviewed by: _____

Office: _____

City, State: _____

FACILITY REVIEW

Does the facility have pre-admission criteria?	( ) Yes ( ) No
Is the facility clean and cheerful?	( ) Yes ( ) No
Does the facility admit only those patients with rehabilitation potential?	( ) Yes ( ) No
Does the facility offer an evaluation program to determine rehab potential?	( ) Yes ( ) No
Does the facility have a designee in the business office to deal with the insurer/case manager?	( ) Yes ( ) No
Do patients look well cared for?	( ) Yes ( ) No
Is there a family education program?	( ) Yes ( ) No
Is there a patient/family information guidebook?	( ) Yes ( ) No
Are there other patients with the same diagnosis? How many? _____	( ) Yes ( ) No
Are there dedicated treatment teams per diagnosis?	( ) Yes ( ) No
Are the facilities and equipment appropriate for the patient's needs?	( ) Yes ( ) No
Do patients have access to dining area, nursing units, grounds, elevators, etc.?	( ) Yes ( ) No
Are there well-defined policies and procedures in place for medical emergencies?	( ) Yes ( ) No
Can the facility adequately treat minor/moderate medical complications on-site?	( ) Yes ( ) No
Will the facility notify insurance representative of upcoming conferences/staffings?	( ) Yes ( ) No
Are goals reset as patient status changes?	( ) Yes ( ) No
If patient no longer shows significant gains, is discharge proposed?	( ) Yes ( ) No
Is there a staff coordinator or internal case manager assigned to each patient who acts as a liaison for family and insurance representative?	( ) Yes ( ) No
Are there well-defined quality assurance programs in place?	( ) Yes ( ) No
Are there outcome criteria? Is the effectiveness of services measured?	( ) Yes ( ) No

Additional questions for subacute facility:

Is this a dedicated environment?	( ) Yes ( ) No
Is there significant use of agency nurses?	( ) Yes ( ) No

Average Length of Stay:
By diagnosis—the figures for preceding year (if available)
CVA _____
SCI (NEW) _____
SCI (OLD) _____
Referral Procedure:

Source: Courtesy of Case Management Society of America, Little Rock, Arkansas.

Appendix 12–B Provider Service Agreements

Initial _____

Renewal _____

CLAIMS NOTIFICATION—PSYCHIATRIC/SUBSTANCE ABUSE SERVICES

To: _____ Date: _____

Re: Patient: _____

    Insured: _____ Group: _____

    S.S. #: _____

    Physician: _____ Phone: _____

    E-mail: _____

    Type of Services:

    Inpatient Services _____

    Outpatient Services _____

    Day-Hospital Services _____

    Long-Term Residential _____

    Other _____

    Date to Start: _____ Date to End or Reevaluation Date: _____

    Provider: Name: _____ Telephone: _____

            Address: _____ Ext: _____

            City, State, Zip Code: _____

            E-mail: _____

            Contact Person: Service: _____ Telephone: _____

                         Billing: _____ Ext: _____

            Billing Address, if Different: _____

            E-mail: _____

            Fees: Per diem: _____ All-Inclusive? Yes _____No _____

                 Per week: _____ If no, state other charges.

                 Per month: _____

Special Arrangements: _____

_____

Claims Person: Name: _____ Phone: _____

Advised: Yes _____ No _____

Arranged by: Case Manager: _____ Phone: _____

            Company: *Options Unlimited on behalf of the Plan identified in the attached Service Agreement.*

Accepted by: _____ Title: _____

Initial _____

Renewal _____

CLAIMS NOTIFICATION—DURABLE MEDICAL EQUIPMENT FORM

To: _____ Date: _____

Re: Patient: _____

    Insured: _____ Group: _____

    S.S. #: _____

    Physician: _____

Equipment:	Purchase Price	Rental Price
Wheelchair: Manual:	_____	_____
Electric:	_____	_____
Hospital Bed:	_____	_____
Walker:	_____	_____
Commode:	_____	_____
Alarm:	_____	_____
Oxygen & Related Equipment:	_____	_____
Other:	_____	_____

Arrangement Made: _____

Length of Time: _____ Date Started: _____

Date to end or reevaluation date: _____

Discussed with claims department: Yes _____ No _____

Name: _____ Phone #: _____

Provider Agency: _____

Contact Person: _____

Address: _____

Telephone #: _____ Fax #: _____

E-mail: _____

Arranged by: Case Manager: _____

      Company: *Options Unlimited on*   Telephone #: _____

      behalf of the Plan identified on the   E-mail: _____

      attached Service Agreement.

Accepted by: _____

Title: _____ Date: _____

Initial _____

Renewal _____

CLAIMS NOTIFICATION—INFUSION SERVICES

To: _____ Date: _____

Re: Patient: _____

     Insured: _____ Group: _____

     S.S. #: _____

     Physician: _____ Phone: _____

     E-mail: _____

Type of Services: _____ Fees: _____

TPN: _____

Chemotherapy: _____

Pentamidine: _____

Antibiotics: _____

Antivirals: _____

Enteral Feedings: _____

Pain Management: _____

Nursing Services Required: (For patient education, site care, etc.)

Describe: _____

Equipment Required: (Pumps, supplies, etc.)

Describe: _____

Frequency of Services:

Continuous: _____ Daily: _____ Hours per Day: _____

Date to Start: _____ Date to End/Reevaluation Date: _____

Provider Agency: _____ Phone #: _____

Address: _____ Fax #: _____

Contact: Service: _____ Billing: _____

E-mail: _____ E-mail: _____

Address: _____

Advised: _____ Yes _____ No

Arranged by: Case Manager: _____

              Company: *Options Unlimited on*   Telephone #: _____

              behalf of the Plan identified on the   E-mail: _____

              attached Service Agreement.

Accepted by: _____Title: _____

Initial _____
Renewal _____

CLAIMS NOTIFICATION—NURSING CARE SERVICES FORM

To: _____ Date: _____

Re: Patient: _____ Group: _____

Insured: _____

S.S. #: _____

Physician: _____

Type of Service:

Nursing:

R.N. _____ L.P.N. _____ Aide _____ Other _____

Hours per Day: _____ Hours per Week: _____ Fees per Hour: _____

Provider: Name: _____ Telephone: _____

Address: _____

City, State, Zip Code: _____

Billing Address, if different: _____

Contact Person: Service: _____ Phone: _____

Fax: _____ E-mail: _____

Billing: _____ Phone: _____

E-mail: _____

Note: If more than one agency will be used, enter identifying information.

Name: _____ Phone: _____

Address: _____ E-mail: _____

Contact Person: Service _____ Billing: _____

Date to Start: _____ Date to End or Reevaluation Date: _____

Claims Person: Name: _____ Phone: _____

Advised: Yes _____ No _____ E-mail: _____

Arranged by: Case Manager: _____

Company: *Options Unlimited on behalf of the Plan identified on the attached Service Agreement.*

Phone #: _____

Accepted by: _____ Title: _____

Initial _____

Renewal _____

CLAIMS NOTIFICATION—THERAPY SERVICES FORM

To: _____ Date: _____

Re: Patient: _____

    Insured: _____

    S.S. #: _____

    Physician: _____

Type of Therapy:

P.T. _____ O.T. _____ Speech _____ Respiratory _____ Other _____

Frequency of Therapy:

Daily _____ Weekly _____

Fees per Hour: _____ Estimated Duration of Therapy: _____

Date to Start: _____

Date to End or Reevaluation Date: _____

Name of Therapist(s): _____

Address: _____

City, State, Zip Code: _____

Phone #: _____ Tax I.D. #: _____

E-mail: _____

Claims Person: Name: _____

              Phone #: _____ Fax #: _____

              E-mail: _____

Advised?: Yes _____ No _____

Arranged by: Case Manager: _____

Company: *Options Unlimited on behalf of the*   Phone #: _____

Plan identified in the attached Service Agreement.

Accepted by: _____ Title: _____

Initial _____
Renewal _____

CLAIMS NOTIFICATION—REHAB HOSPITAL/
SKILLED NURSING FACILITY

To: _____ Date: _____

Re: Patient: _____

    Insured: _____ Group: _____

    S.S. #: _____

    Physician: _____ Phone: _____

    E-mail: _____

Type of Services:

Inpatient Services: _____

Outpatient Services: _____

Therapies: OT: _____ PT: _____ Speech: _____

Other: _____

Date to Start: _____ Date to End or Reevaluation Date: _____

Provider: Name: _____ Telephone: _____

    Address: _____ E-mail: _____

    City, State, Zip Code: _____

Contact Person: Service: _____ Telephone: _____

    Billing: _____ Fax: _____

    E-mail: _____

Billing Address, if Different: _____

    Fees: Per diem: _____ All-Inclusive? Yes ____ No ____

    Per week: _____ If no, state other charges: _____

    Per month: _____

Special Arrangements: _____

Claims Person: Name: _____ Phone: _____

    E-mail: _____

Advised?: Yes _____ No _____

Arranged by: Case Manager _____ Phone: _____

    E-mail: _____

    Company: *Options Unlimited on behalf of the Plan identified in the attached Service Agreement.*

Accepted by: _____ Title: _____

Source: Courtesy of Options Unlimited, Case Management Services Division, 2003, Huntington, New York.

Appendix 12–C Expanded Cost-Benefit Analysis Summary

Summary of Savings for Case Management Services—Calendar Year
Local 123 Welfare Fund
January 1, xxxx-December 31, xxxx Year End Summary

Cases open at beginning of year	7	
Cases referred this year	49	
Cases closed this year	46	
Total cases worked this year	56	
Total fees for the year		$102,335
Average fees per month		$ 8,528
Average fees per case/year		$ 1,827
Average fees per case/month		$ 152
Total savings for the year		
Gross		$816,131
Net		$713,796
Average Savings per Case for the Year		$ 12,746
Ratio of Dollars to Savings	1:8	

Local 123 Welfare Fund
First Half-Year Summary of Cost-Benefit Analysis for Case Management Services
January 1, xxxx–June 30, xxxx

Cases open at beginning of period	7	
Cases referred this period	29	
Cases closed during the period	22	
Total cases worked during period	36	
Total number of open cases	14	
Total fees for the period		$ 61,571
Average fees per month		$ 10,262
Average fees per case/period		$ 1,710
Average fees per case/month		$ 285
Total savings for period		
Gross		$402,990
Net		$341,419
Average savings per case/period		$ 9,484
Ratio of dollars to savings	1:7	

Note: To evaluate the benefits of a program for a client, we use total fees billed for all cases worked and the saving resulting from our intervention, whether savings were realized in every case, one case, or several cases.

SAMPLES OF CASES FROM JANUARY 1, XXXX – JUNE 1, XXXX

CASE MANAGEMENT COST-BENEFIT ANALYSIS REPORT

Re: 0002

Carrier/Client Group: Local 123

Date of Referral: 1/11/xx

Date of Closure: 1/31/xx

Total Weeks/Months of Case Management: 3 weeks

Diagnosis: Cancer of the Colon

Case Management Fees: $1,313

Summary of Intervention:
Options Unlimited conducted a thorough assessment and expedited discharge from acute care to subacute care. Once at subacute level, progress was monitored closely. In this way, discharge to home was expedited 1 week earlier than antici-pated. Home care visits were negotiated and provided to determine if additional services (HHA, PT, OT) would be necessary. A full report from home care RN was obtained by the case manager and evaluated. Through involving claimant and family, additional services were avoided.

Potential Charges:
Expedited discharge from 1 week acute care at $1,500/day × 7 days = $10,500
Surgeon fees at $100/day = $700
Primary MD fees at $100/day = $700
Subacute care nonnegotiated × 8 days at $900/day = $7,200
Expedited discharge of 1 additional week subacute care at $400/day = $2,800
BLS transportation 1 way at $260 + $8 mile = $324
2 home care visits at $150/visit = $300

Total of Potential Charges:
$22,524

Actual Cost and Related Charges:
Subacute care at $400/day negotiated × 8 days = $3,200
BLS transport at $120 + $5 mile = $160
2 skilled RN visits at $100/visit = $200

Total of Actual Charges and Case Management Fees:
$3,560 + $1,313 = $4,873

Net Savings: $17,651

CASE MANAGEMENT COST-BENEFIT ANALYSIS REPORT

Re: 0003

Carrier/Client Group: Local 123

Date of Referral: 2/9/xx

Date of Closure: 5/12/xx

Total Weeks/Months of Case Management: 2 months

Diagnosis: Total Hip Replacement

Case Management Fees: $1,514

Summary of Intervention:
Options Unlimited implemented home health aide, nursing, and DME services. The claimant was discharged unsafely from the hospital without Options Unlimited's knowledge. The claimant had a knowledge deficit regarding her medication and ambulation regime. Through nursing intervention, it was determined that the claimant was taking two medications that cross-reacted. Through prompt intervention, an emergency visit was avoided. The claimant's teenager was taught to be independent with her mother's injections thus avoiding nursing visits. Physical therapy was implemented in a timely manner as client was at high risk for falls. DME was monitored for appropriate discontinuance of services. The physician was not cooperative with returning case management and home care agency calls. No on-call physician was available.

Claimant's physician answering machine instructed all patients "to go to ER if problem arises."

Potential Charges:
ER visit due to cross-reaction between medication = $750
Unnecessary nursing visits for injections at $150/visit × 2 weeks = $1,500
Home Health Aide services at $18/hour × 2/hrs day × 18 days = $648
PT home visit at $150 × 5 visits = $750
PT visit outpatient via Care Provider

Total of Potential Charges:
$5,148

Actual Cost and Related Charges:
Negotiated:
PT visits × 6 at $85 = $510

Home Health Aide at $15/hr × 2 hrs/day × 18 days = $540
Nursing visits at $100/visit × 12 = $1,200

Total of Actual Charges and Case Management Fees:
$2,250 + $1,513 = $3,763

Net Savings: $1,385

CASE MANAGEMENT COST-BENEFIT ANALYSIS REPORT

Re: 0005

Carrier/Client Group: Local 123

Date of Referral: 12/8/xx

Date of Closure: 3/7/xx+1

Total Weeks/Months of Case Management: 3 Months

Diagnosis: Hepatic Encephalopathy

Case Management Fees: $1,064.15

Summary of Intervention:
This quarter, with physician input, case manager formulated a comprehensive plan of care to provide infusion therapy, with skilled nursing, to monitor the claimant's status on a continuous basis during an acute exacerbation of hepatic encephalopathy, thereby providing for a medically safe home environment in lieu of hospitalization. Extensive research was required to select qualitative providers of specific services at cost-effective rates; however, the claimant's husband, a resident physician, strongly objected to home care and maintains that the hospital setting is the only appropriate setting in the event of acute exacerbation. Nutritional counseling was provided in the last quarter. Through the claimant's increased level of understanding of nutritional restrictions and dietary allowances, she has a greater level of compliance to dietary regimen and greater awareness of symptoms of hepatic encephalopathy. As a result, claimant intervenes more readily with oral hydration and complications have been averted. Case closed due to relative stability of status and present refusal to consider option of home infusion therapy.

Potential Charges:
February 1–March 7, xxxx
2 hospital admissions for IV hydration at $1,500/day, 3 days each admission = $9,000
Daily MD visits at $150/day = $900

Total of Potential Charges:
$9,900

Actual Cost and Related Charges:
Nutritional counseling (last quarter) resulted in greater dietary compliance and no acute exacerbations of symptomatology. No hospital admissions since November.

Total of Actual Charges and Case Management Fees:
$1,064 Case Management Fees

Net Savings: $8,836
Lifetime Savings $13,275

CASE MANAGEMENT COST-BENEFIT ANALYSIS REPORT

Re: 0006

Carrier/Client Group: Local 123

Date of Referral: 12/30/xx

Date of Closure: Remains open

Total Weeks/Months of Case Management: 2 months

Diagnosis: Preterm labor, preterm membrane rupture

Case Management Fees: $1,286

Summary of Intervention:
Options Unlimited expedited the claimant's hospital discharge following two hospitalizations through placement of home care services in lieu of prolonged hospital stays. Expedited hospitalization discharge through the placement of home care services for IV hydration, fetal stress testing, and home uterine monitoring at negotiated rates for considerable savings to the benefit provider.

Expedited hospitalization II through the placement of home care services for skilled nursing for wound care and home health aide services due to claimant's C-Section incision opening when wound staples were removed 4 days after surgery. Services were provided at rates negotiated with two providers, Healthcare and Metro Home Care.

Potential Charges:
33 days in hospital at $1,500/day = $49,500
Associated MD visits at $150/day × 33 = $4,950
Nursing visits 2 × day at $150/visit × 14 days = $4,200
Home Health Aide at $160/day × 5 days = $800
Note: Also avoided birth of premature infant

Total of Potential Charges:
$59,450

Actual Cost and Related Charges:
33 days home uterine monitoring at $125/day = $4,125
14 days hydration at $100/day = $1,400
7 days infant nonstress testing at $125/day = $875
14 days wound care at $100/visit × twice day = $2,400
5 days home health aide at 4 hrs/day × $15/hr = $300

Total of Actual Charges and Case Management Fees:
$9,070 + $1,286 = $10,356

Net Savings: $49,094

CASE MANAGEMENT COST-BENEFIT ANALYSIS REPORT

Re: 0009

Carrier/Client Group: Local 123

Date of Referral: 11/27/xx

Date of Closure: 2/6/xx+1

Total Weeks/Months of Case Management: 5 weeks

Diagnosis: Recurrent asthma

Case Management Fees: $652.55

Summary of Intervention:
This claimant has had recurrent hospitalization for asthma. Through case management intervention, the claimant was referred to a pulmonologist and a more aggressive treatment plan was developed. Options Unlimited intervened to coordinate delivery of prescription plan medication. Family and physician were contacted as claimant did not receive medication delivery in a timely manner resulting in noncompliance with medication regime and increasing symptomatology of an asthma attack. Family was directed to contact MD immediately for an interim prescription to obtain medication avoiding an ER visit and hospitalization. Since case management intervention, no further hospitalizations have occurred.

Potential Charges:
Avoidance of ER visit at $750
Avoidance of hospital × 3 days for asthma at $1,500/day = $4,500
Associated MD fees at $100/day × 3 = $300

Total of Potential Charges:
$5,550

Actual Cost and Related Charges:
None

Total of Actual Charges and Case Management Fees:
$652.55 Case Management Fees

Net Savings: $4,897.45

CASE MANAGEMENT COST-BENEFIT ANALYSIS REPORT

Re: 0022

Carrier/Client Group: Local 123

Date of Referral: 12/6/xx

Date of Closure: 2/10/xx+1

Total Weeks/Months of Case Management: 12 weeks

Diagnosis: Coronary Artery Disease/Diabetes

Case Management Fees: $2,430

Summary of Intervention:
During a recent visit to this claimant, this consultant noted that claimant's blood sugars were extremely high. This consultant noted that claimant had stopped taking one of her diabetic medications just prior to a recent procedure, was due to resume taking this following this procedure and never did. Claimant resumed taking this medication after this consultant pointed out this error. This consultant continued to monitor claimant's progress after she resumed her prescribed diabetic medication. Claimant's blood sugars remained moderately high. This consultant recommended that claimant visit her endocrinologist, which she did. Claimant's endocrinologist increased the dosage of claimant's diabetic medication. Claimant had also complained of intermittent midsternal chest pain and did not have a prescription for Nitroglycerine (helps to reduce the workload of the heart, reducing the incidence of heart attack). This consultant directed claimant to contact her cardiologist and notify him of these symptoms, which she did. Cardiologist ordered Nitroglycerine, which relieved the chest pain. This consultant educated, supported, and guided this claimant toward improving her health status. Initially, this claimant had little knowledge of her cardiac or diabetic condition. This consultant was instrumental in the claimant returning to her endocrinologist whom she had not seen in more than 6 months (claimant's blood glucose levels were extremely elevated at this time). This consultant encouraged the claimant to contact her physician when she was experiencing chest pain, which was relieved. Through contact with Dr. M and the Cath Lab, this consultant was able to reschedule this claimant's cardiac cath procedure following a cancellation due to a misunderstanding. This consultant also alerted Dr. M of this claimant's uncontrolled diabetic state. This resulted in better preparation for the catheterization procedure, possibly averting another cancellation.

Potential Charges:
Cardiac Complications:
Two Emergency Room visits at $750 each visit = $1,500
Two admissions to rule out M.I. × 10 days each admission:
C.C.U. × 3 days each admission at $2,000 per day = $12,000
7 days on medical floor each visit to ensure stability on medication at $1,500 per day = $21,000
Diabetic Complications:
Two Emergency Room visits at $750 each visit = $1,500
Two MD Emergency Room charges at $125.00 = $250
Two admissions to stabilize diabetic crisis × 10 days each at $1,500 per day = $30,000

Total of Potential Charges:
$66,250

Actual Cost and Related Charges:
None

Total of Actual Charges and Case Management Fees:
$2,430 Case Management Fees

Net Savings: $63,820

Local 123 Welfare Fund	
Second Half-Year Cost-Benefit Analysis for Case Management Services	
July 1, xxxx–December 31, xxxx	
Cases open at beginning of period	14
Cases referred this period	20
Cases closed during the period	24
Total cases worked during period	34
Total number of open cases	10
Total fees for the period	$ 40,764
Average fees per month	$ 6,794
Average fees per case/period	$ 1,199
Average fees per case/month	$ 200
Total savings for period	
Gross	$413,141
Net	$372,377
Average savings per case/period	$ 10,952
Ratio of dollars to savings	1:10

Note: To evaluate the benefits of a program for a client, we use total fees billed for all cases worked and the savings resulting from our intervention, whether savings were realized in every case, one case, or several cases.

CASE MANAGEMENT COST-BENEFIT ANALYSIS REPORT

Re: 0001

Carrier/Client Group: Local 123

Date of Referral: 3/19/xx

Date of Closure: 7/20/xx

Total Weeks/Months of Case Management: 4 1/2 months

Diagnosis: Liver transplant

Case Management Fees: $1,900 ($4,267 Lifetime Fees)

Summary of Intervention:
Options Unlimited spent a great deal of time on negotiations for hospitalization and transplant services. Initially, the reimbursement manager was noncompliant with this consultant's multiple phone calls. Contact was made with transplant coordinator to resolve this issue. The facility was also initially not open to negotiations. Through persistent intervention by Options Unlimited, a 30% discount was finally obtained for hospitalization and transplant services.

Potential Charges:
Hospitalization at $97,324
Transplant services at $122,391

Total of Potential Charges:
$219,715

Actual Cost and Related Charges:
Negotiated rate of $153,800

Total of Actual Charges and Case Management Fees:
$153,800.50 + $1,900 = $155,800

Net Savings: $64,015
Note: Prior net savings of $2,357 = lifetime savings of $66,372

CASE MANAGEMENT COST-BENEFIT ANALYSIS REPORT

Re: 0002

Carrier/Client Group: Local 123

Date of Referral: 7/3/xx

Date of Closure: 9/30/xx

Total Weeks/Months of Case Management: 12 weeks and 4 days

Diagnosis: Coronary Artery Disease

Case Management Fees: $1,349

Summary of Intervention:
Options Unlimited conducted a thorough assessment and expedited this claimant's discharge from acute care to home in a prompt fashion utilizing safe and medically appropriate plan of home care services. These services included a visiting nurse who specializes in diabetic care and teaching as well as postoperative management of home care patients. Home physical therapy was added to this claimant's home program because he was found to have decreased strength and mobility upon initial visiting nurse assessment. The mentioned services were arranged at a cost-effective rate. All services were monitored closely and discontinued once the claimant was medically stable with MD's approval. Options Unlimited coordinated and negotiated cardiac rehabilitation services at a cost-effective, all-inclusive rate. These services included continued monitoring of diabetes and continued education focusing on preventive measures. This consultant researched and encouraged claimant to have a consultation with an endocrinologist for guidance regarding effective diabetic management. Claimant took our advice and is currently under the care of an in-network endocrinologist for diabetes management. Options Unlimited has reviewed claims on an ongoing basis. Claimant is very grateful toward our intervention.

Potential Charges:
Emergency room visit because of ineffective diabetic management = $750
Nonnegotiated visiting nurse services at $150/visit = $1,200
Nonnegotiated home physical therapy services at $150 per visit for 4 visits = $600
Nonnegotiated cardiac rehab services at $200 per visit × 3 days per week for 12 weeks = $7,200

Total of Potential Charges:
$9,759

Actual Cost and Related Charges:

Negotiated visiting nurse service $100 per visit × 8 visits = $800

Negotiated home physical therapy services at $100 for initial eval and $85 per visit thereafter × 4 visits = $440

Negotiated cardiac rehab services at $100 per visit all inclusive × 3 days per week for 12 weeks = $3,600

Total of Actual Charges and Case Management Fees:
$4,840 + $1,349 = $6,189

Net Savings: $3,561 Lifetime Savings

CASE MANAGEMENT COST-BENEFIT ANALYSIS REPORT

Re: 0003

Carrier/Client Group: Local 123

Date of Referral: 6/18/xx

Date of Closure: 10/4/xx

Total Weeks/Months of Case Management: 15 weeks

Diagnosis: Cerebral Aneurysms

Case Management Fees: $2,989

Summary of Intervention:
This consultant monitored this claimant's progress through contact with Dr. S and Lisa C. The claimant's care was monitored for appropriateness and effectiveness. Suggestions were made for changes when appropriate and necessary.

This consultant was able to expedite this claimant's transfer from Brook Memorial Hospital to St. John Rehabilitation Center as soon as Dr. S wrote orders for the same. This avoided additional hospital days that would have been spent by the social worker in an attempt to have completed all of these arrangements (on short notice) independently.

This consultant arranged cost-effective inpatient rehabilitation services through St. John Rehabilitation Center. This claimant's progress was monitored closely and the services provided were assessed for effectiveness.

This consultant was able to arrange for cost-effective skilled nursing services through St. John. This was for a 2-week period following permission from the group to flex benefits for the same.

This consultant was able to arrange cost-effective ambulance and ambulette transportation services when the claimant was transferred from the hospital to the rehabilitation center and back, and again when the claimant needed transportation for a CT scan. This consultant avoided the need for a more expensive ambulance transport by arranging for the claimant's daughter to accompany her in an ambulette.

Potential Charges:
Three additional hospital days spent while the hospital social worker/discharge
   planner made arrangements for transfer at $2,000 per day = $6,000
Inpatient rehabilitation services at $1,500 per day × 30 days = $45,000
Ambulance Transportation × 2 at $450 each = $900, plus $9.25 per mile × 36
   miles = $333

Total $52,233

Two additional weeks of inpatient rehabilitation services at $550.00 per day = $7,700

Total of Potential Charges:
$59,933

Actual Cost and Related Charges:
Inpatient rehabilitation services at $550 per day × 30 days = $16,500
Ambulance transportation × 1 at $185 plus $3.75 per mile = $252.50
Ambulette transportation × 1 at $25.00 each way plus $1.00 per mile = $68
Two additional weeks of inpatient rehabilitation services at a reduced rate of $300.00 per day = $4,200

Total of Actual Charges and Case Management Fees:
$21,020.50 + $2,989 = $24,009

Net Savings: $35,924 Total Lifetime Savings

CASE MANAGEMENT COST-BENEFIT ANALYSIS REPORT

Re: 0004

Carrier/Client Group: Local 123

Date of Referral: 4/6/xx

Date of Closure: 9/16/xx

Total Weeks/Months of Case Management: 5 1/2 months

Diagnosis: Lung Cancer

Case Management Fees: $332 ($1,051 prior fees = $1,383 Lifetime Fees)

Summary of Intervention:
Options Unlimited worked closely with the claimant's oncologist and encouraged the claimant's chemotherapy be administered in the physician's office, 3 days a month for 3 months, when it was demonstrated that the claimant suffered no severe reaction from same during the first 3 months of treatment when it was administered in a more costly hospital setting. Options Unlimited monitored the claimant closely for chemotherapy side effects and complications.

Potential Charges:
9 days hospitalization at $1,500/day = $13,500
9 MD visits at $100/visit = $900

Total of Potential Charges:
$14,400

Actual Cost and Related Charges:
9 days of chemotherapy at $269.47 = $2,425.23

Total of Actual Charges and Case Management Fees:
$2,425.23 + $332 = $2,757

Net Savings: $11,643.00
Note: Prior savings of $8,100 = $19,743 Total Lifetime Savings

CASE MANAGEMENT COST-BENEFIT ANALYSIS REPORT

Re: 0008

Carrier/Client Group: Local 123

Date of Referral: 11/20/xx

Date of Closure: 8/28/xx+1

Total Weeks/Months of Case Management: 10 months

Diagnosis: Cancer of Nasopharynx

Case Management Fees: $3,075.33 ($4,104 Lifetime Fees)

Summary of Intervention:
As claimant's condition deteriorated, we sought and obtained approval to set up hospice services at home. A per service arrangement was negotiated rather than a per diem as the claimant needs were limited and this was much more cost-effective. Timely and appropriate intervention and support by Options Unlimited case manager avoided hospitalization or the need for inpatient hospice. The claimant expired on 8/26/xx+1.

Potential Charges:
2 hospital stays at 5 days each or 10 days at $2,000/day = $20,000
Associated MD visits at $100/visit × 10 = $1,000
Inpatient hospice at 14 days × $450/day = $6,300
Per diem rate for home hospice = $125/day × 20 days = $2,500

Total of Potential Charges:
$29,800

Actual Cost and Related Charges:
Home hospice at per service rate for a total of services of approximately = $1,500

Total of Actual Charges and Case Management Fees:
$1,500 + $3,075 = $4,575

Net Savings: $25,225
Note: Lifetime Net Savings $21,121

CASE MANAGEMENT COST-BENEFIT ANALYSIS REPORT

Re: 0026

Carrier/Client Group: Local 123

Date of Referral: 6/12/xx

Date of Closure: 7/13/xx

Total Weeks/Months of Case Management: 1 month

Diagnosis: Status Asthmaticus

Case Management Fees: $608

Summary of Intervention:
Options Unlimited expedited the claimant's discharge from the hospital through the placement of skilled nursing visits provided by a Spanish-speaking nurse from a home care agency in order to provide the claimant and her mother with the necessary knowledge base of her disease process and compliance with her plan of treatment in order to prevent unnecessary ER visits and/or hospitalization due to disease exacerbation. The claimant has been compliant and returned to school full-time. Previous to Options Unlimited intervention, the claimant had missed 102 days of school this school year.

Potential Charges:
1 ER visit at $750
3 days hospitalization at $2,000/day = $6,000
3 MD visits at $100/each = $300
4 SNV nonnegotiated rate of $150/visit = $600

Total of Potential Charges:
$9,650

Actual Cost and Related Charges:
4 SNV at negotiated rate of $100/visit = $400

Total of Actual Charges and Case Management Fees:
$400 + $608 = $1,008

Net Savings: $8,642 Lifetime Savings

Source: Courtesy of Options Unlimited, Case Management Services Division, 2003, Huntington, New York.

Appendix 12–D Expanded Cost-Benefit Analysis Summary for Self-Funded Plan

---

July 1, xxxx–September, 30, xxxx
Third Quarter Cost-Benefit Analysis for Case Management Services for Sam's

Cases open at beginning of period	4
Cases referred this period	0
Cases closed during the period	5
Total cases worked during period	7
Total number of open cases	2
Total fees for the period	$ 5,325.00
Average fees per month	$ 1,775.00
Average fees per case/period	$ 761.00
Average fees per case/month	$ 254.00
Total savings for period	
Gross	$59,946.00
Net	$54,621.00
Average savings per case/period	$ 7,803.00
Ratio of dollars to savings	1:11

Note: To evaluate the benefits of a program for a client, we use total fees billed for all cases worked and the savings resulting from our intervention, whether savings were realized in every case, one case, or several cases.

CASE MANAGEMENT COST-BENEFIT ANALYSIS REPORT

Re: 0001

Carrier/Client Group: Sam's

Date of Referral: 1/10/xx

Date of Closure: Open

Total Weeks/Months of Case Management: 9 months

Diagnosis: Congestive Heart Failure; Pulmonary Emboli; Morbid Obesity; Psoriasis

Case Management Fees: $1,475

Summary of Intervention:
Through case management intervention, the claimant continues to be provided with durable medical equipment at negotiated monthly rental. During this quarter, Options coordinated the claimant's relocation to another area in Georgia, without interruption to care or services and by researching quality and cost-effective providers in his area. With our ongoing and continuous support, the claimant has been compliant with all physician visits and his plan of treatment, which has resulted in an additional *27-pound weight loss,* with a total weight loss of 180 pounds in a 9-month period. The claimant continues to work full-time without need for hospitalization since our involvement. Our intervention will continue, although to a lesser extent, in order to ensure that the claimant reaches his target weight.

Potential Charges:
3 months nonnegotiated rate for CPAP respirator @ $475/mo. = $1,425
3 months nonnegotiated rate for Oxygen Concentrator @ $450/mo = $1,350
1 ER visit @ Georgia rate = $500
3 days hospitalization (for respiratory/cardiac complication) @ $1,300/day = $3,900
3 MD visits @ $100 = $300

Total of Potential Charges:
$7,475

Actual Cost and Related Charges:
3 months CPAP Machine rental @ $225/month = $8,675
3 months Oxygen Concentrator @ $175/month = $525

Total of Actual Charges and Case Management Fees:
$1,200 + $1,475 = $2,675

Net Savings: $4,800

CASE MANAGEMENT COST-BENEFIT ANALYSIS REPORT

Re: 0002

Carrier/Client Group: Sam's

Date of Referral: 5/22/xx

Date of Closure: 8/22/xx

Total Weeks/Months of Case Management: 3 months

Diagnosis: Status Asthmaticus; Asthma

Case Management Fees: $398

Summary of Intervention:
This 1-year-old girl was identified for case management during her admission to the hospital for a severe asthma episode. NOTE: This little girl had three hospital admissions last year for the same diagnosis and was identified at that time; however, the mother did not respond to our letter or phone calls. This time, she was more receptive and we have been able to direct her to appropriate medical care as well as advise her of the necessity to rid the home of the causative factors, for example, a cat, smoking adults, etc. Our case manager also reviewed with the parent the importance of seeking treatment at the first signs of respiratory distress. The child appears to be medically stable and the mother more compliant, and our file has been closed. There have been no further episodes.

Potential Charges:
Avoidance of hospital admission for asthma @ $2,000/day @ 5 days = $10,000
MD visits @ $100/visit × 5 = $500

Total of Potential Charges:
$10,500

Actual Cost and Related Charges:
None

Total of Actual Charges and Case Management Fees:
$1,200

Net Savings: $9,300

CASE MANAGEMENT SECOND QUARTER
COST-BENEFIT ANALYSIS REPORT

Note: This second quarter report for case 0003 is included to illustrate previous intervention and savings, which are then added to savings in the third quarter to reflect lifetime savings on this case.

Re: 0003

Carrier/Client Group: Sam's

Date of Referral: 11/17/xx

Date of Closure: Open

Total Weeks/Months of Case Management: 7.5 months

Diagnosis: High Risk Pregnancy; Uncontrolled Diabetes

Case Management Fees: $4,320

Summary of Intervention:
Our case manager was intensely involved with this woman for this 3-month period of time. The patient, because of emotional/marital problems, cultural differences, and lack of education, was extremely noncompliant with prescribed medical appointments. In order to avoid premature delivery of her baby (which was highly likely) and to prevent long-term confinement of this mother in the hospital for the protection of her and the unborn infant, Options arranged for home care visits (with favorable negotiated rates) and visits by a Public Health Nurse (at no cost to the plan) in order to collaborate strategies to manage this case. It was also necessary to research a pediatrician who would work with the treating obstetrician in minimizing the risks for this infant *and* who would be covered by the network and Medicaid. Despite all of this intervention, the patient, after an upset with her husband, did not take her insulin or check her blood sugars and required hospitalization. Options, in discussion with MD and nursing staff, recommended extended stay to allow for medical and emotional stability. Following a nine-day stay, she safely delivered her healthy baby on 5-29-97. Our involvement will continue for a while longer to ensure that the mother's diabetes returns to a safer status and to monitor the infant for diabetes as well.

Potential Charges:
Avoidance of premature delivery of infant 3 months prior to expected date of confinement:
3 months in Neonatal ICU @ $3,000/day = $270,000
MD visits (2 specialists @ $100 ea. × 90 days) = $18,000
OR

Continuous confinement of mother in hospital @ $2,000/day × 90 = $180,000
MD visits @ $100 × 90 = $9,000

Total of Potential Charges:
Range from $189,000 to $288,000

Actual Cost and Related Charges:
Hospital confinement @ $2,000/day × 9 days = $18,000
MD visits × $100 × 9 = $900
Nursing visits @ negotiated $100/visit × 6 = $600

Total of Actual Charges and Case Management Fees:
$19,500 + $4,320 = $23,820

Net Savings: Range from $165,180 to $264,178

CASE MANAGEMENT THIRD QUARTER
COST-BENEFIT ANALYSIS REPORT

Re: 0003

Carrier/Client Group: Sam's

Date of Referral: 11-17-xx

Date of Closure: 8-30-xx+1

Total Weeks/Months of Case Management: 9.5 months

Diagnosis: High-Risk Pregnancy; Diabetes

Case Management Fees: $755 (prior fees of $6,458 results in total fees of $7,213 for life of case)

Summary of Intervention:
During the last 2 months of case management, Options monitored the status of the claimant and her infant daughter to ensure stability and compliance. Because of our case manager's close follow-up, the newborn received appropriate care, and the claimant became much more aware of the need to seek medical treatment for herself. Because of this awareness, the claimant avoided a lengthy hospitalization when she sought treatment after developing a hematoma (collection of blood under the skin surface). The incision and drainage only required an overnight stay instead of a much longer one that would have occurred had she delayed treatment (which had been her usual behavior). Home care services were discontinued in a timely manner. The claimant and infant are receiving the public assistance they are eligible for and the claimant's marital/domestic status appears to be stable. Options was able to contribute significantly to the successful outcome of this extremely medically volatile case, a safe delivery and healthy baby, and *tremendous* savings to the Plan (presented in prior 1st- and 2nd-quarter reports). NOTE: Claimant has expressed a high degree of satisfaction with Options case management services . . . Patient Satisfaction Survey response included.

Potential Charges:
Additional 3 days in hospital due to complications following hematoma @ $2,000/day = $6,000
MD visits @ $100/visit = $300

Total of Potential Charges:
$6,300

Actual Cost and Related Charges:
Overnight hospital admission @ $2,000
MD visit = $100

Total of Actual Charges and Case Management Fees:
$2,100 + $755 = $2,855

Net Savings: $3,445
Note: Prior net savings of $165,180 results in total *net* savings of $168,625 for life of this case.

CASE MANAGEMENT COST-BENEFIT ANALYSIS REPORT

Re: 0004

Carrier/Client Group: Sam's

Date of Referral: 6/6/xx

Date of Closure: 7/30/xx

Total Weeks/Months of Case Management: 7 weeks

Diagnosis: Depression

Case Management Fees: $700

Summary of Intervention:
This file was identified for case management following claimant's admission to a facility for treatment of depression. Options immediately began negotiations in order to maximize the use of available benefits. We were able to expedite the claimant's discharge by 10 days and continued to monitor the effectiveness of the treatment plan as well as his compliance with recommendations. He became medically stable and continued with the necessary outpatient services in a county mental health program.

Potential Charges:
30 days hospitalization at a nonnegotiated daily rate of $1,500 = $45,000 (paid at 80% as per plan would have exhausted his lifetime benefit of $36,000)

Total of Potential Charges:
$45,000

Actual Cost and Related Charges:
21 days @ negotiated rate of $750/day = $15,750

Total of Actual Charges and Case Management Fees:
$15,750 + $700 = $16,450

Net Savings: $28,550

CASE MANAGEMENT COST-BENEFIT ANALYSIS REPORT

Re: 0005

Carrier/Client Group: Sam's

Date of Referral: 5/28/xx

Date of Closure: 8/14/xx

Total Weeks/Months of Case Management: 10 weeks

Diagnosis: Anxiety Disorder

Case Management Fees: $682

Summary of Intervention:
This case was referred directly by Total Plan Administrators, Inc., the TPA, after they received a request to flex inpatient benefits for outpatient benefits. Had benefits not been flexed, the claimant would have been admitted to Willowtree Hospital. After discussion, it was determined that the claimant would benefit from a full-day program in lieu of inpatient hospitalization. This consultant negotiated a cost-effective rate for the day program. Options monitored the claimant's status for effectiveness of her treatment plan and gradually decreased services, working in conjunction with the recommendations of MD. Clinical updates were reviewed on a weekly basis. As the claimant's condition stabilized, this consultant discussed the feasibility of the claimant attending half days in lieu of full days in the program. A cost-effective rate was agreed upon and the claimant transitioned to the three-hour morning program on June 24th. The claimant was discharged from the program on July 5th. Since the claimant's condition has stabilized, this case was closed to case management intervention.

Potential Charges:
Inpatient hospitalization @ $1,500/day × 30 days = $45,000 (exhausting plan limit of $25,000)

Total of Potential Charges:
$25,000

Actual Cost and Related Charges:
Day hospital program @ 300/day × 15 days = $4,500
Partial hospital program @ $150/day × 10 days = $1,500

Total of Actual Charges and Case Management Fees:
$6,000 + $725 = $6,725

Net Savings: $18,275

CASE MANAGEMENT COST-BENEFIT ANALYSIS REPORT

Re: 0006

Carrier/Client Group: Sam's

Date of Referral: 6/12/xx

Date of Closure: 7/2/xx

Total Weeks/Months of Case Management: 3 weeks

Diagnosis: Traumatic eye injury

Case Management Fees: $600

Summary of Intervention:
The claimant, being an adolescent and having lost his left eye secondary to trauma, exhibited emotional problems that impacted his follow-up care. The claimant refused a psychological evaluation. This consultant contacted the claimant's mother and encouraged her to contact the psychologist for strategies in dealing with her son. The claimant refused to see the surgeon postoperatively. This consultant instructed her to inform her son of the potential damage to the "good" eye if an infection develops. She followed the advice resulting in appropriate follow-up care, thus avoiding inpatient hospitalization and treatment secondary to complications.

Potential Charges:
Emergency Room visit due to infection at $700
MD fees at $125
Inpatient treatment to stabilize and treat infection:
   $1,500/day × 5 days = $7,500
   MD fees = $625

Total of Potential Charges:
$8,950

Actual Cost and Related Charges:
None

Total of Actual Charges and Case Management Fees:
$600 Case Management Fees

Net Savings: $8,350

CASE MANAGEMENT COST-BENEFIT ANALYSIS REPORT

Re: 0007

Carrier/Client Group: Sam's

Date of Referral: 1/24/xx

Date of Closure: Remains Open

Total Weeks/Months of Case Management: 8.1 months

Diagnosis: Brain Tumor

Case Management Fees: $896

Summary of Intervention:
This quarter, case manager monitored the claimant's course of recovery since undergoing brain surgery in June; prior to this time, her mother-in-law attended to all the medical issues, as well as assisted the claimant with her ADLs; however, her husband underwent CABG surgery and she returned to her home upstate. Postoperatively, the claimant was seizure and headache free. She underwent surgery for an ovarian cyst with uneventful recovery. Case manager intended to close file, but claimant began experiencing seizure activity again. Claimant has apparently developed a suspicious lesion that will be investigated further. She will also be evaluated by a seizure specialist. Case manager will obtain all pertinent medical data to determine if further surgical intervention is indicated and formulate appropriate level of care if needed. Case manager also intervened when home care agency submitted billing in excess of terms of provider agreement for claims that had already been paid.

Potential Charges:
Home occupational therapy/excess charges = $750

Total of Potential Charges:
$750

Actual Cost and Related Charges:
Occupational therapy paid as per provider agreement.

Total of Actual Charges and Case Management Fees:
$896 Case Management fees

Net Savings: None

CHAPTER 13

Managing a Case Management Department: Your Role as Department Head or Independent Case Manager

REDEFINING CASE MANAGEMENT

In insurance companies, hospital systems, claims departments, and managed care service organizations I have visited across the country, case management is adrift. Many programs lack clear goals, departments manage the distribution of provider services rather than identifying and managing patient problems, and cursory preadmission review masquerades as case management. Effective case management is the foundation for successful managed care. To make it work, we must take stock of our case management programs and get back to the basics.

How Did We Get Off Track?

We stopped—or never began—managing the care of a patient across the continuum of care, in multiple settings, addressing the ongoing needs of the individual. Instead, I see the management of benefits and/or services a patient uses within the system (physicians, infusion, pharmaceutical benefits, rehab, home care); episodic management, in which only a single setting (rehab, home care, hospital) is even recorded, much less managed; nonintegrated programs, where one patient's case is "managed" both by Jane in Home Care, by Alice in Rehab, and by four different precert nurses who log in multiple hospital admissions (so no one is able to say, "Wait, he was only home three days, let's see what the problem is"); or redundant review, in which *all* home care services are tracked, with no distinction made for those patients who only need an occasional skilled visit. Too often in my role as a consultant, I find that the measure of success in some departments is shortening the length of stay.

463

Not every AIDS case or high-risk pregnancy needs a case manager, but every case should be screened by a professional to determine whether it poses a significant health and financial risk. Does this person require an intermediary to make sure she receives appropriate care to prevent potential problems from occurring? By the same token, if cardiac cases are managed in the hospital, but no one reaches beyond discharge to coordinate care outside the hospital or to verify patient compliance, that's not true case management.

The principle behind effective case management remains: Only a *small percentage* of people using expensive services are driving up costs. To provide high-quality, appropriate care, and rein in costs by curtailing clinical risks and dollar exposure, we must address the individual with the problem. Until the patient is contacted, how can one determine what the problems really are?

Nurses have good instincts. They know a problem when they see it, but sometimes corporate structure with its approval requirements makes it impossible for personal insight to have an impact. Overreliance on system-generated "guru guidelines" that make sense to no one also drive up costs. Remember the widely decried mastectomy as a day-op procedure? Or, think of today's day-op prostatectomy. Several red flags indicating a need for further case review and follow-up might well be present, but go unremarked because they don't fit into the boxes to be checked on a survey. What is the incidence of readmission? Infection? Are there signs of bleeding into a catheter or blockage of the catheter?

Back to Basics

Effective case management requires a well-designed case identification methodology, flexibility in management options, the ability to move a person quickly through a system, and prompt decisions and exceptions to benefit plan language as needed. A case manager can begin to realign a case management program by evaluating the group's health care issues and then gradually tailoring a program that targets them. One solution implemented over a wide expanse of cases is not the answer. No one would deluge a patient with multiple drugs and then try to sort out the side effects.

Whether a case manager is heading up a hospital's case management program, an insurance carrier case manager, or a home care agency's case management supervisor, she should consider the organization's mission statement. What are its goals, what is senior management looking for? Are the goals reasonable for her staff? Would they benefit from additional training? As a nurse, she would not intervene with a patient unless she understood his problems and needs. That same principle should be applied in this business/medical environment.

I firmly believe that we need to do more to demonstrate our success for ourselves, our staff, and those supervising our departments. We must define our role and contribution. When management understands the contribution of nurses and case managers, there is no question of their value. Create a report format that shows how case management intervention impacted the health care outcome and the cost of care. Continue to "get smart." The entire health care field has moved into the world of business. We must educate ourselves and our nurses on the clinical, managerial, and financial aspects of health care at the graduate and undergraduate level. We have already waited too long.

Evaluating a CM Department

1. Where are your high-cost cases? Identify the type of cases (diabetes, cancer, high-risk pregnancy) that require management within your employee group, hospital, admissions group, or covered lives.
2. Why are you managing those cases? What is the clinical risk to the patient and financial risk to your group (that is, how much more will it cost if you do not manage this case)? Are you discriminating between long-term, chronic illnesses, and the person who only needs IV antibiotics for 5 to 7 days?
3. Is there a sound system in place to identify cases for case management? Do nurses talk to patients and evaluate their needs? If an administrative assistant scans paperwork, a computer system flags certain diagnoses, services are based on LOS alone, or patients are automatically moved into case management only after they have exhausted their standard contract benefits or require an exception to plan language, you need to revise your mechanism.
4. How flexible are your case management red flags? Is it easy to identify and bring someone into case management? If it takes weeks or months, you do not have an effective case management program. Are multiple layers of people consulted to resolve problems, or do you and your staff have authority and autonomy to act?
5. What have you done to improve patients' overall outcomes? You should be able to record the clinical steps taken and why, and the patients' experiences. You should also see clear contrast in patient care improvement and in benefits spent among cases that are not managed and those that are.
6. Have you set goals? You must know what success looks like in order to implement the steps to achieve it, and then evaluate it. Highly important and often overlooked are the outcomes that are actually communicated to the payer. There is a need for case managers to be willing to be completely accountable; to take credit for our successes, we must continually evaluate our work. The days of an employer thinking, "If I'm paying for it, it must be working" are gone.

BECOMING AN INDEPENDENT CASE MANAGER

As in other entrepreneurial endeavors, there are advantages and disadvantages in "going it alone," and one should evaluate these carefully before hanging out one's shingle. Thanks to some very important changes, both in health care and our economy, small businesses are on the rise. Although many succeed, some do not fare so well. Being given the opportunity for success does not automatically guarantee it, nor does being a truly excellent case manager guarantee profits.

Why then should one consider taking this step? The benefits are numerous. As the statistics bear out, case management has been and will continue to be one of the most effective tools in the growing array of cost-containment and quality assurance tools in the marketplace today. Following mergers and changes in our economy, the large corporate giants are downsizing, and this trend has resulted in the creation and growth of numerous, smaller competitive companies. These companies are facing the same need to contain the costs related to illness and disability and are likely to use the services of smaller case management companies and even independent practitioners. Likewise for the growing number of midsized corporations that are increasingly dissatisfied with lack of attention to their needs and a gap in provision of services. These smaller and midsized companies are facing accelerating concerns; employee ill health and disabilities often have a greater impact and increased risk for these firms, regardless of their funding arrangements. Independents are certainly able to capture a share of this market, as these companies are not necessarily looking for the giants in the case management community.

To case managers who have worked in corporations, hospitals, and health care facilities, some of the problems that characterize large bureaucracies are evident: too many layers of management, too many meetings, too many delays. ("I'll take that suggestion under advisement," "Let's table that for our next meeting.") Are these reasons for becoming an independent practitioner? Perhaps not, but bureaucratic aggravations frequently lead individuals to at least consider starting their own companies.

Autonomy is one advantage, but there are others. Creating and expanding a company provides an opportunity to develop and use talents and skills, including marketing, public relations, financial management, negotiating, risk management, sales, accounting, personnel development, and human resources.

Then there are the financial considerations. No longer is it necessary to wait to be given a raise or a promotion; just write a check! Sound too good to be true? It is, but the opportunity for financial gain is most definitely there.

Given all of these wonderful advantages—autonomy, growth, creativity, and opportunity for success and wealth—what reason could there be for not going it alone? Unfortunately, the disadvantages are almost as numerous as the advantages.

Large organizations may have their problems, but they would not exist if they lacked value entirely. Their very size means that many outstanding professionals work side by side and are able to share their knowledge. When case managers leave this type of environment, they usually miss the camaraderie.

Those individuals were not only colleagues, but many became friends. Friends to have lunch with, discuss goals and dreams with, commiserate with, and have fun with. In addition to those who shared a profession (be it nurse, social worker, rehabilitation counselor), the case managers had other departments and their personnel and resources to draw from while learning and developing an area of expertise. The kind of isolation that comes with independence can truly be overwhelming when cases are not progressing as hoped, when client companies are upset about the time billed on a case, and potential clients, after extensive wooing, select another case management company. These things do happen and sometimes all in one day. Who can one share this with? Not with clients, who would feel anxious if they learned about such problems, nor with colleagues, who may also be competitors. A certain amount of isolation is unavoidable and needs to be addressed. It is easy to keep going when all is well but tougher when it is not.

Although starting a case management company provides an opportunity to create a business from the ground up, it does require learning about things that were of little use before but are now very important. Remember that big company? Aside from the medical staff, it also had departments and services that were probably taken for granted: purchasing, personnel, communications, public relations, and a business office. An independent case manager assumes other roles and performs other functions necessary to keep the business afloat. Remember also the security of knowing that a payroll check will come every 2 weeks? This, too, is no longer a "given." Neither is a 2- or 4-week vacation, paid holidays, or a medical and dental benefits package. In short, the financial security of being an employee has been traded for the opportunity for substantial gains—an opportunity that may never be realized.

FOR YOUR BUSINESS OR DEPARTMENT

So much for the pros and cons of becoming an independent practitioner. After consideration of these factors and others, if there is still a determination to take the next step, what should that be? Whether working to revitalize a case management department or start an independent business, the creation of a business plan should be the first move. Just as in case management, the strategy is to gather all of the necessary information, evaluate the situation, and identify the steps that will ensure a successful outcome. Looking at incorporating long- and short-term goals, strategy is then implemented, progress is monitored, and problems are identified and solved one by one. Why is a business plan necessary, and does it need to be a lengthy, formal document? Not really, especially if in the beginning the company will essentially be a one-person operation or if the plan is being developed for monitoring of progress within the case management department only. But a case manager trying to coordinate care and services on behalf of 20 to 25 cases in different lines of insurance for several different client groups needs to have the structure. Every case management business and all case management department operations require some kind of planning—a framework to provide ongoing direction.

DEVELOPING A BUSINESS PLAN

What should a business plan incorporate? Are there key components that every plan should have? Following is a list of important issues to address.

- **Type of company:** Should it be a full-service company? Should it be restricted to medical case management only? One disease state or one type of insurance only (for example, workers' compensation, liability, group medical)?
- **Location:** Will the company provide services in one town or city? In one or several counties? In the entire state?
- **Size:** Some case managers want to work cases themselves. They have no interest in taking on partners or hiring and supervising other case managers. Others are willing to make that next and very critical move: becoming an employer. Establishing limitations regarding size and number of cases right at the beginning is extremely important. A case manager with 25 cases might be offered 3, 5, or 10 more. Does she say "No, I don't want any more work," take them and be unable to work them, or be spread so thin that the quality of her work suffers? Or, does she start thinking about getting a partner?
- **Financial resources:** Most small businesses require some kind of budget. In addition to salary, there are other expenses: telephone, fax, e-mail, rent, utilities, business and professional liability insurance, postage, office supplies, equipment, and furnishings. Depending on personal finances, a small business loan might need to be considered. A loan assists in defraying some of the start-up costs and keeps the business going until payments from accounts start coming in. If a large portion of business will be with insurance companies, TPAs, and other large groups, payment for services may not be received until 60 to 90 days after invoicing. This kind of delay can certainly result in financial strain, but it can be planned for instead of coming as a worrisome "surprise." As new accounts are acquired, assessing their financial status becomes as crucial as knowing one's own. To illustrate, one of my accounts is a TPA with a consistently expanding client base. Although I was very excited to learn that all their clients would be using our case management

services, that excitement soon turned to anxiety. Two of these accounts went into chapter 11 (filed for bankruptcy). Another small group had their financial office review each payment before authorizing the TPA to release the checks, and still another only funded its account every 60 days. The combination of lost payments and delays in reimbursement had a definite impact on my business, because I had already paid my staff for the work they had done. This example also demonstrates the need to have not only a financial plan, but also some contingency plans.

- **Short- and long-term goals:** In good case management, it is essential to define goals in order to ensure movement of a case toward a successful outcome. The same applies to business planning. Establish some attainable and maybe some not-so-attainable goals for the next year, for the next 5 years, and for the next 10 years. Obviously, changes in the health care industry and the national or local economy may prevent reaching all goals in the planned time frame, but the goals should be set anyway. They will act as "benchmarks" for evaluating and reevaluating the company's direction. Revising a business plan several times in a year or every few years is not a problem. Not having a plan most assuredly will be.

Following is a checklist of assessments to make and needs to consider:

Assess Your Personal Skill Sets
- Skills from nursing and other business experience
- Skills from family finances management
- Skills from life: soccer moms develop excellent organizational and team-building skills

Know Your Strengths and Weaknesses
- What are you good at? You will be doing the work.
- What do you enjoy? You need to enjoy your role to take you through the hard times.
- What are your business and organizational skills?

What Type of Business Do You Envision?
- Do you want a partner—someone to complement or match your skills, for example, one person who is clinically proficient and one with business acumen?
- Will you do consulting work?
- Will you oversee a CM office or department?
- Will you do the case work yourself, maintaining a workable caseload?

Define Your Nature and Personality
- Can you say no?

- Can you sustain your spirit through the early months of potentially uneven returns?
- Do not start a business just because you are a great case manager and/or RN.

What Role Do You Want to Play?
- Where can you make a difference, so your job will be fulfilling?
- What is the need in your community—growing migrant, immigrant, or elder population?
- What is your niche or specialty—oncology, pediatrics, public sector case management?
- Select a clinical niche.
- Select a practice setting.
- Take your CM skills to your company.

Financial and Business Issues
- How will you finance your start-up?
- Do you have 3 to 6 months of assets to tide you over?
- How will you cost-out your services?
- Can you establish a banking relationship?
- Can you hire an accountant?
- How will you create access to legal counsel?
- How will you create contracts for staff and clients?
- Do you know licensing and business regulations for your state?

PRICING THE MARKET

One of the most difficult tasks a new case manager starting a business will have is determining how much to charge for the services provided. Unfortunately, there are no hard-and-fast rules for setting prices. Some may believe that undercutting the competition guarantees business, but this strategy can backfire. It may net a few cases from those who always look for the "cheapest of everything," but more will wonder why the prices are so low. The tendency will be to think services are probably not as good as those provided by other, more established companies. Pricing services closer to the competition is actually a more astute business strategy, especially if the goal is to grow.

To illustrate further, let us say the going rate for case management services in your locale is $75 per hour. You are just starting out, working out of your home. You have no secretary (preparing your reports on your computer) and are managing all the cases yourself. You were making $27 per hour plus benefits in a case management company when you left to start your own business. You really want business, so you decide to charge $35 an hour and are looking forward to considerable profit. You also believe that if you charge $35 and others are charging $75, then you will definitely get business. And you do.

You continue and soon are up to 25 cases, cannot work any more yourself, and decide to hire your first staff case manager. She is perfect, except for one thing: She is not computer literate. So you also hire a secretary. These two additions to your staff cannot work out of your home, so you move into a new office. You have thus, in a short period of time, increased your expenses more than your income. Now what? You need to raise your rates! How do you explain to your new accounts that you will now have to double your rates to $70 an hour or increase even more? An uncomfortable position to be sure—and one indicative of inexperience in business.

Discussions with your accountant or banker will be helpful in deciding a fair market value for your services. Whatever the rate decided upon, it should reflect your costs and allow you to generate a profit. A profit margin is desirable in order for you to continue to be able to upgrade and expand your business, unless, of course, you want to join the not-for-profit organizations or engage strictly in "pro bono" work.

There are various directories and other publications that list companies and provide information about their services and, in many instances, their current rates. The information is fairly reliable, but keep in mind that many of the listed companies may be large, provide several kinds of cost-containment services, or have a national capability, and the costs of any extra services are built into their hourly rates. So although published rates may be helpful, a company's own rates should reflect its cost of doing business rather than being a mirror image of the competition.

LOOKING AT THE COMPETITION

Every case management company and independent practitioner must consider others in the community who are in the same field. This can be intimidating, but it also provides an awareness that case management is a growing industry. Competition is good. It keeps case managers on their toes and helps them stretch toward excellence. Also, "breaking into" the marketplace may be easier if there are others who have gone before. Being the only provider of a service does *not* guarantee a company the entire market and may, in fact, create more problems. Why? Because there is reluctance on the part of purchasers to buy an unknown, no matter how good it may sound. They are inclined to think, "Let the others buy it first, and then we can see how they like it."

Fortunately, case management is already a tried-and-true service. Others have gone before and have demonstrated its worth. The object, then, is to establish a niche among competitors. Rather than being afraid of what they are doing, learn to seek knowledge about what is already out there. This is not difficult to come by. Attending conferences and visiting the exhibitors' area provides firsthand information. The Internet offers fast access to vast amounts of educational, clinical, statistical, operational, and administrative data and resources, and serves as a guide to other books, associations, foundations, and groups. As case managers are now a target market for pharmaceutical and other companies, it is wise to take the time to sort the reliable information from the marketing language. When you place an online request for rheumatoid arthritis information, the pharmaceutical companies with products used to treat the condition are likely to top your search engine list of sites.

Large companies usually print brochures and other handouts that describe their services and list their office locations, areas of specialization, and occasionally even their fees. Smaller regional or local companies also have marketing handouts, and these should be reviewed carefully to discover exactly what these companies are selling to potential clients. Similarities and differences in services can be utilized to help define one's own corporate identity.

Being knowledgeable about the competition and their various activities is part of being in business. Although "hot off the press" information is not always available, information about changes in competitors' client base, rate changes, and innovative services and approaches can be gleaned from various sources. Of most importance is how the competition responds to change. Changes in workers' compensation programs, employer involvement in benefit plans, wellness promotion, management approaches to high-cost and chronic conditions (for example, high-risk pregnancies, cancer, COPD, asthma), and outcomes research influence the direction of case management. How each company responds to these changes will obviously be different, and much can be learned from the successes and the failures of colleagues.

The successful approaches will eventually be described in articles in industry publications (for example, *The Case Manager, Case Management Advisor, Inside Case Management, Business & Health Institute* at www.businessandhealth.com [previously *Business & Health* magazine], *Business Insurance,* and *Risk Management*) or in presentations at various conferences. Keeping abreast, therefore, is as easy as attending conferences and reading industry periodicals. Attending conferences, in addition to updating one's clinical and business knowledge, also affords a wonderful opportunity to interact with competitors in a social environment. Sharing experiences and frustrations frequently results in an enhanced ability to view problems and challenges more objectively and to move toward resolution.

For instance, in a breakout session of a case management conference, there were several case managers representing the national and regional companies as well as independent practitioners. This session was focused on the "business" aspects of case management. There was discussion of billing, including the various approaches used to bill for services and client responses to bills. Interestingly, despite the differences in invoice formats and hourly rates, we learned that we did actually have something in common. Each of us at one time had a client who called to question some aspect of a bill. "Did it really take four tenths of an hour to make that phone call?" "Couldn't you have done it in one tenth or two tenths of an hour?" "Company *X* never charged me for that and you do."

From the conversation, during which we shared the all-too-familiar "war stories" of client objections, it became apparent that case management is being looked at closely. Our results and our costs are being examined. It also was clear that the main cause of client discontent over billing was not skepticism about the efficacy of the services or the reasonableness of the bills but rather lack of documentation. By discussing how to prepare cost-benefit analysis reports, we reviewed how to draft documents that demonstrated the benefits of case management intervention as well as its ability to contain costs. This sharing of information among various case management providers uncovered the solution to a very real problem.

Was this "helping" the competition? Isn't that a business no-no? Aren't we supposed to hope competitors fail and then grab their clients? There was a time when I engaged in that kind of thinking. Although not actively hoping that anyone would fail, I had ambivalent feelings about sharing any of my knowledge with the competition. Experience gained over many years has helped me to view the issue of sharing somewhat differently. If the providers of case management services become better at what they do, then the viability of case management is assured. Because sharing information improves the performance of practitioners, it enhances the status of the entire case management industry and makes it more likely any given practitioner will survive.

A recent example of that kind of thinking put into action was the "Visioneering Case Management's Future" invitational meeting, cohosted by The Academy of Certified Case Managers (ACCM) and CMSA in December 2002. Major players and stakeholders in the case management industry came together to discuss the challenges in health care management and case management in particular, and strategies to ensure the viability of our industry. The success of the meeting and its outcomes was and continues to be dependent on the willingness of the sometimes competing groups to candidly share concerns, perceived shortcomings, and the solutions each has found for specific problems. Attending were representatives from a range of practice settings, provider and payer groups, and associations, including the Academy of Certified Case Managers, American Association of Occupational Health Nurses, American Society on Aging, Association of Rehabilitation Nursing, Blue Cross Blue Shield, CCMC, Health Insurance Association of America, Lippincott's *CM Journal*, Michigan State University, National Association of Social Workers, St. Vincent's Hospital, Trustmark, University of Arizona, and more.

What about those in our industry who, in our judgment, may be doing it a disservice? This includes those who may have different business practices or who may attempt to garner clients by waging a price war or who just may not be good providers. How should one react when potential clients cite these case managers as the norm? Perhaps a client has had a very bad experience with such a provider and now assumes that all case managers are the same. This certainly is a problem and merely dismissing it does not make it go away. We are all part of the good and not so good in this business. Acknowledging that there are good, mediocre, and even bad providers of case management is no different a consideration than in any other product line or area of service. As in other businesses, it is never a good idea to knock the competition. This tactic does not automatically elevate one's own status. When a case manager is confronted with negative comments, her best strategy is to acknowledge the concern without either confirming or denying the information. This enables her to maintain control of the conversation and discuss what must be communicated, which is her ability to provide competent and appropriate case management services.

In reality, competition should be viewed as just another factor in the world of business. Undue importance given to competitors limits an individual's or company's creativity and ability to survive and excel. There are, of course, plenty of large, well-financed, diversified case management companies, but not every client needs that kind of company. For every big client, there are smaller clients just waiting to hear how a small case management company can help them.

NETWORKING AND THE PROFESSIONAL COMMUNITY

Developing and maintaining contacts in the case management and business community are essential for survival. Having the ability to communicate and share information with members of the professional and business sectors enhances one's capabilities. It is often easy within one's own profession (nurse, counselor, social worker) because one shares a common "language" and similar experiences. These become comfortable associations. Reaching outside the case management profession to individuals and organizations not concerned with health care, rehabilitation, or insurance may be somewhat intimidating.

The importance of professional alliances in the workplace is recognized by everyone. In a hospital and other traditional health care settings, a health care provider in one department may need to consult with someone in another department in order to deal with a particular problem. For example, although nurses may possess an understanding of nutritional needs, few would have the extensive dietary education to care for a diabetic without assistance. A call to the dietary department is all that is needed to arrange for a bedside visit, educational materials, and even classes for the patient from a nutritionist or registered dietitian upon discharge. Again, although nurses can assess respiratory function and detect sounds indicative of impending complications, the actual respiratory treatments most often are administered by a respiratory therapist. A social worker on a rehabilitation unit will have a physician and occupational therapist as members of the team who will provide the input needed for appropriate therapeutic service and equipment for a post-CVA patient. Such associations and contacts are inherent to the multidisciplinary approach in rehabilitation facilities and hospitals.

For case managers, especially those outside traditional settings, professional associations are no less important but perhaps more difficult to establish and maintain. It requires time and research to develop a network and creativity to nurture relationships. Furthermore, the networking process needs to be ongoing. Today, one may have two head-injury patients in a caseload, but 6 months from now these cases may be closed. Who should be contacted to assess the needs of the next head-injury patient? Will the neuropsychologist used for the last assessment still be in private practice or will she have joined the staff of a head-injury facility two states away?

Given all of the mergers, acquisitions, and closings of health care organizations, keeping key contacts is a never-ending challenge. Interestingly, however, over the years many of the relationships that I established still exist today. Some of these individuals have moved into new companies or now hold different positions yet continue to be colleagues and invaluable assets.

When I started my own firm in 1983, I was feeling somewhat insecure about its standing as a brand new company. I wondered if any reputable insurance carrier, such as Aetna, would be "allowed" to assign cases to me. The claims manager with whom I had met must have sensed my concern as I nervously inquired, "Don't you have to get this approved?" and "Will your home office have a problem with an unknown?" In reply, he said something that, over the years, has provided me with the confidence to approach potential clients: "We don't do business with Intracorp. We do business with Catherine Mullahy or Jane Doe. A business name may get you in the door but they won't sustain a working relationship." Strong relationships lead to other relationships, and gradually a business network is created and expands. For example, early in my career I was assigned a man who was rendered quadriplegic at the fourth and fifth cervical vertebrae following an automobile accident. When referred to the company that employed me as a rehabilitation specialist, he was on a ventilator in a small community hospital. He had been in its ICU for 2 months, and the referring carrier requested an evaluation. At the time, rehabilitation facilities were few and far between, and those that would even consider accepting a ventilator-dependent patient were very rare.

This 42-year-old man and his family desperately wanted him home, and the carrier obviously did not relish having him endlessly confined in an ICU. An aggressive pursuit of a pulmonary rehabilitation program began. After many telephone calls, evaluation of records by various facilities in surrounding states, and one refusal after another to accept the patient, discouragement and frustration surfaced. I could not, however, forget the visit of this man's wife and their four children to the hospital. I prepared them for the fact that we might not be able to find a suitable facility. They would not accept defeat and said they just "knew" I would help. I was willing to keep trying, but how long would the carrier allow my pursuit of an appropriate placement? On my own time, I continued the search. I made numerous calls to other nurses, to physicians with whom I had worked years before, and to spinal cord programs on the West Coast to see if they knew MDs on the East Coast who specialized in this narrow field.

One night on the evening news, there was a feature highlighting a young spinal cord victim who was treated in a facility headed by a physiatrist who was also a pulmonary specialist. Here might be the answer to my problem. The next morning, I called the news station and found out the name of the physician and the facility and crossed my fingers as I made a call. After giving an overview of the pertinent factors and the family situation, I asked if the physician would at least see my patient to determine if our rehabilitation goals were even feasible. Thankfully, he agreed to see my patient personally and accepted him into the facility.

It was a highly successful intervention and my patient eventually returned home, using the ventilator only during hours of sleep. The discharge planning nurse worked closely with me in transitioning this man back to his community and into the care of his wife and intermittent nursing services. The physician was compassionate, dedicated, and of great assistance to me. Over the years, he changed hospitals several times but continued to do independent medical exams for me and has been a fellow presenter at conferences and a resource to me in countless situations. And the discharge planning nurse? She, too, has moved several times during these past years. We kept in touch, and several years ago she became a regional rehabilitation nurse with a national insurance carrier. A few years later, she was promoted to home office rehabilitation coordinator and became one of my corporate clients. She referred cases to us for case management services. It is indeed a small and interesting world; I never dreamed that these associations started so long ago would continue to be so professionally fruitful.

Many professional associations turn into friendships, and, just as in one's personal life, such relationships deserve extra consideration. This does not mean lavish gifts, expensive lunches, or other such gestures, which may be deemed as potential causes of conflict of interest. Sending a note to an associate expressing appreciation and an acknowledgment to his or her supervisor or company are always acceptable and should become a standard networking plan. In addition, referrals of other patients or colleagues to an associate, as long as there is no monetary payment in return, is a professional way to express recognition of his or her expertise, quality of service, and willingness to work with you in a case management endeavor. Not all case managers have frequent opportunities to refer, but fortunately there are other ways to nurture professional contacts. These include sharing articles of interest, advising associates of seminars, and extending invitations to associates to speak to professional groups or client companies who would welcome their insight. Professional contacts are an important aspect of the case management practice, but when viewed as another link in the process leading to success, they can be both rewarding and enjoyable.

THE BUSINESS COMMUNITY

Most case managers today have some interaction with individuals in the business community and are with increasing frequency being recognized for their contributions toward the attainment of the goals of increasing quality and containing costs. Because the business sector pays the largest share of health care costs, a closer alliance between case managers and this concerned group is essential. The object should be not only to improve individual working relationships, but also to increase the public's awareness of case management in general.

Although most health care professionals know about case management, fewer business people do, despite its proven success. Interestingly, however, when business people are told what case managers do and the results they obtain, their response is usually extremely positive. They then ask, "Why isn't my company using this kind of service?" "How come there aren't more case managers?" and "Why has this been kept a secret?" Why, indeed?

Part of the answer is that case managers have failed to communicate the benefits of their services to those in the business community. The actual providers of case management services are usually linked to business organizations by individuals who are not case managers. For instance, an employer group needs a package of benefits for its employees. Depending on several factors, including economic feasibility, medical benefits will be provided through a plan that is either fully insured, partially funded, or completely self-funded (by the group). The group appoints from within or contracts someone to purchase the kind of plan it feels it can offer and afford. An insurance career, a TPA, or the employer group itself administers the plan and pays the claims. None of the individuals involved thus far in this process is likely to be a case manager.

As the plan design evolves, there maybe discussion of cost-containment techniques, including those of managed care. However, the terms *case management* and *case manager* may never be heard. PPOs, HMOs, pre-cert, utilization review, and second opinion programs will probably come up in conversation, because they have become relatively well-known and well-understood. But case management presents a challenge.

Those who purchase, use, are recipients of, or interact with case management services may be confused. Many assume case management is a given part of TPA services, and automatically credit the TPA with the benefits case management has produced. When there is a change in TPA, neither the employer, consultant, nor broker knows the case management provider as a separate entity. In a more educated health care provider system, carriers and employer groups would know case management is a freestanding service and a working relationship can easily continue beyond the association with a TPA.

Is it any wonder that case management is not a household word? The qualifier that distinguishes case management from other managed care services has not been communicated. Add to this the fact that even though case management finally has been defined, those who market case management services are usually from outside the field. They work in insurance, claims administration, marketing, or finance and tend to tell potential client groups merely that the big cases will be "managed." Unfortunately for the case management professional or company, this kind of characterization falls far short of the representation a case manager would want and is fraught with problems.

Because most managed care tools exist as a system, services are paid for on a capitated basis (per employee per month). Case management services, on the other hand, tend to be billed per hour or per case. In fully insured plans, services such as case management, disease management, and utilization review are often wrapped in a package, with one premium paid on a capitated rate, at x dollars per member per month. When case management services are consolidated into a package, they are no longer as visible as they might be, shining a spotlight on savings. (Of course, the same spotlight illuminates shortfalls, but a well-run case management department will produce more successes and savings than unfavorable results.) Self-funded plans often pay separate rates for services selected from a menu—claims services, reinsurance, an employee assistance program, vision program, and so on.

If employees and their dependents are unaware of a case management program and the case manager role as a health advocate, then when contact with an employee is initiated through a telephone call or a letter, the response might be, "No, thank you" or "I don't think I need you." The employee may call his or her supervisor or the human resource department, who may not know of the program either. The human resource department may then call the broker or insurance company account representative, who will attempt to sort out the confusion. Wouldn't it have been better for everyone to have known about the case management program right from the start? Most assuredly yes, but even knowledge of the program is not enough. What is really needed is communication from case managers.

Case managers should be part of the decision to purchase, marketing directly to the in-between contacts, the consultants and brokers. We must tell our story to the right people, the payers, the human resource managers, the personnel staff overseeing benefits for an employee population. It is the case manager who can best help middle management better position the benefits of our services. We all know that health care is a huge issue that can only be solved via coordination among all concerned parties.

To keep their voices in the forefront regarding health care issues, case managers need to submit articles to business publications, join community and business group coalitions to address health care concerns, and meet with business and health care leaders to tell them about the advantages of case management programs. Case managers need to be more involved in positioning themselves as part of the solution to the country's health care crisis. As health care reform evolves, many segments of society will be examining the details and looking to see how the changes will impact them directly. The business community, too, will be part of this process. Even in small towns, businesses have formed associations and committees. Such groups frequently look for guest speakers or for experts to join a panel discussion on a health care topic. Open exchanges lend themselves readily to the exploration of problems and solutions.

By calling or visiting the local chamber of commerce, one can acquire lists of member organizations and information about any special health or insurance committees. Because case management today is utilized by most lines of insurance, employer groups need to know that case managers understand their concerns and can help prevent continuing escalation of costs.

Local and regional business periodicals are available by subscription or may be reviewed at the local library. They provide insight into particular areas or issues of concern and afford opportunities to respond, such as by sending letters to the editor, to the authors of articles, and to individuals mentioned in articles. Initiating correspondence on a topic or issue can lead to an ongoing dialogue and perhaps will create a new client for case management services.

Besides gaining new clients through involvement with the business community, case managers can enhance their ability to manage a business and ultimately achieve success. Because many case managers do not have a business background, relationships with business people are often invaluable. By observing how others resolve business problems, case managers become more comfortable grappling with them. They can also learn about hiring techniques, computers, financial management, recruitment, training, marketing, and legal issues by attending business seminars and meeting with individuals who provide the services necessary for the business operations.

Case management is much like other businesses and has many of the same requirements. It is necessary to be aware of personal and business limitations and contract or arrange for assistance in dealing with critical day-to-day management issues. Obviously, restrictions (usually financial) may prevent the hiring of appropriate experts. For example, a public relations or marketing consultant could assist in the creation and expansion of a business, but, especially in the early days, hiring such a person may not be feasible. Growth might be slower, but not hiring a consultant is unlikely to create a crisis. On the other hand, a lack of understanding of or comfort with the financial aspects of business can indeed pose a serious threat to the viability of an operation. If expenses exceed income or if taxes or bills are not paid in a timely manner, the consequences can be devastating. In short, whereas some aspects of business can be learned and developed over time, others require immediate attention.

The best place to start finding answers to questions and solutions to problems is right within one's own community. The local chamber of commerce helps businesses to network and is always supportive of new owners. So, too, is SCORE, "Counselors to America's Small Business," a group that provides assistance to start-up businesses. The local branch is listed in the government section of the Yellow Pages, with information also available at state SCORE web sites and at www.scorechapter14.org. There are a myriad of government services and resources available to business owners at the federal, state, and local levels. Contact can be made via the Internet, by e-mail, letter, phone, or a personal appointment. Private-sector services are also available, often for free or for a nominal fee. Most newspapers have business calendars that list dates, times, locations, and fees for a wide variety of seminars, meetings, and discussion groups. Attending such forums provides an opportunity to explore (without serious financial commitment) services that may be of interest and to meet the providers.

Case managers try to empower patients (consumers of health care services) by furnishing the necessary background and describing the alternatives so they can make informed choices. Because owners of case management companies are consumers of business services and products, it makes sense that they should empower themselves through the acquisition of information so that business decisions are sound ones. Information empowers one to be a more astute business manager. All the assistance required to do this is available; you only need to access it, and today it is often only a mouse click away.

GENERATING NEW BUSINESS

Because even successful businesses experience peaks and valleys, having a plan to generate new clients is always important. Relationships with good clients can extend over many years, of course, and this is indeed fortunate, because known entities are usually easier for both the provider of case management services and the recipient company(ies) to work with. Owing to the complexity of case management, the number of players involved, and the need to individualize each case management program, it is highly desirable to maintain longstanding associations. This ideal, however, is not always possible. Occasionally, even the most successful business association ends. For example, a referral source, who is a branch manager of the claims department and a key contact and focal point of referrals to a case management company, receives a promotion to district manager and moves to a different geographic location. Her replacement is a woman who has had a long and successful association with a different case management group, and it is this company that she will continue to utilize. In this era of mergers and acquisitions, it is also possible that a local referral source (an employer group, TPA, or carrier) may be acquired by another entity that may already have a case management program in place with no need to alter that arrangement.

So, what can be done to prepare for the loss of clients? Realize that it can happen tomorrow. Create a plan to generate new business and integrate the plan with the overall business plan. Like the entire business plan, the plan for generating new business needs to be developed thoughtfully, with a budget in mind, with expected goals and time frames in place, and with a way to evaluate the success of the efforts. The process includes many steps, but the following five are probably the most basic.

Establishing Referral Sources

Who exactly are the referral sources for a case management business? Insurance carriers, employer groups, attorneys, TPAs, counties, municipalities, states, the federal government, and individual consumers are current users of case management services. Following the inevitable reform of health care, there are likely to be others.

Various industry and business periodicals provide the names of specific companies that have case management programs. Perhaps there are branch offices or subsidiaries that would be referral sources. Articles citing problems in administering workers' compensation or employee medical plans can be used to identify companies that are probably not aware of the case management solution. It makes sense to get in touch with them and share the good news.

Such an opportunity presented itself to me. I had sent a packet of information to a start-up TPA in my community. With it was a letter congratulating the new company, wishing them success, and providing an overview of case management. I pointed to the win-win scenario that could be created by adding case management to the company's set of tools and even outlined a high-cost case with and without case management. Allowing the claims administrator some time to review my proposal, I followed up with a telephone call about a week later. He thought it was all "very nice" but felt he was dealing with small employer groups with "healthy employees" and probably would not need case management services. He further stated that he had hospital networks and PPOs with "great discounts" and thought he was in great shape. Our discussion continued, but I was unable to change his mind.

However, several months later, the claims administrator saw an article that I had submitted to a publication for self-insurers and TPAs called "The Self-Insurer." He read it over a weekend, thought it made great sense, and intended to try to contact the author when he got into his office on Monday. He looked at the name, thought it looked familiar, and, sure enough, found the author was the very same person who had sent him information months ago. He did, in fact, call me, related the story, and admitted that he was now having "some problems," as I had suspected he would. We arranged a few meetings, and we now enjoy a mutually beneficial association. So, the direct marketing approach did not initially work, but it did pave the way for an eventual business relationship.

Openings like this really are out there, and one needs to be prepared to seize the moment. Although telephone conversations, articles, and letters are all helpful, marketing materials will be important in creating and sustaining an image, which leads to the second step.

Preparing Marketing Materials

Most case managers will want to contract for assistance in designing and implementing a marketing plan and creating a company image. As with most other aspects in the business plan, marketing will likely be done in stages and within certain financial parameters. A new business will probably not be able to afford multipage and multicolor brochures, yet well-designed business cards and stationery are an absolute must for even the smallest of companies. Selecting a company name and corporate logo is a matter of individual preference, but the advice of a public relations or marketing consultant could be extremely helpful. This does not necessarily mean using the largest and most high-profile public relations or advertising firm in one's community. There are many small consulting companies that specialize in the health care market, and they offer many options, even packages of services for discounted fees (for example, a business card, a corporate logo, stationery, and a simple brochure outlining the proposed services). Purchasing a package of services increases the chance that everything will be well-coordinated and focused.

When I first started my company, I only had enough money for the design of my corporate logo, business cards, and stationery. It was almost 2 years later that a corporate brochure was created. At that time, my business was restricted mainly to workers' compensation and auto insurance cases; group medical cases were just starting to be referred. It was my feeling the claimants had minimal understanding of case management and frequently did not hear about us until months after an injury, sometimes only after litigation was also involved. For the group medical insurance referrals, case management was a brand new approach. Because the response to case management by claimants would help make or break us, our first brochure (Figure 13-1) was designed specifically for claimants and their families, not the actual payers. However, I also used it successfully to interest potential clients. It was reader-friendly, had an easy-to-understand question and answer format, and showed us to be proactive (something extremely important to me) and cost-conscious (something extremely important to our clients). It has been modified over the years but remains an integral component of our marketing package. In general, our marketing efforts and direction have evolved and will continue to evolve in response to the ongoing changes in our industry.

Targeting New Business Goals

Although it is important to maintain current business, it is always necessary to identify potential sources of new business. This is a challenging process, one of discovery and innovation. Determining specific new business targets is accomplished through matching one's strengths and areas of expertise with segments of the business community that could utilize such expertise. To be able to capitalize on the many opportunities, one needs to keep current in one's own practice setting (whether this is oncology, AIDS, high-risk pregnancy, etc.) and current within the business community. What are the problems yet to be resolved? How could case management respond? What are the emerging needs that come with our changing population—hospice care, language translation, elder care? What types of partnerships could be created that would facilitate the provision of services? There are immediate targets for case management services today, and on the horizon are potential users waiting to be identified. This is the excitement of our industry!

At my company, we branched out into another area of business, providing Care-at-Home service. Looking to grow this market niche, we created a second marketing piece describing this program and answering the most frequently asked questions for the physicians, social workers, and families with whom we would be interacting.

Since then, we have applied this concept of reaching out to engage the stakeholders in medical care and cost management, whether they are patients, families, physicians, employer groups, TPAs, insurers, brokers, unions, reinsurance carriers, or others. This relationship building serves as a platform to transition into new markets. With information gleaned from questionnaires, we can report that "our patients say. . ." or "brokers say. . ." We have found that a more broad-based appeal leads to greater receptivity.

Figure 13–1 Options Unlimited Patient Brochure

WHAT DO I DO NOW?

Call us. Every case is unique and will be considered in a FREE preliminary screening.

If you decide to contract for our consulting services, you can be assured that OPTIONS offers a personalized service and medically knowledgeable people who will deal with you as an individual. With OPTIONS, you will have a friend and confidant, as well as a medical expert.

HEALTH CARE AND DISABILITY MANAGEMENT SERVICES

HEALTH CARE AND DISABILITY MANAGEMENT SERVICES

(631) 673-1150

Catherine M. Mullahy
President

Catherine Mullahy has thirty-nine years of experience in health care management in both hospitals and corporate settings.

Her diversified nursing experience includes work in multiple trauma, medical/surgical, cardiac, orthopedic, and neurologic conditions.

She is the founder and President of OPTIONS UNLIMITED, a health care and disability management company. Her consulting firm possesses national capability, and works with corporations, private carriers, government agencies, and individuals. She has written for national publications, serves as a consultant to insurance companies and providers, and lectures frequently on a variety of topics in the disability management field.

Catherine Mullahy and OPTIONS UNLIMITED offer you a timely and cost-efficient program whose specialty is caring.

COST-EFFECTIVE
INDIVIDUAL
CASE MANAGEMENT SERVICES
medical, emotional,
and vocational

CATHERINE M. MULLAHY, PRESIDENT
76 EAST MAIN STREET
HUNTINGTON, NEW YORK 11743
(631) 673-1150
FAX (631)-673-8369

Figure 13–1 continued

WHAT IS OPTIONS UNLIMITED?

We are a medically knowledgeable consulting firm that serves the special needs of patients and their families, nationally.

HEALTH CARE AND DISABILITY MANAGEMENT SERVICES

WHAT DOES OPTIONS DO?

We act as the patient advocate to ensure an injured or ill person's return to wellness in the shortest possible time at the lowest possible cost.

HOW DO WE ACCOMPLISH OUR GOALS?

We serve as liaison between the patient, physician, therapist, insurance company, and employer, coordinating all facets in order that each patient may return to a productive life.

WHY DO YOU NEED OPTIONS?

When injury or illness strikes, common reactions of the patient and family are shock, panic, and especially confusion.

They don't know who to talk to, what questions to ask, or where to go for help. They are also insecure with the unfamiliarity of medical language at a time when they become completely dependent on the medical community.

A physician simply cannot spend enough time with the family to help them understand the complex problems involved in catastrophic injury/illness cases.

OPTIONS helps the patient and the family to cope with the medical, insurance, social, emotional, vocational and financial problems related to the injury or illness.

SPECIFICALLY, WHAT DOES OPTIONS DO TO ASSIST YOU?

- Secure proper medical care and equipment
- Prevent inappropriate or excessive treatment
- Expedite facility/home placement and care
- Inform insurance company of your condition and treatment
- Help your family to understand and to adjust
- Find community resources to work on your behalf
- Coordinate and provide necessary follow-up treatment
- Remain available to you and your family for reassurance and counseling

WHO WILL PAY FOR THIS SERVICE?

If your insurance company has referred you to us, they will be billed for our services.

If you contact us directly or if you are referred by your doctor or others involved in your care, we will contact your insurance carrier; if there is no coverage, you will be billed. In all cases, we will outline a clear plan for coordinating your care with an easy-to-understand rate schedule.

WON'T USING OPTIONS JUST CREATE GREATER EXPENSE?

Even if your insurance company does not cover case management services, OPTIONS can usually save you money in medical and related costs. We help you get back to the business of living.

DOES OPTIONS SERVE ONLY SEVERE ILLNESS/INJURY CASES?

Although OPTIONS specializes in catastrophic, chronic, and complex medical problems, we have experience in a wide variety of disabilities—pediatric through geriatric.

Source: Courtesy of Options Unlimited, Case Management Services Division, 2003, Huntington, New York.

Creating and Maintaining Relationships with Referral Sources

Most case management companies initially grow one case at a time and then expand in larger increments as new case management programs are created based on the successful cases. When starting a business, therefore, it is very important to identify and accept the kinds of cases that present the most potential for success, both in terms of medical outcome and savings.

Although we all welcome a challenge and want to be able to demonstrate that we can do what others cannot, we do not want to attempt the "impossible." Some cases are beyond anyone's capabilities—for example, the patient who is 2 years postinjury; who has had two surgical interventions, four hospitalizations, ongoing physical therapy, and psychological counseling; whose employer has no light-duty program; and whose union is in a contract dispute with management. And the claims examiner is already demanding that this case be resolved. This clearly is a challenge to avoid.

This does not mean taking only "easy" cases, because the easy ones do not usually require case management and asking for them sets one up for comments such as "Well, this guy probably would have gone back to work without you." There are, however, many cases in between the two extremes. Case managers also have the potential to create opportunities for success by knowing and then communicating the red flags that indicate the need for case management (see Chapters 9 and 11).

If one referral has been successfully case managed, it should be relatively straightforward to obtain others. Likewise, if one good relationship with a referral source in a company has been established, it should be easier to establish others with individuals in the same company. For instance, following positive outcomes and after proving the value of case management to one claims examiner in a workers' compensation department, a case manager could ask if there were other examiners who might consider using case management services. Does this carrier also write auto or group medical insurance? It would also be a good tactic to ask the initial referral source to write a letter of recommendation or allow him- or herself to be used as a reference. Most individuals who are pleased with the results of case management are only too happy to provide an endorsement, giving credibility to a service that in many cases is still an unknown. Because no one wants to be the first customer, a firm endorsement by one person or company encourages others to try the services being offered.

Expressing appreciation for past and current business is important in maintaining ongoing associations and generating new referrals. If such appreciation is not communicated regularly, client groups soon feel less than valued. Sharing information about conferences or articles that might be of interest is one way to expand relationships. So, too, is seeking expert help from associates, perhaps to clarify a claims matter. I have learned most about the complexities of all the lines of insurance our company is now involved with from individuals who started as clients and over the years have become colleagues.

Initially, I had a need to know, and thankfully there were those who had a desire to share their very specialized knowledge. This collaboration truly was synergistic in that both parties had something to offer and gain from the association; together there was a stronger unit than either possessed as a single entity. With one of these colleagues, I have presented at conferences. She, at my suggestion, was a presenter at a case management conference, and we anticipate coauthoring a book. All these techniques have helped me to expand my own business, and they are quite viable for the new and even established businesses that want to create new markets or expand existing ones.

Reaching Decision Makers

Even the best marketing plan, impressive marketing materials, and savvy marketing strategies do not necessarily generate business unless the individual who can authorize and pay for case management services can be convinced of their value. Case management services, unfortunately, are usually placed in the "loss" column by most companies. Most potential clients are reluctant to pay out additional money for services that, at least until they prove their worth, merely offer the promise of containing costs. Furthermore, the services do not necessarily ease the bureaucratic workload, but may, in fact, require more direct involvement on the part of company staff. Companies also are more inclined to buy products or services that will generate more business and money for them, and case management is not perceived as one of these, at least not in the early stages.

After case management services are established and successful, it is certainly easier to gain work, but what about those first cases? The claims examiner may be a case manager's main contact but is likely not the individual who can create or allow for the expansion of case management programs. How does one identify and get to the decision maker? By keeping alert, asking questions, and paying attention to the market.

Reaching the individual who has overall fiscal responsibility is not always an easy process but is well worth the effort. Start at the very top—by approaching the CEO or president of the group. If the CEO does not have day-to-day responsibility for health care matters but someone else does (for example, the chief financial officer or director of insurance), then this other person is usually directed to respond to the approach. If one starts at the middle-management level, then the person contacted often has to go upward to obtain an okay. Not only that, but requesting assistance (and money) is often perceived as a reflection of poor management. It puts the individual in the position of having to acknowledge a problem and an inability to solve it alone. Few will voluntarily place themselves in this situation, so the decision to use case management will likely be deferred.

HIRING ADDITIONAL STAFF

Success brings with it new questions and new issues. Growth for many reasons can be troublesome, so it requires a good deal of planning. The first issue may be whether to hire another case manager and staff or remain a one-person company. The decision to employ others is possibly one of the most difficult for the entrepreneur case manager. It means relinquishing some of the control over case management activities, delegating some of the responsibilities, and, perhaps the most challenging of all, introducing customers to someone who they may perceive as not quite as good as the expert they have become accustomed to working with.

Another possible issue is whether to accept cases in a broader geographical area than previously covered. Let us assume that a caseload of 18 to 25 is manageable: The case manager can effectively direct and support elements required for each of those cases. She can stay on top of each case, make enough money to pay the bills, and take regular days off and maybe even some vacation time. Perhaps a few more cases can be handled by putting in a few extra hours or a few extra-long days. But then several "quiet" cases all of a sudden become very active. At this point, a prospective client calls and says he has 8 to 10 cases put aside. (Where was he when the caseload was down to 10?) The time is *now;* a decision must be made. Should the case manager accept these cases and plan to work 15 to 18 hours a day? Not if she plans to be around for a few years and certainly not if she plans to continue to be able to provide quality, timely interventions and manage cases rather than be managed by them.

Nothing says the case manager must hire staff and build the company. Some case managers are comfortable setting limits, advising customers that 20 or 25 is the maximum number of cases they want, and then suggesting the name of colleagues who might be able to assist. However, there are good reasons to expand—the challenge, the opportunity to provide services to more people in need, the potential to expand the use of case management, and, of course, the possible financial rewards that might be realized.

Hiring individuals who have the necessary expertise and who share the same philosophy, work ethic, and business goals is highly desirable. Finding such individuals, however, is not always easy. One essential step in the process is to clarify just what it takes to be a case manager. Unfortunately, because case management is evolving, it is difficult to succinctly set out all the job's elements. A standard definition of case management has been created by CCMC, the regulatory body responsible for the CCM designation, as described in Chapter 1. CMSA has also revised its Standards of Practice to more fully describe the role, function, and activities of individual case managers as they practice in today's settings. In addition, URAC has established guidelines for case management organizations and departments. These are all good references.

I have developed three position descriptions, one for a nurse reviewer, one for a medical case manager, and one for a director of case management services position. These appear at the end of the chapter as Appendix 13-A, Appendix 13-B, and Appendix 13-C, and incorporate summaries of each role, principal duties and responsibilities, required knowledge, and qualifications. I use evaluation tools during the course of the year that are matched to these job descriptions when reviewing employees' job performance.

Limiting the search to case managers with the CCM credential, as important as this credential is, would exclude many fine candidates from employment. Experienced case managers who understand all the lines of insurance, have had a diversified clinical background prior to case management, and have worked in a variety of traditional and nontraditional settings would be the best candidates, right? Not necessarily. I have hired case management professionals from competitors and carriers, and I have hired nurses who I thought possessed excellent potential but lacked on-line case management experience. For me, it has been easier, though not always trouble-free, to hire and train individuals who have no case management experience. When bringing in individuals with prior experience, I found it was often difficult to convince them to put aside the business practices (billing, need to attain a set number of hours each week) and philosophies of previous employers. Or, they had only handled workers' compensation or liability cases and could not keep the return-to-work goal out of our group medical insurance cases. It has generally been easier to train rather than retrain.

Further, professional experience, credentials, published papers, and a multitude of degrees do not guarantee success. I used to be intimidated when applicants would submit incredibly impressive résumés, would know what our salary limitations were (as a small company they were restrictive), yet would want to interview for a position. A few PhDs in particular stand out in my mind. It did not take me long to realize they would fail to make it. These candidates had assimilated all of the theory, could quote studies and statistics, but in my judgment would not have been able to understand, nor work within the confines of, the workers' compensation law of our state. Does this mean that no one with a PhD can be a case manager? Not at all, but it does mean that one has to look beyond credentials, impressive résumés, and accomplishments. At the same time, when I interview individuals who are not experienced case managers, this does not mean they are perceived as people with no experience. In my judgment, case management work is complex, demanding, and challenging. Not every individual can do it, even with training. There are professional attainments and personal characteristics that increase the likelihood of success in this field and personal characteristics that almost preclude success.

Professional Background

The type of professional background staff should have depends partly on the type of case management services offered. A company that provides a broad range of medical case management services needs staff members with diversified clinical experience. If it works mainly within the group medical insurance area, it should probably hire mostly nurses. This does not mean that only nurses can provide case management intervention; other allied professionals have much to contribute. However, the typical cases referred to case management are high cost and medically complex, and nurses, in my opinion, are better prepared to handle the many responsibilities that are required.

Of course, not everyone licensed to practice as a nurse has the depth and diversification of educational and clinical background that supports good case management. Although the length of time that one has been a nurse is important, time and grade alone are not sufficient. Perhaps a nurse has been on a spinal cord unit for 8 years or has worked for 10 years in pediatrics; the scope of these practice settings is relatively narrow and would ill-prepare the nurse to work in most case management departments or companies. Only in very large companies might a case manager only be assigned pediatric cases or patients with spinal cord injuries. It is more often that nurses are assigned a wide range of cases. A typical caseload may include a post-CVA patient who needs placement in a rehabilitation facility; a chronic emphysema patient who has become severely compromised; a noncompliant diabetic adolescent; a woman with breast cancer who now, despite aggressive treatment, is a hospice candidate; and a newly diagnosed end-stage renal disease patient who will be on home dialysis. It is evident that a case manager needs a range of skills and expertise in order to manage this kind of caseload.

Although clinical experience is important, so too is the setting in which the knowledge is gained. Because case management is involved in arranging alternate care settings for patients, direct knowledge of nontraditional settings is highly desirable. It affords an understanding of what actually happens beyond the walls of the acute care hospital.

Educational Background

Educational background needs to be considered as well. Nurses can be graduates of diploma schools or have associate or bachelor's degrees. Should only those with bachelor's degrees be allowed to be case managers? The answer for now is no. Many nurses who have graduated from associate and diploma programs have continued to broaden their education. They attend workshops and conferences; subscribe to nursing journals, magazines, and newsletters; and may have also taken college courses in pursuit of a bachelor of science. On the other hand, there are also nurses who, once they get their degree, virtually shut down their education. This illustrates the importance of going beyond what appears on an application or résumé, making no assumptions or exclusions based solely upon schooling and degree(s) held.

Life Experience

Professional experience and educational background most assuredly need to be considered when hiring case managers. Another factor that deserves attention, however, often is not mentioned—the learning one derives from living. When an individual loses a child, spouse, or other family member to illness and goes through the stages of caring, letting go, and grieving, the entire process can be a sobering and, in many ways, enriching occurrence. Coping with life's travails, surprises, and challenges helps one in ways that education and work alone cannot. Adjusting to divorce, job changes, career hurdles, and family problems while maintaining one's sanity (or a reasonable facsimile thereof) actually prepares one very well for the position of case manager.

Because the kinds of cases usually referred for intervention are typically complex and chronic or catastrophic, patients and families will likely have deeply felt and highly personal responses to their illnesses or disabilities. These responses can, if recognition and intervention are lacking, destroy family structures, members, and, on occasion, the individual himself. A case manager's own life experiences can help her detect and deflect dangerous patient and family responses.

One source of stress for case managers is the interaction that occurs between patients and families, physicians, other health care team members, multiple providers, employer groups, and claims staff. Everyone has his or her own needs, priorities, and personality. Taking on the role of "director" of this drama is not easy, not even for experienced case managers. Novice case managers should probably not even attempt this role. To be credible, a case management professional needs sufficient life experience to strike the delicate balance between empathy and efficiency, negotiating and standing fast, providing support and pushing patients to draw on their own inner strength.

Other Intangibles

When I consider what it really takes to be a good case manager, I am still amazed at how many of the qualities are intangible, including the following:

- A sense of humor
- A strong work ethic
- Anger at the system (but not enough to be a hindrance to action)
- A belief in one's ability to make a difference (but not a need for personal power)
- Approachability
- Optimism
- An ability to look at the positives and build on them, tempered by the right amount of reality to prevent "pie in the sky" plans and goals
- An awareness of the business/financial aspects of health care
- A sense of objectivity
- Keenly developed ethical principles
- Energy and creativity
- A commitment to professionalism

The interview process should explore a candidate's personal characteristics, although they are admittedly more difficult to uncover and assess than the candidate's professional experience and educational background. Much of the discovery of these personal qualities depends upon the level of skill of the interviewer and, of course, the structure, philosophy, and goals of the company or department. We always look to use the strengths of each individual, providing our company with a broader skill base.

We have an advantage when conducting interviews, as each candidate is interviewed by a case manager at one stage. Larger corporations might screen potential case managers through the human resources department. Would an HR employee know that a nurse would not say "black and blue" to describe a wound, but rather hematoma or ecchymoses?

The "intangibles" noted previously are important qualities I seek in case manager candidates. To incorporate these areas into interviews, we give all potential case managers five or six scenarios followed by questions that help us understand their approach to issues that might arise (see Table 13-1). In their answers to the questions posed by these scenarios, candidates tell us a bit about their attitude, aptitude, ethics, leadership skills, creativity in strategic planning, and personality.

In addition, we ask candidates to read through case briefs that center on different situations (see Tables 13-2 and 13-3) and then report back to us the issues they

Table 13–1 Scenarios for Potential Case Managers

To assess compassion and the ability to collaborate:

While monitoring the home care plan of a client with AIDS, you find that inadequate pain relief has been achieved and he is at risk of rehospitalization. The home health nurse appears to have limited experience with pain management strategies. What would you do?

To assess consensus building and empowerment:

In attending a rehabilitation team meeting, you find that the rehab team and client's family have differing opinions regarding a discharge plan. How would you approach this to achieve consensus?

To assess planning and organization:

To complete an assessment on a client who is in a rehabilitation hospital, you need to interview the client, family, physician, and the treatment team. You also need to review medical records. How would you approach this efficiently and collaboratively?

To assess advocacy and assertiveness:

In your assessment, you find that the client is not receiving counseling in the hospital as needed because of the counselor's vacation. Would you intervene, and if so, how?

Source: Courtesy of Options Unlimited, Case Management Services Division, 2003, Huntington, New York.

Table 13–2 Case Situation Assessment—Pregnancy

Kim W. is a 37-year-old pregnant female who recently emigrated from Russia and is single. She is in her first trimester and recently had a blood glucose test with a result of 187. She is gravida 3 para 1. Her PMH (prior medical history) includes one miscarriage and a 2 1/2-year-old daughter. The physician at the clinic where she has been receiving prenatal care suggests home glucose testing with glucometer. She is scheduled for a three-hour glucose tolerance test. Her first pregnancy was a C-section due to infant size and claimant's condition at that time. She did not have the same OB/GYN at that time.

1. What risk factors and/or problems do you see in this case?
2. What additional information would you like to obtain?
3. Who would you ask to obtain this information and why?

Source: Courtesy of Options Unlimited, Case Management Services Division, 2003, Huntington, New York.

Table 13–3 Case Situation Assessment—Asthma

Walkirya H. is a 16-year-old female admitted to Bronx Lebanon Hospital with a diagnosis of asthma. She has a PMH of recurrent hospital admits, three for asthma. She lives with her non-English speaking mother. Her parents are divorced. Her PMD is Dr. Diaz, internal medicine. He was not the admitting physician as claimant was admitted through the emergency room. Claimant is currently receiving IV steroids, nebulizer treatments, and ABGs, with peak flow and oxygen saturation monitoring. She was admitted 3 days prior to Options Unlimited being informed of hospitalization.

1. What do you see as problematic in this case?
2. What additional information would you like to obtain?
3. What would you anticipate as the patient's need at the time of discharge?

Source: Courtesy of Options Unlimited, Case Management Services Division, 2003, Huntington, New York.

---

perceive as problematic, and steps they might take to move forward with the case. Responses can provide insight into their thought processes and problem-solving abilities.

A tool to assist interviewers in identifying a potential candidate's knowledge areas and deficits was created by Sandra Lowery, BSN, RN, CCM, CRRN (see Figure 13-2). Offering a starting point, this checklist of care venues, funding sources, resources, and clinical categories can be modified by a case management department or agency, with alternative specialty areas added to address the needs of the group's patient base.

Lowery also offers lines of questioning to assess various skills and traits. For example, to assess assertiveness and problem solving, she suggests asking the candidate, "You find that the patient desires palliative care but is too intimidated by his physician to discuss the physician's plan for further chemotherapy. How would you address this situation?" Another line of questioning to judge resource knowledge, creativity, and planning might be, "You find that your client has a vital need for daily speech therapy. The attending physician agrees but reports that the closest speech therapist is over 75 miles away. What would you do to help this client?"[1]

At the end of this chapter are three additional forms that can be used to ascertain the strengths of potential and staff case managers. They are Appendix 13-D, Interview Evaluation Form, to be used during the first interview; Appendix 13-E, Summary Evaluation Scale, for the second or call-back interview: and Appendix 13-F, Competencies for Unit-Based Nurse Case Manager.

Figure 13–2 Candidate's Knowledge Assessment Tool

KNOWLEDGE ASSESSMENT

Rate your knowledge/familiarity of the following by using a scale of 1 to 5, with 1 indicating the highest level:

	1	2	3	4	5

Levels of care

	1	2	3	4	5
—Acute hospital	[ ]	[ ]	[ ]	[ ]	[ ]
—Rehabilitation	[ ]	[ ]	[ ]	[ ]	[ ]
—Post hospital	[ ]	[ ]	[ ]	[ ]	[ ]

Funding Sources

	1	2	3	4	5
—Private insurance	[ ]	[ ]	[ ]	[ ]	[ ]
—Public insurance	[ ]	[ ]	[ ]	[ ]	[ ]
—Other	[ ]	[ ]	[ ]	[ ]	[ ]

Services/Resources

	1	2	3	4	5
—Home health	[ ]	[ ]	[ ]	[ ]	[ ]
—Home infusion therapy	[ ]	[ ]	[ ]	[ ]	[ ]
—Medical equip./supp.	[ ]	[ ]	[ ]	[ ]	[ ]
—Transportation	[ ]	[ ]	[ ]	[ ]	[ ]
—Outpatient	[ ]	[ ]	[ ]	[ ]	[ ]
—Residential	[ ]	[ ]	[ ]	[ ]	[ ]
—Hospice	[ ]	[ ]	[ ]	[ ]	[ ]

Service Costs

	1	2	3	4	5
—Acute hospital	[ ]	[ ]	[ ]	[ ]	[ ]
—Outpatient	[ ]	[ ]	[ ]	[ ]	[ ]
—Residential	[ ]	[ ]	[ ]	[ ]	[ ]
—Outpatient	[ ]	[ ]	[ ]	[ ]	[ ]
—Home health	[ ]	[ ]	[ ]	[ ]	[ ]

CLINICAL TREATMENT/OUTCOMES

Rehabilitation

	1	2	3	4	5
—Treatment	[ ]	[ ]	[ ]	[ ]	[ ]
—Resources	[ ]	[ ]	[ ]	[ ]	[ ]

continues

Figure 13–2 continued

Neonates	1	2	3	4	5
—Treatment	[ ]	[ ]	[ ]	[ ]	[ ]
—Resources	[ ]	[ ]	[ ]	[ ]	[ ]

Pediatrics

	1	2	3	4	5
—Treatment	[ ]	[ ]	[ ]	[ ]	[ ]
—Resources	[ ]	[ ]	[ ]	[ ]	[ ]

Obstetrics

	1	2	3	4	5
—Treatment	[ ]	[ ]	[ ]	[ ]	[ ]
—Resources	[ ]	[ ]	[ ]	[ ]	[ ]

HIV Disease/AIDS

	1	2	3	4	5
—Treatment	[ ]	[ ]	[ ]	[ ]	[ ]
—Resources	[ ]	[ ]	[ ]	[ ]	[ ]

Oncology

	1	2	3	4	5
—Treatment	[ ]	[ ]	[ ]	[ ]	[ ]
—Resources	[ ]	[ ]	[ ]	[ ]	[ ]

Psychiatric Illness/CD

	1	2	3	4	5
—Treatment	[ ]	[ ]	[ ]	[ ]	[ ]
—Resources	[ ]	[ ]	[ ]	[ ]	[ ]

Transplants

	1	2	3	4	5
—Treatment	[ ]	[ ]	[ ]	[ ]	[ ]
—Resources	[ ]	[ ]	[ ]	[ ]	[ ]

Source: Reprinted from *The Case Manager,* Vol. 3, S. Lowery, "Qualifications for the Successful Case Manager," p. 74, © 1992, with permission from Elsevier.

THE SEARCH FOR CASE MANAGERS

Before candidates can be interviewed and evaluated, they need to be located and be made interested enough to apply for a job. The usual search methods include posting jobs, running classified ads, and contracting with personnel agencies. There are, however, other viable ways of attracting prospective case managers, some of which require only a minimal financial outlay.

Figure 13–3 Recruitment Form Used at Job Fair

HEALTH CARE & DISABILITY MANAGEMENT SERVICES

CASE MANAGEMENT DEPARTMENT

NURSE CASE MANAGERS, MEDICAL/PEDIATRIC
(FULL TIME/PART TIME); LONG ISLAND,
NEW YORK METRO

Position Description:

Care Coordination of High Cost or Complex Cases. Develop and Implement (with treating physician, patient and other medical personnel) treatment plans to maximize patient outcomes while containing costs. Advocate for patients and families. Monitor treatment plans, assess ongoing needs. Patient and family support.

Qualifications:

Professional: RNs (degree preferred - with minimum 5–10 years experience in hospital, home care, infusion care, discharge planning, Insurance Company or Employer selling.

Personal: Caring, high energy, independent, creative, good communication (verbal and written), problem solver, critical analytical skills.

Business: Financial awareness of health care or willingness to get involved in this area, computer skills a plus, bilingual a plus.

Training and supervision is provided, competitive salary, patient contact and case responsibility, small challenging case loads. On-site visits (in patient's home or hospital), car and travel required. Rewarding, challenging dynamic career for the accomplished, confident professional. Professional office, growing corporate environment. **FOR INFORMATION ON POSITIONS AVAILABLE CALL 1-800-457-7685 OR FAX RESUME TO (631)673-8369.**

CATHERINE M. MULLAHY, PRESIDENT • 76 EAST MAIN STREET, HUNTINGTON, NEW YORK 11743 • (631) 673-1150 • FAX (631) 673-8369

Source: Courtesy of Options Unlimited, Case Manaagement Services Division, 2003, Huntington, New York.

For example, writing an article for a professional magazine or local newspaper that gives an overview of the field helps likely candidates envision themselves in the case management role. Organizations, schools, employer groups, insurance carriers, and health care companies and clinics are always looking for speakers. Although the audience may enter the hall expecting to learn about how to work with case managers, an inspirational presentation may lead some listeners to pursue case management as a career. And sometimes merely "spreading the word" about employment openings will attract candidates, as will asking colleagues whether they know of individuals who might be looking to make a move.

Although more costly in dollars and time, attending job fairs and other conferences can be a fruitful method of finding candidates. At a recent CMSA conference, I posted a recruitment form when looking to expand our office's nationwide network of case managers. The posting drew a fair response, and some good contacts were initiated. Attending conferences may actually serve several purposes besides recruitment, such as advertising services, developing a marketing image, garnering insight into needs of the industry, and generating more business through networking.

I've also used regional and local job fairs as opportunities to post similar recruitment forms for our headquarters office in New York (see Figure 13-3).

To fill a key position, such as manager or director, it may make sense to use a recruiting firm (also known as an executive search firm or "headhunter"). Recruiting firms are highly specialized, and there are several that focus entirely on recruitment for the health care and managed care industries. Although the fees can be substantial (often 25 to 30% of a candidate's first-year salary), such firms can make the hiring process almost painless, and most will refund a fee (at least partially) should the candidate not prove suitable once hired.

Case management is already a proven if not yet integral element of the U.S. health care system. To my mind, this is an exciting time to be a case manager, whether employed by a provider or payer or running an independent company. Being independent just gives one that much more visibility and opportunity to shape and build this young industry.

NOTES

1. S. Lowery, "Qualifications for the Successful Case Manager," *The Case Manager* 3, no. 4 (1992): 73.

Appendix 13–A Sample Nurse Reviewer for Prenotification Department Position Description

Options Unlimited

Position Description: Nurse Reviewer for Prenotification Department

Primary Claimants Served:
This position requires that the employee be able to demonstrate the knowledge and skills necessary to provide all aspects of care based on physical, psychological, educational, safety, support systems, and related criteria, appropriate to the claimant served. The skill and knowledge base need to address age-specific issues, cultural diversity, socioeconomic factors, language differences, cultural traditions, spiritual belief systems/practices of the claimant and family members or supportive others. These issues are significant to the Nurse Reviewer's relationship with the claimant and will directly impact on the health care outcome.

Purpose of the Position:
The purpose of the Nurse Reviewer is to assess the medical appropriateness, quality, and cost-effectiveness of proposed hospital, medical, and surgical services in accordance with established criteria. This review activity may be conducted prospectively, concurrently, or retrospectively and in collaboration with claimants, physicians, and other professionals. Through this review process, the Nurse Reviewer will identify those individuals and circumstances that would benefit from the intervention of the case management professional. This position is critical in the maintenance of uniformity, quality, and consistency of benefit determination, administration, and application of the managed care programs. The Nurse Reviewer will provide telephonic case management intervention on behalf of claimants with short-term needs, by monitoring and evaluating options and services to effect an appropriate, individualized plan for the claimant across the continuum of care.

Specific Responsibilities and Duties:
The Nurse Reviewer at Options Unlimited must be able to demonstrate and be accountable for the standards of practice, policies and procedures, quality assurance, and the goals of the organization.

Health Care Management:

1. Manages care of claimants through the health care system based on the individual's needs. Appropriately integrates the individual into the health care

continuum, including procurement of services, health promotion and counseling, disease prevention, health education and screening, and community
resources linkage. Responsibilities include, but are not limited to, the
following:

a. Advocates for the claimant and family throughout the entire episode of
care. Maintains availability to the claimant/family as a resource to facilitate communication among providers and to monitor services rendered.
Remains involved until the claimant achieves the planned level of functional health or closure criteria are met.

b. Using independent judgment and discretion, in addition to consideration
of standards outlined by M & R, Interqual, and others, identifies and
plans strategies to reduce inpatient length of stay and resource consumption. Works in collaboration with physicians and appropriate health care
providers regarding treatment plans required. Provides claimant/family
or significant other with information about such issues as nursing visits,
home care services, appropriate providers, etc.

c. Coordinates/facilitates the claimant's progression throughout the continuum.

d. Works collaboratively and maintains active communication with physicians, nurses, social workers, utilization review staff, and other members
of the multidisciplinary care team to effect timely appropriate claimant
management through the continuum.

e. Makes initial contact with the claimant/family and multidisciplinary
team based on identified needs.

f. Applies knowledge of age-specific, cultural diversity, psycho/social, and
developmental issues during the interview process, documentation, and
intervention with the claimant, their family, or significant others.

g. Remains in communication with claimants and the physicians and other
members of the health care team to identify and resolve variances concurrently, and to assist the claimant in attaining the appropriate care with
positive outcomes.

h. Discusses and educates claimant/family on case management services.
Confirms claimant's understanding of case management intervention and
obtains case management approval when necessary and appropriate.

i. Knowledgeable on new regulations on the federal, state, and local level.

Process and Relationships:

2. Performs Nurse Review by applying clinical criteria to monitor appropriateness of admissions, level of care, and continued stays, and documents
findings based on standards. Responsibilities include, but are not limited to
the following:

a. Collaborates with the physician and the multidisciplinary team to facilitate the plan of care and assist in identification and concurrent resolution of variances.
b. Uses independent judgment and discretion to address, resolve, and process problems impeding the diagnostic or treatment progress. Proactively identifies and resolves delays and obstacles.
c. Seeks consultation from physicians, clinical, and other disciplines and departments as required to expedite care, monitor length of inpatient stay, and facilitate discharge.
d. Collaborates and communicates with all members of the multidisciplinary team to validate information.
e. Identifies potential risk factors.

Service Delivery:

3. Manages aspects of the planning process in anticipation of claimant variances or transitions. Responsibilities include, but are not limited to the following:
   a. Collaborates and communicates with the physician and the rest of the care management multidisciplinary team to facilitate planning for variances or transitions.
   b. Initiates and facilitates referrals for home health care, infusion therapy, hospice, other care facilities, medical equipment, and supplies.
   c. Facilitates transfers to other facilities.
   d. Identifies "at risk" individuals and develops and implements a comprehensive plan of care that addresses the specific need.
   e. Maintains current and appropriate documentation.
   f. Follows department guidelines for utilization of time.

Quality and Performance Improvement:

4. Appropriately identifies potential issues or "at risk" populations and anticipates the need for providing care.
5. Actively participates in clinical performance improvement process.
6. With respect to the individual claimant, analyzes and evaluates the effects of nurse reviewer on quality outcomes, fiscal parameters, customer satisfaction, and systems operations and develops strategies to improve performance.
7. Utilizing problem-solving techniques and conflict resolution skills, develops the plan to provide consistent quality to the claimant and the payer.

Managed Care Regulatory Knowledge:

8. Collaborates with the multidisciplinary team to assist claimant with benefits/resource management to include negotiations with out-of-network providers;

with resolution of payment issues; with developing a more cost-effective plan of care; and with evaluating the appropriateness of the level of care or the use of services. Responsibilities include, but are not limited to the following:

   a. Communicates, as required, with claimants to provide understanding of plan language and/or payer guidelines. Discusses issues for treatment and/or discharge needs with the physicians and relevant staff to provide for appropriate, timely treatment or a safe discharge.

   b. Assists physicians, care providers, and claimant/family in understanding the plan language and benefits as required.

Communication:

9. Maintains open communication with all appropriate parties.

   a. Utilizes problem-solving skills and negotiating techniques to resolve conflict issues.

   b. Identifies, plans, and coordinates aspects of care for the claimant, their family, or significant other.

   c. Communicates with supervisory personnel for problem solving, direction, and planning as well as knowledge issues.

   d. Initiates required forms and/or letters to comply with organizational guidelines.

   e. Completes timely and appropriate assessments, documentation, reports, and cost-benefit analysis.

   f. Interacts with the physicians and members of the entire health care team in appropriate time frames.

10. Maintains strict standards for claimant confidentiality and claimant-related information in addition to security of electronic information; complies with organizational, federal, and state regulations and policy on confidentiality.

Professional Development:

11. Maintains current knowledge of plan language and benefit issues and requirements as it relates to potential denial (whether contractual or utilization related).

12. Attends educational training program to expand job knowledge.

13. Performs other duties as related to case management functions to support and foster an effective, quality case management program.

14. Maintains current knowledge of URAC's standard of practice.

Position Requirements and Qualifications:

Education and Experience:

1. Graduated from an accredited School of Nursing or College: current New York state RN license required, AAS, BSN, Bachelor of Science in Nursing or health-related field preferred.

2. Graduated from an accredited college with a degree and licensure as a Certified Social Worker.
3. Minimum of 3–5 years of relevant clinical medical surgical or specialty experience required as applicable to the position needs.
4. Required to pursue ongoing education, certification, and self-development to remain current with industry standards and business objectives related to case management.

Skills:

1. Basic knowledge of personal computer and software for word processing and/or good keyboard skills preferred, or the ability to enter and retrieve data from relevant computer systems.
2. Ability to effectively communicate with all levels of claimants, TPA, physicians, health care personnel, supervisory staff, and peers.
3. Demonstrates the ability to be organized and efficient in prioritizing and managing assignments with minimal oversight and direction.
4. Demonstrates the willingness to research, learn, and to obtain knowledge for the performance of the position.
5. Demonstrates a courteous, professional demeanor and team spirit and the ability to work in a collaborative, effective manner.
6. Ability to utilize critical thinking and apply sound clinical judgment and assessment skills for decision-making.

Knowledge:

1. Knowledge of JCAHO/CARF (as appropriate) standards and federal and state regulations.
2. Knowledge of acute care, home care, subacute care, long-term care, hospice interventions, and rehabilitation options and requirements.
3. Maintains knowledge of requirement to Third Party Administrators, regulatory agencies, and managed care entities concerning levels of care, continuity of benefits, and medical necessity guidelines.
4. Maintains knowledge of the quality assurance process and determination of positive outcomes.
5. Uses clinical experience, knowledge of managed care and the current standards and trends in health care, best practices, management tools, and familiarity with related resources and literature.

Signature: _____

Date: _____

Director's Signature: _____

Source: Courtesy of Options Unlimited, Case Management Services Division, 2003, Huntington, New York.

Appendix 13–B Sample Medical Case Manager Position Description

Options Unlimited

Position Description: Medical Case Manager

Primary Claimants Served:
This position requires that the employee be able to demonstrate the knowledge and skills necessary to provide care based on physical, psychological, educational, safety, support systems and related criteria, appropriate to the claimant served. The skill and knowledge needs to be able to address age-specific issues, cultural diversity, socioeconomic factors, language differences, cultural traditions, and spiritual belief systems/practices of the claimant, family members, or supportive others. These issues are significant to the case manager's relationship with the claimant and will directly impact on the health care outcome.

Purpose of the Position:
The purpose of the medical case manager is to assess, plan, implement, monitor and evaluate options and services to effect an appropriate, individualized plan for the claimant across the continuum of care. Using independent judgment and discretion, the continuum must be reassessed as an ongoing process for the individual being served by the case manager. This is applied to multiple environments and interactive with the relative components of the claimant's health care system. The process addresses the individual's broad spectrum of needs. The medical case manager utilizes clinical knowledge and competence, positive communication skills, problem solving and conflict resolution techniques, ability to effect change, strong skills in assessment, organization, and time management. The case management process requires a focus on customer service skills, knowledge of setting appropriate goals and measuring outcomes to effectively ensure optimal client outcomes with consideration to payer requirements.

Specific Responsibilities and Duties:
The Medical Case Manager at Options Unlimited must be able to demonstrate and be accountable for the standards of practice policies and procedures, quality assurance, and the goals of the organization.

Health Care Management:

1. Manages care of claimants through the health care system based on the individual's needs. Appropriately integrates the individual into the health care continuum including procuring of services, health promotion and

counseling, disease prevention, health education and screening, and community resources linkage. Responsibilities include, but are not limited to the following:

a. Uses independent judgment and discretion, identifies and plans strategies to reduce in-patient length of stay and resource consumption. Works in collaboration with physicians and appropriate health care providers for changes in plans as required. Provides claimant/family or significant other with information about nursing visits, home care, and appropriate providers.

b. Advocates for the claimant and family throughout the entire episode of care. Maintains availability to the claimant/family as a resource to facilitate communication among providers and to monitor services rendered. Remains involved until the claimant achieves the planned level of functional health or closure criteria are met.

c. Coordinates/facilitates the claimant's progression throughout the continuum.

d. Works collaboratively and maintains active communication with physicians, nurses, social workers, utilization review staff, and other members of the multidisciplinary care team to effect timely, appropriate claimant management through the continuum.

e. As appropriate, meets directly with the claimant/family and multidisciplinary team based on identified needs.

f. Applies knowledge of age-specific, cultural diversity, psycho/social, and developmental issues during the interview process, documentation and intervention with the claimant, their family, or significant others.

g. Remains in communication with claimants and the physicians and other members of the health care team to identify and resolve variances concurrently, and to assist the claimant in attaining the appropriate care with positive outcomes.

h. Knowledgeable of new regulations on the federal, state and local level.

Process and Relationships:

2. Case managers will maintain the integrity of the Code of Professional Conduct for Case Managers. Performs case management by applying clinical criteria to monitor appropriateness of admissions, level of care, and continued stays; and documents findings based on standards. Responsibilities includes but are not limited to the following:

a. Collaborates with the physician and the multidisciplinary team to facilitate the plan of care and assist in identification and concurrent resolution of variances.

    b. Uses independent judgment and discretion to address, resolve, and process problems impeding the diagnostic or treatment progress. Proactively identifies and resolves delays and obstacles.

    c. Seeks consultation from physicians, clinical, and other disciplines and departments as required to expedite care, monitor length of in-patient stay, and facilitate discharge.

    d. Collaborates and communicates with all members of the multidisciplinary team to validate information.

    e. Identifies potential risk factors.

Service Delivery:

3. Manages aspects of the planning process in anticipation of claimant variances or transitions. Responsibilities include but are not limited to the following:

    a. Collaborates and communicates with the physician and the rest of the care management multidisciplinary team to facilitate planning for variances or transitions.

    b. When appropriate, meets directly with the claimant/family based on identified needs. Develops an individualized comprehensive plan of care in collaboration with the physicians and multidisciplinary team.

    c. Initiates and facilitates referrals for home health care, infusion therapy, hospice, other care facilities, and medical equipment and supplies.

    d. Facilitates transfers to other facilities.

    e. Identifies "at risk" individuals and develop and implement a comprehensive plan of care that addresses the specific need.

    f. Completes reports on time.

    g. Remains current on case management documentation.

    h. Writes Cost-Benefit Analysis report and submits by the due date.

Quality and Performance Improvement:

4. Appropriately identifies potential issues or "at risk" populations and anticipates the need to provide care.

5. Actively participates in clinical performance improvement process.

6. With respect to the individual claimant, analyzes and evaluates the effects of case management on quality outcomes, fiscal parameters, customer satisfaction, and systems operations; and develops strategies to improve performance.

7. Utilizes problem-solving techniques and conflict resolution skills, develops the plan to provide consistent quality to the claimant and the payer.

Managed Care and Regulatory Knowledge:

8. Collaborates with the multidisciplinary team to assist claimant with benefits/resource management to include negotiations with out-of-network providers, for resolution of payment issues, to develop a more cost-effective plan of care, and evaluate the appropriateness of the level of care or the use of services. Responsibilities include but are not limited to the following:
   a. Communicates, as required, with claimants to provide understanding of plan language and/or payer guidelines. When it is identified that clients are out of network, discuss issues for treatment and/or discharge needs with the physicians and relevant staff to provide for appropriate, timely treatment or a safe discharge.
   b. Assists physicians, care providers, and claimant/family in understanding the plan language and benefits as required.

Communication:

9. Maintains open communication with all appropriate parties.
   a. Utilizes problem-solving skills and negotiating techniques to resolve conflict issues.
   b. Identifies, plans, and coordinates aspects of care for the claimant, their family, or significant other.
   c. Communicates with supervisory personnel for problem solving, direction, and planning as well as knowledge issues.
   d. Initiates required forms and/or letters to comply with organizational guidelines.
   e. Completes timely and appropriate assessments, documentation, reports, and cost benefit analysis.
   f. Interacts with the physicians and members of the entire health care team in appropriate time frames.
10. Maintains strict standards for claimant confidentially and claimant-related information in addition to security of electronic information; complies with organizational, federal, and state regulations and policy on confidentiality.

Professional Development:

11. Maintains current knowledge of plan language and benefit issues and requirements as it relates to potential denial (whether contractual or utilization related).
12. Attends educational training program to expand job knowledge.
13. Performs other duties as related to case management functions to support and foster an effective, quality case management program.
14. Maintains current knowledge of URAC's standards of practice.

Position Requirements and Qualifications:

Education and Experience:

1. Graduated from an accredited School of Nursing or college: current New York state RN license required, BSN, Bachelor of Science in Nursing or health-related field preferred.
2. Graduated from an accredited college with a degree and licensure as a Certified Social Worker.
3. Minimum of 3–5 years of relevant clinical medical surgical or specialty experience required as applicable to the position needs.
4. Required to pursue ongoing education, certification, and self-development to remain current with industry standards and business objectives related to case management.

Skills:

1. Basic knowledge of personal computer and software for word processing and/or good keyboard skills preferred, or the ability to enter and retrieve data from relevant computer systems.
2. Ability to effectively communicate with all levels of claimants, TPA, physicians, health care personnel, supervisory staff, and peers.
3. Demonstrates the ability to be organized and efficient in prioritizing and managing assignments with minimal oversight and direction.
4. Demonstrates the willingness to research, learn, and obtain knowledge for the performance of the position.
5. Demonstrates a courteous, professional demeanor and team spirit and the ability to work in a collaborative, effective manner.
6. Utilizes critical thinking, and applies sound clinical judgment and assessment skills for decision making.

Knowledge:

1. Knowledge of JCAHO/CARF (as appropriate) standards and federal and state regulations.
2. Knowledge of acute care, home care, subacute care, long-term care, hospice interventions, and rehabilitation options and requirements.
3. Maintains knowledge of requirement to Third Party Administrators, regulatory agencies, and managed care entities concerning levels of care, continuity of benefits, and medical necessity guidelines.
4. Maintains knowledge of the quality assurance process and determination of positive outcomes.

5. Uses clinical experience, knowledge of managed care and the current standards and trends in health care, best practices, management tools, and familiarity with related resources and literature.

SIGNATURE: _____

DATE: _____

DIRECTOR'S SIGNATURE: _____

COB:ja

Source: Courtesy of Options Unlimited, Case Management Services Division, 2003, Huntington, New York.

Appendix 13–C Sample Director of Case Management Services Position Description

Options Unlimited

Position Description: Director of Case Management Services

Primary Claimants Served:
This position requires that the individual is able to demonstrate the ability to monitor, educate, and support the knowledge, skills, and performance of the case management staff. The individual must be able to educate case managers so they remain current to provide comprehensive care based on physical, psychological, educational, safety, support systems, and related criteria, appropriate to the claimants. The Director of Case Management must be able to elevate the knowledge and the recognition to address age-specific issues, cultural diversity, socioeconomic factors, language differences, cultural differences, cultural traditions, and spiritual belief systems/practices of the claimant, family members, or supportive others.

The Director of Case Management supports and implements the CMSA Standards of Practice, URAC guidelines, Code of Professional Conduct for Case Managers, the Federal regulations on confidentiality, and the Options Unlimited policies, procedures, and organizational goals.

The Quality Management Program is developed and implemented by the Director of Case Management Services. It is the role of the Director to assist with the process of identifying the areas of concern within the case management structure and to support the corporate drive toward excellence.

Purpose of the Position:
The Director of Case Management orients, guides, and oversees the case managers within Options Unlimited. The role is to plan, develop, implement, evaluate, and refine case management intervention. This individual supervises the case management personnel; contributes to the hiring and termination decisions; develops job descriptions, competency and performance standards, and schedules; monitors assignments; and assesses activity levels to meet budgetary guidelines. The role provides counseling and training, addresses disciplinary problems, and appraises performance.

The Director of Case Management Services ensures that the case managers assess, plan, and deliver care appropriate to the age specifics of every claimant. The individual must demonstrate sensitivity to the special needs of the claimants, payers, case managers, Options Unlimited personnel, and to all others involved within the job structure.

The individual implements and supports a culture of continuous quality improvement, supports the CMSA standard of practice, URAC guidelines, code of professional conduct, and the federal regulations on confidentiality; all of these are implemented into the philosophy, framework, policy, and procedures of Options Unlimited. The individual in this role contributes to the team objectives and goals with support to the organization and departmental strategic plans.

Specific Responsibilities and Duties:

The Director of Case Management at Options Unlimited must be able to support and empower the case managers in performance of their position description and within the regulations of their licensure. The role fosters and supports accountability for the CMSA Standards of Practice; URAC Guidelines; Code of Case Manager's Conduct; regulations on confidentiality, policy, and procedures; quality management; and the goals of the organization.

Health Care Management:

1. Supervises the case managers in performance of their role and position description.
2. Assists the case managers in the coordination of care and service of a selected client population across the continuum of illness.
3. Empowers the case managers in promoting effective utilization and monitoring of health care resources.
4. Provides leadership for the case management personnel to achieve optimal clinical and resource outcomes.
5. Formulates, implements, and evaluates the knowledge base of the case managers in the performance of their position description.
6. Analyzes the case management goals for the claimants, reviews the plan for its appropriateness, and reviews and identifies anticipated outcomes.
7. Recognizes that all plans of care for the individuals are not successful and the outcomes are not as anticipated; identifies and makes recommendations for a corrective plan.
8. Demonstrates skill and proficiency in applying highly technical principles and concepts.
9. Supports a climate for research and expansion of skill and knowledge.

Process and Relationships:

1. Develops and maintains a positive work climate that supports the overall staff efforts at Options Unlimited.
2. Assists in developing the philosophy, goals, and objectives for concurrent case management performance that meets clinical and financial requirements.

3. Implements the Standards of Practice for Case Management, URAC Guidelines, ethical performance, and functions relevant to the coordination of quality case management.
4. Anticipates, recommends, implements, and evaluates policies and procedures related to the Options Unlimited case management system.
5. Demonstrates knowledge in regard to the case management functions and recommends changes as needed to maintain and upgrade the standards of practice.
6. Demonstrates the ability to work within a team structure.
7. Contributes to the organization's goals and objectives; supports the organizational strategic plans.
8. Actively participates in the consensus building among the Options Unlimited personnel.
9. Empowers the case managers to strive for greater knowledge and promotes professional and personal growth.
10. Maintains strict confidentiality, as written by federal law, in regard to claimants and Options Unlimited personnel.
11. Demonstrates the ability to interact with a wide variety of individuals and to handle complex situations simultaneously.
12. Performs other duties as requested.

Service Delivery:

1. Provides orientation, continuing education, and training on case management.
2. Actively participates in the development of clinician guidelines and incorporates the process into the role of the case managers.
3. Interfaces with external agencies and provides appropriate information, consultation, and recommendations.
4. Supervises case management performance and the implementation of their role.
5. Contributes to the hiring process.
6. Develops job descriptions and performance standards.
7. Monitors the acuity level of the case managers.
8. Provides counseling and training.
9. Addresses disciplinary concerns.
10. Appraises performance.

Quality and Performance Improvement

1. Works within a team environment to manage the functions of the Options Unlimited Case Management Quality Management Committee.
2. Supports a culture of continuous quality improvement.

3. Uses quality improvement tools and strategies in problem-solving activities.
4. Prepares quality, screening abstracts according to current policy and procedure.
5. Identifies patterns or trends in case management that have or had the potential for adverse impact on claimant interventions.
6. Develops corrective action plans and reevaluation of outcomes.
7. Provides reports, summaries, trends, and statistical analysis to the President and Vice President and shares the data with the staff at Options Unlimited.

Managed Care and Regulatory Knowledge:

Collaborates, as required, with the multidisciplinary team to assist the case manager with benefit and resource management, to mentor those who need to negotiate services that are out of network, to resolve payment issues, to institute a more cost-effective plan of care, to evaluate the appropriateness of the level of care or the use of services. Responsibilities include but are not limited to the following:

1. Communicates with the case managers to provide an understanding of Plan language and/or payer guidelines.
2. When identification is made that the claimant is out of network, discusses the issues for treatment/discharge needs with the health care team to provide for an appropriate, timely treatment or a safe discharge.
3. Assists the case manager in assisting the physicians, care providers, and claimant/family in understanding the Plan language and benefits as required.
4. Shares the knowledge of the interventional time factors that impact case management services.

Communication:

1. Maintains open communication with all appropriate individuals.
2. Communicates within and outside Options Unlimited in a timely manner in regard to significant, relevant issues, and follows through with requests.
3. Written communication is clear, concise, well-organized, and follows the approved format of Options Unlimited.
4. Maintains a professional, courteous manner when communicating.
5. Utilizes problem-solving skills to resolve conflict.
6. Identifies, plans, coordinates, and implements the sharing of knowledge.
7. Maintains strict standards for confidentiality and the appropriate dissemination of information.
8. Knowledge of securing electronic information.
9. Complies with organizational, federal, and state regulations, and with policies regarding confidentiality.

Professional Development:

1. Knowledge of legislation that affects the case management process.
2. Attends educational and training programs to expand job knowledge.
3. Performs other duties as related to case management functions to support and implement an effective, quality case management program.

POSITION REQUIREMENTS AND QUALIFICATIONS:

Education and Experience:

1. Graduated from an accredited School of Nursing or college.
2. Current New York state license as a Registered Professional Nurse.
3. Bachelor of Science in Nursing or Health Related field. (Preferred)
4. Minimum of 5–7 years of relevant clinical medical-surgical or specialty experience required. Supervisory experience preferred.
5. Required to pursue ongoing education, certification, and self-development to remain current with industry standards and business objectives related to case management.

Skills:

1. Knowledgeable in the use of personal computers and software for work processing and good keyboard skills.
2. Demonstrates the ability to efficiently enter and retrieve data from relevant computer systems.
3. Demonstrates the ability to communicate effectively.
4. Demonstrates organizational skills and is efficient in prioritizing and managing the case managers and other assignments.
5. Demonstrates the willingness and ability to research, learn, and obtain knowledge for the performance of the position.
6. Demonstrates courteous, professional demeanor and cooperative spirit.
7. Demonstrates the ability to work in a collaborative, effective manner.
8. Demonstrates the ability to utilize critical thinking and apply sound clinical judgment and assessment skills for decision making.

Knowledge:

1. Knowledge of CMSA Standards of Practice for Case Management.
2. Knowledge of URAC Guidelines.
3. Knowledge of the Code of Professional Conduct for Case Managers.
4. Knowledge of the different levels of claimant care and the qualifications required for each level.
5. Knowledge of ERISA regulations and time factors.

6. Knowledge of the plans and their language with the skill to gain interpretation of the specific dialogue.
7. Maintains knowledge of the quality assurance process and the ability to effect positive outcomes.
8. Maintains knowledge of regulatory agencies and managed care entities concerning levels of care, continuity of benefits, and medical necessity guidelines.
9. Uses clinical experience, knowledge of managed care, and the current standards and trends in health care, best practices, management tools, and familiarity with related resources and literature.

Signature: _____

Date: _____

President's/Vice President's Signature: _____

Source: Courtesy of Options Unlimited, Case Management Services Division, 2003, Huntington, New York.

Appendix 13–D Interview Evaluation Form

Employment Selection and Compliance System

Interview Evaluation Form

(Fill Out Immediately After Each Interview)

Name: _____   College: _____

Degree: _____   Major _____   Position Applied For_____

	Appraisal of Candidate				
	Excellent	Good	Average	Below Average	Poor
General First Impression (greeting, self expression, etc.)					
Personal Appearance					
Apparent Drive					
Initiative in Conversation					
Apparent Aggressiveness					
Apparent Ability to Get Along with People					
Attitude					
Speech					
Potential					
ASPIRATIONS - Extent to which the goals and aspirations of the applicant are consistent with available opportunity.					
TRAINING - Extent to which level of educational skills and relevant on-the-job training will enable applicant to cope with the demands of the job.					
WORK HISTORY - Extent to which the applicant's work experience applies to the performance of applicant's duties.					
MANNERS AND APPEARANCE - Extent to which the applicant is able to present and communicate his/her ideas to others.					
COOPERATION - Degree to which the applicant will be able to get along with others in the work environment. Is applicant a team player?					
RESPONSIBILITY - Extent to which applicant will exercise judgment in getting the job done, takes initiative when appropriate, and seeks assistance when required.					
OVERALL FINAL IMPRESSION					

ADDITIONAL COMMENTS

_____

_____

_____

Recommended for Further Interview: ⊕YES   ⊕NO

Recommended for Hire: ⊕YES   ⊕NO

Date: _____   Interviewed By: _____

The First Interview

Source: Reprinted from *Employment Selection and Compliance System,* p. 12, Profiles International Inc., © 2001.

Appendix 13–E Summary Evaluation Scale

Employment Selection and Compliance System

Summary Evaluation Scale

APPLICANT: _____ DATE: _____ JOB: _____

EVALUATION FACTORS	Not Applicable	Unknown	QUALIFICATIONS						
			UNDER QUALIFIED Low Enough To Disqualify The Applicant	POOR Extremely Low But Other Factors Could Compensate	FAIR Low But Acceptable For The Job	AVERAGE The Typical Applicant On This Factor	GOOD Definitely A Cut Above The Average	OUTSTANDING Compares Favorably With Top Applicants	OVER QUALIFIED Interference With Success Is Probable
GENERAL EDUCATION									
SPECIALIZED KNOWLEDGE									
WORK EXPERIENCE									
JOB STABILITY									
GROWTH & DEVELOPMENT									
GENERAL INTELLIGENCE									
PRACTICAL JUDGMENT									
SPECIAL APTITUDES									
MANUAL DEXTERITY									
LEADERSHIP SKILLS									
COMMUNICATION SKILLS									
MOTIVATION									
MANAGEMENT OF TIME									
CHARACTER									
EMOTIONAL MATURITY									
INITIATIVE AND DRIVE									
DEPENDABILITY									
COOPERATIVENESS									
HUMAN RELATIONS									
INTERESTS									
APPEARANCE									
OVERALL QUALIFICATION FOR THE JOB									
JOB SUITABILITY %									

RECOMMENDATIONS:

EVALUATOR _____

The Second Interview

Source: Reprinted from *Employment Selection and Compliance System*, p. 3, Profiles International Inc., © 2001.

Appendix 13–F Competencies for Unit-Based Nurse Case Manager

COMPETENCIES FOR UNIT-BASED NURSE CASE MANAGER

UNIT-BASED NURSE CASE MANAGER'S NAME: _____

COMPETENCIES	COMPETENT BY SELF-ASSESSMENT	EXPLANATION, DEMONSTRATION, OR REVIEW NEEDED	DATE AND INITIAL OF EXPLANATION, DEMONSTRATION, OR REVIEW	DATE AND INITIAL OF OBSERVATION OR DEMONSTRATION OF SKILLS
1. Collaborates with the attending physician to discuss patient progress and achievement of expected day-to-day outcomes defined by the MAP.				
2. Anticipates and identifies variances in the care process related to the patient's individual needs. Makes plans to resolve unexpected care requirements to facilitate returning the patient to the usual progress tract.				
3. Participates in the development and review of case management tools (i.e., MAPs, collaborative case management plans, patient education materials, and discharge instructions for designated patient populations).				
4. Coordinates with other clinical disciplines to facilitate the patient's receiving the required care within the expected time frame.				
5. Participates in nurse case management seminars:				
• Attends				
• Presents				
• Coordinates				
6. Initiates individualized MAP to meet patient needs.				
7. Discusses the collaborative plan of care with physician, associates, and staff from other disciplines.				
8. Initiates patient care conferences when indicated.				

continues

Competencies continued

COMPETENCIES	COMPETENT BY SELF-ASSESSMENT	EXPLANATION, DEMONSTRATION, OR REVIEW NEEDED	DATE AND INITIAL OF EXPLANATION, DEMONSTRATION, OR REVIEW	DATE AND INITIAL OF OBSERVATION OR DEMONSTRATION OF SKILLS
9. Directs and participates in care delivery.				
10. Attends case management workshop.				
11. Initiates or directs teaching plan.				
12. Facilitates posthospitalization follow-up contact. This may include the physician, office staff, and referral agencies when appropriate.				
13. Participates in professional growth and development through publications, seminars, workshops, conferences, and professional affiliations.				
14. Actively serves on case management committee including task force involvement when appropriate.				
15. Actively participates in quality management/ quality improvement activities.				

Source: Reprinted from F. Snowden, ed., *Medical Case Management: Forms, Checklists and Guidelines,* second edition, pp. 2:33, 2:34, Aspen Publishers, Inc., © 2003.

PART IV

Trends and Opportunities in Case Management

CHAPTER 14

Case Manager Credentialing

CERTIFIED CASE MANAGER (CCM)

The Certification of Insurance Rehabilitation Specialists Commission (CIRSC) in Rolling Meadows, Illinois, was the credentialing agency selected by the National Case Management Task Force in February 1992 to develop the case management certification process. This group defined case management and announced the first credentialing process for case managers in September 1992. The report drafted at CIRSC offices and published in 1992 became the basis for the *CCM Certification Guide,* published in 1993 and updated regularly, including basic information regarding application for the Certified Case Manager (CCM) certification. (In 1995, the Interim Commission was incorporated as an independent credentialing body and renamed the Commission for Case Manager Certification [CCMC]. CIRSC is now known as the Certification of Disability Management Specialists Commission [CDMSC]. CCMC continues to publish the *CCM Certification Guide,* revised to meet the changing roles of case managers in numerous practice settings within the evolving managed care industry.) The CCM credential brought into existence a nationally accepted standard for case management practitioners.

THE CCM EXAM

The CCM exam and certification process are administered by the Commission for Case Manager Certification (CCMC). Currently, the CCM is made up of questions across six knowledge domains, further defined into subdomains in the *CCM Certification Guide.* These domains include Processes and Relationships, Healthcare Management, Community Resources and Support, Service Delivery, Psychosocial Intervention, and Rehabilitation Case Management. Although it certainly tests clinical knowledge, the exam is intended to be a tool for the evaluation of the skills necessary for the practice of case management. Factual knowledge is tested, as is the practical application of such knowledge. By having to answer situational test questions, candidates will not be able to merely memorize facts, laws, formulas, and so on, but will need to demonstrate that they have actually engaged in case management activities.

Obviously, those currently in practice will be more comfortable with many of the "hands-on" type of questions, such as the following:

A worker with a reported back injury is referred by his physician for non-invasive diagnostic testing. Which of the following procedures will most likely be performed?

a. Angiogram
b. Myelogram
c. Ultrasound
d. Computerized Axial Tomography

Due to nutritional deficiencies, the chronic alcoholic may develop peripheral neuropathy. This disorder is best described as:

a. A progressive deterioration of sensory and motor functions at the lower extremities which can be reversed if treated early.
b. A disease of the spinal nerves that causes immediate and permanent damage and results in paralysis.
c. Affecting only the most severe, long-term alcoholics who have extensive liver damage.
d. A rapidly progressive loss of sensation and function of the facial and neck muscles.[1]

The correct answers are *d* and *a*.

Are there ways to prepare for this examination? There are several conferences, both local and national, that are useful in obtaining the kind of information and insight required to pass the CCM exam. These include the national conferences sponsored by CMSA, National Association of Rehabilitation Professionals in the Private Sector (NARPPS), and other organizations. Presenters at such conferences are often case management professionals, lawyers, physicians, and others who can share their expertise and the kind of hands-on knowledge that is invaluable to prospective test takers.

Currently, there is no official study guide for the exam, but several of the works listed in Appendix A at the end of the book will be of help. The CCMC also includes a reading list in its *CCM Certification Guide*. The information covered in the exam is always contained in published, readily accessible sources.

Although attending seminars and reading are beneficial, several hours or days of study will not by itself result in a passing grade. Actual working experience and competence are being tested, as well as theory, and although the exam is for entry-level practitioners, it is interesting to note that most case managers have more than 20 years experience in the health care field.[2]

Because there are many clinical areas involved in the practice of case management, individuals who have experience in only one specialty area (for example, neonatology or AIDS) may struggle with certain aspects of the exam. So, too, may allied professionals other than nurses who perform some but not all case management activities or who are members of a case management team but do not have all of the responsibilities. For these individuals, additional preparation may be necessary to round out their knowledge.

BEFORE CCM, TO THE WIDE ARRAY OF CREDENTIALS

Other applicable certification designations, which were in place prior to CCM, are Certified Rehabilitation Registered Nurse (CRRN) from the Rehabilitation Nursing Certification Board and Certified Occupational Health Nurse (COHN) from the American Association of Occupational Health Nurses.

In early 2002, CMSA surveyed a cross section of case management professionals from a wide array of backgrounds. Results showed that the vast majority of case managers that are certified hold the CCM. The second largest group of case managers, approximately half the number of those who have earned the CCM, have some "other" certification. These are followed, from most to least, by case managers with the Certified Disability Management Specialist (CDMS), the Certified Case Manager (Cm) credential from American Nurses Credentialing Center, Certified Occupational Health Nurse (COHN), Certified Rehabilitation Counselor (CRC), Continuity of Care Certification, Advanced (A-CCC), and the Case Manager, Certified (CMC).[3]

A number of new case manager credentialing bodies and credentialing opportunities have been developed, and others increasingly are being applied by case manager professionals. Each of these was designed to meet the needs of case managers in certain settings, and candidates may find it helpful to examine each offering prior to sitting for an exam. Some of the most recognized are included in the following pages, drawn from web sites, articles and papers published in *The Case Manager, Case Management Advisor*, and *Case Management Trends: An Overview of Recent Industry and Regulatory Developments*, published byURAC.[4] The credentialing groups for these programs are included in Appendix A at the end of the book.

CERTIFIED DISABILITY MANAGEMENT SPECIALIST (CDMS)

In place for a number of years as the CIRS credential, the CDMS has six eligibility categories. Each category is specific in its requirements, and it is suggested that interested candidates call the Certification of Disability Specialists Commission to request written materials outlining the categories. Briefly stated, they include a valid registered nurse or certified rehabilitation counselor certification/license plus a minimum of 2 or 3 years, respectively, of acceptable supervised experience; a master's degree in rehabilitation counseling with hours and certified supervision requirements; a bachelor's degree and license or certification, plus a minimum of 2 years acceptable, full-time employment with 1 year under the supervision of a CMS, CCM, or CRC; or a bachelor's, master's, or doctorate degree in any discipline, plus a minimum of 5 years of acceptable, full-time employment under the supervision of a CDMS, CCM, or CRC.

The 1-day exam includes 300 multiple-choice questions covering disability case management, psychosocial intervention, vocational aspects of disability, managed care and disability management concepts, and business knowledge related to disability management. Recertification must occur 5 years after the certification is awarded. The candidate must show completion of 80 hours of approved continuing education and pay a $160 fee.

CERTIFIED OCCUPATIONAL HEALTH NURSE (COHN)

One of three credentials offered by the American Board for Occupational Health Nurses, Inc. (ABOHN), the certifying body for occupational health nurses in the United States, the Certified Occupational Health Nurse (COHN) is offered to registered nurses. Its exam no longer requires a degree, due to a change in requirements of the ABOHN. Its core focus is on the nurse as a clinician, advisor, and coordinator. Any graduate study in occupational health or completion of a baccalaureate program, after basic nursing preparation, can be used toward the experience or education requirement for taking the exam. These options are covered in detail in the application form.

CERTIFIED OCCUPATIONAL HEALTH NURSE–SPECIALIST (COHN-S)

The Certified Occupational Health Nurse–Specialist (COHN-S) credential, also from the ABOHN, reflects the nurse's role in direct care, management, education, and consulting. An applicant must have registered nurse (RN) licensure and a bachelor's degree. It does not require a bachelor of science in nursing. To sit for the COHN-S, an individual must have earned the COHN.

Eligibility criteria for the COHN and the COHN-S require active licensure as a registered nurse or its international equivalent, as well as 4,000 hours experience (or a minimum of 2 years of full-time employment) in occupational health nursing and 50 documented contact hours earned within a 5-year period prior to the application deadline. The continuing education credits that comprise those contact hours must be related to occupational health. An applicant may use professional presentations, nursing leadership, and publications toward meeting this.

CERTIFIED OCCUPATIONAL HEALTH NURSE/CASE MANAGER— COHN/CM AND CERTIFIED OCCUPATIONAL HEALTH NURSE–SPECIALIST/CASE MANAGER (COHN-S/CM)

The Certified Occupational Health Nurse/Case Manager (COHN/CM) and Certified Occupational Health Nurse–Specialist/Case Manager (COHN-S/CM) are both specialty credentials in case management offered by the ABOHN. These case management credentials require current, active status as a COHN or COHN-S, current licensure as an RN or its international equivalent, and 10 documented hours of case management continuing education in the 5 years before the application is submitted.

Recertification for ABOHN credentials is required every 5 years. Available from ABOHN, a candidate handbook covers in depth a variety of topics related to its credentials.

CERTIFIED REHABILITATION COUNSELOR (CRC)

Offered by the Commission on Rehabilitation Counselor Certification (CRCC), the Certified Rehabilitation Counselor (CRC) is designed for rehabilitation professionals practicing rehabilitation counseling, a specialty within the rehabilitation profession, which assists those with physical, mental, developmental, cognitive, and emotional disabilities. There are several rehabilitation disciplines and related processes integral to this credential, including vocational evaluation, job development and job placement, work adjustment, and case management. Created with a number of eligibility levels to sit for the exam, the CRC, its certification standards, a Code of Professional Ethics, its certification guide, and application can be viewed on its web site, www.crccertification.com.

CONTINUITY OF CARE CERTIFICATION, ADVANCED (A-CCC)

Available from the National Board for Certification in Continuity of Care, the Continuity of Care Certification, Advanced (A-CCC) is open to multiple disciplines, including nurses, social workers, therapists, dietitians, and physicians. It can be achieved by those with a baccalaureate degree or higher, licensure in your discipline, and 2 years of full-time experience in continuity of care within the last 5 years prior to sitting for the exam. Candidates without a baccalaureate degree need to verify 8 years of full-time experience in continuity of care within the last 12 years. Documentation of employment, proof that the applicant's job responsibilities include continuity of care functions, and a copy of her current job description must be submitted with her application. Included in the exam content is the continuity of care process, health care delivery systems, professional issues, standards, reimbursement, legal issues, and clinical issues. The certification is valid for 5 years.

CASE MANAGER, CERTIFIED (CMC)

The American Institute of Outcomes Case Management (AIOCM), a membership organization, offers the Case Manager, Certified (CMC) credential. Applicants must be members of the institute who have attained a certain number of points based on education and experience. The AIOCM has established two certification processes: a standard process and a portfolio review process. Using the standard certification process, applicants must meet general education, professional experience, outcomes care, education, and ethical requirements, and pass the 2-hour exam. The portfolio review procedure, by which candidates who do not meet the standard criteria can apply, requires submission of a portfolio of one's education, training, and experience for evaluation by the AIOCM. Only applicants with more than 10 years of related professional experience may utilize the portfolio review application process.

The AIOCM also offers the Advanced Utilization Managers (UMC-A), Clinical Chart Auditing Professionals (CAPC), and Case Manager Associates (CMC-A, described later in this chapter) credentials.

CARE MANAGER CERTIFIED (CMC)

Case managers and case manager candidates should take note that there are two CMC credentials. Care Manager Certified (CMC), from the National Academy of Certified Care Managers (not to be confused with the Case Manager, Certified, also abbreviated CMC, from the AIOCM), requires that applicants meet one of three criteria. They must have a minimum of 2 years of supervised, paid, full-time care management experience that includes face-to-face interviews, assessment, care planning, problem solving, and follow-up. The experience must be subsequent to obtaining a master's degree in a field related to case management, such as social work, nursing, counseling, gerontology, or psychology.

The second criterion is a minimum of 4 years of paid, full-time direct experience with people in fields such as social work, nursing, mental health, counseling, or care management, 2 years of which must be supervised, paid, full-time care management experience that includes face-to-face interaction as described previously. A bachelor's degree in a field related to care management (social work, nursing, counseling, mental health, psychology, or gerontology) is required.

Third, a candidate can sit for the exam if she holds a high school diploma or any degree unrelated to the field of case management and a minimum of 6 years paid, full-time, direct experience with clients in areas such as social work, nursing, mental health, counseling, or care management. Two years of this work must have been supervised, paid, full-time care management experience as noted in the second criterion listing.

CMC certification must be renewed every 3 years.[5]

REGISTERED NURSE-NURSE CASE MANAGER (RN-NCM)

The Registered Nurse-Nurse Case Manager (RN-NCM) credential is administered by the American Nurses' Association through its subsidiary, the American Nurses Credentialing Center. Candidates must hold an active RN license in the United States or its territories, a bachelor's degree, and another ANA certification. They must document a current, nationally recognized core nursing specialty certification, and have worked within the scope of practice for a minimum of 2,000 hours within the 2 years prior to their application for the exam. The RN-NCM certification is valid for 5 years.[6]

CERTIFIED PROFESSIONAL IN HEALTH CARE QUALITY (CPHQ)

Effective January 1, 2004, the Healthcare Quality Certification Board of the National Association for Healthcare Quality voted to eliminate the education and experience criteria that had been required to sit for the Certified Professional in Health Care Quality (CPHQ). The Board suggests that candidates assess their readiness to apply to take the CPHQ exam.[7]

CASE MANAGEMENT ADMINISTRATOR, CERTIFIED (CMAC)

To sit for the Case Management Administrator, Certified (CMAC) exam, sponsored by The Center for Case Management, applicants must meet one of five eligibility requirements. They must hold a master's degree and have 1 year experience in case management administration; a master's degree and 3 years experience as a case manager; a bachelor's degree and 3 years experience in case management administration; a bachelor's degree and 5 years experience as a case manager; or hold one of the following active case manager certifications as entry into the CMAC examination: A-CCC, CRRN, CCM, Certified Social Work Case Manager (C-SWCM), Certified Advanced Social Work Case Manager (C-ASWCM) or CDMS.

This certification is valid for 5 years.[8]

CERTIFIED REHABILITATION REGISTERED NURSE (CRRN)

The Certified Rehabilitation Registered Nurse (CRRN) credential, administered by the Rehabilitation Nursing Certification Board, requires that candidates have a current, unrestricted RN license and have completed within the 5 years preceding the examination: 2 years of practice as a registered professional nurse in rehabilitation nursing, or 1 year of practice as a registered professional nurse in rehabilitation nursing, plus 1 year of advanced study (beyond a baccalaureate) in nursing.

The Rehabilitation Nursing Certification Board also offers the Certified Rehabilitation Registered Nurse-Advanced or CRRN-A certification. It is being phased out. The last opportunities to sit for the exam are December 2003 and June 1–30, 2004. To be eligible to take the CRRN-A exam, an individual must have a master's degree or a doctorate in nursing, current CRRN certification, and an active, unrestricted RN license. Content of the examination is based on a job analysis of advanced practice in rehabilitation nursing.

Both certifications remain active for 5 years until the last day of the month that certification was earned. The CRRN-A program will end on June 30, 2009.[9]

CERTIFIED SOCIAL WORK CASE MANAGER (C-SWCM)

Applicants for the Certified Social Work Case Manager (C-SWCM) credential from the National Association of Social Workers (NASW) must hold active NASW membership in good standing; hold a bachelor's in social work (BSW) degree from a Council on Social Work Education accredited institution, and 1-year (1,500 hours) paid, post-BSW, supervised work experience. (These hours must be accumulated in more than 1 year and less than 5 years.)

Further eligibility criteria include adherence to the NASW Code of Ethics, the NASW Standards for Social Work Case Management, and the NASW Standards for Continuing Professional Education; an NASW Academy of Certified Baccalaureate Social Workers (ACBSW) credential, a current state BSW-level licensure, if applicable, or a passing score on the American Association of State Social Work Boards basic exam; a reference from a BSW- or MSW-level colleague, and an evaluation from an approved supervisor.

The C-SWCM must be renewed every 2 years.[10]

The NASW also offers the Certified Advanced Social Work Case Manager (C-ASWCM) credential for MSW social workers.

CERTIFIED MANAGED CARE NURSE (CMCN)

Certified Managed Care Nurse (CMCN) is offered by the American Board of Managed Care Nursing, an association dedicated to providing training and educational services to nurses in managed care. Eligibility criteria for the CMCN is a Registered Nurse license, Licensed Practical Nurse (LPN) license, or a current license to practice nursing in any American state, territory, or protectorate. The written, 150 multiple-choice question exam is based on the home study course made available by Thomson Prometric. Applicants must qualify under one of four employment experiences listed at "Eligibility Requirements," www.abmcn.org.[11]

CASE MANAGER ASSOCIATE (CMC-A)

The Case Manager Associate (CMC-A) credential from the American Institute of Outcomes Case Management is under development.

OTHER CREDENTIALS AND CREDENTIALING GROUPS

In the late 1990s, the American Nurses Credentialing Center (ANCC), a subsidiary of the American Nurses Association, held its first exam for a case management credential specific to the discipline of nursing, with its primary focus on nurse case management, the Cm. Later this became the Certified Nursing Case Manager (RN,Cm). Now, it is a module called the RN,C or Registered Nurse, Certified.

I am concerned about the number of credentials that have emerged for case managers and the divisiveness they seem to contribute to our industry. Because of interest in case management and its nature as a cross-disciplinary practice, a number of credentials will, of course, evolve. As more companies specify a credential in their employment ads for case managers, and as more case managers enter the field, it will be interesting to note those credentials that move to the top as the most desirable and are recognized as indicators of established professionals. One needs to be informed as to which credential will meet one's needs and serve the industry and our patients well.

In summary, attaining a case management credential should be the goal of each case management professional, and once it is attained, each professional needs to maintain both competency and the credential. Taking the time to get the credential demonstrates both a professional and personal commitment to the case management process and serves to validate its importance for ensuring quality outcomes and the preservation of health care resources. If there are over 23,000 CCMs today, how powerful will our voices be when these numbers continue to expand? We will be firmly positioned for the future, helping our patients, their families, the payers, and the providers. As case managers, we know how valuable our work can be, and the CCM credential will underscore and further promote our contributions.

NOTES

1. Commission for Case Manager Certification, *CCM Certification Guide* (Rolling Meadows, IL: 2003).

2. J. Boling, G. Carneal, "Case Management Trends," in *Case Management Trends: An overview of Recent Industry and Regulatory Developments* (Washington, D.C.: URAC, 2002).

3. J. Boling, G. Carneal, "Case Management Trends," p. 12.

4. L. F. Hoffmann, "Directory of the Top 12 CM Credentials," Supplement to *Case Management Advisor* 11, no. 11 (2000): 1 (For more information, please call 800-688-2421); J. Boling, G. Carneal, "Case Management Trends," in *Case Management Trends: An Overview of Recent Industry and Regulatory Developments* (Washington, D.C.: URAC, 2002), and C. M. Stolte, "The Commission for Case Manager Certification Widens Eligibility Criteria," *The Case Manager* 13, no. 5 (2002): 50.

5. L. F. Hoffmann, "Directory of the Top 12 CM Credentials," p. 7.

6. C. M. Stolte, "The Commission for Case Manager Certification Widens Eligibility Criteria," p. 53 and L. F. Hoffmann, "Directory of the Top 12 CM Credentials," pp. 1–2.

7. Healthcare Quality Certification Board, "2004 Candidate Handbook," pp. 2–3.

8. L. F. Hoffmann, "Directory of the Top 12 CM Credentials," pp. 3–4.

9. Association of Rehabilitation Nurses, "CRRN Certification," www.rehabnurse.org/certification/crrn.html and www.rehabnurse.org/certification/crrna.html.

10. National Association of Social Workers, "Credentials & Specialty Certifications," www.social-workers.org/credentials/specialty/c-swcm.asp.

11. American Board for Managed Care Nursing web site, www.abmcn.org and C. M. Stolte, "The Commission for Case Manager Certification Widens Eligibility Criteria," p. 53.

REFERENCES

L. F. Hoffmann, "Directory of the Top 12 CM Credentials," Supplement to *Case Management Advisor* 11, no. 11 (2000): 1–8.

"Certification—Primary Case Management Certification Options," FAXT Sheet, Case Management Society of America web site, www.cmsa.org, © 2003.

C. M. Stolte, "The Commission for Case Manager Certification Widens Eligibility Criteria," *The Case Manager* 13, no. 5 (2002): 50–54.

American Board for Managed Care Nursing web site:
www.abmcn.org

American Board for Occupational Health Nurses, Inc., Certification Information Kit, web site:
www.abohn.org

American Institute of Outcomes Care Management web site:
www.aiocm.net

American Nurses Credentialing Center web site:
www.ana.org/ancc/

Central Connecticut State University web site:
www.sociology.ccsu.edu/Social Work/NASWbrochure.htm

"Certification Examination for Case Management Administrators Handbook for Candidates"
The Center for Case Management Information Kit

Certification of Disability Management Specialists web site:
www.cdms.org

Commission on Rehabilitation Counselor Certification web site:
www.crccertification.com

Healthcare Quality Certification Board, Certified Professional in Healthcare Quality web site:
www.cphq.org/

National Board for Certification in Continuity of Care web site:
www.nbccc.org

The United States Department of Justice web site:
www.usdoj.gov

CHAPTER 15

Cultural Issues

At the time of the 2000 U.S. Census, the United States had more than 60 distinctive cultural groups.[1] More than 300 different languages are spoken in the country. Beyond the Spanish, Italian, French, Mandarin, German, Japanese, Mexican, Arabic, Russian, Vietnamese, Ukrainian, Sri Lankan, and others, there is the Obispeño of the Chumash near Santa Barbara, California, the Cajun French used in Southern Louisiana, the Crow language of the Missouri Valley, and a multitude of dialects in areas across the nation. At least 80 languages are spoken in New York City alone.

Case managers can rely on translators to bridge the linguistic barriers they might experience with patient population groups, but the variety within our "melting pot" society is not limited to language. America is a rich mix of religion, ethnicity, race, customs, and traditions. A case manager's level of clinical knowledge should now be matched by cultural understanding, or competency.

Before moving on to foreign cultures and the many ways a patient's societal mores and traditions will influence the case manager's approach to intervention, the case manager should honestly evaluate her own feelings and closely held beliefs. What, if any, are her own cultural biases or prejudices? Will she grow impatient when a patient feels an ethnic ceremonial activity must take place before his hospital admission? Can she accept that certain patients will refuse the high-tech Western approach in favor of herbal tinctures and prayer? Is she prepared to assist a diabetic patient who is being asked to remove foods with religious significance from her diet? After she has examined her own thoughts on assisting all manners of people, including those whose customs and beliefs she does not share, she will know more about her strengths and weaknesses as a case manager. To successfully advocate for those of different countries, religions, and races, a case manager will "define culture broadly, value clients' cultural beliefs, recognize complexity in language interpretation, facilitate learning between providers and communities, involve the community in addressing service needs, collaborate with other agencies, hire and train staff professionally, and institutionalize cultural competence."[2]

CULTURAL BELIEFS WILL AFFECT THE DELIVERY OF HEALTH CARE SERVICES

Each society presents its own challenges in providing health care delivery services. According to Nancy Davis, RN, PhD, FACMT, Director, Office of Managed Care, Indian Health Services, Aberdeen, SD, privacy and client confidentiality is a big concern for case managers working among American Indian populations. "The entire community knows everything about the patient almost before the door shuts."

American Indians conceive of individual wellness as harmony and balance among mind, body, and spirit. The same belief that gives him spiritual strength can present a dilemma for a diabetic patient requiring leg amputation. How can he be whole in his afterlife if he is buried without his leg?

Profiled by Jane Gross in *The New York Times*, Chief of Obstetrics and Gynecology at New York University Downtown Hospital, Dr. Iffath Abbasi Hoskins has created a welcoming atmosphere to serve the 65% of the obstetrics patients in the hospital who are Chinese. The staff is bilingual and there are Chinese-language videos for expectant mothers. Sensitivity training for staff members teaches that the cultural resistance to breast-feeding stems from new immigrants feeling that using formula indicates assimilation into the American culture. The suggestion to sooth a sore bottom with an ice pack often is rejected, as it goes against the rules of yin and yang.

During a visit to China, Kathleen Moreo, cofounder of Professional Resources In Management Education, Inc., observed that the Chinese do not say "no," as it is associated with disrespect. When they disagree, they are silent. An American greeted with silence usually assumes there is a misunderstanding, and reiterates their question, position, or statement. Moreo cautions that this is the worst thing a case manager can do when speaking with a Chinese-American. The case manager immediately breaks any developing trust because the patient has made a decision and believes the case manager is trying to force him to change his mind.[3]

Michael J. Demoratz, COO of CareMedical Systems, cites a number of ways in which cultural diversity impacts pain management. He notes that patients from Hispanic, Middle Eastern, or Mediterranean backgrounds generally express pain openly, whereas those from Asian or Northern European lineage tend to underreport pain. In certain cultures, among them Asian and Christian African-American populations, pain and suffering are believed to redeem or purify. Individuals may present a stoic front or refuse medication.[4] For such reasons, a patient might not be able to give an accurate assessment of his pain to the case manager.

Honoring one's elders is integral to the Japanese, Chinese, and Korean cultures. Turning over a loved one's care to a professional, rather than to family members, can be unthinkable to the family. Italian, Greek, French, South-Central American, Middle Eastern, and some Asian societies consider it inhumane to reveal a terminal diagnosis to a patient. Among the Japanese, discussing gastrointestinal conditions is shunned.[5] Most Americans fear death to the point of refusing to consider end-of-life planning.

INTEGRATING LINGUISTIC NEEDS, TRIBAL MEDICINE, AND CULTURAL TREATMENTS

Individuals who are not fluent or comfortable with English are unlikely to seek out services that do not offer translations or address their cultural needs.

A case manager should note that some languages have no words to convey concepts Americans are comfortable with, such as "depression." The Office of Minority Health (OMH), part of the Department of Health and Human Services, published "National Standards on Culturally and Linguistically Appropriate Services in Health Care" (CLAS) in the Federal Register in December 2000. These are 14 benchmarks for "culturally competent care" recommended for adoption or adaptation by the OMH[6] (www.omhrc.gov; 1-800-444-6472).

In South Dakota, the Aberdeen Area Indian Health Services case managers integrate traditional Indian medicine, consultations with Medicine Men, a high degree of family involvement, and the Indian concept of individual wellness as harmony and balance among mind, body, and spirit into their treatment plans. These elements of care are acknowledged and supported, initiated by patients and their families. The beautiful spiritual rooms at the Pine Ridge and Rosebud hospitals are used often.

HEALTH CARE FUNDING

Due to great need, the American Indian and Alaskan Indian cultures, with the highest mortality and morbidity rates in the country, are offered an additional line of health care funding by the federal government. In the Aberdeen Area, South Dakota, the median income is $12,310 and 49.6% of the population lives below poverty level. Life expectancy at birth for both sexes is 11 years less than the United States rate. Three health care systems provide care to these populations: the Indian Health Services (IHS), an agency within the Department of Health and Human Services; Tribal Programs (through contracts with the federal government); and urban clinics. (There are a number of clinics located throughout the United States that have a portion of their funding coming from the IHS.) IHS is not an insurance plan or an entitlement program. There is no universal benefits package.

IHS is the payer of last resort. Alternative resources are Medicare (Part A and Part B), Medicaid (such as the Arizona Health Care Cost Containment System and Medi-Cal in California), Veterans Administration (ChampVA), Crippled Children's Services, Civilian Health and Medical Program of the Uniformed Services, private health insurance, state vocational rehabilitation, workers' compensation, vehicle insurance (for medical coverage), and state maternal and child health programs (the Newborn Intensive Care Program in Arizona and California's Child Health and Disability Prevention Program). Congress funds the IHS program annually.

An Indian can access IHS-funded programs if he is entitled to direct health care services and lives on a federally recognized Indian reservation. An Indian living off reservation must meet several additional criteria to be eligible. Services are most often denied due to lack of documentation of Indian descent, off-reservation occupancy, residency outside of designated off-reservation areas, failure to obtain approval within 72 hours for emergency service, failure to apply for potential or established alternative resources, or a diagnosed problem that is not among established medical priorities.[7]

DEVELOPING CULTURAL COMPETENCY

Know the issues of your patient population and take an active role in improving your cultural competency. To give yourself an idea of where you are on the cultural competency learning curve, take the quiz that appears in Table 15–1. Respond as you are now practicing, not as you hope to be practicing soon.

Case managers can create an assessment tool to help them clarify and evaluate cultural aspects of cases involving patients whose belief systems, language, religion, health care attitudes, and even metabolic reaction to medications will influence their ability to adhere to a treatment plan. This cultural intake sheet should be fashioned with the case manager's patient population in mind, and used during the initial needs assessment phase of the case manager–patient introduction. In all cases, never assume you know the answers. Hinduism is the predominant religion in India, yet individuals also practice Islam, Christianity, Sikhism, Buddhism, Jainism, and other faiths, including Judaism. Questions should be asked to illicit responses concerning the following topics.

Language and Communication

If a language barrier exists, bring in an interpreter, rather than asking a family member to translate. Case management is not customarily needed in the straightforward cases; the family members a case manager meets are at the bedside of a loved one

Table 15–1 A Cultural Competency Self-Test

---

1. Name two diseases/conditions that are influenced by racial/ethnic factors. Explain.
2. Describe two cultural values or beliefs that influence how a cultural group, different from your own, responds to being sick.
3. Do you respect differences in health behaviors practiced by your client?
4. Name two ways in which your practice is responsive to the needs of diverse groups.
5. Do you take culture, gender, and race into consideration when examining risk factors faced by your clients?
6. Do you involve your clients in the decision-making process when considering a course of treatment?
7. What is a question you commonly ask to learn about your clients' ethnic or sociocultural background? How is this information relevant to your practice?

Add up your score. Give yourself one point for each item named on questions 1, 2, 4, and 7. Give yourself one point for a yes on questions 3, 5, and 6.

Score 9–10: Good work, keep it up! Cultural competency is a continuous quality improvement process.

Score 2–8: Keep working, you have a way to go.

Score 0–1: It is time to start developing your competency skills.

Source: Reprinted with permission, *CareManagement* © 2003 Mason Medical Communications, Inc.

---

who is critically or chronically ill. Given their level of emotional involvement, it is not kind or reasonable to expect them to be able to consider the nuances of language while communicating. I have also been involved in cases in which it became obvious that the patient was not getting complete and accurate information. Does the use of body language play a major role in communication? Are there certain gestures commonly used by Americans that are considered offensive? A case manager must be able to pick up on and correctly interpret nonverbal cues.

Culture

What is the patient's country/culture of origin? Spanish-speaking people cannot all be grouped together under a single cultural umbrella. The patient might be from America, Mexico, Puerto Rico, Cuba, the Dominican Republic, Peru, Costa Rica, or a number of other countries, each with its own customs and understanding of health care, physicians, and medical facilities.

Religion

A patient's religious beliefs can greatly impact his attitude to and compliance with a care plan. The case manager should know his religion, whether he is an active practitioner of his beliefs, and whether there are religious dietary restrictions or regimens that are followed. She should also know if and how the patient and family's faith might relate to health care treatment. Is it proper for a female patient to have a male ventilator technician in the home if there is no male family member present? Provisions might need to be made for prayer at certain times of the day, or to accommodate the use of electronically powered medical equipment during the Sabbath.

Family Structure

Gather information that pertains to the family's day-to-day lives, community involvement, and employment. Do both parents work full-time? Do they have a wide network of friends who might offer support with transportation or food preparation? Is the patient's grandmother living with the family and very much the head of the household? These dynamics will shape the family's ability to adhere to a treatment plan.

Table 15–2 Twelve Steps to Cultural Competency

---

1. Find out about the family's internal dynamics, as well as family members' beliefs and what those beliefs mean to them and to the patient.
2. Look at the length of time the family has been in the United States.
3. Don't make an assumption based solely on the country of origin.
4. Don't make assumptions about why people act the way they do.
5. Don't be afraid to ask questions in a respectful manner.
6. If you need an interpreter, find someone who is not a family member, if possible.
7. Compile a list of available translators and have it at your fingertips.
8. Go out of your way as a clinician to learn basic language skills for members of the predominant patient groups you are likely to encounter.
9. Develop a "cheat sheet" of cultural issues that affect case management.
10. List the cultures you may be coming in contact with and do some basic research on their beliefs.
11. Find the resources you need to educate yourself.
12. Above all, treat the families with respect and let them know you care.

Source: Courtesy of *Case Management Advisor* 12, no. 10 (2001): 147.

Dr. Josepha Campinha-Bacote, president of Transcultural C.A.R.E. Associates, created a model to assist health care professionals in providing culturally appropriate services. (See Table 15–2 on the previous page.)

NOTES

1. J. E. Vaughn, "The Importance of Being a Culturally Competent Case Manager," *CareManagement* 9, no. 3 (2003): 28.
2. G. S. Wolfe, "Cultural Competence," *CareManagement* 9, no. 3 (2003): 7.
3. M. B. Thomas, *Case Management Advisor* 12, no. 10 (2001): 147.
4. M. J. Demoratz, "Managing Pain Across Diverse Cultures," *Disease Management Digest* 7, no. 3 (2003): 3.
5. M. J. Demoratz, "Managing Pain Across Diverse Cultures," 2.
6. M. J. Demoratz, "Managing Pain Across Diverse Cultures," 2.
7. Aberdeen Area Indian Health Services, *Aberdeen Area IHS HP/DP Plan* (Aberdeen, SD: 2002).

CHAPTER 16

Behavioral Health

In America, psychiatric disorders affect approximately 25% of the population in a given year. Fifty percent or more of all primary care physician visits are estimated to be due to underlying behavioral problems. Primary care physicians have become stand-ins for a true mental health system, writing more than 70% of all psychiatric prescriptions. Unfortunately, the quality of mental care provided is often inadequate.[1]

A patient struggling with complex medical problems or complex behavioral health issues faces a tough challenge. The patient with multiple diagnoses struggles with medical conditions that affect her mental health and with psychiatric problems that influence her recuperation and healing process. It is known that patients with chronic medical illness exhibit a higher rate of behavioral disorders than the general population, with up to 50% having a concurrent psychiatric diagnosis.[2] Obviously, there is an unmet need in our health care delivery system. Case managers are part of the solution.

To better manage a patient's health care treatment plan, a case manager needs to understand behavioral health issues. Too often, case managers view behavioral health as a concern separate from medical case management, and behavioral health case managers do the same. In the same way that there is often little or no communication among precertification, utilization review, case management, and disease management staff within the same organization, many of us focus on medical or psychiatric issues, but do not consider a case from both standpoints. Behavioral health case management is a special practice; still, no patient, from pediatric to eldercare clients, can adhere to a treatment plan when facing behavioral health problems. Substance abuse, anxiety disorders, incest, depression, schizophrenia, paranoia, delusions, and other behavioral challenges limit a patient's ability to care about her welfare, much less follow a rehabilitative exercise program or schedule and attend physician appointments. The training and background of a case manager make her uniquely prepared to bridge the gap between medical and psychiatric practices and contribute toward improved outcomes for patients.

Building partnerships between case managers and behavioral health care specialists in the United States is only one part of improving care for the mentally ill. Society and Congress are still struggling with the concept of parity in funding and insurance support for behavioral health treatments. There are far more (in number and in acceptable condition) medical facilities and clinics than sites for the mentally ill to receive treatment, find respite, and recover. The good news is that research is showing that illnesses such as depression are physiological and should be treated, rather than an "attitude" that the patient should just "get over." Employers are more aware of lost man-hours because of employees suffering from untreated behavioral health conditions, and have put a spotlight on the problem. These are welcome signs of improvement.

PARTNERING SUCCESSFULLY WITH BEHAVIORAL HEALTH PROFESSIONALS

Many medical case managers do not have a strong knowledge base in psychiatric and behavioral health care issues and treatments. The first steps in preparing for cases to come, and toward building collaborative relationships with behavioral health professionals, are to attend workshops, seminars, and conferences, read books and journals that address behavioral health topics, gather reference materials from associations and agencies that focus on specific mental disease states, and begin to network with colleagues experienced in psychosocial problems. Ask for their opinions on cases you might be working on, and offer to help with any clinical information you can if they have questions regarding a patient.

Social workers can be a valuable resource for insight into behaviors, area treatment facilities and options, and community programs. A number of case managers are social workers, and case managers in general interface with social workers often in the course of handling a medical case. It is beneficial to both practice areas when individuals discuss their various challenges and the solutions they have found.

Case managers can use the same techniques they apply when meeting medical physicians to begin a working association with psychiatrists (see Chapter 9). Introduce yourself as a patient advocate, reiterate that case managers increase patient compliance, and note that case managers intervene to help a patient move successfully through the health care system.

Following are several actions case managers can take to help obtain good outcomes in complex cases:

- Refresh your knowledge base on the behavioral issue or diagnosis the case presents. Update yourself on current treatments and medications, including dosages.
- Request a psychiatric consultation as soon as the patient is alert enough to communicate. Include the consulting psychiatrist and the outpatient psychiatrist after obtaining the appropriate consents.
- Speak with family members to obtain information on the patient's long-term psychological history, as well as her behavior just prior to the event that brought you to the case. This allows you to establish the rapport that will help smooth the case management intervention, discharge planning, and the patient's relocation to another care facility or home.
- Consider early on the possible patient needs following discharge, based on her psychiatric diagnosis. This affords you time to make plans.
- Establish a rapport with the outpatient psychiatrist, treating psychiatrist, and treating medical physician, reinforcing the case manager's role as a communicator, facilitator, and valuable partner in assuring patient adherence to the treatment plan and guiding transitions across the continuum of care.
- Be respectful of the patient as a human being, and be aware of her symptom level to maintain communications with her, as well.[3]

Other techniques a case manager can use to prepare for a medical/behavioral health case include the following:

- Ask an associate who is employed by an outpatient clinic or psychiatric facility if you might, with appropriate permissions obtained, observe at her workplace. Being on the floor with patients or spending an hour at a colleague's side can provide insight on how staff collaborates and patient interaction techniques that work. It will also accustom you to the sometimes odd behavior you may encounter when working behavioral cases.
- Review a patient's insurance plans carefully and thoroughly for psychiatric coverage. As with medical coverage, a number of services may or may not be covered. Case managers should be well-versed in their options when planning for patient discharge or transfer.
- Join the National Alliance for the Mentally Ill organization in your area. Members pay a small fee and receive informative newsletters and insight into how people cope with mental disorders.[4]

BEHAVIORAL HEALTH DISEASE MANAGEMENT PROGRAMS

Behavioral health programs are being incorporated into some disease management programs. This is progress on the face of it, but can become a problem when treatment is provided as a carve-out as part of an EAP health program, and there is no integration with medical case managers. Opportunities for success are missed when case managers do not talk to disease managers or utilization managers. For example, a diabetes patient with multiple hospital admissions who is enrolled in a disease management program should also be referred to a medical case manager and the behavioral health staff. Case managers will assist with compliance issues and follow-through on the physician's treatment plan, and behavioral health specialists can offer support as the patient goes through his grieving process (loss of lifestyle, and, should it come to it, loss of eyesight or limbs).

RESOURCES

National Association of Psychiatric Health Systems
(202) 393-6700
www.naphs.org/

National Alliance for the Mentally Ill
(800) 950-6264
(703) 524-7600
www.nami.org

National Institute of Mental Health
(866) 615-6464 toll free
(301) 443-4513
www.nimh.nih.gov

Anxiety Disorders Association of America
(204) 485-1001
www.adaa.org

Mental Health Infosource
Continuing Medical Education, Inc.
(800) 993-2632
www.mhsource.com

Health Enhancement Research Organization
www.the-hero.org/

World Health Organization
www.who.int/

Medstat
(734) 913-3000
www.medstat.com

NOTES

1. G. V. Gray, "Case Managers and Behavioral Disease Management," *Inside Case Management* 8, no. 9 (2001): 8.

2. G. V. Gray, "Case Managers and Behavioral Disease Management," *Inside Case Management*, 8.

3. R. Happel, "Do the Voices in My Head Bother You?" *The Case Manager* 14, no. 3 (2002): 66.

4. R. Happel, "Do the Voices in My Head Bother You?" *The Case Manager*, 66.

CHAPTER 17

Dying in America

A PERSONAL STORY

From the time of my dad's diagnosis of Alzheimer's disease and over the course of the following 5 years, I tried to prepare him, our family, and myself for the inevitable event, his death. Of course, as a nurse, case manager, and daughter, I experienced the wide range of emotions that one would expect. When I first saw the changes in my dad, the subtle symptoms, I denied their presence. I reasoned that he was disinterested in some conversations or not paying attention because of a hearing loss caused by his years of sirens and bells experienced with the New York City Fire Department. His inability to remember what certain tools were used for, this man who spent so many spare hours tinkering, repairing, crafting wood cabinets and a fiddle to play his beloved Irish music, surely these were just innocent memory lapses. I was having these, too. This man who kept meticulous checkbooks, never needing a calculator, this strong, active, humorous man who was endlessly challenging his mind through daily crossword puzzles and his own inventions, he couldn't possibly have this dreaded disease. He didn't fit the "profile," and of course, as the symptoms grew more pronounced, I refused to accept what I most feared.

At long last, after the diagnostic tests and consultation with a variety of specialists, the diagnosis was made. Because the diagnostic phase spanned a few months, I had a chance to start coming to terms with the reality of the situation. This time also gave me an opportunity to make some plans.

As a case manager, I witness all too many instances of individuals who experience what could only be described as miserable deaths. Their last days are spent in hospitals away from family and friends. They are being probed, tested, and aggressively treated with painful procedures, medications that cause horrendous side effects, and management that only prolongs their suffering.

I wanted to ensure that my dad lived each of his days in a way and manner that was of his choosing and that his final days were peaceful, comfortable, and as dignified and gentle as he was. My experience and knowledge of the workings of the health care system would, I believed confidently, help make that happen. We had many conversations over the years about his end-of-life wishes. Still, death always seemed far removed and these discussions merely hypothetical. To bring the "what ifs" into reality while my dad was highly functional and cognitively capable, I scheduled an appointment for us with a dear friend who was a nurse and elder care attorney. In a thoroughly professional and caring matter, the appropriate advance directives were prepared and executed for my parents. They had very definite and sometimes differing opinions and preferences. Finally, with their three children present, their wishes and directives were notarized. Copies of these documents were provided to their treating physicians, and to us.

The first years of this diagnosis were relatively uneventful and happy as I researched and secured optimum treatment for him and respite for my mom, who became the 24/7 care provider. Eventually, it became evident that he was in the final stages of Alzheimer's. The pivotal event occurred while I was on a business trip one March. My dad appeared to have suffered a CVA. The rescue squad was called and he was admitted to a university hospital on Long Island. After several days at the acute care level and with acknowledgment that he could not return home just yet, he was transferred to a subacute rehabilitation unit. The goal was to optimize his functional capabilities so he could return home.

I realized during this episode of several weeks that each member of my family had quite different perceptions. Some were very realistic, and some were in absolute denial of the reality. Despite the fact that throughout the 5-year duration of this disease I had patiently explained the probable course of Alzheimer's, there were family members who viewed this as a totally unrelated, sudden event, and one that my dad would recover from. Because he was now considerably cognitively and physically impaired, he was unable to actively participate in his rehabilitation and, as per Medicare criteria, would need to be discharged. Now, I would face the challenge of trying to understand and meet everyone's needs on an almost daily basis.

My mom could no longer be a care provider because of her own fragile medical status and emotional state as she watched her loving partner and best friend disappear. He did not know who she was, and she felt rejected and very alone. We had endless discussions and explored a reasonable and safe discharge plan, and brought in round-the-clock home care. None of our planning could prevent my mom's devastation at the painful process of witnessing her husband's continuing deterioration in their home. She felt caring for him at home was her only ethical choice because, "He would never want me to put him in a nursing home."

My brother reinforced her guilt continuously as he became more entrenched in his own feelings of denial. Realizing that his support and acceptance would be key, I had arranged for us to tour a local assisted living facility that offers a wonderful Alzheimer's program. He refused to go, had hurtful conversations with all of us, and made known his strong oppositions to "putting my dad away." Whereas he continued his daily visits with my dad, he cut off all communication with my mom, sister, and me. This most unfortunate action was so stressful for my mom that she was admitted to the hospital on Mother's Day with chest pain and acute anxiety/depression. How did all of this happen, what did I do wrong? What was the best solution or, in this case, the least horrible one?

The emergency admission of my mom had one good outcome. It helped her understand, with reinforcement from her doctor and daughters, that her husband would never want her to suffer any more that she already had, and that his 24/7 care at home was both physically and emotionally exhausting and totally unrealistic for her. My dad was becoming more combative, further heightening the difficulty of securing willing care providers. I, too, realized I had to give up my idea of my home as a possible care setting option.

With tears and regrets, I took my mom and dad for his admission evaluation for the Alzheimer inpatient program. He was deemed a candidate and we planned for his admission within the week. Because life does go on, I tried to resume a limited business schedule. I was in Philadelphia on an appointment when my office contacted me. My dad had suffered a massive GI bleed and was taken from the Skilled Nursing Facility back to the acute care hospital. I rushed home, and my sister arrived soon after from Washington, D.C.

Going straight to the emergency room, I was met by the surgeon-on-call, who explained that they needed to find a location of the bleed and were prepping him for colonoscopy and then the O.R. They had already done a type and cross match and had administered one unit of packed cells. In disbelief, I asked this physician if he was aware or had seen my dad's advance directive, and, if so, why was he being scheduled for surgery? The physician acknowledged that no one had advised him of this (despite the fact that from the very first admit to acute care, then to rehabilitation, then to the SNF unit, I ensured that these documents were part of each record).

In a manner that I had utilized before, I asked the doctor, "If this were your dad, what would you do?" He quite rightly and kindly responded, "Oh no, now you know better. I cannot tell you that. This needs to be your decision." But, I thought, my dad long before had made his decision very clear and no one on staff in this hospital was paying attention to his choice.

Patiently, I reviewed the more pertinent facts with the surgeon; my dad was in the last stages of Alzheimer's, had experienced a CVA, lost more than 40 pounds, did not know anyone, and surely would be an incredible operative risk, to say nothing of potential post-op complications, pain, and his continued suffering. The doctor acknowledged my right to make a decision for my dad and added, "What do you want to do?" Why, I wondered, couldn't he simply admit that surgical procedures were not going to improve my dad's condition or lifestyle, and that it was time to consult his advance directive, prepared for this exact situation. Ah, well, it seems there are those legal issues, so I became my father's voice. I was certain he would not want this procedure, and in fact, it was specifically against his wishes.

My dad was transferred out of the E.R. to a medical unit where, after completing the admission process, I was met by a nurse and another physician exiting my dad's room. They told me they had just hung another unit of packed cells and that they would be checking his hemoglobin/hematocrit to see if he would need more, because "you decided against surgery." I asked why they would be continuing to give him more blood, knowing his situation. The nurse looked me in the eye and said, "You mean you are going to let him bleed to death?"

Feeling as if I had been slapped in the face, I explained to these professionals that rather than viewing it from that perspective, I considered that *not* giving him more blood would result in a gradual decrease in his hgb/hct to a point that would be incompatible with life, and he would peacefully expire. They looked at me, shrugged, and said, "Obviously, you can do what you want," and walked away. They made it clear that they felt I was denying my dad treatment. I wondered why they ignored my dad's directives and virtually accused me of causing his death.

Within a few days, my dad's condition had stabilized enough for him to be transferred back to the SNF unit within the hospital. Fortunately for my dad and for me, I met with a physician assistant within an hour of the admission. Her genuine concern for my obvious distress was evident, and as she kindly put her hand out to pat my shoulder, the weeks and months of inner turmoil were unleashed. Through tears, I related to her the previous events. This woman seemed to instinctively understand my anguish, which now infiltrated so many of my emotions: sadness, confusion, exhaustion, and a powerful feeling of abandonment by my professional colleagues. I found myself protecting my father from a system that disregarded his wishes and was blind to the painful experiences of his last months of life. Somehow, I had believed that they would understand and help me through this incredibly difficult time, as they would wish to be helped in a similar circumstance. Why didn't they? Why did this new professional in her first assignment actively reach out to me and allow me the opportunity to share my frustration, anger, and feelings of guilt and helplessness? With her assistance and at my request, a hospice program for my dad was finally implemented. Despite the fact that Alzheimer's is a terminal illness, not once did any professional ever suggest hospice or even explore our feelings about it. If I had not requested it, I'm certain it would never have been offered.

Creating a hospice program within the SNF was one hurdle. Making certain the facility adhered to the program was another challenge. During the very last weeks of my dad's illness, it was clear that he was experiencing significant pain. His body movements and facial grimaces indicated to me that his pain medications were not being administered every 3 to 4 hours as needed. I would arrive and find him obviously uncomfortable, and suggest that he needed his medication. A nurse would come in, call his name, and ask if he was in pain or if he wanted his pain medication. This to a man who no longer knew his name and was, for the most part, in a semicomatose state.

Continued intervention with the nursing staff was needed as they cautioned me, "We don't want to overmedicate him," or "We don't want to depress his respirations" at the same time my dad was having more frequent episodes of discomfort. I discussed this very odd and upsetting scenario with the hospice physician, and a decision was made for my dad to be medicated every three hours around the clock.

My dad wasn't the only family member who needed assistance. I was on call to help comfort my mother, sister, and brother through these last days. My brother tracked my dad's progress. If our father's temperature was elevated, he wanted him on antibiotics. If dad rejected ice chips, my brother thought his intravenous fluids should be increased. He was clearly unable to come to terms with reality. My mom visited less and less, each time saying good-bye for what she believed would be the last time. The next day my brother would report, "Dad is looking better today."

Throughout the process, I longed for a case manager to lend support and help guide me and my family through this emotionally charged event. I wanted to be a daughter, not the nurse, and definitely not the case manager. Yet, I know that my intervention gave my dad the kind of death he had hoped for, one that was far better than it would have been without my presence. Two months following his admission, he quietly and comfortably passed away.

A peaceful, pain-free death, with final days spent on one's own terms is a wonderful and measurable outcome of individual case management. Advocacy in life and especially in death is at the very heart, or should be, of case management.

DEATH IS NOT AN OPTION

Despite the overwhelming evidence that death is inevitable, most Americans choose to ignore the natural human process that will profoundly affect them and their families. Our nurses and physicians-to-be are not trained on a universal basis as part of their baccalaureate, undergraduate, or graduate studies to address end-of-life (EOL) issues. People feel free to discuss their colonoscopies, but not their feelings about death. Typically, much more research, preparation, and discussion occurs prior to a sweet 16 birthday party than before the final days of one's life. A 1999 National Hospice Foundation survey of Americans age 45 years or older found that more than 50% never discussed their thoughts or feelings about death with family members even when they, or a family member, were terminally ill with less than 6 months to live.[1]

Moliere said, "We die only once—and for so long!" Yes, we do, and case managers, as patient advocates with clinical expertise, are in a good position to help individuals and their loved ones replace misinformation with education, fear with calm resolution, and pain with peace.

Studies conducted on end-of-life issues report that patients are most concerned about being mentally aware, not placing a burden on their family, and feeling at peace with God. A majority of terminally ill patients said that euthanasia and physician-assisted suicide should be available, but very few felt they would ever consider these options themselves.[2]

Passed in 1990 and instituted in December 1991, the Patient Self-Determination Act (PSDA) indirectly encourages individuals to make decisions now about the type and scope of medical care they will want when they are no longer able to make that decision themselves due to incapacitation. Under PSDA, all health care agencies and facilities that receive Medicare and Medicaid funding must recognize livings wills and power of attorney for health care as advance directives. In addition, the Act requires health care agencies (hospitals, long-term care facilities, and home health agencies) to ask patients if they have advance directives, and provides them with educational materials about their rights under state law.

Case managers should note that each state has its own definitions and practices regarding how individual rights to determine one's own health care treatment are guaranteed. For example, a doctor in New York is not required to follow a family's wishes for the patient if they do not have an advance directive naming a health care proxy.[3]

Jeanne Boling, MSN, CRRN, CDMS, CCM, and executive director of CMSA, notes that "case managers enjoy an advantage not shared by any other health care professional; that of working directly with each element impacting the patient over multiple treatment settings and payment sources. Case managers are as vital to insuring a good outcome during a patient's final illness as at any other life stage. The challenge case managers face when it comes to EOL issues is to help health care professionals, patients, and families recognize that a peaceful, dignified death is a good outcome."[4]

EXAMINING YOUR OWN FEELINGS

Patient advocacy is a core function for case managers. Advocating for patients in life and as death approaches is an ethical responsibility. We, as health care professionals, must examine our own feelings, as well as our willingness to allow patients to die and to represent their interests in a proactive and ethical manner. This entails approaching the issues surrounding death straightforwardly, honestly, and kindly.

First, be honest and straightforward with yourself. Do you fear death? Do you feel that requesting pain medication indicates a weakness? You might be the health care professional who needs to tell parents that their child is nearing death. Can you do that and remain objective and strong enough to advocate for and support the family? Are you willing to object to a physician's reluctance to follow a patient's DNR order?

Case management is a demanding role in the health care field. You will need respite, too. You will need to remove yourself from the center of family discussions to retain your ability to assist them effectively. Remember to be as kind to yourself as you are to your patients.

ADDRESSING THE ISSUE OF DEATH

Death and dying present singular problems. This is true whether a spouse is caring for an ill partner, a parent is at the bedside of a child, or an adult is nursing a parent. Sometimes, the patient has accepted the situation and is comfortable with dying but the family cannot let go. Often, the patient and family do not communicate honestly and frankly, especially when death seems imminent. Such dishonesty is not deliberate; it is caused by reluctance to address the issue. In a grim situation (as when a patient has cancer that is metastasizing and may spread to the brain), the case manager might be the person most able to introduce the subject by asking, "Have you thought about a living will? Perhaps you want to discuss this with your physician or your attorney?"

The case manager can make the patient and family aware of support services; help the patient and family come to grips with the reality of the prognosis; and assist in the completion of an estate will, a living will (Table 17–1), a do-not-resuscitate (DNR) order, or a health care proxy (also known as medical directive, a document that clearly states the patient's wishes regarding life-prolonging measures; see Table 17–2). The case manager can also help arrange for a health care surrogate (a person named by the patient to make health care decisions for him in the event of his incapacitation), cremation, a grave plot, or donation of organs. Information on living wills and health care surrogates is accessible through the media, hospitals, attorneys, health care organizations, and lay publications. Many hospitals distribute information on the health care proxy, DNR order, and living will in a printed piece titled, "Advance Directive Information."

Advance directives enable patients and families to confront issues and make decisions prior to a crisis situation, before the stress of an illness weighs heavily

Table 17–1 Living Will

I, *, residing at *, County of Suffolk and State of New York, do hereby make, publish and declare this is my *Living Will* in manner as follows:

First: I willfully and voluntarily make known my desire that no life-sustaining procedures be used to prolong my dying. If at any time I have a terminal condition certified to be such by two physicians who have personally examined me, one of whom is my attending physician, and the physicians have determined that my condition is irreversible and that my death will occur within a relatively short period of time without the use of life-sustaining procedures which would serve only to prolong the dying process, then in that event, I direct that the procedures be withheld or withdrawn, and that I be permitted to die naturally. These procedures shall specifically include but shall not be limited to mechanical respiration, cardiac resuscitation, blood transfusion, feeding and hydration tubes, or organ transplant. I direct that this advanced directive be liberally construed.

I further direct my physicians to take the same action with the same responsibilities and consequences as set forth above in the event that I should become irreversibly senile. To help my physicians to make such determination, I direct that I be deemed senile if I am unable to communicate my name, the place where I am, or the names of my immediate family members.

In addition, I make the same directions and relieve the same persons from any responsibility in the event that I am afflicted by an incurable, fatal, or debilitating disease, and have been judicially declared incompetent.

Second: This *Living Will* is intended to include but is not limited to such life-sustaining procedures as machines that act as substitutes for organs, blood transfusions, feeding tubes and surgical operations. It does not include such procedures or medication that would make me more comfortable and relieve my physical pain.

Third: In the absence of my ability to give directions regarding the use of life-sustaining procedures, it is my intention that this Declaration be honored by my family and physicians and any health facility in which I may be a patient as the final expression of my legal right to refuse medical or surgical treatment and I accept the consequences from the refusal. In this event, I hereby appoint my wife *, as my irrevocable attorney-in-fact, to communicate to the fullest extent possible all of my directions and intentions declared in this my LIVING WILL, to all necessary persons, including but not limited to my physicians, all other health care providers and all members of my family. This power of attorney shall not be affected by my subsequent disability or incompetence. In addition, I hereby nominate my said designated agent as Conservator of my property and Committee of my person and property upon the happening of any of the events named herein. In the event my wife predeceases me, fails to qualify, or ceases to act as my said agent, then I hereby appoint my *, *, to act in her place and stead.

Table 17–1 continued

Fourth: I hereby relieve physicians, any hospital or other institution and my designated agents of any liability for damage or death resulting therefrom, directly or indirectly, including any claim of malpractice by me or my Estate.

Fifth: I direct that if my physician, or my hospital or other institution refuse to obey my wishes in this matter, that my designated agent herein nominated commence suit against such physician and/or hospital or other institution, for all of the hospital costs, drugs, medical expenses, and all other damages flowing from such refusal, and I direct further that neither their bills for subsequent services be paid nor the bills of any other doctors substituted therefore.

Sixth: This *Living Will* may be revoked only by personal service of a revocation executed by me upon all persons in possession of the original or to whom any certified copy hereof has been delivered, or known to be in possession thereof, and is otherwise irrevocable. I understand that the Court of Appeals has held that my family or designated agent(s) must show that "as far as is humanly possible" I have not had a change of mind, and I intend that any change of mind must be shown as directed in this paragraph only, and without such written revocation, it is my direction that it must be permitted that I have not had a change of mind, no matter how long a time has elapsed between the execution of this document and the enforcement of this Living Will. An affidavit by the attorney in possession of the original with regard to the issuance and location of certified copies hereof shall be deemed sufficient.

Seventh: This document must be executed in the same manner as a Will.

Subscribed, this * day of *, 2 .

_____

Living Testator

We, whose names are hereto subscribed, *Do Certify and Attest* that on the date stated above, the Living Testator subscribed his name to this instrument, in our presence and in the presence of each of us and at the same time in our presence and hearing declared the same to be his *Living Will* and requested us and each of us to sign our names thereto as witnesses to the execution thereof, which we hereby do in the presence of the Living Testator and of each other on the said date, and write opposite our names and respective places of residence. We do further attest and affirm that at the time of the execution of this instrument by said Living Testator, it appeared to us that he was a person of sound mind and memory.

_____ residing at _____

_____ residing at _____

Source: Courtesy of Davidow, Davidow, Seigel & Stern, 2003, Islandia, New York.

Table 17–2 Health Care Proxy

---

(1) I, _____ hereby appoint _____
(name, home address and telephone number) _____
_____ as my health care agent to make any and all health care decisions for me, except to the extent that I state otherwise. This proxy shall take
effect when and if I become unable to make my own health care decisions.

(2) Optional instructions: I direct my agent to make health care decisions in
accord with my wishes and limitations as stated below, or as he or she otherwise knows. (Attach additional pages if necessary.)

This Health Care Proxy contains no limitations. I have discussed with my Agent,
and my Agent knows my wishes concerning artificial nutrition and hydration.
(Unless your agent knows your wishes about artificial nutrition and hydration
[feeding tubes], your agent will not be allowed to make decisions about artificial
nutrition and hydration.)

(3) Name of substitute or fill-in agent if the person I appoint above is unable,
unwilling or unavailable to act as my health care agent. _____

(name, home address and telephone number)

(4) Unless I revoke it, this proxy shall remain in effect indefinitely, or until the
date or conditions stated below. This proxy shall expire (specific dates or
conditions, if desired):

_____
_____
_____

(5) Signature _____
Address _____
Date _____

Statement by Witnesses (must be 18 or older)

I declare that the person who signed this document is personally known to me
and appears to be of sound mind and acting of his or her own free will. He or
she signed (or asked another to sign for him or her) this document in my presence.

Witness 1 _____

Address _____

Witness 2 _____

Address _____

Source: Courtesy of Davidow, Davidow, Seigel & Stern, 2003, Islandia, New York. Prepared by: Lawrence Eric Davidow, Esq.

Table 17–3 The Choice in Dying Patient's Advance Directive Checklist

---

✔ Discuss your wishes regarding end-of-life care with your family, friends and health care providers.

✔ Obtain copies of advance directives (a living will and a medical power of attorney) for your state. These are available through Choice In Dying, your state's department of health and sometimes your local hospital.

✔ Choose a trusted family member or close friend who is willing to accept the responsibility to advocate for you if you cannot speak for yourself. Appoint this person as your agent in your medical power of attorney form.

✔ Complete the living will and medical power of attorney forms following your state's law.

✔ Keep the forms in a safe, yet accessible place. Give copies to your agent, physician, family, and friends.

✔ If you enter a hospital or nursing home, have photocopies of your advance directives placed in your medical chart.

✔ Be sure to talk with your agent, physician, family and friends about your wishes regarding medical treatment. Discuss these wishes often, particularly if your medical condition changes.

Source: Reprinted by permission of Choice in Dying, 200 Varick Street, New York, NY 10014-4810. 212/366-5540.

---

on all concerned, making clear thinking more difficult (see Table 17–3). The case manager can assist families by asking questions about treatments and illnesses. Are there medical procedures the patient does not want to undergo? Are there life-saving measures that the patient deems unnecessary or excessive? She can also answer a patient's questions not fully covered by the provider and serve as a strong advocate should the patient wish to decline continued treatment.

DNR ORDERS

In an emergency, it is assumed that all patients would consent to cardiopulmonary resuscitation (CPR). However, this is not the case for some seriously or terminally ill people or for those who are now healthy but prefer not to have CPR should their heart or breathing stop. Case managers can help make patients aware of the processes included in CPR (mouth-to-mouth resuscitation, external chest compression, electric shock, intubation, injection of medication into the heart, heart massage), when and how it is administered, and its benefits and drawbacks. Appendix 17–A shows a guide for patients and their families that is used in a New York teaching hospital.

The importance of making, documenting, and aggressively communicating end-of-life decisions was illustrated earlier by my own experience as my father neared death. The terms of the PSDA were in effect, but ignored in the facility my father entered. The 1995 Study to Understand Prognosis and Preferences for Outcomes and Risks of Treatment (SUPPORT) study, still one of the most far-ranging surveys conducted among terminally ill patients, showed that fewer than half the physicians whose patients had prepared a DNR order stating they did not want cardiopulmonary resuscitation were aware of the DNR order. Further, a *New England Journal of Medicine* study reported that a third of Medicare payments are for care delivered to patients in their last year of life, and that much of this care was for high-tech, high-cost, unwanted interventions.[5] Clear communications and patient-centered care are lacking for those in the last stages of life. Case managers can help patients prepare explicit advance directives and make certain physicians are aware of patients' directives and their contents.

Some of the national groups that can provide assistance to providers, employers, and individuals facing the complexities of advance directives, funeral planning, helping employees manage their grief, and end-of-life care issues include the American Hospice Foundation, Choice in Dying, Funeral and Memorial Societies of America, Grief Encounters Inc., and the National Hospice Foundation. Addresses and phone numbers for these organizations appear in the book's Appendix A.

Case managers not only face the issue of death, but they also face issues of continued "living." How many drugs, unproved treatments, or severe pain will a patient and family endure? Some patients desire treatment even when there is only a 1% chance of success, whereas others with a 75% chance of remaining alive but facing a different way of life choose to forgo treatment. In these difficult situations, the case manager must provide the objective viewpoint.

It is important to impress on the patient and family that decisions should be made in a timely manner; it is too late when the patient is in and out of a coma and family members start arguing over what to do. It might be appropriate to suggest a family meeting early on, especially if there are several adult children and a dying elderly parent. Families need to be told that patients almost always want to be involved in decision making about their care and their future. The case manager should ensure that the patient knows he or she does not have to consent to all forms of treatment. Everyone should be clear about the arrangements that the patient wants and the family is going to be comfortable with. Perhaps a father says he wants to be cremated and have his ashes spread on the ocean. His youngest son objects because he would prefer his father's ashes to remain at a specific site he can visit over the years after his dad's passing. This is an issue to bring into the open.

PAIN MANAGEMENT

According to John Cloud in his 2000 *Time* magazine article, "A Kinder, Gentler Death," nearly one half of Americans die in pain, surrounded and treated by people they do not know. Dr. Diane Meier, head of the Hertzberg Palliative Care Institute at Mount Sinai Medical Center in Manhattan, and her colleagues conducted a nationwide survey of 1,900 physicians regarding their experiences with end-of-life patients, reported in the July 29, 2003 *Newsday*. They found that one in five doctors had been asked by a terminally ill patient to help hasten death. The reason cited most often was unbearable pain. They also noted that doctors were 2.5 times more likely to medicate a patient in severe pain and 4 times more likely if the patient had less than 1 month to live. (And we wonder, what of the cancer pain when they had 2 months to live?) Further, doctors were significantly less likely to help if there was any evidence of depression. (This begs the question: Only happy terminally ill patients are eligible for pain medication?)

In April 2003, legislation was introduced to recognize pain as a priority health problem in the United States. The National Pain Care Policy Act, H.R. 1863, calls for the development of a National Center for Pain and Palliative Care Research at the National Institutes of Health. If passed, the bill would provide for a White House conference on pain care, education and training programs for health care professionals, and the creation of a national outreach campaign to educate consumers.[6]

HOSPICE CARE

Hospice care centers on caring, not curing. Care is provided in the patient's home, in freestanding hospice centers, hospitals, nursing homes, and other long-term care facilities. Hospice services are available to patients of any age, religion, race, or illness, and is covered under Medicare, Medicaid, most private insurance plans, HMOs, and other managed care organizations. (The National Hospice Foundation survey noted earlier in this chapter revealed that 90% of Americans were unaware that hospice care is a covered Medicare service.)[7]

In her own experience, Anne Llewellyn, RNC, BHSA, CCM, CRRN, CEAC, 2003-2004 president of the CMSA board of directors, and whose parents both received hospice care during their final illnesses, has found that it was not the patients who had difficulty "letting go," but the health care professionals who were treating them. "Physicians many times do not want to 'give up'. This means that patients and their families often are left without adequate time to prepare for death. My mother was afraid of dying, and I asked her physician about hospice because I thought it would help her address her fears. Her physician was not supportive. He said, 'Hospice? Why not a psychiatrist?'"[8]

There remains a fear of hospice care in the population at large. "Hospice" is a name, not a place. It is a service that improves the comfort level of people during their final months of life. Pain is treated, and the quality of life is maintained.

PALLIATIVE CARE

Palliative care extends the principles of hospice care to a broader population that could benefit from receiving this service earlier in their illness or disease process. No specific therapy is excluded from consideration. An individual's needs must be continually assessed, and treatment options should be explored and evaluated in the context of the individual's values and symptoms. Palliative care, ideally, would segue into hospice care as the illness progresses.

One problem in creating a strong palliative/hospice care program is the way hospital discharges occur. Under managed care, hospitals feel more pressured to discharge patients promptly. This becomes more complicated when the patient suffers from a chronic condition that will cause his death. Does any discharge planner really want to release a patient 2 or 3 days before his death? To a nursing home far from family members? To a home hospice program if there is no live-in caregiver at home and the patient is very close to death? No one model for hospice care is workable at all hospitals, which adds to the difficulty of assembling model programs and teams.[9]

The obstacles patients and families face in benefiting from hospice care are mirrored in finding and utilizing palliative care. Patients and families are not comfortable discussing death among themselves and with health care professionals, patients are often too close to death to fully utilize the palliative service, and health care professionals are not fully informed regarding the presence and use of palliative care. Again, education in and the creation of palliative care services will offer another option to patients, families, physicians, and the discharge planners who struggle with finding appropriate EOL settings and facilities for terminally ill patients.

It is estimated that approximately 1,000 hospitals nationwide have palliative care teams. This figure leaves us with plenty of room for growth in this area.

CMSA'S 2002 "DYING IN AMERICA" SURVEY

In a 2002 online survey on end-of-life issues conducted by CMSA, case managers reported that 92% of their patients had their advance directives ignored or delayed more than 50% of the time. Ninety-one percent of their clients suffered as their DNR orders were ignored or delayed more than 50% of the time. Similarly, wishes for hospice care were ignored or delayed 50% of the time for 92% of the patients. Roughly 75% of patients received 30 days or less of the 6 months of hospice care available to the terminally ill, and more than 50% spend 14 days or less in hospice.

When asked to expand on their checked responses, anonymously if they preferred, the 142 respondents revealed their frustration and their clients' pain and confusion during the last months of life. Among the pressing challenges they noted:

- "I work in a long-term care setting with a subacute unit. I frequently see patients admitted from the hospital setting with rehabilitation/therapy orders when it is clear that the patient is actively dying. It then becomes my job to discuss the realistic nature of the patient's condition. We frequently hear from families that the hospital/doctor never told them their loved one is dying."
- "Symptom management in end-of-life care has been dismal at best, particularly for pain."
- "I have had patients/families labor over their decision before asking their physicians to withdraw or not pursue further treatment, only to have their physician imply they were making a bad decision."
- "MDs are not willing to refer to hospice early enough for members to get the benefits of hospice care. They are often admitted just days to two to three weeks prior to death and are actively dying at the time of admissions."
- "Oncologists don't seem able to say the word terminal...patients get sent to aggressive rehabilitation hospital rather than hospice...where they fail and have the additional disappointment of expectations being dashed. I work in the rehab hospital and have witnessed firsthand the poor transmission of 'bad news'."
- "More often I find that the clients are not realistic about their disease and cling to any thread of hope the specialist gives them. There also continues to be a fear surrounding hospice."
- "Individual wishes to not be resuscitated are overridden by family members."
- "I believe American society needs much education in end-of-life issues. I work hard with patients and families to get them to understand what resuscitation *really* means and what we do with end-stage patients *after* we save them. Many patients who end up in the nursing home tell me they wish they had never asked for life support if this is the outcome. I make sure that patients and families know this in their decision-making." [10]

The case managers responding to the CMSA survey reiterate what many of us have found in our personal experience; there is a great need for more complete EOL education for providers, patients, and families, and a gaping discrepancy between a patient's wishes for end-of-life care and his actual treatment. This is a clarion call to all case managers, who are in a powerful position to make a significant impact to improve quality of care, one patient at a time.

"It is an inspiring and rewarding experience to see a person die peacefully," notes Llewellyn. "As a case manager, it is important to be the person who gives the family encouragement and 'permission' to talk to the physician about EOL issues such as stopping treatment or providing more pain medication."[11]

NOTES

1. L. F. Hoffmann, "CMSA Finds American Families and Physicians Need Help Addressing End-of-Life Issues," Case Management Society of America press release, June 7, 2002, Little Rock, AR.

2. Associated Press, "Study Shows Priorities at Death," *Newsday* 61, no 74 (2000): A21.

3. T. A. Mercer, "Do Not Resuscitate Orders," *Advance for Nurses* 4, no. 2 (2002): 7.

4. L. F. Hoffmann, "CMSA Finds American Families and Physicians Need Help Addressing End-of-Life Issues," Case Management Society of America press release, June 7, 2002.

5. J. Ziegler, "How Corporations Cope When Death Intrudes," *Business & Health* 14, no. 11 (1996): 40.

6. Burness Communications, *The Last Acts Policy Newsletter* (Bethesda, MD: 2003)

7. L. F. Hoffmann, "CMSA Finds American Families and Physicians Need Help Addressing End-of-Life Issues," Case Management Society of America press release, June 7, 2002.

8. L. F. Hoffmann, "CMSA Finds American Families and Physicians Need Help Addressing End-of-Life Issues," Case Management Society of America press release, June 7, 2002.

9. T. A. Mercer, "Shining Light on Death," *Advance for Nurses* 4, no. 2 (2002): 25.

10. Case Management Society of America, *Dying in America—Preliminary Survey Report* (Little Rock, AR: 2002).

11. L. F. Hoffmann, "CMSA Finds American Families and Physicians Need Help Addressing End-of-Life Issues," Case Management Society of America press release, June 7, 2002.

Appendix 17–A Deciding about CPR: Do-Not-Resuscitate Orders (DNR): A Guide for Patients and Families

What do CPR and DNR orders mean?

CPR (cardiopulmonary resuscitation) refers to the medical procedures used to restart a patient's heart and breathing when the patient suffers heart failure. CPR may involve simple efforts such as mouth-to-mouth resuscitation and external chest compression. Advanced CPR may involve electric shock, insertion of a tube to open the patient's airway, injection of medication into the heart and, in extreme cases, open-chest heart massage.

A do-not-resuscitate (DNR) order tells medical professionals not to perform CPR. This means that doctors, nurses, and emergency medical personnel will not attempt emergency CPR if the patient's breathing or heartbeat stops.

DNR orders may be written for patients in a hospital or nursing home, or for patients at home. Hospital DNR orders tell the medical staff not to revive the patient if cardiac arrest occurs. If the patient is in a nursing home, a DNR order tells the staff and emergency medical personnel not to perform emergency resuscitation and not to transfer the patient to a hospital for CPR.

Why are DNR orders issued?

CPR, when successful, restores heartbeat and breathing and allows patients to resume their previous lifestyle. The success of CPR depends on the patient's overall medical condition. Age alone does not determine whether CPR will be successful, although illness and frailties that go along with age often make CPR less successful.

When patients are seriously or terminally ill, CPR may not work or may only partially work, leaving the patient brain-damaged or in a worse medical state than before the heart stopped. In these cases, some patients prefer to be cared for without aggressive efforts at resuscitation upon their death.

Can I request a DNR order?

Yes. All adult patients can request a DNR order. If you are sick and unable to tell your doctor that you want a DNR order written, a family member or close friend can decide for you.

Is my right to request or receive other treatment affected by a DNR order?

No. A DNR order is only a decision about CPR and does not relate to any other treatment.

Are DNR orders ethically acceptable?

It is widely recognized by health care professionals, clergy, lawyers, and others that DNR orders are medically and ethically appropriate under certain circumstances. For some patients, CPR offers more burdens than benefits, and may be against the patient's wishes.

Is my consent required for a DNR order?

Your doctor must speak to you before entering a DNR order if you are unable to decide, unless your doctor believes that discussing CPR with you would cause you severe harm. In an emergency, it is assumed that patients would consent to CPR. However, if a doctor decides that CPR will not work, it is not provided.

How can I make my wishes about CPR known?

An adult patient may consent to a DNR order orally by informing a physician, or in writing, such as a living will, if two witnesses are present. In addition, the Health Care Proxy Law allows you to appoint someone you trust to make decisions about CPR and other treatments if you become unable to decide for yourself.

Before deciding about CPR, you should speak with your doctor about your overall health and the benefits and burdens CPR would provide for you. A full and early discussion between you and your doctor will assure that your wishes will be known.

If I request a DNR order, must my doctor honor my wishes?

If you don't want CPR and you request a DNR order, your doctor must follow your wishes or:

- Transfer your care to another doctor who will follow your wishes; or
- Begin a process to settle the dispute if you are in a hospital or nursing home.

If the dispute is not resolved within 72 hours, your doctor must enter the order or transfer you to the care of another doctor.

If I am not able to decide about CPR for myself, who will decide?

First, two doctors must determine that you are unable to decide about CPR. You will be told of this determination and have the right to object. If you become unable to decide about CPR, and you did not tell your doctor or others about your wishes in advance, a DNR order can be written with the consent of someone chosen by you, by a family member or by a close friend. The person highest on the following list will decide about CPR for you:

- The person chosen by you to make health care decisions under New York's Health Care Proxy Law
- A court appointed guardian (if there is one)

- Your closest relative (spouse, child, parent, sibling)
- A close friend

How can I select someone to decide for me?

The Health Care Proxy Law allows adults to select someone they trust to make all health care decisions for them when they are no longer able to do so themselves, including decisions about CPR. You can name someone by filling out a health care proxy form, which you can get from your physician or other health care professionals.

Under what circumstances can a family member or a close friend decide that a DNR order should be written?

A family member or close friend can consent to a DNR order only when you are unable to decide for yourself and you have not appointed someone to decide for you. Your family member or friend can consent to a DNR order when:

- You are terminally ill; or
- You are permanently unconscious; or
- CPR will not work (would be medically futile); or
- CPR would impose an extraordinary burden on you given your medical condition and the expected outcome of CPR.

Anyone deciding for you must base the decision on your wishes, including your religious and moral beliefs, or if your wishes are not known, on your best interests.

What if members of my family disagree?

In a hospital or nursing home, your family can ask that the disagreement be mediated. Your doctor can request mediation if he or she is aware of any disagreement among your family members.

What if I lose the ability to make decisions about CPR and do not have anyone who can decide for me?

A DNR order can be written if two doctors decide that CPR would not work or if a court approves of the DNR order. It would be best if you discussed your wishes about CPR with your doctor in advance.

Who can consent to a DNR order for children?

A DNR order can be entered for a child with consent of the child's parent or guardian. If the child is old enough to understand and decide about CPR, the child's consent is also required for a DNR order.

What happens if I change my mind after a DNR order has been written?

You or anyone who consents to a DNR order for you can remove the order by telling your doctor, nurses, or others of the decision.

What happens to a DNR order if I am transferred from a nursing home to a hospital or vice versa?

The DNR order will continue until a doctor examines you and decides whether the order should remain or be cancelled. If the doctor decides to cancel the DNR order, you or anyone who decided for you will be told and can ask that the DNR order be entered again.

If I am at home with a DNR order, what happens if a family member or friend panics and calls an ambulance to resuscitate me?

If you have a DNR order and family members show it to emergency personnel, they will not try to resuscitate you or take you to a hospital emergency room for CPR.

What happens to my DNR order if I am transferred from a hospital or nursing home to home care?

The order issued for you in a hospital or nursing home will not apply at home. You, your health care agent, or family member must specifically consent to a home DNR order. If you leave a hospital or nursing home without a home DNR order, a DNR order can be issued by a doctor for you at home only with your consent or the consent of someone you appointed as a health care agent.

Source: Courtesy of Winthrop University Hospital, 2003, Mineola, New York.

CHAPTER 18

Industry Directions

Case management strategies are being applied nationwide. In the late 1980s, employers were faced with annual health benefit cost increases of more than 20%. In early 1994, a widely reported survey conducted by benefits consultant A. Foster Higgins & Company showed that for the first time since 1987, health benefit expenses rose less than 10%. Nationwide, per employee costs averaged $3,781 in 1993, up only 8% from 1992. The headline-trumpeted news of 1995 was that health costs paid by employers dropped for the first time in a decade, declining 1.1% among companies with at least 10 workers, according to the Foster Higgins survey. In 1996, Foster Higgins tracked active and retired workers' health care expenses separately for the first time and reported that group health care costs for active employees rose a mere 0.2%. (Group health care costs for active and retired employees were up 2.1% in 1996.) Remaining fairly stable, health care costs for active employees increased 1.4% in 1997, as widely reported from the annual Foster Higgins survey. For employers with fewer than 500 employees, costs fell 2.0%. Group health expenses for active and retired employees were up 2.5% in 1997, a huge discount from the double-digit numbers of 10 years earlier.

Today, with various managed care strategies in place, the double-digit increases are back. Employers are addressing their employees' attitude of entitlement to one of responsibility by sharing some of the risks and costs of health care with these employees and passing along more of the risk to those employees who choose unhealthy lifestyles.

Case managers are right in the center of activity as a force for change and as implementors of effective programs that have become our nation's response to the need for health care reform. Case management does not require legislation to be widely accepted and successful; it requires that competent individuals are out there in the field practicing their profession and communicating their success.

Employers, especially self-funded groups, are expecting more from their insurers and Third Party Administrators. They want to see managed care programs in place and they want to see documented outcomes. All of this is good news for case managers who can seize the opportunities to demonstrate their role and effectiveness. Employers and employees are looking for the benefits that case management offers, and insurers and TPAs will need experienced case managers to meet the demands of their client base. CEOs of small and large companies alike no longer say, "Someone's got to do something about rising health care costs"; they are becoming self-insured, forming buying coalitions, and putting case management to work.

We are also beginning to see highly trained nurses taking roles traditionally played by physicians, such as making diagnoses and referring patients to specialists or admitting them to the hospital. In the past few years, laws have been passed in 26 states allowing nurse practitioners to work without the supervision of a physician. Nurse practitioners are setting up their own offices. This new and, according to reports, fast-growing trend will be one to watch. Encouraged by managed care organizations and the public sector, this emerging new role might lead to an increased awareness and use of case managers and nurse case managers.

The promise and potential for case management continues to grow. There are many excellent case management programs across the country and, in fact, as other countries are experiencing concerns with cost, access, and quality within their own health care systems, they are looking to the United States for some of the solutions that they then will modify for adaptation in their respective health care systems. Because of its demonstrated success, case management is attracting a good bit of interest and there already are a few CMSA affiliate international chapters (called Case Management International [CMI]) whose members have attended and presented at conferences in the United States. Obviously, we will need to better define and communicate our success in order to maintain and grow case management, but the future certainly seems bright.

In an effort to solidify the position of case management in the various health care payer and provider systems, CMSA initiated and developed the Center for Case Management Accountability in 1996. The purpose of CCMA is to provide a mechanism or tool for the measurement, evaluation, and reporting of case management outcomes. It marked the beginning of research toward a format to communicate the true value of case management, its benefits, activities central to its practice, and what should be measured. Each customer, whether a patient, employer/payer, or provider perceives the value of case management differently. The patient may not be concerned with the *appropriate* use of available medical services but rather appreciate the information provided by the case manager. The payer, on the other hand, may be looking at the costs but may also be concerned about the quality of that which is paid for. Providers may expect increased efficiency in the delivery of services when case managers are involved, but may also realize improved outcomes for their patients as well. It is the goal of CCMA to go beyond anecdotal evidence to develop measurement tools and strategies to communicate the success of case management to customers and to improve the process and outcomes of case management.

The first CCMA State of the Science paper, "A Framework for Case Management Accountability," was delivered in September 1997. It included the direct outcomes of case management, initial measurements of accountability, and laid out an approach to study and define the elements of accountability, including appropriateness of care, clinical dimensions, coordination of care, cost savings, functional status of the patient, necessity of care, patient compliance, patient empowerment, payer satisfaction, and more. In May 1999, the second State of the Science paper, "Patient Adherence Outcome Indicators & Measurement in Case Management Healthcare," was published. An in-depth examination of patient adherence issues, this paper brought together information on the impact of nonadherence among different patient populations, in various disease states, cultural factors, patient self-reporting, pharmacy records, physiologic parameters, and so forth.

"Coordination of Care," the CCMA's third State of the Science paper clarified definitions, examined mechanisms used to deliver coordinated care, identified outcomes linked to care coordination, and explored how improved measurement, assessment, and program designs can enhance the safety and quality of health care in case management settings.[1]

As the industry continues to evolve and transition, there has been an increase in the number and kinds of credentials and certifications available. This proliferation of credentials is causing confusion among the various consumers of case management and concern among the professionals. There is even discussion and disagreement as to whether our industry should be called care or case management, as if one were perhaps more noble, better, or legitimate than the other. Unfortunately, this kind of "dissension in the ranks" leaves the "ranks" and gets to be viewed as turf battles by those who are looking very closely at us. Instead of using our time, talent, and resources to more productive ends, this creation of still more "sand boxes" diminishes what strength and voice we might have.

Toward working together more collaboratively and to pursue areas of common understanding and purpose, an invitational Visioneering Meeting cohosted by CMSA and the Academy for Certified Case Managers (ACCM) was held in December 2002. Its purpose was to find the thread that united the various stakeholders in the growth of case management and to address the differences and commonalities in case management. Leaders from all practice settings, the government, associations and organizations, disciplines, certifying bodies in case management, and the press attended. That meeting led to the formation of the Case Management Leadership Coalition (CMLC), a group to give voice to collaborative leadership among the broad spectrum of case management practitioners. Hosted by the Health Insurance Association of America (HIAA), the second meeting was conducted in May 2003, with more to follow; in my mind, this is a very positive sign for all of us dedicated to moving the industry forward.

Although we may have our differences and opinions concerning what each of us perceives as "the best," I think we need to look at what is best for our patients and what will help grow the business of case management, for in the end this is all that matters.

Several concepts that were only in discussion stages a few short years ago now appear to be becoming integral components in the managed care arena. Although not without their detractors, those that are discussed in this chapter seem to have strong potential for success and will certainly expand career opportunities for experienced case managers.

An insightful look at health care trends can be found in Dr. Dick Reece's book from Infinity Publishing, *A Managed Care Memoir: A Physician's Whistle-Stop Journey*, under the heading "Eight New Trends for 2004."

E-HEALTH

Broadly defined, e-Health applies to the use of electronic technologies and telecommunications in the practice of clinical health care, patient and professional health-related education, public health, and health medicine. It includes the fields of telemedicine, teleHealth, medical informatics, electronic patient records, supply chain management, and biotechnologies. It can refer to a telephone call between a case manager and a patient seeking a review of instructions, a rural physician conducting an online search for information on a lesser known disease and its presentations, or nurses across the country who individually access continuing education classes via a laptop.[2] *Business and Health* ran an article on e-Health that included a look at opportunities for Information Therapy (see Table 18–1).

Quickly redefining the way patients receive and access health education materials, e-Health is both a boon and a boggart. Using it, patients can communicate with a specialist hundreds or thousands of miles away; however, patients also apply electronic information to self-prescribe, often with poor results. An indication of the felt need to establish some guidelines for web use in health care is the e-Health Ethics Initiative being created and the existing eHealth Code of Ethics developed by the Internet Healthcare Coalition. Whether you see it as a blessing

Table 18–1 Seven Opportunities for Information Therapy

Information can influence health care decisions and behavior at every point along the continuum from prevention and wellness to chronic disease management and end-of-life care.

1. **Prevention:** Routine information prescriptions can extend the preventive services reach of most medical centers from the limited set of immunizations and screenings they now do to a full array of ongoing support in fitness, nutrition, stress management and safety.

2. **Self-care:** This is what a person does to recognize, prevent, treat and/or manage health problems on his or her own. Information prescriptions, whether self-prescribed or otherwise, help people do these things better.

3. **Self-triage:** Decisions to seek medical care focus on three and sometimes four key points: Should I go? When to go? Where to go? And how to go? Getting the right information to the patient at the time of these decisions can save both lives and dollars.

4. **Visit preparation:** A well-prepared patient gains much greater value within the time-constraints of a brief office visit. Information prescriptions that help the patient prepare for what will happen in the visit will lead directly to better decisions, better outcomes and more satisfied patients. Computerized scheduling systems can make this sort of preparation standard procedure for virtually all medical visits.

5. **Self-management of chronic illnesses:** For many chronic diseases like diabetes, arthritis and hypertension, the key to success is adherence to daily self-management behaviors. Regular information prescriptions both to patients and to caregivers can provide valuable and timely encouragement.

6. **Decision-support:** This is the "Holy Grail" of information therapy. In the near future, no major decision for a drug, surgery or invasive medical test will likely be done without information prescriptions to help the patient participate in the decision.

7. **End-of-life care decision support:** Information prescriptions to both patients and caregivers as a part of end-of-life care have both huge potential and complex challenges. Emotionally-sensitive communication of the right information at the right time can help guide families toward decisions that will best meet their needs through the patient's final days of life.

Source: Excerpted from M. Mettler, "Prescribed Information is Powerful Medicine," *Business & Health,* July 1, 2003, www.businessandhealth.com.

or a curse, it is here to stay. In the United States, 6 million individuals per day go to the Internet for health information; 2.25 million U.S. patients per day consult their physician.[3] Sixty-five percent of web users think online health materials should be more accurate, 22% find the information hard to understand, and four of five want a clear distinction between content and advertising.[4]

DEMAND MANAGEMENT: A SELF-CARE CASE MANAGEMENT MODEL

As technology continues to move all of us forward, some of its innovations trouble us. Demand management has sparked some heated debates in medical/legal circles. Its intent has been to provide much-needed advice and information to individuals who then, with this focused knowledge, can make their own decisions regarding the seriousness of their symptoms, whether to seek treatment, or manage the problem themselves. The term *demand management* is almost more controversial than the process; many worry that the impression created is one of patients who are acting out and need to be controlled. To be sure, part of the reason for its early success is that there is still concern by some, including payers and physicians (who are no longer receiving fees on a per-visit basis), that individuals visit emergency departments and doctors for any health care issue and that a high percentage of these visits are unnecessary. It was the hope or goal of demand management that if patients had the right information, they could solve many of the problems themselves.

There are all kinds of demand management/self-care programs, ranging from a type of precertification line (to manage access to services) to a triage line (to direct the level of service; for example, doctor's office tomorrow morning versus emergency department visit now) through to education, information, and advisory programs that are better versions of this concept. At their core, these programs are meant to empower patients with knowledge, to provide early identification *by the patient* of potential problems, and to help patients understand and seek the most appropriate treatment. For many individuals, the services provide emotional support, guidance, advocacy, and a time when questions can be answered in a less stressful environment (via a private telephone call rather than in a busy doctor's office or hospital room).

Many of these programs have highly sophisticated peer-reviewed databases, clinical algorithms, and medical literature abstracts to assist nurses in determining the nature of the condition, the severity of symptoms, the treatment options, and even appropriate providers and locations. This information is given to the caller who then makes his *own* decision regarding self-care or medical treatment. It is important to note and advise that case managers in these programs should not even approach the very fine line between information and diagnosis. Providing a diagnosis to a patient can be a temptation *and* a very real danger, especially when one is armed with all the data and information that leads one so naturally to a conclusion. The experience and competency of case management staff, as well as having current and medically accepted protocols, are key components in a successful program, as is having the program be "user friendly." Although algorithms and decision trees are certainly helpful, there should *always* be an ability to exercise professional judgment as each case warrants, and all such interventions and calls should be well-documented.

Perhaps the greatest contribution that a demand management/self-care program could have would be a first-level review and screening process for referral to a disease management program. Just as a well-designed and integrated preadmission/concurrent review program can identify the potentially high-cost, complex cases for case management intervention, so, too, can a demand management program present us with the same opportunities.

Earlier identification and intervention affords all of us—payers, providers, case managers, and our patients—with much greater potential for achieving improved outcomes, quality and cost-effective use of services, and a true value-added benefit for recipients of these programs.

24-HOUR COVERAGE

Across the country, model programs have been in place, testing the theories of and providing outcomes data for 24-hour managed care. An integration of workers' compensation, group medical, long-term disability, and short-term disability (and in a few cases, dental), 24-hour coverage has been discussed and tried since the early 1990s. Proponents point to its "seamless care" benefits, its potential to significantly speed return-to-work time frames, and its economic and administrative savings. When one case manager or one provider coordinates an individual's occupational and nonoccupational injuries and care, it can help to end much of the confusion and frustration of employees juggling the precert requirements, limits, and benefits of several different insurance lines. The greatest potential of the 24-hour program is that one mind-set governs the various lines of coverage, eliminating the mentality that says that coverage for this condition belongs to the other guy, not to me.

Detractors cite the legal, administrative, and regulatory hurdles of accomplishing fully integrated programs, as well as a lack of interest. In some regions, enrollment in pilot programs has been light. Some states allow employers to arrange managed care contracts with health care providers for occupational medicine, in effect creating ad hoc 24-hour programs. Overall, the success stories indicate that 24-hour coverage will continue to move from its trend status to become an accepted element in management of health care and costs.

Integration of workers' compensation and group health calls not only for administrative shifts, but also for a shift in mind-set. Occupational health care takes a "sports medicine" protocol, focusing on returning workers to the job as soon as possible to reduce indemnity costs. This is because employers pay more for lost-time costs (usually 60% of the total) than for medical fees in workers' compensation cases. For some job profiles, the indemnity/medical ratio can be as high as 75% indemnity to 25% medical. Some employers have had to educate their large HMO providers about the importance of early return to work. Where group health might recommend more treatments over a longer period of time, workers' compensation physical therapy is typically more aggressive.

Herein lies the rub. Attempting to integrate two such diverse models (workers' compensation is state-mandated and group health is voluntary) puts the differences in the delivery and compensation systems into deep relief. Workers' compensation regulations vary from state to state; an employer with workers in several states is already dealing with numerous variables in care and cost management. Adding medical health insurance to the mix adds plan administrators and lines of coverage, accordingly. Still the possible advantages of 24-hour integration outweigh the disadvantages.

Lost productivity due to injury and illness adds up to as much as 15% of payroll. Hughes Electronics, which integrated its workers' compensation and disability care in 1995, has experienced significant savings in short-term disability costs, and lost time has fallen by 30%.[5] Ameritech Corp. integrated its long-term and short-term disability and workers' compensation processes and administrative systems in 1994. Elimination of duplicated claims has decreased disability insurance costs 10% since 1993. Workers' compensation claims fell 28% in the first year and continue to show an annual decrease of 17%. Overall, the integration has saved Ameritech 1% of its total payroll.[6]

CARVE-OUTS

Looking for cost savings and improved outcomes, employers "carve out" certain elements of their health benefit plans and separately administer and manage them. The services targeted are usually expensive due to the volume of users or to the high cost of treatment. Popular carve-outs include pharmaceutical, behavioral health, and vision programs, as well as cardiac and cancer care. Laboratory work, diagnostic services, radiology, imaging, and orthopedics are other areas under consideration for carve-out status. Beneficial in and of themselves, carve-outs can create administrative and management havoc because of the splintering of care. Companies that have different providers in various states, or a range of benefits programs for employees to select from, add another layer of possible provider overload when they carve out selected services from their benefits plans. Case managers can help by tracking an individual through the care maze.

Case managers can be caught in fallout from carve-outs when their services are bundled with other managed care services. TPAs frequently market case management and managed care services to employers, and then contract one vendor for case management, another for precert, and another for utilization review. The employer group is unaware that its benefits management program is fragmented. The number of players and middlemen can make it difficult for case managers to perform as effectively as they might in a fully integrated program.

On the other hand, case managers can take advantage of carve-out opportunities. Employers are exploring creative solutions, including carve-out absentee management programs, disability management, behavioral health programs, complementary and alternative medicine (CAMs; see also Chapter 2), a return to on-site physicians and nurses, as well as revisiting on-site wellness, pregnancy, rehabilitation therapy, physical therapy, and weight reduction programs. They are considering their workforce population and the illnesses presented and looking for ways to keep their employees at their workstations by modifying job and/or worksites and bringing in cardio-treadmills for workouts or medical personnel to help people read their glucometers.

In the same way, smaller companies are looking at their unique needs and contracting with individual physicians, nurses, case managers, and risk management consultants to screen for problems, offer vision plans, create pharmacy benefit management programs, provide risk-management consulting, and supply continuing patient education.

OUTSOURCING

Similar in theory to carve-outs, outsourcing is a term applied when a company farms out benefit functions, seeking technical and regulatory expertise, improved customer service, or to avoid the cost of an in-house systems upgrade. The most frequently outsourced benefits functions according to a survey of employers include health plan claims administration (91% outsource this function), utilization review (91%), record keeping for defined contribution plans (90%), vision care benefits administration (87%), and investments in defined contribution plans (82%).[7] Outsourcing can add another contact for case managers in their communications with administrative or claims-paying personnel, whereas carve-outs add another provider contact.

LOWERING THE COST OF PRESCRIPTION DRUGS

At the same times that the House and Senate consider extending Medicare's coverage of prescription drugs, Governor Rod R. Blagojevich of Illinois is looking to save tens of millions of dollars by purchasing prescription drugs from Canada. The city of Springfield, Massachusetts, is already buying prescription drugs from

Canada for city employees, and officials in California, Connecticut, Indiana, Michigan, Nebraska, and North Carolina are considering the option, according to a *New York Times* article by Monica Davey. This is a trend to watch.

CASE MANAGERS CREATING NEW ROLES

Employer groups, TPAs, and insurers, as well as townships, school districts, and unions, are seeking new solutions to health care challenges. Beyond broadening their markets, case managers need to consider expanding their range of services. They might do well to offer claims management, disease management, pregnancy management, employee wellness programs, and medical bill audits. Corporations are looking at total health care—disability management (24-hour coverage) as another means of maintaining quality care while better managing costs. Further, there are specialties within case management practice: prenatal, pediatric, elder care, AIDS care, facility-based, and home care case management. The health care field will need case managers who can teach; the cities will need case managers who are bilingual. When brainstorming on ways to broaden the scope of case management in the worlds of business and health care, it is useful to consider the stories of case managers who have made a difference.

Karyl Thorn, BSN, MA, CCM, is CEO of Thorn & Associates, a case management firm serving HIV-infected individuals, their employers, and insurers throughout the United States. Ms. Thorn provides expert testimony and life care planning consultation. HIV and AIDS management has become the primary focus of Thorn & Associates. The company goal statement notes that the organization is dedicated to enabling HIV-positive individuals to take control, become their own case managers, and live the fullest and longest life possible. A nationally recognized leader in the field of HIV/AIDS case management, Ms. Thorn also runs a publishing company, Thorn Publishing, which publishes e-books, books, and workbooks designed for those in HIV and AIDS-related practices.

In early 1994, Kathleen Moreo, RN, Cm, BSN, BPSHSA, CCM, CDMS, CEAC, and Anne Llewellyn, RNC, BHSA, CCM, CRRN, CEAC, recognized a great disparity between the continuous learning needs of case managers and the available continuing education for case managers—whether clinical, financial, or business related. After completing a needs assessment (over steaming cappuccinos in a Washington, D.C. café), they decided to take the chance in creating a case management-centered health care educational company. Today, they own an accredited, national health care educational company known formally as Professional Resources In Management Education, Inc., or PRIME. PRIME has a menu of CME and CE educational services sponsored through various educational grants from third parties, including government, for-profit, and not-for-profit entities.

Michael Demoratz, PhD, LCSW, CCM, is president and CEO of CareMedical Systems, Inc., a developer of software and technology solutions for the medical industry. In addition to his work as an IT consultant, he is a nationally recognized lecturer at case management and disease management conferences, where he speaks on a variety of topics, including computer literacy, death, dying, and bereavement, as well as rehabilitation and recovery. He coauthored and published *Dying 101: A Short Course on Living for the Terminally Ill*, a text designed to give patients a voice by fashioning questions to ensure that their end-of-life needs and wishes are addressed and met. It is now presented as a six-CE online course. In 1998, Demoratz created the CM OneList,™ a case management resource and database (www.cmonelist.com) that brings together those invested in case management. Anyone can post a question and receive feedback and answers. Members receive daily updates culled from newspapers, magazines, and web sites, providing news on ethical issues, legislation, medical study results, pharmaceutical benefits, and topical information of the day. Member organizations post flyers, job descriptions, and conference announcements. The *Case Manager's OneList Forum* is a web-based subscription and can be found at the CM OneList site.

Jan Woods, RN, CDMS, CCM, was senior manager of case management services at The St. Paul Companies, an insurer, when she became part of the team that helped extend the application of case management to include general and medical liability cases. Then she went beyond the traditional concept of case management to create St. Paul's liability case management services program. Using concepts and procedures developed by a team of liability claims and case management personnel, the program focuses on evaluating and controlling the damages tied to liability claims. The program proved its efficacy, as utilization of case managers in liability cases almost tripled in 3 years. Woods moved on to become a claim quality consultant on St. Paul's Claim Quality Implementation Team, part of a group responsible for designing and implementing structural and procedural changes that reconfigured the company's entire claims organization.

Linda Greis, RN, BSN, CCM, built a case management service program as part of a larger business organization. As past director of medical case management, she helped develop the Utilization Management Program of the Atlanta Healthcare Alliance, a nonprofit health care coalition of employers, insurers, and providers dedicated to developing and implementing cost-containment strategies. Greis then was named public affairs manager at Visiting Nurse Health System, a nonprofit home health agency providing a full array of home care services and products. Her role was to establish a public affairs initiative to win attention for case management and home health issues, to educate legislators, and to increase awareness of Visiting Nurse Health System, which raised charitable dollars for indigent care in addition to serving its insurer-based clients. Greis was also an adjunct professor at Emory University Graduate School of Nursing, where she helped design a graduate-level case management course.

The days of the pure case management company are gone. To be strategically positioned as professionals, case managers will have to provide a range of services, from analysis of a company's potential problematic cases to case management itself to the documentation of outcomes. I believe case managers at this moment have the opportunity to build the industry, to make it an indispensable part of the U.S. health care delivery system, and to make case management a household term. Challenging times? You bet, but my guess would be that if you have been working as a case management professional already or are just considering a career in case management, you are up to the challenge.

NOTES

1. S. Aliotta, "Coordination of Care," *The Case Manager* 14 no. 2 (2003): 49.

2. Excerpted from "About eHealth International," *eHealth International*, © July 2003.

3. C. Mullahy, "What's Next for Case Management: Ten Trends," session presented at Medical Case Management Conference XV, September 2003.

4. Excerpted from "DataWatch: Weak Links in Health Info," *Business and Health eNews*, www.businessandhealth.com, © September 2003.

5. H. Knight, "24-Hour Care Today," *The Case Manager* 8, no. 1 (1997): 39–42.

6. J. Gemignani, "Still Time for 24-Hour Coverage" *Business & Health* 15, no. 10 (1997): 45.

7. R. Kazel, "Despite Difficulty, Benefits Unification Coming," *Business Insurance* 31, no. 16 (1997): 37.

PART V

Case Management in Action: Cases in Profile

CHAPTER 19

Care at Home

In most cases, home care not only benefits the patient and family, but also is less costly, which is reflected in the recent rapid growth of the home care industry. Over the past several years, there has been increasing recognition of the expense of treatment in the acute care setting. Cost hikes for inpatient and outpatient hospital care were 12% in 2001, accounting for 51% of the overall increase in health care spending, according to the Center for Studying Health System Change (www.hschange.org). Consequently, hospitals, employers, and insurance companies have made serious efforts at cost containment while finding ways to provide patients with the services they need in medically sound alternative settings. For the very ill, appropriate settings include rehabilitation centers with specialized programs and skilled nursing facilities. Although the latter are usually looked on, especially by consumers, as residences for the very old, providing long-term custodial care but no real hope of recovery or improvement, recently they have begun to be perceived as appropriate centers for younger ill patients who need a higher level of care for a finite period of time.

Another alternative treatment location is the patient's home. There is strong evidence that recovery tends to occur more quickly and be more comprehensive when the patient is at home. Also, the patient's quality of life usually improves. Being able to participate in decisions about care imparts to the patient a sense of independence and well-being. Specific treatments and medication needs can be integrated into the family's schedule, minimizing disruption to routines and alleviating the patient's feeling of being a burden. An additional benefit of recuperating at home is the decreased risk of contracting a nosocomial illness (an illness from a hospital-borne infection).

The shift from hospital to home care became possible through advances in technology. Home care has become practical as more and more operations and treatments previously offered only in hospitals were provided on an outpatient basis. Dialysis, intravenous antibiotic therapy, blood transfusions, chemotherapy, HIV-related services, preterm labor infusion therapy, continuous positive airway pressure devices, and ventilator and pain management programs can all be safely administered in the home setting. The National Home Infusion Therapy Association estimates annual revenues for home infusion therapy to be $4.5 billion.

Although technology transfers very well from the hospital to the home, the patient's condition must be relatively stable prior to the switch to home-based care. A patient who is in an acute level ICU or is experiencing one crisis after another is not a candidate for home care. After the patient is transferred from the intensive care unit to a floor, home care may become an option, even if sophisticated equipment and services are required. However, there are some situations in which home care may end up costing as much as hospital care or even more, especially when 24-hour-a-day nursing care and very high-tech services are needed. In such situations, the benefits, expenses, and potential liability of home care must be very carefully weighed.

Home care is particularly appropriate in certain types of cases. Long-term, chronically ill patients—those with chronic neurological problems, such as MS or amyotrophic lateral sclerosis, and those recovering from a complex traumatic brain injury who may still need skilled nursing care while facing a prolonged recuperation—do very well in a home setting. Cancer patients who face the prospect of periodic readmission to the hospital are also home care candidates. Patients undergoing immune system-destroying chemotherapy and AIDS patients with compromised immune systems are highly susceptible to nosocomial infections and may benefit greatly by being transferred to a home setting. Those affected by hemophilia or genetic emphysema can receive replacement therapies at home. Younger children, regardless of the diagnosis, improve well at home, away from the high-tech, impersonal, and often overwhelming atmosphere of a hospital. Even in the case of very ill children, a home setting is preferable, all things being equal, because it supports the nurturing process and the continuing "childhood" of the child.

For these reasons, a movement evolved to keep each patient in the hospital only as long as a coordinated medical team approach is required and then to explore all avenues of removing the patient from the hospital while still providing the quality and comprehensive services needed. Cited as potentially less expensive, home care was tested and proved to be effective for most, but by no means all, recuperating patients. Even so, what started as a cost-containment measure took on new dimensions—home care was felt to be a healthier and more humane alternative for the critically and terminally ill. According to the National Association for Home Care (NAHC), the home health care market grew at an annual rate of 10% from 1987 to 1991, when payers spent $17.1 billion on home care. A $22 billion industry in 1997, home care grew 3% from 1999 to 2000, and revenues reached \$41.3 billion in 2001, as noted by the NAHC (at www.nahc.org). One of the fastest growing segments of the health care industry, home care services were delivered to some 7 million people by more than 17,000 providers in 1994, and to 7.6 million people by more than 22,000 providers in 2001.

CONSUMER DEMAND—AND AMBIVALENCE

At the same time that hospitals and insurance companies are demonstrating increased interest in home health care, consumers, often for different reasons, are demanding it more frequently. When an individual is hospitalized, it can be a very disruptive experience for the entire family. First, many patients and families feel intimidated by the hospital setting. Second, practical concerns, such as scheduling hospital visits or conferences with physicians, taking time off from work, and hiring babysitters, add tension to the worry experienced by the family members. Scheduling difficulties may be especially acute for two-income families with limited time and energy or in situations in which the patient is in a specialized facility distant from the home. Consequently, consumers have welcomed care alternatives, especially home care, which for many is the most attractive option.

There is, however, also some uneasiness among consumers about home care. All patients may not welcome it. The hospital environment provides a sense of security. The patient and family alike may well be heartened as recovery progresses and may look forward to the patient's return home, but there is also concern and fear, especially when a life-threatening problem—a stroke or heart attack, for example—is involved. "How am I going to cope? What happens if there is a problem? I can't push a buzzer and have nurses come running. Can I trust this person hired to give me injections?" Facing the loss of their safety net, patients and their families need to be convinced of the benefits and safety of home care through education and the correction of misconceptions.

Many patients still think of home care simply as consisting of periodic visits by a nurse or other health care provider. They do not perceive it as an ongoing process, a support system that can improve and speed their recovery. In considering and responding to patient reactions, it is important for case managers to remember that patients may receive mixed signals from their families and the medical community. The hospital staff may feel the patient requires a lengthier stay, the spouse may be dreading the responsibility of providing needed care "alone," and the physician might be concerned that he or she will not be kept appropriately informed of the patient's status.

Such fears and concerns are valid and must be recognized and addressed. Many patients, especially older ones, are absolutely bound to this thought: "If I'm sick, I will see the doctor and receive care in the hospital." They worry about the consequences if the doctor is not immediately available. Younger patients, after seeing nurse practitioners and nurse clinicians working with physicians as colleagues, are more willing to consider alternatives. Case managers can play a pivotal role in loosening the hold of long-held beliefs and stereotypes and explaining the benefits of home care.

THE CASE MANAGER AS A PIVOTAL LINK

A case manager must approach each case considered for home care very thoroughly and provide the link between the physician, the discharge plan, the patient, the family, at-home service providers, and the payer. The case manager's concerns lie where medical, nursing, and benefit payment issues dovetail.

First, a home discharge must be safe. Although the primary care physician, in cooperation with any other consulting physicians, has responsibility for discharging a patient, all those involved in the patient's treatment plan, including the nursing staff, the case manager, and home care company employees, share in the responsibility and liability for providing appropriate care. The physician writes the discharge orders stating what medications, services, and ongoing care are required. The nursing staff interprets those orders and their implications and develops a detailed discharge plan. The case manager then takes an active role in determining how the elements of the discharge plan can be best implemented. Is a visiting nurse needed twice a week or daily? Should a physical therapist or a respiratory therapist be requested? What equipment is required? What drugs must be administered and by whom? Using her knowledge of the clinical data included in the discharge orders and plan, the patient's status, area home health care providers, durable medical equipment suppliers, and other community resources, the case manager devises a home care plan that meets all stipulations of the discharge plan.

Often this calls for discretion and creativity. Most benefit policies and discharge plans automatically mention RNs as the most appropriate care support, even when other services from within the home care spectrum might provide more effective help. A home health aide, homemaker, or personal care assistant might tend to the patient's needs very well. Some case managers, for example, have revised plans to incorporate babysitting to tend to an older child and allow an expectant mother with a high-risk pregnancy to get off her feet and get the rest needed to carry the baby full term. For a small amount of dollars, a homemaker can do laundry, go grocery shopping, and prepare meals, enabling a patient to return home rather than remain in the hospital at a daily rate upward of $1,500 minimum. Instead of assuming that a benefits plan or a discharge plan is etched in stone, case managers need to argue for solutions not covered by the plan language to create a better answer. By working the system and then articulating the results in dollars and cents, case managers help promote progressive care and optimum outcomes.

Case managers also need to be able to distinguish cases in which home care is not the best option. Even if a patient is diagnostically suited for home care and medically stable, the family situation or home layout may preclude home care. Case managers need to be acutely aware of the vulnerability of families as they bring patients home. This is especially true when professional assistance is available only part-time. When the patient was in the hospital, the family could come to see the patient, perhaps endure a draining visit, but then leave and recharge. Now, the patient is home and the family must provide physical and emotional support. Suppose the presence of a home health aide for only a 2-, 3-, or 8-hour shift can be justified given the language of the policy, which means the family bears the bulk of the responsibility. When evaluating a patient for home care, the case manager should assess the ability of the family to absorb additional stress.

Another consideration is the geographic setting of the home to which the patient will be discharged. Is it a rural area, suburban neighborhood, or inner-city area? Each type of location has different levels of access to support and emergency services. Reviewing the setting is especially important for patients needing high-tech equipment and services. What are the rescue squad capabilities? What is the response time to a 911 call? Are emergency vehicles capable of reaching the home in 3 minutes or 45 minutes? If a power failure occurs, can the local electric utility provide backup generator support for an individual at home on a ventilator?

A personal visit to the home illuminates conditions that may affect the safety of the discharge. The family may have failed to mention that the home is an apartment five flights up with no elevator and is so small that there is no room for oxygen equipment. How many individuals live in the home; will the patient have any privacy? Are there cultural issues to consider? In a Muslim home, a male nurse or IV technician might be very unwelcome if the patient is female.

A visit also allows a case manager to pick up on the emotional state of the family member who will be the primary caregiver. Is he or she verbally expressing a willingness to care for the patient but also exhibiting fear, hesitation, or reluctance? In an underinsured or poor family, the person providing support might be facing social and financial issues that are more complex than the medical care plan. If the case manager is unable to see the patient and family at home due to her contracted role in a particular case, she should delegate someone on-site to be her eyes and ears and provide her with a mini-home assessment. The home care RN might be a candidate for this.

A case manager must approach each situation individually, evaluating the patient's condition and ongoing needs in consultation with the physician, the family, the family member who will be the main care provider, the availability of respite for the care provider, the range of community services, and so on. Home care may not be the best choice; it may be feasible but require ongoing support. Sometimes, a case manager can be put under pressure to move patients from the hospital into a home setting in order to reduce expenditures and establish credibility. It is important to remember that each case is unique and must be evaluated in light of the particular conditions that exist.

CASES IN PROFILE

Home Care Is Not Always the Answer

As discussed, some medically stable patients may not be candidates for home care because of the family situation. The following case history illustrates this, as well as the problems of paying for needed services that don't appear in the benefit plan, and shows the crucial role a case manager can play in achieving an optimal outcome.

Janet Carr, a 59-year-old mail sorter for a self-funded employer group (an insurance company), was contacted by her employer's disability review program after she had been absent from work for 7 days without submitting a medical report. She explained she had been suffering from severe abdominal pain but had not wanted to "bother" her physician. The following day, the company nurse received a call from a precertification utilization review nurse notifying the disability review program that Mrs. Carr had been admitted to a hospital on an emergency basis for a ruptured bowel and acute peritonitis. Extremely ill, she required emergency surgery, which had high risk due to infection and dehydration. Because she was expected to be in the hospital at least 10 days and because a physician report cited longstanding emotional and psychiatric problems suffered by the patient and possibly her husband, the employer decided to refer Mrs. Carr for case management intervention.

In an initial brief visit with Mrs. Carr several days after her ileostomy and colostomy, the RN case manager noted her debilitated, critical condition and guarded prognosis. In a subsequent visit with Mr. Carr, she noted that he seemed developmentally impaired and, although able to answer certain questions, was tearful and fearful when talking about his wife, who "takes care of us." Seeking further information, the case manager met with Mrs. Carr's primary nurse and surgeon regarding the Carrs' ability to comprehend the extent of Mrs. Carr's illness. The case manager was also able to contact Mrs. Carr's sister, who confirmed that both Mr. and Mrs. Carr suffered from longstanding comprehension problems as well as emotional and psychiatric problems.

During Mrs. Carr's recovery in the hospital, it became clear that Mr. Carr not only did not understand what type of surgery his wife had undergone or the care she would need, but also was unable to perform everyday household chores, such as bill paying and laundry, without his wife's help. He told the case manager that they had no washer or dryer, did not use a laundromat, and that he had left the laundry "soaking in the bathtub so she can take care of it when she comes home." Prior to Mrs. Carr's illness, the couple had been able to manage without assistance from outside agencies. It was apparent that this would no longer be true. Mrs. Carr was unable, physically or mentally, to learn anything about ostomy care. Mr. Carr was insistent that his wife return home immediately but "with no outsiders."

Mrs. Carr became medically stable, and her treating physicians felt that continued hospitalization increased her risk for further infection. The consensus among her medical providers was that she would require continuing medical supervision regarding infection control, nutritional status, electrolyte imbalance, and depression for a prolonged period of time. The Carrs had no family physician. Given Mrs. Carr's need for medication administration, ostomy care, dressing changes, and monitoring, and Mr. Carr's inability to provide any support, she was a candidate for around-the-clock nursing care.

The case manager here was faced with several challenges. The first was Mr. Carr. After being shown his wife's incisions and ostomies and given a brief explanation of the care she needed, he became willing to consider assistance from outside professionals, although his ability to cooperate was minimal. The next difficulty was Mrs. Carr's medical coverage. She had an indemnity plan funded and administered by her employer, an insurance company, that provided for up to 365 days of hospitalization if required, for skilled nursing care in the home if certain criteria were met, for durable medical equipment and supplies, and for 30 days in a rehabilitation facility. There was no coverage for care in a nursing home or for home health aide or homemaker services. After reviewing discharge needs, alternative services, the family situation, the insurance coverage, and available community resources, the case manager proposed the following options to the benefits administrator:

1. Continued hospitalization, which could be justified because of the need for ongoing care, at a minimum cost of $1,500 a day.
2. Twenty-four-hour-a-day skilled nursing care at home at a negotiated cost of approximately $1,080 a day. This option lacked homemaker and housekeeping services assistance the couple needed. In addition, Mr. Carr strongly resisted this option.
3. A skilled nursing facility. This option would require demonstration of cost benefits and approval from the benefits administrator. Negotiated cost was $300 per day.

Following previous successful experiences with case management services, the employer group had instituted a large case management program that allowed modifications to the basic coverage, limiting exceptions to situations suitable for case management intervention and supported by medical and cost justification documentation. Through this program, the case manager received approval to accompany Mr. Carr to three skilled nursing facilities near the couple's home. Mrs. Carr was admitted to a facility within short walking distance, at an all-inclusive cost per day of $300. For a small additional charge, Mr. Carr was able to join Mrs. Carr for lunch and dinner. The insurance company covered the facility's fees under the large case management provision of its policy in lieu of acute hospitalization. Coordinating with the hospital physicians, the case manager arranged to have Mrs. Carr's medical care provided by the surgeon and then by an internist, who would be the couple's primary physician. Next, the case manager assisted in arranging for disability payments from the employer to the couple, contacted the couple's landlord and utility companies and apprised them of the situation, and helped Mr. Carr record and mail the necessary payments.

Mrs. Carr remained in the skilled nursing facility for 2 months, returned to the hospital for reversal of the ostomies, and recuperated at the skilled nursing facility for 2 weeks. She then went home, stronger and healthier and able to care for herself and her husband. This scenario provided the patient with the best care—in this case, not in the home but in an alternative care center—and also resulted in substantial cost savings for the payer. Continuous hospitalization for two months and two weeks would have cost $105,000; 24-hour-a-day nursing care for the same period would have cost $75,600 (at a negotiated $45 an hour; the nonnegotiated fee for this time period would have been $92,400 at the least). Care in the skilled nursing facility cost $21,000 and case management services cost $6,500 over a 7-month period. The savings were substantial, the actual amount being $84,000 less than hospitalization would have cost and $54,600 less than home nursing care would have cost. Unaccounted for are the savings resulting from prevention of complications likely to have occurred if the case manager had not intervened on behalf of the patient and her spouse.

A Home Care Case That Succeeded

James was born 6 weeks prematurely following a maternal infection and premature labor. He developed respiratory distress and was ventilator dependent for several months. After two abdominal surgeries for treatment of an intestinal obstruction and placement of a gastrostomy tube, his condition gradually stabilized, and his parents were given instruction in home care.

Discharged from the hospital at 5 months, James came home with respiratory equipment and medical supplies, including an apnea monitor, oxygen, an oxymeter, suction machines, an ambu bag, and feeding and additional supplies. His home care program incorporated 4 hours per day of RN care.

Shortly after James returned home, the family called our case manager with a request for additional nursing hours. New to the case, the case manager conducted an initial home assessment and found the parents completely overwhelmed by the emotional and physical demands of caring for 6-month-old James, dependent on multiple pieces of sensitive medical equipment, as well as his two siblings, active 2- and 4-year-old preschoolers. The parents were attempting to maintain home care and keeping in contact by telephone with their primary physician, who was 75 miles away at the university hospital. They transported James those same 75 miles in heavy traffic to their hospital's emergency room (rather than their community hospital), even during episodes of respiratory distress. Although the parents were pleased with the quality of nursing care provided by an agency, they were dissatisfied with the service and equipment supplied by their home medical equipment dealer. The case manager determined that the care plan was putting James at risk for a respiratory crisis and rehospitalization.

Consulting with all concerned, she presented a number of recommendations. To avoid rehospitalization and to more properly attend the child at home, RN hours were increased to 16 hours per day. The home medical equipment contract was awarded to a dealer whose personnel were particularly adept at working closely with families and health care professionals. James's oxygen supply system was switched from indoor to outdoor tanks to remove his siblings' temptation to tamper—a potential hazard.

After talking with the family, with the primary treating physician, and with a local hospital, it was agreed that James would be brought to this nearby facility in an emergency, cutting 60 miles off the one-way commute. The case manager negotiated lower fees with the home medical equipment dealer and the nursing agency, and direct payment arrangements were made with the insurance carrier, avoiding co-payment terms for the family and resulting in a significant cost savings to both the carrier and the family.

Because there were limited health care dollars available for James over his lifetime for home nursing care and other services, the case manager referred the family to the Medicaid model waiver program. Participation in this community-based alternative to hospice or institutional care spread expenses between the family, the insurance carrier, and Medicaid. Funded by federal, state, and county sources, the waiver program for chronically ill children extended James's coverage over his lifetime and provided the family with access to other public funding programs.

Timely intervention by the case manager resulted in the stabilization of James's condition and shortened hospital stays (when they were necessary due to distress or infection). A reinforced emphasis on parent education and increased nursing and supportive services reduced the overall number of hospital admissions, and the use of a more accessible hospital helped prevent a catastrophic event such as respiratory arrest. Further, the case manager, who was on-site for regular assessments, was able to intervene in several crises and provide prompt care in situations in which the parents tended to delay medical attention.

Without case management, it is likely that James would have floundered in the medical system and experienced numerous and lengthy hospitalizations at great cost to the family and carrier. His frequent trips to a distant emergency room might well have resulted in respiratory arrest, potential brain damage, and ventilator dependency. Early intervention; referral to physical, speech, feeding, and educational therapies; and enrollment in the Medicaid model waiver program helped prevent developmental delay and mental retardation, optimizing the boy's chances of realizing his full potential. The care-at-home program has prolonged the life of the claims dollars available for James, and prompt case management is now saving his family, the insurer, and Medicaid upwards of $175,000 annually.

ONGOING SUPPORT AT HOME

When a patient is released to home care, the patient and family need ongoing support, and that requires free and frequent communication between all parties involved. After the various elements of home care are successfully established—the necessary medical equipment delivered and set up, the nursing hours arranged, the supplies ordered—regular monitoring and follow-up are essential. The case manager must be alert to the changing needs of the patient, the quality of the care provider service, and signs of family caregiver burnout. Perhaps a family member is providing the primary care with a weekly visit from a nurse to check a catheter. After a few weeks or months, the caregiver will need a respite. A case manager has a responsibility to see that the payer (employer group or insurance company) is convinced of the need, that extra help is temporarily provided, and that the primary caregiver is not punished for being willing and able to care for the patient. The problem of caregiver burnout and need for relief is often most acute in situations in which the parents are primary caregivers for a seriously ill child and are also trying to do the grocery shopping, get their other children to the dentist or to soccer practice, and continue working at their own jobs.

The case manager needs to be aware that the primary caregiver not only must be willing to provide care for the patient, but also must have the physical stamina as well—to get the patient in and out of bed or a wheelchair, for example. Does the caregiver have a chronic back problem or predisposition to back problems? A heart condition? Sometimes, the case manager may need to bring in additional support services so the caregiver is not overburdened. Perhaps a wife has agreed to be the primary caregiver for her husband but has a back condition and requires additional support equipment if she is to be able to care for him. It may be difficult to convince the payer, particularly if the husband and wife are on the same insurance policy, that the extra support is requisite. What has to be made clear to the payer in situations like this is that if the extra support is not provided, the caregiver may be the next casualty, and the payer will have a second claim to reimburse.

IMPORTANCE OF FEEDBACK AND COMMUNICATION

In her combined role as coordinator, troubleshooter, and problem solver, the case manager should actively pursue and receive feedback from all sources—the health care providers, the durable medical equipment suppliers, the patient (if possible), the family member providing the majority of care, and other family members. Specific parameters for communication must be set up: what to communicate, by whom, to whom, and how often. The case manager may request that the nursing service call in weekly reports or submit copies of weekly nursing notes. This regular feedback allows the case manager to follow the patient's condition and evaluate the need for services. It is unfortunate when a case manager learns from a payer that a patient discharged to home care 2 months earlier has been back in the hospital for a week because of a deterioration in his or her condition or the failure of the home care setup to function as planned. The case manager must make sure that she is contacted immediately if a change occurs—if the patient's condition worsens, the caregiver service switches personnel or hours, or any family arrangement that can affect the patient is altered. This is not to say that if a sudden emergency or need arises, the home health care provider or family caregiver should not react and do what is called for. If, for example, increased services are required on a weekend and the case manager cannot be reached, the services should be provided. The case manager should then be informed as soon as possible, at which point she can help decide how the patient's differing status can best be accommodated on a long-term basis—in a cost-effective manner appropriate for the patient, the family, and the payer.

What sometimes happens is that, after a discharge plan is devised and home services arranged for, the case manager may be told by the payer (especially if it has an in-house case management service) or the health care provider service, "We'll track patient progress now and contact you if a problem arises." If the case manager feels that her continuing on-site objective assessments are important, she must communicate that message. When turning a case over to a payer's in-house case management service, the case manager should relay all pertinent case information and acknowledge the ability of the payer's case manager to take on the case, but also make it clear that she is available for interim on-site assessments as needed. If a claims examiner decides to continue tracking a case, the case manager should make certain he or she understands the case manager's role in keeping services in place at the appropriate level. She should also suggest that the claims examiner call her if certain complications arise and leave a list of red flags for his or her reference. When a home care provider case management service offers to take over management of a case, the case manager must be diplomatic. Especially in determining the need to increase or decrease home care services, the case manager is likely to be more objective than the home care service provider. She might review her thoughts on the patient's needs with the home care service and make it clear that she is available for on-site assessments as needed should the patient's status change.

Decisions should not be made arbitrarily by one of the parties. A home health care service may not be the most objective judge of when a change in services is needed. Physicians might not be aware of all the details of the home care arrangement. Ideally, the case manager should be the one to adjust the level of services and then discuss all the ramifications of any changes with the provider services and the payer. For example, the health care service that is providing 8-hour-per-day nursing service at home should not arbitrarily increase the hours to 16 or 24 hours per day. The nursing service can report to the case manager that the patient's condition has worsened and an increase in hours is probably needed, the family caregiver may request additional help, or the physician in charge of the patient may deem more extensive services or medical equipment necessary. In all cases, the case manager should be the pivotal person involved in making the decision and then implementing it.

Follow-up on the use of durable medical equipment is also necessary. Only then will the case manager know whether equipment is actually being used and whether the patient or caregiver is satisfied with it and comfortable using it. There are cases in which equipment remains in the home unused yet is paid for month after month. Perhaps the equipment was part of a standard discharge package, the family caregiver never learned how to use it, the equipment broke, or it was used for a while but is no longer needed. In obtaining information about the use of durable medical equipment, the case manager should speak not only with the health provider, but also with the patients and family members.

The case manager must make it clear to the family that if there is a problem with equipment, if they are not satisfied with the health care provider, or if they are overwhelmed, they should call the case manager. A patient or family may be dissatisfied with the health care provider or with the durable medical equipment but be hesitant to complain simply because they do not know what to expect, feel unable to be assertive, or fear that the patient may not continue to get the best service if they mention a problem. It must be remembered that there may be certain things a health care provider would be reluctant to tell a case manager—that three shifts of care providers failed to show up for work one weekend, for instance. Families need to know that there is someone to turn to if a problem arises.

Although follow-up is often conducted over the phone, there are definite benefits to making personal visits. A visit to the home allows a case manager to pick up on emotional states and to see if there is equipment sitting unused in a corner. Are there signs that the patient is being well cared for by the professional health care service and by the family caregiver? Is the patient progressing? If not, why not?

The case manager should be more than an observer. She should be a catalyst for patient progress. This means giving feedback to all parties—not only recording it, but also troubleshooting and devising answers.

As the pivotal person involved in decisions about needed changes in service and their implementation, the case manager must see that everyone is in the loop—the physician, the home care provider, the therapists, the home medical equipment supplier, the patient (if possible), the primary family caregiver, other family members—and must maintain open communication channels between all involved to ensure that the patient, family, and payer are well served. Only with communication and feedback will come the support that is needed if home care is to be a successful care alternative.

PAYMENT CONCERNS

As stated at the beginning of this chapter, the original impetus for the growth of home care was cost containment. And, in most cases, home care is less expensive than hospital care. However, cost savings are not automatic. Expenses must be calculated, managed, and negotiated intensively.

First, the case manager must determine if and to what extent a benefit plan will allow home care. Today, a provision for home care is included in most benefit plans, but there may be specific limitations. Employers often fear that if too generous a home care benefit is in place, it will be abused and some employees will utilize unneeded home care on a regular basis. Therefore, plans include strict restrictions on home care benefits and tough plan language to eliminate the potential for abuse.

Over the last several years, studies have revealed an increased interest in benefit plan design and have demonstrated that a plan's structure can affect the experience of the employer. An employer or benefit manager can, for example, make the plan language so constrictive that individuals are forced to remain in a hospital or other high-cost facility for longer than is necessary if they are to be eligible for any benefits. Or, plan language can be flexible enough to allow an umbrella of coverage, with limits designed to prevent abuse.

For example, a plan may provide up to one million dollars in benefits per year but, although covering hospital care up to the limit, may allow only 52 four-hour home nursing visits per year. A patient requiring 24-hour care is out of luck. Someone who no longer needs acute care in a hospital but is facing a prolonged recuperation period (for example, 6 months) is going to need two to three visits by a nurse per week and numerous other support services. However, if the plan prohibits that option, the case manager may be forced to utilize the other option—in this case, keeping the patient in the high-cost hospital setting.

Or, perhaps the plan covers skilled nursing services at home but excludes home health aides or homemaker services. What happens if a patient needs a skilled nurse visit only once per week but cannot manage without the support of a home health aide or homemaker services a few hours each day? Is the patient to stay in the more costly and less desirable hospital setting because the plan will not allow needed ancillary services?

Unfortunately, situations like these arise frequently, and case managers are faced with trying to persuade and negotiate with the payers to allow the other services "out of contract"—to make exceptions to the plan language that will meet the needs of patients and at the same time reduce costs. In this type of situation, a case manager should not feel intimidated but should argue the point with the plan administrators and explain that by allowing a full spectrum of services to be provided at home, they will enhance the outcome for the patient and also save money. By presenting concrete examples of improved care and verifiable savings, ideally including an example involving the employer's own plan, the case manager can strengthen her argument.

Sometimes, semantics lies at the crux of an employer's reluctance to permit exceptions. In allowing alternative arrangements, employers and benefit administrators often talk of "out-of-contract" benefits or "contract exceptions"—that is, benefits they are not required to provide. Employers need to learn—and case managers should be prepared to do the informing—that alternative arrangements should be viewed as something done to prevent greater contract exposure. The case manager needs to present the situation clearly, demonstrating that "if you do not allow for and pay for this, then your option is this—which is more costly and may not be the most beneficial step to take." A detailed cost-benefit analysis can be the case manager's most potent tool in presenting the figures.

In addition to investigating and pursuing all of the benefits obtainable through the patient's health plan, the case manager should utilize other resources for providing at-home services to help the patient and payer defray costs. There may be local, county, or state agencies and disease-specific organizations, foundations, or philanthropic groups that can provide services or guidance. The United Way, Meals on Wheels, and "I Can Cope" programs and loaner wheelchairs from the American Cancer Society are examples of available assistance. Food & Friends in Washington, D.C., provides three free meals a day to clients suffering from AIDS, cancer, Alzheimer's, and many other debilitating diseases. Easter Seals offers support services on a sliding scale for children and adults with crippling diseases. For help in seeking financing for home care, case managers can contact hospital social workers and discharge planners, city and county health departments, Social Security and public aid offices, community referral agencies such as United Way, senior citizen centers, local councils on aging, the Department for Aging, and the other social agencies listed in the Yellow Pages and community service directories (available at local libraries). In addition, Gale Research annually publishes the *Encyclopedia of Associations,* a comprehensive source of detailed information on over 135,000 nonprofit membership organizations worldwide, and a resource guide including those established to support individuals with certain diseases or injuries. (This guide is available at local libraries and online.) The Internet is an in-depth source for information, as well.

Even if a benefit plan allows for a particular service, community and other resources should be tapped. The case manager need not spend plan money just because it is there. A plan might allow for transportation assistance for an at-home patient to travel to and from necessary medical appointments; a local disease-specific society (e.g., the Multiple Sclerosis Society) might also provide transportation services for free. Or, a plan might provide for ambulance costs, yet the local volunteer fire department might offer such services for free. By making a one-time donation to an agency, a corporation might secure transportation or other services for an employee for an indefinite period of time. The key is to be cost-effective and not give away the store. This is especially true if there is a ceiling on overall home care expenses in the plan.

The case manager must also hone negotiating skills in order to deal with home health care providers more effectively. When arranging for a home health agency to provide two shifts of nurses for a patient for an expected 2-month period, some negotiation is in order. The case manager need not accept the usual per diem rate but should suggest an appropriate rate. Assuming services are satisfactory, the provider can look forward to a guaranteed income for a specific duration.

In an effort to make the hoped-for positive impact on patient care and cost management, a case manager often will accept responsibility for negotiating a better price on a care package when, in reality, her hands are tied by the Plan language or the timing of case receipt. Even with clear potential for appropriate care and savings, arrangements cannot always be made. When a case manager receives the case 3 months after hospitalization, medication, and DME equipment bills have been paid, she has lost her ability to negotiate on behalf of the client. There is a 2- to 3-day "framework of decision-making" that occurs as a treatment plan is put in place. If the case manager has not been involved from the beginning, thousands of dollars have already been lost. Hopefully, case managers will continue to empower themselves with the financial knowledge and "corporate" skills to become part of the decision-making managed care team. Toward this goal, it is encouraging to see that CEOs and CFOs are beginning to understand the role of case managers and allow it to work for them and their employees.

The growth in home care presents great opportunities for case managers. They are the ones to provide that essential and pivotal link between patient and family, health care providers, and payers—or, in other words, they are the ones to make sure that home care works.

CHAPTER 20

Managing a Long-Term Case

Long-term cases present special challenges to the case managers, to the payers, and, above all, to the patients and families. Among the personal, professional, and business issues for the case manager are explaining the benefits that case management can offer in terms of outcome and cost containment, clearly presenting findings to the referral source, demonstrating concretely how case management can improve the situation overall, and maintaining an objective and encouraging attitude with the patient and family. The single most important contribution the case manager can make is to identify a probable long-term case early on, before numerous services are put in place and before costs start to spiral.

A long-term case is diagnosis driven; long-term care is typically needed for patients with multiple sclerosis, amyotrophic lateral sclerosis, cerebral palsy, cancer, brain or spinal cord injury, multiple trauma (e.g., amputation or burns), and for premature babies. Services may be required for several months, for several years, or for life. To recognize a long-term case, a case manager refers to the diagnosis, all available medical data, and the prognosis. Through use of this information, supported by prior experience and knowledge of the usual length of time for particular types of cases, the case manager can judge how long a case is likely to be open. Educated speculation on the anticipated length and severity of the case is of interest to the client or payer.

The following are five red flags indicating cases that have potential to be long-term:

1. Lack of improvement or complications and setbacks in a seemingly short-term case
2. Terminal illness
3. Six months of treatment (no matter what the type)

4. Multiple medical conditions (e.g., diabetes and hypertension)
5. An increase in complications, indicating possible systemic involvement

INFORMING THE CLIENT

After she has identified a likely long-term case, the case manager should inform the client company as soon as possible. It is important to be frank and make the client aware that a patient will require care and services for an extended period of time and that, consequently, expenses on the case will be ongoing. Just as a claims administrator is responsible for "claims reserving" (determining, at the earliest opportunity, the potential for a claimant to require additional monies and earmarking dollars accordingly), a case manager must evaluate a patient's condition and offer an educated guess as to the care that will be required.

Long-term cases—those that require 6 or more months of case management intervention—are anathema to some clients and payers. A client's perceptions of a patient's probable needs may differ substantially from the case manager's. Therefore, it is very important to clarify the role of case management in long-term cases to the client. Even when the diagnosis identifies a case as long-term and the case manager feels that long-term involvement is necessary or advisable, the client may request that the case manager limit her role. To avoid confusion and unnecessary delays in the provision of care, the case manager must be able to spot potential misunderstandings before they occur and inform the client promptly of changing circumstances to prepare the client for the possibility of a long-term case as soon as that possibility becomes evident.

The case manager's role is often particularly difficult when a referral source has assigned a case that, based on its information, seems not to be problematic. Suppose that during an on-site visit the case manager discovers a situation that does not mesh with what has been relayed to the referral source over the telephone. The patient's condition or the home dynamics may be much more complex than the referral source realizes. Also, in some cases that at first appear to be short-term, unexpected complications or setbacks occur, requiring additional medical attention. A case manager who has established straightforward and forthright communications with the client company and payer will have a stronger foundation to work from when requesting additional funds due to unforeseen circumstances. Such requests become more crucial when specific dollar limits exist in the coverage language or if claims reserving suddenly becomes necessary, because then they have greater potential to negatively impact the case manager's working relationship and ability to put needed treatments in place.

Some case managers, especially those with less experience or those working with a new client or referral source, are reluctant to be totally honest. In an effort to maintain the client relationship, they knowingly overestimate anticipated progress in long-term cases or withhold especially stark information. This strategy can only backfire, diminishing the payer's confidence in case management. By sharing all the information and giving a studied professional opinion, the case manager can help clients appreciate issues of long-term care that they otherwise would not be able to appreciate.

LEVEL OF INVOLVEMENT

For a case manager, the type and level of involvement on a long-term case depends on several factors: the diagnosis, patient's age, prior medical history, current medical situation, treatment plan, and services required, among others. One especially important factor is the nature of the benefit plan. The provisions of the plan may severely limit the specific activities and functions that the case manager can offer, even though the case manager may be confronting a long-term problem in need of attention. The amount of family support may also influence a case manager's participation. Is the family willing and able to care for the patient at home? Will they accept use of an alternative setting—a skilled nursing facility, for example? If problems arise with the services as arranged, is there a family member who can handle the situation? As in home care, the patient's geographic setting and the community resources available are other factors that determine the level of case management needed or advisable.

The timing of a case manager's introduction to a case also affects her role. In general, case management involvement is more time-consuming and labor-intensive in the early stages of a probable long-term case, because on-site visits, telephone calls, numerous written reports (as requested by the client), and written agreements with service providers are required. General tasks include establishing a relationship with the patient, family, care providers, and client; gathering information (e.g., from the physician and hospital discharge plan); assessing patient needs and possible family participation; and arranging for medical care or other assistance.

After the case manager has put the treatment plan into action (i.e., services are in place and the care routine is established), her role usually becomes a less active one. The goal of case management is to enable the people most directly involved with a long-term illness—the patient and family—to live as comfortably and normally as possible. Provided with the appropriate support and the knowledge and resources to manage minor crises (e.g., when a nursing shift fails to show up), the family has been empowered and has become, in effect, its own case manager. The case manager may call once a day in the beginning for purposes of monitoring. Later, she may touch base once a week. After the case manager becomes confident that the family is progressing well, she may only check in every other month, having established the conditions under which she should be called, such as when a minor problem threatens to turn into a major problem.

In a long-term case of 9 months or 2 years in which there are no major changes in the patient's condition or the care provisions, the need for frequent detailed reports to the client diminishes. This is especially true if follow-up at that point is largely telephonic. Then, reports can take the form of a status update letter or an addendum to a previous report, perhaps submitted monthly or quarterly. A telephone update noted in the client's file might be all that is necessary: "Patient's condition is unchanged since last report 3 months ago. Care services put into place remain the same and are still working effectively."

IMPORTANCE OF ONGOING INVOLVEMENT

In long-term cases, ongoing involvement is always advisable. It not only benefits the patient and family, but also benefits the client, providing increased cost containment because problems are addressed early. Continuing contact can be achieved in several ways, depending on the client group, its in-house capabilities, the funds available, and other factors. The contact link might be an in-house case manager. When an insurance company is the original referral source, it sometimes hires a field case manager to help set up services in coordination with its in-house case manager. After the patient's out-of-hospital routine is established, ongoing contact is often managed by the in-house case management service via telephone. The field case manager is only called back in if a problem occurs. Although this is not ideal because on-site visits reveal things not detected through telephone conversations, contact with the patient is maintained. Through experience, a case manager knows which questions will elicit information indicating how the patient's medication and treatment plan are working, whether symptoms are improving or worsening, how the family is coping, and whether there is increasing tension. Picking up on potential trouble spots during phone interviews, the case manager can go back into the field to determine exactly what is going on, what has changed from the original scenario, and what needs to be done to put it all back together before the care plan deteriorates. (Field case managers should make certain they tell in-house case management services that they be called promptly for a detailed in-the-field analysis of a situation if any hint of change is noted during telephonic contact.)

A case manager working with a self-funded employer group bears the responsibility of communicating to the group or the TPA the importance of keeping a case open. The case manager's contribution might be restricted to moving the patient from hospital to home with appropriate services, thereby "closing" the case. When this occurs, the case manager should carefully explain to the client that she will not be visiting every week or even every month and will not be sending unnecessary or overly detailed reports (and not billing for this level of work), but that regular contact will help keep any small difficulties from getting out of hand. What is important is maintaining a link. Case managers need to articulate this to their referral sources. Examples help to prove the point. The case manager can cite a case (preferably one handled by the same referral source) that was closed, seemingly with justification but prematurely, after which point the claims department suddenly discovered that the patient was back in the hospital. This high-cost situation could have been avoided and the problem handled in a more cost-effective manner if case management had been tracking the case.

As in any home-care case, ongoing case management contact also improves the relationship between the patient and family and the physician by keeping the physician "in the loop"—informed about the home situation, the patient's progress, and the patient's adherence to medical directives. And again, the case manager can maintain a liaison with service providers, as the need for particular equipment or support may increase or decrease with improvements or setbacks in the patient's condition. Regular on-site visits also enable the case manager to detect caregiver burnout and suggest temporary changes to handle the immediate situation, thus helping to make the long-term continuation of care feasible.

Premature closing of cases also jeopardizes the effectiveness of the case manager role. The case manager comes to be seen as a person whose function is merely to set up support services after a patient's discharge from a hospital; this view prevents the case manager from becoming an integral member of the care team and reduces the team's ability to provide needed care for the patient in a cost-effective manner.

CHANGES IN LONG-TERM CASES

Solutions that were once workable and cost-effective sometimes become ineffective over the course of a long-term care case. The case manager should expect to modify her plan or renegotiate prices due to staff changes at selected agencies, service that is no longer satisfactory, or a personality clash between a care provider and the patient or family. As mentioned, a change in service or cost often signals a change in the patient's medical condition. Complications occur. A cancer patient is undergoing chemotherapy and/or radiation, with the disease confined to one organ, the stomach. Unfortunately, the disease metastasizes to the liver and lungs and 2 months later to the brain. It might be as "simple" as a rise in body temperature to 101.4, requiring that the patient be rehospitalized for antibiotic treatment because her chemotherapy has so deeply compromised her immune system. The patient who initially was compliant and cooperative develops breathing difficulties and other complications due to the upset of metabolic processes. She might be in pain, uncooperative, combative, hostile, and later comatose. Through these stages of the illness, the case manager must adjust services to fit the need.

In cases like traumatic brain injury or spinal cord injury, rapid gains and improvements in the beginning of treatment are often followed by long stretches of slower, less evident progress—plateaus. Plateaus present problems for the patient, family, and entire care team. They are disheartening and can be the root of both undue despair and false hope. The patient and primary caregiver feel that progress has halted, that they are stuck right where they were months ago. The claims examiner feels that "no news is good news" and that there are no problems. The referral source sees no need to call in a field case manager because the patient is stable. The case manager finds herself asking, "What can I offer here?"

Through phone contact or on-site visits, the case manager should explain what plateaus are, and provide encouragement and support. Because she does not see the individual daily, her perspective is key. Although progress might seem agonizingly slow to the family, the case manager can say, "Wow, since last month I can see such change in the strength of his movements, and now he can lift his arm 6 inches off the bed instead of stopping at 2 inches." By maintaining a journal herself and encouraging the family to jot down notes, the case manager helps lighten the dismay at the slowness of progress and focus attention on the progress being made. By making on-site visits, the case manager can also suggest ways in which the care situation might be changed (e.g., recommending equipment that will encourage more movement and giving the family tips on engaging the patient in his own care). This proactive involvement helps keep a family and its support system intact, provides tools and coping skills, and makes it less likely that more expensive services will be needed to correct a problem that went unnoticed.

Family situations also change. Initially, a family's ability to cope may be very good, and they will insist that they will do whatever it takes to care for the patient and keep him at home. And in the beginning, this is so; everyone is very energetic and involved. But then, the primary care provider gets burned out. The family then requires support—a homemaker, home health aide, or RN.

Another red flag to watch for is financial difficulty. There are a myriad of ways in which monetary affairs can change during a long-term case and affect the long-term care situation and the family's stability. Insurance often pays part of the expenses involved in caring for the ill patient while the family funds the rest—and the financial strain can gradually become overwhelming. A number of factors are at play. The primary caregiver may have left a part-time job because of the need at home, diminishing family income. The primary wage earner in the family may become unemployed. The patient may be coming to the end of a period of salary replacement but still need several months of care. Continuing longer than expected, the case may hit a benefit ceiling. Throughout the course of care, the case manager must track financial resources and make the best use of them. The only way a case manager can monitor the patient and family situation and be able to prevent small, moderate, and major problems from becoming catastrophic is to maintain some degree of ongoing involvement in the case.

NEGOTIATING FOR LONG-TERM CARE

When negotiating for long-term services, case managers often overlook a cost-containment tactic available to them: Long-term cases provide a long-term guaranteed income for service providers. Therefore, case managers should address long-term cost issues with the providers upfront, stating frankly that because they will be billing for a set amount over a period of perhaps 5 or 6 months, negotiating costs is appropriate. This is true whether the provider is a skilled nursing care facility, home health aide service, or nutritional supplement manufacturer. The case manager's job is to get patients the level of service they need at the time they need it in the most cost-effective manner. This means negotiating based on need and fair market value and always holding out for the best price available. It is the case manager's responsibility to be familiar with competitive rates and comfortable with challenging costs and seeking deals while always leaving room to negotiate. For example, a vendor or facility representative should never be told the total amount available through a benefit plan; the release of this information would significantly reduce the case manager's bargaining power.

Intensive negotiation is particularly appropriate when a patient's needs and the required levels of services change during a prolonged period of care. An individual brain injury or multiple trauma patient may demand intense skilled nursing and ancillary services at the outset of treatment but will require less and less care during the later stages of recovery. In situations like this, renegotiation is key so that costs reflect the patient's improved condition and reduced need for many services. Further, other services may be requested. For instance, whereas skilled nursing care may be curtailed, physical or occupational therapy may be started. Overall, the case manager should see to it that changes in the levels and types of services being provided to a patient are reflected in changes in costs.

EMPLOYING ALL POSSIBLE RESOURCES

Financial resources for long-term care are always a concern—whether for a young, long-term patient or for the care of an elderly person. Long-term care insurance policies vary greatly in the type and extent of funding they provide and in the restrictions put on types of services. Resources and benefits may alter as the patient ages, and the family support system and finances may change. In addition to the patient's specific health plan (employer-funded plan, TPA, workers' compensation, or other), long-term care policy, or disease-specific policy, all other possible resources for funding and services should be investigated.

As with home care cases, many disease-specific organizations and groups provide or arrange for services. Further, recognizing the long-term needs of patients, disease-specific groups use a sliding scale, based on the patient's financial resources, for determining reimbursement. (A sliding scale arrangement is usually not available for acute, short-term care.) For example, there may be a dollar limit on a plan's psychological benefits. Depending on the need, arrangements can be made for payment on a sliding scale. In this way, a young person with an eating disorder may pay a minimum predetermined per-visit rate over a longer period of time. Case managers need to be aware of these types of resources and arrangements, including the funding available through grants, foundations, and other organizations, and use them to supplement and even protect the funding available from the insurance plan so it can be reserved for later use.

Again, community resources should also be tapped. Why pay for transportation to a doctor's appointment or for ambulance service if there are local community organizations providing the service free? Because long-term care is always a financial drain, case managers should make every effort to use whatever resources are available and to safeguard the insurance coverage the patient has at his or her disposal.

LONG-TERM CARE OF THE ELDERLY

Case management can also be applied to manage the long-term care of the elderly—those not seriously ill but requiring support services. This is especially true now that long-term care insurance policies are available and companies are calling on case managers to evaluate the medical and emotional condition of elderly individuals. It is especially significant as the cost of the top 50 drugs prescribed to seniors rose 6.1% in the past year, 60% of drug errors come from physicians failing to monitor patients after prescribing a medication, and elderly patients are particularly inclined to skip doses to save money, or take a mix-and-match approach to their drug regimen.

Insurance companies are not the only clients seeking to use case management services in the care of the elderly. Adult sons and daughters of aging parents often recognize the need for help in locating community resources, daycare programs, and other services that address the needs of the elderly at minimal cost. These may include senior day activity programs with bus transportation, meal preparation and delivery, housekeeping services, and shopping services. Expanded professional services can be phased in later. Housing situations can also be assessed. For example, an elderly person may benefit from moving from a two-story domicile to a single-level apartment and possibly later to an adult residence at which services such as transportation, meal preparation, and housekeeping are available.

Figure 20–1 The Geriatric Continuum

At-Risk Geriatric Population—Levels of Case Management

Category	Low risk	Medium risk	High risk
Sample characteristics	• Lifeline or similar service participant • Minimal support system • Compromised financial status	• Newly diagnosed chronic illness • 2–3 co-morbidities • New lifestyle change (e.g., loss of spouse) • No active support system • 3 or more medications • Active treatment by 2 or more physicians	• 75 years or older • In assisted living • 2–3 comorbidities and/or major functional limitations • 2 or more acute care admits within past 12 months • 1 or more ER or observ. admits within past 12 months • Multiple MD interventions • On dialysis • In day treatment • Using home health
Level of case management	Maintenance	Active	Intensive
Case management by:	Social worker (BS)	Social worker (MS) and/or RN	RN
Frequency of contact between case manager and enrollee	Approximately every 6 to 8 weeks	Approximately monthly	Approximately every 2 weeks or more as appropriate

Source: Reprinted with permission from F. J. Fowler and F. L. Machisko, The Geriatric Continuum, *Continuing Care,* Vol. 16, No. 4, p. 24, © 1997, Stevens Publishing Corporation.

Gaining in popularity, geriatric networks or continuums mirror the best case management programs in that they move the elderly population away from fragmented, episodic care into an integrated model that is flexible and offers a range of services designed to meet the needs of the population. Multidisciplinary in nature, these eldercare programs maintain contact with participants. The elder enrollee is able to access available services through a case manager who coordinates communications among the providers, payers, patients, and community. Figure 20–1 is an example of one such continuum designed by Fowler Healthcare Affiliates, Inc.

IMPLICATIONS OF LONG-TERM CARE FOR THE FAMILY

Long-term care has numerous implications for the family, many of them resulting from the patient's illness and prognosis. It is much easier for the family—and for the case manager—when the long-term situation has improvement as an end goal. The more uncertain or grave the future, the more stressful the case becomes. In this type of situation, the case manager cannot say, "It's a bad day; things will get better." When the prognosis is not good, a family may accept the likely death of the patient or refuse to believe the physician's opinion. In most cases, the family sees someone who was once a healthy active member and contributor but is now irreversibly changed.

Attention must also be given to the primary caregiver. Just as the patient should be encouraged to find a disease-specific support group, so too should the caregiver be encouraged to arrange for periods of respite and to talk with people facing similar challenges. There are numerous associations for spouses, parents who have a child with a long-term illness, and for siblings or children of individuals suffering from a long-term illness. The benefits are multiple: for the caregiver, for the long-term patient, and, more practically, for the client who will continue to contain costs.

Quite often in long-term cases, whatever strains there were in the family before the illness become exacerbated and the whole situation seems beyond remedy. I call it the "fractured family syndrome." Divorce, alcoholism, emotional illness, overwhelming depression, adolescent rebelliousness, child abuse—case managers see all of these things in such situations. The combination of horrendous health care problems, personal or family stresses, and real or potential financial difficulties can cause unending emotional turmoil. Tension builds, especially in younger families. It is typical for a young mother to be the care provider for an aging and ill parent while fulfilling the roles of wife and parent. Her husband or children may feel neglected. What case managers sometimes see then is resentful and attention-seeking children who develop behavior problems or start experimenting with drugs. Or, a spouse may start drinking heavily or become totally involved in work, avoiding the home. In some cases, the family falls apart. The primary caregiver cannot manage it any more. There are many examples of the spouse of a person with multiple sclerosis simply leaving, after years of giving caring support and knowing that there are years to come of the same or worse.

What should the case manager do in situations such as these? Following are some tips on helping families through a crisis period:

- Suggest family counseling.
- Suggest the primary caregiver join an appropriate support group.
- Recommend books on coping, such as the *Family Guide to Stroke* (American Heart Association), *The Family Guide to Surviving Stroke and Communication Disorders* (Allyn & Bacon), *Taking Time: Support for People with Cancer*

and the People Who Care about Them (National Cancer Institute, National Institutes of Health, U.S. Department of Health and Human Services), *Right to Die* (Group for the Advancement of Psychiatry), *The AIDS Caregiver's Handbook* (St. Martin's Press), *The Caregiver's Journey* (HarperCollins), *The Forgetting Alzheimer's: Portrait of an Epidemic* (Anchor Books), *There's Still a Person in There: The Complete Guide to Treating and Coping with Alzheimer's* (Perigee), *The Lupus Book: A Guide for Patients and Their Families* (Oxford University Press), *New Hope for People with Lupus: Your Friendly, Authoritative Guide to the Latest in Traditional and Complementary Solutions* (Prima Publishing), and *Guarded Prognosis: A Doctor and His Patients Talk About Chronic Disease and How to Cope with It* (Hill & Wang). (For pertinent guides, check with national associations, which often put together recommended reading lists.)

- Direct families to resources that help them claim some of the billions in untapped public assistance dollars provided by state and federal assistance programs. The web site www.benefitscheckup.org includes information on Supplemental Security Income, Medicaid, state drug benefits, Meals on Wheels, food stamps, health insurance counseling, and veterans' medical care and transportation. The site offers addresses and phone numbers of local government offices, and screens candidates for property tax exemptions, utility bill relief, talking-book programs, an inexpensive lifetime pass to national parks, and home repair and renovation services. The web site www.homeinsteadsolutions.com provides access to a national network of eldercare products and services; Home Instead can also be reached toll-free at 1 (888) 405-4242. Digital Divide Network lists public places where one can get access to a computer and learn about other benefits that may be available. Its toll-free number is 1 (866) 583-1234.
- Remind family members to keep their own appointments and to take care of themselves. Encourage them to go to their gym regularly, or make an appointment for a massage, facial, or manicure.
- Help the family members communicate and achieve some level of comfort with feelings of fear, anxiety, and so on.

Case managers should also remember to get support for themselves through contact with peers. Some case managers try to relive their own experiences through other families, which is detrimental to all involved.

IMPLICATIONS OF A LONG-TERM CASE FOR THE CASE MANAGER

It is important to note that long-term cases have many implications, often hidden at first, for case managers. Case managers react very differently when working on long-term cases than on shorter cases that frequently have positive outcomes. The more problematic the case and the more discouraged and overwhelmed the family becomes, the greater the burden placed on the case manager. Even though the patient's medical condition may become more stable, other long-term problems occur, and the case manager might feel like the only person who is truly attempting to face them. The family may want out and may dump their concerns on the case manager as a way of seeking relief. Frequently, case managers become disheartened and burn out.

Some case managers do a very good job of being compassionate and supportive while keeping themselves from becoming too personally involved. However, others cross the line, which is dangerous because they sacrifice their objective professionalism. There are many reasons or triggers that may lead a case manager to become too personally connected. A 34-year-old case manager, working a case in which a husband is caring for his 34-year-old wife dying of breast cancer, can become too connected. A transference of feelings occurs, and the case manager identifies with the patient. She loses her objectivity and, not realizing it, starts to make decisions based on how she would personally like things done if she were the patient.

There are other circumstances that may obstruct objectivity. Perhaps the husband–caregiver reminds a case manager of her ex-husband, with whom she is fighting for child support payments. Perhaps the patient is dying of Alzheimer's and the case manager's mother has just been diagnosed with Alzheimer's. There may be a personality conflict between the case manager and the caregiver, which can obstruct objectivity as much as feelings of empathy can.

There can also be situations in which the case manager has not lost objectivity but simply is no longer effective or useful on the case. At the beginning stages of the case, her energy level was high, she carefully analyzed all parameters, and she devised a workable and cost-effective plan that met the needs of the patient. After a while, changes occurred and everything she tried in response failed. Now the case manager is running out of ideas. The case begins to haunt her, and there is no end in sight. She is no longer a catalyst for improvement.

When no longer objective or effective, case managers need to be honest concerning their own feelings. They must recognize their worth and their contribution or lack of contribution. They need to have open communication with peers and supervisors.

In fact, I think long-term cases require periodic conferences between case managers and supervisors so that the value of the case management process can be continually assessed. Is the case manager making a difference? Is she just reporting to the client, almost like a journalist? Is she acting as a catalyst for change? Or, is she identifying the same problems month after month but not coming up with any new solutions? Such reevaluations can uncover the need for a fresh perspective on the case—perhaps that of a different case manager.

Confronting a lack of effectiveness can be very difficult for a case manager, particularly if she has a one-person business and substantial income may be lost if she gives up the case. But honesty is absolutely necessary, and if the case manager is not moving toward some positive results, for whatever reason, she does not belong on the case. A supervisor in a larger case management unit or company may have to make such decisions, but ideally each case manager will develop an ability to judge her own contributions accurately. Honesty must also extend to the family and client. If a case manager decides that she is no longer effective, she should discuss this with the client, explaining that although the case still requires case management services, she is not the right person for this particular case at this time. Difficult? Yes, but vital if the case manager is to remain effective and provide real help to patients and families in long-term cases.

FROM ACUTE CARE TO HOME CARE: A CASE HISTORY

Marge Reynolds, a 46-year-old mother of two teens, has a 27-year history of chronic colitis, which she apparently had under control using a combination of medication and diet. In April, she was admitted to the hospital for complaints of abdominal and gastrointestinal distress, vomiting, weight loss, and abdominal pain. Two-and-a-half years earlier, she had developed increasing and unremitting abdominal pains and had entered the hospital at that time for a diagnostic work up. She underwent a colectomy with anastomosis following the discovery of a partial bowel obstruction, but she elected to forgo a colostomy despite the warnings of her physicians. One week after the surgery, Mrs. Reynolds suffered acute abdominal bleeding. Additional surgery and a colostomy were performed. Her recovery progressed well, and she returned to her normal activities.

The next year, Mrs. Reynolds experienced prolonged vaginal bleeding and was diagnosed as having uterine cancer. Based on her medical history, a complete hysterectomy was done, with additional testing to rule out metastatic disease or ovarian cancer. Her chemotherapy treatments were completed just prior to the onset of the pains and vomiting that led to her hospital admission in April.

Twelve days after her admission and diagnostic work ups, which incorporated CAT scans and MRI testing, Mrs. Reynolds's surgeon performed exploratory surgery. The operations included a resection of the bowel and stoma, relocation of the stoma site, resection of the abdominal wall, and insertion of a Teflon mesh to replace an excised section of body wall necessitated by multiple tumors of metastatic origin.

Mrs. Reynolds's timely recovery was compromised by her generally weakened condition from previous chemotherapy treatments and further complicated by the need for the insertion of a Porta-Cath to provide nutritional support, as she was experiencing vomiting, diarrhea (related to short bowel syndrome), dehydration, and malnutrition. The hospital social worker recommended that Mrs. Reynolds be kept in the hospital based on the delay in her stabilization, the fact that she required highly sophisticated intravenous TPN 24 hours a day, and her determined resistance to hospice care.

When a hospital extension was first requested for patient stabilization, a preadmission-utilization review nurse red-flagged Mrs. Reynolds's file for case management. One of our independent case managers visited Mrs. Reynolds in the hospital. Finding her too ill to converse, the case manager consulted her chart and reviewed her progress with Mrs. Reynolds's husband, the treating physicians, the nursing staff, the utilization review nurse, and a hospital social worker. From the family physician and Mr. Reynolds, the case manager learned of Mrs. Reynolds's previous hospital admissions, her fight against colon and ovarian cancer, and her recent chemotherapy treatments.

In her initial report, sent to the insurer just short of 1 month after Mrs. Reynolds entered the hospital, the case manager noted the patient was in a generally weakened condition and was hampered by an underfunctioning ileostomy and episodes of vomiting and frequent diarrhea. The assessment also included detailed descriptions of treatment and medication, the surgeon's planned insertion of a triple lumen, central venous catheter, or Porta-Cath, and the observation that Mrs. Reynolds was able to get out of bed only with assistance and required help with ambulating and hygiene.

During her on-site visit to the hospital, the case manager had been able to discuss the home environment and the potential for home care services with Mr. Reynolds, the hospital nurses, and the social worker. That home care seemed a possibility was welcome news, as Mrs. Reynolds had made it clear that she did not want to be admitted to a hospice. Due to the complexity of Mrs. Reynolds's treatment, the option of home care had not occurred to the treating physician, nurses, or social worker, but the case manager was able to assure the hospital staff and family that home care was a viable alternative for Mrs. Reynolds. In conversation, the case manager confirmed that the insurer would cover the cost of a home health aide, episodic RN attendance, and home IV therapy or hyperalimentation (which was then being considered by the treating physician). The case manager also received word from the treating physicians that home care was a perfectly acceptable medical alternative to hospice care. Discharge was delayed until Mrs. Reynolds's condition improved.

In mid-May, a Porta-Cath was inserted and TPN infusion begun in an effort to stabilize Mrs. Reynolds's condition. She responded well to the nutritional support and experienced less nausea, vomiting, and gastric distress. During the case manager's next visit, Mrs. Reynolds was eating several small meals a day. Working closely with the hospital staff, the case manager continued coordinating discharge planning and home care services.

Mrs. Reynolds's family supported the idea of home treatment, but were unable to be at home during the day to administer that care. Accepting bids from the most qualified suppliers and negotiating for the most cost-effective treatment, the case manager arranged for home nursing services (HNS), a home health aide, and TPN services. In early July, less than 7 weeks after she arrived at the hospital, Mrs. Reynolds was able to go home.

Instead of continuing her acute hospitalization, she was able to receive treatment at home, assisted by a home health aide who helped with bathing, dressing, meal preparation, and other personal activities. An HNS nurse taught Mr. and Mrs. Reynolds how to hang her intravenous fluids, how to perform tubing changes, how to monitor the electrolyte balance and glucose levels, and what to do in an emergency. From her office, the case manager pushed the insurer to allow her to make a home visit a few days after Mrs. Reynolds's discharge. She wanted to see the program in action and make sure her plan was effective. Her visit was timely.

The infusion company had overstocked the Reynolds's home with supplies, making it difficult to move through the house, and charged for unneeded equipment and fluids that could not possibly be used before their expiration date. Reviewing the invoices, the case manager also found that the firm had charged for a period of 28 days when Mrs. Reynolds was still in the hospital, and it was billing for pump rental and infusion nursing visits that it had previously agreed would be included in the per diem cost. The case manager arranged for immediate credits to the account.

She also noted that Mrs. Reynolds was receiving 24 hours of TPN, unusual for homebound patients because it eliminates any freedom of movement the individual might enjoy. Following conversations with the HNS nurse and family physician, approval was given for Mrs. Reynolds to receive her full prescribed volume of TPN Intralipids over a 20-hour period. The case manager's aim was to allow Mrs. Reynolds to move about her home, increasing her stamina and independence. To boost her mobility, the case manager got carrier approval for a rental wheelchair (no loaner wheelchairs were available from community loan closets). The allowed interruption in infusion therapy and the wheelchair enabled Mrs. Reynolds to attend her son's high school graduation later that month, an important emotional and physical outing that boosted her spirits and reinforced the family's sense of wholeness.

The case manager continued monitoring the home infusion therapy and TPN, Mrs. Reynolds's medical condition, and the need for nursing and home health aide services. In subsequent visits, the case manager noticed that Mrs. Reynolds appeared to have gained strength and a little weight and was pleased with her increased mobility. With her TPN and other infusions now being completed in 18 hours, she was able to take showers, sit outside during good weather, and attend family gatherings. Mrs. Reynolds was also independent in setting up her TPN solutions, tubing, and changing infusion bottles. Her daily life was a far stretch from the acute hospitalization she could well have been experiencing.

Unfortunately, due to the onset of severe back pain and other complications from previous battles with cancer, Mrs. Reynolds was subsequently readmitted to the hospital. With ongoing intervention by the case manager, her hospital stay was of short duration, and she was able to return home. The case manager's continued home visits proved invaluable when the case manager found Mrs. Reynolds in a medical crisis that the attending home health aide was unable to manage. After contacting the treating physician and conducting a reevaluation of Mrs. Reynolds's home situation in light of her deteriorating condition, the case manager arranged for additional RN support. She also suggested family counseling to help ease the stress felt by Mr. Reynolds and the two teenagers, who were trying unsuccessfully to cope with terminal illness and death.

Through the case manager's early involvement, Mrs. Reynolds was able to experience increased self-reliance and to live the last months of her life at home with her family. Although the wheelchair rental was a very small item in the whole home care picture, it gave Mrs. Reynolds and her family a highlight to remember. Because of the case manager's attention to detail and knowledge of the latest technologies, Mrs. Reynolds received a preferred alternative to hospital or hospice care, and the insurer paid fewer and less expensive claims.

The value of case management to Mrs. Reynolds and her family might be incalculable, but a review of one quarter's cost-benefit analysis report sent by our case manager to the insurer shows exactly what case management meant to the bottom-line. Under "avoidance of potential charges," there are 70 days in the hospital at $1,750 per day, plus pharmacy and physician charges totaling $132,500. Total actual charges for case management fees, reduced-rate TPN, and negotiated fees for home health aide and nursing services came to $54,500, for a net savings of $78,000. The case manager also discovered $12,500 in overcharges submitted by the TPN vendor; this amount would have boosted actual charges to $67,000.

CHAPTER 21

Techniques for AIDS Cases

AIDS REMAINS WITH US

In the space of 3 weeks during the summer of 2003, significant news about HIV and its treatment hit the headlines. A rapid-result HIV test, used overseas for years, became available to the public in the United States (California). The Centers for Disease Control and Prevention (CDC) announced plans to buy approximately 250,000 of the 20-minute tests, called OraQuick, and provide them to state health departments as part of a larger HIV-prevention initiative. (The CDC had already put $35 million toward prevention efforts reaching out to those most at risk.) Then, at an international AIDS conference in Paris, it was announced that the largest study to date examining resistance to AIDS drugs found that 10% of all newly infected European patients carried drug-resistant HIV strains.

"AIDS continues to thrive," comments Karyl Thorn, BSN, MA, CCM, CEO of Thorn Associates, a case management firm serving HIV-infected individuals, their employers, and insurers throughout the United States, "HIV/AIDS is clearly the defining medical and public health issue for our generation. It has emerged from viral obscurity to become the most devastating pandemic in history, eclipsing both the Black Death, which decimated Europe in the 14th century, and the 1918 Influenza.

"Since we first became aware of AIDS in the summer of 1981, the disease has spread in successive waves around the globe. By 2003, HIV had infected a cumulative total of more than 60 million people, over 20 million of whom have died. More than 13 million children globally have experienced a parent's death to AIDS. By 2010, the number is expected to exceed 25 million. In some African countries, every sixth child is an orphan. Unfortunately, the catastrophic potential of this pandemic has not yet been realized. HIV and AIDS continue to exact an enormous toll throughout the world, most notably in sub-Saharan Africa. The incidence of HIV and AIDS is rising dramatically in China, India, parts of eastern Europe and central Asia, and Russia.

"There are currently 800,000 to 900,000 people in the U.S. living with HIV, and approximately 40,000 new cases annually. AIDS deaths to date in the U.S. are 467,910. The incidence of risky behavior (any sexual behavior, drug sharing), noncompliance, drug resistance, and the *denial* syndrome continue to fuel this disease."

Thorn introduces information that clarifies the news that 10% of all newly infected European patients carried drug-resistant HIV strains. Two percent of all those diagnosed with HIV are resistant to all known AIDS drugs at the time of their diagnosis. In the United States, 25% of the HIV/AIDS population is resistant to one or more drugs. When you look at that statistic, remember that it isn't exactly the whole story. Within that statistic, a patient might have a resistance to only one drug in the class. It is important to consider the various substrains of the virus. Those who have the disease Type B HIV subtype are showing higher resistance levels. Drug-resistant strains were first confirmed in the United States in 1992. The news reinforces what we have known; the longer a patient is on HIV/AIDS mediation, the more likely she is to become resistant because of the incredible rate at which the virus replicates, at 10 to 30 billion virions a day. Every 30 minutes, the virus turns over in the patient's body. Consider then, the number of wild, "new" strains of viruses that are spawned.

Further, 40% of those infected with HIV in the United States are also positive for hepatitis C, with two diseases running through their bodies. Hepatitis C requires a drug regimen just as toxic and just as rigid in terms of adhering to time and dosage.

THE DISEASE PROGRESSION IS UNIQUE

Because the disease progression is unique, Thorn believes case managers need to augment their knowledge base for greater efficacy. She states, "While case managers can build upon their comprehension of other chronic illnesses, in fact, *must* be able to build on their knowledge base of cardiovascular disease, lipodystrophy, tuberculosis (TB), liver disease including but not limited to hepatitis C virus (HCV), transplantation, opportunistic diseases, the aging process, and the unique problems for women with invasive carcinomas, the process of immune compromise with HIV overlays these complications and exacerbates the processes. It is almost a given that with certain medications you'll have or are very likely to have a problem. For example, if a person is taking a protease inhibitor, you have to watch for insulin resistance and signs of hypoglycemia, to be able to address this so you don't have to address a diabetic coma. Without a clear understanding of the underlying process, case management services become as fragmented as our healthcare system, ever chasing the tail of the dragon and never seeing the entire creature."

"HIV causes progressive immune compromise," notes Thorn, as an example. "The case manager who would be cost effective must be proactive in watching for signs of progression, such as diabetes, hyperlipidemia, lipodystrophy, hyper-bilirubinemia, anemia, protein-calorie malnutrition, drug noncompliance, drug side effects, nausea, vomiting, diarrhea, abdominal pain, somnolence, insomnia, and fever."

Further, Thorn continues, "Case managers who do build a relationship with someone living with HIV disease may well be asked to provide information as that person and their family (of origin and/or of choice) makes decisions about switching or even discontinuing antiretroviral therapies. This is not only a medical decision since these regimens require strict adherence in dosing and eating, often with regimens requiring 15 to 30 medications daily."

Case managers working with HIV-positive patients face all the challenges of other types of long-term, catastrophic care cases plus additional elements that do not present themselves in other diagnoses. These include issues of confidentiality, access to information, social stigmatization, prejudice against certain lifestyles, and benefits manipulation.

AIDS carries a social weight attached to no other diagnosis or disease I or my case managers at Options Unlimited have encountered. There are numerous barriers and roadblocks we run into while trying to reach out to AIDS patients and attempting to gain for them the most benefit from the health delivery system. Without a doubt, the greatest hindrance to our work is the "fear and loathing" that the affliction can generate. Some families and friends remain supportive; others fear they will catch it, think the individual somehow "deserved it," and desert the person with the disease. In one case our office managed, the family "welcomed" the patient back into their home only so that they could profit from his disability checks. They did not prepare food for him; they did not help attend to his needs. He moved into an apartment and died alone.

A secondary hurdle is the issue of confidentiality. Because of the stigma attached to the disease, concern about confidentiality is understandable. Patients do not want to be shunned at the office or fired. Neither do they want to see their health benefits disappear. Under the guise of preserving benefit dollars for the group (heeding their fiduciary responsibility), employers have been known to suddenly limit benefit payouts for claims associated with HIV and AIDS. In one instance, we were working on behalf of an AIDS patient whose employer assured us that they valued this person's contributions and planned to take good care of him. Our case manager negotiated, in good faith, excellent contracts for IV therapy services. Months later, the providers began calling the case manager to report unpaid bills. The claims administrator said that claims were being processed and passed along to the employer for final approval. Too late, we discovered that not only had the employer decided to place a retroactive cap on claims to be paid out for HIV-associated claims, but they also had been holding all our patient's claims from the onset of care until costs accumulated to reach that mark. The employer had no intention of "taking good care" of the patient who, unfortunately, lived long enough to get that message clearly, facing the added worry of how his caretakers were going to be paid. (Under ERISA, employers have up to 270 days, or nine months, to notify benefit plan members or insureds that their contract has been changed.)

Care providers have been less than forthcoming as well. One doctor absolutely refused to return any calls. In another case, our case manager introduced herself, faxed over her consent authorization, assured the medical records administrator that she knew the patient and the patient's HIV status, yet was denied access to any information until the patient called and said that the information should be released to her.

All such barriers need to be broken down. AIDS is an epidemic that cuts across gender, age, race, and social strata. In nursing or medical school, students are taught to be nonjudgmental; some obviously slept in the day that lecture was given. Prior to taking an HIV-positive case, a case manager should carefully examine her own feelings on the issues. What are her thoughts on gay and lesbian lifestyles? AIDS is not a gay or lesbian disease, but much of the media coverage and emotional reaction to AIDS revolves around the issue of homosexuality. Can the case manager separate the disease from the person she is helping? For so many tangible and intangible reasons, HIV infection seems to stand apart from all other diagnoses. Can she be unbiased in her management of the patient's care? Has she addressed her own feelings about death? Some patients suffering with AIDS are in total denial regarding their demise. Others have accepted the proximity of death but cannot conquer their fear of dependence on others. How will the case manager react when a patient—a person she has been working with for 2 years, a person who has shared with her intimate details of his life—tells her that he plans to commit suicide if he becomes blind? How does she feel about suicide? Is she prepared for the angry reactions from some family members, the "it's his own fault" response that a few feel is appropriate?

I asked case management supervisors who have worked a number of HIV cases what they would tell a case manager preparing to meet her first HIV-positive patient. They emphasized that the case manager should examine her own response to the prospect of taking the case, and if she has strong adverse feelings, she should explore the option of giving the case to another case manager. (After a case is taken on, the case manager should avoid turning over the patient to another person if at all possible; the case manager–HIV patient relationship, more than others, requires stability.) They suggested that she know the diseases related to AIDS very well, gathering information by reading and by attending lectures and conferences. Over the course of involvement, the case manager should educate the patient and help the patient become his own case manager. This is a good idea in any case, but HIV patients in particular can benefit greatly by taking an active role in their case management. Many HIV-positive patients are extremely knowledgeable and alert to the subtle changes in their condition that might signal a problem; when accustomed to alerting their case managers and physicians of impending difficulties, their care becomes 100% improved and they maintain a much better overall condition and spirit.

The case management supervisors further emphasized that AIDS patients need consistency in the relationship, and case managers should develop a strong rapport with their patients. To do this, they need patience, patience, and more patience. Building trust may be the biggest hurdle. For multiple reasons, HIV-positive patients are wary and skeptical, more so than cancer, MS, or other patient groups. They are very reluctant to open up and allow themselves to rely on any new person. Sometimes, establishing a relationship is a slow process; sometimes, it is almost impossible. The case manager needs to be able to approach the patient at the level at which intervention becomes acceptable. There might be 30 or 40 things the case manager can suggest that will help; the patient might be willing to listen to only one. The case manager might have to present the options and return to them in 3 months. In 3 months, the patient might be willing to discuss certain topics (such as a living will or medical directive) but be unwilling to act until another 3 months have passed. More than any other patient–case manager relationship, this one requires continued nurturing and effort.

Karyl Thorn augments this thought and takes it a step further: "Case managers with strong relationships may also be told important information about alternative medicines and medical practices. Unless that case manager is looking for such information, it is often undisclosed and drug-drug interactions occur without warning." This highlights the responsibility a case manager has to ask the leading questions, even as she is building a connection with the patient.

Just as she leads the way in gathering vital information and insights while talking with the patient, case managers need to be vocally active in conversations with physicians. Ask questions about the disease status, and inquire about possible new therapies or drug interactions. Thorn observes, "Some case managers are well versed in symptom management but many still take a passive posture and wait for the physician to tell them how their mutual charge is doing. This is monitoring rather than managing."

It should also be said that it is sometimes difficult for case managers to maintain their objectivity in HIV cases because they do become so involved. They learn much about their patients' lives, sometimes more than they expected to ever know about a patient. It can be a tough job to build the rapport needed to help a patient and still be able to step back and assess the patient's condition and needs in an impartial manner.

LIVING WITH AIDS

The HIV infection leads to AIDS and death, as it did in the late 1980s and early 1990s; however, there are many long-term survivors and long-term nonprogressors. With significant advances in antiretroviral drug and protease inhibitor combinations, and increased understanding of the importance of nutrient-dense calories, protein, nutritional supplements, and viral load testing, HIV infection is now managed as a chronic disease requiring long-term care, in which case managers focus on wellness and prevention strategies and can include return-to-work planning.

Viral load testing is becoming so specific that physicians can detect even small changes and know whether a person is moving toward resistance. Genotyping and phenotyping testing have made their way into clinical practice, giving physicians knowledge of the exact strain of the disease and exactly which drug to use. In addition, physicians can apply peak and trough regimens, matching the concentrations of drugs for contact levels in the body.

Survival is possible, and people can live very long lives depending on the following:

- Early HIV diagnosis and initiation of therapy
- Use of viral load indicators and CD4+ T-cell counts
- Aggressive HIV treatment with combination therapy (a minimum of three drugs)
- Measures to prevent and treat opportunistic infections
- Prevention of protein-calorie malnutrition
- Restoration of the immune system
- Support and use of the mind-body connection
- Empowering the HIV-infected individual to become his own case manager[1]

According to Thorn, HIV patients who maintain their ideal body weight can live 10 years or more without progressing to AIDS. However, should that patient lose 10% of his ideal body weight, his life expectancy drops. Even a 5% drop in body weight has negative effects. Wasting syndrome, which is treatable and reversible, claims over 30% of all AIDS patients. Thorn notes that it is vital that case managers work on nutritional issues with their HIV and AIDS patients because the virus itself consumes calories. Careful and continuous nutrition monitoring, and the low fat, low saturated fat, and protein diet have dramatically decreased the incidences of wasting that case managers had been seeing. A nutritional assessment and consultation with a dietitian who understands AIDS can help a patient fight malnutrition and significantly extend his life.[2]

Case managers can also assist their HIV/AIDS patients by helping them obtain and track serum albumin tests that screen the body's protein stores and blood counts, review the dangers of raw or uncooked food and unfiltered tap water, educate them on wellness practices, and promote muscle-building exercise, dental and vision screenings, and stress management.[3]

NEW DRUG THERAPIES—EVERY DOSE, EVERY DAY

Multiple antiretroviral drug combinations are used to reduce HIV virus levels to undetectable elevations. When kept below detection levels, the incidence of opportunistic diseases and other signs of progression slows considerably. The drugs are expensive. Drug treatment is challenging because medications must be taken in a sequence difficult for many patients to track, can have debilitating side effects, affect different patients in a variety of ways, and are only effective in about 30% of patients. (Nonadherence due to the complicated daily medication sequences is perhaps the largest contributor to that rate.) Further, because early intervention is vital, these complex drug therapies are often given to people who felt perfectly fine until they began taking the "cure." Patients who don't follow the dosing schedules often exhibit earlier resistance to cocktails, another reason that the case manager's role in patient understanding and compliance with "every dose, every day" is so important.

Thorn feels it's smart for case managers to suspect that people are not being adherent. The regimen is so very time- and dose-specific, and makes many feel worse than does the disease itself. If your client is not between 95% to 100% adherent to his dosing regimen, he is already facing increased resistance. The majority of HIV/AIDS patients are adherent only 85% to 95% of the time. Case managers need to remind patients that sticking to specific dosages at the exact times they must be taken is a "must"; no exclusions.

The commitment to stay adherent, knowing that the drug regimens are not effective for the long haul, is a challenge in itself. HIV/AIDS is a disease of the immune system, a long-term assault on the body. It invades and gradually destroys, all the while keeping the immune system at a high level of activity. Any disease one might be predisposed to (liver, cardiovascular) is more likely to develop.

When an individual starts on a new drug regimen, the viral load is high. The case manager needs to be supportive and say, "we have to wait 24 weeks, or 6 months, to know how well these drugs are fighting the virus." How will a case manager know when a patient is on a failed medication regimen? Thorn encourages case managers to look for three things:

First, a virologic failure means that the virus is continuing to replicate despite the appropriate use of medications. If an HIV patient's RNA count is not less than 400 copies after 24 weeks on therapy, that regimen is probably not working. If her RNA count is not less than 50 copies after 48 weeks, then the drug combination is not effective.

Second, another strong indicator is immunological failure, when the client's CD4+ T-cell count is less than 25–50 cells/mm^3 in the first year of therapy. If the medication hasn't reduced the viral load sufficiently to allow the body to produce new T cells, even if the patient feels great, the regimen is failing.

Third, a case manager should be on alert if her patient experiences an opportunistic infection, such as a herpes outbreak. Hoping the onset of herpes, shingles, or diarrhea will contain itself and just go away, patients often do not report these problems to their physicians. Here again, the case manager serves as an important link to the treating physicians. As a patient advocate, coach, and counselor, the case manager can encourage the patient to share this with his doctor, and if needed, alert the doctor. In such cases, the patient needs to be reevaluated, and the physician obviously needs to know.

She also emphasizes that the standard of care includes the use of medications that are highly toxic and can lead to toxicity and resistance, so case managers should always be looking for signs of both, as well as other adverse events. With certain medications, it's very likely, almost a given, that a complication will occur. The drugs can cause insulin resistance leading to diabetes, hypoglycemia, and a possible diabetic coma, if unchecked. Dyslipidemia is a problem when the high triglyceride levels from long-term use of protease inhibitors put the patient at cardiac risk. Nucleoside analog reverse transcriptase inhibitors including ddi and AZT, two basics of an HIV therapy regimen, can lead to lactic acidosis. The high levels of carbon dioxide in the client's system will cause him to appear confused or act demented. This is the time for the case manager to take a look at his lab work and check his medications.

With any nonnucleoside or protease inhibitor, hepatotoxicity is a problem. These drugs dramatically challenge the liver. The case manager must continually review lab reports for evidence of increases in liver enzymes.

The use of nucleoside analog reverse transcriptase inhibitors also can bring on horrible peripheral neuropathies. The patient can feel leg, arm, hand, and feet pain so intense that morphine is required. If a client mentions feeling cramps in her legs or soreness in her feet, the case manager should ask, "Are you still taking these medications?" The patient might answer, "Yes, but I feel like I've aged 40 years overnight."

If a patient with HIV is a hemophiliac, protease inhibitors will cause breakthrough bleeding. A patient might also have problems with osteonecrosis, which causes the bones to die, or osteoporosis and demineralization of the bones leading to pathological fractures. The case manager will have to work with her patient to ensure she gets adequate amounts of calcium in her diet.

In addition to the drug-drug and drug-food interactions, a patient is likely to have some type of metabolic complication. Protease inhibitors can cause underlying metabolic disturbances, such as the maldistribution of body fat causing patients to appear disproportioned.

The protease inhibitors range in cost from $12,000 to $15,000 annually. Viral load tests, which measure the effectiveness of the drug therapies, are also expensive, and less than 50% of all HIV-infected individuals are using this test. According to health economists, the annual cost of HIV per year of life saved is low compared to other types of specialized care for the chronically ill, such as a leukemia patient.[4]

Table 21–1 shows FDA-approved HIV drugs. Table 21–2 offers a list of HIV drugs and brief descriptions. The version appearing here is valuably expanded on the web site coreynahman.com, as a database with an AidsMeds Q&A, fact sheet, insite monography, prescribing information, Medline search, and price comparison culled from AIDSINFONYC.org, HIV InSite, and Rx List, and offered "in a more user-friendly form."

Table 21–1 FDA-Approved HIV Drugs

Drug	Approval date
Retrovir (zidovudine, AZT)	March 1987
Videx (didanosine, ddI)	October 1991
Hivid (zalcitabine, ddC)	June 1992
Zerit (stavudine, d4T)	June 1994
Epivir (lamivudine, 3TC)	November 1995
Invirase (saquinavir-HGC)	December 1995
Norvir (ritonavir)	March 1996
Crixivan (indinavir)	March 1996
Viramune (nevirapine)	June 1996
Viracept (nelfinavir)	March 1997
Rescriptor (delavirdine)	April 1997
Combivir (AZT and 3TC)	September 1997
Fortovase (saquinavir-SGC)	November 1997
Sustiva (efavirenz)	September 1998
Ziagen (abacavir)	December 1998
Agenerase (amprenavir)	April 1999
Kaletra (lopinavir and ritonavir)	September 2000
Trizivir (AZT + 3TC + abacavir)	November 2000
Viread (tenofovir)	October 2001
Fuzeon (enfuvirtide, T-20)	March 2003
Emtricitabine (Emtriva, FTC)	July 2003

Source: Reprinted from Medscape.com, www.medscape.com, © 2003.

Table 21–2 Anti-HIV Drugs

Agenerase (amprenavir) – protease inhibitor

Combivir – combination of Retrovir (300mg) and Epivir (150mg) together in the same tablet for convenience

Crixivan (indinavir) – protease inhibitor

Epivir (3tc/lamivudine) – nucleoside analog reverse transcriptase inhibitor

Emtriva [emtricitabine (FTC)] Emtriva.com – mechanism of action animation, full PI

Fortovase (saquinavir) – protease inhibitor

Fuzeon (enfuvirtide) – fusion inhibitor

Hivid (ddc/zalcitabine) – nucleoside analog reverse transcriptase inhibitor

Hydrea (hydroxyurea) – may increase efficacy of Videx (ddi)

Invirase (saquinavir) – protease inhibitor

Kaletra (lopinavir) – protease inhibitor

Lexiva (fosamprenavir) – protease inhibitor approved 10/20/03

Norvir (ritonavir) – protease inhibitor

Rescriptor (delavirdine) – non-nucleoside analog reverse transcriptase inhibitor

Retrovir, AZT (zidovudine) – nucleoside analog reverse transcriptase inhibitor

Reyataz (atazanavir; BMS-232632) – protease inhibitor

Sustiva (efavirenz) – non-nucleoside analog reverse transcriptase inhibitor

Trizivir (3 non-nucleosides in one tablet; abacavir, zidovudine, and lamivudine)

Videx (ddI/didanosine) – nucleoside analog reverse transcriptase inhibitor

Videx EC (ddI/didanosine) – nucleoside analog reverse transcriptase inhibitor; same exact active ingredient as Videx in a delayed-release formulation

Viracept (nelfinavir) – protease inhibitor

Viramune (nevirapine) – non-nucleoside analog reverse transcriptase inhibitor

Viread (tenofovir disoproxil fumarate) – nucleotide reverse transcriptase inhibitor (Adenosine Class)

Zerit (d4t/stavudine) – nucleoside analog reverse transcriptase inhibitor

Ziagen (abacavir) – nucleoside analog reverse transcriptase inhibitor

Source: Excerpted from www.coreynahman.com, © 2003.

Figure 21–1 Harmful Drug Interactions for AIDS Patients

Drugs to avoid using in combination with ritonavir include:

Demerol	Enkaid
Feldene	Quinidine
Darvon	Propulsid
Hismanol	Tambocor
Seldane	Rythmol
Cordarone	Vascor
Prozac	

Drugs to avoid using in combination with indinavir include:

Hismanol	Propuisid
Seldane	Halcion
Versed	

Drugs to avoid using in combination with saquinavir include:

Mycobutin	Phenobarbital
Seldane	Dilantin
Hismanol	Decadron
Tegretol	

Source: This copyrighted material was reprinted with permission from *Case Management Advisor,* an American Health Consultants publication. For more information please call 800-688-2421.

Note: The antibiotic drugs rifabutin (Mycobutin) and rifampin can lower the amount of Retrovir in the blood. Retrovir should be used with caution in combination with other drugs that can suppress the bone marrow, such as ganciclovir. Retrovir and stavudine (d4T, Zerit) do not work well together and should not be combined.

Source: The Simple Facts Project, AIDS Treatment Data Network, 2002, www.atdn.org.

This information does not intend to promote or endorse any specific treatment for any health-related condition.

As promising as the new drug therapies are, case managers should note that ritonavir, indinavir, and saquinavir can cause harmful, and sometimes fatal, drug interactions when taken in combination with certain prescriptions or over-the-counter medications. When taking ritonavir and indinavir, patients may have to adjust the dosage of other drugs.[5] Figure 21–1 lists drug combinations that should be avoided. Figure 21–2 recommends the various ways to use Retrovir (AZT) in combination with other anti-HIV drugs. (This information does not intend to promote or endorse any specific treatment for any health-related condition.)

An excellent web site to check for HIV/AIDS drug interactions is hivmedicationguide.com, at which one can plug in any drug or combination of drugs to check for potential problems or side effects.

Figure 21–2 Public Health Service HIV Treatment Guidelines

Public Health Service HIV treatment guidelines say that the best way to use Retrovir is in combination with other anti-HIV drugs. The guidelines recommend combinations of three or four anti-HIV drugs as first treatment for HIV. The recommended combinations should take one drug or combo from column A and one combo from column B. (Drugs are listed in alphabetical, not priority order.)

Recommendation	*Column A*	*Column B*
Strongly Recommended	Sustiva	Videx + Epivir
	Crixivan	Videx + Zerit
	Viracept	Epivir + Zerit
	Norvir + Crixivan	Videx + Retrovir
	Kaletra	Epivir + Retrovir
	Norvir + Fortovase	
Recommended as Alternatives	Ziagen	Retrovir + HIVID
	Agenerase	
	Rescriptor	
	Viracept + Fortovase	
	Viramune	
	Norvir	
	Fortovase	
Not recommended because of insufficient data	hydroxyurea in combination with ARVs	
	Norvir + Agenerase	
	Norvir + Viracept	
	Viread	
Not Recommended and should not be offered	Invirase	Zerit + Retrovir
		HIVID + Videx
		HIVID + Epivir
		HIVID + Zerit

Source: The Simple Facts Project, AIDS Treatment Data Network, © 2002, www.atdn.org.

This information does not intend to promote or endorse any specific treatment for a health-related condition.

There are additional resources that case managers can tap for information and assistance regarding AIDS; in New York, these include Gay Men's Health Crisis Inc. (212-337-3530) and the Long Island Association for AIDS Care. The New York State Department of Health sponsors care programs for New York State residents with HIV infection who are uninsured or underinsured. These include the AIDS Drug Assistance Program (ADAP), ADAP Plus, and the HIV Home Care Uninsured Fund. Designed for people with partial insurance or subject to a

Medicaid spend-down requirement, ADAP provides free medications to treat HIV/AIDS and opportunistic infections. ADAP Plus covers free primary care services at selected clinics and hospital outpatient facilities. Supplementing or replacing medical insurance for AIDS patients, the HIV Home Care Uninsured Fund covers home care services, such as home health aides, IV therapy, medications, supplies, lab tests, and durable medical equipment for chronically dependent individuals as ordered by their physicians. Community Prescription Service (800-842-0502) provides financing for prescription drugs, offers drugs at reduced prices, and assists with insurance claims filing. It also publishes *Infopack,* an AIDS treatment newsletter, free of charge. Some experimental drugs are available through FDA programs, whereas nontraditional, nonapproved medications can be obtained out-of-country and via underground AIDS drug networks.

CASES IN PROFILE

A Noncooperative Physician

When he was referred to one of our case managers, Mr. Jackson* had been HIV-positive for 2 years. He was 48 years old, had no AIDS diagnosis, and had been hospitalized for dizziness, loss of consciousness, and questionable seizure. Because of his HIV status, his hospitalization claim was marked for case management intervention. His significant other, an alcoholic, had died 6 months prior. His difficulty in dealing with the death of his partner, along with his HIV status, had led him to retire. With absolutely no family and no support system, Mr. Jackson had paid a neighbor, Mr. Miller, to serve as his guardian and executor of his will. He lived in a fourth-floor, walk-up apartment, and climbing the stairs became a problem as his illness progressed.

Wasting syndrome and fatigue were Mr. Jackson's most visible symptoms. He also had herpes and chronic fungal infection in his mouth, making it difficult for him to eat. But the greatest problem with this individual was his physician. The doctor was generally noncommunicative and noncooperative with every member of the health care team. He did not return phone calls and did not return the case manager's questionnaire. He did not respond to the social worker and was nasty to the nurses on the floor. When reached by phone or met at the hospital and asked a question, he would give only rude answers or no response at all. He would answer no questions about Mr. Jackson and provided no diagnostic information. Although Mr. Jackson was aware of the problem ("I know my doctor won't do anything," he said) and friends encouraged him to change physicians (the case

---

*All case history names have been changed.

manager even researched and made referrals of other physicians), he would not change. The case manager was new to case management and this was her first HIV case, making the situation a greater challenge to her personally.

The patient gradually started to decline. He became more and more cachexic as a result of the wasting syndrome common to HIV patients, and his fatigue increased. He had limited benefits for a home health aide and nursing visits (40 visits per year). Through research, the case manager was able to get Mr. Jackson into the New York State HIV Uninsured Care Program, which provided for daily attendance by a home health aide and weekly nursing visits. Because Mr. Jackson refused to allow the aide to cook for him, she implemented a Meals on Wheels plan for him. The case manager believed that perhaps dementia was starting to evolve at this point; the patient's responses and attitudes were becoming slightly strange. When she tried to discuss all of these things with the physician, he was completely unresponsive. He never responded to questions about TPN, which would have been appropriate to treat his patient's cachexia. The patient himself also hindered treatment by refusing any drugs or therapies that might have improved his condition, such as AZT. He was willing to go on supplemental oral feedings but was able to drink only one can per day.

For the 6 months he was in case management, the patient remained very private and enigmatic. When asked if he had told his doctor that he did not want certain treatments, he said, "No, but I won't go on AZT." He had a will but did not have a DNR order.

Four months after initial case management involvement, Mr. Jackson's condition deteriorated. Following a nursing assessment, he was admitted to the hospital suffering from a change in mental status, headaches, disorientation, and neck stiffness. His dementia increased and his temperature spiked to 104; he was diagnosed with meningitis and was treated with antibiotics.

To counteract the lack of a support system, the case manager researched hospice facilities for Mr. Jackson. He expressed a desire to enter the facility in which his significant other had stayed. When the case manager tried to place Mr. Jackson in hospice, the physician did not answer the facility's questions regarding the patient and his diagnosis. Further, the employer, which had affirmed to Mr. Miller that it would take care of Mr. Jackson's needs, denied that it had said anything of that nature when the time came to respond. The employer did not decrease Mr. Jackson's benefits but refused to go out of benefits on the patient's behalf when that became necessary.

As difficult as it was, the case manager talked with Mr. Jackson in order to plan for the future. He again confided that if his condition worsened, he wanted to be admitted to the facility in which his partner had died. He could not be sent home because that would have required backup care in addition to the 24-hour nursing service, and Mr. Miller, the guardian, was not willing to be responsible for that care. The physician went on vacation; he did not respond to the case manager, the social worker, or to the facility in which the patient had expressed an interest. The patient remained in the hospital until the day he died 2 months later. There were absolutely no savings in this case, and the case manager offered her opinion that the physician hastened the demise of his patient.

Turning the Tables

In contrast, Mr. Davis, a 35-year-old man who is HIV-positive, was referred to us when he was admitted to the hospital for diarrhea and abdominal pains. When the case manager met him, Mr. Davis had been HIV-positive for 3 years, was fairly healthy and active, and was employed as the head of the sales department for a computer company. His employer was and is extremely supportive and has extended his benefit package beyond the plan contract. Surrounded by a family that is both financially and emotionally supportive, he has been welcomed into his mother's home when he needed additional care (his father recently passed away). A sister in particular has been very involved in learning more about HIV and AIDS and has been in regular contact with the case manager concerning her brother.

Approximately a year after the case manager had been introduced to Mr. Davis, he was diagnosed with CMV (cytomegalovirus) retinitis, which destroys the retina, and therefore, over time, vision. Treated with high-tech infusion therapy (ganciclovir or DHPG), the patient is able to give himself infusions without assistance. He is very conscious of the costs associated with his care. He has had no nursing visits; he refuses them. In his case, because his family and a very compassionate physician attend him, savings through case management have probably been greater than 50%.

His physician is very caring and monitors Mr. Davis closely, and although it did take a while to develop a relationship with the case manager (because she was referred by "an insurer"), the physician does respond to her calls. ("He is very soft spoken," she jokes, "but he does talk to me.") He is also very willing to work with the case manager to minimize costs. As an example, Mr. Davis has limited home nursing visits available—40 per year. Those visits could have been used up swiftly for laboratory draws because Mr. Davis has a central line. When the physician heard about the situation, he allowed the patient to come into his office and have his lab draws taken there. That alone accounts for tremendous savings per year. The physician is also excellent at coordinating Mr. Davis's care with other quality physicians, including an ophthalmologist.

In general, the patient has been stable but does have a problem with CMV retinitis. When relating this case history, the case manager remembered a patient visit that stood out because Mr. Davis, unlike his usual state, was very depressed.

Her skills in creating and sustaining rapport while retaining professional poise were put to the test. The patient–case manager discussion revolved around Mr. Davis's psychological status. She wanted to help pinpoint his fear so they could address it together. She found that death did not threaten him; however, he found blindness unacceptable.

Before he had become sick, the case manager had applied to all potential sources of financial assistance. Mr. Davis made it clear that he was not a believer in the value of psychological counseling. The antidepressant Prozac was suggested. The case manager utilized the New York State AIDS Drug Assistance Program as a supplement to his medical insurance; it covers the co-payment and deductible for the patient. Mr. Davis also is already enrolled in the state's HIV uninsured program. He also has 18 months of COBRA coverage on a contingency basis, should he require it.

Continuing to do well despite a T-cell count that is barely perceptible, Mr. Davis is maintaining a more positive attitude, has gained weight, and is staying healthier. He and the case manager decided to ignore his T cells for now; based on the numbers alone, he should not be as well as he is. When he was depressed, he developed more problems. Now on Prozac, he is in better shape overall and has been out of the hospital for 7 months. He does have Kaposi's sarcoma the size of a half-dollar on his foot. Due to increasing severity of the CMV retinitis, he has had to stop working. The drugs he is taking for retinitis have severe side effects, decreasing his white blood cell count and making him more susceptible to other infections. His physician has considered admitting Mr. Davis to the hospital to treat him with foscarnet sodium, but because it is a more toxic medication than ganciclovir and causes additional side effects, they are trying to hold off as long as possible on that decision. Fairly stable, Mr. Davis suffers from fatigue and sweats, but there is no dementia, and diarrhea has diminished.

He and his case manager discuss his change in attitude openly. He knows that psychological problems take their toll, and his health is better when he can live as fully and joyfully as possible. They also periodically discuss the need for a living will and an estate will. Mr. Davis has had a will for his estate drawn up but has not been able to finalize the paperwork. He continues to avoid preparation of a living will, and his case manager has decided to table conversation on that topic for a few months.

On her most recent quarterly cost-benefit analysis report, the case manager noted in her summary of intervention that she had monitored the claimant's medical status via phone and personal visits to the patient and his physicians to prevent complications. She was able to negotiate cost-effective pricing for ganciclovir and filgrastim (G-CSF) and also negotiated fees for medication changes, resulting in lowered fees for days when medications were wasted. Total potential charges for Mr. Davis during the quarter were $71,128.00. Through alternative care and case management, actual fees were only $28,863.40, for a net savings of $42,264.60.

Significant Support and Lack of Support

Mr. Taylor was a 42-year-old who had never had a major illness before his admittance to the hospital in September with a diagnosis of pneumonia. He had been experiencing fatigue, especially after exercise, increasing body aches, and other flu-like symptoms. A sudden shortness of breath brought him to the emergency room. The staff inquired about his HIV status; Mr. Taylor was tested and told that he was HIV-positive.

At the time of referral, the case manager was unaware of his HIV status; the case was flagged for the diagnosis of pneumonia. Initially, the case manager had a tremendous amount of trouble getting in touch with the patient. The physician who had admitted him was very uncooperative. Following his discharge, Mr. Taylor switched to a physician who was well-known in AIDS treatment circles and who did cooperate with the case manager, at least when he wanted services put in place. With strong support from his partner, Mr. Taylor remained well and stable for a few months and lived comfortably at home.

After the first symptoms appeared, however, the effects of the disease became severe fairly rapidly. The case manager was able to put IV therapy services in place for him at home at a good negotiated rate. (He required no other services—no home health aide or hospice care.) Within 3 to 4 months, he was no longer able to work because he was physically unable to be at the job site owing to complications (Kaposi's sarcoma and CMV retinitis). In poor shape, he was admitted to the hospital in July with pneumonia and required a ventilator. The physician became uncommunicative and never did return the case manager's calls regarding Mr. Taylor's condition. She found out through the medical records department that he had expired.

Unfortunately, the employer group had decided midway through the course of treatment to limit HIV reimbursement to $25,000 lifetime. As it stands now, the company that provided IV services for Mr. Taylor has billed out in excess of $39,000 and has been paid less than $3,000. This was an extremely difficult situation for the case manager, who had negotiated in good faith, and a nightmare for Mr. Taylor. Just prior to his demise, he saw that his bills were going unpaid, and he was visibly concerned about how his caretakers would be paid. It has now become a concern of his estate.

During the course of intervention, the case manager provided support and information, arranged for assistance from compassionate organizations, facilitated initiation of home infusion services to expedite hospital discharge, and renegotiated for infusion services as changes in therapy occurred. Medications applied were Cytovene (ganciclovir) and Foscavir (foscarnet sodium). Without case management intervention, the cost of Cytovene and related services and supplies would have been $10,676.37 (customary charges), and the cost of Foscavir therapy and related services and supplies would have been $50,975.58 (customary charges). At $800 a day, hospitalization expenses for medication adjustments could have been $16,000.00. Total potential charges came to $77,651.95. Because of initial negotiations and renegotiations for IV services, alternative care and related actual charges were only $32,298.88, for a net savings of $45,353.07.

Fear of Living

Mr. Abatale was referred to our office in November 1990. We had received claims regarding AZT prescriptions and the infectious disease specialists who had seen him. Contact with Mr. Abatale was attempted on several occasions; he never replied. A letter was written to him in January 1991, followed by another in March. The case manager continued to request a meeting. She was able to reach him finally by telephone and saw him for the first time in April 1992. At that point, he was living with his parents, Italian immigrants who spoke no English. This man was vice president of a company, traveled extensively, and until very recently had been actively employed and living on his own. An only son, he was his parents' link to society in this country, had handled all their needs for them, and was worried about what would happen to them after he died.

He had been healthy until 18 months prior to first contact with the case manager. For the last 4 to 5 months of this period, he had difficulty moving, became anemic, and complained of muscle weakness. Having been to several physicians, he was dissatisfied with the medical care he had received; he felt the physicians lacked compassion and that he had been shuttled around. He also went to see a psychotherapeutic counselor and was unhappy with his treatment there. He felt that no one was doing anything to help him.

When the case manager finally met with Mr. Abatale, the first words out of his mouth were, "I am just waiting to die." He said he was putting his affairs in order and making arrangements for himself and, as he could, for his parents. Very much a loner, he had been abandoned by fair-weather friends, many of whom did not want to socialize with him after they found out what his problem was. The case manager asked if he had any interests; he responded that he could not pursue any interests due to his fatigue. Unwilling to become involved in any new pursuits or relationships, he did not want to meet people. He refused counseling, saying it served no purpose. He would sleep late in the morning and occasionally go to the physician. He exhibited no interest in doing anything and did not do anything. The case manager was struck by his despondency. "Here was a man who traveled the world and loved it, and he was sitting in his house in the darkness; literally, the drapes were drawn. As far as he was concerned, the only thing left for him was to die."

Ironically, this was a person who had none of the problems and complications customary with AIDS. He complained of minor aches and pains and suffered from poor affect and feelings of depression, but although his T-cell count would drop, he did not develop diarrhea or retinitis or wasting syndrome.

The case manager met with him for a year and a half. Over time, his attitude did change. He expressed appreciation to the case manager for her visits; he said he enjoyed the meetings, that the contact was positive, and that her interest in him made a difference. He began taking small trips, and his outlook improved. Following a vacation in Hawaii with his parents, he traveled to South America to visit old friends. When his file was closed in September 1993 (his company changed claim administrator companies, which unfortunately meant that his case had to be turned over to another case manager), Mr. Abatale was basically stable mentally and physically. The case manager felt the benefits from her involvement were less a matter of financial savings and more in the region of quality of life. Her client had been able to bring himself "back from the dead" and continue to experience a full, fairly active life.

These are only a few examples of the complexities and considerations involved when a case manager is working with an HIV-positive or AIDS patient. What is difficult to relate is the cold indifference of some family members, employers, and providers and the contrasting enthusiastic, steady support of others. There is much that can be done to help prolong and ease the lives of AIDS patients, and case managers have the opportunity to truly make a difference.

RESOURCES

For most recent standards of care:

www.aids-etc.org

www.aidsinfo.nih.gov

All standards of care are on this site: adult, adolescent, pediatric, maternal–child transmission, perinatal, five post-exposure prophylaxis, health care worker exposure, nonoccupational exposure guidelines, and management of HIV complications, including TB and opportunistic infection guidelines (signs, symptoms, treatments).

For drug interactions:

HIV Medication Guide
www.hivmedicationguide.com

Canadian AIDS Treatment Information Exchange
www.catie.ca/comp_e.nsf
Private and confidential toll-free line: 1-800-263-1638

National AIDS Hotline
1-800-342-AIDS (342-2437)

AIDS Treatment Information Services (ATIS)
1-800-HIV-0400 (448-0400)

AIDS Treatment Data Network (ATDN)
www.atdn.org
1-800-734-7104

AIDSINFONYC.org

AIDS Project Los Angeles (APLA)
HIV Resource Center
213-993-1612

CoreyNahman.com
www.coreynaham.com

GayHealth.com

Project Inform Treatment Information Hotline
1-800-822-7422

For women with HIV:

The Well Project
www.thewellproject.com

NOTES

1. K. Thorn, "The Watershed Years in HIV: Mainstreaming Information," *The Case Manager* 8, no. 4 (1997): 6.
2. L. F. Hoffmann, "Early, Aggressive CM Gives Patients the Key to Survival with HIV," *Case Management Advisor* 7, no. 1 (1996): 1–2. (For more information, please call 800-688-2421.)
3. L. F. Hoffmann, "Early, Aggressive CM," 2–3.
4. L. F. Hoffmann, "New Drugs Shift Thinking on AIDS Management," *Case Management Advisor* 8, no. 9 (1997): 154–156, 161. (For more information, please call 800-688-2421.)
5. L. F. Hoffmann, "New Drugs," 161.

CHAPTER 22

Public Sector
Case Management

NEW DIRECTIONS IN PUBLIC SECTOR CASE MANAGEMENT

Just as the private sector of health care payers has realized the effects of increased costs, of a longer living population, and of a changing and more convoluted health care delivery system, so, too, has the public sector. As case management has become an integral part of efforts to promote quality of care, improve patient outcomes, and contain costs for the private payers, we are seeing a real growth of case management in the public sector.

The government has been a payer of health care for the elderly and economically disadvantaged for many years, and it has been in the forefront with some initiatives to contain costs. An example of this is the early DRG reimbursement system, whereby hospitals are reimbursed based on a given diagnosis or condition and a predetermined length of stay (LOS). Although this and other cost control methods may have focused efforts on acute care hospital utilization, they did little to address the issues and problems of individuals who could benefit from case management intervention.

The government contracts with various organizations to administer its health insurance programs and has been actively involved in the last several years in moving many of those participants into managed care organizations. At the federal and state levels, the government became increasingly concerned that monies to care for the growing numbers of elderly would be insufficient. These public payers also realized, as did those in the private sector, that not everyone uses the available dollars to the same degree. They recognized that several diagnostic conditions use the largest proportion of resources, which, in turn, has a direct correlation to the dollars that are expended.

Response to this has led to initiatives that address the most costly problems and target the population groups most likely to benefit from these efforts. To reduce costs by more effective intervention, government case management programs have typically looked at several of the following: high-risk pregnancy, high-risk newborn, sickle cell anemia, AIDS, psychiatric, cancer, and drug and alcohol patients. The Centers for Medicare and Medicaid Services (CMS, the former HCFA or Health Care Financing Administration) is in the midst of one such initiative, a comprehensive study called the Medicare Coordinated Care Demonstration Project. As in private sector, public sector studies have shown that a relatively small number of recipients with certain chronic illnesses account for the larger portion of Medicare fee-for-service costs. The demonstration project, authorized by the Balanced Budget Act of 1997, is being conducted to determine whether private sector case management tools used by HMOs, MCOs, insurers, and providers could be applied to the fee-for-service population.

Sherry Aliotta, RN, BSN, CCM, President and CEO, S.A. Squared, Inc., who works predominantly in the public sector, finds that demand for case management is increasing notably, as it has proven to be effective in helping to secure more cost-effective care without a decline in good outcomes and the provision of services. Case management has drawn growing recognition for its success with the public sector populations, Aliotta notes. With today's tremendous financial pressures and decreasing federal and state budgetary resources, the government is turning to case management and population management to help keep Medicare and Medicaid functioning at appropriate levels.

This interest in and demand for case management has opened up new opportunities for case managers to be involved in different aspects of case management and population management, including taking their place at the table as decision makers. "Our services are perceived as value-added," comments Aliotta. "There is the clear perception that case managers have a lot to offer in terms of designing health management programs that work for these very heterogeneous and diverse populations. Medicare and Medicaid together are meant to encompass all types of people, young and old, and case managers are the key to delivering good outcomes for them."

Her mantra is, "Finding solutions that work." Aliotta has found that some strategies that are effective in the commercial environment cannot be applied to the same degree for Medicare/Medicaid populations. Her solution is to build a plan that accepts outright that persons will vary in their ability to adhere to a plan, and design accordingly, with measures to promote a quick response to events that may occur as a result of noncompliance.

This is not to infer that most of her client base is noncompliant. Rather, a majority of the people she sees are very motivated to take the best steps, to follow the suggested plan, but are challenged and sometimes thwarted by lack of access to the financial and transportation resources to achieve their goal. "If someone in my family is ill, we make the doctor's appointment, arrange for any needed testing or support equipment, pick up the medications, and address the problem," notes Aliotta. Not all of her clients can follow suit. Still, one of her public sector clients has a departmental mission statement to "Do the Right Thing": to provide for the right care at the right time in the right environment.

According to Aliotta, there is room in public sector case management to do the right things through use of alternatives to the generally accepted plan. For one client, her company designed a program that utilized a 24-hour home companion to monitor the administration of IV antibiotics and assist with tasks of daily living, rather than seeking admission to a nursing home. The option does have to be reviewed and approved, like out-of-plan solutions in the private sector, but the system is flexible enough to put such options in place.

The level of scrutiny of and accountability for case management services has increased significantly over the years. During her first review, Aliotta recalls the reviewer saying, "Case management isn't even mentioned in our survey materials," they were so far below the radar. Today, the government is looking to address regulations and standards to the practice of case management in the public sector. There is a great deal of oversight from the state and local government on any communication that goes out to the Medicare/Medicaid population, and all policies and procedures are thoroughly and stringently reviewed. The case managers work with their Compliance Departments on a daily basis to make sure they are in accordance with regulations. In her previous job, Aliotta had 2 manuals of standards; in public sector case management, there are 17 manuals.

The upside to all this is that case management has demonstrated its success with public sector clients, and now is not only requested (demanded, even), but is also one of the major players in determining and administering the health care programs.

AN OVERVIEW

In the 1990s, there were increasing and somewhat aggressive marketing efforts to move the elderly and economically disadvantaged individuals to managed care companies, as the government sought to find resolution to its monetary concerns. These efforts, although initially met with resistance, became more successful, and the numbers of Medicare and Medicaid enrollees in managed care groups increased. Then, double-digit inflation in health care costs returned, prompting MCOs and HMOs to move out of the Medicare/Medicaid markets.

Because case management finds many of its solutions in the creative use of available benefits, such strategies are sometimes more difficult to implement in public plans. When the government is the payer, whether federal or state, approval of exceptions can be hindered due to the review process. Not being able to move cases more quickly through the system drives up costs for the government and until recently, no one in the government seemed to care.

Because Medicaid/Medicare is at risk to lose money because of unmanaged or poorly managed high-cost cases, just as private companies are, it has become a mandate for them to resolve the problems, inclusive of contract language exceptions or paying for benefits in lieu of greater exposure (costs) to the plan. In keeping with their efforts to remain profitable, today, the government actively seeks case management input in determining the management and use of public monies.

COMPLICATIONS THAT REMAIN

Although some of the cost issues are being addressed in the public sector, still others seem to be caught up in the bureaucracy and regulations that have been its historical dilemma. In our company, for instance, we are case management providers in the Medicaid model waiver program for infants and children who have complex and often life-threatening medical conditions. In addition to having medical and care need requirements, these children also must have private health insurance through a parent in order to be deemed eligible for this waiver program. Whereas most state Medicaid programs are for those in economic need, these waiver programs require that the child is denied regular Medicaid assistance, and, in fact, the family must secure this denial before being considered for the waiver program.

Each child in the program is assigned to a county-appointed case manager; the county, in turn, directs the parent to select another case manager from an approved vendor listing who will actually assume ongoing responsibility to manage the care that will be required. Our case managers face many challenges in trying to develop plans for these children. In addition to the usual activities of assessing, implementing, coordinating, evaluating, and monitoring, they need to develop detailed budgets that delineate not only each aspect of care, service, and equipment that the child will require (from MD visits, nursing care, PT, OT, and special feedings, to transportation, oxygen, and ventilators), but also enumerate just what kind of funding is expected (such as private insurance, state or county funds, or parental contribution) and the amount of dollars for each.

These care plans and the proposed budget (including the hours and dollars for the case manager's planned intervention) are then submitted for approval. The budgets are revised every three months and represent just a *portion* of the other required reports and forms. Because Medicaid reimbursement is often considerably lower than what providers can obtain from private insurance, it can be difficult to find quality providers who will accept these cases.

Although funding issues certainly complicate the management of these individuals whose benefits are derived from public funds, there are other issues that have a much greater impact on whether a case will have a successful outcome. For example, in traditional Medicare programs, the insureds are typically over the age of 65, and although there certainly are exceptions, many of them have several medical conditions. Because senior citizens are concurrently dealing with medical challenges *and* potential challenges in the health care system, the frustration and confusion are certainly understandable.

These frustrations, combined with other issues, place many of the elderly at significant risk for complications and poor outcomes. A good number of seniors are living alone, having lost a life partner or, perhaps, never marrying. With loss of loved ones through death or the geographic relocation of many to the warmer climates, to senior citizen communities, or to children's and friends' homes, many seniors are isolated or have little reliable, ongoing support. Homes or apartments that served them well when they were younger and stronger now present architectural barriers. Financial limitations can also be significant, with individuals making choices between food and other necessary living expenses and medical care and related expenses.

We hear of individuals who, although they have insurance through Medicare, need to pay for all of their oral prescriptions themselves (unless their plan has a drug program). Even with prescription coverage, we see growing members of the elderly who become so used to having to watch their dollars due to lowered incomes that they economize in this area as well. Instead of taking their medication three times a day, they reduce it to one or two times a day or take it a few times a week, thus making the drugs "last longer." Getting refills for medications is also a problem for many because of an inability to get to the pharmacy or waiting too long.

Another area of concern is one that we are seeing with growing frequency as our society ages and that is the condition of dementia and the related diagnoses of Alzheimer's and Parkinson's. Often difficult to diagnose, these disorders truly complicate the management and safety of individuals affected by them. In all but the later phases of the illness, the patient may appear and, in fact, may be physically functional. However, the individual's ability to consistently comprehend, remember, and follow medical care instructions; remember medication and dosing requirements; understand and adhere to dietary restrictions and nutrition needs; or coordinate and keep medical appointments is impaired. One can readily appreciate that the aforementioned problems would put a patient at risk, yet getting resolution is difficult because of the many restrictions, exclusions, and limitations in Medicare and Medicaid (as well as in many private insurer and payer plans). Most Alzheimer and dementia-diagnosed patients need support services rather than skilled care services, which are typically *not* covered. Yet if patients do *not* take their medications or become malnourished and dehydrated, they most assuredly will develop a medically "covered" condition.

As more seniors are moving into managed care arrangements or risk-based contracts and as it becomes financially feasible to manage the needs of individuals in the most cost-effective way and to decrease the utilization of hospital and other costly services, such problems are being addressed and resolved by case managers with improved outcomes and savings as a result. Even in situations in which the "flexing" of benefits is not possible and such support services remain uncovered, case managers are often able to serve as a broker of services by referring the frail elderly to community-based programs, such as Meals on Wheels, Alzheimer day programs, transportation, homemaker/companion assistance, and others. Such programs are often available on an "as needed" basis with payment on a sliding scale according to available funds from each citizen. More cooperation is being evidenced at the federal, state, and community levels across the country in an effort to provide care and support in the most cost-effective, least restrictive environment.

Although the elderly represent the largest group of Medicare enrollees, there are others who, because of their medical disabilities and Social Security eligibility, also qualify for medical benefits through this federal program. Because of the complexity, chronicity, and long-term needs, these individuals may also be involved in case management programs. Understandably, the issues for case managers, in addition to illness issues, will need to be addressed and resolved in this more challenging population group.

NONMEDICAL CHALLENGES INFLUENCE OUTCOMES

Perhaps the most difficult cases for case managers active in public sector programs are those we face when working with the underinsured, economically disadvantaged individuals who are in the various state-funded Medicaid programs. When children and adults have Medicaid as their insurance, they already are facing many obstacles and roadblocks in obtaining medical care. Choice of hospitals, physicians, and other providers may be limited because not all will accept Medicaid patients or because limits are placed on the number of patients to be treated for the lower reimbursement. These services are often available in clinic settings where waiting is long, care is fragmented, and follow-up is less than ideal.

Even when there is a good health care system in place, however, there are many other issues with Medicaid enrollees that cannot be addressed by medical care alone. Because economic need is the major criteria used for Medicaid eligibility, it seems reasonable to accept that certain other factors place many of its beneficiaries at risk. Those who are unemployed or underemployed may also have need for food, housing, clothing, and transportation. When housing is available, it is frequently substandard and unsafe due to crowding; bathroom facilities are shared by several families; there are unsanitary, often nonworking fixtures; there are no heat and limited lighting; and there is no phone service because of non-payment. When there are also cultural differences, language barriers, and educational deficiencies, including illiteracy, one can begin to appreciate the many obstacles that would preclude a good outcome. When recipients are in rural areas, these same problems may exist but without a concentration of agencies and resources to provide the necessary assistance.

Most case managers today have some experience with these public forms of insurance and occasionally are working within several lines of insurance on the same patient. Because many people today are employed beyond the Medicare-eligible age of 65, they may be covered by their employer's health plan as their primary coverage, with Medicare as a secondary payer. A retiree over the age of 65 may have Medicare as primary coverage and the employer-sponsored plan as secondary coverage. In patients with end-stage renal disease, Medicare becomes primary 30 months following the diagnosis of this condition even if the individual is under the age of 65. Coordinating care and services for individuals with multiple lines of insurance can be confusing and frustrating, and it is extremely important to know "who's on first . . . what's on second." When the state is the payer, through Medicaid (in California, Medi-Cal), knowledge of its various regulations and requirements is also critical.

Just as in private sector case management, there is a need to identify those individuals and conditions that have potential for complex and costly problems and then develop a process of proactive intervention. Because of the conditions and factors just discussed, case managers working with these individuals will need to be especially skilled and experienced not just clinically but, equally important, in the social welfare, community resource, and financial areas. In public sector case management, there really needs to be a team approach with social workers as integral members of the team.

Perhaps the biggest challenge with the economically disadvantaged who, because of their complex medical conditions, become involved in a case management program is keeping them in the program. In conversations with case managers across the country who are struggling with this issue, "disenrollment" is becoming a major deterrent in the successful implementation of case management programs. Enrollees move from plan to plan, and many have never heard of or received case management intervention. They are often mistrustful of any efforts to "direct" or "control" them. Case management, if it is to be successful, will have to be able to meet the many challenges that these recipients present; however, the opportunities to truly make a difference with this very special population group are growing in their potential.

CHAPTER 23

Cases in Profile

HIGH-RISK PREGNANCY

Case Overview

Mrs. K, a pregnant 39-year-old, was identified for case management during her hospital admission for a cerclage for an incompetent cervix. This procedure was performed at the 17th week, when it was also discovered that the patient had developed gestational diabetes, requiring the administration of insulin twice daily. Further complicating her condition was morbid obesity, her weight was 339 pounds, and this was her ninth pregnancy. She had had five elective terminations and two spontaneous abortions. Her only child, an 18-year-old, was in college in North Carolina, and the patient lived in Brooklyn with her fiancé, also a diabetic.

Problems Identified

In addition to the aforementioned, the following problems were identified and resolved by the case manager:

1. The patient was to use a glucometer and test strips; however, the plan covered the glucometer only, with supplies to be paid for by the claimant. She was on disability with markedly decreased income and could not afford the test strips. Intervention: Case manager contacted plan administrator, obtained approval for reimbursement, following exploration of risks and potential costs without the necessary supplies.
2. Claimant was to maintain bed rest, except for bathroom privileges and visits to high-risk obstetrician every 2 weeks. Case manager learned that the

claimant had walked three blocks to MD because fiancé had his driver's license suspended. Intervention: Case manager referred to social worker for funding assistance for transportation, which was obtained.

3. Claimant's blood sugars continued to be very unstable. Case manager learned claimant often skipped breakfast and then felt no need to take insulin. Also, not compliant with calls to MD three times a week to report blood sugar readings. Intervention: Case manager reinforced MD instructions, discussed risks to claimant and baby, and contacted nurse practitioner in MD office to have calls made to claimant that provided more support and closer monitoring.

4. During the sixth month, the claimant experienced cramping, diagnosed as contractions, and was not a candidate for home uterine monitoring (due to excess weight, monitor would not detect contractions). Started on Brethene with further instructions for hydration and bed rest. Case manager learned the claimant was snacking more since she was home all the time. Intervention: Case manager provided more education, and in discussion of hobbies and interests, asked if the claimant ever knitted, crocheted, etc., and learned the claimant used to "years ago." Case manager suggested resuming this hobby to keep hands and mind busy, making a baby blanket or sweater as early gift for baby (promoting commitment to unborn child).

5. Late in the sixth month, during a call to the claimant, this case manager learned she is not feeling well, had a cold several days ago, and, upon further questioning, case manager learned the claimant was having more frequent urination and some burning (did not mention during call from nurse practitioner, thought it might be from Brethene). Intervention: Case manager contacted MD's office to have claimant seen. Urinary tract infection was diagnosed; claimant was placed on antibiotics.

6. During 34th week, in weekly call to claimant, case manager learned the claimant was retaining fluid and always thirsty. To quench thirst during hot weather, she was drinking more tomato juice, adding more salt to foods, etc. Blood sugars also more unstable. Intervention: Case manager contacted MD's office and suggested nursing visits for closer monitoring of blood pressure, blood sugars, and fetal assessments; MD in agreement. Case manager arranged for services, negotiated fees, and continued to monitor claimant with calls to her, MD, and nursing agency.

Outcome

Claimant's cerclage released during 37th week and several days later delivered a healthy six-pound, two-ounce baby girl. Claimant and infant went home in 2 days (baby blanket knitted by mom finished "just in time").

Potential Charges and Savings

Without case management intervention, this patient would have had at least three hospital admissions, each one of 3 to 5 days' duration, to treat diabetic complications, urinary tract infection, premature labor episodes, or toxemia. Without our intervention, it is highly likely that a premature baby would have been born and at the very least, mother would have been hospitalized for monitoring for the last 3 to 4 weeks of her pregnancy.

> 3 hospital admissions @ 3 days each @ $1,500/day = $13,500 for various complications
> 3-week hospital admission @ $1,500/day for monitoring = $31,500
> Total savings if premature baby was avoided = $45,000
> If premature baby had been the result, costs would be higher with a length of stay of 45 days in Neonatal ICU @ $2,500/day = $112,500
> Total savings if preemie baby was born = $157,500

Analysis

As can be seen with this case, continuous intervention by the case manager allowed for early identification and resolution of many problems, which prevented more costly complications to the claimant and her child. The case manager was creative, persistent, and focused on the goal of a healthy baby and a safe pregnancy. This woman presented many challenges (aside from her medical problems), and the advocacy role assumed by the case manager resulted in better quality of care, excellent outcome, and demonstrated savings to the plan.

LONG-TERM CASE MANAGEMENT FOR CHRONIC DISEASE MANAGEMENT

Case Overview

An 18-year-old female was identified for case management during an admission to the hospital for seizure disorder, deliberate overdosing with Tegretol (antiseizure medication), depression, lupus, and kidney failure. Past history included cardiac surgery at age 8 and the diagnosis of lupus with progression of symptoms since age 10. This young girl's mother had died 1 year ago; her father was also hospitalized during this girl's admission for treatment of coronary disease and diabetes. He would be unable to be a care provider for his daughter, who would need home care following treatment of her serious conditions. Although this young girl had multiple problems, she was in a university children's hospital, whose health care team was most receptive to case management intervention.

Problems Identified

The following problems were identified and resolved by the case manager during the initial 6 months of intervention:

1. After treatment for her acute medical conditions, and before she could go home, she required inpatient treatment for her severe depression. The facility recommended was not a provider within the father's medical plan; if she were admitted here, reimbursement would be limited to 70% of the charges. The father would be unable to pay the 30% co-payment. Intervention: Case manager obtained approval from the plan administrator for reimbursement at 100% if case manager was able to negotiate a network fee. Case manager worked with CFO of facility and negotiated the approved rate.

2. After inpatient treatment of her medical and psychological conditions, it was determined that there was much anger/stress between the father and daughter, especially since the death of her mother. Counseling was recommended for both; however, the father refused to partake in sessions. There was no network provider within walking distance from the girl's home, and the father was unwilling to commit to providing the necessary transportation. Intervention: Case manager was able to locate a therapist with expertise in treating adolescents with chronic conditions, negotiated with her to accept network fee reimbursement, and negotiated with the plan to approve her in the network. In addition, the claimant was referred to a support group, located by case manager, for persons with lupus.

3. The claimant's progression of symptoms had already resulted in a kidney failure and, in an effort to reduce the severity of the progression, she would need monthly infusions of Cytoxan and weekly lab work. This girl was in her senior year of high school, had already missed much school, and further absences would jeopardize her graduation. Intervention: Case manager arranged for infusion and laboratory services after school hours and at negotiated rates.

Outcome

This girl's situation eventually stabilized and the file was closed; however, because of her prior history of noncompliance as well as low IQ, the therapist and physician were advised to contact the case manager for any further problems. Within 4 months, the claimant's symptoms had become more severe, she was having two to three seizures per day, her blood pressure had become elevated, she was showing subtherapeutic levels of medications in laboratory findings, and she was not keeping medical appointments. Both the physician and therapist contacted the case manager and the file was reopened. The case manager identified and resolved the following problems during the second phase of case management intervention, which took place over 5 months:

1. The claimant, no longer needing Cytoxan, was placed on a complex medication regimen and was being seen by a rheumatologist, neurologist, nephrologist, and psychiatrist, all of whom were changing and adjusting medications. Case manager, in reviewing medications and in conversation with MDs, patient, and her father, determined that patient once again was very depressed, overwhelmed with diet and medications, and was now dating a "nice boy" and just "wanted to be normal." Intervention: Case manager scheduled a meeting with patient, father, therapist, rheumatologist (who, at the request of case manager, agreed to act as coordinator of care with all medication changes going through him), and case manager for a Saturday morning (to accommodate patient's school requirements and father's need to not miss any more days from work with the risk of loss of medical benefits). Patient's IQ of 85 with possible neurological compromise secondary to increased seizure activity and complex medication schedule (some different doses on alternate days) were all determined to be factors contributing to noncompliance. The patient was encouraged to verbalize her concerns and desire to be "normal." She agreed to resume counseling and keep all medical appointments. Case manager worked with MD, patient, and patient's father regarding medication schedule. Dispenser/calendar system was developed and used successfully.

2. Patient's father, also experiencing medical complications, was feeling overwhelmed with care responsibilities for his daughter and had not really grieved since the death of his wife (who was closer to his daughter and was his "best friend"). Case manager learned this during calls to him and realized that he, too, needed intervention. Intervention: Case manager located a therapist near father's place of work and secured his agreement to attend "just one visit." The session was a good one and he agreed to continue. He became more compliant with his medication, diet, and visits to MD and began working in strategies to assist his daughter.

Potential Charges and Savings

For this young girl, at best several hospital admissions for seizure disorder, kidney failure, acute depression, and lupus exacerbations were avoided. Prior to our involvement, she had five hospital admissions with length of stay ranging from 7 to 19 days each. Conservative estimate of savings from her would be a minimum of $100,000. Additional savings could be realized from the minimal intervention with the father, as well.

Analysis

This case presented multiple and serious medical psychosocial and financial issues that, without the assistance of a case manager, would have resulted in further deterioration and possible death of this young girl. Case managers should also understand from this presentation how vitally important it is to discover and address the psychosocial factors as well as family issues. Working as a member of the health care team, but also as a key negotiator and patient advocate, the case manager became the individual responsible for the success of this case.

PEDIATRIC ASTHMA

Case Overview

A 7-year-old boy was identified for case management when he was admitted to the hospital for the third time in 5 months for asthma, this time with an additional complication of pneumonia. This child is the oldest of three children and lives in a rural area of Mississippi with his parents. The family had just moved from Georgia, the father disabled since 1995, and the mother (the insured) employed 9 months with the current employer and provider of benefits. Prior history indicates a 5-year history of frequent asthma episodes treated in urgent care centers and emergency departments with several hospital admissions each year. The case management goal was to obtain stability of this medical condition with child and parents and to increase knowledge and compliance.

Problems Identified

During the 6 months of case management intervention, the following problems were identified and resolved by the case manager:

1. Initially, parents were very resistant to assistance from case manager. The mother, especially, was concerned that her employer might know about all the admissions and bills, and that she might now be in danger of losing her job and medical coverage for her family. She also stated that she could not afford case management. Intervention: Case manager spent much time explaining how her son was identified for intervention, that this was part of her benefit coverage and was offered at no cost to her, and that her supervisor or managers were not involved nor would any of this be discussed with them. Finally, she provided consent, and an appointment for a visit to their home was scheduled.

2. During the home visit, the case manager noted the presence of a cat and dog as family pets, as well as carpeting in the child's room, a down comforter and pillow on his bed, and a father who smokes although he acknowledged that he was trying to stop. Intervention: Case manager discussed with parents and child that the aforementioned factors were highly probable in triggering child's asthma episodes. She recommended that nonallergic bedding be used, carpet be removed, that pets at least for the time be given to a friend, and that any smoking be done outdoors. Parents agreed and complied with requests.

3. Child had been treated by many pediatricians and family practitioners at several centers. As the case manager discussed the importance of continuity of care, the parents with much embarrassment informed her of the reason for this. Their prior insurance company required a 20% co-payment and, with the increased number of doctor visits and emergency room and hospital admissions, they were having financial problems with doctors who refused further treatment unless a payment was made at the time of their visit. Hospital emergency rooms did not require this payment, which is why the family used them more. Intervention: Case manager explained that current insurance would have a $10 co-pay for network MDs and that the case manager would intervene and arrange for assistance with the billing department. She also stressed the importance of ongoing involvement with one physician for continuity and for a better ability to evaluate and modify treatment, medications, etc.

4. The child was having clusters of episodes that the mother acknowledged she tried to treat herself with over-the-counter medications. When his temperature would start to go up, she would use the antibiotics that she "saved" from the last episode (or from another child in the family). She explained that because the antibiotics were so expensive, she tried to make them last. Intervention: Case manager explained the process of therapeutic blood levels of antibiotic steroids, bronchodilators, etc., what occurs when medications are not taken as directed, reasons why over-the-counter preparations are contraindicated for children with asthma, etc. She also stressed that until the child's condition could be evaluated further, prompt attention by a physician needed to occur sooner rather than later. The parents related that no one had ever explained all of this to them.

5. The child had been seen by many different doctors but had never been evaluated by a pediatric pulmonologist. Because of the increasing severity of episodes, the case manager discussed this with parents and suggested that they request a referral from the present pediatrician. The parents were very reluctant to do this, because they were afraid of making the doctor angry.

Intervention: Case manager, after determining parents' interest in obtaining this consult, offered to intervene on their behalf with current pediatrician. This was done and arrangements were made.

6. Following child's evaluation by a pediatric pulmonologist, it was determined that he would be a good candidate for an asthma disease management program that this group practice had available. The plan, however, had language that did not cover "educational services." Intervention: Case manager contacted plan administrator, explained child's history, financial risks to the plan (i.e., costs of continuing hospital admissions, emergency room visits, etc.), and emphasized the parents' willingness and demonstrated cooperation to date. Also advised that fees for program could be negotiated. Approval was obtained, and child and parents completed the program's initial phase of risk analysis and education and will continue to be followed indefinitely at minimal cost.

Outcome

Many escalating and potential problems were addressed during this time. Coordination among physicians, corrections of medication misuse, and asthma education all contributed to an improved and healthier lifestyle.

Potential Charges and Savings

Had case management not been involved, child had strong probability of continuing with multiple emergency department visits and several hospital admissions. Each emergency department visit was averaging $600 with 10 per year (this per mother) and 5 admissions varying in length from 5 to 10 days each. Potential charges for this child could have been between $50,000 to $60,000. For the year that included case management involvement, there were only two emergency department visits and no hospital admissions.

Analysis

With the illustration of this child's situation, case managers should be able to appreciate the value of getting "up close and personal." This was clearly a case that was being lost in the health care system and the financial difficulties of a family. Too often, we do not stop to uncover the reasons behind the problems and costs. As demonstrated in this case, each problem (once identified) had a relatively easy solution. Success can be attained using the sound principles of case management throughout the process. Improved outcomes, quality of care, and savings were measurable in this case, as was the parents' satisfaction as measured by a positive response to a survey sent to them.

AIDS MANAGEMENT

Case Overview

This 51-year-old male was identified for case management during his admission to the hospital for weakness of the left upper extremity and slurred speech. No definitive diagnosis was made at the time of this admission or at a subsequent admission to a different hospital 5 weeks later for the same symptomatology. His prior history was a diagnosis of HIV 10 years ago secondary to IV use of heroin. The claimant stopped the use of heroin at the time of the HIV diagnosis and up until 1 year prior to the hospital admission had received no consistent medical care. Throughout those many years, he took AZT but acknowledged that he did not take it as prescribed. There were frequent changes in physicians because of "personality clashes and other differences." Recent blood tests showed the toxoplasmosis, but CAT scans and MRIs of the brain were "inconclusive." The claimant was married. His wife was stated to be very supportive but under increasing stress because of his mood swings and angry outbursts, including threats to sign himself out of the hospital against medical advice. This man was employed as a supervisor of a trucking firm, had been working continuously (other than during these two hospital admissions), and was determined to return to work so as not to lose his benefits. Although seen by an infectious disease specialist while hospitalized, the claimant was anxious to return to his internist for ongoing care, citing that his condition was not "serious enough" to require a specialist.

Problems Identified

This case has been open for more than 1 year, and it is expected that case management intervention will be beneficial and warranted for the foreseeable future. The following illustrates just some of the problems that were identified and resolved by the case manager.

1. Claimant was being treated in local hospitals, by multiple physicians without the benefit of currently recommended drug protocol for AIDS, including protease inhibitors. Due to less-than-optimum treatment and symptoms highly probable of toxoplasmosis, his continued deterioration was likely. Claimant was extremely fearful, controlling, and in denial about his condition. He

preferred to believe that he had had a mild stroke, saying, "All I need is some physical and speech therapy." Intervention: Case manager spent time establishing rapport and gaining trust of this very frightened man. She provided him with information and educational materials about the advances in the treatment of AIDS from a renowned university hospital with acknowledged expertise in this condition. She asked him to at least consider a consultation visit in order for him to be able to make an informed decision, including the option to remain with the current physician. The claimant did agree and the case manager made the arrangements and attended the appointment with him and his wife.

2. Claimant was pleased with consultation visit and treatment and attended several visits. In a follow-up call to the physician, case manager learned that he had not kept most recent appointment. Intervention: Case manager called claimant's home and was told that the trips into the city were taking too long, requiring at least a half-day from work. He was concerned that his boss was becoming less understanding and asking questions about his condition. Case manager called the physician group, explained concerns of claimant and asked for names of university-affiliated infectious disease specialists nearer to the claimant's home or place of work. Obtained names of three MDs; however, none were in the employer's plan's network. Case manager contacted plan administrator and obtained approval for physician selected by claimant.

3. Before setting an appointment with this MD, his office requested copies of hospital records (from the second most recent admissions) including MRIs, CAT scans, and laboratory tests. Claimant and his wife had difficulty in speaking to the appropriate person at each of the hospitals, and then were told that there would be charges (payable in advance). When they called the plan's claims department to see if this would be covered, they were told "no." Intervention: Case manager contacted plan administrator, explained that not getting records would necessitate duplication of tests, further delay in treatment. Approval was obtained from the plan administrator and the hospitals agreed to submit claims for prompt payment through the case manager, who would expedite process.

4. Claimant was started on the recommended drug protocol including a protease inhibitor. His condition began to improve; however, in one of her follow-up calls to the claimant, the case manager learned that he had abruptly discontinued the protease inhibitor because of pain and left side abdominal bloating. Intervention: Remembering from her review of claimant's medical records a finding of a left adrenal tumor 1 year ago (felt to be benign but with advisory for reevaluation in order to monitor size, etc.), the case manager contacted the infectious disease specialist to discuss her concerns as

well as to alert him about claimant's discontinuance of Crixovan (the protease inhibitor). Referral to an endocrinologist was made. The tumor had changed minimally but did not require surgical intervention. The claimant was placed on Viracept (another protease inhibitor, felt to have fewer side effects), which has been well-tolerated. Both MD and case manager have explained dangers involved in claimant's adjusting dosage, times, and medications without MD consultation. (The concern is that the HIV will develop immunity to these drugs, especially with the abrupt starting and stopping of the drugs.)

Outcome

Many other problems were resolved during this time. These included assisting with a return to work, referral to a support group, and ongoing advocacy for the claimant and his wife as they coped with the realities of this disease.

Potential Charges and Savings

Case management was definitely responsible for the avoidance of many charges that most certainly would have occurred. These included at least two hospital admissions (secondary to noncompliance and the resulting complications or deterioration of his condition) and duplication of testing and doctor visits as the claimant continued his pursuit of treatment from multiple physicians without appropriate expertise.

Analysis

The problems illustrated in this case are somewhat typical of those of patients dealing with life-threatening medical conditions. The desire to be in control, feelings of anxiety, and mistrust sometimes to the point of self-destruction are often seen. Patients need to be accepted where they are, and we must acknowledge their feelings while at the same time keeping them from harm's way. Continuous involvement by the case manager allowed for prompt intervention and resulted in improved, more appropriate care for this patient. Because of ongoing problems with noncompliance and real potential for further problems, this case will remain open. Activity of the case manager will be determined by the stability of the patient. Although the addition of protease inhibitors has greatly improved life expectancy for HIV patients and has changed case management, it is still more cost-effective to prevent problems than resolve them. Case management will continue to be an effective strategy in improving outcomes and demonstrating savings.

DIABETES

Case Overview

Mrs. S, a 58-year-old Caucasian female, was identified for case management during her hospital admission for a left thalamic CVA. She presented to the emergency room with complaints of numbness to the face, jaw, and right arm; dizziness; and right hemiplegia. It was noted that she had been diagnosed with type 2 diabetes 3 years prior, had not seen a physician in 1 year, and had a blood sugar on admission of 525. Mrs. S was a smoker, had a cholesterol of 221, and her triglycerides were 450. Her blood pressure in the ER was 149/99. She was not taking any medications or following any diet plan. She was divorced, and lived with her daughter, son in-law, and grandchildren in rural Tennessee. Prior to the event, she was employed as a loader in a factory on the evening shift.

Problems Identified

The following problems were identified and resolved by the case manager:

1. Mrs. S was in need of extensive rehabilitation in order to return to her baseline functioning and return to work. Intervention: The case manager worked closely with her health care team and arranged for timely transition from acute care to their network participating rehabilitation unit. When able, she was transitioned to a three times weekly outpatient program. Prior to returning to work, the case manager arranged for the occupational therapist to visit the patient's employer and evaluate her workstation and duties for safety in light of her minor residual limitations.

2. The patient had not followed a diabetic or low cholesterol meal plan in the past and did not understand the importance of it. She was started on Glucophage at the time of diagnosis, but stopped this on her own believing it to be the cause of occasional diarrhea. She was not checking her blood sugar at home. She continued to smoke and had not been educated regarding the relationship between smoking and coronary artery disease. Mrs. S was obese at 179 lbs. and a height of 5'. She had not seen a physician nor taken any medications in over 1 year. Intervention: The attending neurologist was contacted by the case manager and he agreed to consult with a network participating endocrinologist. The case manager requested the hospital's dietitian see the patient for an assessment, recommendations, and to begin teaching. The case manager obtained a prescription and letter of medical necessity for a glucometer and testing supplies, which the family picked up and brought to the rehab unit prior to discharge. This intervention allowed

the claimant and her daughter to become proficient with blood sugar testing while nursing support was available. She was also instructed on drawing up and administering insulin prior to discharge. Her progress was monitored closely by communicating regularly with the dietitian and diabetes educator.

3. Mrs. S was diagnosed with coronary artery disease resulting from cardiovascular system compromise due to hyperlipidemia and hyperglycemia. A combination of high blood pressure, insulin resistance, and high levels of fats in the blood had increased her risk of heart disease and stroke significantly. If all three conditions were not brought under control, she would continue to be at high risk for future complications. The patient had never received any diabetic education, did not understand the relationship of her coronary artery disease and hypertension to diabetes, and it was felt this was the major reason for her past noncompliance. Intervention: The case manager contacted the patient at the bedside and discussed the importance of self-management education and following her physician's plan of care in order to reduce future risks. The patient verbalized understanding and a willingness to learn. The case manager, therefore, arranged for bedside education from the registered dietitian and diabetes educator to continue on a daily basis while in the rehab unit. The patient's daughter was included in several training sessions. One follow-up skilled nursing visit was arranged by the case manager to evaluate the patient in her home environment, reinforce teaching, and answer any questions. The case manager continued to monitor the patient closely by contacting her twice weekly by phone and maintaining communication with her health care team.

Outcome

Upon completion of her 14-day inpatient rehab stay and several-week outpatient rehab program, the patient was able to demonstrate the ability to safely perform her work duties without modification to her employer and the occupational therapist. She was allowed to return to work 4 hours per day initially and gradually transitioned to a full shift. Because she was her sole source of support, it was vital she be able to return to gainful employment.

The endocrinologist started the patient on a multidrug regimen including insulin. The physician made continuing adjustments until her blood sugars were well-controlled. After discharge, the case manager contacted the hospital's diabetes center and learned patients newly diagnosed with diabetes in their facility could attend a 2-day class free of the usual $480 fee. Orders were received and the claimant was enrolled in the class that she attended with a family member. The patient continued to see her endocrinologist every 3 months for follow-up care. She was compliant with her dietary and medication regimen, lost 14 pounds in 3 months, began a walking program, and joined a diabetes support group. The patient stopped smoking while hospitalized and remains smoke free to date. Most significantly, Mrs. S reduced her baseline HbA1c from 14.3% (goal = <7%) to 7.8% 3 months after her CVA.

Potential Charges and Savings

Without case management intervention, the claimant would have likely been discharged from rehab without having received the much needed diabetes education that was the key to her future compliance with her plan of care and avoidance of readmission to date (2 years later). It is unlikely she would have received the specialized endocrinology care, which resulted in bringing her blood sugars under control and keeping them stable, lowering her risk for repeat strokes, heart attack, and other diabetic complications. Had case management not been involved to arrange her formal diabetes class, the plan would have been billed for the class. In addition, the patient certainly would have been discharged prematurely from rehab without achieving adequate diabetes control that would have placed her at great risk for a diabetic emergency and multiple future readmissions.

Diabetes class = $480
3 hospital admissions for various complications, 5 days each @
   $1,500/day = $22,500
Associated MD fees of $100/day x 15 days = $1,500
5 emergency room visits for diabetic complications @ $750/visit = $3,750
Total avoided charges = $28,230

Analysis

This case demonstrates the positive outcomes that can be achieved when the diabetes patient is motivated, a window of opportunity is seized, and the appropriate self-management tools are made available. Further, continuous monitoring and intervention by the case manager allowed for resolution and prevention of multiple interrelated problems that improved the patient's quality of life and reduced exposure to the plan.

ONCOLOGY MANAGEMENT

Case Overview

Mrs. H, a 58-year-old Hispanic female, was identified for case management when she was scheduled to undergo an abdominal perineal resection with creation of a permanent colostomy for adenocarcinoma of the colon. The claimant lived with her husband in Woodhaven, New York. Her husband was the insured and worked nights. She had an adult daughter living outside the home who was very supportive. The claimant was contacted and offered case management, but she declined.

Four months after her surgery, she continued to experience significant abdominal pain. She saw her surgeon for this problem and was prescribed anti-inflammatory and pain medications. He advised the claimant the pain was due to adhesions. A CAT scan was negative for tumor and did not reveal any significant pathology. The surgeon recommended she see her gynecologist for an evaluation. Meanwhile, she continued to take pain medicines. The patient saw her gynecologist 7 months after her initial surgery. She was diagnosed with a urinary tract infection and started on antibiotics. The gynecologist could find no reason for her chronic pain other than psychological issues related to the radical surgery and her husband's aversion to the colostomy. He suggested she seek counseling for this problem and started Mrs. H on antidepressants. She was scheduled for a hysteroscopy in order to visualize the uterine vault and also referred to an urologist for evaluation. The hysteroscopy with biopsies ruled out any uterine pathology.

Nine months after her initial surgery, she continued to complain of significant pain that was causing problems with her mobility. The patient began to walk with a cane. The pain was initially described as being low in the pelvis. Later, she began to complain of a burning pain in her thighs. She was referred to a neurologist who diagnosed the patient with degenerative disc disease and arthritis, which he felt was the source of her pain.

Eleven months following her initial surgery, she developed back pain in addition to the persistent burning sensations in her thighs. She was referred to a rheumatologist for evaluation. He performed an MRI, which was negative. In the interim, she was referred to an orthopedic surgeon who specialized in spinal problems. He could find no answer for the patient's chronic pain. A routine follow-up colonoscopy was performed 1 year after her surgery. The results were negative. She continued to see her urologist for worsening bladder function.

One month later, the claimant was admitted with urinary retention. She was again contacted regarding case management and this time she agreed. During this admission, a mass was identified that was compressing a ureter. Further study revealed widespread metastasis of her cancer. The case manager worked with the urologist to locate a network participating oncologist who specialized in colon cancer at a well-known metropolitan cancer center.

The case manager coordinated arrangements for a visit a few days after discharge. At that visit, participation in a clinical trial was discussed. However, after consideration, the claimant and her daughter declined. Alternatively, a plan to proceed with traditional chemotherapy was decided upon. Case management worked closely with the oncologist and his staff to arrive at a plan that allowed each chemotherapy treatment to be initiated at the cancer center and continued for 48 hours at home. The case manager made arrangements for the daughter to be trained to discontinue the infusion and perform line care. This avoided the need for an inpatient stay or skilled nursing visits. When the patient's red blood count dropped as a result of her chemotherapy, Epoetin therapy was initiated. The case manager contacted the oncologist who agreed to allow the expensive drug to be purchased through the patient's pharmacy plan and delivered to her home, as opposed to purchasing it from the cancer center at a much higher price. This intervention resulted in conservation of the patient's limited benefits and significant savings to the plan. She was started on an effective pain management regimen by the oncologist, who was familiar with her type of pain, and currently reports she is pain free. Unfortunately, the patient's prognosis is poor.

Problems Identified

The following problems were identified and resolved by the case manager:

1. Mrs. H received fragmented care for 1 year, which did not identify the source of her pain. During this time, she did not receive appropriate care for her cancer, which was spreading. In addition to pain and suffering, her benefit dollars were not used efficiently. Had the patient agreed to case management when initially offered, this unfortunate scenario might have been prevented. Intervention: After the patient agreed to case management, the admitting urologist was contacted promptly and a plan agreed upon to have the patient evaluated at a Center of Excellence by a specialist in her type of cancer.

2. The patient's chemotherapy needed to be infused over 48 hours. Intervention: To prevent an inpatient stay or skilled nursing visit, the case manager arranged for the daughter to be trained to discontinue the infusion and perform her line care.

3. The patient required expensive medication to address her low blood counts. Intervention: As an alternative to purchasing the drug at the cancer center at a price 100% above AWP, the case manager arranged to obtain the drug through a pharmaceutical house participating with the patient's pharmacy network. The drug was delivered to the patient's home, and she brought it with her to her cancer center visits for administration. This intervention resulted in significant savings to the plan and conservation of the patient's limited benefit resources.

Outcome

The patient's care became prompt, efficient, and cost-effective as a result of case management intervention. Her much needed benefit dollars were spent only for medically necessary care that was expertly coordinated through one physician and facility. Past problems with poor communication between multiple physicians were eliminated.

Potential Charges and Savings

Without case management intervention, the patient would have required, at minimum, one skilled nursing visit every 2 weeks for discontinuation of her chemotherapy infusion and line care. Over the 6-month regimen, this would amount to twelve visits. In addition, the Epoetin she received twice monthly (12 doses) would have been purchased from the cancer center at a cost 100% above AWP ($4,129.44 per dose) as opposed to 14% below AWP ($1,775.66 per dose).

Skilled nursing visits × 12 avoided @ $130/visit = $1,560
Drug costs avoided = $28,245.36
Total avoided charges = $29,805.36

Analysis

This case demonstrates the value of care coordinated by a case manager to avoid fragmentation, poor communication, wasted benefit dollars, and to facilitate prompt identification and intervention for health problems. Unfortunately, the patient did not have case management services for 1 year after her initial cancer surgery. If she had, it is likely the outcome would have been different and would have greatly affected her quality of life and the amount of health care dollars spent.

MORBID OBESITY/GASTRIC BYPASS

Case Overview

Mrs. C, a 39-year-old female, was identified for case management during precertification for a planned gastric bypass procedure. The claimant was 5'9" and weighed 370 pounds, giving her a body mass index (BMI) of 46 (a BMI of 20–25 is the ideal range for an adult, and a BMI of greater than 40 indicates a serious weight problem and carries the greatest risk for medical complications). The claimant had been overweight her entire life, and had tried numerous diets, including use of prescription weight-loss medication without demonstrable success. She had a medical comorbidity of hypertension for which she takes one prescription agent with marginal control.

She reported frequent daytime headaches and somnolence, which she attributed to poorly controlled blood pressure. The claimant also told of severe bouts of hunger during the day despite eating three full meals, often binging on high carbohydrate snacks and fast foods, and drinking approximately one liter of full calorie soda per day. Upon exertion, she experienced shortness of breath and demonstrated bilateral pitting edema to her lower extremities.

She experienced recurrent vaginal and urinary tract infections, which she suggested were caused by poor hygiene due to her large body habitus. However, she avoided medical intervention due to embarrassment about her weight and shame discussing this issue with her male primary care physician. In addition, Mrs. C stated that her physician was not supportive of her plan to undergo gastric bypass surgery, as he felt that she was a poor surgical risk and should continue conservative weight-loss measures.

Employed as a laboratory technician, she said she suffered from social anxiety for fear of ridicule and had never sought psychological counseling for treatment. She had never married and had limited social supports. The main caregiver for her elderly parents who live nearby, she lived alone in a condominium apartment.

Problems Identified

The following problems were identified and resolved by the case manager during the 12 months of intervention:

1. Of concern was the claimant's untreated social anxiety, which if not immediately addressed, would hinder her attempts at independent health management. Intervention: The case manager provided an on-site visit to the claimant's home to develop a trusting relationship with the claimant. Mrs. C voiced her frustration over many failed weight-loss attempts, and spoke of the cycle of continued weight gain and using food to self-soothe her dissatisfaction with her health and appearance. The case manager researched a psychotherapist with experience in counseling food addictions, the claimant was referred to a psychiatrist to address her anxiety disorder, and was placed on appropriate short-term medication. With ongoing telephonic support from the case manager during the initial trial of medication, the patient showed improvement in her overall mood and increased work productivity in the weeks following psychiatric intervention.

2. Referred to a bariatric surgeon by a coworker, the patient underwent an initial surgical consultation and was advised to undergo an extensive medical evaluation prior to surgical consideration. For this, she needed support and direction to locate appropriate physicians for medical clearance. Intervention: Working collaboratively with the claimant's primary care physician, the case manager researched and recommended appropriate specialists to address the claimant's medical issues, and researched a cardiologist for the

claimant. Mrs. C underwent baseline cardiac testing including a Thallium Stress Test, which did not reveal any cardiac abnormalities. She was placed on a second blood pressure medication, which effectively controlled her blood pressure.

Noting that her daytime headaches and somnolence were suggestive of sleep apnea, the case manager researched a pulmonologist for the claimant and ensured appropriate scheduling of an outpatient sleep study, which confirmed a sleep apnea diagnosis. The case manager then found a DME company that offered sleep apnea classes to assist patients with use of the equipment in a small group setting. Although initially fearful of meeting with other patients, Mrs. C received emotional backing and encouragement from the case manager to foster compliance with group attendance. She also was given appropriate training and education in appropriate CPAP use, and suitable in-home follow-up by the DME company respiratory therapist. The claimant reported compliance with use, with resultant improved sleep and decreased headaches.

3. The case manager recognized that Mrs. C's frequent vaginal and urinary tract infections countered with her increased hunger might be indicative of an underlying diagnosis of diabetes. Intervention: She collaborated with the claimant's primary care physician, who ordered a glucose tolerance test for the claimant. The test confirmed a diagnosis of type 2 diabetes mellitus, and demonstrated a Hemoglobin A1C of 8.0. The patient was referred to an endocrinologist for further intervention, placed on appropriate oral medication, and given an appropriate carbohydrate-restricted diet. The case manager started blood glucose monitoring and recommended a Nutritionist consultation to provide in-depth diabetes education. Following Nutritionist collaboration, she provided extensive dietary support to Mrs. C, recommending lifestyle modifications, including substituting diet soda and water for full-calorie soda, and reading food labels to assist with carbohydrate monitoring. She also suggested a switch to a female gynecologist, who prescribed appropriate antibiotic medication to treat the patient's urinary tract infection. The case manager also promoted good health habits by reinforcing the need for monthly breast self-examinations and an annual pap smear.

4. Excluded from consideration for the less-risky laparoscopic gastric bypass procedure due to her extremely high BMI, Mrs. C was considered for the open surgical procedure, which would have resulted in a large abdominal incision and placed her at risk for wound infection and dehiscence due to her large protuberant abdomen. As bariatric surgery has significant peri- and postoperative risks, the case manager recommended preoperative weight loss for the claimant to decrease her BMI, decrease her risk for surgical complications, and allow for consideration of a laparoscopic procedure.

With improvement in the patient's social anxiety, the case manager also recommended a second try with Weight Watchers for additional support with weight loss and meal planning. At the recommendation of the case manager, Mrs. C began attending a bariatric support group to provide further information and insight regarding her planned gastric bypass surgery. Intervention: The case manager accompanied Mrs. C to her initial Weight Watchers and bariatric support group meetings, and provided ongoing encouragement to her and assistance with appropriate meal planning. The patient regularly attended both Weight Watchers and the bariatric support group meetings, and kept a written log of her meals.

When the case manager suggested that she identify her triggers to overeating, including frustration, anger, and sadness, the patient reported that she felt overwhelmed with caring for her parents, and that her siblings were not sharing in the responsibilities. Through collaboration with the patient's treating psychotherapist, the case manager worked on solutions to empower Mrs. C to confront her siblings on parental support issues, and assisted her with developing a schedule to delegate her parents' weekly shopping excursions and medical visits equitably with her siblings.

Following a group effort with the claimant's primary care physician and cardiologist, the case manager assisted Mrs. C in designing a realistic exercise regimen of daily walking, advising her to park her car a further distance from her office and use the stairs to her third-floor apartment instead of the elevator. Through identification of triggers to stress, a support system with weight loss, and an achievable exercise program, the patient lost 50 pounds over the course of 5 months, successfully decreasing her BMI and making possible the less risky laparoscopic surgical procedure.

5. The case remained open during the peri- and postoperative period for Mrs. C's gastric bypass procedure. Intervention: The case manager educated the claimant regarding surgical expectations and potential postoperative complications, recommending an additional Nutritionist visit for individualized information on meal size and necessary modifications in chewing and swallowing food to prevent vomiting postoperatively. The Nutritionist's teaching was reinforced with in-depth information on the necessary protein and vitamin requirements during the initial postoperative period and beyond.

6. The patient lacked postoperative home support. Intervention: With Mrs. C's permission, the case manager contacted her sister, who offered to help her sister during her initial hospital recovery, and arranged a home care visit to instruct the patient and her sister on management of her surgical drain and surgical incision sites. Mrs. C underwent laparoscopic gastric bypass surgery as scheduled, did not experience any postoperative complications, and was able to return to full-time employment 3 weeks after her surgery.

Outcome

This case was monitored for 6 months after the successful surgery. The case manager remained in close collaboration with Mrs. C's bariatric surgeon to monitor laboratory values and identify potential hemolytic and electrolyte imbalances that might occur postoperatively and taught the patient to interpret her lab data. She was compliant with ongoing physician follow-up on a monthly basis.

The patient lost 96 pounds after her surgery, representing a total weight loss of 146 pounds since case management intervention. She no longer suffered from sleep apnea and donated her purchased CPAP machine to her local church outreach program. She continues to demonstrate an ideal Hemoglobin A1C value of 5.5 and no longer requires medication to treat diabetes. Her disease is appropriately controlled through strict carbohydrate avoidance and ongoing endocrinology management, and she has no need for blood pressure medication now. She has joined a gym, practices aerobic exercise and strength training three times per week, and anticipates reaching her target weight of 150 pounds within the next 6-to-8 months. She continues to attend Weight Watchers and a bariatric support group, and has made new friends who have shared similar experiences. On a comparably limited basis, she has stayed with psychotherapy; her antianxiety medication has been discontinued and she makes good use of her stress management system. Mrs. C has several companions with whom she often meets socially, and is building a relationship with a man. She and her siblings have placed their parents in an assisted-living facility where they enjoy socialization with senior citizens and medical monitoring.

Potential Charges and Savings

For this claimant, several hospitalizations were avoided. Prior to case management intervention, the claimant had undiagnosed sleep apnea and diabetes mellitus, and severe social anxiety that inhibited her ability to seek appropriate medical intervention. Had her medical issues not been addressed, she would have certainly experienced hospitalization due to potential problems of sleep apnea, which include cardiac arrhythmias, narcolepsy, and stroke, and her diabetes would have gone undetected for an indeterminate period of time. Conservative hospital costs would have totaled approximately $75,000. Had morbid obesity not been addressed, she would have faced increased morbidity and mortality, with lifelong costs certainly totaling at least $1 million for treatment of preventable, obesity-related complications.

In addition, had case management not been involved to provide support and direction to the claimant with regard to preoperative weight loss, the claimant likely would have undergone the more risky open surgical procedure, and been at risk for postoperative complications because of her large body habitus, and for infection due to diabetes, all while lacking social support. Case management addressed the patient's potential complications, making possible the less-invasive surgical procedure and avoiding additional hospital costs for postoperative complications of approximately $20,000.

Analysis

This case presented multiple medical and psychosocial issues that, without the assistance of a case manager, would have resulted in further deterioration and possibly death of the claimant from preventable medical issues. Instead, through development of a trusting case management relationship, the patient was able to take control of her weight and fears with resultant medical, social, and spiritual success.

PEDIATRIC: LONG-TERM FEEDING DISORDER

Case Overview

This female claimant was born at 37 weeks gestation via Cesarean section with a birth weight of 3 pounds 5 ounces and had both cardiac problems (PDA) and a diaphragmatic hernia. She remained in the NICU for nearly 3 months. Among her medical issues were having only one functioning lung, failure to thrive due to gastroesophageal reflux, and persistent retching and other feeding difficulties. She was demonstrating developmental delays.

Before entering case management, the claimant had required and undergone surgical repair of hernia, ligation of the Patent Ductus Arteriosis (PDA), Nissan Fundoplication (surgery to address chronic issues of gastric reflux) for G.I. reflux and placement of a gastrostomy button (which became her sole source for feeding and hydration). When the claimant was 20 months of age and still totally dependent on gastrostomy feedings, as well as having become completely intolerant of any food, fluid, or objects placed in her mouth (other than her pacifier), the child's parents contacted the insurer seeking approval for her inpatient admission into Columbia Presbyterian Medical Center for a high-dollar 5-day intensive behaviorally based feeding program.

The insurer wanted the program and the potential outcomes of attendance and nonattendance researched; therefore, they requested case management services. They were seeking the input of the medical case manager and the entire medical team, and recommendations provided by the case manager for approval or denial of the requested admission.

The claimant's parents had become very stressed about the child's inability to "eat normally" and were rushing in any and all directions where they believed they would find quick answers to what was potentially becoming a lifelong problem. There had been repeat hospitalizations (high dollar) related to respiratory and feeding issues. The child's parents were insistent that the insurer cover the costs of each attempt at "fixing the problems" and had threatened legal action if denial of benefits was even suggested.

The insurer was concerned that there had been duplication of services and that benefit dollars had been spent on other unsuccessful attempts to improve this child's situation. Clearly, case management was needed to oversee needs, care, and costs.

In addition, the claimant's very limited DME coverage was quickly being depleted as the physicians had put in place at home an oximeter, oxygen, and feeding pump (all nonnegotiated), prior to case management being brought into the case. This needed to be addressed in retroactive negotiation to maximize the claimant's DME benefit dollars.

Problems Identified

1. The claimant's oral intolerance had become so severe that it was projected by the G.I. team that she would require gastrostomy tube feedings for an undetermined number of years and possibly into adulthood unless there were more aggressive interventions made (beyond the Early Intervention Program services that she had already been receiving without improvement in this area).

2. Immediate research into the history of this feeding program, its clinical outcomes, and its potential for success with this claimant needed to be undertaken by the case manager so that recommendations could be made to the insurer almost immediately (as the opening in the program was made available within a short window of time and would not occur again for many months).

3. The DME providers were initially resistant to retroactive negotiations, but due to outstanding claims were eventually persuaded by the case manager to negotiate to maintain the accounts ongoing on this potentially long-term case.

4. The Columbia Presbyterian Medical Center Feeding Program was designed as an intensive "learn to eat" program with a feeding/behavioral specialist taking on the total role of teacher. The parents, although able to be present, were strictly forbidden from interfering with the process. This, like many interventions before and after this program, caused great stress for the claimant's mother as she saw this as a failure in her role as mother and caregiver to her young child.

5. The insurer requested this case manager attend a feeding session at this program for observation and recording of the quality of the intervention, etc. There was some tolerance of formula via syringe introduced into the patient's mouth, but there was also much distress on the part of the claimant and her parents. There was "some" improvement per her gastroenterologist, but the claimant was a "long way from becoming an oral eater."

6. The claimant went on to require additional interventions and other short- and long-term feeding training (all of which the insurer wanted thoroughly researched and monitored for appropriateness prior to their approval of same).

7. The claimant's slow (but generally steady) feeding and developmental progress met with some concerns by the insurer as the case continued to be high-dollar because of the costs of the DME and supplies, as well as admissions for several attempts at feeding training in various settings because the Columbia Program was no longer an appropriate site to meet her changing needs.

8. The case manager was required to monitor and process claims, research all interventions, make appropriate recommendations to the insurer, monitor height and weight via physicians, and monitor all therapies involved in the claimant's care. The case manger was required to work closely with the family on home-based follow-up of often difficult and emotionally draining feeding sessions.

9. At one point, the mother's frustration with the time it was taking and the slowed progress in her child's accepting oral feedings caused her to over-stuff her daughter's mouth with food, leading to a potential choking episode and the acute need for emergent supportive intervention with the parents. The case manager expedited a report of same to the medical team and facilitated sensitive support and teaching with the mother to avoid future episodes related to her frustration.

10. Eventually, the claimant was deemed a candidate for admission into a multiweek Intensive Feeding Program. This would train her to eat, and prepare her caregivers (both parents and extended family, as needed) to feed her, monitor her caloric intake, and break through the rigid refusal process she had developed over the years of gastrostomy feedings, still her major source of hydration and nutrition.

11. This long-term program at the Kennedy Krieger Institute was very costly and required much in the way of negotiation by the case manager to make it a program the insurer would consider. The case manager did obtain a considerable discount for the program, and the claimant was enrolled. The case manager monitored and supported the family throughout the length of the program, and for the several months of home-based follow-up required for this child's successful accomplishment of oral feeding skills.

Outcome

This child was in case management for nearly 3 years and had the benefit of the continuity of one case manager throughout that time. When the case was closed to case management, the child was attending a regular preschool with her twin brother, where she was bringing in her own choices of snack and lunch items. She remained sensitive to certain textures and taste combinations. It was believed that she would work those things out as she continued to grow, thrive, and gain weight, all by oral intake. Before closing the case, the medical team and case manager saw her through an entire winter as there was potential for complications due to respiratory problems. She did well and did not require feeding supplementation via the gastrostomy tube, and her parents had a family celebration when she "said goodbye to tubey" after all those years of dependence on it for her survival.

Potential Charges and Savings

    Psychological therapy services = $14,231
    Emergency room visits = $3,000
    Additional hospital admissions = $26,410
    Associated hospital MD charges = $7,789.75
    Costs of inpatient feeding program (multiweek hospital stay) = $103,320
    Feeding program physicians fees = $7,745
    Total Potential Charges = $162,495.75

Note: There were likely additional charges related to family issues that resulted from this child's feeding issues, which are not documented as the family members were not the "official case management client."

Analysis

As demonstrated with this case, sometimes case management services are not only needed early in the life of a child, but also may be necessary for quite a length of time. The interventions may be necessarily continuous, the case can be closed and reopened as the child grows and the needs change, or the case may be maintained on an extended-diary basis.

The case manager was able to avoid duplication of services, entry into less than clinically successful programs and settings by this vulnerable family, repeated hospitalizations, and the potential for injury to the child due to the severity of parental frustration, which often occurs in long-term feeding disorder cases. As demonstrated, there were very high potential charges for this child, and the continued and diligent involvement of this case manager kept the family, the medical team, and the insurer all focused upon the goal of teaching this child to eat like others and to be able to gain and maintain a normal weight for her growth and development. Although the case was often challenging and frustrating because it took so long to reach the goals, the dedication of the child's family, the provision of excellent case management, and the willingness of the insurer to flex some benefits, as needed, resulted in an outstanding outcome and high-dollar savings to the insurer.

PEDIATRIC: LONG-TERM RARE RESPIRATORY DISORDER

Case Overview

This 9-month-old female infant was a direct referral for case management from a private insurer (an indemnity plan) as they sought the case manager's pediatric expertise in assessing, intervening, and monitoring the present and projected long-term needs of this young child with a rare respiratory disorder. The infant resided at home with her parents and one older sibling.

Problems Identified

1. The claimant required mechanical ventilation during any periods of sleep. Her diagnosis of Congenital Central Hypoventilation Syndrome meant that whenever she was asleep, her neurological system would "forget" to trigger spontaneous breathing. She would simply stop breathing, leaving her at risk for respiratory failure and death.
2. The claimant's father traveled the country for business much of the time and was not available as a regular care provider, further necessitating home care nursing to assist this overwhelmed mother. The case manager immediately began to form a close working relationship with the health care providers and the claimant's mother (primary caregiver) to gain their trust. To avoid repeated hospitalizations or a catastrophic home care event to the claimant, she began telephonic teaching to the parent regarding home care management.
3. At the time of referral for case management, the insurer had been providing home nursing care services to the young patient because physicians would not discharge her to home without home care nurses in place day and night. The claimant's insurance benefits plan did not include a home care nursing benefit but, due to the complexity of the case, the insurer provided home care nursing on a temporary basis. When the insurer attempted to decrease the number of home care nursing hours provided, the parents threatened a lawsuit. The insurer sought a medically feasible way to meet this claimant's needs while decreasing the high-dollar costs of the case.

4. To maximize the claimant's existing benefit dollars in view of the anticipated long-term nature of this medically complex case, the insurer requested that case management negotiate out-of-network charges with the only nursing agency geographically available to provide home care nursing to this child. The case manager accomplished such negotiations, as well as retroactive negotiations of nursing care, equipment, and supply claims, and the cost of the new ventilator equipment needed to meet the needs of this growing child.

5. This case was telephonic, as the claimant and the case manager were many states apart. This case manager had to rely upon the home care nurses, physicians, and specialty caregivers, as well the claimant's parents to accurately portray the child's medical and developmental status and needs.

6. The parents were initially distrustful of the case manager, because the insurer had brought her onto the team. Soon, they came to rely on her ability to negotiate a better quality of home care nursing while teaching them (and the extended family of caregivers) how to manage on their own for those hours being slowly weaned down by the insurer.

7. The case manager was a conduit of much important information between the parents, medical team, and insurer. Case management interventions at times took considerable hours, but resulted in better educated and less angry parents who became increasingly skilled at caring for their child at home during the nonnursing shifts. This resulted in a decrease in rehospitalizations of the child, a decrease in costs to the insurer, and freed the parents to relocate to a state where their child would be eligible for the Medicaid Model Waiver Program. During the protracted period of the parents' planned relocation, the case manager negotiated a slow tapering off of the home care nursing hours, as medically appropriate. Close support and teaching, as well as troubleshooting among all involved parties, enabled the case manager to decrease nursing care costs to the insurer without the high number of repeat hospitalizations that had been evident early in the case.

8. As the child's insurance plan did not cover air transport of the child to the new state of residency, the case manager made every attempt to secure a donated, medically safe flight for the claimant with her ventilators and all other necessary equipment. Due to legal aeronautic regulations, this was not feasible. The case manager then assisted the parents in planning medically and emotionally for the car trip, arranging for the insurer to provide rented backups to the ventilators and all the necessary precautions to expedite the claimant's safe travel across several states to her new home.

9. Home care nursing and respiratory services, provision of respiratory supplies, and all related equipment had to be put into place in the new state by the case

manager in time for the family's arrival. Close contact between the insurer and the case manager regarding the vendors involved (in-network wherever possible and negotiation of nonnetwork services, as needed) resulted in a smooth transition for this medically complex child and her family.

Outcome

Shortly after the case manager became involved in dialogue with the health care team and the claimant's parents, there was a decrease in the rate of the child's rehospitalizations. This and the carefully managed decrease of home care nursing hours achieved considerable insurer savings. After the child was safely cared for more frequently by her parents, they became more secure in their abilities. The case manager's skill in arranging for a flexible number of home care nursing hours each week over a period of time enabled all members of the child's health care circle to better tolerate change and benefit limits, thus decreasing animosity while increasing compliance. By providing concrete support, education, and medically relevant relocation assistance to the parents, the case manager was able to expedite their move out of state and enroll them in the Medicaid Model Waiver Program. This resulted in a very substantial dollar savings to the insurer as the Medicaid Waiver Program then assumed the costs of all home care nursing services.

After the claimant established residency in her new state, the case manager advocated for home care nursing with the local Medicaid Waiver Program Coordinator. She secured sufficient hours to allow the parents respite and the time to care for other family members' needs, as well as those of their child with the unique respiratory issues.

After the case manager and the insurer effectively addressed home care, nursing, and supply needs, and helped establish a good relationship between the claimant and an appropriate new medical team, the client's family was able to further research the technological advances in treating their child's disorder. They have seen a medical specialist in this rare respiratory syndrome and are currently awaiting DNA assessment of the involved gene with hopes of gene manipulation to eradicate the disorder.

Potential Charges and Savings

Without case management intervention, there would likely have been a significant number of avoidable MD office visits, emergency room visits, and likely rehospitalizations. It is likely the insurer's high-dollar expenditure for 24 hour/day home care nurses would have continued, and potentially multiplied, due to the costs of a legal battle over the insurer's attempts to cut home care nursing hours had the case manager not assisted, educated, and supported the parents. Potential charges included:

Home care nursing services (avoided 8,967 hours @ $38/hr) for savings = $340,764
Reduced hospital stays and/or hospital admissions avoided = $47,500
Associated MD hospital fees = $6,300
Emergency room treatments avoided = $8,550
Avoidance of unnecessary MD visits = $850
Savings on medical equipment and supplies = $22,850
Detection and elimination of erroneous billing = $2,380
Negotiation of additional out-of-network costs = $36,213
Total savings to date = $465,407

Analysis

On this case, the case manager employed many skills to manage several multi-faceted problems. The family alone presented numerous challenges. To create a working foundation, the case manager needed to gain both the trust and the cooperation of the family, as well as all members of the health care team. She needed to keep them focused on the goal of maintaining this very fragile girl at home with her family in a medically safe, developmentally conducive, and positive environment. The case manager had to advocate for the child, parents, insurer, medical team, and home care providers, all the while keeping a close eye on the optimal care of this young child. This required great patience, skill, creativity, attention to detail, tenacity, and persuasion skills to encourage all involved to participate in what would ultimately be a win/win situation.

TRANSPLANT REJECTION OF SMALL BOWEL WITH PSYCHOLOGICAL COMPONENT

Case Overview

This 13-year-old Caucasian female was identified for on-site case management intervention during her hospital admission for transplant rejection of her small bowel with Post Transplant/Lymphoma Prolyphic Disease secondary to anti-rejection immunosuppression. She required Remicade IV to treat colitis. On admission to the hospital, she also presented with a urinary tract infection (UTI). Her neurogenic bladder places her at high risk for frequent UTIs. Her prior history is complex with multiple medical, financial, and socio/environmental issues identified.

At age 4, the claimant had a colon resection and ileostomy due to pseudo-obstruction of her small bowel and was evaluated for a small bowel transplant (experimental at that time but presently an approved procedure). In 1996, she subsequently developed cancerous lesions on her ribs, diagnosed as Post Transplant Lymphoma Prolyphic. In addition, she has multiple food allergies and is lactose intolerant. Our goal was to provide the child with as optimal an outcome as possible while preventing and decreasing hospital stays as they occurred.

Problems Identified

In addition to the aforementioned, the following problems were identified:

1. The claimant needed intravenous infusion of Remicade to treat her colitis; however, Remicade was not FDA-approved for her specific diagnosis. The case manager was successful in obtaining funding via the drug manufacturer for Remicade. Had case management not been involved, the claimant would have either remained hospitalized or would have been rehospitalized for colitis-related symptoms and/or continued rejection of her small bowel transplant. The medication, even though not approved for her diagnosis, was the only treatment available to place her in remission.

2. Due to the chronicity of this child's condition and other family members' medical problems, financial concerns are an ongoing issue. The claimant needed Pedialyte as an enteral supplement at night. Pedialyte was not covered by her Plan. The claimant's mother was giving it to her every other day because of financial constraints. This resulted in a hospitalization due to dehydration. Community resources were researched and funding was obtained for many of the claimant's needs (Pedialyte, diapers, food, clothing). This resulted in decreased hospitalizations as the child was provided with adequate hydration.

3. The claimant remains at high risk for rehospitalizations because of her complex medical problems. The case manager monitored each hospital stay for medical appropriateness and provided timely implementation of services, thus decreasing length of hospital stay. The claimant required IV infusion, enteral feeding equipment, and diabetic supplies within the home setting. Home care services were implemented for both child and parental education.

4. There is a strong psychological component in this case. The claimant is depressed. Family and individual counseling is needed for all members of this family on an ongoing basis. The case manager attempted to address these issues in several ways. An extensive amount of time was spent on researching an inpatient facility that could address both the child's medical and psychological needs. The child was hospitalized and mother initially

attended counseling. Unfortunately, the mother became dissatisfied with the facility and requested discharge from the facility. She eventually was non-compliant with responding to the case manager's phone calls.

Outcome

Continued case management intervention did provide early identification and timely intervention of medical problems. Hospitalizations were not only avoided, but were also decreased in length. Community resources were utilized to prevent recurrent hospitalizations for nutrition- and dehydration-related problems. Funding was obtained for Remicade. Had case management not been involved, the claimant would have been rehospitalized for colitis-related symptoms or remained hospitalized. Case management attempted to attend to the strong psychological issues but, regrettably, was not completely effective. Many of the child's problems were addressed and resolved, but without complete parental collaboration with case management, it was difficult to obtain a successful outcome for this child and, sadly, this case was closed to case management.

Potential Charges and Savings

Without case management intervention, this child would have remained hospitalized for longer lengths of stay and experienced at least one emergency room visit due to dehydration. She entered the hospital three times. CM intervention and monitoring reduced her total hospital stays by 8 days.

Decreased hospital stays by 8 days @ $1,500/day = $12,000
Eliminated associated MD fees x 2 (PCP and Specialist) @ $200/day x 8 days = $1,600
Avoided minimum of one ER visit = $750
Avoided rehospitalization for dehydration x 4 days = $6,000
Plus MD fees = $800
Case management monitoring of services for appropriateness, unnecessary long-term use of DME equipment (wheelchair), and associated rental fees were avoided = $850
Other savings were realized through use of in-network providers.
Total potential charges/savings = $22,000

Analysis

The problems identified in this case are typical of an individual with chronic life-threatening conditions. This child remains at high risk for complications. Both the child and family require ongoing psychological intervention and support in order to ensure a successful outcome for this child.

Unfortunately, although the psychological issues were identified and addressed, the case manager was unable to obtain a successful outcome for this child without complete parental collaboration. The child's mother refused to cooperate with the psych facility and discharged her daughter from therapy. Because of the mother's termination of contact with the case management company, the case was not open to case management, and a recommendation was made to close it. Continuous intervention by the case manager, advocating for the claimant, would have made a great difference in this outcome, and it becomes difficult and often frustrating for a case manager to let go of a case like this one.

Appendix A

Additional Resources

ACADEMIC/EDUCATIONAL RESOURCES

The following offer case management certificate programs, majors, or graduate level programs:

Adelphi University
School of Nursing
Garden City, NY
Veronica L. Conners, RN, EdD, PhD
Associate Dean for Graduate Studies
(516) 877-4564
conners@adelphi.edu

Baylor University
School of Nursing
3700 Worth Street
Dallas, TX 75246
Dr. Pauline T. Johnson
Director of Graduate Studies
(214) 820-4191
Pauline_Johnson@baylor.edu

Brigham Young University
550 SWKT, PO Box 25436
Provo, UT 84602-5436
Joan Baldwin
Associate Professor, College of
  Nursing
(801) 378-6066

Carlow College
3333 Fifth Avenue
Pittsburgh, PA 15213
Ms. Sue Sterrett, MSN, MBA
Graduate Program Director
Division of Nursing
(800) 333-2276
www.carlow.edu/

Detroit College of Business
4801 Oakman Blvd.
Dearborn, MI 48126
Carole Gdula
(313) 581-4400 ext. 444

George Mason University
College of Nursing & Health Science
4400 University Drive
Fairfax, VA 22030
Dr. Roberta Conti
Assistant Professor
(703) 993-1000
cnhs@gmu.edu

Grand Valley State University
CM Certificate Program
1 Campus Drive
Allendale, MI 49401
(616) 331-5000
www.gvsu.edu/

Greenville Technical College
Buck Mickel Center
216 S. Pleasantburg Drive
Greenville, SC 29607
Abbe Fass
Program Manager, Instructor
Continuing Education/Health
  Sciences-Nursing
(864) 250-8800
www.greenvilletech.com

Indiana University-Purdue University Fort Wayne
IPFW Continuing Education
2101 E. Coliseum Blvd.
Fort Wayne, IN 46805-1499
Continuing Studies
(219) 481-6607
ww.ipfw.edu/ce/catalog/health

Lewis University
One University Pkwy
Romeoville, IL 60446-2200
Laura Kiran
(815) 836-5291

Michigan State University
College of Nursing
A100 Life Sciences Building
East Lansing, MI 48824-1317
Joan Bowman, RN, MPA, CCM
(517) 432-8135
http://nursing.msu.edu/continuing
  education.asp

Pace University
Case Management Institute
School of Nursing
961 Bedford Road, Room L17
Pleasantville, NY 10570
Geraldine Colombraro
Assistant Dean
(914) 773-3359

Pacific Lutheran University
School of Nursing
Tacoma, WA 98447-0003
Celo Massicotte Pass
Associate Dean, Graduate Nursing
  Education
(253) 535-7324
gradnurs@plu.edu
Patsy Maloney
(253) 535-7685

Saint Peter's College
Dept. of Nursing
2641 Kennedy Blvd.
Jersey City, NJ 07306
Dr. Marylou Yam, Director
(201) 915-9216

Samuel Merritt College
College of Nursing
370 Hawthorne Avenue
Oakland, CA 94609
Audrey Berman
Graduate Coordinator & Associate
Professor of Nursing
(510) 869-6511
aberman@samuelmerrit.edu

San Francisco State University
School of Nursing
1600 Holloway Avenue
San Francisco, CA 94132
Dr. Charlotte Ferretti
Director, Case Management & Long-
  Term Program
(415) 338-2371
ferretti@sfsu.edu
Dr. Mary Ann Haw
mahaw@sfsu.edu

Seton Hall University
S. Orange Avenue
South Orange, NJ 07079
Phyllis Shanley Hansell, Dean
hanselph@shuy.edu

Sonoma State University
Department of Nursing
1801 E. Cotati Avenue
Rohnert Park, CA 94928
Greg Crow
Graduate Coordinator
(707) 664-2643
Greg31@pacbell.net

**State University of New York-
  HSCB**
Box 22
Brooklyn College of Nursing
450 Clarkson Avenue
Brooklyn, NY 11203-2098
Dr. Lalia Sedhom
Professor, Director of the Center for
  Nursing Research
(718) 270-7605
lsedhom@netmail.hscbklyn.edu

University of Alabama
Capstone College of Nursing
Box 870358
504 University Blvd.
Tuscaloosa, AL 35487-0358
(800) 313-3591
Marietta Stanton
Professor, Graduate Coordinator
(205) 348-1020
mstanton@bama.ua.edu
www.ua.edu/academic/colleges/
  nursing

University of Arizona
College of Nursing, Bldg 203
1305 North Martin
PO Box 210203
Tucson, AZ 85721-0203
Pamela G. Reed, FAAN
Professor, Associate Dean for
  Academic Affairs
(520) 626-6154
preed@nursingarizona.edu
Dr. Rose Gerber
(520) 626-2406

University of Kentucky
College of Nursing
315 College of Nursing Building
Lexington, KY 40536-0232
Dr. Julie Sebastian
Assistant Dean for Advanced Practice
(859) 323-7581
jgseba00@uky.edu

**University of Maryland/Baltimore
  County**
4815 Maple Grove Road
Hampstead, MD 21074
Harriet Moore
hmoore1@chpdm.umbc.edu

University of St. Francis
500 Wilcox Street
Joilet, IL 60435
Robin Nash, Director of Health
(815) 740-5039
nash@stfrancis.edu

University of San Diego
Philip Y. Hahn School of Nursing
5998 Alaca Park
San Diego, CA 92110-9885
Dr. Patricia Roth
Professor
(619) 260-4572
roth@sandiego.edu

University of Southern Indiana
School of Nursing and Health
  Professions
8600 University Boulevard
Evansville, IN 47712-3597
(877) 874-4584
http://healthce.usi.edu/

University of Virginia
McLeod Hall
Charlottesville, VA 22903-3395
Dr. Sharon Utz
Chairman, Adult Health Division
(804) 924-2743
swi29@virginia.edu

University of Wisconsin-Madison
School of Nursing
600 Highland Avenue-K6/340
Madison, WI 53792-2455
Dr. Mary Ellen Murray
(608) 263-6945

Vanderbilt University
2305 West End Avenue
Nashville, TN 37203-1700
Patty Peerman
Director of Admissions
(615) 343-3802
paddy.peerman@mcmail.vander
  bilt.edu

Villanova University
College of Nursing
800 Lancaster Avenue
Villanova, PA 19085-1690
Dr. Claire Manfredi
Professor and Director, Graduate
  Program
(610) 519-4907
claire.manfredi@villanova.edu

Canada

McMaster University
1280 Main Street W
Hamilton, Ontario
Canada
L8S 4L8
Dr. Andrea Baumann
(905) 525-9140 ext. 24321
baumanna@mcmaster.ca

University of Toronto
Department of Nursing
50 George Street
Toronto, Ontario
Canada
M5S 3H4
(416) 978-8713
inquiry.nursing@utoronto.ca

Australia

University of Melbourne
Level 1, 723 Swanston Street
Carlton, Victoria, 3053
Australia
011 (613) 8344-0800
www.nursing.unimelb.edu.au/gdcm

University of South Australia
GPO Box 2471
Adelaide, South Australia, 5001
Australia
011 (618) 8302-0114
international.office@unisa.edu.au,
CM courses offered external mode

ADDITIONAL CREDENTIALS (SEE CHAPTER 14)

Certified Professional Utilization Review (CPUR)
McKesson HBOC
Interqual Products Group
293 Boston Post Road W., Suite 180
West Marbourough, MA 01752
(800) 522-6738, x 3136 or 2954
www.interqual.com

Certified Rehabilitation Counselor (CRC)
Commission on Rehabilitation Counselor Certification
1835 Rohlwing Road, Suite E
Rolling Meadows, IL 60008
(847) 394-2104
www.crccertification.org

Certified Brain Injury Specialist (CBIS)
American Academy for the Certification of Brain Injury Specialists
Brain Injury Association
1776 Massachusetts Ave., NW, Suite 100
Washington, DC 20036
(202) 296-6443

OTHER PROGRAMS

CARE2LEARN.COM
www.care2learn.com

CMSA WebED
www.cmsa.org/Education/WebED/

CEUs4CaseManagers
www.CEUs4CCM.com
(866) 543-2273

CEUs4RehabNurses
www.CEUs4CRRN.com

Registered Nurse Case Manager
www.RNCaseManager.com

Social Worker Case Manager
www.SWCaseManager.com

The Center for Case Management (CCM)
6 Pleasant Street
South Natick, MA 01760
(508) 651-2600
www.cfcm.com

Consultants in Case Management Intervention Associates (CCMI Associates)
1163 New Boston Road
Francestown, NH 03043
(603) 547-2245
Sandra Lowery, President
CCMI@lowery.mv.com

Creative Health Care Management Inc.
1701 East 79th Street, Suite 1
Minneapolis, MN 55425
(800) 728-7766
www.chcm.com

DVDiBenedetto & Associates, Ltd.
PO Box 738
Yonkers, NY 10710-0738
(914) 771-5152
Deborah V. DiBenedetto, President
www.dvd-associates.com
dvdaltd@aol.com

HealthCare Resource Group
12525 Lambert Road
Whittier, CA 90606
(562) 945-7224
www.hcrg.com
CM certificate course

International Foundation of Employee Benefit Plans
18700 W. Bluemound Road
PO Box 69
Brookfield, WI 53008-0069
(414) 786-6710
Offers videotapes, audio cassettes

Professional Resources in Management Education (PRIME)
1820 SW 100 Avenue
Miramar, FL 33025
(954) 436-6300
www.primeinc.cc/

Note: Also check into educational symposia presented at regional and national conferences.

ASSOCIATIONS

Agency for Health Care Research and Quality
2101 E. Jefferson St., Suite 501
Rockville, MD 20852
(301) 594-1364
www.ahcpr.gov

The ALS Association
185 Madison Avenue
New York, NY 10016
(212) 679-4016
Also 15300 Ventura Boulevard, Suite 315
Sherman Oaks, CA 91403
(818) 990-2151

Alzheimer's Disease and Related Disorders Association, Inc.
700 East Lake Street
Chicago, IL 60601
(312) 853-3060
(800) 621-0379

American Association of Occupational Health Nurses, Inc.
2920 Brandywine Road, Suite 100
Atlanta, GA 30341
(770) 455-7757
www.aaohn.org

American Association of Preferred Provider Organizations
1101 Connecticut Avenue, NW, Suite 700
Washington, DC 20036
(202) 429-5133

American Board for Occupational Health Nurses
201 East Ogden, Suite 114
Hinsdale, IL 60521
(630) 789-5799
www.abohn.org

American Board of Disability Analysts
345 24th Avenue No., Suite 200
Nashville, TN 37203
(615) 327-2984

American Burn Association
c/o Cleon W. Goodwyn, MD
Secretary, American Burn Association
New York Hospital
Cornell Medical Center
525 E. 68th Street, Room L-706
New York, NY 10021
(800) 548-2876

American Cancer Society
90 Park Avenue
New York, NY 10016
(212) 599-8200

American Diabetes Association
1660 Duke Street
Alexandria, VA 22314
(703) 549-1500
(800) 232-3472

American Heart Association
7272 Greenville Avenue
Dallas, TX 75231-4596
(214) 373-6300

American Hospice Foundation
1130 Connecticut Avenue, NW
Washington, DC 20038-4101
(202) 223-0204

American Hospital Association
1 North Franklin
Chicago, IL 60606
Phone: (312) 422-3000
Fax: (312) 422-4796
www.aha.org

American Institute of Outcomes Care Management
1215 Lambert Road
Whittier, CA 90606
Phone: (562) 945-9990
Fax: (562) 698-2339
www.aiocm.net

American Lung Association
1740 Broadway
New York, NY 10019
(212) 315-8700

American Managed Care and Review Association
1227 25th Street, NW, Suite 610
Washington, DC 20037
(202) 728-0506

American Medical Association
515 North State Street
Chicago, IL 60610
(800) 621-8335 (copies)
(312) 464-4706 (information)

American Nurses Association
600 Maryland Avenue, SW, Suite 100 West
Washington, DC 20024
1-800-274-4ANA
www.ana.org

American Organization of Nurse Executives (AONE)
Washington, DC Headquarters
Liberty Place
325 Seventh Street, NW
Washington, DC 20004
Ph: (202) 626-2240
Fax: (202) 638-5499
Alternate phone: (312) 422-2800
(Chicago office)

Association of Rehabilitation Nurses
5700 Old Orchard Road, First Floor
Skokie, IL 60077-1057
(708) 966-3433

Blue Cross and Blue Shield Association
676 North St. Clair Street
Chicago, IL 60611
(312) 440-6345

Case Management Society of America
8201 Cantrell, Suite 230
Little Rock, AR 72227
(501) 225-2229
www.cmsa.org

Certification of Disability Management Specialists Commission
1835 Rohlwing Road, Suite E
Rolling Meadows, IL 60008
(847) 394-2106

Choice in Dying
200 Varick Street
New York, NY 10014-4809
(212) 366-5540

Commission on Rehabilitation Counselor Certification
1835 Rohlwing Road, Suite E
Rolling Meadows, IL 60008
(847) 394-2104
www.crccertification.com

Commission for Case Management Certification
1835 Rohlwing Road, Suite D
Rolling Meadows, IL 60008
(847) 818-0292
www.ccmcertification.org/index.html

Disease Management Association of America
1129 20th Street, NW, Suite 850
Washington, DC 20036-3421
Phone: (202) 861-1490
Fax: (202) 861-1477
www.dmaa.org

Employee Benefit Research Institute
2121 K Street, NW, Suite 600
Washington, DC 20037-1896
(202) 659-0670

Funerals & Memorial Societies of America
PO Box 457
Hinesburg, VT 05481

Grief Encounters, Inc.
5021 Vernon Avenue, #209
Edina, MN 55436
(612) 922-3489

Health Insurance Association of America
1201 F Street, NW, Suite 500
Washington, DC 20004-1204
Phone: (202) 824-1600
Fax: (202) 824-1722
www.hiaa.org

Health Research and Educational Trust (HRET)
1 North Franklin
Chicago, IL 60606
Phone: (312) 422-2600
Fax: (312) 422-4568

Joint Commission on Accreditation of Healthcare Organizations (JCAHO)
One Renaissance Blvd.
Oakbrook Terrace, IL 60181
(630) 792-5800 for CM seminars/ cities
www.jcaho.org

The Leapfrog Group
c/o AcademyHealth
1801 K Street, NW, Suite 701-L
Washington, DC 20006
(202) 292-6713
www.leapfroggroup.org/

National Academy of Certified Case Managers
3389 Sheridan Street, Suite 170
Hollywood, FL 33021
(800) 962-2260

National AIDS Hotline
(800) 447-AIDS (specific information)
(800) 342-AIDS (general information, recording)

National Association for Healthcare Quality (NAHQ)
PO Box 1880
San Gabriel, CA 91778
(818) 286-8074

National Association for Home Care
519 C Street, NE
Washington, DC 20002-5809
(202) 547-7424

National Association of People with AIDS
1413 K Street, NW, 8th Floor
Washington, DC 20005
(800) 808-8060

National Association of Rehabilitation Professionals in the Private Sector
313 Washington Street, Suite 302
Newton, MA 02158
(508) 820-8889
www.narpps.org (in development)

National Association of Social Workers
750 First Street, NE
Washington, DC 20002
(202) 408-8600
www.naswdc.org

National Board for Certification in Continuity of Care
7313 Southview Court
Fairfax Station, VA 22039
(860) 586-7525

National Cancer Institute
International Cancer Information Center
Building 82, Room 123
Bethesda, MD 20892
(301) 496-2794
(800) 422-6237

National Center for Policy Analysis
12655 N. Central Expressway,
Suite 720
Dallas, TX 75243-1739
(972) 386-6272
www.ncpa.org/

National Committee for Quality Assurance
2000 L Street NW, Suite 500
Washington, DC 20036
(202) 955-3500
www.ncqa.org

National Head Injury Foundation
1140 Connecticut Avenue, NW,
Suite 812
Washington, DC 20036
(202) 296-6443

National Hospice Foundation
1901 N. Moore, #901
Arlington, VA 22209
(703) 516-4928

National Institutes of Health
900 Rockville Pike, Building 31
Bethesda, MD 20892
(301) 496-4000
www.nih.org

National Insurance Consumers Helpline
(800) 942-4242

National Multiple Sclerosis Society
205 East 42nd Street
New York, NY 10017
(212) 986-3240

National Organization for Rare Disorders, Inc.
PO Box 8923
New Fairfield, CT 06812-8923
(203) 746-6518

National Rehabilitation Association
633 South Washington Street
Alexandria, VA 22314
(703) 836-0850

National Viatical Association
1200 G Street, NW, Suite 760
Washington, DC 20005
(202) 347-7361

New York Business Group on Health
386 Park Avenue South, Suite 703
New York, NY 10016-8804
(212) 252-7440

Office of Minority Health Resource Center
PO Box 37337
Washington, DC 20013-7337
(800) 444-6472
www.omhrc.gov

Rehabilitation Nursing Certification Board
4700 W. Lake Avenue
Glenview, IL 60025-1485
(800) 229-7530
www.rehabnurse.org

Susan G. Komen Breast Cancer Foundation
5005 LBJ Freeway, Suite 270
Dallas, TX 75244
(800) 462-9273

URAC (American Accreditation HealthCare Commissions)
1220 L Street, NW, Suite 400
Washington, DC 20005
(202) 216-9010

Viatical Association of America
1200 19th Street, NW, Suite 300
Washington, DC 20036

Washington Business Group on Health
Y-Me National Breast Cancer Organization
212 West Van Buren, 5th Floor
Chicago, IL 60607
(800) 221-2141

JOURNALS AND MAGAZINES

AAOHN Journal
6900 Grove Road
Thorofare, NJ 08086-9447
(609) 848-1000

Advance for Nurses
2900 Horizon Drive
King of Prussia, PA 19406
(800) 355-5627
www.advancefornurses.com

Alternative Healthcare Management
2082 SE Bristol Street, Suite 217
Newport Beach, CA 92660-1740
(949) 477-2402
www.althealthcaremag.com

Alternative Therapies in Health and Medicine
169 Saxony Road, Suite 104
Encinitas, CA 92024-6779
(760) 633-3910

Alzheimer's Care Quarterly
7201 McKinney Circle
Frederick, MD 21704
(800) 638-8437

Business & Health (electronic version only)
Five Paragon Drive
Montvale, NJ 07645
(201) 358-7200
www.businessandhealth.com

Business Insurance
740 North Rush Street
Chicago, IL 60611-2590
(800) 678-9595

CareManagement
256 Post Road East, Suite 204
Westport, CT 06880-3617
(203) 454-1333

Caring
228 7th St, SE
Washington, DC 20003-4306
(202) 547-5277

Case Management Advisor
3525 Piedmont Road, NE, Bldg. Six, Suite 400
Atlanta, GA 30305
(770) 934-1440
www.ahcpub.com

The Case Manager
10801 Executive Center Drive, Suite 509
Little Rock, AR 72211
(501) 223-5165
www.mosby.com/casemgr

Case Review
4676 Admiralty Way, #202
Marina del Rey, CA 90292
(310) 306-2206

CE-Today for Nurse Practitioners
CEU-Online, Inc.
6 Partridge Lane
Londonderry, NH 03053
(603) 432-7099
www.np.ce-today.com

Continuing Care
5151 Beltline Road, 10th Floor
Dallas, TX 75254
(972) 687-6700
www.ccareonline.com

Employee Benefit News
1325 G Street NW, Suite 970
Washington, DC 20005
(202) 504-1122
www.benefitnews.com

*Group Practice Managed Healthcare
News*
201 Littleton Road, Suite 100
Morris Plain, NJ 07950-2932
(201) 285-0855

Harvard Women's Health Watch
10 Shattuck Street, Suite 612
Boston, MA 02115-6011
(617) 432-2876
www.health.harvard.edu

Health monitor
21 West 38th Street, 4th Floor
New York, NY 10018
(212) 997-9800
www.healthmonitor.com

HomeCare
23815 Stuart Ranch Road
Malibu, CA 90265-8987
(310) 317-4522
www.homecaremag.com

Home Health Care Consultant
666 Plainsboro Road, Bldg. 300
Plainsboro, NJ 08536-3026
(609) 275-3800
www.mmhc.com/hhcc

Home Healthcare Nurse
3904 Therina Way
Louisville, KY 40241-1542
(502) 339-9005
www.nursingcenter.com

Home Health Care Dealer/Provider
6701 Center Drive W, #450
Los Angeles, CA 90045-1535
(310) 642-4400
www.hhcdealer.com

Hospice
1901 N. Moore St., #901
Arlington, VA 22209-1706
(703) 243-5900

Hospice Forum
228 Seventh St, SE
Washington, DC 20003-4306
(202) 547-7424

Infusion
205 Dangerfield Road
Alexandria, VA 22314-2833
(703) 549-3740
www.nhianet.org

Journal of Case Management
43 Enterprise Drive
Bristol, CT 06011
(860) 589-6226

*The Journal of Hospice and Palliative
Nursing (JHPN)*
www.jhpn.com

*Journal of Pain and Palliative Care
  Pharmacotherapy: Advances in
  Acute, Chronic and End of Life
  Symptom Control*
30 S. 2000 E, Room 258
University of Utah
Salt Lake City, UT 84112-5820
Editor: Arthur G. Lipman, Pharm.D.
alipman@pharm.utah.edu

Journal of Rehabilitation
633 S. Washington Street
Alexandria, VA 22314-4109
(703) 836-0850

Managed Care Interface
66 Palmer Avenue, Suite 49
Bronxville, NY 10708-3420
(914) 337-7878

Managed Care Quarterly
200 Orchard Ridge Drive
Gaithersburg, MD 20878
(800) 638-8437
www.aspenpublishers.com

Medical Economics
Five Paragon Drive
Montvale, NJ 07645
(201) 358-7200
www.memag.com

Modern Healthcare
360 N. Michigan Avenue
Chicago, IL 60601
(312) 280-3173
www.modernhealthcare.com

McKnight's Long-Term Care News
2 Northfield Plaza
Northfield, IL 60093
(847) 441-3700
www.mcknightsonline.com

The NIH Record
Bldg. 31, Room 2B03
Bethesda, MD 20892
(301) 496-2125

The Nations Health
1015 15th St, NW, #300
Washington, DC 20005-2605
(202) 789-5600

Nursing Economics
East Holly Avenue
Box 56
Pitman, NJ 08071-0056
(609) 256-2300
www.ajj.com/services/pblshng/nej/

Nursing Management
1111 Bethlehem Pike
Spring House, PA 19477-1114
(215) 646-8700
www.nursingmanagement.com

Rehabilitation Nursing
4700 W. Lake Avenue
Glenview, IL 60025-1468
(847) 375-4710
www.rehabnurse.org

Rehab Management
6701 Center Drive W., Suite 450
Los Angeles, CA 90045-1556
(310) 642-4400
www.rehabpub.com

*Rehab & Community Care
  Management*
101 Thorncliffe Park Drive
Toronto, Ontario, M4H 1M2, Canada
(416) 421-7944

The Remington Report
30100 Town Center Drive, Suite 0-421
Laguna Niguel, CA 92677-2064
(800) 247-4781
www.remingtonreport.com

RNdex Information Products
Information Resources Group, Inc.
El Dorado Hills Business Park
5000 Windplay Drive, Suite 4
El Dorado, CA 95762
(800) 200-6040

Risk & Insurance
747 Dresher Road, Suite 500
Horsham, PA 19044-0980
(215) 784-0860

Risk Management
205 East 42nd Street
New York, NY 10017
(212) 286-9364

TeamRehab Report
23815 Stuart Ranch Road
Malibu, CA 90265-8987
(310) 317-4522

The Self-Insurer
PO Box 15466
Santa Ana, CA 92735
(714) 508-4920

NEWSLETTERS

AAPPO Journal
One Bridge Plaza, Suite 350
Fort Lee, NJ 07024
(201) 947-5545

AAOHN Case Management Advisory
50 Lenox Pointe
Atlanta, GA 30324-3176
(404) 262-1162

AAOHN News
50 Lenox Pointe, NE
Atlanta, GA 30324-3176
(404) 262-1162

Case Management
13343 NW Old Germantown Road
Portland, OR 97231
(503) 283-8797
NursingCM@aol.com

The Case Report
CMSA
8201 Cantrell, Suite 230
Little Rock, AR 72227
(501) 225-2229
www.cmsa.org

CMSA @ At Work For You
CMSA
8201 Cantrell, Suite 230
Little Rock, AR 72227
(501) 225-2229
www.cmsa.org

Disease Management Advisor
1123 Zonolite Road, Suite 17
Atlanta, GA 30306-2016
(800) 597-6300
www.nhionline.net

Disease Management Digest
256 Post Road East, Suite 204
Westport, CT 06880-3617
(203) 454-1333

*EBRI Issue Brief and Employee
    Benefit Notes*
The Johns Hopkins University Press
701 West 40th Street, Suite 275
Baltimore, MD 21211
(410) 516-6964

The Elder Care Connector
www.homeinstead.com

E-News (electronic newsletter)
End of Life Physician Education
  Resource Center
Medical College of Wisconsin,
  MEB Room 3235
8701 Watertown Plank Road
Milwaukee, WI 53226
(414) 456-4353
www.eperc.mcw.edu

Health Business
Faulkner & Gray
PO Box 27758
Washington, DC 20077-1343
(800) 848-1153

Home Care Case Management
3525 Piedmont Road, NE, Bldg. Six,
  Suite 400
Atlanta, GA 30305
(800) 688-2421

Inside Case Management
4343 North Clarendon, Unit 1616
Chicago, IL 60613
(773) 281-8492

Joint Commission Perspectives
One Renaissance Boulevard
Oakbrook Terrace, IL 60181
(800) 346-0085 Ext. 558
www.jcrinc.com

Intramural Research Highlights
U.S. Department of Health and
  Human Services
2101 East Jefferson Street, Suite 501
Rockville, MD 20852
(301) 594-1400

Last Acts Policy Newsletter
  (e-newsletter)
7910 Woodmont Avenue, Suite 1340
Bethesda, MD 20814-3015
(301) 652-1558
Ben Milder, Editor
Bmilder@burnesscommunications.com
Colleen Chapman, Editor
cchapman@burnesscommunications
  .com
www.lastacts.org

Lifeline Connections
111 Lawrence Street
Framingham, MA 01702-8156
(800) 543-3546
www.lifelinesys.com

Managed Care Outlook
Capitol Publications
1101 King Street
PO Box 1453
Alexandria, VA 22313-2053
(800) 327-7203

Medical Benefits
108 5th Street, SE
Charlottesville, VA 22902-5284
(804) 979-4947

NAHC Report
519 C Street, NE
Washington, DC 20002
(202) 547-7424

NARPPS Newsletter
313 Washington Street, Suite 302
Newton, MA 02158
(508) 820-8889

NRA Newsletter
633 South Washington Street
Alexandria, VA 22314
(703) 836-0850

On Workers' Compensation
2875 Northwind Drive, Suite 210 A
East Lansing, MI 48823
(517) 332-5266

PharmaFacts for Case Managers
256 Post Road East, Suite 204
Westport, CT 06880-3617
(203) 454-1333

Rehabilitation Review
313 Washington Street, Suite 302
Newton, MA 02158
(508) 820-8889

Orphan Disease Update
P O Box 8923
New Fairfield, CT 06912
(203) 746-6518

Research Activities
Agency for Health Care Research and
   Quality
U.S. Department of Health and
   Human Services
2101 East Jefferson Street, Suite 501
Rockville, MD 20852
(301) 594-1364

Reference Guides

Aventis Pharmaceuticals Inc. 2003. *Managed Care Digest.* Bridgewater, NJ. (www.managedcare digest.com/HMOPPO.jsp)

Banja, J. 2004. *Medical Errors and Medical Narcissism: Bioethical Explorations* (working title). Sudbury, MA: Jones and Bartlett Publishers.

Benefits Source Book. Updated annually. (Annual guide to research data, products, and services for employee benefit management.) Marietta, GA: Employee Benefit News, Enterprise Communications.

Berkow, R., and A. Fletcher, eds. 1987. *The Merck Manual of Diagnosis and Therapy.* 15th ed. Rahway, NJ: Merck Sharp & Dohme.

Blancett, S., and Flarey, D. 1996. *Handbook of Nursing Care Management.* Gaithersburg, MD: Aspen Publishers, Inc.

Blum, L. 1993. *Free Money for Health Care: A Financial Aid Directory for Patient Care and Patient Services.* Gaithersburg, MD: Aspen Publishers.

Carpenito, L. J. 1993. *Handbook of Nursing Diagnosis.* 5th ed. Philadelphia, PA: J.B. Lippincott.

Castle Connolly Staff (Compiler) et al. 2003. *America's Top Doctors: The Best in American Medicine (America's Top Doctors,* third edition), Castle Connolly Medical, Ltd.

Castleman, M. 2000. *Blended Medicine: The Best Choices in Healing.* Emmaus, PA: Rodale Press.

Cohen, E. L., and T. Cesta. 1997. *Nursing Case Management: From Concept to Evaluation.* 2d ed. St. Louis, MO: Mosby-Year Book.

Complete Directory of People with Learning Disabilities, 1997/98. Updated annually. Lakeville, CT: Grey House Publishing.

Conner, C., ed. 1997. *Health Care Fraud and Abuse Compliance Manual.* Gaithersburg, MD: Aspen Publishers.

Crimando, W., and T. F. Riggar, eds. 1996. *Utilizing Community Resources: An Overview of Human Services.* Boca Raton, FL: St. Lucie Press.

Curaflex Health Services, 1991. *Home Infusion Therapy Resource Guide.* Ontario, CA.

D'Avanzo, C. E., and E. M. Geissler. 2003. *Cultural Health Assessment,* third edition. St. Louis, MO: Mosby-Year Book.

Dell Orto, A. E., and P. W. Power. 1994. *Head Injury and the Family: A Life and Living Perspective.* Boca Raton, FL: St. Lucie Press.

Dietrick, H. J., and V. H. Biddle. 1990. *The Best in Medicine: Where to Find the Best Health Care Available.* New York, NY: Harmony Books.

Driving Down Health Care Costs: Strategies and Solutions 1997. Updated annually. New York, NY: Panel Publishers.

Edelstein, E., ed. 1992. *Blue Book American Druggist: Annual Directory of Pharmaceuticals.* New York, NY: Hearst Corporation.

The Editors of Prevention Magazine Health Books (Editor) et al. 1997. *New Choices in Natural Healing: Over 1,800 of the Best Self-Help Remedies from the World of Alternative Medicine.* Emmaus, PA: Rodale Press.

Field, T. F., and L. P. Norton. 1990. *ADA Resource Manual for Rehabilitation Consultants.* Athens, GA: Elliott & Fitzpatrick.

Fiesta, J. 1983. *The Law and Liability: A Guide for Nurses.* New York, NY: John Wiley & Sons.

Fincham, J. E. and A. I. Wertheimer, eds. 2000. *Pharmacy and the U.S. Health Care System,* second edition. Binghamton, NY: Haworth Press.

Garner, J. C. 1998. *Health Insurance Answer Book.* New York, NY: Panel Publishers.

Goor, R., and N. Goor. 1992. *Eater's Choice.* 3rd ed. Boston, MA: Houghton Mifflin Co.

Griffin, K. 1995. *Handbook of Subacute Health Care.* Gaithersburg, MD: Aspen Publishers, Inc.

Griffith, P.D.M. 1993. *The Managed Care Resource Manual for Obstetrics.* Marietta, GA: Healthdyne Perinatal Services.

Health and Medical Care Directory. 1988. Niagara Falls, NY: Yellow Pages of America.

Health Insurance Association of America. Updated annually. *Source Book of Health Insurance Data.* Washington, DC.

Healthcare Consultants of America. 2003. *2003 Physicians Fee and Coding Guide.* Augusta, GA.

Hilden, J. M., D. R. Tobin, and K. Lindsey. 2003. *Shelter from the Storm: Caring for a Child with a Life-Threatening Condition.* Boulder, CO: Perseus Publishing.

HMO/PPO Directory. 1995. Montvale, NJ: Medical Economics Co.

Inlander, C. B., and K. Morales. 1993. *Getting the Most for Your Medical Dollar.* New York, NY: Pantheon Books.

Isaacs, S. L., and A. C. Swartz. 1992. *Consumer's Legal Guide to Today's Health Care.* New York, NY: Houghton Mifflin.

Jenkins, M. and Henne, R., eds. 1996. *The National Directory of Managed & Integrated Care Organizations.* Wall Township, NJ: Health Resources Publishing.

Karaffa, M. C., ed. 1992. *ICD-9-CM: International Classification of Disease.* 9th rev., 4th ed. Los Angeles, CA: Practice Management Information Corporation.

Kirschner, C. G., et al. 1992. *Physicians' Current Procedural Terminology (CPT).* 4th ed. Chicago, IL: American Medical Association.

Kongstvedt, P. R. 2001. *The Managed Health Care Handbook.* 4th edition. Sudbury, MA: Jones and Bartlett Publishing, Inc.

Larson, D. E., ed. 1990. *Mayo Clinic Family Health Book.* New York, NY: William Morrow. Updated annually.

Lesko, M., et al. 1993. *What to Do When You Can't Afford Health Care.* Kensington, MD: Information USA.

MacKenzie, L., and A. Lignor, eds. 1993. *The Complete Directory for People with Learning Disabilities*. Lakeville, CT: Grey House Publishing.

The Managed Care Yearbook. 1994. Wall Township, NJ: American Business Publishing.

Medical Interface. 1993. *Executive Managed Care Directory*. Bronxville, NY: Medicom International.

Medical Society of the State of New York. 1990. *Medical Directory of New York State*. 62d ed. Lake Success, NY. (Check local library for state organizations publishing similar directories.)

Melonakos, K. 1990. *Saunders Pocket Reference for Nurses*. Philadelphia, PA: W. B. Saunders.

Mercier, L. R. 1991. *Practical Orthopedics*. 3rd ed. St. Louis, MO: Mosby-Year Book.

Meyer, D., and P. Vadasy. 1996. *Living with a Brother and Sister with Special Needs*. 2d ed. Seattle, WA: University of Washington Press.

National Association of Rehabilitation Professionals in the Private Sector. Updated annually. *National Directory of NARPPS*. Brookline, MA.

National Association of Social Workers. Updated annually. *NASW Register of Clinical Social Workers*. Washington, DC.

National Cancer Institute. 1997. Washington, DC.

  Breast Cancer Screening Program Makes Good Business Sense (F370)

  Establishing Workplace Breast Cancer Screening Programs: Blueprint for Action (F368)

  What You Need to Know About Breast Cancer (95–1556)

  Advanced Cancer: Living Each Day (93–856)

  Chemotherapy and You: A Guide to Self-Help During Treatment (94–1136)

  Facing Forward: A Guide for Cancer Survivors (3-2424)

The 2003–2004 National Directory of Brain Injury Rehabilitation Services. 2003. McLean, VA: Brain Injury Association.

The National Housing Directory for People with Disabilities. 1993. Lakeville, CT: Grey House Publishing.

Nicholl, L. H., 2001. *Nurses' Guide to the Internet*, 3rd edition. Philadephia, PA: Lippincott Williams & Wilkins.

The Official ABMS Directory of Board Certified Medical Specialists 1998. 30th ed. 1998. New Providence, NJ: Reed Elsevier, Inc.

PDR: Physician's Desk Reference. Updated annually. Montvale, NJ: Medical Economics Co.

PDR Drug Interactions and Side Effects Index. Updated annually. Montvale, NJ: Medical Economics Co.

PDR for Nonprescription Drugs. Updated annually. Montvale, NJ: Medical Economics Co.

Pell, A. R. 1987. *Making the Most of Medicare: A Guide Through the Medicare Maze*. New York, NY: Prentice Hall.

Raymond, F. 1997. *Surviving Alzheimer's: A Guide for Families*. Forest Knolls, CA: Elder Books.

Reed, P. 1998. *The Medical Disability Advisor: Workplace Guidelines for Disability Duration*. 3d ed. Denver, CO: Reed Group, Ltd.

Robbins, D. A. 1996. *Ethical and Legal Issues in Home Health and Long-term Care*. Gaithersburg, MD: Aspen Publishing, Inc.

Roche, L. 1997. *Coping with Caring: Daily Reflections for Alzheimer's Caregivers*. Forest Knolls, CA: Elder Books.

Romano, J. 1998. *Legal Rights of the Catastrophically Ill and Injured: A Family Guide*, 2d edition. Norristown, PA: Rosenstein & Romano, P.C.

Rossi, P. 1999. *Case Management in Healthcare.* Philadelphia, PA: W. B. Saunders Company

Rothenberg, M. A., and C. F. Chapman. 1989. *Dictionary of Medical Terms.* 2d ed. Hauppauge, NY: Barron's Educational Series.

Sapienza, J. 2002. *Urgent Whispers: Care of the Dying.* Eugene, OR: LLX Press.

St. Coeur, M., ed. 1996. *Case Management Practice Guidelines.* St. Louis, MO: Mosby-Year Book.

Schull, P., ed. 1996. *Professional Guide to Symptoms.* 2d ed. Springhouse, PA: Springhouse Publishing.

Schneider, J. S., and Lidsky, T. I. 1999. *The Doctor's Always In: A Guide to 1000+ Best Health and Medical Information Sites on the Internet.* Cherry Hill, NJ: Neuroinformatics Inc.

Schwartz, G. E. et al. 1989. *The Disability Management Sourcebook.* Washington, DC: Washington Business Group on Health and Institute for Rehabilitation and Disability Management.

Shephard, B. D., ed. 1997. *The Complete Guide to Women's Health.* 3d rev. ed. New York, NY: Plume Books.

Sherman, B. S., ed. 1988. *Directory of Residential Facilities for Emotionally Handicapped Youth.* 2d ed. Phoenix, AZ: Oryx Press.

Sherman, C. D., Jr., ed. 1990. *World Oncology Directory and Source Book.* Milan: World Directories Ltd. (Contact Charles D. Sherman, Jr., Highland Hospital, Rochester, NY 14620)

Shrey, D. E., and M. Lacerte. 1995. *Principles and Practices of Disability Management in Industry.* Boca Raton, FL: St. Lucie Press.

Spratt, J. R. Hawley, and R. Hoye, eds. 1997. *Home Health Care.* Boca Raton, FL: St. Lucie Press.

Stanhope, M., and R. N. Knollmueller. 1992. *Handbook of Community and Home Health Nursing.* St. Louis, MO: Mosby-Year Book.

Substance Abuse Residential Treatment Centers for Teens. 1990. Phoenix, AZ: Oryx Press.

Taber, C. W. 1961. *Taber's Cyclopedic Medical Dictionary.* 8th ed. New York, NY: McGraw-Hill.

Thorn, K. 1990. *Applying Medical Case Management: AIDS.* Canoga Park, CA: Thorn Publishing.

Tierney, L. M., Jr. et al., eds. 1997. *Current Medical Diagnosis and Treatment.* Updated annually. Norwalk, CT: Appleton & Lange.

Tobin, D. R. 1998. *Peaceful Dying: The Step-by-Step Guide to Preserving Your Dignity, Your Choice, and Your Inner Peace at the End of Life.* Boulder, CO: Perseus Book Group.

Wolinsky, H., and Wolinsky, J. 2001. *Healthcare Online for Dummies.* New York, NY: Hungry Minds, Inc.

U.S. Department of Health and Human Services. 1990. *AIDS and the Workplace: Resources for Workers, Managers, and Employers.* Washington, DC: U.S. Government Printing Office.

U.S. Department of Health and Human Services. Updated annually. *Guide to Health Insurance for People with Medicare.* Washington, DC: U.S. Government Printing Office.

Wasserman, D. 1996. *Physician's Fee Reference.* 13th ed. West Allis, WI: Yale.

Weiner, R.S., ed. 1997. *Pain Management.* Boca Raton, FL: St. Lucie Press and the American Academy of Pain Management.

Wong, M. M., ed. 1995. *1995 National Directory of Bereavement Support Groups and Services.* Forest Hills, NY: ADM Publishing.

Note: For ICD-9 and other code references, see Chapters 9 and 11; for ethics references, see Chapter 6; for provider references, see Chapter 2; for special camps and facilities for specific disease states, see Chapter 2; for end-of-life references, see Chapter 17.

SEMINARS/
CONFERENCE SPONSORS

(Also see Other Program section in
Appendix A)
    Call for upcoming offerings.

Academy of Certified Case
Managers
PO Box 210
Green's Farms, CT 06838-0210
(203) 454-1333, ext. 2

American Association of Health
Plans
1129 20th Street, NW, Suite 600
Washington, DC 20036-3403
(202) 778-3200

American Association of Managed
Care Nurses
4435 Waterfront Drive, Suite 101
Glen Allen, VA 23060
(804) 747-9698

American Health Consultants
PO Box 71266
Chicago, IL 60691-9986
(800) 688-2421

Annual National Managed Health
Care Congress
NMHCC
100 Winter Street, Suite 4000
Waltham, MA 02154
(617) 487-6700
    (There are also regional managed
health care conferences offered
throughout the year.)

Casa Colina Centers for
Rehabilitation
2850 North Garey Avenue
Pomona, CA 91767
(909) 596-7733

Center for Bio-Medical
Communication, Inc.
80 West Madison Avenue
Dumont, NJ 07628
(201) 385-8080

Conference Development, Inc.
100 Winter Street, Suite 4000
Waltham, MA 02154
(617) 487-6700

CMSA Annual Conference and
Educational Forum
Case Management Society of America
8201 Cantrell, Suite 230
Little Rock, AR 72227
(501) 225-2229

Federal Publications, Inc.
1120 20th Street, NW
Washington, DC 20036
(800) 922-4330
(202) 337-7000

Global Business Research, Inc.
151 West 19th Street, 8th Floor
New York, NY 10011
(212) 645-4226

Institute for International Research
437 Madison Avenue, 23rd Floor
New York, NY 10022
(212) 826-1260
(800) 345-8016

International Business
Communications
USA Conferences, Inc.
225 Turnpike Road
Southborough, MA 01772-1749
(508) 481-6400

International Business Forum
7 Penn Plaza, Suite 901
New York, NY 10001
(212) 279-2525

Joint Commission on Accreditation
of Healthcare Organizations
1 Renaissance Blvd.
Oakbrook Terrace, IL 60181
(630) 792-5000

Magee Rehabilitation Hospital
Education Department, Six Franklin
Plaza
Philadelphia, PA 19102
(215) 587-3424

Medical Case Management
Conference Series
Mosby-Year Book Inc.
11830 Westline Industrial Drive
St. Louis, MO 63146
(314) 872-8370

National Health Lawyers
Association
1120 Connecticut Avenue, NW,
Suite 950
Washington, DC 20036
(202) 833-1100

Rehabilitation Hospital of Colorado
Springs
325 Parkside Drive
Colorado Springs, CO 80910
(719) 630-8000

Rehabilitation Institute of Chicago
Education and Training Center
345 East Superior
Chicago, IL 60611
(312) 908-6179

Rehabilitation Management, Inc.
7144 North Harlem, Suite 241
Chicago, IL 60631
(312) 763-5600

Rehabilitation Training Institute
PO Box 4116
Winter Park, FL 32793-4116
(800) 431-6687

Self-Insurance Exchange, Inc.
25251 Paseo de Alicia, Suite 200
Laguna Hills, CA 92653
(714) 768-0334

Self-Insurance Institute of America,
Inc.
PO Box 15466
Santa Ana, CA 92735
(714) 261-2553

SkillPath Seminars
6900 Squibb Road
PO Box 2768
Mission, KS 66201-2768
(800) 873-7545

Strategic Research Institute
500 Fifth Avenue
New York, NY 10110
(212) 302-1800
(800) 599-4950

The University of Vermont
Burlington, VT 05405
(802) 656-3131
www.uvm.edu/
Continuing Education

URAC
1220 L Street NW, Suite 400
Washington, DC 20005
(202) 216-9010
www.uraq.org

**Washington Business Group on
  Health**
777 North Capitol Street, NE,
  Suite 800
Washington, DC 20002
(202) 408-9320

Zitter Group
90 New Montgomery Street, Suite 820
San Francisco, CA 94105
(415) 495-2450

Glossary

MEDICAL AND INSURANCE TERMINOLOGY

accident and health (A & H). Accident and health coverage is a feature of all group insurance except group life insurance. It is also referred to as accident and sickness, casualty, and disability coverage. The insurance industry's new general term is *health insurance.*

accident and sickness (A & S). Accident and sickness coverage, although sometimes used as synonymous with accident and health coverage, usually refers to weekly indemnity insurance (loss-of-time, short-term disability income coverage). See loss-of-time benefits.

accumulation period. The maximum length of time an individual has to incur covered expenses that satisfy a required deductible.

active life reserve. The reserve for potential disability claims on currently insured active (not disabled) lives.

actively-at-work requirement. A form of individual evidence of insurability, because the insured's health must be at least sound enough for him or her to be actively at work at his or her usual place of employment on the date the insurance takes effect. Because this definition is impractical for dependents, there is usually a provision that if a dependent is confined in a hospital on the date the insurance would otherwise become effective, the effective date of his or her insurance will be deferred until his or her release from the hospital.

activities of daily living (ADLs). Activities in the nonoccupational environment arising from daily living needs (e.g., mobility, personal hygiene, dressing, sleeping, eating, and skills required for community living).

adjustor. A person who handles claims (also referred to as a *claims service representative*).

appeal. A formal request to reconsider a determination not to certify an admission, extension of stay, or other medical service.

appeal committee. A management group not involved in initial claims decisions; it reviews denials (partial or full) when appealed by the claimant. It is an employee's right (as mandated by ERISA) to have a full and fair review of his or her case when a service is denied. The appeal committee reviews the claims file, the documentation of the denial, and the plan provision that was used to deny. It is the "court of last resort" and requires complete documentation to uphold a denial.

appropriateness of care. Care is considered appropriate if it is the right kind of care rendered in a proper setting.

assessment. The ongoing process of analyzing and integrating data obtained from the patient and family, relevant treatment providers, caregivers, and funding sources in order to identify the present plan of care, current and anticipated needs, and problems or obstacles that may be resolved through case management intervention.

assurance (insurance). The spreading of risk among many, with the likelihood that some will suffer a loss. The term *assurance* is more common in Canada and Great Britain; the term *insurance* is more common in the United States.

attending physician. The physician with primary responsibility for the care provided to a patient in a hospital or other health care facility.

authorization to pay benefits. A provision in a medical claim form by which the insured directs the insurance company to pay any benefits directly to the provider of care on whose charges the claim is based.

automatic reinsurance. A type of reinsurance in which the insurer must cede and the reinsuring company must accept all risks within certain contractually defined areas (also called *treaty reinsurance*). The reinsuring company undertakes in advance to grant reinsurance to the extent specified in the agreement in every case in which the ceding company accepts the application and retains its own limit.

benefits. The amount payable by an insurance company to the claimant, assignee, or beneficiary under a specific coverage.

bill audit. The review of hospital, physician, durable medical equipment, and health care service provider bills for inaccuracies or overbilling.

business alliances. Groups of business companies allied together to reduce health care costs by jointly purchasing medical services.

capitation. A method of payment for health services in which the health care provider is paid a fixed amount for each person over a specific amount of time regardless of the actual number or nature of services provided to each person.

caregiver. A family member, volunteer, or medical professional charged with providing care in the home setting.

carrier. The insurance company or other entity that agrees to pay the losses. A carrier may be organized as a company (stock, mutual, or reciprocal) or as an association of underwriters (e.g., Lloyds of London).

case reserve. The dollar amount stated in a claims file that represents an estimate of the amount still unpaid.

certification. A determination by a utilization review organization that an admission, extension of stay, or other medical service has been provided and qualifies as medically necessary and appropriate under the medical review requirements of the applicable health benefit plan.

claim. A request for payment of reparation for a loss covered by an insurance contract.

claimant. The person filing the claim to whom benefits are to be paid by the claims administrator.

claims administrator. Any entity that reviews and determines whether to pay claims to enrollees, physicians, or hospitals on behalf of the health benefit plan. Payment determinations are made on the basis of contract provisions, including those regarding medical necessity, and other factors. Claims administrators may be insurance companies, self-insured employers, management firms, Third Party Administrators, or other private contractors.

claims cost control. Efforts made by an insurer both inside and outside its own organization to restrain and direct claims payments so that health insurance premium dollars are used as efficiently as possible.

claims reserves. Funds reserved by an insurer to settle incurred but unpaid claims; may also include reserves for potential claims fluctuation.

claims service representative. A person who investigates losses and settles claims for an insurance carrier or the insured. *Adjustor* is a synonymous, although less preferred, term.

clinical experience. Expertise gained through professional clinical practice (e.g., any combination of direct patient care in a specialty area, home health, or general clinical area for which the applicant is licensed or certified).

coinsurance. A provision under a health insurance policy whereby the consumer assumes a percentage of the costs of covered services.

complementary and alternative medicine (CAM). The use of complementary and alternative care treatments is still considered controversial or "unorthodox" in some quarters; however, especially given the increased cultural diversity of our patient populations, they are among the most appropriate healing techniques for certain patients. Classified as mind/body/spirit treatment, holistic medicine, and Eastern medicine, these alternative approaches can refer to acupuncture, guided imagery, dietary therapy, Chinese medicine, spiritual healing, herbal remedies, homeopath, meditation, craniosacral therapy, chiropractic care, massage including Reiki, fertility treatments, paranormal healing, Tai Chi, and Yoga, among others.

comprehensive major medical insurance. A form of major medical expense insurance (written with an initial deductible) that can substitute for separate policies providing basic hospital, surgical, and medical benefits.

concurrent insurance. Insurance of a person under two or more policies providing similar or identical coverages (usually avoided in group insurance).

concurrent review. A form of utilization review that tracks the progress of a patient during treatment; conducted on-site or by telephone.

contingency reserve. A reserve established to share among all policyholders the cost to the insurer of unpredictable catastrophic losses.

coordination of benefits (COB). A method of integrating benefits payable under more than one group health insurance plan so that the insured's benefits from all sources do not exceed 100% of his or her allowable medical expenses. Another method, based on a strict benefit-by-benefit (or "carve-out") calculation, could result in zero payment by an insurer other than the one that pays benefits first.

co-payment. The portion of a claim or medical expense that a claimant must pay out of pocket.

cost-based or cost-related reimbursement. One method of payment of medical care programs by third parties, typically Blue Cross plans or government agencies, for services delivered to patients. In cost-related systems, the amount of the payment is based on the costs to the provider of delivering the service. The actual payment may be based on any one of several different formulas, such as full cost, full cost plus an additional percentage, allowable costs, or a fraction of costs. Other reimbursement schemes are based on the charges for fraction of costs, on the charges for the services delivered, or on budgeted or anticipated costs for a future time period (prospective reimbursement).

cost containment. The control of the overall cost of health care services within the health care delivery system. Costs are contained when the value of the resources committed to an activity are not considered to be excessive.

coverage. (1) The aggregate of risks insured by a contract of insurance; (2) a major classification of benefits provided by a group policy (e.g., term life, weekly indemnity, major medical); (3) the amount of insurance or benefits stated in the group policy for which an insured is eligible.

covered charges. Charges for medical care or supplies that, if incurred by an insured or other covered person, create a liability for the insurance under the terms of a group policy.

defensive medicine. The increased use of laboratory tests, hospital admissions, and extended lengths of stays in hospital by physicians for the principal purpose of forestalling the possibility of malpractice suits by patients and providing a good legal defense in the event of such lawsuits.

diagnosis-related groups (DRGs). Groupings of patients by discharge diagnosis to measure a hospital's output. These are used for analysis and monitoring of the hospital's resource utilization performance and costs.

direct contract model. A health plan that contracts directly with private practice physicians rather than through an independent practice association or medical group.

direct costs. Administration costs directly attributable to particular group cases and excluding any share of overhead expenses.

disability. A condition that makes an individual unable to earn full wages by doing the work performed when the individual was last employed.

disability benefit. A payment that arises because of total or permanent disability of an insured; a provision added to a policy that provides for a waiver of premium in case of total and permanent disability.

disability income insurance. A form of health insurance that provides periodic payments to replace income when an insured person is unable to work as a result of illness or injury.

discharge planner. The individual who assesses a patient's need for treatment after hospitalization in order to help arrange for the necessary services and resources to effect an appropriate and timely discharge.

discharge planning. The process that assesses a patient's need for treatment after hospitalization in order to help arrange for the necessary services and resources to effect an appropriate and timely discharge.

e-Health. A term that applies to the use of electronic technologies and telecommunications in the practice of clinical health care, patient and professional health-related education, public health, and health medicine. It includes the fields of telemedicine, teleHealth, medical informatics, electronic patient records, supply chain management, and biotechnologies.

enrollee. The individual who has elected to contract for or participate in a health benefit plan for him- or herself or his or her dependents.

exclusion. A specific illness or treatment that is expressly not covered by a plan or insurance contract.

exclusive provider organization (EPO). A form of PPO in which any services rendered by a nonaffiliated provider are not reimbursed, and the entire cost must be paid out of pocket by the claimant. EPO providers are usually reimbursed on a fee-for-service basis according to a negotiated discount or fee schedule.

fee-for-service. A form of reimbursement in which physicians and hospitals are paid a "reasonable or customary" fee for a unit of service; also, a system for the payment of professional services in which the practitioner is paid for the particular service rendered rather than receiving a salary for services provided during scheduled work or on-call hours.

gatekeeper. A primary care provider who authorizes all specialist referrals. Use of gatekeepers is an essential feature of HMOs.

group model HMO. An HMO that contracts with a group of physicians who are paid a set salary per patient to provide a predetermined range of services.

group practice. Three or more physicians who deliver patient care, jointly use medical equipment and personnel, and divide income by a predetermined formula.

health benefit plan. Any public or private organization's written plan that insures or pays for specific health or medical expenses on behalf of enrollees and/or covered persons.

Health Care Financing Administration (HCFA). An administrative body of the federal government that oversees all aspects of health financing.

health insurance. Protection that provides payment of benefits for covered sickness or injury; includes various types of insurance, such as accident protection, disability income, medical expenses, and accidental death and dismemberment coverage.

health maintenance organization (HMO). An organization that provides health care for a geographic area and that accepts responsibility for delivering an agreed-upon set of health maintenance and treatment services to a voluntarily enrolled group. An HMO collects a predetermined periodic payment paid in advance on behalf of each individual enrolled.

holistic medicine. A trend in medicine that emphasizes that the system must extend its focus beyond the physical aspects of disease or particular organs. It is concerned with the whole person and the interrelationships between the emotional, social, spiritual, and physical implications of disease and health.

home health care. Health care provided in the home to aged, disabled, sick, or convalescent individuals who do not need institutional care. The most common types of home care include visiting nurse services and speech, physical, occupational, and rehabilitation therapy. These services are provided by home health agencies, hospitals, or other community organizations.

home health services. Health care services provided to a patient in his or her own home by health care personnel.

hospice. A health care program whose purpose is to provide care, compassion, and support for those patients in the final stages of illness and close to death.

hospital alliances. Groups of hospitals allied together to reduce costs by sharing common services and developing group purchasing programs.

impairment. An inability or lessened ability to perform work duties because of a work-related injury or disease.

indemnity. The security against possible loss or damage; a predetermined reimbursement amount paid in the event of a covered loss.

independent medical exam (IME). A medical exam used by insurers to determine an individual's diagnosis, need for continued treatment, degree and permanency of disability, or ability to return to work.

independent practice association (IPA). An HMO that contracts with physicians who see HMO patients in their own private offices. Physicians are reimbursed on a capitated or a fee-for-service basis.

initial evaluation. The assessment conducted by a case manager following case referral. Medical, psychological, social, vocational, educational, and economic factors are explored to ascertain the best course of action for achieving rehabilitation and the feasibility of rehabilitation.

injury. Harm to a worker that requires treatment and/or compensation under workers' compensation.

inside limits. Internal control limits within the structure of overall benefits or the benefit plan; they are utilized to establish a maximum amount for a procedure, service, confinement, disability, calendar year, and so on.

job description. A detailed description of the duties, tasks, and requirements of a job, including specific physical and mental qualifications for performance. A job description is an important tool for analyzing an insured's potential to return to his or her pre-injury job and for ascertaining transferable skills.

legal reserve. The minimum reserve a company must keep to meet future claims and obligations as calculated under a state insurance code.

long-term care. The health care provided to individuals who do not require hospital care but who do need nursing, medical, and other health care services provided over time.

long-term disability income insurance. The insurance issued to a group or an individual to provide a reasonable replacement of a portion of income lost due to a serious, prolonged illness.

loss control. The efforts by insurers and insureds to prevent accidents and reduce losses through the maintenance and upgrading of health and safety procedures.

loss expenses. The part of an expense (such as legal allocation fees) paid by an insurance company directly to the plaintiff in settling a particular claim.

loss-of-time benefits. The benefits paid to help replace earned income lost through inability to work because of a disability caused by accident or illness. Weekly indemnity insurance is the type of insurance that provides such benefits.

loss ratio. The ratio of losses to premiums for a given period.

loss reserve. The dollar amount designated as the estimated cost of an accident at the time the first notice is received.

malingering. The practice of feigning illness or inability to work in order to collect insurance benefits.

malpractice. Improper care or treatment by a physician.

managed care. A system of health care delivery aimed at managing the cost and quality of access to health care. Managed care is used by HMOs, PPOs, and managed indemnity plans to improve the delivery of services and contain costs.

maximum benefit (overall maximum benefit). The maximum amount any one individual may receive under an insurance contract.

Medicaid. The state public assistance programs open to persons of any age whose financial resources are insufficient to pay for health care. Provided under Title XIX of the Social Security Act of 1986.

Medicare. The hospital insurance and supplementary medical insurance systems for the aged and disabled created in 1965 by amendments to the Social Security Act.

modified job. The predisability job adapted for the insured in such a manner that it can be performed within prescribed physical or mental limitations.

modified open panel plan. A service approach to the provision of group legal insurance in which any lawyer who agrees to accept a predetermined fee schedule and other procedural requirements may provide covered legal services to a member of a plan.

network model HMO. An independent practice association of group practices as opposed to solo physicians.

nondisabling injury. An injury that may require medical care but does not result in loss of working time or income.

nonduplication clause. A clause that excludes expenses incurred to the extent that an employee or dependent receives benefits under any type of policyholder-sponsored insurance plan.

nonexempt (nonexempt employees). A classification of employees designating those employees subject to overtime compensation and working time limits under the federal Labor Standards Act.

nonoccupational insurance. Insurance that does not provide benefits for an accident or sickness arising out of a person's employment.

occupancy rate. A measure of inpatient health facility use determined by dividing available bed days by patient days. It measures the average percentage of a hospital's beds occupied and may be institutionwide or limited to one department or service.

occupational therapy (OT). A program of prescribed activities that focuses on coordination and mastery and is designed to assist the insured to regain independence, particularly in activities of daily living.

orthotics. The field that specializes in using orthopedic appliances, braces, and other devices to support weight, prevent or correct deformities, or improve the function of movable parts of the body.

overinsurance. Insurance exceeding in amount the probable loss to which it applies. Overinsurance, which can be a serious problem, is controlled in group medical care coverage by the contractual use of nonduplication of benefits provisions (e.g., coordination of benefits).

partial disability. A condition resulting from an illness or injury that prevents an insured from performing one or more regular job functions.

per diem cost. Literally, cost per day. Refers, in general, to hospital or other inpatient institutional costs for a day of care. Hospitals occasionally charge for their services using a per diem rate derived by dividing total costs by the number of inpatient days of care given. Per diem costs are, therefore, averages and do not reflect the true cost for each patient. Thus, the per diem approach is said to give hospitals an incentive to prolong hospital stays.

period of disability. The period during which an employee is prevented from performing the usual duties of his or her occupation or employment or during which a dependent is prevented from performing the normal activities of a healthy person of the same age and sex. More than one cause (accident or sickness) may be present during or contribute to a single period of disability.

permanent and total disability. A disability that will presumably last for the insured's lifetime and that prevents him or her from engaging in any occupation for which he or she is reasonably fitted.

physician advisor. A physician who represents a claims administrator or utilization review organization and who provides advice on whether to certify an admission, extension of stay, or other medical service as being medically necessary and appropriate.

point-of-service (POS) plan. Evolved from the preferred provider organization concept, point-of-service plans are customized managed care plans often offered by larger companies. These plans combine employee choice and customized care with tight medical management and local utilization.

preadmission authorization (or precertification). The practice of requiring those covered by a health care plan to telephone a claims department prior to hospitalization, outpatient surgery, or other significant medical procedure. In most cases, a two-week notification period is requested, with allowances made for emergency treatment, for which a report within 48 hours of hospital admission is generally required.

preexisting condition. A physical or mental condition of an insured that manifested itself prior to the issuance of the individual policy or for which treatment was received prior to such issuance.

preferred provider organization (PPO). A system of health care delivery in which a third-party payer contracts with a group of medical care providers who furnish services at lower than usual fees in return for prompt payment and a certain volume of patients. The discounted fee structure is usually of a fee-for-service type.

preventative care. Care directed at preventing disease or its consequences (e.g., through immunization and early detection). Promotion of health through improving the environment or altering behaviors, especially through health education, has gained prominence and is an important strategy used, for example, by HMOs, primary care centers, and others.

primary care. Basic health care provided by physicians, general practitioners, internists, obstetricians, pediatricians, and midlevel practitioners that emphasizes a patient's general health needs as opposed to specialized care. Includes basic or initial diagnosis and treatment, health supervision, management of chronic conditions, and preventative health services. Appropriate referral to consultants and community resources is an important facet of primary care.

probationary period. The length of time a person must wait from the day of his or her entry into an eligible class or application for coverage to the date his or her insurance becomes effective. Also sometimes referred to as the *service period* or *waiting period.*

profile. A longitudinal or cross-sectional aggregation of medical care data. A patient profile lists all of the services provided to a particular patient during a specified period of time. Physician, hospital, or population profiles are statistical summaries of the pattern of practice of individual physicians or hospitals or the medical experience of specific populations. Diagnostic profiles, a subcategory of physician, hospital, or population profiles, focus on a specific condition or diagnosis.

proposal. A quotation submitted to a prospective group insurance policyholder by the insurance company through an agent, broker, or group representative.

This quotation outlines the benefits available under the proposed plan and the costs to both employer and employee. This is an important visual sales aid.

protocols. The generally accepted procedures and methods for the delivery of medical care.

provider. A licensed health care facility, physician, or other health care professional that delivers health care services.

rate. The charge per unit of payroll used to determine workers' compensation or other insurance premiums. The rate varies according to the risk classification of the policyholder.

rating. The application of the proper classification rate and other factors that may be used to set the premium rate for a policyholder. The three principal forms are manual, experience, and retrospective rating.

reconsideration. An initial request for additional review of a utilization review organization's determination not to certify an admission, extension of stay, or other medical service. A reconsideration request is called an *expedited appeal* by some utilization review organizations.

rehabilitation. The restoration of a totally disabled person to a meaningful occupation. A provision in some long-term disability policies provides for a continuation of benefits or other financial assistance while a totally disabled insured is being retrained or attempting to resume productive employment.

reinsurance carriers. Insurers for the insurers. See stop-loss insurance.

reserve general. (1) An amount representing actual or potential liabilities that is kept by an insurer to cover debts to policyholders; (2) an amount allocated for a special purpose. Note that a reserve is usually a liability and not an extra fund. On occasion, a reserve may be an asset, such as a reserve for taxes not yet due.

retrospective review. Another form of utilization review that allows insurers and employers to maintain records of physicians' practice patterns, hospital length of stay averages, and typical treatment patterns for specific diagnoses and thereby build a database to help analyze "standard and reasonable" procedures and costs.

review criteria. The written policies, decision rules, medical protocols, or guides used by a utilization review organization to determine certification (e.g., appropriateness evaluation protocols [AEPs] and intensity of service, severity of illness, discharge and appropriateness [ISD-A] screens).

second surgical opinion (SSO). When there is a complex medical picture, when questionable treatment is under way, or when elective surgery is recommended, a second surgical opinion is often requested by the insurer, employer, or patient. Some of the elective surgeries leading to an SSO request are often unnecessary, such as the removal of adenoids, bunions, gallbladder, and tonsils or open-heart, knee, or hip surgery.

settlement options. The provisions (stated or intended) in insurance contracts that allow an insured or beneficiary to receive benefits in other than a lump sum payment.

short-term disability income insurance. The insurance that pays benefits during the time a disability exists to a covered person who remains disabled for a specified period not to exceed 2 years.

staff model HMO. An HMO that employs physicians who operate out of their own facilities or clinics but who receive a salary from the HMO.

stop-loss insurance. The insurance taken by employer groups to cover the financial responsibility of health benefit payments that exceed an established threshold. A company might have health care benefits of $1,000,000 per covered life, with a threshold set at $100,000 with a reinsurer. This means there is coverage for a patient with claims of $150,000 or $250,000, but the company only pays the first $100,000 out of its group coverage and is reimbursed dollar for dollar by the stop-loss carrier for any costs over the threshold up to $1,000,000.

subrogation. In the health insurance context, subrogation is the contractual right of the plan or carrier, where state law permits, to succeed to the rights of the covered person in relation to a claim against a third party. This means that the insured party gives up the right to sue the negligent party. This right is given to the insurance company because it has paid a claim on the insured's behalf. If the insured suffers damages over and above those covered by his or her policy, he or she can sue the third party.

targeted review. A review process that focuses on specific diagnoses, services, hospitals, or practitioners rather than on all services provided or proposed to be provided to enrollees.

third-party administration. The administration of a group insurance plan by some person or firm other than the insurer or the policyholder.

Third Party Administrator (TPA). The companies that work with insurance firms, handling all the administrative tasks involved in processing claims. Employers who have become self-insurers, taking on the responsibility of funding their own benefit plans, may use a TPA or they may oversee the payment of claims themselves, via a self-insured, self-administered plan.

third-party payment. The payment of health care by an insurance company or other organization so that the patient does not directly pay for his or her services.

transferable skills. The skills an insured has acquired through occupational or vocational endeavors that may be applied with minimal training in another occupation.

usual, customary, and reasonable (UCR). Health insurance plans often pay a physician's full charge if it does not exceed his or her usual charge, if it does not exceed the amount customarily charged for the service by other physicians in the area, or if it is otherwise reasonable.

utilization. Utilization is commonly examined in terms of patterns or rates of use of a single service or type of service (hospital care, prescription drugs, physician visits). Measurement of utilization of all medical services in combination is usually done in terms of dollar expenditures. Use is expressed in rates per unit of population at risk for a given period (e.g., number of admissions to a hospital per 1,000 persons over 65 years of age per year).

utilization review (UR). The process of reviewing medical services for necessity, appropriateness, and efficiency to ensure that a patient is not given care that exceeds medical need and, thereby, reduces the number of unnecessary or inappropriate health care services. It includes review of admissions, length of stay, discharge, and services ordered and provided and is conducted on a preadmission, concurrent, and retrospective basis.

utilization review organization. An entity that conducts utilization review and determines certification of an admission, extension of stay, or other medical service.

vocational evaluation. A professional analysis of the insured's work potential, integrating information about physical capabilities, mental aptitudes, interests, personality motivation, transferable skills, and environmental considerations.

workers' compensation. The social insurance system for industrial and work injuries regulated in certain specified occupations by the federal government.

workers' compensation law. A statute imposing liability on employers to pay benefits and furnish care to employees injured and to pay benefits to dependents of employees killed in the course of and because of their employment.

LEGAL TERMINOLOGY

agency. A relationship between two parties in which the first party authorizes the second to act as agent on behalf of the first. It usually implies a contractual arrangement between two parties managed by a third party, an agent.

agent. A party authorized to act on behalf of another and to give the other an account of such actions.

appeal. The process whereby a court of appeals reviews the record of written materials from a court proceeding to determine if errors were made that might lead to a reversal of the trial court's decision.

assumption of risk. A doctrine based on voluntary exposure to a known risk. It is distinguished from contributory negligence (which is based on carelessness) in that it involves the comprehension that a peril is to be encountered as well as the willingness to encounter it.

claimant. One who asserts a right or demand in a legal proceeding.

claims-made policy. A professional liability insurance policy that covers the holder for a period in which a claim of malpractice is made. The alleged act of malpractice may have occurred at some previous time but the policy insures the holder when the claim is made.

compensation. An act that a court orders (including money that a court or other tribunal orders to be paid) by a person whose acts or omissions have caused loss or injury in order to recompense the injured party with respect to the loss.

confidential communications. Certain classes of communications that the law will not permit to be divulged; in general, such communications pass between persons who stand in a confidential or fiduciary relationship to each other (or who, because of their relative situation, owe a special duty of secrecy and fidelity).

cross-examination. The questioning of a witness during a trial or deposition by the party opposing those who asked the person to testify.

damages. The money awarded by the court to someone who has been injured (plaintiff) that must be paid by the party responsible for the injury (defendant). Normal damages are awarded when the injury is considered to be slight. Compensatory damages are awarded to repay or compensate the injured party for the loss that was incurred. Punitive damages are awarded when the injury is found to have been committed maliciously or in wanton disregard of the plaintiff's interests.

defendant. The person against whom an action is brought because of an alleged responsibility for violating one or more of the plaintiff's legally protected interests.

deposition. A sworn pretrial testimony given by a witness in response to oral and written questions and cross-examination. The deposition is transcribed and may be used for further pretrial investigation. It may also be presented at the trial if the witness cannot be present.

disability. In a legal context, the term means incapacity for the full enjoyment of ordinary legal rights.

discovery. A pretrial procedure that allows the plaintiff's and defendant's attorneys to find out about matters relevant to the case, including information about what evidence the other side has, what witnesses will be called, and so on. Discovery devices for obtaining information include depositions and interrogatories to obtain testimony, requests for documents and other tangible evidence, and requests for physical or mental examinations.

evidence. Any species of proof or probative matter, legally presented at the trial of an issue, by the act of the parties and through the medium of witnesses, records, documents, tangible objects, and the like, for the purpose of inducing beliefs in the minds of the court or jury as to the truth of their contention.

expert witness. A person who has special knowledge of a subject about which a court requests testimony. Special knowledge may be acquired by experience, education, observation, or study but is not possessed by the average person. An expert witness gives expert testimony or expert evidence. This evidence often serves to educate the court and the jury in the subject under consideration.

fiduciary relationship. A legal relationship of confidentiality that exists whenever one person trusts or relies on another, such as a doctor–patient relationship.

fraud. A false representation of a matter of fact (whether by words or conduct, by false or misleading allegations, or by concealment of that which should be disclosed) that deceives and is intended to deceive another so that person shall act upon such representation to his or her legal injury.

guardian ad litem. A person appointed by the court to safeguard a minor's legal interest during certain kinds of litigation.

imputed negligence. Malpractice due to negligent practice of a person taught.

in loco parentis. The Latin phrase meaning "in the place of the parent." The assumption by a person or institution of the parental obligations of caring for a child without adoption.

indemnify. To secure against loss or damage; to give security for the reimbursement of a person in the event of an anticipated loss to that individual.

injury. Any wrong or damage done to another, either to the individual's person, rights, reputation, or property. Consists of damages of a permanent nature.

interrogatories. A series of written questions submitted to a witness or other person having information of interest to the court. The answers are transcribed and are sworn to under oath.

liability. The legal responsibility for failure to act, thus causing harm to another person, or for actions that fail to meet standards of care, so causing another person harm.

liaison. A nurse who acts as an agent between a patient, the hospital, and the patient's family and who speaks for the entire health care team.

litigation. A contest in a court for the purpose of enforcing a right.

malfeasance. The performance of an unlawful, wrongful act.

malpractice. A professional person's wrongful conduct, improper discharge of professional duties, or failure to meet standards of care, which results in harm to another person.

misfeasance. An improper performance of a lawful act, especially in a way that might cause damage or injury.

motion. A request to the court to take some action or a request to the opposing side to take some action relating to a case.

negligence. The failure to act as an ordinary prudent person; conduct contrary to that of a reasonable person under similar circumstances.

nonfeasance. A failure to perform a task, duty, or undertaking that one has agreed to perform or that one had a legal duty to perform.

petition. An ex parte application to a court asking for the exercise of the court's judicial powers in relation to some matter that is not the subject for a suit or action, or a request for the authority to undertake an action that requires the sanction of the court.

plaintiff. A person who brings a suit to court in the belief that one or more of that individual's rights have been violated or that a legal injury has occurred.

professional corporation (PC). A corporation formed according to the law of a particular state for the purpose of delivering a professional service.

professional liability. A legal concept describing the obligation of a professional person to pay a patient or client for damages caused by the professional's act of omission, commission, or negligence. Professional liability better describes the responsibility of all professionals to their clients than does the concept of malpractice, but the idea of professional liability is central to malpractice.

professional liability insurance. A type of liability insurance that protects professional persons against malpractice claims made against them.

release. The relinquishment of a right, claim, or privilege by a person in whom it exists or to whom it accrues, to the person against whom it might be demanded or enforced.

remedy. The means by which a right is enforced or the violation of a right is prevented, redressed, or compensated.

res ipsa loquitur. Literally, "the thing speaks for itself." A legal doctrine that applies when the defendant was solely and exclusively in control at the time the plaintiff's injury occurred, so that the injury would not have occurred if the defendant had exercised due care. When a court applies this doctrine to a case, the defendant bears the burden of proving that he was not negligent.

respondeat superior. Literally, "let the master respond." This maxim means that an employer is liable in certain cases for the consequences of the wrongful acts of its employees while the employee is acting within the scope of his or her employment.

right of conscience law. A legal equivalent to freedom of thought or of religion.

right of privacy. The right of individuals to withhold their person and property from public scrutiny, if so desired, as long as it is consistent with the law of public policy.

right to access law. A law that grants a patient the right to see his or her medical records.

right to die law. A law that upholds a patient's right to choose death by refusing extraordinary treatment when the patient has no hope of recovery. Also referred to as the *natural death law* or *living will law.*

settlement. An agreement by the parties to a transaction or controversy that resolves some or all of the issues involved in a case.

standards of care. In a malpractice lawsuit, those acts performed or omitted that an ordinary, prudent person in the defendant's position would have done or not done; a measure by which the defendant's alleged wrongful conduct is compared.

statute. The written act of a legislative body declaring, commanding, or prohibiting an action (in contrast to unwritten common law).

statute of limitations. A statute that sets forth limitations of the right of action for certain described causes (e.g., declaring that no suit can be maintained on such cases of action unless brought within a specified period of time after the right came into existence).

subpoena. A process commanding a witness to appear and give testimony in court.

tort. A private or civil wrong outside of a contractual relationship.

tort-feasor. A wrongdoer who is legally liable for the damage caused.

uniform anatomical gift act. A law of the type existing in all 50 states that allows anyone over 18 to sign a donor card willing some or all of his or her organs after death.

waiver. The intentional or voluntary relinquishment of a known right.

wrongful death statute. A statute of the type existing in all states that provides that the death of a person can give rise to a cause of legal action brought by the person's beneficiaries in a civil suit against the person whose willful or negligent acts caused the death. Prior to the existence of these statutes, a suit could be brought only if the injured person survived the injury.

wrongful life action. A civil suit usually brought against a physician or health facility on the basis of negligence that resulted in the wrongful birth or life of an infant. The parents of the unwanted child seek to obtain payment from the defendant for the medical expenses of pregnancy and delivery, for pain and suffering, and for the education and upbringing of the child. Wrongful life actions have been brought and won in several situations, including malpracticed tubal ligations, vasectomies, and abortions. Failure to diagnose pregnancy in time for abortion and incorrect medical advice leading to the birth of a defective child have also led to malpractice suits for a wrongful life.

ACRONYMS AND ABBREVIATIONS

A & H	accident and health
A & S	accident and sickness
AAOHN	American Association of Occupational Health Nurses
ABOHN	American Board for Occupational Health Nurses
A-CCC	Continuity of Care Certification, Advanced
ACCM	Academy for Certified Case Managers
ADA	Americans with Disabilities Act of 1990

ADB	accelerated death benefit
ADEA	Age Discrimination in Employment Act
ADL	activities of daily living
AEP	appropriateness evaluation protocol
AIDS	acquired immunodeficiency syndrome
AMA	American Medical Association
ANA	American Nurses Association
ANYOCC	any occupation (used in long-term disability policies)
ASO	administrative services only
CAM	complementary and alternative medicine
CARF	Certification Association of Rehabilitation Facilities
CAT	computerized axial tomography
CCM	Certified Case Manager
CCMC	Commission for Case Management
CDC	Centers for Disease Control
CDH	consumer-driven health care
CDMS	Certified Disability Management Specialist
CDMSC	Certification of Disability Management Specialists Commission
CIRS	Certified Insurance Rehabilitation Specialist
CIRSC	Certification of Insurance Rehabilitation Specialists Commission
CLAS	National Standards on Culturally and Linguistically Appropriate Service in Health Care
CM	Case Manager
CMAC	Case Management Administrator, Certified
CMC	Care Manager Certified (from NACCM)
CMC	Case Manager, Certified (from AIOCM)
CMC-A	Case Manager Associate
CMCN	Certified Managed Care Nurse
CMS	Centers for Medicare and Medicaid Services (formerly HCFA, Health Care Financing Administration)
CMSA	Case Management Society of America
COB	coordination of benefits
COBRA	Consolidated Omnibus Budget Reconciliation Act of 1986
COHN	Certified Occupational Health Nurse
COHN/CM	Certified Occupational Health Nurse/Case Manager
COHN-S	Certified Occupational Health Nurse-Specialist
COHN-S/CM	Certified Occupational Health Nurse-Specialist/Case Manager
CPHQ	Certified Professional in Health Care Quality
CPT	Current Procedural Terminology (used in code designations)

CRC	Certified Rehabilitation Counselor
CRRN	Certified Rehabilitation Registered Nurse
C-SWCM	Certified Social Worker Case Manager
DME	durable medical equipment
DRG	diagnosis-related group
EPO	exclusive provider organization
ERISA	Employee Retirement Income Security Act of 1974
FDA	Federal Drug Administration
FMLA	Family and Medical Leave Act of 1993
FRER	Foundation for Rehabilitation Certification Education & Research
HBV	Hepatitis B virus
HCFA	Health Care Financing Administration (now CMS, Centers for Medicare and Medicaid Services)
HCO	health care organization
HEDIS	Health Plan Employer Data and Information Set
HHA	home health agency
HHC	home health care
HIA	health insurance alliance
HIPAA	Health Insurance Portability and Accountability Act of 1996 (also called the Kassebaum-Kennedy Act)
HIPCs	health insurance purchasing cooperatives
HISOCC	his occupation (used in long-term disability policies)
HIV	human immunodeficiency virus
HMO	health maintenance organization
ICD-9	International Classification of Disease, 9th edition
IDFN	integrated delivery and financing network (an IDS)
IDFS	integrated delivery and financing system (an IDS)
IDN	integrated delivery network (an IDS)
IDS	integrated delivery system
IOM	Institute of Medicine
IPA	independent practice arrangement
ISD-A	intensity of service, severity of illness, discharge and appropriateness
Joint Commission	Joint Commission on Accreditation of Healthcare Organizations
LPN	Licensed Practical Nurse
LTD	long-term disability
LVN	Licensed Vocational Nurse
MCO	managed care organization
MSA	Medical Savings Account
MSO	managed services organization

OMH	Office of Minority Health
OT	occupational therapist or occupational therapy
PBM	pharmacy benefits management
PCP	primary care physician
PHO	physician–hospital organization
PhRMA	Pharmaceutical Research and Manufacturers of America
PIP	personal injury protection (auto policy clause)
POS	point-of-service
PPO	preferred provider organization
PPS	prospective payment system
PRO	professional review organization
PSDA	The Patient Self-Determination Act
PSRO	professional standards review organization
PT	physical therapist or physical therapy
R&C	reasonable and customary
RN-NCM	Registered Nurse-Nurse Case Manager
SNF	skilled nursing facility
SNV	skilled nursing visit
SHMOs	social health maintenance organizations
SPD	summary plan description
STD	short-term disability
TEFRA	Tax Equity and Fiscal Responsibility Act of 1982
TPA	Third Party Administrator
TPN	total parenteral nutrition
URAC	Utilization Review Accreditation Commission, also doing business as the American Accreditation HealthCare Commission
WC	workers' compensation

The glossary includes terms adapted or reprinted from *A thru Z: Managed Care Terms,* with permission of Medicom International and Novartis, © 2001; *Managed Healthcare,* with permission of Logical Health Care Solutions Corporation, © 2000; *Managed Care: What It Is and How It Works,* second edition, by Peter R. Kongstvedt, with permission of Jones and Bartlett Publishers, Inc., © 2004; *Home Care: An Emerging Solution to the Nation's Health Care Crisis,* with permission of Olsten Kimberly QualityCare, © 1993; *CCM Certification Guide,* with permission of the Foundation for Rehabilitation Certification, Education and Research, © 1993; *Health Insurance Answer Book: 1994 Cumulative Supplement* by Thomas A. Darold, with permission of Panel Publishers, a division of Aspen Publishers, Inc., 36 West 44th Street, Suite 1316, New York, NY 10036, © 1994; and *Case Management Practice,* with permission of the Foundation for Rehabilitation Certification, Education and Research, © 1993.

Case Management and Health Care Web Sites

Alternative Medicine

Alternative Medicine Foundation
http://www.amfoundation.org/

Alternative Health News Online
http://www.altmedicine.com/

CAMline
http://www.camline.org/index2.htm

Complementary Medical Association
http://www.the-cma.org.uk/

Health Care Information Resources
Alternative Medicine section
http://www-hsl.mcmaster.ca/
    tomflem/altmed.html#gen

Behavioral Health

www.dementia.com

www.depression.about.com

Cultural Competency

Agency for Health Care Research and
    Quality Minority Health Research
www.ahcpr.gov/research/minorix.htm

Cross Cultural Health Program
www.xculture.org

Diversity RX
www.diversityrx.org

Office of Minority Health
www.ohmrc.gov

Transcultural Nursing Society
www.tcns.org

Death and Dying/End of Life

Choice in Dying
www.choices.org

DignityResources.com is a new web
site that provides financial education
and related resources for people facing
serious or life-threatening illness.
www.dignityresources.com

Dying Well
www.dyingwell.org

End of Life Education for Nurses
www.aacn.nche.edu/elnec

Growth House
www.growthhouse.org
Resources for bereavement and grief,
death and dying, death with dignity,
euthanasia, hospice, palliative care,
suicide, terminal illness, AIDS, and
HIV

Last Acts
http://www.lastacts.org

Partnership for Caring
www.partnershipforcaring.org

Promoting Excellence in End-of-Life
  Care
www.promotingexcellence.com

e-Health

eHealth Initiative
www.ehealthinitiative.org

eHealth International
The Journal of Applied Health
  Technology
www.ehealthinternational.org

eHealth Magazine
www.ehealthmag.com

E-Health Terms
www.aishealth.com/EHealthBusiness/
  EHTerms.html

Internet Health Coalition
www.ihealthcoalition.org

Today in E-Health Business
www.aishealth.com/TodayEHealth
  Business.html

HIV/AIDS

AIDSINFONYC.org

www.AidMeds.com
For people living with HIV, to help
make empowered treatment decisions;
AIDS drug database

AIDS Treatment Data Network
  (ATDN)
www.atdn.org
1-800-734-7104

HIV Drug Database
http://coreynahman.com

For most recent Standards of Care

www.aids-etc.org

www.aidsinfo.nih.gov

For drug interactions

HIV Medication Guide
www.hivmedicationguide.com

Canadian AIDS Treatment
  Information Exchange
www.catie.ca/comp_e.nsf

www.GayHealth.com

Hospice/Palliative Care

American Academy of Hospice and
  Palliative Medicine
www.aahpm.org/

American Board of Hospice and
  Palliative Medicine
www.abhpm.org/

The Hospice Association of America
www.hospice-america.org

Hospice Net
www.hospicenet.org

International Association for Hospice
and Palliative Care
www.hospicecare.com

The National Hospice and Palliative
Care Organization
www.nhpco.org/

Palliative Education Resource Center
www.eperc.mcw.edu/

The Zen Hospice Project
www.zenhospice.org

Other Sites

www.aishealth.com

Alzheimer's Association
www.alz.org

Alzheimers.com
www.alzheimers.com

America's Doctor
www.americasdoctor.com

CareGiver Zone
www.caregiverZone.com

Case Manager's OneList
www.cmonelist.com

Centers for Disease Control and
Prevention
www.cdc.gov

Center for Medicare & Medicaid
Services
www.cms.hhs.gov

The Ferguson Report
Newsletter of Online Health
www.fergusonreport.com

Health Care Information Resources
www.hsl.mcmaster/ca/tomflem/altmed
.html#gen

Healthcare Online for Dummies
www.dummies.com

Health monitor
www.healthmonitor.com

Healthy.net

Mayo Clinic Health Oasis
www.mayohealth.org

Medline
ww.medline.com

MedScape
www.medscape.com

National Family Caregivers
Association (NFCA)
www.nfcacares.org

National Institutes of Health
www.nih.gov/health

National Organization for Rare
Disease
www.rarediseases.org

Partnership for Solutions (PFS)
For people with chronic conditions
www.partnershipforsolutions.org

Public Agenda Online (health care
issues)
www.publicagenda.org/issues

Strength for Caring
www.strengthforcaring.com

Index

About the Author

Catherine M. Mullahy, RN, BS, CRRN, CCM, is a nationally recognized case management consultant and a spokesperson for the case management industry. She is founder and president of Options Unlimited, a medical case management and benefits consulting firm in Huntington, New York, serving individuals, corporations, insurers, managed care organizations, unions, and Third Party Administrators nationwide since 1983. Recipient of the national award, 1999 Distinguished Case Manager of the Year, presented by the Case Management Society of America (CMSA), Mullahy was 2001-2002 National President of the CMSA board. She is Past-Chair of the Commission for Case Manager Certification (CCMC) and is the CCMC representative to the Foundation for Rehabilitation Education and Research. She has served on ongoing expert panels in connection with the development of the CCM credential since its inception, and was Chair of the CCMC committee that developed the case management Code for Professional Conduct.

Editor of *The Case Manager* magazine and on the editorial board of *Case Management Advisor*, Mullahy is a frequent lecturer and writer, and she has contributed to numerous magazines and books. Her popular book, *The Case Manager's Handbook, Second Edition*, was named a 1998 "Book of the Year" by the *American Journal of Nursing* magazine and is on the CCMC and American Board of Quality Assurance Utilization Review (ABQAURP) reading lists. In 1997, the Professional Rehabilitation Association named her Rehabilitation Professional of the Year.

In addition, she is the author of *The Case Manager's Handbook Forms & Letters on CD-ROM* and *The Case Manager's Handbook Study Guide.* Mullahy has contributed chapters to *Best Practices in Medical Management* ("Case Management and Managed Care"), *The Persons Served: Ethical Perspectives on CARF's*

Accreditation Standards (Commission on Accreditation of Rehabilitation Facilities), and *The Managed Health Care Handbook,* 3d ed. ("Case Management and Managed Care"). She served as editor for *Essential Readings in Case Management* and was contributing editor for *Medical Case Management—Forms, Checklists & Guidelines.*

Mullahy is a member of the Case Management Society of America, National Head Injury Association, National Association of Rehabilitation Professionals in the Private Sector, Professional Rehabilitation Association, Foundation for Rehabilitation Education and Research, Self-Insurance Institute of America, National Benefits Association, New York Business Group on Health, American Association for Managed Care Nurses, Association for Rehabilitation Nurses, Association of Benefit Administrators, Commission for Case Manager Certification, Long Island Association, and the Hauppauge Industrial Association.

Options Unlimited, founded by Mullahy in 1983, provides a comprehensive array of services: CareWatch™ utilization review, including preadmission review, concurrent review, discharge planning, and outpatient review; CareSolutions™ medical case management; GroupHealth™ case management for insured or self-funded groups; DisAbilities™ short- and long-term disability management; First Breath™ high-risk pregnancy management; Elder Options™; disease management programs such as Living with Diabetes and Living with Asthma; CompSolutions™ workers' compensation case management; and AccuClaim™ medical claims analysis and review. Options Unlimited also offers corporate wellness programs, return-to-work programs, and family support and education in cases of catastrophic illness. It is based in Long Island, New York.

The firm's current client base consists of Third Party Administrators representing employers, municipalities, manufacturers, school districts, insurers, union benefit trusts, and businesses; major health care carriers; long-term and short-term disability carriers; as well as workers' compensation and auto carriers, among others.

With over 34 years of experience managing health care delivery in home, hospital, hospice, and critical care settings, Mullahy's diversified nursing background includes treatment of multiple trauma, cardiac, orthopedic, and neurological conditions.

Deborah K. Jensen is president of An In-House Associate, Inc. In collaboration with a range of specialists, she has written for the *Journal of Care Management, Continuing Care, National Real Estate Investor, Practical Lawyer,* and other trade magazines. A freelance writer, her work has appeared in *The New York Times, The Self-Insurer, The Case Manager, Health monitor, Medical Interface,* and *The Winged Foot.* In addition, her New York-based company provides writing services to corporations, individuals, public relations firms, and other organizations.